Lecture Notes in Computer Science 3312

Commenced Publication in 1973
Founding and Former Series Editors:
Gerhard Goos, Juris Hartmanis, and Jan van Leeuwen

T0223734

Alan J. Hu   Andrew K. Martin (Eds.)

Formal Methods in Computer-Aided Design

5th International Confrence, FMCAD 2004
Austin, Texas, USA, November 15-17, 2004
Proceedings

 Springer

Volume Editors

Alan J. Hu
University of British Columbia
Department of Computer Science
2366 Main Mall, Vancouver, BC V6T 1Z4, Canada
E-mail: ajh@cs.ubc.ca

Andrew K. Martin
IBM Austin Research Laboratory
11400 Burnet Rd, MS 904-6H004
Austin, TX 78758-3493, USA
E-mail: akmartin@us.ibm.com

Library of Congress Control Number: 2004115344

CR Subject Classification (1998): B.1.2, B.1.4, B.2.2-3, B.6.2-3, B.7.2-3, F.3.1, F.4.1, I.2.3, D.2.4, J.6

ISSN 0302-9743
ISBN 3-540-23738-0 Springer Berlin Heidelberg New York

Springer is a part of Springer Science+Business Media

springeronline.com

© Springer-Verlag Berlin Heidelberg 2004
Printed in Germany

Typesetting: Camera-ready by author, data conversion by Olgun Computergrafik
Printed on acid-free paper   SPIN: 11342083   06/3142   5 4 3 2 1 0

Preface

These are the proceedings of the fifth international conference, Formal Methods in Computer-Aided Design (FMCAD), held 15–17 November 2004 in Austin, Texas, USA. The conference provides a forum for presenting state-of-the-art tools, methods, algorithms, and theory for the application of formalized reasoning to all aspects of computer-aided system design, including specification, verification, synthesis, and testing.

FMCAD's heritage dates back 20 years to some of the earliest conferences on the subject of formal reasoning and computer-aided design. Since 1996, FMCAD has assumed its present form, held biennially in North America, alternating with its sister conference CHARME in Europe. We are delighted to report that our research community continues to flourish: we received 69 paper submissions, with many more high-quality papers than we had room to accept. After a rigorous review process, in which each paper received at least three, and typically four or more, independent reviews, we accepted 29 papers for the conference and inclusion in this volume. The conference also included invited talks from Greg Spirakis of Intel Corporation and Wayne Wolf of Princeton University.

A conference of this size requires the contributions of numerous people. On the technical side, we are grateful to the program committee and the additional reviewers for their countless hours reviewing submissions and ensuring the intellectual quality of the conference. We would also like to thank the steering committee for their wisdom and guidance. On the logistical side, we thank Christa Mace for designing our website and attending to countless organizational tasks. And we thank our corporate sponsors – AMD, IBM, Intel, and Synopsys – for financial support that helped make this conference possible.

September 2004

Alan J. Hu
Vancouver, British Columbia

Andrew K. Martin
Austin, Texas

Program Committee

Mark Aagaard (University of Waterloo, Canada)
Dominique Borrione (Laboratoire TIMA and Université Joseph Fourier, France)
Randy Bryant (Carnegie Mellon University, USA)
Jerry R. Burch (Synopsys, USA)
Ed Clarke (Carnegie Mellon University, USA)
Nancy Day (University of Waterloo, Canada)
David Dill (Stanford University, USA)
Hans Eveking (Darmstadt University of Technology, Germany)
Masahiro Fujita (University of Tokyo, Japan)
Daniel Geist (IBM, Israel)
Steven German (IBM, USA)
Ganesh Gopalakrishnan (University of Utah, USA)
Mike Gordon (Cambridge University, UK)
Susanne Graf (VERIMAG, France)
Ravi Hosabettu (Sun Microsystems, USA)
Alan J. Hu, Co-chair (University of British Columbia, Canada)
Warren Hunt (University of Texas, USA)
Steve Johnson (Indiana University, USA)
Robert B. Jones (Intel, USA)
Thomas Kropf (Bosch, Germany)
Andreas Kuehlmann (Cadence, USA)
Tim Leonard (Intel, USA)
Andy Martin, Co-chair (IBM, USA)
Ken McMillan (Cadence, USA)
Tom Melham (University of Oxford, UK)
Paul S. Miner (NASA, USA)
John O'Leary (Intel, USA)
Laurence Pierre (University of Nice, France)
Carl Pixley (Synopsys, USA)
Shaz Qadeer (Microsoft Research, USA)
Sriram Rajamani (Microsoft Research, USA)
David Russinoff (Advanced Micro Devices, USA)
Jun Sawada (IBM, USA)
Eli Singerman (Intel, Israel)
Satnam Singh (Microsoft, USA)
Anna Slobodova (Intel, USA)
Enrico Tronci (Università di Roma "La Sapienza", Italy)
Matthew Wilding (Rockwell Collins, USA)
Jin Yang (Intel, USA)
Tomohiro Yoneda (National Institute of Informatics, Japan)

Additional Reviewers

Jason Baumgartner
William Bevier
Ritwik Bhattacharya
Per Bjesse
Menouer Boubekeur
Annette Bunker
Pankaj Chauhan
Jared Davis
Arthur Flatau
Kiran Gallapally
Eric Gascard
Mark Greenstreet
David Greve
Alex Groce
Anubhav Gupta
John Harrison
Tamir Heyman
Pei-Hsin Ho
Priyank Kalla
Sharon Kcidar
Raihan Kibria

Alfred Koelbl
Malte Krieger
Robert Krug
Flavio Lerda
Jens Levihn
Hanbing Liu
Tony Ma
Jean-Christophe Madre
Freddy Mang
In-Ho Moon
Silvia Mueller
Traian Muntean
Chris Myers
Ziv Nevo
Volker Nimbler
Joel Ouaknine
Sudhindra Pandav
Sandip Ray
Erik Reeber
Sitvanit Ruah
Ingo Schaefer

Martin Schickel
Sanjit A. Seshia
Ohad Shacham
Radu I. Siminiceanu
Robert de Simone
Ed Smith
Marielle Stoelinga
Rob Sumners
Matyas Sustik
Muralidhar Talupur
Michael Theobald
Tayssir Touili
Alex Tsow
Rachel Tzoref
Serita Van Groningen
Tatyana Veksler
Viswanath Vinod
Yue Yang
Karen Yorav
Reto Zimmermann

Steering Committee

Mark D. Aagaard
Alan J. Hu

Warren A. Hunt, Jr.
Steven D. Johnson

Andrew K. Martin
John W. O'Leary

Table of Contents

Challenges in System-Level Design 1
    Wayne Wolf

Generating Fast Multipliers Using Clever Circuits 6
    Mary Sheeran

Verification of Analog and Mixed-Signal Circuits
Using Hybrid System Techniques.................................... 21
    Thao Dang, Alexandre Donzé, and Oded Maler

A Methodology for the Formal Verification of FFT Algorithms in HOL ... 37
    Behzad Akbarpour and Sofiène Tahar

A Functional Approach to the Formal Specification of Networks on Chip .. 52
    Julien Schmaltz and Dominique Borrione

Proof Styles in Operational Semantics 67
    Sandip Ray and J. Strother Moore

Integrating Reasoning About Ordinal Arithmetic into ACL2 82
    Panagiotis Manolios and Daron Vroon

Combining Equivalence Verification and Completion Functions 98
    Mark D. Aagaard, Vlad C. Ciubotariu, Jason T. Higgins,
    and Farzad Khalvati

Synchronization-at-Retirement for Pipeline Verification 113
    Mark D. Aagaard, Nancy A. Day, and Robert B. Jones

Late Design Changes (ECOs)
for Sequentially Optimized Esterel Designs 128
    Laurent Arditi, Gerard Berry, and Michael Kishinevsky

Non-miter-based Combinational Equivalence Checking
by Comparing BDDs with Different Variable Orders 144
    In-Ho Moon and Carl Pixley

Scalable Automated Verification
via Expert-System Guided Transformations 159
    Hari Mony, Jason Baumgartner, Viresh Paruthi, Robert Kanzelman,
    and Andreas Kuehlmann

Simple Yet Efficient Improvements
of SAT Based Bounded Model Checking 174
    Emmanuel Zarpas

Simple Bounded LTL Model Checking 186
    Timo Latvala, Armin Biere, Keijo Heljanko, and Tommi Junttila

QuBE++: An Efficient QBF Solver 201
    Enrico Giunchiglia, Massimo Narizzano, and Armando Tacchella

Bounded Probabilistic Model Checking with the Murφ Verifier........... 214
    *Giuseppe Della Penna, Benedetto Intrigila, Igor Melatti,
    Enrico Tronci, and Marisa Venturini Zilli*

Increasing the Robustness of Bounded Model Checking
by Computing Lower Bounds on the Reachable States 230
    Mohammad Awedh and Fabio Somenzi

Bounded Verification of Past LTL 245
    Alessandro Cimatti, Marco Roveri, and Daniel Sheridan

A Hybrid of Counterexample-Based and Proof-Based Abstraction 260
    Nina Amla and Ken L. McMillan

Memory Efficient All-Solutions SAT Solver and Its Application
for Reachability Analysis... 275
    Orna Grumberg, Assaf Schuster, and Avi Yadgar

Approximate Symbolic Model Checking for Incomplete Designs 290
    Tobias Nopper and Christoph Scholl

Extending Extended Vacuity 306
    Arie Gurfinkel and Marsha Chechik

Parameterized Vacuity... 322
    Marko Samer and Helmut Veith

An Operational Semantics for Weak PSL 337
    Koen Claessen and Johan Mårtensson

Accepting Predecessors Are Better than Back Edges
in Distributed LTL Model-Checking 352
    Luboš Brim, Ivana Černá, Pavel Moravec, and Jiří Šimša

Bloom Filters in Probabilistic Verification 367
    Peter C. Dillinger and Panagiotis Manolios

A Simple Method for Parameterized Verification
of Cache Coherence Protocols 382
    Ching-Tsun Chou, Phanindra K. Mannava, and Seungjoon Park

A Partitioning Methodology for BDD-Based Verification 399
  Debashis Sahoo, Subramanian Iyer, Jawahar Jain, Christian Stangier,
  Amit Narayan, David L. Dill, and E. Allen Emerson

Invariant Checking Combining Forward and Backward Traversal 414
  Christian Stangier and Thomas Sidle

Variable Reuse for Efficient Image Computation 430
  Zijiang Yang and Rajeev Alur

Author Index 445

Challenges in System-Level Design

Wayne Wolf

Dept. of Electrical Engineering, Princeton University
wolf@princeton.edu
http://www.princeton.edu/~wolf

Abstract. This paper summarizes some of the challenges presented by very large integrated circuits. Today's embedded applications require not just complex algorithms but multi-tasking systems that perform several different types of operations on the data. Those applications are run on systems-on-chips that embody complex, heterogeneous architectures. Furthermore, systems-on-chips are connected into even larger systems. The large amounts of state in systems-on-chips, along with the interactions between traditional functionality and performance, mean that we must expand the scope of system design and verification activities. We still need to solve all the traditional design problems, but we must also develop new methodologies that allow us to design and verify the long-term behavior of the system.

1 Introduction

Modern integrated circuits can embody hugely complex systems. Successfully designing these systems-on-chips (SoCs) requires mastering not only all the traditional hardware design problems, but new types of hardware and software design problems as well. This paper surveys the nature of systems-on-chips and identifies some important new problems that SoC designers face.

2 Characteristics of Applications

Systems-on-chips enable new applications for integrated circuits. However, applications have a life of their own. Systems-on-chips must be designed to satisfy the requirements of applications as they evolve. As a result, it is useful to consider the sorts of applications that are destined to be implemented on systems-on-chips.

SoC applications are becoming more and more complex in at least two ways. First, modern applications are composed of many algorithms. Early systems for multimedia, communications, etc. tended to use one or a few basic building blocks. As our knowledge of these applications grows, experts tend to add new functions to the block diagram to improve the quality of the system. Both the size of the block diagram and its interconnectivity tend to grow over time. One of the implications of this trend is that applications tend to include more types of algorithms over time. For example, modern video compression algorithms generally use three very different types of algorithms: motion estimation, which is very memory intensive; discrete cosine transform (DCT), which is numerically complex; and Huffman coding, which is bit-intensive.

A.J. Hu and A.K. Martin (Eds.): FMCAD 2004, LNCS 3312, pp. 1–5, 2004.
© Springer-Verlag Berlin Heidelberg 2004

Second, the blocks in the block diagram tend to become more complex as well. Consider motion estimation in video compression. Early systems used full search which tested a large number of locations in a fixed order. Modern video compression systems use motion estimation algorithms that use frequent tests to reduce the number of points searched. Using more control-intensive algorithms reduces the number of data values that must be fetched from memory but makes the memory access patterns much harder to predict. This data dependent behavior makes the underlying machines harder to specify, design, and verify.

Audio encoding is another domain in which algorithms have become more complex, making system design and verification more complex. Modern audio encoders, such as Ogg Vorbis [Vor04], set the size of the window for frequency transformations on-the-fly, based upon audio characteristics. Large windows offer better fidelity but require considerably more computation; smaller windows can be used without much audible effect in some cases. The coders monitor the audio statistics and select the appropriate window size for the current segment of audio. Although reducing the number of multiplications required, this approach makes the software considerably more complex. We no longer know at design time how many iterations that will be performed in the transform loop (though we do know at run time before we start to execute the loop). Dynamic loop bounds cause difficulties for verification and run-time analysis. At the microarchitecture level, they also change the branch prediction statistics and, more important, change the program's cache behavior.

Algorithms will continue to become more complex. Hardware and software designers will have to develop more powerful methods that can handle the dynamic behavior of modern algorithms for signal processing, communication, networking, and other important applications.

3   Multiprocessor Systems-on-Chips

Multiprocessor systems-on-chips (MPSoCs) [Wol04,Jer04] are increasingly popular as platforms for advanced applications. MPSoCs are custom, heterogeneous multiprocessors designed for specific applications. Unlike chip multiprocessors, which are components of larger systems, MPSoCs are designed to be complete systems. The complexity of MPSoCs makes them significant design challenges.

All the traditional digital design problems still manifest themselves in MPSoC design. But the greater complexity of these chips brings new problems to the fore. Some of these problems are due to the large amounts of memory in MPSoCs. The large state space in MPSoCs makes behavior much more difficult to describe and verify.

The complexity enabled by memory is embodied in both code and data. For example, the reference implementation for the H.264 codec, a relatively new video compression standard, is about 100,000 lines of C code. Complex applications often require large buffers and intermediate storage. The behavior of these systems cannot be fully described as the sum of small transactions; these systems must be modeled in ways that describe their large-scale, long-term behavior.

Figure 1 shows the results of some network-on-chip experiments performed at Princeton University and NEC. [Xu04]. This plot shows the network traffic over time for a multiprocessor designed to support real-time, high-speed gesture analysis

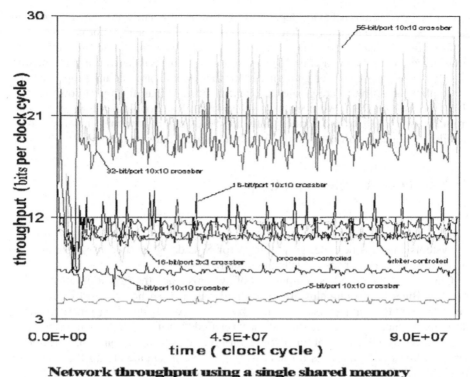

Network throughput using a single shared memory

Fig. 1. Traffic within a network-on-chip (Xu et al. [Xu04] © 2004 IEEE).

[Wol02]. Video computing is often characterized as "streaming" – performing a predictable set of operations on periodic data. This application performs real-time video, but the simulation shows that the system behavior does not fit the stereotype of streaming. This application includes several types of algorithms, ranging from color classification through floating-point hidden Markov model analysis. Several of the phases use control-intensive applications. As a result, the amount of data per frame varies and the times at which the data are produced varies.

The characteristics of modern applications make for several challenges in MPSoC design. First, buffer sizes are harder to predict. Checking for buffer overflow is very important, but the task becomes harder when the amount of data varies considerably during the course of execution. Second, computational loads become harder to predict. This may in some cases lead us to dynamically allocating tasks to processing elements in the MPSoC.

One of the implications of the complex nature of applications is that we have to look at behavior over longer intervals. The large amounts of memory in an MPSoC hold a huge number of states. Transaction-level modeling, while important for verifying elements of system behavior, doesn't really capture all the behavior of a complex system. Applications perform sequences of transactions and the MPSoC hardware and software design must ultimately be verified on that application-level behavior. Some of the verification can be performed on an abstract model of the system, but to the extent that the system behavior depends upon timing, the hardware and software may need to be modeled together to determine both functionality and performance.

Traditionally, hardware and software design have been considered separate. With multiprocessor systems-on-chips, we must learn to design hardware and software together. The chances of designing hardware that doesn't provide the proper features for application software are greater in a multiprocessor than for a traditional embedded processor or DSP. We need to develop design methodologies that let us work from abstract, platform-independent software development environments down to the detailed timing and power consumption of traditional hardware design.

4   Networks of Systems-on-Chips

Systems-on-chips are themselves complex, but we are increasingly connecting together systems-on-chips to create even larger, more complex systems. These networks of systems-on-chips pose design problems for SoC designers because the chip must be verified to work as part of this larger system.

Chips have been used as components of systems since the invention of integrated circuits. But systems-on-chips are increasingly used in ad hoc networks, presenting very different design and verification problems. A fixed system configuration can be designed to meet certain criteria and then verified that it meets those criteria. However, ad hoc systems present much more variety. SoCs may be connected together in large numbers such that it is difficult or impossible to enumerate all the configurations. The SoCs in the network may also receive new software during the operation of the network. The cell phone network is a prime example of this phenomenon: huge numbers of nodes connected in a constantly changing pattern and subject to software changes in the field.

Sensor networks are an emerging example of networks of systems-on-chips. The networking sections of today's sensor networks are complex, offering ad-hoc connectivity, but they often provide only low data rates with simple processing within the sensor network nodes. We should expect to see more sensor networks that perform more processing on higher-rate data, since it is often more power efficient to process data in the field than to transmit it to a central server. As the computations on the nodes become more complex, some of the problems we encounter in MPSoCs – for example, dynamic task allocation becomes even more important.

We need better methods for dealing with networks of SoCs. We need to be able to specify the networks, including what configurations are valid. We must be able to verify the properties of our specifications. And we must be able to verify that our implementations continue to satisfy those properties.

Acknowledgments

This work has been supported in part by the National Science Foundation under grant CCR-0325119.

References

[Jer04] Ahmed Jerraya and Wayne Wolf, eds., *Multiprocessor Systems-on-Chips*, Elsevier, 2004.

[Vor04] http://www.vorbis.com

[Wol02] Wayne Wolf, Burak Ozer, and Tiehan Lv, "Smart cameras as embedded systems," *IEEE Computer*, 35(9) September 2002, pp. 48-53.

[Wol04] Wayne Wolf, "The future of multiprocessor systems-on-chips," in *Proceedings, 41st Annual Design Automation Conference*, ACM Press, 2004, pp. 681-685.

[Xu04] J. Xu, W. Wolf, T. Lv, J. Henkel, and S. Chakradhar, "A case study in networks-on-chip design for embedded video," in *Proceedings, DATE 04*, IEEE Computer Society Press, 2004.

Generating Fast Multipliers
Using Clever Circuits

Mary Sheeran

Chalmers University of Technology
ms@cs.chalmers.se

Abstract. New insights into the general structure of partial product reduction trees are combined with the notion of clever circuits to give a novel method of writing simple but flexible and highly parameterised data-path generators.

1 Introduction

In this work, our original intention was to describe and analyse a number of different multipliers, and to account for the effects of choices about layout and wire length. We concentrated on the central component of most multipliers, the reduction array that converts the partial products into a pair of binary numbers to be added by a final fast adder. To our surprise, we found a very general way to describe a large class of reduction arrays. They all have the form of the triangular array of cells shown in Fig. 3, and varying just two small wiring patterns inside the cells allows us to cover a range of slow and fast multipliers. This insight into the structure of reduction trees in general led us to the idea of building an adaptive reduction array, in which those two small wiring cells are (repeatedly) instantiated to appropriate wiring patterns *during circuit generation*, based on information about delay on the inputs gained by the use of models of the half and full adder cells and of the wires connecting them. This is a neat application of the idea of *clever circuits* [12]. The resulting reduction tree seems to have rather good performance, at least according to our abstract analyses. Much work will need to be done to confirm that the adaptive array is indeed superior to standard arrays. We will need to experiment with different approaches to the layout of the array. Further, we were able to use clever wiring cells also to take account of restrictions in the availability of tracks for cross-cell wiring.

We became increasingly interested in methods of writing simple but powerful circuit *generators* that look exactly like structured circuit *descriptions* but that produce circuits that are adapted to a given context and so are not as regular as might first appear. We believe that the move to deep sub-micron necessitates new design methods in which lower level details are exposed early in the design, while, at the same time, there is a move to design at higher levels of abstraction and with a greater degree of reuse. Thus, methods of getting low level information up through levels of abstraction will become increasingly important. The method of writing generators for adaptive circuits presented here is an approach to this

A.J. Hu and A.K. Martin (Eds.): FMCAD 2004, LNCS 3312, pp. 6–20, 2004.

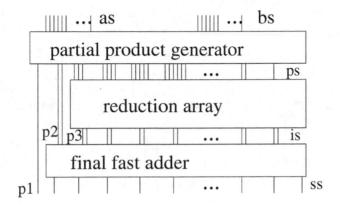

Fig. 1. The structure of a multiplier, as defined in `multBin`

problem. It is presented via a running example, including the actual code of the generators. Readers who are not familiar with Haskell or Lava are referred to the Lava tutorial [4].

2   A General Multiplier

A binary multiplier consists of a partial product generator, a reduction array that reduces the partial products to two bits for each bit-weight, and a final adder that produces the binary result (see Fig. 1). Thus, transcribing from the picture, the top level of a Lava description of a multiplier is

```
multBin comps (as,bs) = p1:ss
   where
      ([p1]:[p2,p3]:ps) = prods_by_weight (as,bs)
      is                = redArray comps  ps
      ss                = binaryAdder     ([p2,p3]:is)
```

Binary numbers are represented by lists, least significant bit first. (In Haskell, [] is the empty list, [a,b,c] is a list of length 3, and (a:as) is a list whose first element is a and the remainder of which is the list as.) The three equations correspond to the three components of the multiplier, and indicate what their inputs and outputs are. For example, the partial product generator has as inputs the two binary numbers to be multiplied, least significant bit first, and produces a list of lists of bits. The first of these is of weight one and is the singleton list [p1]. The second is of weight two and contains two bits: [p2,p3]. The remainder, ps, is a list of lists of increasing weight, and is input to the reduction tree. This description works only for 3 by 3 bit multiplication and above. The comps parameter to both the multiplier contains a tuple of the building blocks, such as full- and half-adders, used to construct the multiplier. We postpone the decision as to what exactly it should contain.

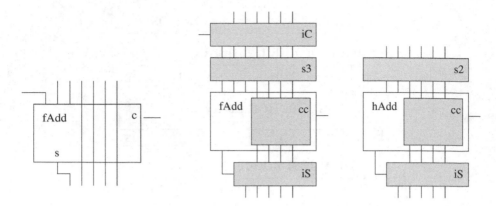

Fig. 2. (a) A specific fcell (b) A general fcell showing building blocks (c) hcell

In this paper, we concentrate entirely on the design of the reduction array. It is implemented as a linear array (a `row`) of `compress` cells, each of which reduces the partial products at its bit-weight to two.

```
redArray comps ps = is
  where (is,[]) = row (compress comps) ([],ps)
```

Carries flow from left to right through the array, with an empty list of carries entering on the left and exiting on the right. Here, again, the `comps` parameter will later contain a tuple of building blocks. That we use a linear array means that we are considering the so-called column-compression multipliers. However, as we shall see, this class of multipliers is large, encompassing a great variety of well-known structures.

It remains to design the `compress` cell. It takes a pair of inputs, consisting of a list of carries on the left, and a list of partial products at the top. It should produce two bits at the bottom, and on the right a list of carries to be passed to the next column, which has weight one higher. All of the input bits to `compress` have the same weight. It must produce two bits of the same weight, and any necessary carries.

If we had a building block that reduced the number of product bits by one, with a carry-in and a carry-out, we would be well on the way. An example of such a `fcell` (in this case with six inputs at the top and five outputs at the bottom) is shown in Fig. 2(a). It is a kind of generalised full-adder, made from a full-adder and some wiring. Fig. 2(a) shows a specific instance, but we can make a general `fcell` by parameterising the component not only on the full adder but also on the wiring, as shown in Fig. 2(b).

The wiring component `iC`, for *insert Carry*, determines how the carry input, which comes from the left, is placed among the $n + 1$ outputs of the `iC` block. If it is placed in the leftmost position, then that part of the cell looks like the particular cell shown in Figure 2(a). But there are many other choices, as we shall see later. Similarly, there are many choices for how the *insert Sum* component,

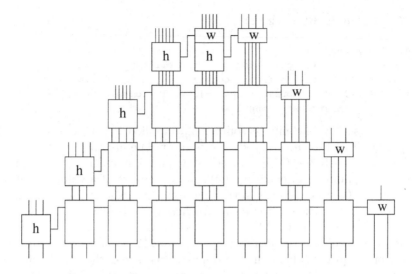

Fig. 3. The reduction array for 6 by 6 bit multiplication

iS, can look. In experimenting with wire-aware design, we have found that it makes sense to include *all* of the wiring as explicit components. One should think of tiling the plane, not only when building regular arrays of cells, but even inside the cells. So, we add two further components. s3 divides $n + 3$ wires into 3 that are passed to the full-adder and n that cross it. cc is the wiring by means of which those values cross the cell. fcell is defined using layout-oriented combinators, following the pattern shown in Figure 2(b).

A column of fcells is exactly what we want for compress in the special case where the number of carries is exactly two less than the number of partial product bits. Then, the fcells, reduce the partial products to two, one bit at a time. If this difference in length is greater than 2, we can rescue the situation by topping a recursive call of compress with a generalised half-adder cell that does not have a carry-in, using the combinator |-. The half-adder cell is called hcell, and is illustrated in Fig. 2(c). The hcell reduces the length difference by one, and can be thought of as handing the remaining problem to the smaller recursive call below it (see also the columns on the left in Fig. 3). It uses the same iS, iC and cc cells as the full-adder, and needs an s2 cell that passes two of its inputs to the half-adder. (For a more precise analysis, it would be better to have different building blocks for the half- and full-adder, but we choose to reuse building blocks for simplicity.)

On the other hand, if the length difference is less than two, removing the topmost carry input and placing it among the partial products, using the *insert Carry* wiring that we have already seen adds two to the length difference. The wcell selects this piece of wiring from the tuple of building blocks. The recursive call that is placed below wcell again takes care of solving the remaining problem.

```
wcell (hAdd,fAdd,iS,iC,cc,s2,s3) = iC

compress comps (as,bs)
   | (diff >  2)  = (compress comps |- hcell comps)   (as,bs)
   | (diff == 2)  = column (fcell comps)              (as,bs)
   | (diff <  2)  = (compress comps -| wcell comps)   (as,bs)
  where diff = length bs - length as
```

Fig. 3 shows a row of compress components, applied to partial products of the shape produced by the partial product generator. The instances of compress on the left have a length difference of three (between the number of partial product inputs and the number of carry inputs), and so consist of a column of fcells below a hcell. (Unmarked cells in the diagram are fcells; those marked h are hcells, and those marked w are wcells.) Then, there is one instance where the difference is one, so it is wcell above a recursive call in which the difference is 3, that is is a column of fcells topped by hcell. Finally, there are several instances of compress where the difference is zero, and these are columns of fcell topped by wcell. This triangular shape contains the minimum hardware (in terms of half- and full-adder cells) needed to perform the reduction of partial products. To multiply two n-bit binary numbers, one needs $(n-1)(n-2)$ half- or full-adder cells in the reduction array, $n-1$ of them half-adders.

A row of compress cells can adapt itself to the shape of its inputs, as the definition of compress causes the right number of full or half-adders to be placed in each column. So such a row can function as a multi-operand adder, or function correctly with different encodings of the inputs. For the particular case of the reduction tree for a standard multiplier, there is no need to define a special triangular connection pattern to achieve the desired triangular shape. Such a specialised connection pattern would have lacked the flexibility of this approach.

A reduction array defined by the function redArray is also very general in another sense. By varying iS and iC wiring cells in the tuple of building blocks called comps, a great variety of different multipliers can be constructed, ranging from simple slow arrays to fast logarithmic Dadda-like trees. This surprisingly simple but general description of reduction arrays is, as far as we know, new. We had not expected to find such regularity even among the so-called irregular multipliers.

3 Making Specific Reduction Arrays

A reduction array built using the function redArray is characterised by the tuple of building blocks: (hAdd,fAdd,iS,iC,cc,s2,s3) that is the comps parameter (see Figs. 2 and 3). For now, we fix cc to be the identity function, and s2 and s3 to be the functions sep2 = splitAt 2 and sep3 = splitAt 3 that split the list without performing any permutation. What we will vary between multipliers are the iS and iC wiring cells. Their role is to insert a single bit into a list of bits, to give a new list whose length is one longer than that of the original input list. The full-adder or half-adder that consumes some of the resulting list always works from the beginning, that is from the left in Fig. 2. So by choosing where to place the single bit, we also choose where in the array it will be processed.

3.1 A Simple Reduction Array

If we place the single bit at the beginning of the list for both the sum and the carry case, the choice shown in Fig. 2(a), we make a reduction array that consumes carries and sums as soon as possible. A carry-out is consumed by the next rightmost cell, and a sum output is consumed by the next cell down in the column. This is the reduction array that forms the basis of the standard linear array multiplier. It has only nearest neighbour connections between the full and half adder cells [6].

3.2 The Regular Reduction Tree Multiplier

Postponing sums, by choosing iS to be toEnd, the function that places a value at the end of a list, but consuming carries immediately as before gives the Regular Reduction Tree multiplier proposed by Eriksson et al. [7].

3.3 A Dadda Multiplier

A better choice, though, is to postpone both sums and carries, using the toEnd wiring function for both iS and iC. This gives a Dadda-like multiplier with both good performance and pleasing regularity. It is very similar to the modified Dadda multiplier proposed by Eriksson [6], but adds a simple strategy for layout.

3.4 A Variety of Arrays

If carries are consumed not in the current cell but in the cell below, and if sums are consumed as soon as possible, we get a variant on the carry-save array, called CCSA [6]. Similarly, other choices of the wiring cells give different arrays. We could easily describe yet more reduction arrays if we divided the triangular shape into two, roughly down the middle, and used different versions of the wiring cells in each half. Instead, we turn our attention to the problem of estimating gate and wire delays in data-paths like the reduction arrays.

4 Calculating Gate Delays

The description of the array is parameterised on the tuple of building blocks. This allows us to calculate gate delays simply by simulating a circuit made from versions of those cells that, instead of operating on bits, operate on integers representing delays. The non-standard cells model the delay behaviour of the real cells. For example, the delay-model of the half-adder is

```
halfAddI (as, bs, ac, bc) [a1,a2] = [s,cout]
    where
    s    = max (as+a1) (bs+a2)
    cout = max (ac+a1) (bc+a2)
```

It has four parameters representing the delay between each input and the sum and each input and the carry. The delay version of the full-adder is similar. Here, `max` and `+` are overloaded functions that work on both Haskell integers and the integers that flow in circuits; as a result, `halfAddI` is also overloaded. A standard approach to the analysis of partial product reduction trees is to count delays in terms of *xor* gate delay equivalents [11]. For the half-adder, this would give cross-cell delays of (1,1,0.5,0.5), for instance. Since we will simulate circuits carrying delay values, we are restricted to integer delays, and so must multiply all of these numbers by 10. Thus, we define half- and full-adder delay estimation circuits as

```
hI as = halfAddI (10,10,5,5) as
fI as = fullAddI (20,20,10,10,10,10) as

Main> fI [0,5,5]
[25,15]
```

`hI` and `fI` are again overloaded to work both at the Haskell level and the circuit level. This overloading will prove useful later, when these delay-modelling cells will be used first at the circuit level, that is during simulation, and then at the Haskell level, that is during generation. This is a standard and simple delay model, giving worst-case delays without taking account of false paths. For the moment, it is sufficient for our purposes, though in future work we will want to look at more complex delay estimation.

To make a delay estimation version of a reduction array, we simply replace the half- and full-adder in its component tuple by `hI` and `fI`. We leave the wiring cells alone; they are polymorphic and so can operate on either bits or integers as required. To find the gate delay leading to each output, we feed zeros into the resulting circuit, and simulate. The function `ppzs n` produces a list of lists of zeros of the shape expected by the array.

```
dDadG n = simulate (redArray (hI,fI,toEnd,toEnd,id,sep2,sep3)) (ppzs n)

Main> dDadG 16
[[0,10],[5,20],[20,30],[30,40],[40,50],[50,50],[50,60],[60,70],[70,70],
[70,70],[70,80],[70,80],[80,90],[90,90],[90,90],[90,90],[90,90],[90,90],
[80,90],[80,80],[70,80],[70,80],[70,70],[60,70],[60,60],[50,60],[50,50],
[40,20],[0,20]]
```

The Dadda array has a maximum delay of 9 xor-gate delays at size 16 by 16. By comparison, the linear array (from section 3.1) of the same size has a maximum delay of 41 xor-gate delays. The next step is to take account of wire delays.

5   Taking Account of Wire Delays

The wires whose delays are of interest to us are those that cross the cells, that is they correspond to the `cc` parameter in the tuple of functional and wiring components (see Fig. 2). So, in our delay calculation, we can just replace this parameter, which was the identity function before, with a function that adds a fixed value `d` to the incoming delay. The gate delay models are `hI` and `fI`, as before. However, this is not quite right. When we check the various delay profiles using this approach, we find that *all* of the array topologies incur long wire delays. Why is this? It is because our triangular shaped array takes all of the input partial products at the top, and allows them to flow down to the cell that processes them. So, for example, in the linear array, there is a long wire carrying a partial product bit right from the top of the array to the bottom. But the delay on these partial product carrying wires is not of interest to us in the current analysis (though we would want to count these delays if we implemented the array in exactly this form). The standard approach to comparing reduction arrays in the literature is to ignore the problem of getting each partial product bit to the cell that processes it. In real arrays, the partial product production is typically mixed with the reduction array, and the problem of distributing the multiplier inputs to the right positions is handled separately. We would like, at a later date, to tackle the analysis of such a mixed partial product production and reduction array, including all wire delays. Here, though, we will analyse just the reduction array, and will count delays only in the inter-cell wires, that is the sum and carry wires that run across cells from top to bottom.

To achieve this, we tag each wire that might contribute delays in the simulation with a Boolean, indicating whether it is a partial product or is an output from a full- or half-adder. The partial product inputs are tagged with `True`. Those wires do not contribute to the delay, while wires tagged with False do.

```
wireIB d (m,b) = if b then (m,b) else (m+d,b)

cross d = map (wireIB d)
```

So now, in the tuple used in delay simulation, we can replace the `cc` wiring cell by `cross d`. As a result, the half- and full-adder cells must also change, to be able to accommodate the new Boolean tags. For instance, to make the hybrid full-adder circuit, `fIB`, we combine `fI` with an abstract half-adder, `fB`, that takes Booleans as input and outputs `[False, False]`, indicating that the corresponding wires do not carry partial product bits. The two full-adder variants operate completely independently, one working on delay values, and the other on Boolean tags.

```
fIB as = (fI // fB) as

Main> fIB [(0,True),(5,True),(5,True)]
[(25,False),(15,False)]
```

The hybrid half-adder, `hIB`, is constructed similarly. The `sep2` and `sep3` wiring cells are polymorphic, and so do not need to change, even though the types of values that flow along their wires are now different. To study the gate and wire delay behaviour of a particular array, we construct a component tuple with `hIB` in the half-adder position, `fIB` in the full-adder position, and `cross d` as the cross-cell wiring. The necessary Boolean tags are inserted and removed by the functions `markTrue` and `unmark`, while `getmax` returns the largest delay. For larger sizes, the effects of wire delay become significant. For 53 bit multiplication, the maximum delays for the Dadda reduction array range from 15 xor-gates for zero cross-cell wire delay to 32 for a wire delay of 4.

```
maxDel f n = simulate (markTrue ->- f ->- unmark ->- getmax) (ppzs n)

mDad d = maxDel (redArray(hIB, fIB, toEnd, toEnd, cross d, sep2, sep3))

Main> [(i,mDad i 53) | i <- [0..4]]
[(0,150),(1,189),(2,230),(3,275),(4,320)]
```

It would be interesting to develop further analyses to help in understanding the different delay behaviours of the multipliers, as well as to repeat these calculations with different settings of the cell and wire delays, for various sizes, and perhaps in a more symbolic way. Here, we continue our series of multiplier descriptions by considering a multiplier in which the wiring depends, in a systematic way, on the estimated delay in the cells and the wires.

6   A Cleverer Multiplier

In simpler circuit descriptions, it is usual to use a Haskell integer variable to control the size of the generated circuit. *Clever circuits* is a more sophisticated programming idiom in which Haskell values that are more closely tied to the circuit structure are used to guide circuit generation [12]. In the previous section, we used this idea to build a circuit to perform delay calculations. The Boolean tags were what we call *shadow values* – Haskell-level values that were used to guide the generation of the delay-estimation circuit. The shadow values could be seen as controlling the production of a net-list containing wire-modelling components that add d to their inputs as well as fI and hI components. This ensured that only certain wires of the original circuit contributed to the delay estimation.

Here, we apply the same idea one step earlier, during the initial circuit generation. In this case, though, we use clever circuits to control the generation of *wiring* rather than of components. We have shown how multipliers can be parameterised on the iS and iC cells, and we made various decisions about their design, always choosing a fixed piece of wiring for each of these cells, for each array. But why not make these cells react to the delays on their inputs during circuit generation, and configure themselves accordingly, resulting in possibly different choices throughout the multiplier? This appealing idea is similar to that used in the TDM multiplier, and in related work [11, 13, 1]. Here, we show how well it fits into our general reduction array description, giving an adaptive array that can depend not only on gate delays (as in the TDM), but also on delays in the wires crossing cells.

The first step is to make a cell that becomes either the identity on two bits, or a crossing (or swap), depending on the values on its shadow inputs. If the predicate p holds of x and y, the swap is performed; otherwise the output is the same as the input.

```
cswap p ((a,x),(b,y)) = if (p x y) then ((b,y),(a,x)) else ((a,x),(b,y))
```

Now, during circuit generation, if `cswap` receives, on its shadow inputs, two values for which p holds, then it becomes a crossing, otherwise it is the identity. And once the circuit has been generated, all record of the shadow values that influenced its shape have disappeared.

The clever wiring cells should (like `iC` and `iS`) have a pair of inputs, consisting of a single value and a list. We assume that the list of inputs is in increasing order of delay. Then, we want to insert the single value into the correct position in the list, so that the resulting list is also in increasing order of delay, and so presents the wires with the least delay for use by the next half- or full-adder. We do this using a row of `cswap` components, and then sticking the second output of the row onto the end of the first, using append right (`apr`):

```
cInsert = row (cswap p) ->- apr
  where p (g1,b1) (g2,b2) = g1 > (g2::Int)
```

This is similar to the row of comparators that is the insertion component of insertion sort. The predicate p compares the integer delay values. Depending on the delays of the input wires, various wirings can be formed, ranging from the simplest `apl`, in which no swaps are made, to `toEnd`, in which all the possible swaps are made, placing the single input at the end of the list. The important point is that the wiring adapts to its position in the array, based on the delay information that it receives during circuit generation. We replace `iS` and `iC` by `cInsert`.

What remains to be done is to make shadow versions of all of the other components, and to combine them with their concrete counterparts. These shadow versions must work on Haskell-level (integer, Boolean) pairs. We have, however, already constructed `hIB` and `fIB` cells that work on such pairs; we simply reuse them here (exploiting the fact that `hI` can also work on Haskell integers).

```
adapt (hAdd, fAdd, cc) (d,pds)
  = mmark pds ->- redArray (hAdd // hIB,
                            fAdd // fIB,
                            cInsert, cInsert,
                            cc // cross d,
                            sep2, sep3)  ->- unmark
```

`adapt` defines the adaptive reduction array. It is just a call of the `redArray` function with a suitable tuple of building blocks. The `mmark pds` function sets up the shadow values correctly, based on the input delay profile pds, and `unmark` removes the shadow values on the outputs. Thus, `adapt` is parameterised not only on the half-adder, full-adder and the cross-cell wiring, but also on the delay d in that wiring and on the delay profile of the incoming partial products, pds. The latter two parameters influence the formation of the circuit, that is they control exactly what wiring pattern each instance of `cInsert` becomes in the final circuit. Each sublist of pds is assumed to be in delay sorted order (and this could, if necessary, be achieved by further use of clever wiring).

If, during generation, we choose the cross-cell wire delay to be zero, and the input delay profile to be all zeros, we get a basic TDM-style multiplier [11].

Measuring both gate and wire delays, with a cross-cell delay of 2, for 16 by 16 bit multiplication, the TDM array has a maximum delay of 116 units (where 10 units is one xor-gate delay). If the same wire delay is used during the generation of the array, the maximum delay reduces to 100. We call the resulting array wire-adaptive. For comparison, the modified Dadda array has a maximum gate and wire delay of 122 units for this size. For 64 bit multiplication, the delays for the wire-adaptive, TDM and Dadda arrays are 234, 258 and 266 respectively, while the corresponding figures for 80 bits are 270, 300 and 302. So it makes sense to take account of wire delay while generating reduction arrays. Making use of the input delay profile during circuit generation further improves the resulting array.

7   Taking Account of Constraints on Available Tracks

In real circuits, there are typically constraints on the number of tracks available for cross-cell wiring. Here, again, we are concerned only with the sum and carry wires, and we do not consider the problem of routing the partial product wires to the correct positions. The circuits that we have seen so far took no account of constraints on wiring tracks. Here, we demonstrate the versatility of our approach to writing array generators by incorporating such a constraint.

In each cell, we would like to limit the number of sum and carry wires that can cross the cell to be a maximum of tr, the number of available tracks. This can be done by using clever wiring in new versions of the s2 and s3 wiring cells (see Fig. 2). Let us consider the case of s3. When the number of sum or carry wires crossing the cell below it is in danger of becoming too large, fcon tr moves one or two such wires leftwards, as necessary, so that they are consumed by the cell, instead of crossing it. The function move (m,n) p ensures that there are at least n elements satisfying p in the first output list, which should be of length m. The new version of s2 is hcon tr, which is similar to fcon tr.

```
fcon tr as
  | (1 <  tr+1)  = move (3,0) p as
  | (1 == tr+1)  = move (3,1) p as
  | (1 == tr+2)  = move (3,2) p as
 where
   l = length (filter p as)
   p (c,(i,b)) = not b
```

adaptC is the same as adapt, apart from the addition of the tr parameter and the replacement of sep2 and sep3 by the two adaptive wiring cells, hcon tr and fcon tr, in the tuple of building blocks. The result is a remarkably powerful reduction array generator. Varying the available number of tracks gives us even more variety in the arrays produced, and allows us to trade off delay against wiring resources. The function mAdCon takes as parameters the number of cross-cell tracks, the wire delay to use during generation and simulation, and the size of the two numbers being multiplied; it returns the maximum delay on an output in the reduction tree, for zero input delay. For 18 bits, and ignoring wire delays, having zero tracks gives a linear array with 42 xor-gate delays, and the delay decreases as more tracks are made available, reaching the minimum 9 gate delays for 7 or more tracks.

```
mAdCon tr d1 d2 n = maxDel (adaptC tr (hIB,fIB,cross d2) (d1,pps 0 n)) n

Main> [(i,mAdCon i 0 0 18) | i <- [0..8]]
[(0,420),(1,235),(2,155),(3,125),(4,110),(5,100),(6,100),(7,90),(8,90)]
```

Finer delay modelling, for example the use of calls to external analysis tools, would give better multiplier performance. Here, we assumed that delay increases linearly with wire length. We will investigate a model in which delay is proportional to the square of the length. This would be easy to incorporate. We will also consider the automatic generation of buffers on long wires.

8   Related Work

The most widely used partial product reduction tree is the Wallace tree [15]. It can be thought of as being made from horizontal blocks that are carry-save adders, rather than from vertical compress blocks as here. However, the Dadda tree [5], particularly in the modified form shown here, gives comparable performance in both delay and power [6].

Luk and Vuillemin presented, analysed and implemented a family of fast recursively-defined multiplication algorithms [8]. One of these is a linear array of bit-convolver circuits, where the bit-convolver has the same function as our compress cells. The bit-convolvers were recursively defined as binary trees, and laid out with the root in the middle and the two smaller trees above and below it (as is standard in adder trees). This corresponds, also, to implementing the entire multiplier as a rectangular array with two half-sized recursive calls sandwiching the final adder. The corresponding implementation compared well with Wallace trees for smaller sizes. The emphasis in the work of Luk and Vuillemin is also on the generation of multipliers from readable descriptions containing some geometric information. The importance of parameterised generators is stressed, and formal verification (of fixed size circuits) is also considered. This work is an important inspiration for ours. An adaptive tree should be faster than a static binary one, but it may be that we need to lay out the tree with the root in the middle. This needs to be investigated in future work.

The original TDM multiplier generation method considers gate delay in choosing how to wire up a partial product reduction array to minimise maximum gate delay [11]. When our adaptive array works with the standard gate delay model and zero input and wire delay, it is mimicking exactly the original TDM method, and achieves identical gate delays. The original TDM uses what the authors call a 3-greedy algorithm; the three fastest wires are chosen for connection to the next full-adder. Like our adaptive array, the basic TDM method can be adapted to take account of the input delay profile. Later work showed that the 3-greedy method produces near-optimal results for maximum delay, but that a more sophisticated 2-greedy method produces better delay profiles because it allows a more global optimisation [13]. The analysis and the new generation algorithms are elegant, but the resulting method uses expensive search, which neither the basic TDM nor our approach requires. We are interested in seeing how far we can get with symbolic evaluation, which requires no search and so scales up well.

The TDM method and its more sophisticated successors do not currently take account of wire delay and the authors mention that this is a natural next step. The methods do not either take account of constraints on tracks. They could, presumably, be adapted to do so. Al-Twaijry et al present a partial product reduction tree generator that aims to take account of both wire delay and constraints on available tracks [1]. This work seems close to ours. The big difference is in the method of writing the generators. Ours are short, and retain the structure of the array, with parameterisation coming from local changes inside the cells, whereas the standard approach is to write C code that generates the required net-list. We are hopeful that our generators will be more amenable to formal verification.

Our approach can be seen as deciding on the placement of the hcells, fcells and wcells in advance, and then making a multiplier with the required properties by forming the wiring inside those cells during generation, making use of context information such as input delay and constraints on tracks. Thus, it is important to keep that placement when producing the final circuit. Some approaches aim, instead, to produce unplaced net-lists that will give short wires when given to a synthesis tool that does the placement [14]. Both our approach and the TDM methods use half- and full-adders as the building blocks. The work of Um and Kim uses entire carry-save adders as building blocks, arguing that this gives more regular interconnections. A final adjustment phase aims to get some of the advantages of using a finer granularity. Our approach is very different because we aim to give the writer of the generator control over placement, and thus over degree of regularity. We are not restricted to the triangular placement described here, and intend to experiment with other layouts.

To our knowledge, the best approach to the design of reduction trees under constraints on tracks is based on the over-turned stairs (OS) trees [10]. The OS trees are a sequence of increasingly sophisticated recursive constructions of delay-efficient trees of carry-save adders that are designed to minimise cross-cell tracks. Although the method of counting cross-cell tracks is not identical to ours (since we consider a carry-in that is not used by the current cell to cross the cell), we believe that our simple constrained reduction trees have longer delay than the reported results (which give only gate delays) for higher order OS trees for larger sizes. We will consider ways to improve our algorithm, and will do a more detailed comparison.

9   Discussion

We have given a short parameterised structural description of a partial product reduction tree made from hcells, fcells and wcells (see Figs. 2 and 3). We then showed how a great variety of multipliers can be obtained by varying the building blocks (iS, iC etc.) of those cells, while retaining the same overall structure. First, we made standard arrays, including a modified version of the Dadda tree. Because of the surprising regularity of the Dadda array, a colleague, Henrik Eriksson, was able to lay it out with ease in a manual design flow. The measured results for delay and power consumption are promising and a paper is in preparation. It is usual to dismiss both Dadda and Wallace trees as difficult to lay out. We have shown that a Dadda tree can be made regular. In Lava, we performed a simple delay estimation on the various arrays by using non-standard interpretation. We replaced circuit components, including wires, by non-standard versions that estimated their delay, and then performed simulation.

The next step was to use the same kind of delay modelling *during circuit generation*. The idea of *clever circuits*, that is circuits that can adapt to context information, was combined with the delay modelling to control the production of *wiring cells*. This allowed us to produce fast arrays that can adapt to gate and wire delay, and to the delay profile of their inputs. Next, we showed that further use of clever wiring allowed the generator to adapt to constraints on wiring resources. A very high degree of parameterisation is achieved by *local* changes in the cells. This was made possible by the initial insights into the general structure of reduction arrays. The result is a powerful circuit generator that looks exactly like a structural description of a simple multiplier, and so is very small. We consider this to be a very promising approach to the writing of data-path generators. The combination of clever circuits with the connection pattern approach that we have long used in Lava seems to give a sudden increase in expressive power. Here, we used clever wiring to get parameterisation, but in other applications, we will need to control the choice of components, or even of recursive decompositions. The latter arises, for example, in the generation of parallel prefix circuits, where different recursive decompositions give different area, delay and fanout tradeoffs. We are currently investigating ways to choose recursion patterns dynamically during circuit generation, partly because we plan to use these methods to make the fast adder that is needed to complete a multiplier design. Such an adder must adapt to the delay profile of the reduction tree that feeds it.

We would like to verify the generators once and for all, for all sizes and parameters. Our hope is to be able to verify a generator as though it were a circuit description, exploiting the fact that the generator is structured as a circuit (and is short and simple). To do this, we expect to build on the seminal work by Hunt and his co-workers on the use and verification of circuit generators [3] and on recent work on the verification of parameterised circuits [2]. We will probably have to develop verification techniques that are specialised to our style of writing circuit generators. We are interested in investigating the use of a first order theorem prover to automatically prove the base case and step of the necessary inductive proofs.

The ideas presented here could be used to implement module generators that provide designers with access to a library of highly flexible adaptive data-paths, without demanding that the designer construct the modules himself. This would allow the incorporation of these ideas into more standard design flows. This vision is compatible with the timing-driven module-based design flow that was outlined recently by Mo and Brayton [9].

Our next step will be to implement and analyse a fast adaptive multiplier in our Wired system, in which geometry is considered, and the exact placement of each wire is accounted for.

Acknowledgements

This work is supported by the Semiconductor Research Corporation (task id. 1041.001), and by the Swedish funding agency Vetenskapsrådet. We gratefully acknowledge an equipment grant from Intel Corporation.

References

1. H. Al-Twaijry and M. Aloqeely: An algorithmic approach to building datapath multipliers using (3,2) counters, *IEEE Computer Society Workshop on VLSI*, IEEE Press, Apr. 2000.
2. C. Berg, C. Jacobi and D. Kroening: Formal verification of a basic circuits library, *IASTED International Conference on Applied Informatics*, ACTA Press, 2001.
3. B. Brock and W. A. Hunt Jr.: The DUAL-EVAL Hardware Description Language and Its Use in the Formal Specification and Verification of the FM9001 Microprocessor. *Formal Methods in System Design*, 11(1), 1997.
4. K. Claessen and M. Sheeran: A Tutorial on Lava: A Hardware Description and Verification System, Apr. 2000. http://www.cs.chalmers.se/~koen/Lava/tutorial.ps
5. L. Dadda: Some Schemes for Parallel Adders, *Acta Frequenza*, vol. 34, no. 5, May 1965.
6. H. Eriksson: Efficient Implementation and Analysis of CMOS Arithmetic Circuits, PhD. Thesis, Chalmers University of Technology, Dec. 2003.
7. H. Eriksson, P. Larsson-Edefors and W.P. Marnane: A Regular Parallel Multiplier Which Utilizes Multiple Carry-Propagate Adders, *Int. Symp. on Circuits and Systems*, 2001.
8. W. K. Luk and J. E. Vuillemin: Recursive Implementation of Optimal Time VLSI Integer Multipliers, *VLSI'83*, Elsevier Science Publishes B.V. (North-Holland), Aug. 1983.
9. F. Mo and R.K. Brayton: A Timing-Driven Module-Based Chip Design Flow, *41st Design Automation Conference*, ACM Press, 2004.
10. Z.-J. Mou and F. Jutand: "Overturned-Stairs" Adder Trees and Multiplier Design, *IEEE Trans. on Computers*, Vol. 41, No. 8, Aug. 1992.
11. V.G. Oklobdzija, D. Villeger and S.S. Liu: A Method for Speed Optimized Partial Product Reduction and Generation of Fast Parallel Multipliers Using an Algorithmic Approach. *IEEE Trans. on Computers*, vol. 45, no. 3, Mar. 1996.
12. M. Sheeran: Finding regularity: describing and analysing circuits that are not quite regular, *12th Advanced Research Working Conference on Correct Hardware Design and Verification Methods, CHARME*, LNCS 2860, Springer-Verlag, 2003.
13. P.F. Stelling, C.U. Martel, V.G. Oklobdzija and R. Ravi: Optimal Circuits for Parallel Multipliers, *IEEE Trans. on Computers*, vol. 47, no. 3, Mar. 1998.
14. J. Um and T. Kim: Synthesis of Arithmetic Circuits Considering Layout Effects, *IEEE Trans. on Computer-Aided Design of Integrated Circuits and Systems*, vol. 22, no. 11, Nov. 2003.
15. C. S. Wallace: A suggestion for a fast multiplier, *IEEE Trans. on Computers*, EC-13, 2, Feb. 1964.

Verification of Analog and Mixed-Signal Circuits Using Hybrid System Techniques*

Thao Dang, Alexandre Donzé, and Oded Maler

VERIMAG
Centre Equation, 2 avenue de Vignate
38610 Gières, France
{tdang,donze,maler}@imag.fr

Abstract. In this paper we demonstrate a potential extension of formal verification methodology in order to deal with time-domain properties of analog and mixed-signal circuits whose dynamic behavior is described by differential algebraic equations. To model and analyze such circuits under all possible input signals and all values of parameters, we build upon two techniques developed in the context of hybrid (discrete-continuous) control systems. First, we extend our algorithm for approximating sets of reachable sets for dense-time continuous systems to deal with differential algebraic equations (DAEs) and apply it to a biquad low-pass filter. To analyze more complex circuits, we resort to bounded horizon verification. We use optimal control techniques to check whether a Δ-Σ modulator, modeled as a discrete-time hybrid automaton, admits an input sequence of bounded length that drives it to saturation.

1 Introduction

Formal verification has become part of the development cycle of digital circuits. Its advantage relative to more traditional simulation methods lies in its *exhaustiveness*: It can guarantee that a system behaves correctly in the presence of *all* its possible inputs, whose number can be infinite or too large to be covered by individual simulations. Of course, this advantage does not come for free and verification algorithms are more complex and costly than simple simulation. The extension of verification methodology to deal with analog and mixed-signal circuits is far from being straightforward due to the following reason. Digital circuits are modeled as discrete event dynamical systems (automata, transition systems) where the inputs are sequences of binary values, and the behaviors of the circuit induced by these inputs are binary sequences corresponding to paths in the transition graph. Hence digital verification can be realized using graph search algorithms. In contrast, the mathematical model of an analog circuit is

---

* This work was partially supported by the European Community projects IST-2001-33520 CC (Control and Computation) and IST-2003-507219 PROSYD (Property-based System Design) and by the US Army Research Office (ARO) contract no. DAAD19-01-1-0485.

A.J. Hu and A.K. Martin (Eds.): FMCAD 2004, LNCS 3312, pp. 21–36, 2004.

that of a continuous dynamical system defined typically by differential algebraic equations where inputs are real-valued signals defined over the real time axis, and the behaviors they induce are trajectories in the continuous state space of the system.

A typical verification task is to prove that a circuit behaves correctly for all possible input signals and that none of them drives the system into a bad state, for example a state where one of the components reaches saturation. Even if we are satisfied with checking the circuit against a *finite* number of typical input signals, something that can be done using numerical simulation, we still have a problem because of the possible variations in system parameters which are determined only *after* low-level synthesis is complete. To account for such variations during high-level design, symbolic analysis methods that compute symbolic expressions characterizing the behavior of a circuit have been developed and successfully applied to linear or linearized circuits [14]. Extensions of these methods to non-linear circuits are mainly based on simplification and reduction to linear or weakly non-linear systems, which are often limited by accuracy trade-offs (see, for example, [32, 31]). Consequently, numerical simulation with a finite number of input signals is the commonly used validation tool, albeit its inadequacy for systems with under-specified parameters.

In this paper we focus on verifying *time-domain properties*[1] of analog and mixed-signal circuits with dynamics described by a system of differential algebraic equations with parameters. To analyze such a circuit under all possible input signals and parameter values, we use techniques developed in the context of hybrid (discrete-continuous) control systems (see the conference proceedings [17, 25, 2] for a sample of recent hybrid systems research). In particular we extend the forward reachability analysis technique that we have developed for linear [5] and non-linear [4] *ordinary* differential equations to deal with differential *algebraic* equations. The case of mixed-signal circuits is investigated through the modeling and analysis of a Δ-Σ modulator, a widely used circuit, for which stability analysis remains a challenging problem [29, 20, 12]. We tackle this problem using the approach advocated in [8] for the verification discrete-time hybrid systems. The idea is to formulate bounded horizon reachability as a hybrid constrained optimization problem that can be solved by techniques such as mixed-integer linear programming (MILP), in the same sense that bounded verification of digital systems can be reduced to solving a Boolean satisfiability (SAT) problem.

There have been several previous works on formal verification of analog circuits (see [22, 15, 19, 27] and references there in). The work closest to this paper is [22, 19], in which an analog system is approximated by a discrete system in which classical model-checking algorithms can be applied. The discrete system is obtained by partitioning the state space into boxes (each of which corresponds to a state of the discrete model). In [19] the transition relation is determined by reachability relation between the boxes which is approximated by simulating trajectories from some test points in each box.

---

[1] Frequency-domain properties which are often used in analog design are outside the scope of this paper. Properties used in digital verification, such as those specified in *temporal logic* are, using this terminology, time-domain properties.

The rest of the paper is organized as follows. In Section 2 we present our approach to the verification of non-linear analog circuits using reachability computation for differential algebraic equations. The approach is then illustrated with a low-pass filter circuit. In Section 3 we formulate the bounded horizon verification problem for a mixed-signal Δ-Σ modulator and solve it using an MILP solver. Some discussions and future research directions close the paper.

2   Verification of Non-linear Analog Circuits

2.1   Approach

Mathematically, the behavior of a non-linear analog circuit can be described by a set of differential algebraic equations (DAE):

$$F(x(t), \dot{x}(t), u(t), p) = 0, \tag{1}$$

where $x \in \mathbb{R}^n$ denotes the state variables (internal voltages, currents, and outputs), $\dot{x}$ denotes their time derivatives, $p \in P \subset \mathbb{R}^m$ is the parameter vector, and $u : \mathbb{R}^+ \to U$ is the input signal. We assume a set $\mathcal{U}$ of admissible input signals consisting of piecewise-continuous functions taking values in a bounded and convex set $U \subset \mathbb{R}^l$. In this model the input is uncertain, which allows one to model external disturbance and noise. A parameter can be a resistor value, a transistor saturation current, etc. The equations (1) result from applying Kirchhoff laws to the whole circuit and the characteristics equations to the basic elements. Such circuit equations can be automatically generated by techniques such as Modified Nodal Analysis (MNA) [13].

To verify time-domain properties of the circuit, such as those related to the transient behavior, one needs to characterize the set of solutions of (1) under all possible inputs $u(\cdot)$ and all parameter values p. For reachability properties (the circuit never reaches a bad state), it suffices to compute the set of states reachable by all possible trajectories of the system that we define formally below.

We denote by $\gamma(t, x_0, u(\cdot), p)$ the value at time t of the solution of (1) with the initial condition $x(0) = x_0$ under the input signal $u(\cdot) \in \mathcal{U}$ and a parameter $p \in P$. Given a set of initial conditions X_0 and $T > 0$, the reachable set from X_0 during the time interval $[0, T]$ is defined as:

$$\Phi(X_0, T) = \{\gamma(t, x_0, u(\cdot), p) \mid t \in [0, T] \ \wedge \ x_0 \in X_0$$
$$\wedge \ u(\cdot) \in \mathcal{U} \ \wedge \ p \in P\}.$$

Note that, unlike simulation, reachability computations can also handle uncertainty in initial conditions. The extension of reachability techniques for ordinary differential equations (ODEs) to handle DAEs is not straightforward since these classes of equations differ in both theoretical and numerical properties, and this is captured by the *index* concept (for an introduction see [9]). The differential index of (1) is the minimal number of differentiations required to solve for the derivatives $\dot{x}$. In general the problem of numerically solving DAEs with index

2 or higher is ill-posed [7]. DAEs that model practical electronic circuits are typically of index 1 or 2 and in this work we focus on the former. In particular, we will study the equivalent semi-explicit form of (1):

$$\dot{x}(t) = f(x(t), y(t), p), \tag{2}$$
$$0 = g(x(t), y(t), p). \tag{3}$$

Note that the implicit DAE system (1) can be trivially transformed into the above form as follows: By letting $z(t) = \dot{x}(t)$, $y = (z, u)$ and substituting in (1) we obtain $0 = F(x(t), y(t), p)$. Thus the resulting system in the above semi-explicit form is: $\dot{x}(t) = z(t)$ and $0 = F(x(t), y(t), p)$.

Coupling the ODE (2) with the non-linear equation (3) means that the solution of (2) has to lie on the manifold defined by (3). If the Jacobian $g_y(x, y) = \partial g/\partial y$ is invertible in a neighborhood of the solution, then by differentiating the algebraic equation we obtain

$$\dot{y} = -g_y^{-1} g_x f, \tag{4}$$

and in this case, the DAE system is of index 1. In a simpler case, where $\partial F/\partial \dot{x}$ in (1) is regular, the algebraic equation (3) disappears, and (1) is a DAE of index 0, i.e. an ODE [9].

A trivial way to compute reachable sets for index 1 DAEs is to transform it into an ODE composed of (2) and (4) using the above-described differentiation and then apply the existing techniques for ODEs. However, the drawback of this approach is that the solution may drift away from the algebraic constraint. We will retain the algebraic constraint (3) and interpret the original DAE as the ODE, composed of (2) and (4), on the manifold defined by (3). We will combine the commonly-used technique of geometric integration using projection [11], with our reachability algorithm, to compute the reachable set.

2.2   Computing Reachable Sets of ODEs on Manifolds

We summarize below the approach we have developed over the years for reachability computation of ODEs and hybrid automata. We start with an algorithm for linear ODEs of the form $\dot{x}(t) = Ax(t)$, first presented in [5] and implemented in the tool **d/dt** [6]. Many other techniques for computing reachable sets can be found in the hybrid systems literature. In particular, those developed independently by Chutinan and Krogh and implemented in the tool CheckMate [10] are very similar to ours. We use $\gamma(t, x_0)$ for the solution and $\Phi(X_0, T)$ for the states of the solutions at any $t \in T$ starting from any $x_0 \in X_0$. Basically we compute a polyhedral over-approximation of the reachable states on a step-by-step basis as in numerical integration, that is, we compute a sequence of polyhedra that over-approximates the sequence

$$\Phi(X_0, r), \Phi(\Phi(X_0, r), r) \dots$$

Given a convex polyhedron R, the set R' of states reachable from R at time r can be computed as the convex hull of the points reachable at time r from the vertices of R. Then, the set of states reachable during the whole time interval $[0, r]$ is approximated by the convex hull $conv(R \cup R')$ which is enlarged by an appropriate amount to ensure conservative approximation[2].

This basic algorithm is then extended in various directions. When the system admits an input and is of the form $\dot{x}(t) = Ax(t) + bu(t)$, the computation can still be done by applying optimization techniques to find "extremal" values for u that push the set "outwards" [30]. Another important extension handles systems that admit mode switching and are modeled by *hybrid automata* [1], automata that have a distinct differential equation in each state, depending on the values of the continuous state variables. As long as the automaton remains in the same discrete state, the reachability computation proceeds as for simple ODEs but when the reachable polyhedron intersects the switching surface, it needs to be split and parts of it undergo reachability computation under the new dynamics. We will come back to this in the next section and the reader is referred to [5, 6] for more details.

The analysis of hybrid automata with under-specified inputs is part of the more recent methodology [4] for analyzing non-linear systems of the form $\dot{x}(t) = f(x(t)) + bu(t)$ using a piecewise-affine approximation. This method is based on partitioning the state space into simplices and assigning a distinct discrete state to each of them. The dynamics at each state is specified by an affine function obtained by interpolation on the values of f on the vertices the corresponding simplex. This approximation is conservative since the interpolation error is included in the model as an input. In addition, if the derivative $\dot{x}$ is a C^2 function, the reachable set approximation error is quadratic in the size of the underlying simplicial partition.

Before proceeding let us remark that the potential contribution of ideas coming from hybrid systems to the design of analog circuits is not restricted to verification. In particular, the modeling of non-linear systems by piecewise-linear ones, called *hybridization* in [4, 3], offers an alternative modeling style that was often avoided because it does not fit into the analytical and numerical framework of continuous systems. On the contrary, many discontinuous phenomena that could have been modeled naturally as discrete transitions, are often "smoothened" to avoid numerical instability. Hybrid modeling and analysis can treat such phenomena directly.

We can now return to ODEs on a manifolds and combine reachability with projection. For the sake of clarity we omit u and p and work with

$$\dot{x}(t) = f(x(t)), \tag{5}$$
$$0 = g(x(t)). \tag{6}$$

The following algorithmic scheme, illustrated in Figure 1, computes an approximation of the reachable states where Φ is the reachability operator and $\Pi_{\mathcal{M}}$ denotes projection onto the manifold $\mathcal{M}$ defined by (6).

---

[2] Note that this part of the algorithm is not needed for discrete-time systems.

Algorithm 1 Computation of $\Phi(X_0, .)$ with time step r.

$R_0 = X_0$
repeat $k = 0, 1, \ldots,$
　　$\hat{R}_{k+1} = \Phi(R_k, r)$
　　$R_{k+1} = \Pi_{\mathcal{M}}(\hat{R}_{k+1})$
until $R_{k+1} = \bigcup_{i=1}^{k} R_i$

The projection of a point $x \in \mathbb{R}^n$ onto the manifold $\mathcal{M}$ is computed as

$$\Pi_{\mathcal{M}}(x) = \arg \min_{\bar{x}} |x - \bar{x}| \text{ subject to } g(\bar{x}) = 0,$$

where $| \cdot |$ is the Euclidean norm. In the special case where g is linear, this optimization problem can be easily solved using linear algebra. The projection of a convex polyhedron $\hat{R} = conv(v^1, \ldots v^m)$ is approximated as the convex hull of the projected vertices, $R = conv(\bar{v}^1, \ldots \bar{v}^m)$. Although R does not always lie entirely on $\mathcal{M}$, its distance to $\mathcal{M}$ can be made as small as desired. Indeed, we can prove that the convergence order of this approximate reachability method for DAEs is that of the reachability method for ODEs used to compute Φ, which is *quadratic* [6, 4]. To see this consider a point $x \in \mathcal{M}$ and its successor $\hat{x} = \Phi(\{x\}, r)$ computed by Φ. The distance between $\hat{x}$ and $\mathcal{M}$ is bounded by the local error of the method for computing Φ. Hence, the distance between $\Pi_{\mathcal{M}}(\hat{x})$ and the exact successor of x is of the same order.

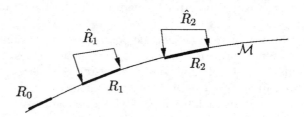

Fig. 1. Combining projection and reachability computations for ODEs.

2.3   Example: A Biquad Low-Pass Filter

We now illustrate the approach with a second order biquad low-pass filter circuit, shown in Figure 2. This example is taken from [19]. The circuit equations are as follows:

$$\dot{u}_{C1} = \frac{u_{C2} + u_o - u_{C1}}{C_1 R_2}, \tag{7}$$

$$\dot{u}_{C2} = \frac{U_i - u_{C2} - u_o}{C_2 R_1} - \frac{u_{C2} + u_o - u_{C1}}{C_2 R_2}, \tag{8}$$

$$u_o - V_{max} \tanh(\frac{(u_{C2} - u_o)V_e}{V_{max}}) + U_{om} = 0, \tag{9}$$

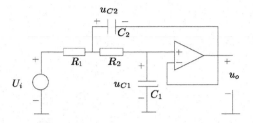

Fig. 2. A low-pass filter.

$$i_o = -C_2 \dot{u}_{C2}, \tag{10}$$

$$U_{om} = \mathcal{V}(i_0), \tag{11}$$

$$\mathcal{V}(i_o) = K_1 i_o + 0.5\sqrt{K_1 i_o^2 - 2K_2 i_o I_s + K_1 I_o^2 + K_2}$$
$$- 0.5\sqrt{K_1 i_o^2 + 2K_2 i_o I_s + K_1 I_s^2 + K_2}. \tag{12}$$

The state variables are (u_{C1}, u_{C2}), the voltages across the capacitors C_1 and C_2 (the reference directions of which are indicated by the $+$ and $-$ signs in Figure 2). The algebraic constraints (9-12) come from the characteristics of the operational amplifier where u_o is the output voltage and U_{om} corresponds to the output voltage decrease caused by the output current i_o. In this circuit, U_i (input voltage), V_{max} (maximal source voltage), V_c, I_s, C_1, C_2, R_1, and R_2 are parameters. Denoting $x = (u_{C1}, u_{C2})$ and $y = u_o$, the circuit equations can be put in the semi-explicit form (2-3). Assuming that the Jacobian $g_y(x, y)$ has bounded inverse in a neighborhood of the solution (which can indeed be verified for a concrete circuit), by differentiating (9) the circuit equations can be transformed into a non-linear ODE on a manifold as in (5-6) with state variables $z = (u_{C1}, u_{C2}, u_o)$.

As mentioned earlier, to reduce the complexity of reachability computation, we will use the hybridization idea. First, the non-linear characteristics $U_{om} = \mathcal{V}(i_o)$ in equation (11) can be approximated by a piecewise-affine function of the form:

$$\mathcal{V}(i_o) = \begin{cases} K_1 i_o + K_3 & \text{if } i_o \leq I_s, \\ 0 & \text{if } -I_s < i_o < I_s, \\ K_1 i_o - K_3 & \text{if } i_o \geq I_s. \end{cases} \tag{13}$$

Therefore, the original system is approximated by a hybrid automaton with 3 discrete states (modes). The conditions for staying in a mode and for switching between modes are determined by the value interval of i_o. For example, in order to stay in the mode corresponding to the first equation of (13) the state variables (u_{C1}, u_{C2}, u_o) should satisfy $i_o \leq I_s$. Using (10) this condition becomes: $-C_2 \dot{u}_{C2} \leq I_s$, which together with (8) gives

$$-\frac{U_i - u_{C2} - u_o}{R_1} - \frac{u_{C2} + u_o - u_{C1}}{R_2} \leq I_s.$$

Note that the hyperbolic tangent function in (9) is retained because it can be observed from simulation results that this non-linearity is important for the accuracy of the model. In general, the designer's knowledge of the the circuit can help to choose appropriate simplifications and approximations. As a result, the continuous dynamics of each mode is defined by a DAE which remains non-linear and is transformed automatically to a piecewise-affine dynamics using the hybridization technique of [4].

The property to verify is the absence of overshoots. For the highly damped case (where $C_1 = 0.5e - 8$, $C_2 = 2e - 8$, and $R_1 = R_2 = 1e6$), Figure 3 shows the projection of the reachable set on u_{C1} and u_{C2}. The initial set is defined by a box: $u_{C1} \in [-0.3, 0.3]$, $u_{C2} \in [-0.3, 0.3]$ and $u_o \in [-0.2, 0.2]$. From the figure, one can see that u_{C1} indeed remains in the range $[-2, 2]$. This computation took **d/dt** 3 minutes until termination. We are currently working on making this process more systematic and efficient. In particular we investigate the automatic transformation of circuit equations into ODEs on a manifold.

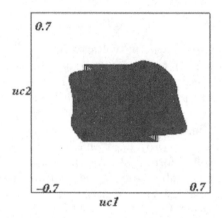

Fig. 3. The reachable set for the filter projected on variables u_{C1} and u_{C2}.

3   Verification of Mixed-Signal Circuits

3.1   Optimal Control Based Verification Approach

Mixed-signal circuits that exhibit both logical and continuous behaviors can be naturally modeled as hybrid automata and verified using the reachability techniques described in the previous section. However, as it also happens in digital verification, reachability algorithms may explode in time and space before termination and less exhaustive methods should sometimes be used. One popular approach is to restrict the verification to behaviors of *bounded* length and ask whether the set of such behaviors contains one that violates the property in question. A positive answer demonstrates a "bug" in the system while a negative one is generally not a proof of correctness unless the length bound is very large. Bounded horizon reachability for digital systems is typically formulated as Boolean satisfiability. For dynamical systems over a continuous state space, bounded horizon problems were used in the context of optimal control, where one looks for a finite input signal that induces a behavior which is optimal according to some performance criterion. In discrete-time, this problem reduces to a finite-dimensional optimization of a continuous function subject to continuous constraints (see a unified treatment of the discrete and continuous case in [23]). The application of these ideas to the verification of hybrid systems has been advocated by Bemporad and Morari [8]. In verification the input is interpreted as a disturbance and the search for a bad behavior becomes a search for the *worst* input sequence with respect to the property in question (see also [30] for the applicability of optimal control to reachability-based verification). The discrete part of the system makes the optimization problem hybrid, and one of the popular methods for solving it is mixed integer-linear programming (MILP).

In this section we focus on circuits that can be modeled by a discrete-time hybrid system of the form:

$$F(x(k), x(k+1), u(k), \delta(k), p) = 0, \ k \in \mathbb{N}, \tag{14}$$

where $\delta(k) \in \{0,1\}^s$ is a binary vector of dimension s describing the logical part of the dynamics. For convenience, we will use notation similar to the continuous-time case. We use $x(k) = \gamma(k, x(0), u(\cdot))$ to denote the state at time k of the solution of (14) with initial state $x(0) \in X_0$ and input $u(\cdot) \in \mathcal{U}$ which is a sequence ranging over a closed bounded set $U \subset \mathbb{R}^l$ (i.e., $u(\cdot) = (u(k))_{k \in \mathbb{N}}$).

To prove safety over a finite horizon $N \in \mathbb{N}$ we compute a set of *worst* trajectories whose safety implies the safety of all the other trajectories. The formulation of verification as an optimal control problem is done via an objective function J such that $J(x)$ is positive iff x is outside the safe set. Then for each $k \leq N$, we maximize J for the trajectory $x(t)$ with $t = 0, \ldots, k$ by solving the following constrained optimization problem:

$$\max \ J(x(k)), \tag{15}$$
$$s.t. \ F(x(t), x(t+1), u(t), \delta(t), p) = 0, \tag{16}$$
$$u(t) \in \mathcal{U}, \ t \in \{0, 1, \ldots, k-1\}, \tag{17}$$
$$x(0) \in X_0. \tag{18}$$

We then check whether the worst trajectories obtained satisfy $J(x(k)) \leq 0$ for all $k \leq N$, meaning that the property is true over horizon N. We illustrate this approach through the stability analysis of a Δ-Σ modulator.

3.2   The Δ-Σ Modulation: Principles and Hybrid Modeling

We describe briefly the principles of Δ-Σ modulation, a very popular technique for analog to digital conversion. Basically, a Δ-Σ modulator processes an analog input through four steps [29]: (1) *Anti-aliasing* in order to be sure that the signal bandwidth lies within a given range $[-f_b, f_b]$; (2) *Oversampling* or sampling at a frequency greater than the Nyquist rate $2 \times f_b$; (3) *Noise shaping* so that the quantization error is "pushed" toward high frequencies outside the bandwidth of interest; (4) *Quantization,* typically on few bits. In the following examples quantization is done on one bit. We use an input-output plot of a simple model, shown in Figure 4, to explain intuitively how Δ-Σ modulation works. When the input sinusoid is positive and its value is less than 1, the output takes the $+1$ value more often and the quantization error which is the difference between the input and the output of the quantizer is fed back with negative gain and "accumulated" in the integrator $\frac{1}{z-1}$. Then, when the accumulated error reaches a certain threshold, the quantizer switches the value of the output to -1 for some time, which reduces the mean of the quantization error. This model is called a first order Δ-Σ modulator since it uses a first order filter to process noise.

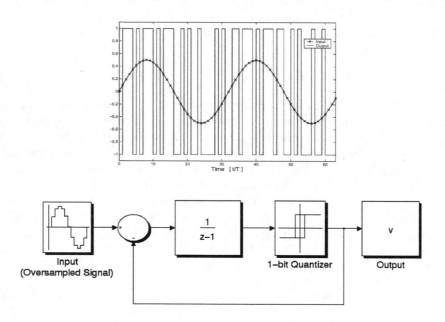

Fig. 4. A first order Δ-Σ modulator and an example of an input-output plot.

We now describe a hybrid model of a third-order Δ-Σ modulator (shown in Figure 5), generated using the standard MATLAB **delsig** toolbox [28] which provides practical models used by designers. Higher order Δ-Σ modulators achieve better performance but induce stability problems [12]. A modulator is said to be stable if its integrators values remain bounded under a bounded input. This property is of a great importance since integrator saturation can deteriorate circuit performance. Stability analysis for such circuits is still a challenging research problem [12] due to the presence of two sources of non-linearities: saturation and quantization.

The circuit is modeled as a discrete-time hybrid automaton. When none of the integrators saturates, the dynamics of the system can be represented in the following state-space form:

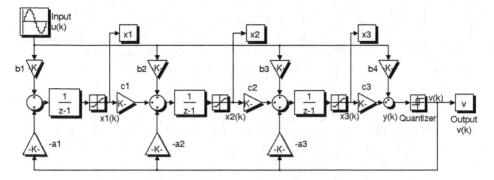

Fig. 5. A model of a third-order modulator with integrators that may saturate.

$$x(k+1) = Ax(k) + bu(k) - sign(y(k))a, \tag{19}$$

$$y(k) = c_3 x_3(k) + b_4 u(k), \tag{20}$$

where matrix A, vectors a and b are constants depending on the various gains of the model, $x(k) \in \mathbb{R}^3$ represents the integrator states, $u(k) \in \mathbb{R}$ is the input and $y(k) \in \mathbb{R}$ is the input to the quantizer. The output of the quantizer $v(k) = sign(y(k))$ is the only discrete state variable and as long as it remains constant, the dynamics is continuous and affine. Figure 6 gives the usual graph representation of the corresponding hybrid automaton. Note that the discrete state variable can be made Boolean by letting $\delta(k) = \frac{sign(y(k))+1}{2}$ which transforms (19-20) to the general form of (14).

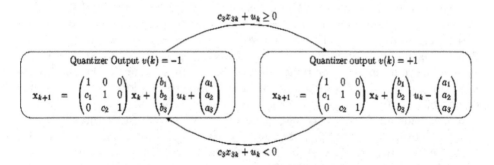

Fig. 6. A hybrid automaton model of the Δ-Σ modulator.

3.3   Stability Analysis: Formulation and Results

The stability property of the modulator is stated as follows: For a given bounded set $X_0 \subset \mathbb{R}^3$ of initial states and a range of input values $U = [u_{min}, u_{max}]$, the system is stable if and only if for any $x(0) \in X_0$ and any sequence $u(\cdot) \in \mathcal{U}$ the sequence $\gamma(k, x(0), u(\cdot))$ is bounded, that is, there exists a *bounded* set $\mathcal{S}$ such that

$$\forall k \in \mathbb{N} \; \forall x(0) \in X_0 \; \forall u(\cdot) \in \mathcal{U} : \gamma(k, x(0), u(\cdot)) \in \mathcal{S}.$$

In the following, we apply the method described in Section 3.1 to check this property over a horizon N where the safe set $\mathcal{S}$ is the rectangular set $[-x_1^{sat}, x_1^{sat}] \times [-x_2^{sat}, x_2^{sat}] \times [-x_3^{sat}, x_3^{sat}]$, the set of states where no integrator saturates. Since we want x to remain inside $\mathcal{S}$, we define the objective function J as:

$$J(x(k)) = \max_{i=1,2,3}(|x_i(k)| - x_i^{sat}).$$

Solving this optimization problem means finding an input sequence that drives the integrators as close as possible to their saturation limits. By symmetry it can be easily shown that if $\gamma(\cdot, x(0), u(\cdot))$ is a sequence obtained from $x(0)$ with input $u(\cdot)$, then we have $\gamma(k, x(0), u(\cdot)) = -\gamma(k, -x(0), -u(\cdot))$ for all k. Thus, if X_0 and U are symmetric sets with respect to the origin, maximizing $|x_i(k)|$ is the same as maximizing $x_i(k)$; hence, we can define J as: $J(x(k)) = \max_{i=1,2,3}(x_i(k) - x_i^{sat})$.

We transform this problem into 3 MILP problems (one for each i) by rewriting the function F, given by (19-20), as a set of linear constraints over real and binary variables. To get rid of the *sign* function, we use the standard "big-M" trick. Given bounds $m < 0$ and $M > 0$ on $y(k)$, we introduce two new constraints for all k:

$$y(k) \leq \delta(k)M, \tag{21}$$

$$y(k) > (1 - \delta(k))m. \tag{22}$$

Thus, it holds that $\delta(k) = 1 \Leftrightarrow y(k) \geq 0$, and we can replace $sign(y(k))$ in (19) by $2\delta(k) - 1$. With the above definitions and constraints, the problem (15-18) is put in MILP form.

We used the efficient solver MOSEK [26] to solve the resulting MILP problem for various bounds on initial states $x(0)$ and input signals u over a finite horizon N ranging from 1 to 30. The results are shown in Figure 7, where the curves depict the maximal obtained value of $x_1(N)$ as a function of N (note that for each N the maximum might be obtained by another input sequence). The qualitative behavior exhibited by x_2 and x_3 is similar. From these plots one can see, for example, that for $x(0) \in [-0.1, 0.1]^3$ and any *constant* sequence $u(k) = c \in [-0.5, 0.5]$ for all N the maximal value of $x_1(N)$ never leaves the safe set $\mathcal{S}$ and, moreover, it converges quite fast towards a constant value, which shows that the $\Delta\text{-}\Sigma$ modulator is stable up to $N = 30$ and most likely forever after. This also holds for $x(0) \in [-0.01, 0.01]^3$ and *any* $u(k) \in [-0.1, 0.1]$ but not for $u(k) \in [-0.5, 0.5]$. Note furthermore that the bad input signals the we found are generally non-trivial, and could not have been found easily by simulation with initial states and input values that are simply on the boundaries of their domains.

3.4   Reachability Versus Optimal Control

Safety verification of piecewise affine hybrid systems can also be achieved by computing a so-called *robustly positively invariant set* (RPI), which has already been used in the context of $\Delta\text{-}\Sigma$ modulators [21, 16]. An RPI set Ω is such that

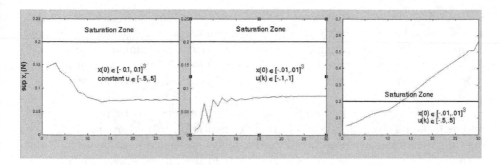

Fig. 7. The curves show $\sup x_1(N)$ as a function of the horizon N for various bounds on initial states $x(0)$ and input signals u.

if $x(k) \in \Omega$ then $x(k+1) \in \Omega$ regardless of $u(k)$. Indeed, if such a bounded set containing X_0 is found, the boundedness of $x[k]$ is guaranteed. It is easy to see that the reachable set is an RPI set and therefore, we can prove the stability of the Δ-Σ circuit by computing (or over-approximating) the reachable set using a discrete-time version of the algorithm of Section 2. Nevertheless, two characteristics of the Δ-Σ modulator render the reachability computation very expensive:

- Switching between modes is very frequent, which makes the reachable set highly non convex admitting an exponentially growing number of polyhedra.
- The fundamental instability introduced by the integrators makes the system particularly sensitive. Hence, while the use of over-approximations of the reachable set (such as using convex hull) can reduce the computational complexity, the results are often too coarse to prove the property.

One can observe similar phenomena in a recent application of reachability techniques to the same circuit (but under more restricted input signals) reported in [18]. The optimization procedure just described is not immune to these problems although it can reach larger horizons (the computation for horizon 30 took more than two hours on a 2.4GHz machine). On the other hand, efficient algorithms for computing RPI sets, such as those described in [21], require the affine modes to be stable and thus cannot be used for this example. Indeed, the instability of the integrators (the A matrix) implies the instability of each mode of the affine system and the stability of the modulator relies only on switches between the modes.

4   Conclusion and Future Work

We have presented a framework for modeling and verification of analog and mixed-signal circuits using hybrid system techniques. These results are much more modest, both in terms of rigor (approximate computation, non guaranteed termination) and of size (systems with few state variables) than the state-of-the-art in digital hardware verification, but this is not surprising given the inherent complexity of the problems and the current practices in the domain. Fortunately, the accumulated experience in hybrid systems will be useful in accelerating the progress in analog verification, especially by avoiding dead ends that have already been explored.

Some innovative ideas are needed in order to extend the scope of our techniques to larger systems. As in discrete verification, abstraction and model reduction techniques are necessary in order to facilitate compositional reasoning. Although the circuit structure may give hints for useful decompositions, the nature of interaction between analog devices will probably not make this task easy. Another research direction would be to develop reachability techniques that take into account some more refined constraints on the input signals such as bounds on their frequency or on their average value. Current reachability algorithm for systems with input are essentially "breadth-first" and are not adapted for excluding individual input signals that violate such constraints. Additional work that will be needed in order to integrate formal methods in the design process includes the automatic translation from circuit descriptions (such as those expressed in VHDL-AMS) to hybrid automata, as well as the definition of an expressive formalism for specifying properties of analog signals. First steps in this direction are reported in [24].

Acknowledgment

We thank Lars Hedrich for his help in modeling the biquad filter and for providing us with a lot of information about various techniques used for validating analog circuits. All that we know about Δ-Σ modulation is the result of our interactions with Rob Rutenbar, Bruce Krogh and Smriti Gupta at CMU during the summer of 2003. Goran Frehse provided many useful comments on previous versions of this paper.

References

1. R. Alur, C. Courcoubetis, N. Halbwachs, T.A. Henzinger, P.-H. Ho, X. Nicollin, A. Olivero, J. Sifakis, and S. Yovine. The algorithmic analysis of hybrid systems. *Theoretical Computer Science* 138:3–34, 1995.
2. R. Alur and G.J. Pappas (eds). *Hybrid Systems: Computation and Control*. LNCS 2993, Springer, 2004.
3. E. Asarin and T. Dang. Abstraction by projection. In *Hybrid Systems: Computation and Control*, LNCS 2993, 32–47, Springer, 2004.
4. E. Asarin, T. Dang, and A. Girard. Reachability analysis of nonlinear systems using conservative approximation. In *Hybrid Systems: Computation and Control*, LNCS 2623, 20–35. Springer, 2003.
5. E. Asarin, O. Bournez, T. Dang and O. Maler, Reachability analysis of piecewise-linear dynamical systems, In *Hybrid Systems: Computation and Control*, LNCS 1790, 20-31, Springer, 2000.

6. E. Asarin, T. Dang, and O. Maler. The d/dt tool for verification of hybrid systems. In *Computer Aided Verification*, LNCS 2404, 365–370, Springer, 2002.
7. U.M. Ascher and L.R. Petzold. Stability of computational methods for constrained dynamics systems. *SIAM Journal on Scientific Computing* 14:95–120, 1993.
8. A. Bemporad and M. Morari. Control of systems integrating logic, dynamics, and constraints, *Automatica* 35:407-427, 1999.
9. K.E. Brenan, S.L. Campell, and L.R. Petzold. *Numerical Solution of Initial Value Problems in Ordinary Differential-Algebraic Equations*. North Holland, 1989.
10. A. Chutinan and B.H. Krogh. Verification of polyhedral invariant hybrid automata using polygonal flow pipe approximations. In *Hybrid Systems: Computation and Control*, LNCS 1569, 76-90, Springer, 1999.
11. C. Lubich and E. Hairer and G. Wanner. *Geometric Numerical Integration. Structure-Preserving Algorithms for Ordinary Differential Equations.*, volume 31 of *Series in Comput. Mathematics*. Springer, 2003.
12. B. Pérez-Verdú and F. Medeiro and A. Rodríguez-Vázquez. *Top-Down Design of High-Performance Sigma-Delta Modulators*, chapter 2. Kluwer Academic Publishers, 2001.
13. U. Feldmann and M. Günther. The DAE-index in electric circuit simulation. In *Proc. IMACS, Symposium on Mathematical Modelling* 4:695–702, 1994.
14. H. Floberg. *Symbolic Analysis in Analog Integrated Circuit Design*. Kluwer, 1997.
15. A. Ghosh and R. Verumi. Formal verification of synthesized analog circuits. In *Int. Conf on Computer Design* 4:40–45, 1999.
16. M. Goodson R. Schreier and B. Zhang. An algorithm for computing convex positively invariant sets for delta-sigma modulators. *IEEE Transactions on Circuits and Systems I* 44:38–44, January 1997.
17. M. Greenstreet and C. Tomlin (eds). *Hybrid Systems: Computation and Control*. LNCS 2289. Springer-Verlag, 2002.
18. S. Gupta, B.H. Krogh, and R.A. Rutenbar, Towards formal verification of analog designs, *Proc. ICCAD 2004* (to appear), 2004.
19. W. Hartong, L. Hedrich, and E. Barke. On discrete modelling and model checking for nonlinear analog systems. In *Computer Aided Verification*, LNCS 2404, 401–413, Springer, 2002.
20. S. Hein and A. Zakhor. On the stability of sigma delta modulators. *IEEE Transactions on Signal Processing* 41, 1993.
21. K. Kouramas S.V. Rakovic, E.C. Kerrigan and D.Q. Mayne. Approximation of the minimal robustly positively invariant set for discrete-time LTI systems with persistent state disturbances. In *42nd IEEE Conference on Decision and Control*, 2003.
22. R.P. Kurshan and K.L. McMillan. Analysis of digital circuits through symbolic reduction. *IEEE Trans. on Computer-Aided Design* 10:1350–1371, 1991.
23. O. Maler. On optimal and sub-optimal control in the presence of adversaries. *Workshop on Discrete Event Systems (WODES)*, (to appear), 2004.
24. O. Maler and D. Nickovic. Monitoring temporal properties of continuous signals. *Proc. FORMATS/FTRTFT'04*, (to appear), 2004.
25. O. Maler and A. Pnueli (eds). *Hybrid Systems: Computation and Control*. LNCS 2623, Springer, 2003.
26. MOSEK ApS. The Mosek Optimization Toolbox for Matlab version 3.0 (revision 19) user's guide and reference manual, November 2003.
27. A. Salem. Semi-formal verification of VHDL-AMS descriptors. *IEEE Int Symposium on Circuits and Systems*, 5:V–333–V–336, 2002.

28. R. Schreier. The delta-sigma toolbox version 6.0, January 2003.
29. H.V. Sorensen P.M. Aziz and J.V.D. Spiegel. An overview of sigma-delta converters. *IEEE Signal Processing Magazine*, 61–84, January 1996.
30. P. Varaiya. Reach set computation using optimal control. In *Proc. KIT Workshop*, Verimag, Grenoble, 1998.
31. T. Wichmann. Computer aided generation of approximate DAE systems for symbolic analog circuit design. In *Proc. Annual Meeting GAMM*, 2000.
32. T. Wichmann, R. Popp, W. Hartong, and L. Hedrich. On the simplification of nonlinear DAE systems in analog circuit design. In *Computer Algebra in Scientific Computing*. Springer, 1999.

A Methodology for the Formal Verification of FFT Algorithms in HOL

Behzad Akbarpour and Sofiène Tahar

Dept. of Electrical & Computer Engineering, Concordia University
1455 de Maisonneuve W., Montreal, Quebec, H3G 1M8, Canada
{behzad,tahar}@ece.concordia.ca

Abstract. This paper addresses the formal specification and verification of fast Fourier transform (FFT) algorithms at different abstraction levels based on the HOL theorem prover. We make use of existing theories in HOL on real and complex numbers, IEEE standard floating-point, and fixed-point arithmetics to model the FFT algorithms. Then, we derive, by proving theorems in HOL, expressions for the accumulation of roundoff error in floating- and fixed-point FFT designs with respect to the corresponding ideal real and complex numbers specification. The HOL formalization and proofs are found to be in good agreement with the theoretical paper-and-pencil counterparts. Finally, we use a classical hierarchical proof approach in HOL to prove that the FFT implementations at the register transfer level (RTL) implies the corresponding high level fixed-point algorithmic specification.

1 Introduction

The fast Fourier transform (FFT) [6, 9] is a highly efficient method for computing the discrete Fourier transform (DFT) coefficients of a finite sequence of complex data. Because of the substantial time saving over conventional methods, the fast Fourier transform has found important applications in a number of diverse fields such as spectrum analysis, speech and optical signal processing, and digital filter design. FFT algorithms are based on the fundamental principle of decomposing the computation of the discrete Fourier transform of a finite-length sequence of length N into successively smaller discrete Fourier transforms. The manner in which this principle is implemented leads to a variety of different algorithms, all with comparable improvements in computational speed. There are two basic classes of FFT algorithms for which the number of arithmetic multiplications and additions as a measure of computational complexity is proportional to $N \log N$ rather than N^2 as in the conventional methods. The first proposed by Cooley and Tukey [10], called decimation-in-time (DIT), derives its name from the fact that in the process of arranging the computation into smaller transformations, the input sequence (generally thought of as a time sequence) is decomposed into successively smaller subsequences. In the second general class of algorithms proposed by Gentleman and Sande [13], the sequence of discrete Fourier transform coefficients is decomposed into smaller subsequences, hence its

A.J. Hu and A.K. Martin (Eds.): FMCAD 2004, LNCS 3312, pp. 37–51, 2004.

name, decimation-in-frequency (DIF). In a theoretical analysis of the fast Fourier transform, we generally assume that signal values and system coefficients are represented with real numbers expressed to infinite precision. When implemented as a special-purpose digital hardware or as a computer algorithm, we must represent signals and coefficients in some digital number system that must always be of finite precision. There is an inherent accuracy problem in calculating the Fourier coefficients, since the signals are represented by a finite number of bits and the arithmetic operations must be carried out with an accuracy limited by this finite word length. Among the most common types of arithmetic used in the implementation of FFT systems are floating- and fixed-point. Here, all operands are represented by a special format or assigned a fixed word length and a fixed exponent, while the control structure and the operations of the ideal program remain unchanged. The transformation from real to floating- and fixed-point is quite tedious and error-prone. On the implementation side, the fixed-point model of the algorithm has to be transformed into the best suited target description, either using a hardware description or a programming language. This design process can be aided by a number of specialized CAD tools such as SPW (Cadence) [27], CoCentric (Synopsys) [8], Matlab-Simulink (Mathworks) [22], and FRIDGE (Aachen UT) [20].

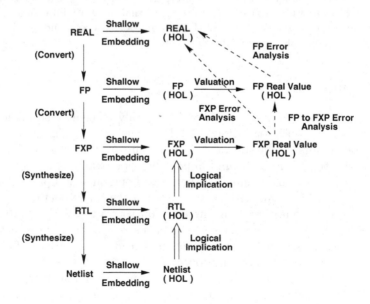

Fig. 1. FFT specification and verification methodology

In this paper, we describe a methodology for the formal specification and verification of FFT algorithms based on shallow embedding technique [5] using the HOL theorem proving environment [14]. The overall methodology is depicted in the commutating diagram shown in Figure 1. We first focus on the transition from real to floating- and fixed-point levels. Here, we model the ideal real specification of the FFT algorithms and the corresponding floating- and fixed-point implementations as predicates in higher-order logic. For this, we make use of existing theories in HOL on the construction of real [15] and complex [18] numbers, the formalization of IEEE-754 standard based floating-point arithmetic [16, 17], and the formalization of fixed-point arithmetic [1, 2]. We use valuation functions to find the real values of the floating- and fixed-point FFT outputs and define the error as the difference between these values and the corresponding output of the ideal real specification. Then we establish fundamental lemmas on the error analysis of floating- and fixed-point roundings and arithmetic operations against their abstract mathematical counterparts. Finally, based on these lemmas, we derive, for each of the two canonical forms of realization, expressions for the accumulation of roundoff error in floating- and fixed-point FFT algorithms using recursive definitions and initial conditions. While theoretical work on computing the errors due to finite precision effects in the realization of FFT algorithms with floating- and fixed-point arithmetics has been extensively studied since the late sixties [19], this paper contains the first formalization and proof of this analysis using a mechanical theorem prover, here HOL. The formal results are found to be in good agreement with the theoretical ones.

After handling the transition from real to floating- and fixed-point levels, we turn to the HDL representation. At this point, we use well known techniques to model the FFT design at the RTL level within the HOL environment. The last step is to verify this level using a classical hierarchical proof approach in HOL [23]. In this way, we hierarchically prove that the FFT RTL implementation implies the high level fixed-point algorithmic specification, which has already been related to the floating-point description and the ideal real specification through the error analysis. The verification can be extended, following similar manner, down to gate level netlist either in HOL or using other commercial verification tools as depicted in Figure 1, which is not covered in this paper.

The rest of this paper is organized as follows: Section 2 reviews some related work. Section 3 describes the details of the error analysis in HOL of the FFT algorithms at the real, floating-, and fixed-point levels. Section 4 describes the verification of the FFT algorithms in the transition from fixed-point to register transfer levels. Finally, Section 5 concludes the paper.

2   Related Work

Analysis of errors in FFT realizations due to finite precision effects has traditionally relied on paper-and-pencil proofs and simulation techniques. The roundoff error in using the FFT algorithms depends on the algorithm, the type of arithmetic, the word length, and the radix. For FFT algorithms realized with fixed-point arithmetic, the error problems have been studied extensively. For instance, Welch [30] presented an analysis of the fixed-point accuracy of the radix-2 decimation-in-time FFT algorithm. Tran-Thong and Liu [28] presented a general approach to the error analysis of the various versions of the FFT algorithm when fixed-point arithmetic is used. While the roundoff noise for fixed-point arithmetic enters into the system additively, it is a multiplicative component in the case of floating-point arithmetic. This problem is analyzed first by Gentleman and Sande [13], who presented an upper bound on the mean-squared error for floating-point decimation-in-frequency FFT algorithm. Weinstein [29] presented a statistical model for roundoff errors of the floating-point FFT. Kaneko and Liu [19] presented a detailed analysis of roundoff error in the FFT decimation-in-frequency algorithm using floating-point arithmetic. This analysis is later extended by the same authors to the FFT decimation-in-time algorithm [21]. Oppenheim and Weinstein [26] discussed in some detail the effects of finite register length on implementations of digital filters, and FFT algorithms.

In order to validate the error analysis, most of the above work compare the theoretical results with experimental simulation. In this paper, we show how the above error analyses for the FFT algorithms can be mechanically performed using the HOL theorem prover, providing a superior approach to validation by simulation. Our focus will be on the process of translating the hand proofs into equivalent proofs in HOL. The analysis we develop is mainly inspired by the work done by Kaneko and Liu [19], who proposed a general approach to the error analysis problem of the decimation-in-frequency FFT algorithm using floating-point arithmetic. Following a similar idea, we have extended this theoretical analysis for the decimation-in-time and fixed-point FFT algorithms. In all cases, good agreements between formal and theoretical results were obtained.

Prior work on error analysis and theorem proving was done by Harrison [17], who verified floating-point algorithms against their abstract mathematical counterparts using the HOL Light theorem prover. His error analysis is very similar to the type of analysis performed for DSP algorithms. The major difference, however, is the use of statistical methods and mean square error analysis for DSP algorithms which is not covered in the error analysis of the mathematical functions used by Harrison. To perform such an analysis in HOL, we need to develop a mechanized theory on the properties of random processes. This type of analysis is not addressed in this paper and is a part of our work in progress.

Related work on the formalization and mechanical verification of the FFT algorithm was done by Gamboa [12] using the ACL2 theorem prover. The author formalized the FFT as a recursive data-parallel algorithm, using the powerlist data structure. He also presented an ACL2 proof of the correctness of the FFT algorithm, by translating the hand proof taken from Misra's seminal paper on powerlists [24] into a mechanical proof in ACL2. In the same line, Capretta [7] presented the formalization of the FFT using the type theory proof tool Coq. To facilitate the definition of the transform by structural recursion, Capretta used the structure of polynomial trees which is similar to the data structure of powerlists introduced by Misra. Finally, he proved its correctness and the correctness of the inverse Fourier transform (IFT).

Bjesse [4] described the verification of FFT hardware at the netlist level with an automatic combination of symbolic simulation and theorem proving using the Lava hardware development platform. He proved that the sequential pipelined implementation of the radix-4 decimation-in-time FFT is equivalent to the corresponding combinational circuit. He also proved that the abstract implementation of the radix-2 and the radix-4 FFT are equivalent for sizes that are an exponent of four. While [12] and [7] prove the correctness of the high level FFT algorithm against the DFT, the verification of [4] is performed at the netlist level. In contrast, our work tries to close this gap by formally specifying and verifying the FFT algorithm realizations at different levels of abstraction based on different data types. Besides, the definition used for the FFT in [12, 7] is based on the radix-2 decimation-in-time algorithm. We cover both decimation-in-time and decimation-in-frequency algorithms, and radices other than 2. The methodology we propose in this paper is, to the best of our knowledge, the first project of its kind that covers the formal specification and verification of integrated FFT algorithms at different abstraction levels starting from real specification to floating- and fixed-point algorithmic descriptions, down to RT and netlist gate levels.

3   Error Analysis of FFT Algorithms in HOL

In this section, the principal results for roundoff accumulation in FFT algorithms using HOL theorem proving are derived and summarized. For the most part, the following discussion is phrased in terms of the decimation-in-frequency form of radix-2 algorithm. The results, however, are applicable with only minor modification to the decimation-in-time form. Furthermore, most of the ideas employed in the error analysis of the radix-2 algorithms can be utilized in the analysis of other algorithms. In the following, we will first describe in detail the theory behind the analysis and then explain how this analysis is performed in HOL.

The discrete Fourier transform of a sequence $\{x(n)\}_{n=0}^{N-1}$ is defined as [25]

$$A(p) = \sum_{n=0}^{N-1} x(n) \, (W_N)^{np}, \qquad p = 0, 1, 2, \ldots, N-1 \qquad (1)$$

where $W_N = e^{-j2\pi/N}$ and $j = \sqrt{-1}$. The multiplicative factors $(W_N)^{np}$ are called twiddle factors. For simplicity, our discussion is restricted to the radix-2 FFT algorithm, in which the number of points N to be Fourier transformed satisfy the relationship $N = 2^m$, where m is an integer value. The results can be extended to radices other than 2. By using the FFT method, the Fourier coefficients $\{A(p)\}_{p=0}^{N-1}$ can be calculated in $m = \log_2 N$ iterative steps. At each step, an array of N complex numbers is generated by using only the numbers in the previous array. To explain the FFT algorithm, let each integer p, $p = 0, 1, 2, \ldots, N-1$, be expanded into a binary form as

$$p = 2^{m-1}p_0 + 2^{m-2}p_1 + \cdots + 2p_{m-2} + p_{m-1}, \qquad p_k = 0 \text{ or } 1 \qquad (2)$$

and let p^* denote the number corresponding to the reverse bit sequences of p, i.e.,

$$p^* = 2^{m-1}p_{m-1} + 2^{m-2}p_{m-2} + \cdots + 2p_1 + p_0 \qquad (3)$$

Let $\{A_k(p)\}_{p=0}^{N-1}$ denote the N complex numbers calculated at the kth step. The decimation-in-frequency FFT algorithm can then be expressed as [19]

$$A_{k+1}(p) = \begin{cases} A_k(p) + A_k(p + 2^{m-1-k}) & \text{if } p_k = 0 \\ [A_k(p - 2^{m-1-k}) - A_k(p)] \, w_k(p) & \text{if } p_k = 1 \end{cases} \quad (4)$$

where $w_k(p)$ is a power of W_N given by $w_k(p) = (W_N)^{z_k(p)}$, where

$$z_k(p) = 2^k \left(2^{m-1-k} p_k + 2^{m-2-k} p_{k+1} + \cdots + 2p_{m-2} + p_{m-1}\right) - 2^{m-1} p_k \quad (5)$$

Equation (4) is carried out for $k = 0, 1, 2, \ldots, m-1$, with $A_0(p) = x(p)$. It can be shown [13] that at the last step $\{A_m(p)\}_{p=0}^{N-1}$ are the discrete Fourier coefficients in rearranged order. Specifically, $A_m(p) = A(p^*)$ with p and p^* expanded and defined as in equations (2) and (3), respectively.

There are three common sources of errors associated with the FFT algorithms, namely [19]:

1. **input quantization:** caused by the quantization of the input signal $\{x_n\}$ into a set of discrete levels.
2. **coefficient accuracy:** caused by the representation of the coefficients $\{w_k(p)\}$ by a finite word length.
3. **round-off accumulation:** caused by the accumulation of roundoff errors at arithmetic operations.

Therefore, the actual array computed by using equation (4) is in general different from $\{A_k(p)\}_{p=0}^{N-1}$. We denote the actual floating- and fixed-point computed arrays by $\{A_k'(p)\}_{p=0}^{N-1}$ and $\{A_k''(p)\}_{p=0}^{N-1}$, respectively. Then, we define the corresponding errors of the pth element at step k as

$$e_k(p) = A_k'(p) - A_k(p) \quad (6)$$
$$e_k'(p) = A_k''(p) - A_k(p) \quad (7)$$
$$e_k''(p) = A_k''(p) - A_k'(p) \quad (8)$$

where $e_k(p)$ and $e_k'(p)$ are defined as the error between the actual floating- and fixed-point implementations and the ideal real specification, respectively. $e_k''(p)$ is the error in transition from floating- to fixed-point levels.

In analyzing the effect of floating-point roundoff, the effect of rounding will be represented multiplicatively. Letting $*$ denote any of the arithmetic operations $+, -, \times, /$, it is known [11, 31] that, if p represents the precision of the floating-point format, then

$$fl\,(x * y) = (x * y)(1 + \delta), \quad \text{where } |\delta| \leq 2^{-p} \quad (9)$$

The notation $fl\,(.)$ is used to denote that the operation is performed using floating-point arithmetic. The theorem relates the floating-point arithmetic operations such as addition, subtraction, multiplication, and division to their abstract mathematical counterparts according to the corresponding errors.

While the rounding error for floating-point arithmetic enters into the system multiplicatively, it is an additive component for fixed-point arithmetic. In this case the fundamental error analysis theorem for fixed-point arithmetic operations against their abstract mathematical counterparts can be stated as

$$fxp\ (x * y)\ =\ (x * y)\ +\ \epsilon,\ \text{where}\ |\epsilon|\ \leq\ 2^{-fracbits\ (X)} \tag{10}$$

and *fracbits* is the number of bits that are to the right of the binary point in the given fixed-point format X. The notation $fxp\ (.)$ is used to denote that the operation is performed using fixed-point arithmetic. We have proved equations (9) and (10) as theorems in higher-order logic within HOL. The theorems are proved under the assumption that there is no overflow or underflow in the operation result. This means that the input values are scaled so that the real value of the result is located in the ranges defined by the maximum and minimum representable values of the given floating-point and fixed-point formats. The details can be found in [3].

In equation (4) the $\{A_k(p)\}$ are complex numbers, so their real and imaginary parts are calculated separately. Let

$$\begin{aligned} B_k(p) &= Re\ [A_k(p)] & C_k(p) &= Im\ [A_k(p)] \\ U_k(p) &= Re\ [w_k(p)] & V_k(p) &= Im\ [w_k(p)] \end{aligned} \tag{11}$$

where the notations $Re\ [.]$ and $Im\ [.]$ denote, respectively, the real and imaginary parts of the quantity inside the bracket $[.]$. Equation (4) can be rewritten as

$$\left. \begin{aligned} B_{k+1}(p) &= B_k(p) + B_k(q) \\ C_{k+1}(p) &= C_k(p) + C_k(q) \end{aligned} \right\} \quad \text{if}\ p_k = 0 \tag{12}$$

$$\left. \begin{aligned} B_{k+1}(p) &= [B_k(r) - B_k(p)]\ U_k(p) - [C_k(r) - C_k(p)]\ V_k(p) \\ C_{k+1}(p) &= [C_k(r) - C_k(p)]\ U_k(p) + [B_k(r) - B_k(p)]\ V_k(p) \end{aligned} \right\} \quad \text{if}\ p_k = 1$$

where $q = p + 2^{m-1-k}$ and $r = p - 2^{m-1-k}$. Similarly, we can express the real and imaginary parts of $A'_{k+1}(p)$, $B'_{k+1}(p)$ and $C'_{k+1}(p)$, and $A''_{k+1}(p)$, $B''_{k+1}(p)$ and $C''_{k+1}(p)$, using the floating- and fixed-point operations, respectively. The corresponding error flowgraph showing the effect of roundoff error using the fundamental floating- and fixed-point error analysis theorems according to the equations (9) and (10), respectively, is given in Figure 2, which also indicates the order of the calculation.

Formally, a flowgraph consists of nodes and directed branches. Each branch has an input signal and an output signal with a direction indicated by an arrowhead on it. Each node represents a variable which is the weighted sum of the variables at the originating nodes of the branches that terminate on that node. The weights, if other than unity, are shown for each branch. Source nodes have no entering branches. They are used to represent the injection of the external inputs or signal sources into the flowgraph. Sink nodes have only entering branches. They are used to extract the outputs from the flowgraph [25, 3].

The quantities $\gamma'_{k,p}$, $\gamma''_{k,p}$, $\delta'_{k,p}$, $\delta''_{k,p}$, $\epsilon'_{k,p}$, $\epsilon''_{k,p}$, $\zeta'_{k,p}$, $\zeta''_{k,p}$, $\eta'_{k,p}$, $\eta''_{k,p}$, $\lambda'_{k,p}$, and $\lambda''_{k,p}$ in Figure 2 are errors caused by floating-point roundoff at each arithmetic step. The corresponding error quantities for fixed-point roundoff are $\gamma_{k,p}$, $\gamma_{k,p}'''$, $\delta_{k,p}$, $\delta_{k,p}'''$, $\epsilon_{k,p}$, $\epsilon_{k,p}'''$, $\zeta_{k,p}$, $\zeta_{k,p}'''$, $\eta_{k,p}$, $\eta_{k,p}'''$, $\lambda_{k,p}$, and $\lambda_{k,p}'''$. Thereafter, the actual real and imaginary parts of the floating- and fixed-point outputs $A_{k+1}'(p)$ and $A_{k+1}''(p)$, respectively are seen to be given explicitly by

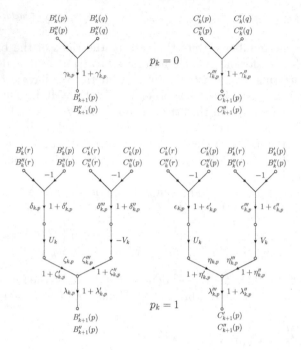

Fig. 2. Error flowgraph for decimation-in-frequency FFT

$$
\left.
\begin{aligned}
B_{k+1}'(p) &= [B_k'(p) + B_k'(q)](1 + \gamma_{k,p}') \\
C_{k+1}'(p) &= [C_k'(p) + C_k'(q)](1 + \gamma_{k,p}''')
\end{aligned}
\right\} \quad \text{if } p_k = 0 \qquad (13)
$$

$$
\left.
\begin{aligned}
B_{k+1}'(p) &= [B_k'(r) - B_k'(p)]\, U_k(p)(1 + \delta_{k,p}')(1 + \zeta_{k,p}')(1 + \lambda_{k,p}') \\
&\quad - [C_k'(r) - C_k'(p)]\, V_k(p)(1 + \delta_{k,p}'')(1 + \zeta_{k,p}'')(1 + \lambda_{k,p}'') \\
C_{k+1}'(p) &= [C_k'(r) - C_k'(p)]\, U_k(p)(1 + \epsilon_{k,p}')(1 + \eta_{k,p}')(1 + \lambda_{k,p}'') \\
&\quad + [B_k'(r) - B_k'(p)]\, V_k(p)(1 + \epsilon_{k,p}'')(1 + \eta_{k,p}'')(1 + \lambda_{k,p}'')
\end{aligned}
\right\} \quad \text{if } p_k = 1
$$

and

$$
\left.
\begin{aligned}
B_{k+1}''(p) &= [B_k''(p) + B_k''(q)] + \gamma_{k,p} \\
C_{k+1}''(p) &= [C_k''(p) + C_k''(q)] + \gamma_{k,p}'''
\end{aligned}
\right\} \quad \text{if } p_k = 0 \qquad (14)
$$

$$
\left.
\begin{aligned}
B_{k+1}''(p) &= [B_k''(r) - B_k''(p) + \delta_{k,p}]\, U_k(p) + \zeta_{k,p} - \\
&\quad ([C_k''(r) - C_k''(p) + \delta_{k,p}''']\, V_k(p) + \zeta_{k,p}''') + \lambda_{k,p} \\
C_{k+1}''(p) &= [C_k''(r) - C_k''(p) + \epsilon_{k,p}]\, U_k(p) + \eta_{k,p} + \\
&\quad ([B_k''(r) - B_k''(p) + \epsilon_{k,p}''']\, V_k(p) + \eta_{k,p}''') + \lambda_{k,p}'''
\end{aligned}
\right\} \quad \text{if } p_k = 1
$$

The errors $e_k(p)$, $e_k'(p)$, and $e_k''(p)$ defined in equations (6), (7), and (8) are complex and can be rewritten as

$$e_k(p) = B'_k(p) - B_k(p) + j[C'_k(p) - C_k(p)] \tag{15}$$

$$e'_k(p) = B''_k(p) - B_k(p) + j[C''_k(p) - C_k(p)] \tag{16}$$

$$e''_k(p) = B''_k(p) - B'_k(p) + j[C''_k(p) - C'_k(p)] \tag{17}$$

$$k = 1, 2, \ldots, m, \; p = 0, 1, \ldots, N-1$$

with

$$e_0(p) = e'_0(p) = e''_0(p) = 0, \qquad p = 0, 1, \ldots, N-1 \tag{18}$$

From equations (12), (13), (14), (15), (16), and (17), we derive the following error analysis cases:

1. *FFT Real to Floating-Point:*

$$e_{k+1}(p) = \begin{cases} e_k(p) + e_k(q) + f_k(p) & \text{if } p_k = 0 \\ [e_k(r) - e_k(p)] \, w_k(p) + f_k(p) & \text{if } p_k = 1 \end{cases} \tag{19}$$

where $f_k(p)$ is given by

$$f_k(p) = \begin{cases} \gamma'_{k,p}[B'_k(p) + B'_k(q)] + j\gamma''_{k,p}[C'_k(p) + C'_k(q)] & \text{if } p_k = 0 \\ [(1 + \delta'_{k,p})(1 + \zeta'_{k,p})(1 + \lambda'_{k,p}) - 1][B'_k(r) - B'_k(p)]U_k(p) \\ -[(1 + \delta''_{k,p})(1 + \zeta''_{k,p})(1 + \lambda'_{k,p}) - 1][C'_k(r) - C'_k(p)]V_k(p) \\ +j[(1 + \epsilon'_{k,p})(1 + \eta'_{k,p})(1 + \lambda''_{k,p}) - 1][C'_k(r) - C'_k(p)]U_k(p) \\ +j[(1 + \epsilon''_{k,p})(1 + \eta''_{k,p})(1 + \lambda''_{k,p}) - 1][B'_k(r) - B'_k(p)]V_k(p) \\ \hspace{8cm} \text{if } p_k = 1 \end{cases} \tag{20}$$

2. *FFT Real to Fixed-Point:*

$$e'_{k+1}(p) = \begin{cases} e'_k(p) + e'_k(q) + f'_k(p) & \text{if } p_k = 0 \\ [e'_k(r) - e'_k(p)] \, w_k(p) + f'_k(p) & \text{if } p_k = 1 \end{cases} \tag{21}$$

where $f'_k(p)$ is given by

$$f'_k(p) = \begin{cases} \gamma_{k,p} + j\gamma'''_{k,p} & \text{if } p_k = 0 \\ \delta_{k,p}U_k(p) + \zeta_{k,p} - \delta'''_{k,p}V_k(p) - \zeta'''_{k,p} + \lambda_{k,p} + \\ j(\epsilon_{k,p}U_k(p) + \eta_{k,p} + \epsilon'''_{k,p}V_k(p) + \eta'''_{k,p} + \lambda'''_{k,p}) & \text{if } p_k = 1 \end{cases} \tag{22}$$

3. *FFT Floating- to Fixed-Point:*

$$e''_{k+1}(p) = \begin{cases} e''_k(p) + e''_k(q) + f'_k(p) - f_k(p) & \text{if } p_k = 0 \\ [e''_k(r) - e''_k(p)] \, w_k(p) + f'_k(p) - f_k(p) & \text{if } p_k = 1 \end{cases} \tag{23}$$

where $f_k(p)$ and $f'_k(p)$ are given by equations (20) and (22).

The accumulation of roundoff error is determined by the recursive equations (19), (20), (21), (22), and (23), with initial conditions given by equation (18). In HOL, we first constructed complex numbers on reals similar to [18]. We defined in HOL a new type for complex numbers, to be in bijection with $\mathbb{R} \times \mathbb{R}$. The bijections are written in HOL as *complex* : $\mathbb{R}^2 \to \mathbb{C}$ and *coords* : $\mathbb{C} \to \mathbb{R}^2$. We used convenient abbreviations for the real (*Re*) and imaginary (*Im*) parts of a complex number, and also defined arithmetic operations such as addition, subtraction, and multiplication on complex numbers. We overloaded the usual symbols $(+, -, \times)$ for $\mathbb{C}$ and $\mathbb{R}$. Similarly, we constructed complex numbers on floating- and fixed-point numbers. Then we defined the principal N-roots on unity $(e^{-j2\pi/N} = cos\,(2\pi n/N) - j\,sin\,(2\pi n/N))$, and its powers $(OMEGA)$ as a complex number using the sine and cosine functions available in the transcendental theory of the HOL reals library [15]. We specified expressions in HOL for expansion of a natural number into a binary form in normal and rearranged order according to the equations (2) and (3). The above enables us to specify the FFT algorithms in real $(REAL\_FFT)$, floating- $(FLOAT\_FFT)$, and fixed-point (FXP_FFT) abstraction levels using recursive definitions in HOL as described in equation (4). Then we defined the real and imaginary parts of the FFT algorithm (FFT_REAL, FFT_IMAGE) and powers of the principal N-roots on unity $(OMEGA\_REAL, OMEGA\_IMAGE)$ according to the equation (11). Later, we proved in separate lemmas that the real and imaginary parts of the FFT algorithm in real, floating-, and fixed-point levels can be expanded as in equation (12). Then we proved lemmas to introduce an error in each of the arithmetic steps in real and imaginary parts of the floating- and fixed-point FFT algorithms according to the equations (13), and (14). We proved these lemmas using the fundamental error analysis lemmas for basic arithmetic operations [3] according to the equations (9) and (10). Then we defined in HOL the error of the pth element of the floating- $(REAL\_TO\_FLOAT\_FFT\_ERROR)$ and fixed-point $(REAL\_TO\_FXP\_FFT\_ERROR)$ FFT algorithms at step k, and the corresponding error in transition from floating- to fixed-point $(FLOAT\_TO\_FXP\_FFT\_ERR OR)$, according to the equations (6), (7), and (8). Thereafter, we proved lemmas to rewrite the errors as complex numbers using the real and imaginary parts according to the equations (15), (16), and (17). Finally, we proved lemmas to determine the accumulation of roundoff error in floating- and fixed-point FFT algorithms by recursive equations and initial conditions according to the equations (18), (19), (20), (21), (22), and (23).

4   FFT Design Implementation Verification

In this section, we describe the verification of the transition from fixed-point specification to RTL implementation for FFT algorithms. We have chosen the case study of a radix-4 pipelined 16-point complex FFT core available as a VHDL RTL model in the Xilinx Coregen library [32]. Figure 3 shows the overall block diagram of the design. The basic elements are memories, delays, multiplexers, and dragonflies. In general, the 16-point pipelined FFT requires the calculation of two radix-4 dragonfly ranks. Each radix-4 dragonfly is a successive combination of a radix-4 butterfly with four twiddle factor multipliers. The FFT core accepts naturally ordered data on the input buses in a continuous stream, performs a complex FFT, and streams out the DFT samples on the output buses in a natural order. These buses are respectively the real and imaginary components of the input and output sequences. An internal input data memory controller orders the data into blocks to be presented to the FFT processor. The twiddle factors are stored in coefficient memories. The real and imaginary components of complex input and output samples and the phase factors are represented as 16-bit 2's complement numbers. The unscrambling operation is performed using the output bit-reversing buffer.

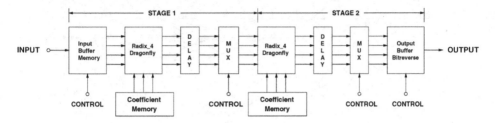

Fig. 3. Radix-4 16-point pipelined FFT implementation

To define the radix-4 FFT algorithm [6, 25], we represent the indices p and n in equation (1) in a base 4 (quaternary number system) as

$$p = 4p_1 + p_0, \qquad p_1, p_0 \;=\; 0, 1, 2, 3 \qquad (24)$$
$$n = 4n_1 + n_0, \qquad n_1, n_0 \;=\; 0, 1, 2, 3 \qquad (25)$$

It is easy to verify that as n_0 and n_1 take on all possible values in the range indicated, n goes through all possible values from 0 to 15 with no values repeated. This is also true for the frequency index p. Using these index mappings, we can express the radix-4 16-point FFT algorithm recursively as

$$A_1(p_0, n_0) \;=\; \sum_{n_1=0}^{3} x(n_1, n_0)\, (W_{16})^{4p_0 n_1} \qquad (26)$$

$$A_2(p_0, p_1) \;=\; \sum_{n_0=0}^{3} A_1(p_0, n_0)\, (W_{16})^{(4p_1+p_0)n_0} \qquad (27)$$

The final result can be written as

$$A(p_1, p_0) = A_2(p_0, p_1) \qquad (28)$$

Thus, as in the radix-2 algorithm, the results are in reversed order. Based on equations (26), (27), and (28) we can develop a signal flowgraph for the radix-4 16-point FFT algorithm as shown in Figure 4, which is an expanded version of the pipelined implementation of Figure 3. The graph is composed of two successive radix-4 dragonfly stages. To alleviate confusion in this graph we have shown only one of the radix-4 butterflies in the first stage. Also, we have not shown the multipliers for the radix-4 butterflies in the second stage since they are similar to the representative butterfly of the first stage. Figure 4 also illustrates the unscrambling procedure for the radix-4 algorithm.

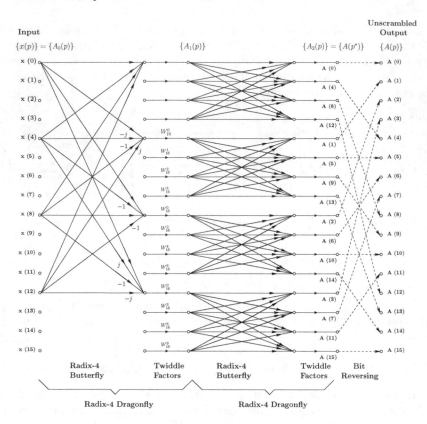

Fig. 4. Signal flowgraph of radix-4 16-point FFT

In HOL, we first modeled the RTL description of a radix-4 butterfly as a predicate in higher-order logic. The block takes a vector of four complex input data and performs the operations as depicted in the flowgraph of Figure 4, to generate a vector of four complex output signals. The real and imaginary parts of the input and output signals are represented as 16-bit Boolean words. We defined separate functions in HOL for arithmetic operations such as addition, subtraction, and multiplication on complex two's complement 16-bit Boolean words. Then, we built the complete butterfly structure using a proper combination of these primitive operations. Thereafter, we described a radix-4 dragonfly block ($DRAGONFLY\_RTL$) as a conjunction of a radix-4 butterfly and four 16-bit twiddle factor complex multipliers as shown in Figure 4. Finally, we modeled the complete RTL description of the radix-4 16-point FFT structure (DIF_FFT_RTL) in HOL. The FFT block is defined as a conjunction of 8 instantiations of radix-4 dragonfly blocks according to Figure 4, by applying the proper time instances of the input and output signals to each block. Following similar steps, we described a fixed-point radix-4 16-point FFT structure (DIF_FFT_FXP) in HOL using complex fixed-point data types and arithmetic operations.

For the formal verification, we first proved that the FFT RTL description implies the corresponding fixed-point model.

$$
\begin{aligned}
\vdash_{thm} \; & \forall \, N \, X_r \, X_i \, W_r \, W_i \, A_r \, A_i. \\
& DIF\_FFT\_RTL \, N \, X_r \, X_i \, W_r \, W_i \, A_r \, A_i \implies \\
& DIF\_FFT\_FXP \, N \, FXP\_VECT\_COMPLEX \, (X_r, X_i) \qquad\qquad (29) \\
& \qquad\qquad FXP\_VECT\_COMPLEX \, (W_r, W_i) \\
& \qquad\qquad FXP\_VECT\_COMPLEX \, (A_r, A_i)
\end{aligned}
$$

The proof of the FFT block is then broken down into the corresponding proof of the dragonfly block, which itself is broken down to the proof of butterfly and primitive arithmetic operations.

$$
\begin{aligned}
\vdash_{thm} \; & \forall \, N \, A_r \, A_i \, W_r \, W_i \, Q_r \, Q_i. \\
& DRAGONFLY\_RTL \, N \, A_r \, A_i \, W_r \, W_i \, Q_r \, Q_i \implies \\
& DRAGONFLY\_FXP \, N \, FXP \, (A_r) \, FXP \, (A_i) \qquad\qquad (30) \\
& \qquad FXP \, (W_r) \, FXP \, (W_i) \, FXP \, (Q_r) \, FXP \, (Q_i)
\end{aligned}
$$

We used the data abstraction functions FXP and $FXP\_VECT\_COMPLEX$ to convert a complex vector of 16-bit two's complement Boolean words into the corresponding fixed-point vector. We have also described the radix-4 16-point fixed-point FFT algorithm ($FXP\_FFT\_ALGORITHM$) using the defining equations (26), (27), and (28). Then we proved that the expanded fixed-point description based on the flowgraph of Figure 4 implies the corresponding closed form fixed-point algorithmic description.

$$
\begin{aligned}
\vdash_{thm} \; & \forall \, N \, X \, W \, A. \\
& DIF\_FFT\_FXP \, N \, X \, W \, A \implies \qquad\qquad\qquad (31) \\
& \forall \, p. \, A \, (p) \, = \, FXP\_FFT\_ALGORITHM \, N \, X \, W \, p
\end{aligned}
$$

In this way we completed the verification of the RTL implementation to fixed-point algorithmic specification of a radix-4 16-point FFT algorithm.

5   Conclusions

In this paper, we described a comprehensive methodology for the verification of generic fast Fourier transform algorithms using the HOL theorem prover. The approach covers the two canonical forms (decimation-in-time, and decimation-in-frequency) of realization of the FFT algorithm using real, floating-, and fixed-point arithmetic as well as their RT implementations, each entirely specified in HOL. We proved lemmas to derive expressions for the accumulation of roundoff error in floating- and fixed-point implementations compared to the ideal real specification. As a future work, we plan to extend these lemmas to analyse the worst-case, average, and variance errors. Then we proved that the FFT RTL implementation implies the corresponding specification at fixed-point level using classical hierarchical verification in HOL, hence bridging the gap between hardware implementation and high levels of mathematical specification. In this work we also have contributed to the upgrade and application of established real, complex real, floating- and fixed-point theories in HOL to the analysis of errors due to finite precision effects, and applied them on the realization of the FFT algorithms. Error analyses since the late sixties used theoretical paper-and-pencil proofs and simulation techniques. We believe this is the first time a complete formal framework has been constructed in HOL for the verification of the fast Fourier transform algorithms at different levels of abstraction. The methodology presented in this paper opens new avenues in using formal methods for the verification of digital signal processing (DSP) systems as complement to traditional theoretical (analytical) and simulation techniques. We are currently investigating the verification of complex wired and wireless communication systems, whose building blocks, heavily make use of several instances of the FFT algorithms.

References

1. B. Akbarpour, S. Tahar, and A. Dekdouk, "Formalization of Cadence SPW Fixed-Point Arithmetic in HOL," In Integrated Formal Methods, LNCS 2335, pp. 185-204, Springer-Verlag, 2002.
2. B. Akbarpour, S. Tahar, "Modeling SystemC Fixed-Point Arithmetic in HOL," In Formal Methods and Software Engineering, LNCS 2885, pp. 206-225, Springer-Verlag, 2003.
3. B. Akbarpour, S. Tahar, "Error Analysis of Digital Filters using Theorem Proving," In Theorem Proving in Higher Order Logics, LNCS 3223, pp. 1-16, Springer-Verlag, 2004.
4. P. Bjesse, "Automatic Verification of Combinational and Pipelined FFT Circuits," In Computer Aided Verification, LNCS 1633, pp. 380-393, Springer-Verlag, 1999.
5. R. Boulton, A. Gordon, M. Gordon, J. Harrison, J. Herbert, and J. Van-Tassel, "Experience with Embedding Hardware Description Languages in HOL," In Theorem Provers in Circuit Design, pp. 129-156, North-Holland, 1992.
6. E. O. Brigham, "The Fast Fourier Transform," Prentice Hall, 1974.
7. V. Capretta, "Certifying the Fast Fourier Transform with Coq," In Theorem Proving in Higher Order Logics, LNCS 2152, pp. 154-168, Springer-Verlag, 2001.
8. Synopsys, Inc., "CoCentric^{TM} System Studio User's Guide," USA, Aug. 2001.
9. W. T. Cochran et. al., "What is the Fast Fourier Transform," IEEE Transactions on Audio and Electroacoustics, AU-15: 45-55, Jun. 1967.
10. J. W. Cooley, J. W. Tukey, "An Algorithm for Machine Calculation of Complex Fourier Series," Mathematics of Computation, 19: 297-301, Apr. 1965.
11. G. Forsythe, C. B. Moler, "Computer Solution of Linear Algebraic Systems," Prentice-Hall, 1967.
12. R. A. Gamboa, "The Correctness of the Fast Fourier Transform: A Structural Proof in ACL2," Formal Methods in System Design, Special Issue on UNITY, Jan. 2002.
13. W. M. Gentleman, G. Sande, "Fast Fourier Transforms - For Fun and Profit," In AFIPS Fall Joint Computer Conference, Vol. 29, pp. 563-578, Spartan Books, Washington, DC, 1966.
14. M. J. C. Gordon, T. F. Melham, "Introduction to HOL: A Theorem Proving Environment for Higher-Order Logic," Cambridge University Press, 1993.
15. J. R. Harrison, "Constructing the Real Numbers in HOL," Formal Methods in System Design 5 (1/2): 35-59, Kluwer, 1994.

16. J. R. Harrison, "A Machine-Checked Theory of Floating-Point Arithmetic," In Theorem Proving in Higher Order Logics, LNCS 1690, pp. 113-130, Springer-Verlag, 1999.
17. J. R. Harrison, "Floating-Point Verification in HOL Light: The Exponential Function," Formal Methods in System Design 16 (3): 271-305, Kluwer, 2000.
18. J. R. Harrison, "Complex Quantifier Elimination in HOL," In Supplemental Proceedings of the International Conference on Theorem Proving in Higher Order Logics, pp. 159-174, Edinburgh, Scotland, UK, Sep. 2001.
19. T. Kaneko, and B. Liu, "Accumulation of Round-Off Error in Fast Fourier Transforms," Journal of Association for Computing Machinery, 17 (4): 637-654, Oct. 1970.
20. H. Keding, M. Willems, M. Coors, and H. Meyr, "FRIDGE: A Fixed-Point Design and Simulation Environment," In Proceedings Design Automation and Test in Europe Conference, pp. 429-435, Paris, France, Feb. 1998.
21. B. Liu, T. Kaneko, "Roundoff Error in Fast Fourier Transforms (Decimation in Time)," Proceedings of the IEEE (Proceedings Letters), 991-992, Jun. 1975.
22. Mathworks, Inc., "Fixed-Point Blockset User's Guide (ver. 2.0)," 1999.
23. T. Melham, "Higher Order Logic and Hardware Verification," Cambridge Tracts in Theoretical Computer Science 31, Cambridge University Press, 1993.
24. J. Misra, "Powerlists: A Structure for Parallel Recursion," In ACM Transactions on Programming Languages and Systems, 16 (6): 1737-1767, Nov. 1994.
25. A. V. Oppenheim, R. W. Schafer, "Discrete-Time Signal Processing," Prentice-Hall, 1989.
26. A. V. Oppenheim, C. J. Weinstein, "Effects of Finite Register Length in Digital Filtering and the Fast Fourier Transform," Proceedings of the IEEE, 60 (8): 957-976, Aug. 1972.
27. Cadence Design Systems, Inc., "Signal Processing WorkSystem (SPW) User's Guide," USA, Jul. 1999.
28. T. Thong, B. Liu, "Fixed-Point Fast Fourier Transform Error Analysis," IEEE Transactions on Acoustics, Speech, and Signal Processing, ASSP 24 (6): 563-573, Dec. 1976.
29. C. J. Weinstein, "Roundoff Noise in Floating Point Fast Fourier Transform Computation," IEEE Transactions on Audio and Electroacoustics, AU-17 (3): 209-215, Sep. 1969.
30. P. D. Welch, "A Fixed-Point Fast Fourier Transform Error Analysis," IEEE Transactions on Audio and Electroacoustics, AU-17 (2): 151-157, Jun. 1969.
31. J. H. Wilkinson, "Rounding Errors in Algebraic Processes," Prentice-Hall, 1963.
32. Xilinx, Inc., "High-Performance 16-Point Complex FFT/IFFT V1.0.5, Product Specification," USA, Jul. 2000, http://xilinx.com/ipcenter.

A Functional Approach
to the Formal Specification of Networks on Chip

Julien Schmaltz* and Dominique Borrione

TIMA Laboratory, VDS Group
Joseph Fourier University
46 avenue Felix Viallet
38031 Grenoble Cedex, France
{Julien.Schmaltz,Dominique.Borrione}@imag.fr

Abstract. We present a functional approach, based on the ACL2 logic, for the specification of *system on a chip* communication architectures. Our decomposition of the communications allows the method to be modular for both system definition and validation. When performed in the context of the ACL2 logic, all the definitions and theorems are not only reusable, but also constitute an executable and proven valid specification for the system. We illustrate the approach on a state of the art network on chip: the *Octagon*. We prove that messages travel over this network without being modified and eventually reach their expected destination.

1   Introduction

The design of a production quality *system on a chip* (SoC), involving several processor-like modules, and several memories and peripherals is well supported by a variety of simulation and formal verification tools at the register transfer level (RTL) and below, where ninety percent of the design time is spent [1]. In contrast, the initial phase when concepts are first written down, and which involves critical decisions on the number of units, their communication, the main pipelines, memory size and global system performances, is only supported by simulation tools taking as input relatively *ad hoc* formalisms. It is far from obvious that the RTL implementation is ever checked compliant with the description model produced at the concept phase. Yet, as systems increasingly reuse preexisting processor and memory cores, which have been verified intensively in isolation, an essential aspect of an overall system functional correctness relies on the correctness of their communications. In this context, the work reported here focuses on the specification of the communications on a chip, specified at a high-level of abstraction, and involving generic network components where the number of interconnected modules is finite, but possibly not fixed. Our objective is to develop a high-level specification and verification method for the concept

---

* Part of this work was done while visiting the Department of Computer Sciences of the University of Texas at Austin. This visit was supported by an EURODOC scholarship granted by the "Région Rhône-Alpes", France.

A.J. Hu and A.K. Martin (Eds.): FMCAD 2004, LNCS 3312, pp. 52–66, 2004.

Table 1. Summary of Communications

Type of message	Structure	Between
Order	(operation location item) operation ∈ {read, write, no_op}	application ↔ interface
Result	(Rstat RiTem) Rstat ∈ {OK, inv_addr, inv_op, ... }	application ↔ interface
Request	(r/w addr data) r/w ∈ {r, w}	interface ↔ interface
Response	(Status Rdata) Status ∈ {OK, inv_addr, inv_op, ... }	interface ↔ interface

phase, that will support validating that the intended communication module is correct. Simulation, semi-formal and formal validation techniques are all considered complementary, and therefore targeted by our study. Formal efforts in protocol verification ([8] [9] [10] [11]) are connected to our work, but in contrast to them, our approach focuses on the modeling and the validation of the routing and the travel of messages over an interconnect. Our goal is to prove that a token travels correctly, and arrives to its destination on a *parameterized* communication structure.

In this paper, we present the formal specification, in the ACL2 logic [2], of a state of the art network on chip developed by *ST Microelectronics* and named *Octagon*. Our purpose is the translation of the informal descriptions presented in the scientific literature ([3] and [4]), into a formal description in a computational logic, where the formal model is both executable and can be validated by the proof of theorems. Our modeling style is functional, *i.e.* components and their interconnections are represented by sets of functions. Our approach is *modular* for both the modeling and the validation process, which eases the elaboration of models and proofs. Our contribution is a specification and functional verification methodology for the very first design steps of parameterized communication virtual modules. To our knowledge, the application of automatic theorem proving to on-chip communication hardware is new. To this end, we have developed a specific library of functions and theorems, most of which will be reusable for circuits of similar functionality.

In the next section, we introduce the functional formalism used for the specification of *Octagon*. We present the functional definition of the transfer of messages and the general theorems that express its correctness. Section three introduces the main features of the *Octagon* and of the interconnected nodes. In section four, the overall memory structure and the functional specification of a node system are presented. Within a node system, we prove that the local communications are correct according to the formalism of section two. The functional definition of the *Octagon*, and the main theorems that validate this model are given in section five. We prove that messages eventually reach their expected destination without being modified. In the final section, we discuss the experimental results, and present our conclusions.

Fig. 1. Point to point interconnection scheme

2   Functional Specification of Communication Systems

2.1   Principles of Communications

We consider communications between a master - typically a processor (DSP, MCU...) - and a slave - typically a co-processor or a memory (ASIC, DMA...). In this configuration, a master starts the communication by sending an *order* to the slave, which replies with a *result* (see Table 1). For the purpose of this paper, we assume masters to be processors and slaves to be memories. Consequently, an *operation* is a *read* or *write* to a given location, or *no_op* to indicate an idle state of the master. *Rstat* takes the value *OK* if the communication is successful. For a memory, it can be *inv_addr* to indicate a wrong address or *inv_op* to indicate an unknown operation. Communication operations are *orthogonal* to the computation operations [5]. They are separated in two classes of components: the interfaces and the applications (Figure 1). To distinguish between interface-application and interface-interface communications, the former dialogue is denoted by *orders* and *results*, the latter by *requests* and *responses*. In this paper, the need for the distinction between *orders* and *requests* on the one side, *results* and *responses* on the other side, is not obvious, due to the simplicity of the interface protocol. In more elaborate cases, *e.g.* Ethernet, the encapsulation of orders/results with protocol information produces messages of a quite distinct structure.

For the purpose of this paper, a *request* has the same structure as an order. Parameter *data* is meaningful for a write request, in the case of a read it takes value '-' to denote a "don't care". Likewise, a *response* is similar to a *result*. *status* corresponds to *Rstat*, and takes the same possible values: *OK*, *inv_addr*, *inv_op* . . .

In the following, we use the element name for the function that returns an element of a communication event. For instance, *Operation, Location, Item* are the functions that return the first, second and third element of an *order*.

2.2   Functional Modeling of Communications

Our formalism is pictured on Fig. 2. An interface communicates with two components, an application and another interface, and is thus modeled by two functions. For the master interface: MI_{req} computes a *request* from an *order*; MI_{res} computes a *result* from a *response*. For the slave interface: SI_{ord} computes an *order* from a *request*; SI_{resp} computes a *response* from a *result*. Master and slave interfaces are not directly connected. A communication medium, bus or

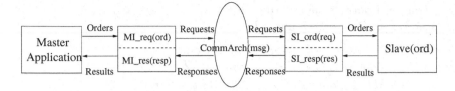

Fig. 2. Formalization of Communications

network, determines how requests and responses are transferred between them. The medium is modeled by a function *CommArch* which takes and returns a *response* or a *request*, *i.e.* a *message*. Communications are modeled by the composition of these functions.

In practice, the slave interface functions take an additional input: a flag *select*. If *select* is *true* then the interface is active and each function computes an order or a response. Otherwise, the functions return error values meaning that they are not ready to operate. Consequently, the composition of these "concrete" functions is not exactly a mathematical composition. Let us consider the functions MI_{req} and SI_{ord}:

Definition 1. *Master Interface*

$MI_{req}(order)$ *returns Request* $\overset{def}{=}$
  if $Operation(order) = read$ **then**   *; read request*
   $list(r, Location(order), Item(order))$
 else   *; write request*
   $list(w, Location(order), Item(order))$
  endif

Definition 2. *Slave Interface*

$SI_{ord}(request, select)$ *returns Order* $\overset{def}{=}$
 if *select* **then**   *; slave interface is active*
   if $r/w(request) = r$ **then**   *; read operation*
    $list(read, Addr(request), Data(request))$
  else   *; write operation*
    $list(write, Addr(request), Data(request))$
  endif
 else   *; slave is not active*
  $list(not\_ready, no\_loc, no\_item)$.
 endif

The transfer of an order from the master to the slave application is defined as the composition of MI_{req}, $CommArch$ and SI_{ord}:

Definition 3. *Transmission of an Order via a medium*

 $Trans\_ord(order, select)$ *returns Order* $\overset{def}{=}$
  $SI_{ord}(CommArch(MI_{req}(order)), select)$

A transfer from the slave to the master application is defined as the composition of MI_{res}, $CommArch$ and SI_{resp}:

Definition 4. *Transmission of a Result via a medium*

$$Trans\_res(result, select)\ returns\ Result \stackrel{def}{=}$$
$$MI_{res}(CommArch(SI_{resp}(result, select)))$$

Let function *Slave* model the slave application; a complete transfer between the master and the slave is defined by the composition of $Trans\_res$, *Slave* and $Trans\_ord$:

Definition 5. *Transfer*

$$Transfer(order, select)\ returns\ Result \stackrel{def}{=}$$
$$Trans\_res(Slave(Trans\_ord(order, select)), select)$$

The correctness of the transmission of an order is achieved if the order received by the slave application is "equal" to the order sent by the master application. Generally, the function *Addr* used in the SI_{ord} function will modify the *location* of the original order to satisfy a specific mapping of the slave application addresses. Consequently, the order received by the slave application is not strictly equal to the sent order, but equal *modulo* a given address mapping. This is noted $ord_1 \simeq ord_2$, defined by: (1) $Operation(ord_1) = Operation(ord_2)$; (2) $Item(ord_1) = item(ord_2)$; (3) $Location(ord_1) \simeq_{map} Location(ord_2)$, where $\simeq_{map}$ defines the address mapping. If we can establish that $CommArch(msg) = msg$ then the following holds obviously:

Theorem 1. *Trans_Ord Correctness*
$$\forall\ order,\ Trans\_ord(order,\ true)\ \simeq\ order$$

The correctness of the transmission of a result is achieved if the result received by the master application is equal (generally strictly) to the result sent by the slave application. Similarly to Theorem 1, the following holds:

Theorem 2. *Trans_Res Correctness*
$$\forall\ result,\ Trans\_res(result,\ true)\ =\ result$$

The correctness of a transfer is achieved if its result is equal (again *modulo* an address mapping) to the application of the function *Slave* to the order produced by the master application.

Theorem 3. *Transfer Correctness*
$$\forall\ order,\ Transfer(order,\ true)\ \simeq\ Slave(order)$$

Proof. Follows from theorems 1 and 2. □

The remainder of this paper concentrates on the modeling and proof of these theorems on the Octagon architecture. We used the same interface functions and our goal is to prove that Theorem 3 holds. To this aim, specific properties must be satisfied by the Octagon communication architecture: (a) it must not modify a message (this is proved by Theorem 6); (b) it must convey a message between the correct source and destination (this is proved by Theorems 4 and 5).

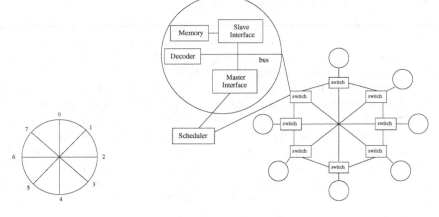

Fig. 3. Basic Octagon Unit

Fig. 4. Node System connected to a switch and the scheduler

3   Overview of the Octagon

3.1   Architecture and Routing

A basic Octagon unit consists in eight nodes and twelve bidirectional links (Figure 3). It has two main properties: two-hop communication between any pair of nodes and simple, shortest-path routing algorithm ([3] and [4]).

An *Octagon packet* is data that must be carried from the source node to the destination node as a result of a communication request by the source node. A scheduler allocates the entire path between the source and destination nodes of a communicating node pair. Non-overlapping communication paths can occur concurrently, permitting spatial reuse.

The routing of a packet is accomplished as follows. Each node compares the tag (*Packet_addr*) to its own address (*Node_addr*) to determine the next action. The node computes the relative address of a packet as:

$$Rel\_addr \; = \; (Packet\_addr \; - \; Node\_addr) \; mod \; 8 \qquad (1)$$

At each node, the route of packets is a function of *Rel_addr* as follows:

- *Rel_addr* = 0, process at node
- *Rel_addr* = 1 or 2, route clockwise
- *Rel_addr* = 6 or 7, route counterclockwise
- route across otherwise

Example 1. Consider a packet *Pack* at node 2 sent to node 5. First, $5-2\ mod\ 8 = 3$, *Pack* is routed across to 6. Then, $5 - 6\ mod\ 8 = 7$, *Pack* is routed counterclockwise to 5. Finally, $5 - 5\ mod\ 8 = 0$, *Pack* has reached its final destination.

3.2 Node and System Structure

Each node of the network is a small system built around a bus architecture. It contains an address decoder, a master and a slave interface and a memory unit. This system is connected to *Octagon via* a switch (Figure 4). Master interfaces and switches are connected to the scheduler.

Nodes and Octagon work as follows. If the memory unit and the master interface involved in a communication belong to the same node, the request is said to be *local* and the output flag of the decoder is set to *true*. It is said to be *non-local* otherwise, and the output flag of the decoder is set to *false*. Suppose a non-local transaction is pending at several master interfaces. The scheduler determines the set of transactions that can be done concurrently, *i.e.* those that do not share communication paths. A path is allocated for each one of them and carries both the request and the response. When every concurrent transaction is finished, the system is ready for a new set of transactions.

In the next two sections, we present the functional specification and validation of the network, in algorithmic notation for readability. The actual model is written in LISP and can be found in [6] which also contains the ACL2 theorems. All proofs have been performed mechanically with the ACL2 theorem prover, and the reader interested in the detailed proof steps can run the certified "book" available on the web [7].

4 Functional Specification of the Node System

4.1 Memory Structure

The overall system memory is equally distributed over the nodes. Let ms be the size of a memory in a node, and Num_Node be the number of nodes (8 for the Octagon, but the argument is more general). The size of the global memory is $global\_ms = Num\_Node \times ms$.

During transfers, the master uses the global address, which ranges from 0 to $global\_ms - 1$ and the slave selected by the decoder reads or writes the data to its local address $local\_addr$. The local and global addresses are related by: $local\_addr = global\_addr \bmod ms$.

Conversely, the destination node possessing a given global address $global\_addr$ is the node i, such that

$$i = global\_addr \ div \ ms \tag{2}$$

From the above, a definition of relation $\simeq_{map}$ that preserves the validity of Theorem 1 is given by:

$$x \simeq_{map} y \Leftrightarrow y = x \bmod ms$$

4.2 Functional Memory Model

The memory unit of a node is modeled by a list *memo* of items and a function *Memory* that operates on *memo*. The address of an item is its position in the list.

Definition 6. *Memory*

$Memory(order, memo)$ *returns* $(Status\ Item\ Memo)$ $\overset{def}{=}$
  if $Location(order) < Len(memo)$ **then**   *; valid address?*
   if $Operation(order) = read$ **then**
    $list(OK, Memo[Location(order)], memo)$
   elsif $Operation(order) = write$ **then**
    $list(OK, Item(order), Update(memo, Location(order), Item(order)))$
   else   *; invalid operation*
    $list(inv\_op, no\_item, Memo)$
   endif
  else   *; invalid address*
   $list(inv\_addr, no\_data, Memo)$
  endif
where $L\,[i]$ denotes the i'th element of L,
Update(L, a, v) returns a list where the element at position a is v

The global memory $Glob\_Mem$ is represented by the ordered concatenation of all local memory lists $Memo$, starting from 0.

$$Glob\_Mem = (d_0\ d_1\ ...\ d_{ms-1}\ d_{ms}\ d_{ms+1}\ ...\ d_{num\_node \times ms-1}) \tag{3}$$

Two functions are defined on $Glob\_Mem$: get_local_mem extracts the memory unit number $node\_nb$ from the global memory, and $update\_local\_mem$ returns a global memory containing an updated local memory.

Definition 7. *Get Local Memory*

$get\_local\_mem(Glob\_Mem, node\_nb, ms)$ *returns* $Memo$ $\overset{def}{=}$
  $first(ms, nthcdr(node\_nb \times ms, Glob\_Mem))$
        where first(n,L) returns the n first elements of L and
         nthcdr(n, L) returns L without its first n elements

Example 2. Consider $Glob_Mem = $ (a b c d e f), $ms=2$ and $Num\_Node=3$. The memory of node 1 is $first(2, nthcdr(1 \times 2, Glob_Mem)) = first(2, (c\ d\ e\ f)) = $ $(c\ d\ )$.

Definition 8. *Update Local Mem*

$update\_local\_mem(Glob\_Mem, memo, node\_nb, ms)$ *returns* $Glob\_Mem$ $\overset{def}{=}$
  $concatenate(first(node\_nb \times ms, Glob\_Mem), memo,$
    $nthcdr((node\_nb + 1) \times ms, Glob\_Mem))$

Example 3. The memory of node 1, as of example 2, is updated as follows:
$update_local_mem((a\ b\ c\ d\ e\ f), (g\ h), 1, 2) = concatenate((a\ b), (g\ h), (e\ f)) = $
$(a\ b\ g\ h\ e\ f)$.

4.3   Specification of the Node System

We define a function *Node* which represents a generic node system. Its execution models either one local communication or a step in a distant communication.

Priority is given to the communication started by the local master. It takes three architectural parameters: $Glob\_Mem$, ms, and the own node number $node\_nb$. The other arguments are the pending order of the local master ord, the request req and the response $resp$ coming from a distant node, and two Boolean flags stating the validity of these last two arguments. $Node$ returns a list composed of the result of a local communication (the constant *no_result* if none), the emitted request (*no_message* if none), the response to the incoming request (*no_response* if none), and the new value of the global memory.

Definition 9. *Node System*
$Node(ord, req, resp, Glob\_Mem, ms, validRequest, validResponse, node\_nb)$
$\quad returns\ (Result\ Request\ Response\ Glob\_Mem)\ \overset{def}{=}$
$\quad\quad$ **if** $Operation(ord)\ =\ no\_op$ **then**
$\quad\quad\quad$ **if** $validRequest$ **then**
$\quad\quad\quad\quad (*no\_result * *no\_message *$
$\quad\quad\quad\quad\quad Netw\_transfer(req, Glob\_Mem, ms, node\_nb))$
$\quad\quad\quad$ **elsif** $validResponse$ **then**
$\quad\quad\quad\quad (MI_{res}(resp)\ * no\_message * *no\_response *\ Glob\_Mem)$
$\quad\quad\quad$ **else**
$\quad\quad\quad\quad (*no\_result * *no\_message * *no\_response *\ Glob\_Mem)$
$\quad\quad\quad$ **endif**
$\quad\quad$ **elsif** $Decoder(Location(ord), ms)$ **then**
$\quad\quad\quad (Bus\_transfer(ord, true)\ * no\_message * *no\_response *\ Glob\_Mem)$
$\quad\quad$ **else**
$\quad\quad\quad (*no\_result *\ MI_{req}(ord)\ * no\_response *\ Glob\_Mem)$
$\quad\quad$ **endif**

Local communications are represented by function $Bus\_transfer$ which is defined similarly to definitions 9 and 10 of section 2. Function $CommArch$ is replaced by function Bus, which is here modeled by the identity function: $Bus(x) = x$. Consequently, the correctness of local operations follows from Theorems 1, 2, and 3.

At the beginning of a distant communication initiated by the master of node nb_1, the local order is $read$ or $write$ and function $Node$ with parameter $node\_nb$ $= nb\_1$ calls MI_{req}. This produces a request which is sent over the network. At the destination node nb_2, the $validRequest$ is set to "true" by the scheduler. This is modeled to a second call to function $Node$ with $node\_nb = nb\_2$ that calls function $Netw\_transfer$ below to compute the response. The response is sent back to the source node nb_1, with a third call to $Node$ with parameters $node\_nb = nb\_1$ and $validResponse = $ "true", that invokes function MI_{res} to compute the final result of the distant communication.

Definition 10. *Network Transfer*
$Netw\_transfer(req, Glob\_Mem, select, node\_nb)$
$\quad\quad returns\ (Response\ Glob\_Mem)\ \overset{def}{=}$

let ord **be** $SI_{ord}(req, select, ms)$ **in**
   let $(res\ mem)$ **be**
         $Memory(ord, get\_local\_mem(Glob\_Mem, node\_nb, ms))$ **in**
     $list(SI_{resp}(res, select),$
         $update\_local\_mem(Glob\_Mem, mem, node\_nb, ms))$

Distant communications are completed by function $Octagon$, presented in the next section.

5 Functional Specification of Octagon

5.1 Routing Function

We define a function $Route$ which represents the routing algorithm of section 3.1 for an arbitrary number Num_Node of nodes. Num_Node is a natural number, that is a multiple of 4. It computes the path - a list of node numbers - between nodes $from$ and to.

Definition 11. *Routing Function*

$Route(from,\ to,\ Num\_Node)\ returns\ Path \stackrel{def}{=}$
  $let\ Rel\_addr\ be\ (to - from)\ mod\ Num\_Node\ in:$
  if $Rel\_addr = 0$ **then** $list(from)$
  elsif $0 < Rel\_addr \leq \frac{Num\_Node}{4}$ **then**
    $list(from, Route(Clockwise(from, Num\_Node), to, Num\_Node))$
  elsif $Num\_Node - \frac{Num\_Node}{4} \leq Rel\_addr < Num\_Node$ **then**
    $list(from, Route(Counterclockwise(from, Num\_Node), to, Num\_Node))$
  else
    $list(from, Route(Across(from,\ Num\_Node),\ to,\ Num\_Node))$
  endif
$where$
  $Clockwise(from,\ n) \stackrel{def}{=} (from + 1)\ mod\ n$
  $Counterclockwise(from,\ n) \stackrel{def}{=} (from - 1)\ mod\ n$
  $Across(from,\ n) \stackrel{def}{=} (from + \frac{n}{2})\ mod\ n$

The following properties establish the correctness of function $Route$: a) it terminates; b) it computes a path consistent with the network topology; and c) the number of hops is less than or equal to $\frac{Num\_Node}{4}$.

In ACL2, a new recursive function must be proven to terminate before it can be added to the logic. This is done by exhibiting a measure (an ordinal) that decreases according to a well-formed relation based on the ordinals up to ϵ_0 (chapter 6 of [2]). The measure used for $Route$ is $Min[(dest - from)\ mod\ n, (from - dest)\ mod\ n]$.

The second property is divided in three parts. First, we prove that each move is part of the available ones: clockwise, counterclockwise or across. Second, $Route$ produces a non-empty path that contains no duplicate. Finally, we prove that a path starts with node $from$ and ends with node to.

The following theorem states the properties b) and c) on *Route*. Predicates *noDuplicatesp* and *AvailableMovesp* are obvious, and not spelled out for brevity.

Theorem 4. *Correctness of Route*
$\forall$ *from, to, Num_Node* $\in \mathcal{N}$ *such that Num_Node* mod $4 = 0$
$$0 < len(Route(from, to, Num\_Node)) \leq \tfrac{Num\_node}{4} + 1$$
$\land$ *noDuplicatesp*($Route(from, to, Num\_node)$)
$\land$ *AvailableMovesp*($Route(from, to, Num\_node), Num\_Node$)
$\land$ *First*($Route(from, to, Num\_Node)$) $= from$
$\land$ *Last*($Route(from, to, Num\_Node)$) $= to$

5.2 Scheduler

In the rest of the paper, we consider that an order is pending at each master (a *no_op* operation standing for the absence of order). Master 0 is given the highest priority, and master $Num\_Node - 1$ the lowest. The pending orders are represented by a list *op_lst* which has the following form:

$$op\_lst = (... \; (i \; op_i \; loc_i \; item_i) \; ... \; (j \; op_j \; loc_j \; item_j) \; ...) \tag{4}$$

where i is a node number, *op* an operation, and *loc* a global address.

The role of the scheduler is to identify all the pending orders that can be concurrently executed, taking into account their priority. The local communications are always executed, removed from *op_lst*, and their results are stored. The other requests involve distant communications, and their route is computed. A priority ordered *travel list* is built, where each travel is a request followed by its route. It has the following form:

$$tl = (... \; (\; (r/w_k \; addr_k \; dat_k) \; k \; n_1 \; n_2 \; ... f) \; ...) \tag{5}$$

where k is the source node and f is the final node computed by: $f = addr\_k$ *div ms*. By a simple induction, we prove that Theorem 4 holds for every route in tl.

We define a function *Scheduler* which extracts a set of non-overlapping routes from tl, i.e. such that a node may appear in at most one route. It takes three arguments: 1) the travel list tl; 2) a list *non_ovlp*, initially empty, that contains the non-overlapping communications at the end of the computation; 3) the list *prev*, initially empty, of the nodes used by the communications in *non_ovlp*. Each computation step processes one request route, and adds it to *non_ovlp* if the intersection of its node set with *prev* is empty; then *prev* is updated. For brevity, overlapping communications are dropped in function *Scheduler* below. In the full model, they are stored in another travel list, for later processing.

Definition 12. *Scheduler*
$Scheduler(tl \; non\_ovlp \; prev) \; returns \; Travel\_List \stackrel{def}{=}$
   if $tl = \emptyset$ **then**
      non_ovlp
   else

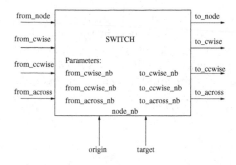

Fig. 5. Generic Switch

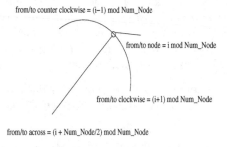

Fig. 6. A step in a travel

if $getroute(car(tl)) \cap prev = \emptyset$ **then**
$$Scheduler(cdr(tl), car(tl) \cup non\_ovlp,$$
$$getroute(car(tl)) \cup prev)$$
　　else
$$Scheduler(cdr(tl), non\_ovlp, prev)$$
　　endif
endif

Let *Grab_nodes(tl)* be a function that creates the list of the nodes used by every route in a travel list *tl*. The correctness of *Scheduler* is expressed by the following theorem:

Theorem 5. *Correctness of Scheduler*
$\forall tl, noDuplicatesp(grab\_nodes(Scheduler(tl, nil, nil)))$

5.3   Traveling Functions

We define a function *Switch* which represents a generic switch component (Figure 5). It takes as arguments: the four inputs (*from_x*), two commands (*origin* and *target*) and the parameters. It produces a new value for every output. The switch reads a message on the input selected by the value of *origin*, and writes the message on the output selected by the value of *target*. The other outputs are set to a default "no message" value.

In our model, a message travels on its route r as a result of iterative calls to function *Switch*, until every node of r has been visited. Let i be the current node at a given travel step in route r. *Switch* is called with i as *node_nb*. *origin* and *target* take the previous and next node numbers w.r.t. i in r. The other parameters are numbered as pictured on Figure 6. If i is the first node of r, *origin* is equal to i. If i is the last node of r, *target* is equal to i. The values assigned to the outputs of *Switch*, as a result of executing one travel step, are used in the next call to *Switch* where i is replaced by its successor in r. These calls to *Switch* represent the structure of the interconnected nodes effectively involved in the travel along route r. The set of concurrent travels over the structure are represented by function *Trip*, which takes as arguments a travel list *tl* and the parameter *Num_Node* and executes the travel of every request in the travel list. To validate this function, we check that the theorem below is true if and only if every route in *tl* contains no duplicate and satisfies the predicate *AvailableMovep*. For space reasons, the definitions of functions *Switch* and *Trip* are not given.

Theorem 6. *Correctness of the Interconnection Structure*
$$\forall tl, Num\_Node, \ Trip(tl, Num\_Node) = tl$$

5.4 Correctness of Distant Communications

Function *Octagon* represents the overall system. It takes as arguments the list *op_lst* containing the orders pending at every node, the two parameters *Num_Node* and *ms* and the global memory *Glob_Mem*. It first recursively calls function *Node* for every order of *op_lst*. Every such call either produces a result, which is stored in a list *LocRes*, or produces a request, which is put, together with its route, in a travel list *tl*. Second, it calls *Scheduler* to extract the non-overlapping communications from *tl*. Then, a first call to *Trip* moves every request to its destination node. Function *Node* is recursively called for each one of the requets to compute the response of every one of them. The responses are carried back to their respective source node by a second call to *Trip*. Finally, a third recursive call to *Node* is made to compute the result of every response. Function *Octagon* returns the list *LocRes* of the local orders, the list *NetwDone* of the results of the distant orders and the final memory.

Definition 13. *Octagon*
$Octagon(op\_lst, Num\_Node, ms, Glob_Mem)$
$\qquad returns(LocRes \ NetwRes \ Memory) \overset{def}{=}$
$\quad$ **let** *(LocRes tl Glob_Mem1)* **be**
$\qquad Rec\text{-}Node\text{-}MakeTravelList(op\_lst, Nun\_Node, ms, Glob\_Mem)$ **in**
$\qquad\quad tl1 = Scheduler(tl, \emptyset, \emptyset)$
$\qquad\quad tl2 = Trip(tl1 \ N)$
$\qquad\quad$ **let** *(RespTl Glob_Mem2)* **be**
$\qquad\qquad Rec\text{-}Node\text{-}Response(tl2, Glob\_Mem1, ms)$ **in**
$\qquad\qquad RespTl\_back = Trip(RespTl, Num\_Node)$
$\qquad\qquad$ **let** *(NetwDone Glob_Mem3)* **be**
$\qquad\qquad\quad Rec\text{-}Node\text{-}Result(RespTl\_back, Glob\_Mem2, ms)$
$\qquad\qquad\quad list(LocRes \ NetwDone \ Glob\_Mem3)$

To validate this function, we need to prove that Theorem 3 still holds. Let us consider distant communications. The theorem below states the correctness of distant communication in a very general case. Let *Scheduled* be a set of scheduled orders:

Theorem 7. *Correctness of Octagon for Distant Communications*
$\forall op\_lst \in Scheduled, Num\_Node, ms, Glob\_Mem$
$NetwDone(Octagon(op\_lst, Num\_Node, ms, Glob\_Mem))[i] =$

$Memory(Order(op\_lst)[i],$

$\qquad get\_local\_mem(Glob\_Mem, Last(Route(op\_lst)[i]), ms))$

Proof. First, Theorem 4 and 5 relieve the conditions of the validity of Theorem 6 which allows us to remove the calls to *Trip*. Then, for every order of *op_lst* three calls to *Node* are made which reconstitute the definition of a transfer, *i.e.* calls to MI_{req}, SI_{ord}, *Slave*, SI_{resp} and MI_{res}. □

In practice, we decompose this final proof in a litany of theorems which consider separately the correctness of the returned status, data and memory. We also split read orders from write orders. For instance, we prove that if *op_lst* contains only distant read orders then the memory is not changed.

Theorem 8. *Correctness of the Memory for Read Orders*
$\forall op\_lst, Glob\_Mem, ms, Num\_Node$
$all\_distant\_read\_ordersp(op\_lst) \implies$
$GetMemory(Octagon(op\_lst, Num\_Node, ms, Glob\_Mem)) = Glob\_Mem$

Similarly, we prove that every write order is equal to a direct update of the memory.

Theorem 9. *Correctness of the Memory for Write Orders*
$\forall op\_lst \in Scheduled, Glob\_Mem, ms, Num\_Node, i$
$all\_distant\_write\_ordersp(op\_lst) \wedge 0 \leq i < Num\_Node \implies$
$GetMemory(Octagon(op\_lst, Num\_Node, ms, Glob\_Mem))[i] =$
$Update(Glob\_Mem, Location(Orders(op\_lst)[i]), Items(Orders(op\_lst)[i]))$

6   Conclusion and Future Work

In this paper, we have presented an original approach to model and analyse master/slave based communication architectures in the ACL2 logic. We have illustrated this approach on the *Octagon*, for which we built a functional model that can be executed on test cases. Using the ACL2 theorem prover, the functional correctness of the network routing and scheduling algorithm were established. We proved that tokens travel correctly over this structure: messages eventually reach their expected destination without being modified. In reality, our results hold on a generalization of the *Octagon*: we model an *unbounded* interconnection structure as of Fig. 3, where the number of switches is a multiple of 4.

The model and its proof were developed in three months but the proof can be replayed in less than ten minutes on a Pentium IV at 1.6 GHz with 256 Mb of main memory, under Linux. The overall model [7] contains around one hundred definitions and the proof requires more than two hundred lemmas and theorems.

Most of the human effort was spent on building the foundations for the modeling methodology, ensuring that the functional definitions for the interconnected hardware modules are compositional, and identifying the key theorems. The result is a specification infrastructure for scalable network modules. Thanks to the modularity of our methodology, most of the functions may be redefined; provided the essential theorems still hold for them, the overall proof is not changed.

For instance, the scheduling function may implement a different priority policy: if Theorem 5 still holds on the new scheduling, Theorems 6 and 7 remain valid. Likewise, the routing algorithm of another network structure may be redefined: if it can be proved to satisfy Theorem 4, the final theorems remain valid.

In the near future, we are planning to apply the above ideas to other network on chip designs, in the context of the European "EuroSoC" network.

Acknowledgements

We are thankful to J Strother Moore, Warren A. Hunt, Jr, their research group and Matt Kaufmann for their precious help on ACL2 and many discussions. We also thank Robert Krug for his help on the arithmetic packages.

References

1. W. Roesner: What is Beyond the RTL Horizon for Microprocessor and System Design. Invited Speaker. *Correct Hardware Design and Verification Methods(CHARME)* LNCS 2860 (2003)
2. M. Kaufmann, P. Manolios and J Strother Moore: Computer-Aided Reasoning: An Approach. Kluwer Academic Publisher (2000)
3. F. Karim, A. Nguyen and S. Dey: An Interconnect Architecture For Networking Systems On Chip. *IEEE Micro* (Sept-Oct 2002) pp. 36–45
4. F. Karim, A. Nguyen, S. Dey and R. Rao : On-Chip Communication Architecture for OC-768 Network Processor. *Design Automation Conference* (2001)
5. J. A. Rowson and A. Sangiovanni-Vincentelli: Interface-Based Design. *Design Automation Conference* (1997)
6. J. Schmaltz: Functional Specification and Validation of the Octagon Network on Chip Using the ACL2 Theorem Prover. *TIMA Technical Report* ISRN TIMA-RR–04/01/02–FR (2004)
7. http://tima.imag.fr/VDS/ProjectValidation.asp (2004)
8. J. Strother Moore: A Formal Model of Asynchronous Communication and Its Use in Mechanically Verifying a Biphase Mark Protocol, *Formal Aspects of Computing* (1993)
9. E. A. Emerson and V. Kahlon: Rapid Parameterized Model Checking of Snoopy Cache Coherence Protocols, in *Proc. of the 9th Conference on Tools and Algorithms for the Construction and Analysis of Systems (TACAS'03)*, pp 144-159, LNCS 2619 (2003)
10. K. Havelung and N. Shankar: Experiments in Theorem Proving and Model Checking for Protocol Verification in *Proc. of Formal Methods Europe (FME'96)*, LNCS 1051 (1996)
11. A. Roychoudhury, T. Mitra and S.R. Karri: Using Formal Techniques to Debug the AMBA System-on-Chip Bus Protocol, in *Proc. of the Design Automation and Test in Europe (DATE'03) Conference*, pp 828-833 (2003)

Proof Styles in Operational Semantics

Sandip Ray and J. Strother Moore

Department of Computer Sciences
University of Texas at Austin
{sandip,moore}@cs.utexas.edu
http://www.cs.utexas.edu/users/{sandip,moore}

Abstract. We relate two well-studied methodologies in deductive verification of operationally modeled sequential programs, namely the use of
inductive invariants and *clock functions*. We show that the two methodologies are equivalent and one can mechanically transform a proof of a
program in one methodology to a proof in the other. Both partial and
total correctness are considered. This mechanical transformation is compositional; different parts of a program can be verified using different
methodologies to achieve a complete proof of the entire program. The
equivalence theorems have been mechanically checked by the ACL2 theorem prover and we implement automatic tools to carry out the transformation between the two methodologies in ACL2.

1 Background

This paper is concerned with relating strategies for deductive verification of sequential programs modeled operationally in some mathematical logic. For operational models, verifying a program is tantamount to characterizing the "initial"
and "final" states of the machine executing the program and showing that every
"execution" of the program starting from an initial state leaves the machine in
a final state satisfying some desired "postcondition".

Deductive verification of sequential programs has traditionally used one of
two reasoning strategies, namely the *inductive invariant* approach [1], and the
clock functions or *direct* approach [2] respectively. While both the strategies
guarantee correctness, to our knowledge no formal analysis has been performed
on whether the theorems proved using one strategy are in any sense stronger
than the other. However, it has been informally believed that the two strategies
are fundamentally different and incompatible.

This paper analyzes the relation between these two strategies. We show that
the informal beliefs are flawed in the following sense: In a sufficiently expressive logic, a correctness proof of a program in one strategy can be mechanically
transformed into a proof in the other strategy. The result is not mathematically deep; careful formalization of the question essentially leads to the answer.
But the question has been asked informally so often that we believe a formal
answer is appropriate. Further, this equivalence enables independent verification of components of a program to obtain a proof of the composite whole. The

A.J. Hu and A.K. Martin (Eds.): FMCAD 2004, LNCS 3312, pp. 67–81, 2004.
© Springer-Verlag Berlin Heidelberg 2004

equivalence has been mechanically checked by the ACL2 theorem prover and such transformation tools implemented in ACL2.

To provide the relevant background, we first summarize the operational approach to modeling and reasoning about sequential programs, and describe the two strategies. We then discuss the contributions of this paper in greater detail. For ease of understanding, we adhere to traditional mathematical notations in this section. We later show how the concepts are made precise in the ACL2 logic.

1.1   Operational Program Models

Operational semantics involves characterization of program instructions by their effects on the states of the underlying machine. For simplicity, assume that a program is a sequence of instructions, and a state of the machine is a tuple describing the values registers, memory, stack, and so on. For every state s, let $pc(s)$ and $prog(s)$ denote the values of two special components in state s, the program counter and the current program respectively. These two components specify the "next instruction" executed by the machine at state s, which is the instruction in $prog(s)$ that is pointed to by $pc(s)$.

Meaning is assigned to an instruction by specifying, for every state s and every instruction i, the effect of executing i on s. This is formalized by a function $effect : S \times I \to S$, where S is the set of states, and I is the set of instructions. If the instruction is a LOAD its effect might be to push the contents of some specific variable on the stack and advance the program counter by some specific amount.

A special predicate *halting* characterizes the final states. A state s of M is *halting* if s is poised to execute an instruction i whose effect on s is a no-op, that is, $effect(s, i) = s$. Most programming languages provide explicit instructions like HALT whose *effect* on every state s is a no-op. In such cases, the machine halts when the instruction pointed to by the pc is the HALT instruction.

To reason about such operationally modeled programs, it is convenient to define a "next state function" $step : S \to S$. For every state s in S, the function $step(s)$ is the state produced as follows. Consider the instruction i in $prog(s)$ that is pointed to by $pc(s)$. Then $step(s)$ is defined to be $effect(s, i)$. Further, one defines the following iterated step function:

$$run(s, n) = \begin{cases} s & \text{if } n = 0 \\ run(step(s), n - 1) & \text{otherwise} \end{cases}$$

Program correctness is formalized by two predicates on the set S, namely a specified precondition *pre* characterizing the "initial" states, and a desired postcondition *post* characterizing the "final" states. In case of a sorting program, *pre* might specify that some machine variable contains a list l of integers, and *post* might specify that some (possibly the same) machine variable contains a list l' of integers that is an ordered permutation of l.

- **Partial Correctness:** Partial correctness involves showing that if, starting from a state that satisfies *pre*, the machine ever reaches a *halting* state, then *post* holds for such a *halting* state. Nothing is claimed if the machine does not reach a *halting* state. Partial correctness can be formally expressed as the following formula:

$$\forall s, n : pre(s) \land halting(run(s, n)) \Rightarrow post(run(s, n))$$

- **Total Correctness:** Total correctness involves showing, in addition to partial correctness, that the machine, starting from a state satisfying *pre*, eventually halts:

$$\forall s : pre(s) \Rightarrow (\exists n : halting(run(s, n)))$$

1.2   Inductive Invariants

Inductive invariants constitute one strategy for proving the correctness theorems. The idea is to define a predicate that (i) is implied by the precondition, (ii) persists along every *step*, and (iii) implies the postcondition in a *halting* state. Thus, predicate *inv* is defined on the set S of states with the following properties:

1. $\forall s : pre(s) \Rightarrow inv(s)$,
2. $\forall s : inv(s) \Rightarrow inv(step(s))$, and
3. $\forall s : inv(s) \land halting(s) \Rightarrow post(s)$.

Then we can prove that for every state s satisfying *inv* and for every natural number n, $run(s, n)$ satisfies *inv*. This follows from property 2 by induction on n. The proof of partial correctness then follows from properties 1 and 3.

Total correctness is proved by a "well-foundedness" argument. A *well-founded structure* is a pair $\langle W, \prec \rangle$ where W is a set and $\prec$ is a partial order on the elements of W, such that there are no infinitely decreasing chains in W with respect to $\prec$. One defines a mapping $m : S \rightarrow W$, where $\langle W, \prec \rangle$ is well-founded, and proves the following property, in addition to 1, 2, and 3 above.

4. $\forall s : inv(s) \land \neg halting(s) \Rightarrow m(step(s)) \prec m(s)$.

The termination proof in the total correctness statement now follows from properties 2 and 4 as follows. Assume that the machine does not reach a *halting* state starting from some state s, such that $pre(s)$ holds. By property 2, each state in the sequence $\langle s, step(s), step(step(s)) \ldots \rangle$ satisfies *inv*. Then, by property 4, the sequence $\langle m(s), m(step(s)), m(step(step(s))) \ldots \rangle$ forms an infinite descending chain on W with respect to $\prec$. However, by well-foundedness, no infinitely descending chain can exist on W, leading to a contradiction.

An advantage of *inductive invariants* is that all the conditions involve only single steps of the program. The proofs are typically dispatched by case analysis without resorting to induction, once the appropriate *inv* is defined. However, the definition of *inv* is often cumbersome, since by condition 2, *inv* needs to be preserved along *every* step of the execution.

1.3   Clock Functions

A direct approach to proving total correctness is the use of *clock functions*. Roughly, the idea is to define a function that maps every state s satisfying *pre*, to a natural number that specifies the number of *steps* required to reach a *halting* state from s. Formally, $clock : S \rightarrow \mathbb{N}$ has the following two properties:

1. $\forall s : pre(s) \Rightarrow halting(run(s, clock(s)))$
2. $\forall s : pre(s) \Rightarrow post(run(s, clock(s)))$

Total correctness follows from these properties as follows. Termination proof is obvious, since for every state s satisfying pre, there exists an n, namely $clock(s)$, such that $run(s, n)$ is halting. Further, since by definition of $halting$, running from a $halting$ state does not change the state, the state $run(s, clock(s))$ uniquely specifies the $halting$ state reachable from s. By property 2 of $clock$, the state also satisfies $post$, showing correctness.

For specifying partial correctness, one weakens the properties 1 and 2 above so that $run(s, clock(s))$ satisfies $halting$ and $post$ only if a halting state is reachable from s. This can be achieved by adding the predicate $(\exists n : halting(run(s, n)))$ as a conjunct in the antecedent of each property. The partial correctness theorem follows using exactly the correctness argument for total correctness.

Proofs involving *clock functions* typically require induction on the length of the execution. However, the definition of *clock* follows the control flow of the program [2,3]; a user familiar with the branches and loops of a program can often define *clock* with relative ease, and the definition of *clock* provides a hint on the induction to be used in proving the correctness theorems.

1.4   Contributions of This Paper

Both *inductive invariants* and *clock functions* guarantee the same correctness theorems. However, the arguments used by the two strategies are different. The question, then, arises whether the theorems proved using one strategy are in any sense stronger than the other.

Why does one suspect that one strategy might be stronger than the other? Consider the total correctness proofs using the two strategies. In the *clock functions* approach, the function $clock(s)$ gives for every state s satisfying pre, the exact number of *steps* required to reach a *halting* state from s. One normally defines *clock* so that $clock(s)$ is the *minimum* number of *steps* required to reach a halting state from s. But that number is a precise characterization of the time complexity of the program! The *inductive invariant* proof, on the other hand, does not appear to require reasoning about time complexity, although it requires showing that the program eventually terminates.

Use of *inductive invariants* is a popular method for program verification. However, in the presence of a formally defined operational semantics, *clock functions* have been found useful. This method has been widely used in Boyer-Moore community, especially in ACL2 and its predecessor, Nqthm, to verify specialized architectures or machine codes [4–6]. Note that relatively few researchers outside this community have used *clock functions*; the reason is that relatively few researchers have pursued code-level mechanized formal proofs with respect to operational semantics. Operational semantics has been largely used by Nqthm and ACL2 since it permits the use of a general-purpose theorem prover for first-order recursive functions. Criticisms for *clock functions* have been typically expressed informally in conference question-answer sessions for the same reason:

given that no extant system supported code proofs for the specialized language presented, there was no motivation for comparing *clock functions* to other styles, but there was a nagging feeling that the approach required more work, namely reasoning about complexity when "merely" a correctness result is desired. The absence of written criticism of *clock functions* and the presence of this "nagging feeling" have been confirmed by an extensive literature search and discussions with authors of other theorem provers.

In this paper, our goal is to clarify relations between *inductive invariants* and *clock functions*. We show by mechanical proof that in the context of program verification, the two styles are equivalent in the sense that a proof in one style in one can be mechanically transformed into a proof in the other.

Besides showing the logical connection between the two proof styles, the equivalence theorems have an important practical implication: our results enable mechanical composition of proofs of different components of a program verified using different styles. Notwithstanding the logical equivalence of the two strategies as shown in this paper, one style might be simpler or more natural to derive "from scratch" than the other in a specific context. As an example, consider two procedures: (1) initialization of a Binary Search Tree (BST), and (2) insertion of a sequence of elements in an already initialized BST. Assume that in either case the desired postcondition specifies that a BST structure is produced. A typical approach for verifying (1) is to define a *clock* that specifies the number of steps required by the initialization procedure, and then prove the result by symbolic simulation; definition of a sufficient *inductive invariant* is cumbersome and requires a detailed understanding of the semantics of the different instructions. On the other hand, an *inductive invariant* proof might be more natural for verifying (2), by showing that each insertion in the sequence preserves the tree structure. However, traditional verification of a sequential composition of the two procedures (initialization followed by insertion) has had to adhere to a single style for both the procedures, often making proofs awkward and difficult. The results of this paper now allow verification of each component in the style most suitable for the component alone, by a trivial and well-known observation that *clock functions* can be naturally composed over different components.

Our equivalence theorems have been mechanically checked by the ACL2 theorem prover. Note that ACL2 (or indeed, any theorem prover) is not critical for proving the equivalence. ACL2 is used merely as a mechanized formal logic in deriving our proofs. However, since ACL2 routinely uses both strategies to verify operationally modeled programs, our theorems and the consequent proof transformation tools we implement, are of practical value in simplifying ACL2 proofs of large-scale programs. Our work can be easily adapted to any other mechanized logic like HOL [7] or PVS [8], that is expressive enough to specify arbitrary first-order formulas, and analogous tools for proof transformation can be implemented for theorem provers in such logics.

The remainder of this paper is organized as follows. In Section 2, we briefly discuss rudiments of the ACL2 logic. In Section 3, we formalize the two proof styles in ACL2 and discuss the mechanical proof of their equivalence. In Section 4, we elaborate the framework to allow composition of proof strategies. In

Section 5, we describe two macros for translation between proof strategies in ACL2. Finally, in Section 6, we discuss related work and provide some concluding remarks. The ACL2 proof scripts for all the theorems described here are available from the home page of the first author and will be distributed with the next version of the theorem prover. Note that although we adhere to the formal notation of ACL2 in the description of our theorems, this paper assumes no significant previous exposure to the ACL2 logic, and only a basic familiarity with Lisp.

2   The ACL2 Logic

In this section, we briefly describe the ACL2 logic. This provides a formal notational and reasoning framework to be used in the rest of the paper. Full details of the ACL2 logic and its theorem proving engine can be found in [9, 10].

ACL2 is essentially a first-order logic of recursive functions. The inference rules constitute propositional calculus with equality and instantiation, and well-founded induction up to ϵ_0. The language is an applicative subset of Common Lisp; instead of writing $f(a)$ as the application of function f to argument a, one writes (f a). Terms are used instead of formulas. For example, the term:

(implies (natp i) (equal (nth i (update-nth i v l)) v))

represents a basic fact about list processing in the ACL2 syntax. The syntax is quantifier-free; formulas may be thought of as universally quantified over all free variables. The term above specifies the statement: "For all i, v and l, if i is a natural number, then the i-th element of the list obtained by updating the i-th element of l by v is v."

ACL2 provides axioms to reason about Lisp functions. For example, the following axiom specifies that the function car applied to the cons of two arguments, returns the first argument of cons.

Axiom:
(equal (car (cons x y)) x)

Theorems can be proved for axiomatically defined functions in the ACL2 system. Theorems are proved by the defthm command. For example, the command:

(defthm car-cons-for-2 (equal (car (cons x 2)) x))

directs the theorem prover to prove that for every x, the output of the function car applied to the cons of x and the constant 2, returns x.

ACL2 provides three *extension principles* that allow the user to introduce new function symbols and axioms about them. The extension principles constitute (i) the *definitional principle* to introduce total functions, (ii) the *encapsulation principle* to introduce constrained functions, and (iii) the *defchoose principle* to introduce Skolem functions. We briefly sketch these principles here. See [11] for a detailed description of these principles along with soundness arguments.

Definitional Principle: The *definitional principle* allows the user to define new total functions in the logic. For example, the following form defines the factorial function fact in ACL2.

```
(defun fact (n) (if (zp n) 1 (* n (fact (- n 1)))))
```
The effect is to extend the logic by the following *definitional axiom*:

Definitional Axiom:
```
(fact n) = (if (zp n) 1 (* n (fact (- n 1))))
```
Here (zp n) returns nil if n is a positive natural number, and otherwise T. To ensure consistency, ACL2 must prove that the recursion terminates [12]. In particular, one must exhibit a "measure" m that maps the set of arguments in the function to some set W, where $\langle W, \prec \rangle$ forms a well-founded structure. The proof obligation, then, is to show that on every recursive call, this measure "decreases" according to relation $\prec$. ACL2 axiomatizes a specific well-founded structure, namely the set of ordinals below ϵ_0: membership in this set is recognized by an axiomatically defined predicate e0-ordinalp, and a binary relation e0-ord-< is axiomatized in the logic as an irreflexive partial order in the set.

Encapsulation Principle: The *encapsulation principle* allows the extension of the ACL2 logic with partially defined constrained functions. For example, the command below introduces a function symbol foo with the constraint that (foo n) is a natural number.

```
(encapsulate (((foo *) => *))
  (local (defun foo (n) 1))
  (defthm foo-returns-natural (natp (foo n))))
```
Consistency is ensured by showing that some (total) function exists satisfying the alleged constraints. In this case, the constant function that always returns 1 serves as such "witness". The effect is to extend the logic by the following *encapsulation axiom* corresponding to the constraints. Notice that the axiom does not specify the value of the function for every input.

Encapsulation Axiom:
```
(natp (foo n))
```
For a constrained function f the only axioms known are the constraints. Therefore, any theorem proved about f is also valid for a function f' that also satisfies the constraints. More precisely, call the conjunction of the constraints on f the formula ϕ. For any formula ψ let $\hat{\psi}$ be the formula obtained by replacing the function symbol f by the function symbol f'. Then, a derived rule of inference, *functional instantiation* specifies that for any theorem θ one can derive the theorem $\hat{\theta}$ provided one can prove $\hat{\phi}$ as a theorem. In the example, since the constant 10 satisfies the constraint for foo, if (bar (foo n)) is provable for some function bar, functional instantiation can be used to prove (bar 10).

Defchoose Principle: The *defchoose principle* allows introduction of Skolem functions in ACL2. To understand this principle, assume that a function symbol P of two arguments has been introduced in the ACL2 logic. Then the form:

```
(defchoose exists-y-witness y (x) (P x y))
```

extends the logic by the following axiom:

Defchoose Axiom:
`(implies (P x y) (P x (exists-y-witness x)))`

The axiom states that *if* there exists some y such that `(P x y)` holds, then `(exists-y-witness x)` returns such a y. Nothing is claimed about the return value of `(exists-y-witness x)` if there exists no such y. This provides the power of first-order quantification in the logic. For example, we can define a function `exists-y` such that `(exists-y x)` is true if and only if there exists some y satisfying `(P x y)`. Notice that the theorem `exists-y-suff` below is an easy consequence of the defchoose and definitional principles.

```
(defun exists-y (x) (P x (exists-y-witness x)))
(defthm exists-y-suff (implies (P x y) (exists-y x)))
```

ACL2 provides a construct `defun-sk` that makes use of the defchoose principle to introduce explicit quantification. For example, the form:

```
(defun-sk exists-y (x) (exists y (P x y)))
```

is merely an abbreviation for the following forms:

```
(defchoose exists-y-witness y (x) (P x y))
(defun exists-y (x) (P x (exists-y-witness x)))
(defthm exists-y-suff (implies (P x y)  (exists-y x)))
```

Thus `(exists-y x)` can be thought of specifying as the first-order formula: $(\exists y : (P\ x\ y))$. Further, `defun-sk` supports universal quantification `forall` by exploiting the duality between existential and universal quantification.

3   Proof Strategies

Operational semantics have been used in ACL2 (and other theorem provers) for modeling complex programs in practical systems. For example, formal models of programs in the Java^{TM} Virtual Machine (JVM) have been formalized in ACL2 [3, 13]. Operational models accurately reflecting the details of practical computing systems are elaborate and complex; however such elaborations are not of our concern in this paper. For this presentation, we assume that a state transition function `step` of a single argument has been defined in the logic, possibly following the approach described in Section 1.1, which, given the "current state" of the underlying machine, returns the "next state". We also assume the existence of unary predicates `pre` and `post` specifying the preconditions and postconditions respectively, and the predicate `halting` below specifying termination.

```
(defun halting (s) (equal s (step s)))
```

We now formalize the *inductive invariant* and *clock function* proofs in this framework. The theorems we describe here are straightforward translations of our descriptions in Sections 1.2 and 1.3. In particular, an *inductive invariant* proof of partial correctness constitutes the following theorems for some function `inv`.

```
(defthm pre-implies-inv (implies (pre s) (inv s)))
(defthm inv-persists (implies (inv s) (inv (step s))))
(defthm inv-implies-post
  (implies (and (inv s) (halting s)) (post s)))
```

A total correctness proof also requires a "measure function" m and the following theorems[1]:

```
(defthm m-is-ordinal (e0-ordinalp (m s)))
(defthm m-decreases
  (implies (and (inv s) (not (halting s)))
           (e0-ord-< (m (step s)) (m s))))
```

Analogously, a *clock function* proof in the logic comprises a definition of the function clock and theorems that express an ACL2 formalization of our discussions in Section 1.3. A total correctness proof constitutes the following theorems:

```
(defthm clock-run-is-halting
  (implies (pre s) (halting (run s (clock s)))))
(defthm clock-run-is-post
  (implies (pre s) (post (run s (clock s)))))
```

where the function run is simply the iterated application of step as defined below:

```
(defun run (s n) (if (zp n) s (run (step s) (- n 1))))
```

Finally, a partial correctness theorem is the "weakening" of the above theorems, requiring them to hold only if there exists a halting state reachable from s.

```
(defthm clock-run-is-halting
  (implies (and (pre s) (halting (run s n)))
           (halting (run s (clock s)))))
(defthm clock-run-is-post
  (implies (and (pre s) (halting (run s n)))
           (post (run s (clock s)))))
```

To prove equivalence between the two proof styles we use the encapsulation principle; that is, we encapsulate function symbols step, inv, m, clock, constrained to satisfy the corresponding theorems, and show that the constraints associated with *inductive invariants* can be derived from the constraints associated with *clock functions* and vice-versa. In Section 5, we will use these generic proofs to implement tools to translate proofs in one style to the other.

3.1   Equivalence Theorems

To obtain a *clock function* proof from *inductive invariants* we will define a clock that "counts" the number of steps until a halting state is reached. Recall from

---

[1] We have used the set of ordinals below ϵ_0 with the relation e0-ord-< instead of a generic well-founded structure $\langle W, \prec \rangle$, since this is the only well-founded set axiomatically defined in ACL2. However, the structure of the ordinals is of no consequence here, and our proofs can be translated in terms of any well-founded structures.

our discussions in Section 1.2 that if `inv` is an inductive invariant that holds for some state s then `inv` holds for all states reachable from s. In ACL2, such a statement is formalized by the theorem `inv-run` below and can be proved by induction on n.

```
(defthm inv-run (implies (inv s) (inv (run s n))))
```

Hence if `clock` can be defined to count the number of `steps` to `halting`, then the obligations for a *clock function* proof will follow from the properties of *inductive invariants*, in particular, `pre-implies-inv` and `inv-implies-post`. For total correctness, the following recursive definition provides such a count.

```
(defun clock (s)
  (if (or (not (inv s)) (halting s)) 0
      (+ 1 (clock (step s)))))
```

The crucial observation is that the function `clock` above is admissible to the ACL2 logic under the definitional principle. The recursion is justified by the theorems provided by the termination proofs in the *inductive invariants* approach, namely, that there exists a "measure", in this case m, that maps the arguments of `clock` to some well-founded set (ordinals) and decreases (according to `e0-ord-<`) in the recursive call.

The situation is a bit more subtle for partial correctness, since there may be no such measure. In this case, therefore, we use the defchoose principle to define the appropriate `clock` as follows:

```
(defun-sk exists-pre-state (s)
  (exists (init i j)
          (and (pre init) (natp i) (natp j) (equal s (run init i))
               (halting (run init j)))))
(defun clock (s)
  (if (exists-pre-state s)
      (mv-let (init i j) (exists-pre-state-witness s)
              (nfix (- j i)))
  0))
```

The function `nfix` above is the identity function if its argument is a natural number; otherwise it returns 0. The function `clock` can be interpreted as follows. If there is a state `init` satisfying `pre` and numbers i and j such that s is reachable from `init` in i `steps` and a `halting` state in j `steps`, then *clock* returns `(- j i)`; otherwise it returns 0. But if s is indeed reachable from some state satisfying `pre`, and a `halting` state is reachable from s, then `(- j i)` represents the number of `steps` to reach a `halting` state from s. Thus in this case the proof obligations for *clock functions* follow from the *inductive invariants* constraints analogous to total correctness. The return value of 0 is arbitrary when no `halting` state is reachable from s, and can be replaced by any value.

To obtain an *inductive invariant* proof from *clock functions*, we define the predicate `inv` expressing the following property: A state s satisfies `inv` if and only if s is reachable from some state `init` satisfying `pre`. Notice that the obligations `pre-implies-inv` and `inv-persists` are trivial for such a predicate. Further, the *clock functions* proofs guarantee that a `halting` state reachable from some `pre` state must also satisfy `post`: Recall that the theorem `clock-run-is-post` guarantees that for every state s satisfying `pre`, the `halting` state (`run s (clock s)`) reached (for partial correctness under the hypothesis that some `halting` state is reachable) from s must satisfy `post`. Since by definition of `halting`, stepping from a `halting` state does not change the state, it follows that *any* `halting` state reachable from s must satisfy `post`. We formalize this using defchoose principle as follows:

```
(defun-sk inv (s)
  (exists (init n)
          (and (pre init) (natp n) (equal s (run init n)))))
```

For total correctness, we define the measure m by determining the number of `steps` to reach the first `halting` state:

```
(defun m-aux (s i clk)
  (if (or (halting s) (>= i clk) (not (natp i)) (not (natp clk)))
      (nfix i)
    (m-aux (step s) (+ i 1) clk)))
(defun m (s) (m-aux s 0 (clock s)))
```

The function m returns a natural number (and hence an ordinal). Further, for any state s reachable from some `pre` state init, if s is not `halting`, then (m (step s)) is exactly 1 less than (m s), since m merely counts the number of `steps` to reach the first `halting` state. Hence m decreases along a `step`, justifying termination.

4   Verifying Program Components

We now show how to generalize our framework to allow different components of a program to be verified using different strategies. The thorny issue in verifying components of a program separately arises from the use of the predicate `halting` in the framework. Recall that the predicate `halting` specifies termination in a very strong sense, specifying that (step s) must be equal to s! However, when a program completes a specific procedure, it merely returns control to the calling procedure. Our verification framework is modified as follows in order to be meaningful for verification of program components.

1. In *clock functions*, for a state s poised to execute a program component of interest, (clock s) must precisely characterize the number of `steps` from s to the "corresponding" exit.
2. In *inductive invariants*, inv needs to "persist" only along the `steps` which execute the instructions in the component of interest.

To formalize this, we introduce a new predicate `external` to indicate the "exit" of the program control from the component of interest, and modify the proof obligations for each style. For technical reasons, we first restrict the predicate `pre` so that `pre` states also do not satisfy `external`:

```
(defthm pre-not-external (implies (pre s) (not (external s))))
```

The restriction, though introduced for technical reasons, is natural, as the subsequent discussions will show. We now "strengthen" the *clock functions* strategy, so that `clock` specifies the *minimum* number of `steps` to reach an `external` state. This is achieved by adding the following constraints to `clock`.

```
(defthm clock-is-natural (natp (clock s)))
(defthm clock-is-minimal
  (implies (and (pre s) (natp n) (external (run s n)))
           (<= (clock s) n)))
```

These constraints, along with those described in Section 3 modified to use `external` instead of `halting`, comprise the *clock function* proof of an individual component. Notice that `(clock s)` now characterizes the number of `steps` to reach the *first* `external` state from `s`. A casual reader might complain that this is not general enough to characterize proofs of complicated program components like recursive procedures. After all, if `external` specifies the return from a procedure, then for a state `s` poised to invoke a recursive procedure, the first `external` state reached from `s` does not represent the "corresponding" return! However, notice that `external` can be an *arbitrary* function of state; for example, a legitimate definition of `external` for a recursive procedure is that *pc* points to the instruction after the return and the stack of recursive calls is empty.

To capture the notion of *first* `external` state in the *inductive invariants* framework, we first attach the constraint that `inv` does not hold for `external` states. The intuition, then, is that `inv` should hold for every state starting from a `pre` state "until" an `external` state is encountered. We can then decide if `(step s)` is the first `external` state, by checking if both `(inv s)` and `(external (step s))` hold. The proof obligations for *inductive invariants* are modified as follows:

```
(defthm inv-persists
  (implies (and (inv s) (not (external (step s)))) (inv (step s))))
(defthm inv-implies-post
  (implies (and (inv s) (external (step s))) (post (step s))))
(defthm m-decreases
  (implies (and (inv s) (not (external (step s))))
           (e0-ord-< (m (step s)) (m s))))
```

We have surveyed several proofs of system models, including JVM proofs in ACL2 [3]. For all non-trivial programs, the verification has been decomposed into "component proofs", and the proof of each component could always be described in terms of the frameworks above.

In this generalized framework again, one can derive the proof obligations in one approach from a proof in the other. Space does not permit a thorough discussion of the generalized equivalence proofs, but the informal intuition is the same as in Section 3. The complete ACL2 script for the proof of this equivalence is available to the interested reader from the web-page of the first author.

An immediate nice consequence of the generalized equivalence results is the capability of mechanically composing proofs of different components of a program obtained using different styles into a proof of the complete program. Consider, for example, *sequential composition*, that is, a program composed of two sequential code blocks A and B. An important, though trivial, observation about *clock functions* is that when two blocks of code are sequentially executed, the clock for the composite program is given by summing the clocks for each component. Thus if clock-A and clock-B are used in deriving *clock function* proofs of A and B respectively, then the composite clock is as given below:

```
(defun clock (s) (+ (clock-A s) (clock-B (run s (clock-A s)))))
```

More involved and complicated compositions involving branches, loops, and recursion are possible and can be built out of sequential compositions.

5   Switching Proof Strategies

Since the equivalence theorems have been proved using the encapsulation principle, functional instantiation can be used to automatically transform proofs from one style to another. Assume that for a specific program modeled by the "step function" c-step, and functions c-pre, c-external and c-post, an *inductive invariant* proof has been constructed for total correctness by introducing some invariant predicate c-inv and measure c-m. The following directive then proves the equivalent of clock-run-is-post for the concrete system.

```
(defthm c-run-post
  (implies (c-pre s) (c-post (c-run s (c-clock s))))
  :hints (((''Goal'':use ((:functional-instance clock-is-post
                          (inv c-inv) (pre c-pre) ....)))))
```

Thus c-run-post is proved by instantiating the "abstract" functions in theorem clock-run-is-post with the "concrete" functions provided. Recall that to use functional instantiation, ACL2 must prove that the concrete functions, namely c-pre, c-step, etc., satisfy the constraints imposed by the abstract counterparts. But such constraints are exactly the proof obligations for *inductive invariants*, which have been already dispatched for the concrete functions.

We have developed two macros inv-to-clock and clock-to-inv to transform proofs from one strategy to another, along with basic tools for automatic composition of sequential blocks. While the actual implementation is more elaborate, the basic approach is to automatically generate "concrete" theorems like the one above and prove them by functionally instantiating the abstract proofs.

6   Conclusion

Operational semantics for modeling programs was proposed by McCarthy [1]. The *inductive invariants* framework is often regarded as the "classical approach" in formal verification of programs. Numerous operational system models have since been mechanically verified using inductive invariants in theorem provers like ACL2 [9, 10], HOL [7], and PVS [8], and tools implemented to facilitate such proofs. On the other hand, in the presence of operational models, especially in Boyer-Moore theorem provers, *clock functions* have found greater success, at least for total correctness proofs. Similar proofs have been done using other theorem provers too, though less frequently [14].

We do not advocate one proof style over another. Our goal is to allow the possibility of going "back and forth" between the two styles; thus a program component can be verified using the strategy that is natural to the component, independent of other components. This is particularly important in theorem proving, where a user needs to guide the theorem prover in the proof search. Avoiding the necessity to adhere to a monolithic strategy solely for composition makes the user-dependent aspect of theorem proving simpler and more palatable. Note however, that the definition of `clock` becomes complicated when proofs of a number of components are composed. This complication is of no consequence for correctness; however, to reason about efficiency it is imperative to obtain a "simpler" `clock`. Our work does not address that issue. For reference, Golden [private communication] uses the simplification engine of ACL2 to produce simpler `clocks`, which can provide effective solutions to such concerns.

Our techniques are applicable to operational models alone. Another approach called *denotational semantics* [15–17] models programs in terms of transformation of predicates rather than states as we described. Our framework cannot be directly applied to that approach. Indeed, the notion of *invariants* we use is tied to an operational view, and cannot be formally reconciled with the denotational approach without an extra-logical *verification condition generator*. However, [18] gives a way of proving partial correctness using *inductive invariants* incurring exactly the proof obligations for a denotational approach. Consequently, this work shows that *clock functions* can be derived using the same proof obligations as well. But operational models are requisites for both results.

Our work also emphasizes the power of quantification in ACL2. The expressiveness of quantification has gone largely unnoticed in ACL2, the focus being on "constructive" definitions using recursive equations. The chief reasons for this focus are executability, and amenability for induction. However, in practical verification, it is useful to be able to reason about a generic model of which different concrete systems are "merely" instantiations. Quantifiers are useful for reasoning about generic models. For example, for some state s, assume we want to consider the property of "some state p from which s is reachable". It is then convenient to posit that "some such p exists", and use the `witness` as the specific p to reason about. We and others have found this convenient in diverse contexts, in formalizing *weakest precondition*, and reasoning about pipelined machines [19].

Acknowledgements

The authors benefitted from discussions with the ACL2 group at UT Austin. We particularly thank Jeff Golden, Matt Kaufmann, Robert Krug, Erik Reeber, Rob Sumners, and Vinod Vishwanath for several comments and suggestions.

References

1. McCarthy, J.: Towards a Mathematical Science of Computation. In: Proceedings of the Information Processing Congress. Volume 62., North-Holland (1962) 21–28
2. Boyer, R.S., Moore, J.S.: Mechanized Formal Reasoning about Programs and Computing Machines. In Veroff, R., ed.: Automated Reasoning and Its Applications: Essays in Honor of Larry Wos, MIT Press (1996) 141–176
3. Moore, J.S.: Proving Theorems about Java and the JVM with ACL2. In Broy, M., Pizka, M., eds.: Models, Algebras, and Logic of Engineering Software, Amsterdam, IOS Press (2003) 227–290
4. Bevier, W.R.: A Verified Operating System Kernel. PhD thesis, Department of Computer Sciences, The University of Texas at Austin (1987)
5. Young, W.D.: A Verified Code Generator for a Subset of Gypsy. Technical Report 33, Computational Logic Inc. (1988)
6. Flatau, A.D.: A Verified Implementation of an Applicative Language with Dynamic Storage Allocation. PhD thesis (1992)
7. Gordon, M.J.C., Melham, T.F., eds.: Introduction to HOL: A Theorem-Proving Environment for Higher-Order Logic. Cambridge University Press (1993)
8. Owre, S., Rushby, J.M., Shankar, N.: PVS: A Prototype Verification System. In Kapoor, D., ed.: 11th International Conference on Automated Deduction (CADE). Volume 607 of LNAI., Springer-Verlag (1992) 748–752
9. Kaufmann, M., Manolios, P., Moore, J.S.: Computer-Aided Reasoning: An Approach. Kluwer Academic Publishers (2000)
10. Kaufmann, M., Manolios, P., Moore, J.S., eds.: Computer-Aided Reasoning: ACL2 Case Studies. Kluwer Academic Publishers (2000)
11. Kaufmann, M., Moore, J.S.: Structured Theory Development for a Mechanized Logic. Journal of Automated Reasoning **26** (2001) 161–203
12. Boyer, R.S., Moore, J.S.: A Computational Logic. Academic Press (1975)
13. Liu, H., Moore, J.S.: Executable JVM Model for Analytical Reasoning: A Study. In: ACM SIGPLAN 2003 Workshop on Interpreters, Virtual Machines, and Emulators, San Diego, CA (2003)
14. Wilding, M.: Robust Computer System Proofs in PVS. In Holloway, C.M., Hayhurst, K.J., eds.: Fourth NASA Langley Formal Methods Workshop. Number 3356 in NASA Conference Publication (1997)
15. Floyd, R.: Assigning Meanings to Programs. In: Mathematical Aspects of Computer Science, Proceedings of Symposia in Applied Mathematcs. Volume XIX., Providence, Rhode Island, American Mathematical Society (1967) 19–32
16. Hoare, C.A.R.: An Axiomatic Basis for Computer Programming. Communications of the ACM **12** (1969) 576–583
17. Dijkstra, E.W.: Guarded Commands, Non-determinacy and a Calculus for Derivation of Programs. Language Hierarchies and Interfaces (1975) 111–124
18. Moore, J.S.: Inductive Assertions and Operational Semantics. In Geist, D., ed.: 12th International Conference on Correct Hardware Design and Verification Methods (CHARME). Volume 2860 of LNCS., Springer-Verlag (2003) 289–303
19. Ray, S., W. A. Hunt, Jr: Deductive Verification of Pipelined Machines Using First-Order Quantification. In Alur, R., Peled, D.A., eds.: Computer-Aided Verification (CAV). Volume 3114 of LNCS., Boston, MA, Springer-Verlag (2004) 31–43

Integrating Reasoning
About Ordinal Arithmetic into ACL2

Panagiotis Manolios and Daron Vroon

Georgia Institute of Technology, College of Computing
801 Atlantic Drive, Atlanta, Georgia, 30332, USA
{manolios,vroon}@cc.gatech.edu
http://www.cc.gatech.edu/~{manolios,vroon}

Abstract. Termination poses one of the main challenges for mechanically verifying infinite state systems. In this paper, we develop a powerful and extensible framework based on the ordinals for reasoning about termination in a general purpose programming language. We have incorporated our work into the ACL2 theorem proving system, thereby greatly extending its ability to automatically reason about termination. The resulting technology has been adopted into the newly released ACL2 version 2.8. We discuss the creation of this technology and present two case studies illustrating its effectiveness.

1 Introduction

Termination arguments play a critical role in the design and verification of computing systems. We are interested in providing support for reasoning about the termination of arbitrary programs written in actual programming languages. To that end, we develop a powerful and extensible framework – based on our previous work on ordinal arithmetic [15, 16] – for reasoning about termination in the ACL2 theorem proving system [11, 12].

Our choice of ACL2 for this project was based on two criteria. Since termination is unsolvable, we wanted a system with theorem proving support and in which termination plays a key role. ACL2 meets both of these criteria. It is a powerful theorem proving system which has been applied to several large-scale industrial projects by companies such as AMD, IBM, Motorola, Rockwell Collins, and Union Switch and Signal. Termination is a centerpiece of reasoning in ACL2, as all functions admitted using the definitional principal must be proved to terminate before ACL2 will admit them. This is accomplished by providing a measure function that maps the function parameters into the ordinals and showing that recursive calls decrease according to the measure.

In previous work we developed and verified algorithms for ordinal arithmetic. In this paper, we discuss how we integrated this work with ACL2 version 2.8 [12] to create a powerful, extensible, general framework for reasoning about termination. It is extensible in that new techniques and theorems can be added to ACL2 to enhance its ability to automatically reason about termination, *e.g.*, we proved the well-foundedness of the lexicographic ordering over lists of natural numbers, which enables ACL2 to use measure functions that instead of mapping into the ordinals, map into lists of natural numbers.

A.J. Hu and A.K. Martin (Eds.): FMCAD 2004, LNCS 3312, pp. 82–97, 2004.

The generality of our approach is a byproduct of our focus on providing support for proving arbitrary termination arguments, not on automatically proving termination for a decidable fragment of the termination problem. As an example of this generality, our work has been used to prove Dickson's Lemma [21], which plays a crucial role in proving the termination of Buchberger's algorithm for finding Gröbner bases of polynomial ideals (see Section 6.2).

Our work can also be used to reason about *reactive systems*, nonterminating systems that participate in ongoing interactions with their environments (*e.g.*, networking protocols and operating systems). In this context, termination arguments are used to prove liveness properties, which assert that a desired behavior of the system is not postponed forever. For example, imagine a complicated bus protocol operating on a system with a dynamic topology. Suppose this protocol partitions long messages into packets that are sent according to a priority-based scheme. The property stating that the protocol will never result in deadlock or livelock is a liveness property, which is proved with termination arguments.

While the current literature on termination is vast, most of the related work is focused on various restricted instances of the termination problem. For example, much of the current research on termination is aimed at providing termination proofs for Term Rewriting Systems (TRSs) [2, 1, 8]. Most of the remaining research is focused on developing algorithms and heuristics for the automatic generation of appropriate well-founded measure functions [14, 19, 7, 6, 5]. Since termination is an undecidable problem, this research focuses on solving decidable fragments and is generally presented in terms of toy languages that lack the full functionality of programming languages used in practice. The work we present here, on the other hand, focuses on automating the process of verifying termination arguments and not on guessing measure functions.

In sections 2 and 3, we give an overview of ACL2 and the ordinals. In Section 4 we briefly review our previous work on developing efficient algorithms for ordinal arithmetic. In Section 5, we present the changes we made to ACL2 in integrating our ordinal arithmetic work. Section 6 contains two case studies illustrating the use of our new technology. In Section 7, we discuss some lessons we learned in the course of this project. Finally, we cover the related work in more detail and conclude in Sections 8 and 9.

2   ACL2 Overview

ACL2 stands for "A Computational Logic for Applicative Common Lisp." It comprises a programming language, a first-order mathematical logic based on recursive functions, and a mechanical theorem prover for that logic.

The programming language can best be thought of as an applicative ("side-effect-free" or "pure functional") subset of Common Lisp. We assume basic knowledge of Common Lisp syntax. Because it is a programming language, ACL2 is executable, and execution can reach speeds comparable to programs written in C [22].

The logic of ACL2 is a first-order predicate calculus with equality, recursive function definitions, and mathematical induction. The primitive built-in functions are axiomatized. For example, one axiom is (car (cons x y)) = x and another is x $\neq$ nil $\Rightarrow$ (if x y z) = y. After axiomatizing the basic data types, a representation of the ordinals up to ε_0 is introduced along with an ordering relation, "less than," defined recursively on this definition. This forms the basis for the principle of mathematical induction in ACL2. To prove a conjecture by induction one must identify some ordinal-valued measure function. The induction principle then allows one to assume inductive instances of the conjecture being proved, provided the instance has a smaller measure according to the chosen measure function.

The ACL2 theorem prover is an example of the so-called Boyer-Moore school of inductive theorem proving [3, 4]. It is an integrated system of ad hoc proof techniques that include simplification, generalization, induction and many other techniques. Simplification is, however, the key technique and includes the use of evaluation, conditional rewrite rules, definitions (including recursive definitions), propositional calculus, a linear arithmetic decision procedure for the rationals, user-defined equivalence and congruence relations, user-defined and mechanically verified simplifiers, a user-extensible type system, forward chaining, an interactive loop for entering proof commands, and various means to control and monitor these features. See the ACL2 online user's manual for the full details [12].

ACL2 has been applied to a wide range of commercially interesting verification problems. We recommend visiting the ACL2 home page [12] and inspecting the links on Tours, Demo, Books and Papers, and for the most current work, The Workshops and Related Meetings. See especially [10].

3   Ordinal Overview

Ordinals can most easily be thought of as a transfinite extension of the natural numbers $(0, 1, 2, \ldots)$. The first infinite ordinal is ω, which is the least ordinal that is greater than all the natural numbers. The next ordinal is $\omega + 1$, then $\omega + 2$, and so on until we reach $\omega + \omega$, which is denoted $\omega \cdot 2$. We can continue this process to get $\omega \cdot 2 + 1, \omega \cdot 2 + 2, \ldots$, $\omega \cdot 2 + \omega = \omega \cdot 3$, and so on. Eventually, we get to $\omega \cdot \omega$, which is denoted ω^2. Likewise, we can keep on counting to ω^3 and ω^4, and so on. The ordinal $\omega^{\omega^{\omega^{\cdots}}}$ is denoted ε_0 and is the ordinal on which termination reasoning in ACL2 is based.

Not surprisingly, set theorists define the ordinals in terms of sets. Each ordinal is simply the set of all ordinals less than itself. Thus, the ordinal denoted as 0 is the empty set, $\emptyset$. The ordinal corresponding to 1 is the set containing 0, $\{0\} = \{\emptyset\}$. The ordinal denoted by 2 is $\{0, 1\} = \{\emptyset, \{\emptyset\}\}$. The other natural numbers are defined similarly. The ordinal ω is just the set of all natural numbers, $\{0, 1, 2, \ldots\}$. Note that this implies that the "element of operator", $\in$, the proper subset operator, $\subset$, and the "less than" operator, $<$, are all equivalent on the ordinals.

For the purposes of termination, the most interesting property of ordinals is that they are *well-founded*. That is, there is no infinite sequence of ordinals, $(\alpha_1, \alpha_2, \ldots)$, such that $\alpha_i > \alpha_{i+1}$ for all $i > 0$. Thus, for any ordinal α, the pair $\langle \alpha, < \rangle$ is what is known as a *well-founded structure*. In fact, it is a *well-ordered structure*, which means α is well-founded under $<$ and for any ordinals $\beta, \gamma \in \alpha$, either $\beta < \gamma, \gamma < \beta$, or $\beta = \gamma$.

Proving termination means showing that a program has no infinite computations. This is generally done by assigning a value to each program state and showing that this value decreases with each step of the program. If these values range over a well-founded structure, then by definition, the values cannot decrease infinitely, which proves that the program terminates. Any well-founded structure can be extended to a well-ordered structure by making the relation total while preserving well-foundedness. The termination argument based on the original well-founded structure then directly transfers to this well-ordered extension. A basic result of set theory is that any well-ordered structure is order-isomorphic to a unique ordinal. In this sense, ordinals are the most general setting for termination arguments. This is why Turing says that for proving termination, "it is natural to give an ordinal number" [18].

3.1   Ordinal Arithmetic

Given a well-ordered structure, $\langle A, <_A \rangle$, we denote the unique ordinal that is isomorphic to this structure as $Ord(A, <_A)$.

Ordinal addition is defined as follows. Given two ordinals, α and β, $\alpha + \beta = Ord(A, <_A)$, where $A = (\{0\} \times \alpha) \cup (\{1\} \times \beta)$, and $<_A$ is the lexicographic ordering on A. Thus addition corresponds to starting with the elements of α and then tacking on the elements of β.

Ordinal multiplication is defined as follows. Given two ordinals, α and β, $\alpha \cdot \beta = Ord(A, <_A)$, where $A = \beta \times \alpha$ and $<_A$ is the standard lexicographic ordering. In other words, we create β copies of α.

Ordinal exponentiation is defined by transfinite recursion. Given an ordinal, $\alpha \neq 0$, $\alpha^0 = 1$, $\alpha^{\beta+1} = \alpha^\beta \cdot \alpha$, and $\alpha^\beta = \bigcup_{\gamma < \beta} \alpha^\gamma$. For the case where $\alpha = 0$, we have $0^0 = 1$, and $0^\beta = 0$ for all ordinals $\beta \neq 0$.

Although the finite ordinals correspond to the natural numbers and therefore enjoy all the algebraic properties we expect, the infinite ordinals behave differently. For example, addition and multiplication are not commutative: $2 + \omega = \omega < \omega + 2$ and $2 \cdot \omega = \omega < \omega \cdot 2$. Also, multiplication only distributes from the left. That is, $\alpha \cdot (\beta + \gamma) = (\alpha \cdot \beta) + (\alpha \cdot \gamma)$, but it is not the case that $(\beta + \gamma) \cdot \alpha = (\beta \cdot \alpha) + (\gamma \cdot \alpha)$. This makes reasoning about ordinal arithmetic more interesting.

4   Algorithms for Ordinal Arithmetic

In previous work we developed algorithms for ordinal arithmetic based on a notation for the ordinals up to ε_0. We developed efficient algorithms on succinct notations that are now used by ACL2 to reason about ordinal expressions in the ground (variable-free) case. We present here a brief overview of this work.

4.1   Ordinal Notations

The basis for the ordinal notation used in ACL2, for versions prior to version 2.8, is the following variant of Cantor's Normal Form Theorem.

Theorem 1. *For every ordinal $\alpha \in \varepsilon_0$, there are unique $\alpha_1 \geq \alpha_2 \geq \cdots \geq \alpha_n > 0$ such that $\alpha > \alpha_1$ and $\alpha = \omega^{\alpha_1} + \cdots + \omega^{\alpha_n} + p$.*

Table 1. Ordinal Arithmetic Complexity Results

Function	Complexity
(ocmp a b)	$O(\min(\#a, \#b))$
(o-p a b)	$O(\#a(\log \#a))$
(o+ a b)	$O(\min(\#a, |a| \cdot \#(\text{o-first-expt b})))$
(o- a b)	$O(\min(\#a, \#b))$
(o* a b)	$O(|(\text{o-first-expt a})||b| + \#(\text{o-first-expt a}) + \#b)$
(o^ a b)	$O((\text{natpart b})[|a||b| + |(\text{o-first-expt a})||a| + \#a]$
	$+\#(\text{o-first-expt}\,(\text{o-first-expt a}))|b| + \#b)$

With this notation, the ACL2 representation of the ordinal $\alpha \in \varepsilon_0$, with normal form $\omega^{\alpha_1} + \cdots + \omega^{\alpha_n} + p$, is:

$$ACL2(\alpha) = (ACL2(\alpha_1)\ ACL2(\alpha_2)\ \ldots\ ACL2(\alpha_n)\,.\,p)$$

For example, $\omega + 2$ is (1 . 2) in ACL2 and $\omega^\omega + \omega^\omega + \omega^2 + 3$ is ((1 . 0) (1 . 0) 2 . 3) in ACL2.

The basis for our ordinal notation, which is used in the newly released ACL2 version 2.8, is based on the following variant of Cantor's Normal Form Theorem. The idea is to collect terms with the same exponent using the left distributive property of ordinal multiplication over addition.

Theorem 2. (Cantor Normal Form) *For every ordinal $\alpha \in \varepsilon_0$, there are unique $n, p \in \omega, \alpha_1 > \cdots > \alpha_n > 0$, and $x_1, \ldots, x_n \in \omega\backslash\{0\}$ such that $\alpha > \alpha_1$ and $\alpha = \omega^{\alpha_1} x_1 + \cdots + \omega^{\alpha_n} x_n + p$.*

With this notation, the ACL2 representation of the ordinal α, with normal form $\omega^{\alpha_1} x_1 + \cdots + \omega^{\alpha_n} x_n + p$, is:

$$CNF(\alpha) = ((CNF(\alpha_1)\,.\,x_1)\ (CNF(\alpha_2)\,.\,x_2)\ \ldots\ (CNF(\alpha_n)\,.\,x_n)\,.\,p)$$

The difference between the notations is conceptually trivial, but important because the notation based on Theorem 2 is exponentially more succinct than the one based on Theorem 1, where the *size* of an ordinal under a given representation is the number of bits needed to denote the ordinal in that representation. To see this, consider $\omega \cdot k$: it requires $O(k)$ bits with the representation in Theorem 1 and $O(\log k)$ bits with the representation in Theorem 2.

4.2   Algorithms for Arithmetic

Despite the fact that ordinals have been studied for over 100 years, and that ordinal notations play a critical role in several fields of mathematics, we could not find a complete set of algorithms for the standard arithmetic operators on ordinal notations. We therefore defined efficient algorithms for ordinal ordering ($<$), addition, subtraction, multiplication, and exponentiation for our ordinal notation. Analysis of the correctness and complexity of these algorithms can be found in [15], and the complexity results are summarized in Table 1. Complexity is given in terms of the length (denoted | |) and size

```
(defun natp (x)              (defun o-first-expt (x)
  (and (integerp x)            (if (o-finp x)
       (<= 0 x)))                  0
                                 (caar x)))
(defun posp (x)
  (and (integerp x)          (defun o-first-coeff (x)
       (< 0 x)))               (if (o-finp x)
                                  x
(defun o-finp (x)                (cdar x)))
  (atom x))
                             (defun o-rst (x) (cdr x))

(defmacro o-infp (x)         (defun make-ord (fe fco rst)
  '(not (o-finp ,x)))          (cons (cons fe fco) rst))
```

Fig. 1. Basic Ordinal Functions

(denoted $\#$) of the arguments. The length of an ordinal is the length of its list representation, and the size is 1 for natural numbers and the sum of the sizes of the ordinal's exponents for infinite ordinals. The complexity of o^ is given in terms of natpart, which returns the natural number at the end of the list representation of an ordinal.

Here we present the ordinal addition algorithm as an example. The basic ordinal functions on which our arithmetic algorithms are based are given in Figure 1. Note that natp and posp are recognizers for natural numbers and positive integers, respectively. The function finp and macro infp recognize whether or not an ordinal is finite. Note that (make-ord a b c) constructs an ordinal in our representation where a is the first exponent, b is the first coefficient, and c is the rest of the ordinal: ((a . b) . c). The functions o-first-expt, o-first-coeff, and o-rst deconstruct an ordinal, returning the first exponent, first coefficient, and rest of an ordinal, respectively.

Given these definitions, binary addition of two ordinals in our notation is defined as follows:

```
(defun ob+ (x y)
  (let* ((fe-x (o-first-expt x)) (fco-x (o-first-coeff x))
         (fe-y (o-first-expt y)) (fco-y (o-first-coeff y))
         (cmp-fe (ocmp fe-x fe-y)))
    (cond
      ((and (o-finp x) (o-finp y)) (+ x y))
      ((or (o-finp x) (eq cmp-fe 'lt)) y)
      ((eq cmp-fe 'gt) (make-ord fe-x fco-x (ob+ (o-rst x) y)))
      (t (make-ord fe-y (+ fco-x fco-y) (o-rst y)))))))
```

where (ocmp a b) is a function that returns lt, gt, or eq if a is less than, greater than, or equal to b, respectively.

The correctness of this algorithm relies heavily on the properties of so-called *additive principal ordinals*, which are ordinals of the form ω^β where β is an ordinal greater than 0. There are two properties of these ordinals that concern us. The first is that they are closed under addition. That is, $\alpha < \omega^\gamma$ and $\beta < \omega^\gamma$ implies that $\alpha + \beta < \omega^\gamma$.

The second is the additive principal property, which states that $\alpha < \omega^\beta$ implies that $\alpha + \omega^\beta = \omega^\beta$. Here we give several examples to illustrate ordinal addition. Multiplication and exponentiation are much more complex.

The first is $(\omega 5 + 8) + (\omega^2 3 + \omega 7 + 1)$. By associativity and the closure of additive principal ordinals, we have $(\omega 5 + 8) + (\omega^2 3 + \omega 7 + 1) = \omega 5 + (8 + \omega^2 3) + \omega 7 + 1 = (\omega 5 + \omega^2 3) + \omega 7 + 1 = \omega^2 3 + \omega 7 + 1$. This corresponds to the second case of our algorithm. For the second example, consider $(\omega^2 + \omega 5 + 8) + (\omega^2 3 + \omega 7 + 1)$. This is equal to $\omega^2 + (\omega^2 3 + \omega 7 + 1)$ by our last example. By the left distributive property of multiplication, this is equal to $\omega^2 4 + \omega 7 + 1$, which corresponds to the last case of our algorithm. Finally, consider $(\omega^3 + \omega^2 + \omega 5 + 8) + (\omega^2 3 + \omega 7 + 1)$. By our last example, this is equal to $\omega^3 + \omega^2 4 + \omega 7 + 1$, which is already in normal form. This corresponds to the third case of our algorithm.

5   Changes to ACL2

In this section, we discuss how we integrated our new ordinal arithmetic results with ACL2 to make a powerful, extensible, general tool for reasoning about program termination. We partition this discussion into two sections. In Section 5.1, we give an overview of the *interface changes*, the changes that users of ACL2 will notice. This includes alterations to the core ACL2 logic and our library. In Section 5.2, we discuss the internals of our library, including how we tuned it to maximize its efficiency and effectiveness.

5.1   Interface Changes

The first and most fundamental change we made was to the ACL2 logic itself, which now uses our ordinal representation as its foundation for reasoning about induction, well-foundedness, and termination. This involved adding the helper functions in Figure 1, the ordering function, `o<`, the ordinal recognizer predicate, `o-p`, and the macros `o<=`, `o>`, and `o>=`. Once the new ordinal functions were added, we updated the affected sections of the logic to use our ordinal notation. We did not add our arithmetic functions to the base "ground-zero" ACL2 theory, but included them in a library so as to maintain the simplicity and minimality of the ground-zero theory.

The next change to ACL2 was to improve its ability to reason about arithmetic over the natural numbers and positive integers using the `natp` and `posp` functions. This was crucial for our ordinal arithmetic library, and in order to better integrate these results into ACL2, we created a library, `natp-posp`, based on these results and added it to the arithmetic module, a collection of theorems about arithmetic over the integers, rationals, and complex rationals. The result is an arithmetic module with better support for reasoning about natural numbers and positive integers.

Our library is comprised of several *books*, files of definitions and theorems. Here we review the top-level books that a typical ACL2 user might want to use. The `ordinals` and `ordinals-without-arithmetic` books provide an easy way to access all of our results about ordinal arithmetic. The difference between these books is simply that `ordinals-without-arithmetic` does not include ACL2's arithmetic module, which is useful for users who use different arithmetic modules.

The `lexicographic-ordering` book contains a proof of the well-foundedness of lists of natural numbers under the lexicographic ordering, allowing ACL2 to use the lexicographic order on naturals to prove termination, instead of the ordinals. This book is valuable for two reasons. First, it is a good tool for teaching new ACL2 users, as the lexicographic order on the naturals is simpler to explain than the ordinals. This allows new users to more quickly and easily start reasoning about termination. Second, it provides an example for more experienced users of how to use our library to prove that an ordering is well-founded.

The `e0-ordinal` book is useful for transfering legacy results to the new version of ACL2. It includes the predicate recognizing the old ordinals, `e0-ordinalp`, the corresponding ordering function, `e0-ord-<`, and functions for converting ordinals in this notation to and from ordinals in our notation (`atoc` and `ctoa` respectively). These functions are proved to be order-isomorphisms and inverses of each other.

We used our ordinal arithmetic library to certify the ACL2 regression suite, which is a collection of hundreds of books that formalize mathematical concepts in ACL2 and provide case studies illustrating how to model and verify large systems such as microprocessors. To deal with books that explicitly mention the old ordinals only in termination proofs, this requires simply using the old ordinal representation, which, given the isomorphism result in the `e0-ordinal` book, involves one call to `set-well-founded-relation`. However, some books contain more significant reasoning about the old ordinals and therefore require the full power of the ordinal isomorphism result; an example appears in Section 6.1.

5.2   Internal Engineering of the Books

Creating an efficient and robust library required a considerable amount of effort and in this section we discuss some of the issues.

First, we configured ACL2 to reason about the representation of the ordinals and the basic operations on them in an algebraic fashion. While ACL2 is a typeless language, it is still possible to use algebraic specifications by defining constructors and destructors for the ordinals, proving that they satisfy the appropriate properties, and then disabling the definitions. Since ACL2 is not able to use the definitions of the functions, it is forced to reason using only the algebraic theory. We did this for the functions `make-ord`, `o-first-expt`, `o-first-coeff`, and `o-rst` (see Figure 1). Besides the obvious advantages of algebraic specifications, this approach is more efficient, as otherwise the rewrite rules for manipulating ordinals are in terms of lists (which is how the ordinals are represented), but these rules interact with ACL2's rules for reasoning about lists, leading to inefficiencies.

Next, we related the most efficient version of our algorithms [15] with a simpler but less efficient version [16] using a new feature of ACL2 called mbe ("must be equal"). This feature allows the user to give two definitions for a single function, which must be proved to be equivalent under some *guard conditions* that characterize the intended domain of application. The `logic` definition is used by ACL2 during proof attempts. The `exec` definition is used as the executable version of the function, when the function is applied to the intended domain. This allows us to execute using efficient definitions, but to reason using simpler, cleaner definitions. We used mbe for ordinal multiplication and exponentiation.

Finally, we profiled the books. We used proof analysis tools provided by ACL2 to find sources of inefficiency in proof attempts. Theorems proved by the user cause the ACL2 system to behave differently depending on how they are tagged. Thus, as one can imagine, a large collection of theorems such as those in the ordinal library can interact in very subtle and complex ways. This makes finding sources of inefficiency difficult. For example, we originally had the following rule.

```
(defthm fe-o-p
  (implies (o-p a) (o-p (o-first-exp a)))
  :rule-classes ((:forward-chaining)))
```

Once this rule is admitted, ACL2 will add (o-p (o-first-exp a)) to the *context*, the set of things it knows, when (op a) appears in the context. Note that this will not cause an infinite loop since ACL2 has heuristics for applying forward chaining rules that avoid this. Therefore, this seemed like a harmless rule to us. However, when combined with other forward chaining rules triggered by (o-p (o-first-exp a)), this rule gave us a significant slowdown in the verification of our books. In order to fix this, we changed the theorem to this.

```
(defthm fe-o-p
  (implies (o-p a) (o-p (o-first-exp a)))
  :rule-classes ((:forward-chaining
                    :trigger-terms ((o-first-exp a)))
                   (:rewrite :backchain-limit-lst (5))))
```

The new trigger term insures that (o-first-exp a) is mentioned somewhere in the theorem before the rule is used. This significantly cuts down on the number of times this rule, and the rules that are triggered by it, are used. We also tagged this theorem to be used as as rewrite rule, but only if the hypothesis can be proved in 5 or less steps. Profiling is a crucial part of engineering an effective library of theorems. We therefore carefully profiled our library, and the result was an order of magnitude improvement in performance.

6   Using the New Ordinals: Two Case Studies

In this section we provide two case studies illustrating the use of our ordinal library in ACL2. The first demonstrates how existing libraries making significant use of the ordinals in the old representation can easily be altered to use our new representation. The second case study illustrates how other users have used our ordinal arithmetic library to mechanically prove complex termination arguments.

6.1   Legacy Books: Multiset Case Study

ACL2's multiset ordering library [20] makes significant use of the ordinals. A *multiset* is a set in which items can appear more than once. For example, $\{1, 3, 2, 2, 4\}$ is a multiset over the natural numbers which contains two 2's. Given a set, A, with an order $<$, the *multiset order*, $<_{mul}$, of multisets over A is defined as follows. $N <_{mul} M$ iff there exist multisets X and Y (over A), such that $\emptyset \neq X \subseteq M$, $N = (M - X) \cup Y$,

```
(encapsulate ((mp (x) booleanp)
              (rel (x y) booleanp)
              (fn (x) e0-ordinalp))
  ...

  (defthm rel-well-founded-relation-on-mp
    (and (implies (mp x) (e0-ordinalp (fn x)))
         (implies (and (mp x) (mp y) (rel x y))
                  (e0-ord-< (fn x) (fn y))))
    :rule-classes :well-founded-relation))

  ...

(defthm multiset-extension-of-rel-well-founded
  (and (implies (mp-true-listp x)
                (e0-ordinalp (map-fn-e0-ord x)))
       (implies (and (mp-true-listp x)
                     (mp-true-listp y)
                     (mul-rel x y))
                (e0-ord-< (map-fn-e0-ord x)
                          (map-fn-e0-ord y))))
  :rule-classes :well-founded-relation)
```

Fig. 2. Original Multiset Results

and $\forall y \in Y$, $\exists x \in X$ such that $y <_A x$. If we restrict ourselves to finite sets, then if $<_A$ is well-founded, it can be shown that so is $<_{mul}$. The multiset library provides a macro called defmul which, given a well-founded relation over a set and a recognizer for that set, automatically generates the corresponding multiset relation and proves it to be well-founded.

The defmul macro depends on results proved in another book, called multiset, which provides useful lemmas about multisets, and uses ACL2's encapsulate feature to prove in general that a multiset extension of a well-founded relation is well-founded (See Figure 2). The encapsulated code hides the details of the functions from the rest of the book. All that is known outside the encapsulate is that mp and rel return boolean values, fn returns an ordinal in the old representation, and rel has been proved to be well-founded on the set recognized by mp using the embedding fn. Following this encapsulate, there are a number of lemmas about these functions based only on that information, which culminate in the proof of the well-foundedness of the multiset extension of rel.

There are two problems in certifying this book using the new version of ACL2. The first is that the original theorem declaring the well-foundedness of rel is no longer a proof of well-foundedness. The embedding, fn must return an ordinal in the new representation in an order-preserving way. The second problem is that the final theorem about the well-foundedness of the multiset extension must also be altered to use our new ordinals.

The solution is relatively simple, and relies on the results of our e0-ordinal book. Using our conversion functions, ctoa and atoc, we transfered the results of the multiset book to results about the new ordinal notation. First, we altered the encapsulate so that fn and the well-foundedness result were in terms of the new ordinals. This simply required replacing e0-ordinalp and e0-ord-< by o-p and o<, respectively.

Next, we added the following macro.

```
(defmacro fn0 (x) '(ctoa (fn ,x)))
```

This simply converts the ordinal in the new notation given by fn into the corresponding ordinal in the old representation. The theorems involving fn were changed to use fn0 instead. After the final result (which we renamed and retagged as a rewrite rule), we added the following lines of code to convert the results into a valid well-founded-relation argument using the new ordinal notation.

```
(defun map-fn-op (x)
  (atoc (map-fn-e0-ord x)))

(defthm multiset-extension-of-rel-well-founded
  (and (implies (mp-true-listp x) (o-p (map-fn-op x)))
       (implies (and (mp-true-listp x)
                     (mp-true-listp y)
                     (mul-rel x y))
                (o< (map-fn-op x) (map-fn-op y))))
  :rule-classes :well-founded-relation)
```

Finally, we changed the defmul macro so that it uses the new theorem and function names. With this approach, we did not have to alter the lemmas about the old ordinals in multiset. Doing so would have required essentially modifying the entire book. This "wrapping" method can be used to quickly and easily update old libraries so that they can be certified using the new ordinals.

6.2   New Results: Dickson's Lemma Case Study

Our library was used by Sustik to give a constructive proof of Dickson's Lemma [21]. This is a key lemma in the proof of the termination of Buchberger's algorithm for finding a Gröbner basis of a polynomial ideal, and is therefore an important step toward the larger goal of formalizing results from algebra in ACL2 [17]. Sustik made essential use of the ordinals and our library, as his proof depends heavily on the ordinals and could not have been proved in older versions of ACL2 without essentially building up a theory of ordinal arithmetic similar to our own. Our library was able to automatically discharge all the proof obligations involving the ordinals.

Dickson's Lemma states that, given an infinite sequence of monomials, m_0, m_1, $m_2, \ldots$, there exists $i, j \in \mathbb{N}$ such that $i < j$ and m_i divides m_j. Sustik's argument involves mapping initial segments of the monomial sequence into the ordinals such that if Dickson's lemma fails, the ordinal sequence will be decreasing. Thus, the existence of an infinite sequence of monomials such that no monomial divides a later monomial implies the existence of an infinite decreasing sequence of ordinals, which is not possible due to the well-foundedness of the ordinals.

This proof relies heavily on ordinal addition and exponentiation. For example, sets of monomials, which are represented as lists of tuples of natural numbers, are mapped to the ordinals by the following function.

```
(defun tuple-set->ordinal-partial-sum (k S i)
  (cond ((or (not (natp k)) (not (natp i))) 0)
        ((zp k) 0)
        ((equal k 1)
         (tuple-set-min-first S))
        ((<= (tuple-set-max-first S) i)
         (o^ (omega) (o+ (tuple-set->ordinal-partial-sum
                            (1- k) (tuple-set-projection S) 0)
                         1)))
        (T (o+ (o^ (omega)
                   (tuple-set->ordinal-partial-sum
                    (1- k) (tuple-set-filter-projection S i) 0))
               (tuple-set->ordinal-partial-sum k S (1+ i))))))
```

Key lemmas about this function therefore required sophisticated reasoning about the behavior of ordinal addition and exponentiation. One such lemma is as follows.

```
(defthm map-lemma-3.2
  (implies (and (tuple-setp k A) (natp k) (< 1 k) (natp i))
           (o< (o^ (omega) (tuple-set->ordinal-partial-sum
                             (1- k)
                             (tuple-set-filter-projection A i)
                             0))
               (tuple-set->ordinal-partial-sum k A i))))
```

This and other similar theorems require results about ordinal arithmetic including the following: (1) $\alpha < \beta \Rightarrow \gamma + \alpha < \gamma + \beta$, (2) $\alpha \le \beta \Rightarrow \alpha + \gamma \le \beta + \gamma$, (3) $\alpha \le \beta \wedge \gamma \le \delta \Rightarrow \alpha + \gamma \le \beta + \delta$, (4) $\alpha < \beta \Rightarrow \gamma^\alpha < \gamma^\beta$, and (5) $\alpha \le \beta \Rightarrow \alpha^\gamma \le \beta^\gamma$.

Initially, Sustik used a preliminary version of our library, and he needed 26 additional theorems about ordinal arithmetic for his proof. After streamlining our library, no additional ordinal arithmetic lemmas were required, and the results specific to Dickson's Lemma, such as those above, were discharge twice as quickly. The overall result was a 70.5% speedup in the verification of the Dickson's Lemma library. This is an example of the kind of termination proof that would be quite difficult to fully automate.

7   Lessons Learned

During this project we learned several lessons that we believe will be of benefit to users working on large projects in ACL2 and similar systems. These include lessons about the features and shortcomings of ACL2, as well as lessons about effectively designing and implementing large projects in ACL2. Here, we share some of these lessons.

One invaluable feature of ACL2 is its regression suite. This large collection of books includes the formalization of many mathematical theories and industrial case studies, making it a valuable testbed for new features. Running the regression suite on our altered version of ACL2 stressed our library and helped us maximize its efficiency and effectiveness. Along the way we learned two valuable lessons. The first is that it is important to have a general way of integrating results into the regression suite. In our case, we used the ordinal isomorphism results, as we illustrate in Section 6.1, to transfer results about the old ordinals to the new ordinals; this saved us from having to understand the details of existing books. The second lesson we learned is that the regression suite can reveal patterns in the use of ACL2 that can inspire new improvements. For example, we did not originally plan on integrating our results about `natp` and `posp` with the arithmetic module. However, when working with the regression suite, we found that many libraries contained functions similar to `natp` and `posp`, and this prompted us to create a separate book that we added to the arithmetic module.

Another feature of ACL2 is its extensive documentation [12]. It describes each ACL2 feature and function in detail, and an important part of integrating our work into ACL2 was updating the documentation. This included describing our functions, but, more importantly, it required us to reason at the meta-level, providing a hand-written proof of the well-foundedness of our ordinal notation (which does not appeal to the ordinals), in order to demonstrate the soundness of our new additions to ACL2. Thus, updating the documentation is important both for keeping users up-to-date with the current features of ACL2 and for arguing at a meta-level about the soundness of the ACL2 logic.

As we mentioned earlier, profiling was a crucial step in making our library more efficient. What we found is that this is actually very difficult to do in ACL2. There is a mechanism called `accumulated-persistance` that allows the user to gauge the performance of each individual rule. However, many performance problems come from the interaction among the rules, not from each rule's individual performance. We think that ACL2 users would benefit from a mechanism for analyzing this interaction. For example, one can imagine having a mechanism for reporting the amount of time spent on rules of each class (*e.g.*, forward chaining rules versus rewrite rules). Since rules of one class often trigger other rules of the same class, this could prove to be useful.

Another shortcoming of the ACL2 system is the naming scheme, which it has borrowed from Lisp. Namespace collisions can be avoided in ACL2 by creating new packages. For example, we could have created a package called ORD, and defined all our functions in that package (*e.g.*, `ORD::o<`). In fact, this would have been useful for us, since we found functions called `op` (the original name of our predicate function) and `natp` in several libraries in the regression suite. However, referring to one package from another involves either prefixing symbols with package names or importing symbols into the current package (thus causing namespace issues again). It usually takes several iterations to determine which symbols a package should import, but the ACL2 implementation requires restarting ACL2 for every such change. In the end, we found it easier to rename our predicate function to `o-p` and to rename or delete the `natp` functions found in other books. ACL2 users would benefit from a better mechanism for dealing with namespace issues.

Our use of algebraic specifications to deal with `make-ord`, `o-first-expt`, `o-first-coeff`, and `o-rst` sped up our books, but it took several iterations to discover where abstraction should be used. We found that algebraic specifications are often more trouble than they are worth. When in doubt, we recommend starting with little or no abstraction, and adding more based on how functions are being used in proof attempts. If the theorem prover seems to be struggling with the underlying representation, then perhaps abstraction can help.

Finally, we learned the value of recording lessons learned while working on a big project in ACL2. We have noticed through past experience that users (including us) often make the same mistakes repeatedly. They have to rediscover ways to improve their libraries or avoid pitfalls. Having a record of these tips, tricks, and lessons can potentially be a valuable time-saver when working on new projects. They are also valuable for finding difficulties with ACL2 such as the ones we presented here, which can be used to improve the theorem-proving system and may provide insight that will help developers of other theorem proving systems as well.

8   Related Work

There has been a significant amount of work dealing with the problem of termination in recent years. Much of it has focused on the termination of term rewriting systems (TRSs). Current techniques for proving the termination of TRSs can be found in [2]. One such method is the *interpretation method*, which involves mapping terms into a well-founded set and showing that the left-hand-side of rewrite rules map to a bigger value than the corresponding right-hand-side for all rules. Another method involves *simplification orders* which are orders over terms such that terms are always greater than their subterms. This often involves extending a well-founded order on the signature of the TRS to apply to all terms. Popular simplification orders include the *lexicographic path ordering* and *Knuth-Bendix orderings*. One method for proving termination of TRSs using simplification orders is called the *dependency pair method* [1]. Recent work focusing on automating this method has met with some success [8]. These methods, while useful in the context of theorem proving and optimization in compilers, are designed for TRSs rather than programming languages used in practice. They therefore have not been shown to scale to the complexities of actual programming languages.

Another approach to termination is the size-change principal [14]. This method involves using a well-order on function parameters, analyzing recursive calls to label any clearly decreasing parameters. All possible infinite sequences of function calls are then checked to be sure that there are infinite decreases and only finitely many possible increases in the values of arguments to recursive function calls. This is similar but much less sophisticated than ACL2's termination reasoning. For example, there is no explicit description on how to determine if a function parameter "decreases." The examples are based on a simple toy language, and the analysis of arguments of the form (f x), where f is a user-defined function, is not considered. Only primitive operations are dealt with. The conditions under which recursive calls are made are not taken into account, *e.g.*, if a recursive call is made in the else branch of an if statement, we know that the test of the if statement is false at that point. This information is often *necessary* for establishing termination.

There are many other methods that can potentially be extended to deal with full programming languages. Podelski and Rybalchenko give a complete method for proving termination of non-nested loops with linear ranking functions [19]. Dams, Gerth, and Grumberg give a heuristic for automatically generating ranking functions [7]. Colón and Sipma give two algorithms for proving termination, one which synthesizes linear ranking functions, but is limited to programs with few variables, and one which is more heuristic in nature and converges faster on the invariants it can discover [6, 5].

What is novel about our approach is that we focus on extendability and generality. The result is a system into which new heuristics and techniques (such as the ones cited above) can be incorporated in order to improve automation. However, when these techniques fail (as they eventually must, since termination is undecidable), the user can interact with the theorem prover to find a proof.

9   Conclusions and Future Work

We have developed a general framework based on the ordinals for proving program termination, which has been incorporated into ACL2 v2.8. The resulting system allows us to prove termination in a general context for arbitrary programs and in a highly automated fashion, as we demonstrated with the case study of Dickson's Lemma. For future work, we plan to add decision procedures and heuristics to our framework to further automate ACL2's ability to reason about termination. We also plan to use ACL2 as a back-end reasoning engine, combined with a front-end system containing static analysis techniques in order to reason about the termination of programs written in imperative languages such as C and Java.

Acknowledgments

We would like to thank the authors and maintainers of ACL2, J Moore and Matt Kaufmann for their help and support of our project. We also wish to thank Mátyás Sustik for providing us with the Dickson's Lemma book, which proved very helpful as a testbed for our library.

References

1. T. Arts and J. Giesl. Termination of term rewriting using dependency pairs. *Theoretical Computer Science*, 236:133–178, 2000.
2. F. Baader and T. Nipkow. *Term Rewriting and All That*. Cambridge University Press, 1998.
3. R. S. Boyer and J. S. Moore. Proving theorems about pure lisp functions. *JACM*, 22(1):129–144, 1975.
4. R. S. Boyer and J. S. Moore. *A Computational Logic*. Academic Press, New York, 1979.
5. M. A. Colón and H. B. Sipma. Synthesis of linear ranking functions. In *TACAS01: Tools and Algorithms for the Construction and Analysis of Systems*, volume 2031 of *LNCS*, pages 67–81, 2001.
6. M. A. Colón and H. B. Sipma. Practical methods for proving program termination. In *International Conference on Computer Aided Verification, CAV'02*, volume 2404 of *LNCS*, pages 442–454, 2002.
7. D. Dams, R. Gerth, and O. Grumberg. A heuristic for the automatic generation of ranking functions. In *Workshop on Advanced Verification*, July 2000. See URL
   http://www.cs.utah.edu/wave/.
8. N. Hirokawa and A. Middledorp. Automating the dependency pair method. In *Automated Deduction – CADE-19*, LNAI, pages 32–46. Springer-Verlag, 2003.
9. A. J. Hu and M. Y. Vardi, editors. *Computer-Aided Verification – CAV '98*, volume 1427 of *LNCS*. Springer-Verlag, 1998.

10. M. Kaufmann, P. Manolios, and J. S. Moore, editors. *Computer-Aided Reasoning: ACL2 Case Studies*. Kluwer Academic Publishers, June 2000.
11. M. Kaufmann, P. Manolios, and J. S. Moore. *Computer-Aided Reasoning: An Approach*. Kluwer Academic Publishers, July 2000.
12. M. Kaufmann and J. S. Moore. ACL2 homepage. See URL
    http://www.cs.utexas.edu/users/moore/acl2.
13. M. Kaufmann and J. S. Moore, editors. *Fourth International Workshop on the ACL2 Theorem Prover and Its Applications (ACL2-2003)*, July 2003. See URL
    http://www.cs.utexas.edu/users/moore/acl2/workshop-2003/.
14. C. S. Lee, N. D. Jones, and A. M. Ben-Amram. The size-change principle for program termination. *ACM Symposium on Principles of Programming Languages*, 28:81–92, 2001.
15. P. Manolios and D. Vroon. Algorithms for ordinal arithmetic. In F. Baader, editor, *19th International Conference on Automated Deduction – CADE-19*, volume 2741 of *LNAI*, pages 243–257. Springer–Verlag, July/August 2003.
16. P. Manolios and D. Vroon. Ordinal arithmetic in ACL2. In Kaufmann and Moore [13]. See URL http://www.cs.utexas.edu/users/moore/acl2/workshop-2003/.
17. F.-J. Martín-Mateos, J.-A. Alonso, M.-J. Hidalgo, and J.-L. Ruiz-Reina. A formal proof of Dickson's Lemma in ACL2. In M. Y. Vardi and A. Voronkov, editors, *Logic for Programming, Artificial Intelligence and Reasoning (LPAR 2003)*, volume 2850 of *LNCS*, pages 49–58. Springer Verlag, 2003.
18. F. Morris and C. Jones. An early program proof by Alan Turing. *IEEE Annals of the History of Computing*, 6(2):139–143, April–June 1984.
19. A. Podelske and A. Rybalchenko. A complete method for the synthesis of linear ranking functions. In B. Steffen and G. Levi, editors, *Verification, Model Checking, and Abstract Interpretation, VMCAI 2004*, volume 2937 of *LNCS*, pages 239–251, 2004.
20. J.-L. Ruiz-Reina, J.-A. Alonso, M.-J. Hidalgo, and F.-J. Martin. Multiset relations: A tool for proving termination. In M. Kaufmann and J. S. Moore, editors, *Proceedings of the ACL2 Workshop 2000*. The University of Texas at Austin, Technical Report TR-00-29, November 2000.
21. M. Sustik. Proof of Dixon's lemma using the ACL2 theorem prover via an explicit ordinal mapping. In Kaufmann and Moore [13]. See URL
    http://www.cs.utexas.edu/users/moore/acl2/workshop-2003/.
22. M. Wilding, D. Greve, and D. Hardin. Efficient simulation of formal processor models. *Formal Methods in System Design*, 18(3):233–248, May 2001.

Combining Equivalence Verification
and Completion Functions

Mark D. Aagaard, Vlad C. Ciubotariu, Jason T. Higgins, and Farzad Khalvati*

University of Waterloo

Abstract. This work presents a new method for verifying optimized register-transfer-level implementations of pipelined circuits. We combine the robust, yet limited, capabilities of combinational equivalence verification with the modular and composable verification strategy of completion functions. We have applied this technique to a 32-bit OpenRISC processor and a Sobel edge-detector circuit. Each case study required less than fifteen verification obligations and each obligation could be checked in less than one minute. We believe that our approach will be applicable to a large class of pipelines with in-order execution.

1 Introduction

Formal verification techniques and tools have advanced to the point where a high-level model of a superscalar processor with out-of-order execution and exceptions is a common case study. Despite these advances, the techniques and tools developed for processor verification have generally been limited to experts working on high-level models. In contrast, equivalence checking of register-transfer-level designs is now standard practice in most design flows.

Among the variety of strategies for verifying processors, Hosabettu's completion functions approach [3] is one of the most appealing, because it is general, intuitive, and compositional. In this paper, we describe a technique that uses combinational equivalence verification and completion functions to verify register-transfer-level implementations of pipelined circuits. We have applied our technique to verify VHDL implementations of a 4-stage, in-order, 32-bit OpenRISC [4] processor implementing 47 instructions and an eight-stage Sobel edge detector. Each of the circuits required less than fifteen verification obligations. Each verification obligation was checked in less than a minute using Synopsys Formality [5] as the equivalence verifier.

The overall goal of this work was to use off-the-shelf software to formally verify register-transfer-level implementations of pipelined circuits. We wanted to avoid abstracting the implementation, because many bugs are introduced at lower levels of the design as the code gets larger and more complex. Optimizations for clock speed and area often transform the implementation in ways that obscure the original clean and modular high-level design. Both of our case studies had been validated extensively, yet we still found two bugs in the edge detector. Both of the bugs resulted from low-level performance optimizations that would be unlikely to appear in high-level models.

* This research was supported in part by Semiconductor Research Corporation, Natural Sciences and Engineering Council of Canada, and Intel Corporation.

A.J. Hu and A.K. Martin (Eds.): FMCAD 2004, LNCS 3312, pp. 98–112, 2004.
© Springer-Verlag Berlin Heidelberg 2004

We chose to use combinational equivalence verification as our verification tool because of its high capacity, high degree of automation, and widespread usage. Combinational equivalence verification is limited to comparing the next-state equations of signals based only on the combinational circuitry driving the signal. As such, combinational equivalence verification cannot verify even retiming optimizations, let alone verify a pipelined implementation against a non-pipelined specification. Sequential equivalence checking can verify some retiming optimizations, but quickly escalates to reachability analysis and all of the typical state-space explosion problems. The key to our approach is that completion functions verify pipelines one stage at a time, which makes the task amenable to combinational equivalence verification and significantly reduces computational complexity.

2   Background on Completion Functions

This section provides background information on completion functions and how they are used to decompose the verification of pipelined circuits. The verification engineer writes one completion function for each in-flight instruction in the pipeline. There is typically one in-flight instruction per stage in the pipeline, hence there is typically one completion function for each stage.

The completion function for a stage describes the effect on the architectural state of completing the partially executed instruction in the stage. Executing a completion function for a stage has essentially the same effect as flushing the instruction in the stage. Executing all completion functions flushes the entire pipeline. For in-order pipelines, completion functions are composed in a linear fashion, starting from the last stage of the pipeline and working incrementally upstream to the first stage.

Figure 1 shows a contrived, but illustrative, pipeline along with its commuting diagrams for Burch-Dill flushing [2] and completion functions. The pipeline contains three architectural registers (R_1, R_2, and R_3) and three stage registers (S_1, S_2, and S_3). In the starting state (q_i), the pipeline contains three instructions (A, B, and C). The implementation step (N_i) and specification step (N_s) fetch the instruction D. In the flushing commuting diagram, bubbles enter the pipeline as the pipeline is flushed. In the completion function diagram, each completion function (C_i) completes the execution of the instruction in stage i by writing to downstream architectural registers (e.g., C_2 writes to R_2 and R_3).

The end result of verification with completion functions is the same as verification by flushing. The difference between the two approaches is that the commuting diagram for flushing is a monolithic verification obligation, while the commuting diagram for completion functions enables a stage-by-stage decomposition into multiple verification obligations. For our contrived example, there are four verification obligations, represented by the dotted lines in Figure 1d. Working from bottom to top, each obligation verifies a single pipeline stage. Shaded cells represent the subset of the architectural registers that are involved in each proof obligation.

In the first obligation, we verify the third (bottom) stage by comparing the value of R_3 produced by completing the instruction in the last stage of the pipeline to the value of R_3 produced by taking an implementation step. Similarly, in the second obligation

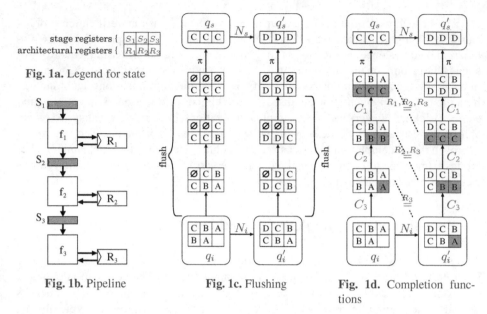

Fig. 1a. Legend for state

Fig. 1b. Pipeline

Fig. 1c. Flushing

Fig. 1d. Completion functions

Fig. 1. Simple pipeline with flushing and completion-function commuting diagrams

we verify the second (middle) stage. We prove that the composition of C_3 and C_2 is equivalent, with respect to R_2 and R_3, to taking an implementation step and running C_3. Verification obligations can often be simplified by using previously proven results from lower obligations. We work our way up the commuting diagram incrementally, gradually verifying all of the stages. For the fourth (top) obligation, we compare the specification against the completion function for the first stage. This last obligation catches any mistakes that were made in the completion functions, such as reproducing an implementation bug in a completion function.

Stalls, bypass paths, and speculative execution are quite specific to individual pipelines, so we present these features in the context of our OpenRISC processor in Section 5.2. Often, verifying completion function correctness statements requires invariants to restrict the set of implementation states. Finding and verifying invariants is done the same as with other verification techniques.

3   Background on Equivalence Verification

The equivalence verification process can be divided into three main steps. In the first step, the specification and implementation are matched by identifying pairs of related signals or points in the two circuits. Typically, the match points are the inputs, flip-flops, and outputs of the circuit. Depending on the details of the specification and implementation, it may be possible to perform this matching step automatically either through naming conventions or through signature analysis of nodes in the circuit.

In the second step, a subset of the match points, called the compare points, are identified. The compare points represent the points in the specification and implementation for which one wants to verify equivalence.

In the third step, the next-state function of each compare point in the specification is verified against the next-state function of the corresponding compare point in the implementation. If this comparison is successful for each pair of compare points, then the specification and implementation are considered to be equivalent. If there is a pair of corresponding compare points that are not equivalent, then the logic cones for those compare points can be examined to isolate the implementation error.

Verifying the equivalence of a pair of compare points is accomplished mainly with the use of BDD- and SAT-based techniques. Equivalence verification also uses structural matching heuristics and cut-points to handle multipliers and other circuits that are beyond the capacity of BDDs and SAT.

The appeal of equivalence verification is the highly automated nature of the verification – for many circuits no user interaction is required. This automation is achieved at the expense of the range of properties that can be verified: usually point-by-point equivalence of next-state functions for flip-flops and outputs.

Equivalence verification algorithms can be characterized as either combinational or sequential. Combinational equivalence verification compares only combinational logic and cannot handle retiming optimizations. Sequential equivalence verification attempts to verify implementations where the circuitry to be compared crosses flip-flop boundaries, which is a substantially more difficult challenge than combinational equivalence verification.

As with most verification problems, some implementations satisfy their specification (i.e., have equivalent next-state equations) only when the implementation is in a reachable state. In these situations, equivalence verification can quickly escalate into general reachability analysis and invariant finding. Equivalence checkers provide mechanisms for users to assume preconditions when performing the verification, but there is rarely support for verifying that the preconditions are invariants.

To be as general as possible in the equivalence checkers that can be used with our approach, we limit ourselves to combinational equivalence verification. In some of our verifications, we use of both predefined and user-defined preconditions.

Sometimes, black boxes are required to model components in a circuit. These black boxes are needed when the component leads to state explosion, when the component is external to the part of the circuit being verified, or when the component is analog. Black boxes allow equivalence verification to be performed by removing the problematic component from the circuit. When matched black boxes appear in the specification and the implementation, the inputs to the black boxes are verified for equivalence and the outputs from the black boxes are assumed to be equivalent.

4   Approach

In this section, we describe our approach for casting completion-function verification as a combinational equivalence verification problem. We begin with the intuition behind our approach, and then explain how we handle pipeline stages that stall, memory arrays, and initial states.

In Figure 2, we use the third verification obligation from Figure 1d to illustrate the combination of completion functions and equivalence checking. This obligation verifies the first stage of the pipeline by comparing the composition of C_3, C_2, and C_1 against taking an implementation step and then executing the composition of C_3 and C_2. We implement the completion functions as combinational logic and tell the equivalence verifier to compare the output architectural variables (R_1', R_2'', and R_3''').

We create two circuits, one for the left side of the completion function diagram (Figure 2b) and one for the right side (Figure 2c). Each completion function C_i reads its stage register S_i and, through the downstream completion functions, reads the downstream architectural registers. The outputs of each completion function are updated values for the downstream architectural registers. On the right side, to mimic the effect of taking an implementation step, each completion function reads from the *next* value of its stage register (S_i'), which is done by reading from the *input* to the stage register.

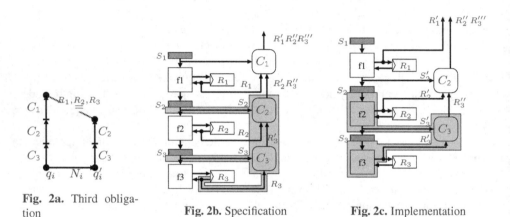

Fig. 2a. Third obligation

Fig. 2b. Specification

Fig. 2c. Implementation

Fig. 2. Third step of simple example

The large gray polygons represent the second verification obligation and illustrate how we take advantage of the compositional nature of completion functions. Because we have verified the second obligation, we know that the two large gray polygons are equivalent. We can simplify the third verification obligation by replacing the output of each gray polygon (R_2' and R_3'') with a new primary input and telling the equivalence checker that these inputs will always have the same value in both models. We further illustrate this technique in Section 5.2.

Pipeline stages that can stall require chip-enables on their stage register. For registers with chip enables, we need to model the chip-enable circuitry in the next-state equation for the register. To use combinational equivalence verification to compare an implementation with chip enables against an unpipelined specification, we replace each register that has a chip enable with an equivalent circuit that uses a multiplexer to reload the previous contents of the register in the event of a stall.

Equivalence verification has no knowledge of the contents of memory arrays. We model each memory array with combinational circuitry that has the same behaviour as the memory array for a bounded number of read and write operations. Our combinational model of memory is based on the anonymous-function model of memory, where a memory array is an anonymous function from addresses to data values. Mathematically, reading from memory (Equation 1) is simply function application. Writing to memory (Equation 2) returns a new anonymous function that compares the read address ($rdaddr$) with the write address to determine whether the read should get the written data or should read from the prior contents of memory.

$$Rd \ addr \ mem \equiv mem \ addr \tag{1}$$

$$Wr \ wr\_en \ wraddr \ data \ mem \equiv \lambda rdaddr. \tag{2}$$
$$\textbf{if} \ wr\_en \wedge (rdaddr = wraddr)$$
$$\textbf{then} \ data$$
$$\textbf{else} \ Rd \ rdaddr \ mem$$

To compare the contents of two memory arrays, M_1 and M_2, we test that, for all addresses $tstaddr$, reading from $tstaddr$ returns the same data for M_1 and M_2. To use equivalence verification to verify reading from and writing to memory, we need combinational circuits that model Equations 1 and Equation 2. Our model (Figure 3) uses the M-block circuit to model the initial values of a memory array and the W-block circuit to model write operations. Our model is bisimilar via the simulation relation $\mathcal{B}$ in Equation 3 to a conventional memory array with respect to a bounded number of read and write operations.

$$\mathcal{B} \ M_1 \ M_2 \equiv \forall a, d. \ (Rd \ a \ M_1 = d) \iff (Rd \ a \ M_2 = d) \tag{3}$$

An M block (Figure 3a) with n pairs of address and data inputs captures the initial state of a memory, where up to n unique addresses will be read. The data inputs to an M block are primary inputs to the two circuits subject to equivalence verification while the address inputs are wires coming from all the possible expressions that are used to read from memory. We do not need to know the total number of memory elements in the actual memory array.

Each W block (Figure 3b) represents one write operation. For a read operation that occurs after n writes we cascade an initial M block with n subsequent W blocks, as shown in Figure 3c for three unique addresses and two write operations.

For each read operation that is performed in an implementation step, we need an M/W-block cascade. Two factors mitigate the potential complexity of this configuration. First, because we verify only the inductive step, we can replace the M blocks with black boxes. Second, equivalence checkers often exploit heuristics based on matching signal names and circuit structures to decompose the verification task and reduce computational complexity.

Our memory circuits match the anonymous function model by having an unconnected input ($tstaddr$) for the address to read from. Our technique for modeling memory supports both read-before-write and write-before-read memory arrays by either including or removing a W block for a write that happens in the same clock cycle as a read.

A commuting diagram is the inductive step of a proof of trace containment. The base case of trace containment shows that each initial state of the implementation corresponds to an initial state in the specification. Initial states typically correspond to when the circuit is reset. Verifying the base case corresponds to verifying that when

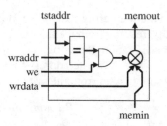

Fig. 3b. W-block circuit

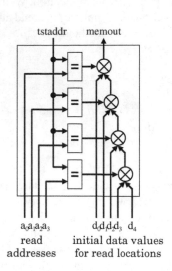

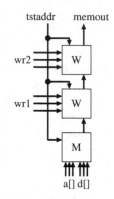

a₀a₁a₂a₃
read
addresses

d₀d₁d₂d₃ d₄
initial data values
for read locations

Fig. 3a. M-block circuit for 4 unique read
addresses

Fig. 3c. Cascade of initial state and two write
operations

Fig. 3. Building blocks for memory model

the circuit is reset, it will transition to a proper reset state. Many of the bugs related to
reset occur because of low-level synchronization and timing problems that appear only
in timing simulation and other abstraction layers below the register-transfer level. Our
approach does not directly address verifying the base case, because we feel that reset
verification is best done via timing simulation with uninitialized values for inputs and
internal state.

5   OpenRISC

In this section we describe our implementation and verification of an OpenRISC processor. We use this example to illustrate how completion functions handle stalls, bypass
paths, and speculative execution and how we accommodate these behaviours in our
equivalence-verification-based approach.

5.1   OpenRISC Implementation

OpenRISC is a load/store RISC instruction set architecture created by the OpenCores
group. The OpenRISC architecture contains thirty-two general-purpose registers and a

condition-code register with carry, overflow, and flag fields. Our case study is based on an implementation of the ORBIS32 instruction set, using the OpenRISC 1200 microarchitecture definition (OR1200) as a guide. This instruction set contains fifty-two instructions and two addressing modes: register-indirect with displacement and PC-relative. We implemented all of instructions, except for five that require either operating-system support or access to special-purpose registers. Figure 4 shows a block diagram of our implementation and summarizes some of the implementation statistics.

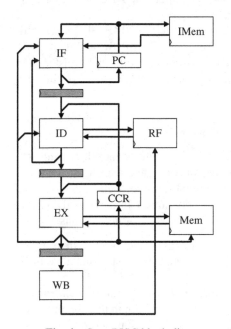

Fig. 4a. OpenRISC block diagram

Architectural State		
Pc	Program counter	32 bits
Ccr	Condition code reg	3 bits
Rf	Register file	32 32-bit words
Mem	Data Memory	1024 32-bit words

Implementation State		
Id_R	Decode stage	64 bits
Ex_R	Execute stage	175 bits
Wb_R	Writeback stage	49 bits
Mult	Multiplier	175 bits
Misc	Misc. control	3 bits

Fig. 4b. Architectural and implementation state

	Multiply	Shift	All Others
Number of instrs.	3	7	37
Latency	8	5	4

Fig. 4c. Instruction latencies

Fig. 4. OpenRISC implementation

The fetch stage computes the next program counter value based on stall and mis-predict information. It also receives the next instruction from IMem and passes this to the decode stage. In the fetch stage, all branches are statically predicted not-taken.

The decode stage fetches the operands for the instruction and determines if the instruction is of ALU, memory, or branch type. Branches are resolved in the decode stage. Taken branches assert a mispredict signal and the target PC is sent to the fetch stage. Branch conditions test the flag field of the condition code register, which is set by ten instructions that perform relational tests on general-purpose registers.

The execute stage performs the ALU and memory operations. The latency of different instruction types is shown in Figure 4c. In the case of multicycle instructions, bubbles are inserted into the writeback stage. On a cache miss, the pipeline stalls until the new cache line has been loaded.

The execute stage updates the condition code register, which becomes available to the decode stage in the next clock cycle. If the instruction in the execute stage sets a flag and there is a branch instruction in decode that reads the flag, the fetch and decode stages stall. Updates to the register file are forwarded to the decode stage. The only data-dependent stalls are branches dependent on a flag-setting instruction.

The execute stage uses a 5-cycle 32-bit multiply. The multiply datapath is one of the critical paths in our design, and is far slower than the register-file access. Because the time to do a register file read is much less than the overall clock period, we chose to calculate our addresses for memory operations in the decode stage, after the operands have been read. This allowed us to access memory in parallel with ALU operations, and thereby reduce the latency through the pipeline.

Our implementation was synthesized for an Altera APEX20KE FPGA. On this FPGA device, our 4-stage pipelined implementation of the OpenRISC architecture required 2676 four-input logic cells and 629 flip flops (not including the register file); it ran at 33 MHz. With the exception of the register file and memory, all of the state signals in Figure 4b appear in our verification.

5.2   OpenRISC Case Splits and Commuting Diagrams

When a stage is stalled, an instruction is killed, or a bubble is introduced into the pipeline, instructions do not follow the normal flow from one stage stage to the next. The commuting diagram and intermediate verification obligations must reflect the expected flow of instructions, or else false negatives will be encountered. In our OpenRISC implementation, there are three events that cause an irregular flow of instructions:

1. A multicycle instruction in the execute stage remains in the execute stage in the next clock cycle. In this situation, the decode and fetch stages stall and a bubble is introduced into the writeback stage.
2. A branch instruction in the decode stage is stalled because of a data dependency on the condition code register caused by a flag-setting instruction in the execute stage. In this situation, the decode and fetch stages stall. When the flag-setting instruction leaves the execute stage, a bubble is inserted into execute.
3. A branch instruction in the decode stage signals that it was mispredicted. In this situation, the instruction in the fetch stage is killed and a bubble appears in the decode stage in the next clock cycle.

Figure 5 illustrates the normal flow of instructions as well as the irregular conditions just described. For example, in clock cycle 4, the branch instruction asserts the mispredict signal, which kills the instruction α in the fetch stage and causes a bubble to appear in the decode stage in the next clock cycle. Figure 5 also serves as a bridge between completion-function commuting diagrams (bottom half of the figure) and the conventional reservation-table style of drawing pipeline behaviour (top-half of figure). As demonstrated by the Karnaugh map of case splits in Figure 5, the three commuting diagrams in Figure 6 are sufficient to characterize all behaviours of the processor.

Based upon the Karnaugh map for case splits, we know that we have three cases to verify: multicycle stalls in the execute stage, a branch stalling because of a condition code dependency, and normal flow of instructions. We did one verification run for each equality line in the three commuting diagrams. We imposed each case split using assumptions in equivalence verification.

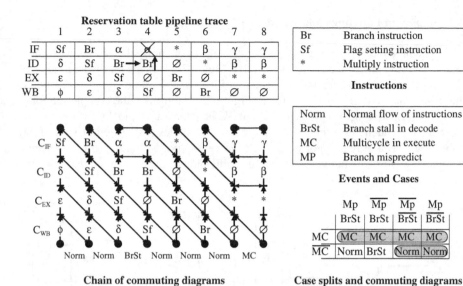

Reservation table pipeline trace

	1	2	3	4	5	6	7	8
IF	Sf	Br	α	✗	*	β	γ	γ
ID	δ	Sf	Br→Br	∅	*	β	β
EX	ε	δ	Sf	∅	Br	∅	*	*
WB	φ	ε	δ	Sf	∅	Br	∅	∅

Br	Branch instruction
Sf	Flag setting instruction
*	Multiply instruction

Instructions

Norm	Normal flow of instructions
BrSt	Branch stall in decode
MC	Multicycle in execute
MP	Branch mispredict

Events and Cases

	Mp	$\overline{\text{Mp}}$	$\overline{\text{Mp}}$	Mp
	BrSt	BrSt	$\overline{\text{BrSt}}$	$\overline{\text{BrSt}}$
MC	MC	MC	MC	MC
$\overline{\text{MC}}$	Norm	BrSt	Norm	Norm

Chain of commuting diagrams

Case splits and commuting diagrams

Fig. 5. Sample pipeline trace and chain of commuting diagrams

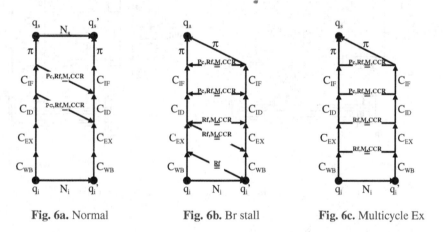

Fig. 6a. Normal

Fig. 6b. Br stall

Fig. 6c. Multicycle Ex

Fig. 6. OpenRISC commuting diagrams

An attractive feature of equivalence verification is the use of black boxes to abstract complex circuitry. We originally did our verification with black boxes for the adder, shifter, and multiplier in the execute stage. After our verification runs passed, we replaced the black boxes of the adder and shifter with their real circuitry and experienced an almost negligible increase in runtime. We hypothesize that the fast run times are due to a heavy reliance upon structural matching between the specification and implementation. (We were unable to verify the multiplier due to a VHDL coding restriction in the equivalence checker that we used, with a bit of effort we can rewrite the implementation to avoid this problem.)

5.3   Completion Functions and Hardware Models

We now examine the verification of the decode stage in the normal case, as an example of one of the more intricate conditions to verify. Figure 7 shows the hardware models of the specification and implementation for this verification obligation, which corresponds to the lowest diagonal line in Figure 6a. In Figure 7, we unfolded the completion functions C_{Id}, C_{Ex}, and C_{Wb} to reveal the use of W blocks and M blocks for one of the register file dependencies – the other architectural variables (PC, IMem, CCR, Mem) are not shown. The gray polygons represent the verification obligation for the execute stage, which was proven before tackling the verification of the decode stage.

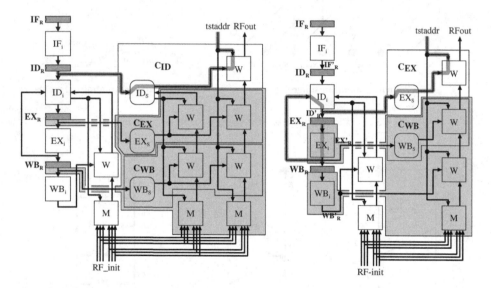

Fig. 7a. Specification   **Fig. 7b.** Implementation

Fig. 7. Hardware model of verification obligation for decode

On the implementation side of Figure 7, there is one cascade of M/W blocks to represent the register file, while on the specification side, there are two cascades. On the implementation side, the cascade of M/W blocks is used to verify the contents of the register file after the writeback stage has written its result. On the specification side, one cascade is used to verify the contents of the register file and one cascade is used by the decode stage to read a source operand. Recall that Figure 7 shows only one of the two register-file dependencies. We could show the dependency for the second operand by including another cascade of M/W blocks that was read by the decode stage. On the specification side, both cascades of M/W blocks in the gray polygon have the same inputs for initial memory values, write addresses, write enables, and write data. Thus, both cascades are for the same memory array. Both cascades are needed, because a single cascade represents a single read operation.

To demonstrate the effect of a bypass path on verification with completion functions, we have highlighted the path through the circuit seen by *tstaddr* if we use the second verification obligation to replace the gray polygons with primary inputs. If we make this simplification, the bypass path allows the right-side *tstaddr* to see the effect that the instruction in execute has on the register file, while on the left side, *tstaddr* sees the effect of only the instruction that is in decode. This difference results in a false negative. If we include the circuitry in the gray polygons, the left side includes C_{Ex}, which mimics the behaviour of the bypass path on the right side. In general, completion functions are unable to take full advantage of previously proven obligations when there are non-architectural locations in the implementation (such as bypass paths) where instructions can read their data.

6   Sobel Edge Detector

Monochrome edge-detector circuits transform grey-scale images into black-and-white images where white pixels indicate the location of edges (high gradients of brightness) in the original image. We have implemented and verified a Sobel edge detector algorithm for a 256×256 image. The input to the circuit is the stream of 8-bit pixels for the image. The input is buffered in an intermediate 3×256 memory array. The overall computation of the circuit is described in Figure 8. The Table stage holds a 3×3 table of pixels, as shown in Figure 8b. On each clock cycle, a new column of three pixels is read from the memory array and shifted into the table. The nine pixels in the table are passed to the filtering stage to calculate horizontal, vertical, and diagonal direction derivatives. The maximum of the absolute value of the derivatives is used to calculate the magnitude, which is then compared to a threshold value. When the magnitude is greater than the threshold, the output of the circuit is 1, indicating an edge at the pixel in the centre of the 3×3 table. The direction of the detected edge is calculated using the outputs of the filter (the derivatives). Our implementation is an eight-stage pipeline. It contains 664 flip-flops and 678 4-input FPGA cells and operates at a maximum clock speed of 134MHz on a Xilinx Virtex II Pro.

It was quite straightforward to apply completion functions and equivalence verification to check our edge detector. We started by verifying the implementation of the Magnitude stage against its completion function. Once this was complete, we combined the implementation of the Max4 stage with the specification of the Magnitude stage and verified this against the combined specification of the Magnitude and Max4 stages. We worked systematically up the pipeline stage by stage until we had verified the pipeline from the table to the output.

Despite a significant amount of simulation-based debugging using test vectors and real images, the formal verification found two bugs. Both bugs were corner cases. The first bug was a synchronization problem between the valid bits for the different directions of edges. The second bug was an incorrect optimization where we thought two signals would always have the same value, and so the implementation tested only one of the signals.

Figure 9 illustrates a retiming optimization that we performed in the derivative stage to reduce area and to allow the synthesis tool to rebalance the computation tree so as

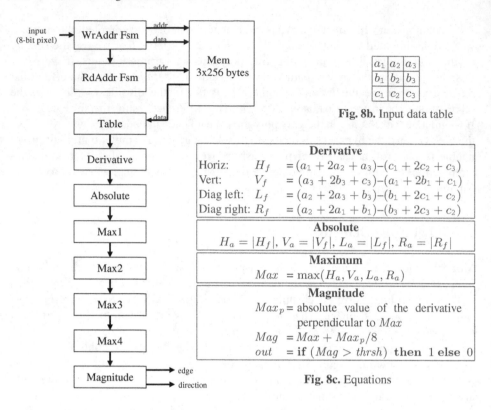

Fig. 8b. Input data table

Derivative		
Horiz:	H_f	$= (a_1 + 2a_2 + a_3) - (c_1 + 2c_2 + c_3)$
Vert:	V_f	$= (a_3 + 2b_3 + c_3) - (a_1 + 2b_1 + c_1)$
Diag left:	L_f	$= (a_2 + 2a_3 + b_3) - (b_1 + 2c_1 + c_2)$
Diag right:	R_f	$= (a_2 + 2a_1 + b_1) - (b_3 + 2c_3 + c_2)$

Absolute
$$H_a = |H_f|, \ V_a = |V_f|, \ L_a = |L_f|, \ R_a = |R_f|$$

Maximum
$$Max = \max(H_a, V_a, L_a, R_a)$$

Magnitude
Max_p = absolute value of the derivative perpendicular to Max
$Mag = Max + Max_p/8$
out = if $(Mag > thrsh)$ **then** 1 **else** 0

Fig. 8c. Equations

Fig. 8a. Block diagram

Fig. 8. Sobel edge detector circuit

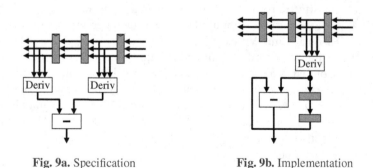

Fig. 9a. Specification   **Fig. 9b.** Implementation

Fig. 9. Retiming optimization in derivative stage

increase clock speed. We were able to use completion functions to verify that the two circuits have equivalent behaviour, and then use this assumption in the verification of the entire circuit.

7   Conclusion

The goal of the work presented here was to explore the use of off-the-shelf software to formally verify register-transfer-level pipelines against a high-level correctness statement. We chose combinational equivalence verification as our verification technology and completion functions as our verification strategy. We chose combinational equivalence verification because it is used widely, requires minimal user input, and can handle reasonably large circuits. To realize our goal, we developed a combinational circuit based on the anonymous-function model of memory that is bisimilar to conventional memory arrays up to a bounded number of read and write operations.

We have used our approach to verify a 32-bit OpenRISC processor with 47 instructions, four-stages, and in-order execution. We have also verified an eight-stage implementation of monochrome Sobel edge detection, where we used completion functions to verify each pipeline stage and to verify a retiming optimization within a stage. Despite a significant amount of prior debugging with test vectors and real images, our formal verification found two rather subtle bugs in the edge detector. One bug was a synchronization corner case and the other involved two signals that we previously thought had identical behaviour. The OpenRISC case study involved 14 verification obligations and the edge detector required 9 obligations. Each obligation required less than a minute of computation.

Hosabettu *et al* proposed the idea of completion functions and have used them in an interactive theorem prover to verify abstract models of out-of-order processors with a variety of complex features [3]. Berezin *et al* have used completion functions with symbolic model checking to verify an abstract model of Tomasulo's algorithm [1]. Velev has used completion functions and automated first-order decision procedures to verify abstract models of out-of-order processors [6]. These previous efforts have demonstrated that completion functions can be beneficial with automated verification techniques. Our work extends the range of application of completion functions, by applying them in the context of the quite restrictive "logic" of combinational equivalence. Our work also demonstrates an extension to the scope of verification to which combinational equivalence verification can be applied.

For OpenRISC, much of the effort in verifying the circuit was in the one-time cost to map pipeline features, such as stalls and branch mispredictions, into the appropriate completion functions. Our approach could be heavily reused in future verification efforts and we estimate that for a pipeline of similar complexity, the completion functions could be created and the verification performed in one week. Similarly, by reusing the approach for the Sobel edge detector, we estimate four days would be required to create the completion functions and verify a circuit with complexity similar to the Sobel edge detector. In verifying both of our examples, we did not need any invariants.

Currently, the one cumbersome aspect of our approach is manipulating the implementation to connect the completion functions to the internal signals. We have been working purely at the source code level, which requires bringing internal signals, such as stage registers, up through layers of structural hierarchy, which can be quite tedious. Because of this, it would be preferable to work on a flattened netlist that was annotated with structural information so as to easily develop semi-automated tools to connect completion functions to the implementation. With a flattened netlist, we estimate the effort to perform the verification would be halved.

Putting aside the effort to connect the stage registers to the completion functions, we were pleased both with the ease of using completion functions with equivalence verification and with the verification power. The ability to verify a retiming optimization was an unanticipated but pleasant surprise. Our results so far are quite promising with respect to the computational complexity of the verification. We hypothesize that the approach is best suited to pipelines with in-order execution, but we do not view this as a serious restriction. Applications such as image processing, encryption, and compression contain many large, deep, and in-order pipelines.

Acknowledgements

This paper benefited from many discussions with Hazem Shehata, the comments of Robert Jones, and the comments of the anonymous referees.

References

1. S. Berezin, E. M. Clarke, A. Biere, and Y. Zhu. Verification of out-of-order processor designs using model checking. *Formal Methods in System Design*, 20(2):159–186, March 2002.
2. J. R. Burch and D. L. Dill. Automatic verification of pipelined microprocessor control. In *CAV*, pages 68–70. Springer Verlag, July 1994.
3. R. Hosabettu, G. Gopalakrishnan, and M. Srivas. Formal verification of a complex pipelined processor. *Formal Methods in System Design*, 23(2):171–213, September 2003.
4. OpenCores. *OpenRISC 1000 Architecture Manual*, 2003.
5. Synopsys, Inc. *Synopsys Formality Data Sheet*, 2004.
6. M. Velev. Using rewriting rules and positive equality to formally verify wide-issue out-of-order microprocessors with a reorder buffer. In *DATE*, pages 28–35, Mar. 2002.

Synchronization-at-Retirement for Pipeline Verification

Mark D. Aagaard[1], Nancy A. Day[2], and Robert B. Jones[3]

[1] Electrical and Computer Engineering, University of Waterloo, Waterloo, ON, Canada
markaa@swen.uwaterloo.ca
[2] Computer Science, University of Waterloo
nday@cs.uwaterloo.ca
[3] Strategic CAD Labs, Intel Corporation, Hillsboro, OR, USA
rjones@ichips.intel.com

Abstract. Much automatic pipeline verification research of the last decade has been based on some form of "Burch-Dill flushing" [BD94]. In this work, we study *synchronization-at-retirement*, an alternative formulation of correctness for pipelines. In this formulation, the proof obligations can also be verified automatically but have significantly-reduced verification complexity compared to flushing. We present an approach for systematically generating invariants, addressing one of the most difficult aspects of pipeline verification. We establish by proof that synchronization-at-retirement and the Burch-Dill flushing correctness statements are equivalent under reasonable side conditions. Finally, we provide experimental evidence of the reduced complexity of our approach for a pipelined processor with ALU operations, memory operations, stalls, jumps, and branch prediction.

1 Introduction

Many different strategies to verify pipelines have been documented in the literature. The capacity of verification strategies tends to decrease with the amount of automation. Yet, automation makes formal verification more practical and extends its "reach" in practice. A seminal paper in 1994 by Burch and Dill [BD94], introduced *flushing*, an approach that computes automatically an abstraction function from a pipelined implementation to a specification that executes instructions as atomic operations. The essential idea is that partially-completed instructions in the pipeline can finish executing by introducing *bubbles* (NOPs that don't increment the program counter) into the front of the pipeline until the pipeline is empty. At that point, the architectural state of the pipeline can be compared against the specification.

Two primary difficulties with Burch-Dill flushing have emerged. First, the computational complexity of flushing a pipeline full of symbolic instructions quickly becomes prohibitive as pipelines grow in size and complexity. The complexity arises because the implementation must be stepped until all in-flight instructions have retired. Second, finding invariants to characterize the reachable pipeline states is a difficult and mostly manual process. Much of the recent research on pipeline processor verification has used manual decomposition to circumvent the computational complexity of flushing. A common approach is to prove a collection of invariants that guarantee *flushpoint equality*: when the implementation is in a flushed state, the architectural state agrees with the specification state.

A.J. Hu and A.K. Martin (Eds.): FMCAD 2004, LNCS 3312, pp. 113–127, 2004.

Specifications execute instructions atomically, while pipelined implementations execute several instructions simultaneously. When verifying a single step of the implementation, embedded in the correctness statement is a choice about which one of the in-flight instructions should be compared against the specification. This choice defines the *synchronization point* between the implementation and specification. The difficulty in choosing a synchronization point is that an instruction writes to different pieces of architectural state at different stages in the pipeline. For example, the program counter for fetching instructions and the register file are consistent only if the pipeline is flushed.

The two common synchronization points are fetch (*sync-at-fetch*) and retire (*sync-at-retire*). Burch-Dill flushing is a sync-at-fetch approach: the effects of the instruction that is fetched are compared to the result of executing the instruction sequentially in the specification. In this paper, we study sync-at-retire: only instructions that retire will be compared to the specification. At first glance, this may appear to be vacuous – how can a pipeline be verified if the correctness statement ignores the pipeline contents? The answer lies in the assumptions that we must make to prove sync-at-retire.

Determining the assumptions and proving that they are invariant is where the reasoning about the rest of the pipeline occurs. We present an approach in which these invariants are generated systematically based on the structure of the pipeline using history variables and completion functions [HGS03]. The verification of the individual invariants is modular and regular, and the validity of the decomposition is visible by inspection.

Using sync-at-retire as a correctness statement addresses both of the weaknesses of Burch-Dill flushing. First, because the sync-at-retire correctness statement and the necessary invariants do not require the entire pipeline be flushed, the verification complexity is significantly reduced. Second, our approach provides a method for the systematic creation of invariants.

This paper contains three main contributions:

1. A systematic technique for generating and proving the invariants necessary to prove sync-at-retire so that all proof obligations involve taking only a single-step of the implementation, extending the reach of automatic verification tools,
2. Proving that sync-at-retire is an equivalent correctness statement to sync-at-fetch under reasonable conditions about the flushing function, and
3. Demonstrating on several pipeline variants that verifying sync-at-retire (and the necessary invariants) is computationally more efficient than verifying sync-at-fetch.

Our approach is applicable to safety verification for the control logic of pipelines. By safety, we mean that any step of the implementation corresponds to a step of the specification. We use a simple processor and processor-related terms to illustrate our approach. Processor pipelines provide good pedagogical examples for this class of verification techniques, but these techniques are certainly not limited to processors. Realistic applications for our approach include simple embedded processors or sub-pipelines within processors.

The paper is organized as follows. Section 2 provides formal definitions for sync-at-fetch and sync-at-retire. In Section 3, we detail our sync-at-retire approach and demonstrate how we derive and verify the needed invariants in a systematic way. In Section 4, we prove that, under reasonable side conditions, verifying sync-at-retire is equivalent to verifying sync-at-fetch. Section 5 reports results of verifying example pipelines with both sync-at-fetch and sync-at-retire. The discussion of related work is deferred to Section 6, where it is presented in the context of our results. Section 7 summarizes the paper and considers future directions.

2   Synchronize, but Where?

The specification of a processor is described by an instruction set architecture (ISA) that executes instructions atomically. The goal of pipelined processor safety verification is to show that all execution traces of a pipeline correspond to a trace of the specification. A commonly-used method of demonstrating this correspondence is to find a simulation relation between pipeline and specification states such that one step of the pipeline corresponds to one step of the specification [Mil71].

The novelty of the Burch-Dill approach was in creating a simulation relation automatically using an abstraction function that maps pipeline state to ISA state. The abstraction function first completes the execution of every operation in the pipeline (flushing) and then projects only the ISA state elements from the implementation to compare with the specification. We characterize this correctness statement as synchronization-at-fetch (*sync-at-fetch*) because it compares the effects of executing the *fetched* instruction with ISA execution of the same instruction. Figure 1 shows the commuting diagram for the sync-at-fetch correctness statement. Table 1 shows the notation used in our descriptions. For a deterministic implementation and specification, sync-at-fetch reduces to:

$$\forall\, q_i.\ \pi_f(\mathit{flush}\,(n_i\,q_i)) = n_s\,(\pi_f\,(\mathit{flush}\,q_i)).$$

To facilitate verification, the processor datapath is usually abstracted away with *uninterpreted functions*, leaving the datapath verification to be handled separately. The correctness statement is typically checked using decision procedures such as UCLID [LSB02], CVC Lite [BB04], and SVC [BDL96]. For deep and/or complex pipelines, Burch-Dill flushing suffers from rapid growth in the complexity of the terms that arise from completing the execution of every operation in the pipeline.

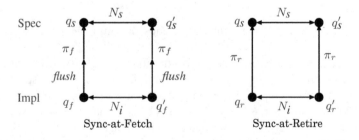

Fig. 1. Correctness Statements

An alternative correctness formulation, synchronization-at-retirement (*sync-at-retire*), compares only the result of executing the instruction about to *retire* (complete) with the specification executing the same instruction. The benefit of this correct-

Table 1. Notation

Q_i, Q_s	Sets of implementation and specification states
$N_S : Q_s \rightarrow Q_s \rightarrow Bool$	Next-state relation for specification
	(Relations are shown as two-way arrows in commuting diagrams.)
$n_S : Q_s \rightarrow Q_s$	Next-state function for specification
$N_i : Q_i \rightarrow Q_i \rightarrow Bool$	Next-state relation for implementation
$n_i : Q_i \rightarrow Q_i$	Next-state function for implementation
$\pi_f : Q_i \rightarrow Q_s$	Project at fetch
$flush : Q_i \rightarrow Q_i$	Flush an implementation state
$isFlushed : Q_i \rightarrow Bool$	Implementation state has no in-flight instructions
$numFetch : Q_i \rightarrow Q_i \rightarrow nat$	Number of instructions fetched in a step
$\pi_r : Q_i \rightarrow Q_s$	Project at retire
$kill : Q_i \rightarrow Q_i$	Kill all in-flight instructions
$numRetire : Q_i \rightarrow Q_i \rightarrow nat$	Number of instructions retired in a step
$numWillRetire : Q_i \rightarrow nat$	The number of in-flight instructions that will eventually retire.
π	$= \pi_f = \pi_r$ when in a flushed state
pc, rf, mem, pc_r	Fetch program counter, register file, memory, retirement program counter

ness statement is that the simulation relation involves simply discarding all partially-completed operations, and projecting the specification state elements from the implementation to compare with the specification. To implement precise exceptions, pipelines can only write results to programmer-visible (specification) state when instructions complete. Hence, the contents of specification state elements in the pipeline, excepting the program counter, should correspond exactly to the contents of specification state elements prior to the execution of the instruction about to retire. In the sync-at-retire approach, the program counter for the specification is set to be the program counter for the instruction about to retire, denoted pc_r. Figure 1 also shows the sync-at-retire correctness statement. Specialized for a deterministic implementation and specification, it is:

$$\forall q_i. \ \pi_r \, (n_i \, q_i) = n_S \, (\pi_r \, q_i)$$

where π_r is similar to π_f except that it matches the implementation's pc_r with the specification pc.

At first glance, sync-at-retire seems like a dubious correctness statement, for it only compares the completion of a single instruction with one step of the specification. In fact, the above formula simply ensures only that the last stage of a pipeline's execution is correct. The key, however, is that to prove this correspondence, we must assume that the instruction has been correctly executed up to the final stage of the pipeline. This assumption is an invariant that characterizes the reachable state space of the last stage of the implementation. To prove this invariant, we must make assumptions about the reachable state space of the previous stage, and so on. This *back-chaining* continues until the first stage of the pipeline, where invariants must hold under environmental constraints. In this way, a sync-at-retire correctness statement sets up a natural decomposition of the verification problem into proving that each stage executes correctly. The resulting invariants can all be verified automatically and are significantly less complex than using flushing to prove sync-at-fetch. In the next section, we describe in detail how the invariants for sync-at-retire can be systematically constructed using history variables and completion functions.

For implementations that can stall, both of these correctness statements add a case verifying that when no instructions is fetched (or retired), then the externally visible state does not change.

A potential difficulty occurs with both sync-at-retire and sync-at-fetch if architectural state is committed after instruction retirement. For example, some microarchitectures delay committing store operations. In this situation, a structural decomposition with a separate proof about the memory hierarchy can be needed.

3   Synchronization-at-Retirement

In this section, we describe verifying sync-at-retire for deterministic implementations and specifications, and present a systematic process for creating and verifying the necessary invariants. The overall strategy is to prove that the invariants imply sync-at-retire and then that the invariants are indeed invariant.

The experience of the authors, along with results detailed in the literature, indicates that invariant finding is likely the most difficult aspect of this type of verification. We describe a novel invariant-generation process based on the use of history variables and completion functions. Our approach decomposes the proof by pipeline stages; each stage is further decomposed into individual data elements of instructions.

3.1   Parcels and History Variables

For the systematic creation of invariants, we capture the movement of an instruction through the pipeline using *parcels* – information about the instruction at each stage of the pipeline. After instruction decode, every pipeline register contains a parcel with the following fields:

valid	pc	pc_next	opcode	src1	data1	src2	data2	dest	result

The valid field indicates whether or not the parcel is a bubble. The pc and pc_next fields contain the program counter (address) for the current instruction and the program counter for the next instruction. The opcode, src1, src2, and dest fields are the opcode, and register addresses for the operand sources and instruction result. The data1, data2, and result fields contain the actual operands and result. When used, immediate data is placed in the data2 field.

In the early stages of the pipeline, many of these fields contain don't cares. For example, the value of data1 does not matter until after the instruction operands have been read from the register file. As an instruction moves through the pipeline, many parcel fields become history variables. For example, once values have been read, the source addresses are never read again. Our approach only requires history variables for in-flight instructions; we need no record of instructions that have retired.

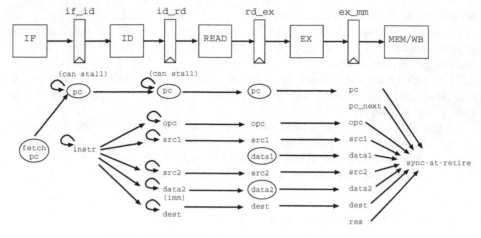

Circles show invariants that require completion functions.

Fig. 2. Example Pipeline, Invariants, and Invariant Dependencies

3.2   Proof Decomposition

We decompose the necessary set of invariants by stage and by parcel element. Each invariant states that a parcel element is correct in a given stage. We prove sync-at-retire by assuming that the parcel contents in the last pipeline register have been computed correctly. Then we chain backward, proving each invariant by relying only on the invariant describing the correctness of the corresponding parcel element in the previous stage.

We explain our approach for generating invariants using the pipeline in Figure 2. This pipeline executes NOPs, ALU instructions, loads, stores, jumps with direct addressing, and branches with offset addressing. We use uninterpreted functions to represent operations on data.

Figure 2 also shows the parcel fields at each stage in the pipeline that have invariants associated with them, and the dependencies between invariants (more on this later). We provide an overview of the invariants, starting with the last stage of the pipeline.

For the sync-at-retire correctness statement to be valid, the parcel in ex_mm must have been correctly calculated and the MEM/WB (memory/writeback) logic must write correct values to memory and the register file. The table below describes the invariants that characterize a correct ex_mm parcel; all have as an antecedent that the parcel is valid. These invariants are sufficient to prove sync-at-retire.

ex_mm_pc_ok	pc matches pc_r
ex_mm_pc_next_ok	pc_next is either ex_mm.pc + 4 or the branch/jump target
ex_mm_opc_ok	opcode matches instruction memory at ex_mm.pc
ex_mm_src1_ok	src1 matches instruction memory at ex_mm.pc
ex_mm_data1_ok	data1 matches ex_mm.src1 in register file
ex_mm_src2_ok	src2 matches instruction memory at ex_mm.pc
ex_mm_data2_ok	data2 matches ex_mm.src1 in register file or immediate data
ex_mm_dest_ok	dest matches instruction memory at ex_mm.pc
ex_mm_res_ok	result matches branch target or result of ALU operation

Moving back, we prove the ex_mm invariants by assuming that the parcel in the previous stage (rd_ex) was computed correctly. Proofs of the invariants are sliced by data element: to prove ex_mm_data1_ok, we need only rd_ex_data1_ok. These verification obligations check that the EX logic is correct. The EX logic computes branch targets and the results of ALU instructions. If the branch is mispredicted, earlier stages will squash parcels in its shadow and reset the fetch program counter.

Because instruction memory never changes, the invariants for opc, src1, src2, and dest are the same in every stage after instruction decode. These invariants are proved by back-chaining one stage at a time until the front of the pipeline is reached. In contrast, pc_next does not have to be correct until it is determined by the EX logic. In stages prior to ex_mm, no invariants are required for pc_next, because it may not be correct. In general, as we move back in the pipeline, fewer invariants about parcel fields are required. The next table describes the invariants necessary for the rd_ex pipeline register, omitting the ones related to instruction memory.

rd_ex_pc_ok	pc matches pc_next of completing ex_mm
rd_ex_data1_ok	data1 matches rd_ex.src1 in register file *after* instruction in ex_mm is completed
rd_ex_data2_ok	original immediate data, or data2 matches rd_ex.src2 in register file *after* instruction in ex_mm is completed

To state some of the invariants about the rd_ex stage, we need to refer to a future specification state, namely the specification state that results from completing the instruction in the ex_mm stage. For example, if the pipeline's bypass logic is correct, the data1 field should be the value in register src1 after the instruction in ex_mm is completed. To calculate the specification state that results from completing the parcels downstream from a stage, we use completion functions [HGS03]. The completion function for a stage describes the result that the instruction currently in that stage will eventually have on the specification state.

A completion function takes an specification state and a parcel and returns the specification state that results from committing this parcel. A completion function is similar to running the specification except that some of the results (such as fetching the operands) have already been computed and are present in the parcel. Figure 3 shows the register file completion function for the ex_mm parcel and illustrates how the invariant rd_data1_ok uses this completion function. Hosabettu *et al.* [HGS03] used completion functions as a decomposition technique for a proof of sync-at-fetch; our use differs significantly as we use completion functions to construct a set of invariants decomposed by stage and parcel elements.

The other invariants are constructed similarly. All invariants are proved inductively; Figure 2 shows the dependencies between invariants. When a stage can stall, the proof of an invariant must assume both the invariant for the parcel element in the previous stage and for the parcel element in the current stage. The circled invariants in Figure 2 use completion functions. We compose the completion function of a given stage with the composition of the completion functions from the downstream stages. Note that in the if_id stage, the instruction has not yet been decoded, so there are no parcel fields.

The most complex invariant for our pipeline is the one about fetch_pc. This is because the pipeline might contain bubbles in any stage. This invariant includes a com-

```
// instruction in ex_mm updates rf of specification state correctly
ex_mm_cf_rf ex_mm (_,rf,mem) =
  if (valid ex_mm)
  then if (is_ld ex_mm)
    // if load op, read data from memory and write to register file
    then write rf (ex_mm.dest) (read mem (ex_mm.data1))
    else (is_alu ex_mm)
      // write computed result for ALU operations
      (write rf (ex_mm.dest) (ex_mm.result))
      // otherwise, no change to register file
      rf
  // otherwise, no change to register file
  else rf

// if instruction in rd_ex is valid, then data1 field matches src1 in rf
rd_ex_data1_ok rd_ex (_,rf,_) =
  (valid rd_ex) ==> (rd_ex.data1 == read rf rd_ex.src1)

// invariant instantiation
rd_ex_data1_ok rd_ex (ex_mm_cf ex_mm (pc_r,rf,mem))
```

Fig. 3. Example Completion Function, Invariant Definition, and Invariant Instantiation

position of completion functions to determine the program counter that results from executing all the instructions currently in the pipeline. These completion functions must determine whether a given instruction in the pipeline will retire, which in turn depends on whether there are any mispredicted branches ahead of this instruction.

We conclude this section with a brief, but formal description of our approach for a three stage pipeline with no stalls. We use the following sets and functions:

P_j Type of parcel at state j
$\pi_j : Q_i \to P_j$ Project pipeline register j
$c_j : P_j \to Q_s \to Q_s$ Completion function for stage j
$I_j : P_j \to Q_s \to Bool$ Invariant for stage j

Using the definitions $q_s = \pi_r\ q$, $q'_s = \pi_r\ (n_i\ q)$, $p_j = \pi_j\ q$, and $p'_j = \pi_j\ (n_i\ q)$, the proof steps are:

$$I_3\ p_3\ q_s \quad \vdash \quad n_s\ q_s = q'_s$$
$$I_2\ p_2\ (c_3\ p_3\ q_s) \quad \vdash \quad I_3\ p'_3\ q'_s$$
$$I_1\ p_1\ (c_2\ p_2\ (c_3\ p_3\ q_s)) \quad \vdash \quad I_2\ p'_2\ (c_3\ p'_3\ q'_s))$$
$$\vdash \quad I_1\ p'_1\ (c_2\ p'_2\ (c_3\ p'_3\ q'_s))$$

Note that the conclusion of the first obligation is the sync-at-retire correctness statement. These proof obligations are further decomposed by parcel element as described in Figure 2. The history variables used in this approach do not add to verification complexity because the pipeline never reads history variables.

In summary, we create an invariant for each computed parcel field in each stage of the pipeline. Earlier in the pipeline, fewer fields have been computed, so fewer invariants are needed. Our decomposition checks the correctness of each stage of the pipeline individually, significantly reducing the complexity of the formula to be verified and usually making it easier to isolate an error for debugging. All of the proof obligations require taking only a single-step of the implementation. *No flushing of the implementation pipeline ever occurs with our approach.* The only multi-step computation contained in our approach is the composition of completion functions, a much simpler task than reasoning about flushing the entire pipeline.

4 Equivalence of Correctness Statements

We have proved the equivalence of the sync-at-retire and sync-at-fetch correctness statements for superscalar non-deterministic implementations and deterministic specifications. Our proof establishes that sync-at-retire implies sync-at-fetch, and that sync-at-fetch implies sync-at-retire. Our proof relies on minor conditions describing the relationship between *flush*, *kill*, π, and other functions used in the correctness statements.

Of the two directions, the proof that sync-at-retire implies sync-at-fetch was substantially more difficult. The difficulty arose in discovering conditions that do not require flushing an implementation state, so they are computationally less expensive to check than the sync-at-fetch correctness statement. Because sync-at-fetch relies on flushing, we used conditions that rely on flushing when proving sync-at-fetch implies sync-at-retire. In this section, we focus on the more difficult of the two proofs (sync-at-retire implies sync-at-fetch, Theorem 1), but limit our presentation to scalar implementations for clarity. The details of the other proofs appear in a technical report [ADJ04].

Theorem 1. *Sync-at-retire implies sync-at-fetch*
$$[\forall\, q_r, q_r'.\ N_i\ q_r\ q_r' \implies \pi_r\ q_r' = n_s\ (\pi_r\ q_r)]$$
$$\implies$$
$$\left[\forall\, q_f, q_f'.\ N_i\ q_f\ q_f' \implies \pi_f(\text{flush } q_f') = n_s\ (\pi_f(\text{flush } q_f))\right]$$

Each of sync-at-fetch and sync-at-retire compare an implementation step against a specification step. But, for the same implementation step, the two correctness statements choose different specification steps. Sync-at-fetch chooses the specification step that executes the instruction that the implementation fetches, while sync-at-retire chooses the specification step that executes the instruction that the implementation retires. The essence of our proof is to establish a relationship between the implementation step that fetches an instruction and the implementation step that retires the instruction. We introduce the notion of a *serial execution* of the implementation to bridge the gap between the fetching step and retiring step. In a serial-execution step, the implementation starts in a flushed state, takes a single step to fetch an instruction, then flushes the single fetched instruction, to result in a flushed state.

Figure 4 outlines the proof that sync-at-retire implies sync-at-fetch. The rightmost column illustrates the justification for each step. Solid lines denote relations that are known (e.g., the left-hand-side of an implication); dashed lines denote relations on the right-hand-side of an implication; solid circles denote universally quantified states; and hollow circles denote existentially quantified states.

Theorem 1 is of the form $(A \implies B) \implies (C \implies D)$. The proof of such a theorem proceeds by assuming C, then using $A \implies B$ and other lemmas to prove D. For Theorem 1, we begin in Step 1 by assuming the antecedent of sync-at-fetch. In Step 2, we use Lemma 1 to prove that the implementation step from q_r to q_r', which fetches the instruction i, corresponds to a serial-execution step from q_e to q_e'. In Step 3, we use Lemma 3 to prove that the serial-execution step from q_e to q_e' corresponds to the step from q_r to q_r', which retires the instruction i. The correspondence is achieved by killing all in-flight instructions (denoted as *kill* in the diagram). In Step 4, we use sync-at-retire to prove that q'_e is equivalent to the specification state q'_s. Step 5 concludes the proof by showing that sync-at-fetch holds between $q_f \rightarrow q'_f$ and $q_s \rightarrow q'_s$.

Lemma 1 says that each step of fetching an instruction corresponds to a serial-execution step. The lemma could be proved easily by flushing q_f and q'_f, but in the proof of sync-at-retire implies sync-at-fetch, we wish to avoid flushing. The purpose of Lemma 1 is to prove that the two paths of the commuting diagram, $q_f \rightarrow q_e \rightarrow q'_e$ and $q_f \rightarrow q'_f \rightarrow q'_e$, both result in the same state q'_e. The proof proceeds in two phases: first, we prove that both paths retire the same number of instructions; then we prove that any pair of paths that start from the same state and retire the same number of instructions will result in the same state. The proof relies on Lemma 2 and Condition 1.

Lemma 2 says that each step that retires an instruction corresponds to a serial-execution step. The proof of this lemma involves applying sync-at-retire correctness to the state one step prior to the flushed state q'_e. Applying the *kill* function to q_e and all states prior to q'_e results in the same implementation step because no instructions are retired in these steps.

Lemma 2. *Retire implies serial execution*

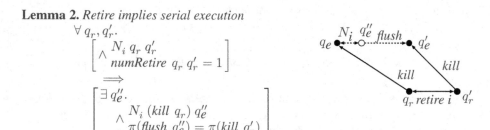

$$
\forall q_r, q'_r.
$$
$$
\left[\wedge \begin{array}{l} N_i \ q_r \ q'_r \\ numRetire \ q_r \ q'_r = 1 \end{array} \right]
$$
$$
\Longrightarrow
$$
$$
\left[\begin{array}{l} \exists q''_e. \\ \wedge \begin{array}{l} N_i \ (kill \ q_r) \ q''_e \\ \pi(flush \ q''_e) = \pi(kill \ q'_r) \end{array} \end{array} \right]
$$

Condition 1 says that from a flushed state, a fetched instruction will never be killed (i.e., its execution is not speculative and it should eventually retire). Such a condition may not be necessary in practice for the correctness of a pipeline, but we require it to prove that sync-at-retire implies sync-at-fetch. The condition can be verified by proving invariants about *numRetire* and *numWillRetire*. In Section 5, we demonstrate that checking Condition 1 is computationally less expensive than using sync-at-fetch.

Condition 1. *From a flushed state, a fetched instruction will always retire*

$$
\forall q, q'.
$$
$$
\left[\begin{array}{l} \wedge \ isFlushed \ q \\ \wedge \ N_i \ q \ q' \\ \wedge \ numFetch \ q \ q' = 1 \end{array} \right] \Longrightarrow \left[\vee \begin{array}{l} numRetire \ q \ q' = 1 \\ numWillRetire \ q' = 1 \end{array} \right]
$$

Lemma 3 is used in Step 3 of Figure 4. The lemma says that for each serial-execution step, there exists an implementation step that retires the instruction and is related to the serial-execution step via the *kill* function. This lemma is the opposite of Lemma 2, which says that each retiring step corresponds to a serial-execution step. To prove Lemma 3, note that a witness for the implementation state q_r can be computed by starting in the flushed state q_e, taking a step to fetch an instruction, and then stepping the pipeline until the instruction is about to retire.

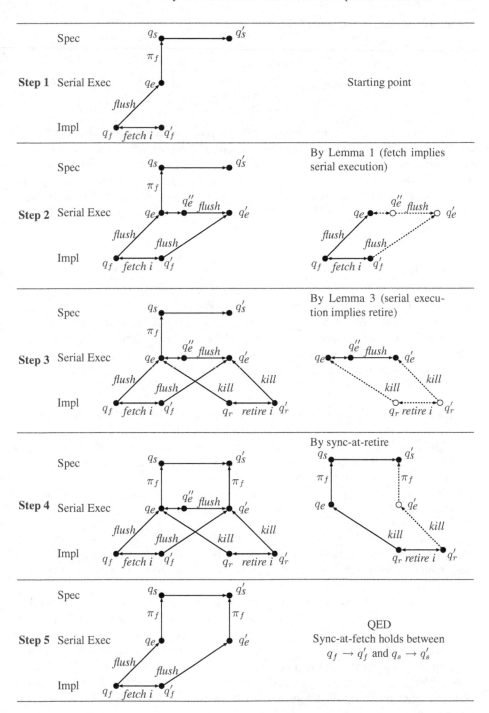

Fig. 4. Overview of proof that sync-at-retire implies sync-at-fetch

Lemma 3. *Serialized implementation implies retire*
$$\forall\, q_e, q_e''.$$

$$
\left[\wedge\ \begin{array}{l} N_i\ q_e\ q_e'' \\ isFlushed\ q_e \end{array}\right]
\Longrightarrow
\left[\begin{array}{l} \exists\, q_r, q_r'. \\ \quad\wedge\ \begin{array}{l} N_i\ q_r\ q_r' \\ q_e = kill\ q_r \\ \pi(flush\ q_e'') = \pi(kill\ q_r') \end{array} \end{array}\right]
$$

The proof that sync-at-fetch implies sync-at-retire proceeds symmetrically to Figure 4: we show that every step that retires an instruction corresponds to a step in serial execution, and that every step in serial execution corresponds to a step that fetches that same instruction. In the superscalar proofs [ADJ04] multiple instructions might be fetched or retired in a single clock cycle. This generalization means that a single fetching or retiring step corresponds to multiple steps of serial execution and multiple steps of the specification.

5   Results

We used SVC [BDL96] to compare the verification complexity and time of three example pipelines to demonstrate that sync-at-retire is computationally more efficient than sync-at-fetch. Complete proof scripts are available at [Mic]. Table 2a shows the case splits, expressions generated and run-times for the three pipelines, each of which is an extension of the previous, and has the stages shown in Figure 2 and the following features:

- **pipe1:** executes loads and stores; no branches; stalls for dependencies on load instructions; includes icache misses and bubble squashing.
- **pipe2:** adds branch and jump instructions with branch prediction; the branch target is resolved in the READ stage meaning two instructions can be in the shadow of a mispredicted branch.
- **pipe3:** moves branch target resolution to the EX stage, meaning that three instructions can be in the shadow of a mispredicted branch.

The row labeled "total time" is the sum of the time for checking sync-at-retire and all invariants needed for sync-at-retire. No invariants were required by sync-at-fetch for these simple pipelines. Both methods require environmental assumptions that opcodes are distinct.

We expect that this result is independent of proof engine – similar results should be found using a different validity checker such as UCLID [LSB02] or CVC Lite [BB04]. Sync-at-retire does involve the manual work of creating the invariants, however these are systematically created and not iteratively discovered based on counter-examples. While in theory our approach requires more manual work (to construct the invariants), we found in practice that debugging the pipeline was often significantly easier because of the systematic nature of the invariant construction, which isolate bugs to a single pipeline stage.

To guarantee that proving sync-at-retire is equivalent to proving sync-at-fetch, we also checked the proof obligation required by the proof outlined in Section 4. Table 2b

Table 2. Run-time results

Pipeline	pipe1	pipe2	pipe3
Sync-at-retire			
Case splits	44	78	78
Exprs. generated	252	530	532
Time (s)	<1	<1	<1
Largest invariant:			
Case splits	4.5k	374k	527k
Exprs. generated	15.0k	7.72M	9.28M
Time (s)	<1	44	54
Total time (s)	7	115	141
Sync-at-fetch			
Case splits	10.4k	615k	852k
Exprs. generated	1.48M	72.6M	77.6M
Time (s)	9	674	651

(a) sync-at-retire vs. sync-at-fetch

Pipe3	Condition 1
Case splits	95.0k
Exprs. generated	624k
Time (s)	4.5

(b) sync-at-retire implies sync-at-fetch

shows the complexity of checking Condition 1 for pipe3. It is considerably less expensive than checking sync-at-fetch. Note again that sync-at-retire is an acceptable correctness criteria by itself, and this condition is only necessary to guarantee that sync-at-fetch is also satisfied.

6 Related Work

In earlier work, we surveyed many of the different approaches to safety verification of microprocessors, and compared their correctness statements [ACDJ03]. In the body of work that we surveyed, most verification efforts used sync-at-fetch. In this section, we limit the discussion to prior work that has used sync-at-retire.

Fox and Harman [FH96,FH03] suggested the idea of relating a pipeline to a specification at the time of retirement with *retiming functions*. A retiming function maps an implementation state to the specification state that corresponds to the retiring instruction. There is a separate data abstraction function. They verify a single-step commuting diagram, but there is no discussion of invariants. They use term rewriting systems for verification.

Arons and Pnueli [PA98,AP00] have used synchronize-at-retire with theorem proving. They use a program counter similar to ours, where the externally-visible program counter is the address of the next instruction to be retired. They do not discuss invariant generation other than to mention that it was the most difficult part of the proof.

Arvind and Shen [AS99] reported using term rewriting systems (TRS) in the verification of pipelined processors. In their paper, they discuss applying rewrites until the system reaches a *drained* (flushed) state, an approach similar to flushing. They also mention the possibility of "rolling back" pipeline execution by killing all partially-completed instructions, but do not discuss it in enough detail for a meaningful comparison.

Manolios [MS04] uses a *commitment* approach that maintains history variables with parcels. Unlike our application, Manolios uses history variables that keep track of the state of the pipeline before a given operation executed. He uses the history variables to "rewind" the pipeline to revert to a previous state. He reports that using commitment to verify safety properties is computationally more complex than using flushing. However, with commitment, the incremental cost of verifying liveness is less than with flushing.

Arons and Pnueli [AP98], Jhala and McMillan [JM01], and Lahiri and Bryant [LSB02] use a set of invariants (refinement maps), rather than a simulation relation, as their correctness statement. The typical approach is to augment the implementation with history variables. When an instruction is fetched, issued, or dispatched, the specification is executed to compute the correct values for any architectural state variables that the instruction will write. When the instruction writes to architectural state, the actual values written are compared to those in the history variables. Each architectural state variable has its own refinement map, and so there is no unique synchronization point in the verification. The lack of a synchronization point usually prevents the direct comparison of an implementation state with the specification state. In some cases, it is possible to do a direct comparison when the implementation is in a flushed state.

7 Conclusion

In this paper, we demonstrated that verifying a correctness formulation based on sync-at-retire can have significant advantages over a formulation based on sync-at-fetch because no verification step requires more than a single step of the implementation. Further, we proved that the two formulations are equivalent in the bugs that they will detect. We did not attempt to show that sync-at-retire can verify a more complex pipeline than any previously verified with sync-at-fetch, but instead focused on the comparison of the approaches. We are interested in comparing our work with Hosabettu's approach to decomposing the sync-at-fetch correctness statement with completion functions [HGS03], but must first map his approach to an automated verification environment.

For processor pipelines, a significant advantage of sync-at-retire as opposed to sync-at-fetch is dealing with precise interrupts, where instructions ahead of the interrupt in the pipeline may be killed. The sync-at-fetch approach would require a complex "informed flushing" function to decide how many instructions should be flushed before comparing with the specification state. In contrast, sync-at-retire requires no such function, and any reasonable interrupt handling scheme can be encoded in the invariants. We are currently studying and quantifying this observation.

We plan to study sync-at-retire with other kinds of pipelines: very deep pipelines used in digital signal processors and parallel pipelines, such as those used in graphics engines. We are also interested in exploring the applicability of our approach to superscalar pipelines with out-of-order instruction execution and in-order retirement.

Acknowledgments

We thank the anonymous reviewers for their insightful comments. We thank Jun Sawada for an idea that helped us discover proofs for two out of the conditions in the paper. The first and second authors are supported in part by the Natural Sciences and Engineering Research Council of Canada (NSERC). Aagaard is supported in part by Intel Corporation, and the Semiconductor Research Corporation. The third author thanks Intel Corporation's Strategic CAD Labs for providing a work environment that supports external research collaboration.

References

[ACDJ03] M. D. Aagaard, B. Cook, N. A. Day, and R. B. Jones. A framework for superscalar microprocessor correctness statements. *Software Tools for Technology Transfer*, 4(3):298–312, 2003.

[ADJ04] M. D. Aagaard, N. A. Day, and R. B. Jones. Equivalence of sync-at-fetch and sync-at-retire correctness for pipeline circuits. Technical Report CS2004-31, University of Waterloo, School of Computer Science, September 2004.

[AP98] T. Arons and A. Pnueli. Verifying Tomasulo's algorithm by refinement. Technical report, Dept. of Computer Science, Weizmann Institute, October 1998.

[AP00] T. Arons and A. Pnueli. A comparison of two verification methods for speculative instruction execution with exceptions. In *TACAS*, vol 1785 of *LNCS*, pp 487–502. Springer, 2000.

[AS99] Arvind and X. Shen. Using term rewriting systems to design and verify processors. *IEEE Micro*, 19(3):36–46, 1999.

[BB04] C. Barrett and S. Berezin. CVC Lite: A new implementation of the cooperating validity checker. In *CAV*, vol 3114 of *LNCS*, pp 515–518. Springer, 2004.

[BD94] J. Burch and D. Dill. Automatic verification of pipelined microprocessor control. In D. L. Dill, editor, *CAV*, vol 818 of *LNCS*, pp 68–80. Springer, 1994.

[BDL96] C. Barrett, D. Dill, and J. Levitt. Validity checking for combinations of theories with equality. In *FMCAD*, vol 1166 of *LNCS*, pp 187–201. Springer, 1996.

[FH96] A. Fox and N. Harman. Algebraic models of correctness for microprocessors. In *FMCAD*, vol 1166 of *LNCS*, pp 346–361. Springer, 1996.

[FH03] A. Fox and N. Harman. Algebraic models of correctness for abstract pipelines. *The Journal of Algebraic and Logic Programming*, 57:71–107, 2003.

[HGS03] R. Hosabettu, G. Gopalakrishnan, and M. K. Srivas. Formal verification of a complex pipelined processor. *Formal Methods in System Design*, 23(2):171–213, September 2003.

[JM01] R. Jhala and K. L. McMillan. Microarchitecture verification by compositional model checking. In *CAV*, vol 2102 of *LNCS*, pp 396–410. Springer, 2001.

[LSB02] S. K. Lahiri, S. A. Seshia, and R. E. Bryant. Modeling and verification of out-of-order microprocessors in UCLID. In *FMCAD*, vol 2517 of *LNCS*, pp 142–158. Springer, 2002.

[Mic] http://www.cs.uwaterloo.ca/~nday/microbox.

[Mil71] R. Milner. An algebraic definition of simulation between programs. In *Joint Conf. on AI*, pp 481–489. British Computer Society, 1971.

[MS04] P. Manolios and S. K. Srinivasan. Automatic verification of safety and liveness for Xscale-like processor models using web refinements. In *DATE*, pp 168–175, 2004.

[PA98] A. Pnueli and T. Arons. Verification of data-insensitive circuits: An in-order-retirement case study. In *FMCAD*, vol 1522 of *LNCS*, pp 351–368. Springer, 1998.

Late Design Changes (ECOs)
for Sequentially Optimized Esterel Designs

Laurent Arditi[1], Gerard Berry[1], and Michael Kishinevsky[2]

[1] Esterel Technologies
679 av. Julien Lefèbvre, 06270 Villeneuve Loubet, France
{Laurent.Arditi,Gerard.Berry}@esterel-technologies.com
[2] Strategic CAD Labs, Intel Corp.
2111 NE 25th Ave. Hillsboro, OR, USA 97124
Michael.Kishinevsky@intel.com

Abstract. Late changes in silicon design (ECO) is a common although undesired practice. The need for ECO exists even in high-level design flows since bugs may occur in the specifications, in the compilation, or due to late specification changes. Esterel compilation deploys sequential optimization to improve delay and area of the netlist. This makes it harder to find in the netlist where manual changes should be done and to trace circuit changes back to the high-level specification. We show that all sequential optimizations used in Esterel compilation can be made reversible and demonstrate that an ECO problem can be reduced to a commonly solved combinational ECO problem. This is achieved by reconstructing some of the suppressed registers in order to backannotate to the original code. We demonstrate that the cost of reversibility is negligible.

1 Introduction

Late changes in silicon design, sometimes called ECO (Engineering Change Order), is a common although undesired practice[1]. They happen due to last minute changes in the specifications or due to design bugs found at a late stage, sometimes after the tapeout. At these stages going through the top-down design flow is infeasible, because it would take too long and lead to undesirably large perturbations to the physical layout. Therefore, the change is made manually in a late-stage design representation. High-level design flows generally reduce the number of bugs. However, the need for ECO still exists since there is no guarantee that all bugs are eliminated and since the specification may change late in the game. Since high-level design often deploys more powerful optimization than manual design flows, it becomes harder to find the place in the final circuit where manual changes should be made in order to correct the behavior. It is also

---

[1] The exact definition of an ECO may vary from one organization to another, and it does not necessarily imply a late change. However, in the rest of the paper, we use ECO to refer to a late design change.

A.J. Hu and A.K. Martin (Eds.): FMCAD 2004, LNCS 3312, pp. 128–143, 2004.

harder to trace circuit bugs and changes back to the high-level specification. A software analogy would be to perform manual changes in an executable compiled from C with -Ox options, while back-annotating these changes to the original C code.

We will illustrate this general high-level design problem by an Esterel example, with heavy sequential circuit optimization performed by the Esterel compiler backend. The desired ECO flow is as follows. The original specification S is compiled by the Esterel compiler to a circuit netlist C_0, which is further optimized to the final implementation C using combinational and sequential optimization. If late changes are required this circuit is transformed manually into another netlist C^* such that perturbations to C are minimal. To maintain the high-level specification consistent with the modified implementation and to verify the manual change to the implementation, the original Esterel specification S is also modified into S' to reflect the late changes. S' is then compiled to a new netlist C'. Finally, C^* is verified against C'. To debug mismatches, it is necessary to understand if the fault is in the manual changes to the implementation or in the changes to the Esterel spec, iterating until there is a perfect match. The circuit C' can be used exclusively for verification or to provide hints for modifications of the original implementation C. In the first case, optimization of C' is optional but can speed up verification. The ECO flow is illustrated in Figure 1.

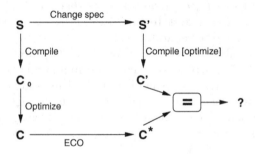

Fig. 1. ECO flow

Three capabilities are required for the described above ECO flow:

– *A sequential equivalence checker* to formally compare C^* and C' since sequential optimization is involved in producing C and possibly C'. Esterel Studio has two embedded sequential equivalence checking engines that are based on BDD [6] and SAT [14]. Capacity of these tools typically matches the capacity of sequential optimization, and it is rarely an issue in the modular compilation flow for control-dominated designs. Recent work demonstrated that the capacity of sequential verification can be further improved, e.g., by using a combination of ATPG (or SAT) and BDD approaches [9], structural equivalence [20], and multiplexing the state of the FSMs under verification [11]. More research in this direction is required to support high-level design flows.

- *Traceability tools* to zoom into the parts of the implementation netlist C, where manual changes corresponding to the modified spec S' should be done. Traceability has been implemented in Esterel Studio 5.0.1. It supports forward linking of every source construct (state, transition, textual Esterel statement) with HDL objects (variables, signals, logic equations) and backward linking of any generated HDL object to its Esterel source. Traceability is presented in Section 2. Notice that traceability is also the basis of critical software and hardware certification, see the DO178B and DO254 directives from the Federal Aviation Administration.
- *Modular compilation* is necessary to confine changes to relatively small circuit blocks. The next version of Esterel Studio will support modular compilation, with only minor limitations. The user will be able to control the grouping of modules, and hence to choose the granularity at which to optimize the design and perform ECOs.

Sequential optimization used in the Esterel backend includes a few transformations: redundant latch removal, re-encoding of exclusive latches, retiming moves, re-encoding of sequential threads, and code migration [16]. We distinguish between reversible and irreversible optimization transformations. In a reversible transformation, one can reconstruct removed registers from the registers of the final circuit and some extra information kept inside the design. All transformations that are bijective or injective on the state space of a circuit are reversible. Surjective transformations (like state minimization) are irreversible: if two states are collapsed they cannot be separated.

Exploiting reversibility, we will show how an ECO problem for the reversible sequential transformations can be reduced to a combinational one by reconstructing some of the suppressed registers in order to backannotate to the original code and to perform division between the logic of an actual design and the logic supporting backannotation. The combinational ECO problem is solved in standard design practice and is supported by some automation (e.g. by the ECO Compiler of Synopsys).

Related Work. There have been a significant body of work in developing methods for incremental logic synthesis and physical design with a focus on automatic algorithms for minimizing perturbations to an existing design in presence of the design changes at the gate or RTL-level, e.g. [21, 4, 13, 10]. [12, 7, 8] addressed some aspect of late changes in the context of high-level or architectural synthesis. In particular [12] allows one to repair a schedule if a data-path has changed and [7] attempts to coordinate design optimization across multiple steps of behavioral synthesis. For the best of our knowledge, our work is the first attempt to address late design changes in presence of sequential optimization.

The rest of the paper is organized as follows. Section 2 presents basics of the Esterel compilation flow and explains how traceability is supported. Section 3 discusses interaction of sequential optimization with the ECO. ECO by examples is presented in Sections 4 for the unoptimized case and 5 for the optimized case. We conclude in Section 6.

2 Traceability in Esterel Compiler

2.1 A Basic Esterel Example

We illustrate the traceability between the Esterel source code and the generated circuit using the following simple program:

```
main module Main :
 input A, B;
 output X, Y;
 abort
     await A; emit X
 when B;
 sustain Y
end module
```

2.2 First Step: Building Esterel Assembly Code

The above program is first translated into an intermediate Esterel assembly code, yielding (approximately) the following sequence of instructions:

```
0: 0 Root: (4) %lc: 0 1 1%
1: 0 Present: [B] (7, 2 %lc: 0 4 1%) %lc: 0 7 1%
2: 0 Resume: <6> %lc: 0 4 1%
3: 0 Present: [A] (5 ,4 %lc: 0 5 4%) %lc: 0 5 4%
4: 0 Pause: (3) <2> %lc: 0 5 4%
5: 0 Emit: [X] (7) %lc: 0 6 4%
6: 0 Watch: {1} <0> %lc: 0 4 1%
7: 0 Emit: [Y] (8) %lc: 0 8 1%
8: 0 Pause: (7) <0> %lc: 0 9 1%
```

The statements are indexed. The number after the index is a module instance index telling by which module instantiation the statement is generated. Here, there is only one module and all indexes are 0. Pragmas such as %lc: 0 5 4% are source code backannotations, telling that a statement or part of a statement is generated from line 5, column 4 of file indexed 0, pointing here to the await keyword.

The flow of control is fully explicit, making statement ordering irrelevant. Direct continuations always appear between parentheses, while statement referenced between angle brackets serve for statement resumptions as explained below.

Here, the Root instruction is the start point, with immediate continuation the Pause statement 4. Therefore, when the program is started, it immediately pauses at 4. Resumption from this point at next tick is based on the indexes between angle brackets, which determine the selection father of a statement, as explained in full details in [2,3]. Here, the Pause statement 4 signals that it is alive to its Resume father 2, which itself signals that it is alive to its Watch abortion father 6, which in turn signals aliveness to the Root statement. Resumption

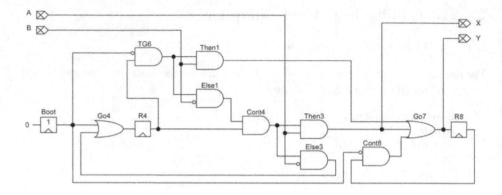

Fig. 2. Esterel generated circuit

follows the reverse path. The `Root` statement resumes its `Watch` son, which implements the `abort` behavior by immediately triggering its associated `Present` test 1 whose index is given between curly brackets. The `Present` statement conditionally triggers the following behaviors:

- If B is present, the continuation 7 is taken, Y is emitted, and the program pauses at 8.
- If B is absent, control is transferred to the `Resume` statement, which resumes its son 4. Resumption of the Pause statement passes control to its continuation 3, which tests for A. If A is present, control is passed to 5, which emits X, and then to 7 to emit Y and pause. If A is absent, control comes back to the Pause statement that pauses again until the next instant, realizing the "await A" behavior.

The assembly code is notably more complex for full-fledged programs, with `Fork` and `Parallel` (join) statements to deal with synchronous concurrency and `Exit` statements to deal with the `trap-exit` Esterel exception mechanism. We give no more details here, since the handling of all statements is pretty similar as far as traceability and ECOs are concerned.

2.3   Second Step: Translation to Circuit

From the above generated Esterel assembly code, the Esterel compiler generates the circuit pictured in Figure 2. The gate names are abbreviated in the picture, with the real full names and associated traceability pragmas as follows:

```
Boot   :  Boot_0_0       %go: 0%
Then1  :  Then_1_0       %then: 1%
Else1  :  Else_1_0       %else: 1% %go: 2%
Then3  :  Then_3_0       %then: 3% %go 5% %emit: X%
Else3  :  Else_3_0       %else: 3%
```

```
Go4     : Go_4_0          %go: 4%
R4      : PauseReg_4_0    %pause: 4%
Cont4   : Cont_4_0        %go: 3%
TG6     : ToGuard_6_0     %go: 1% %go: 6%
Go7     : Go_7_0          %go: 7% %go: 8% %emit: Y%
R4      : PauseReg_4_0    %pause: 8%
Cont8   : Cont_8_0
```

Long names are useful since they are printed in HDL or C and thus propagated down the synthesis chain. The name tells which function a gate is performing and where it comes from. The first number it contains is the index of the statement which generated the gate, while the second number is the module index that identifies to which instance of which submodule the statement belongs, see Section 2.5.

Pragmas add more traceability information to highlight source code at simulation time, to report error messages, and to perform ECOs. Notice that a gate can bear several pragmas. For instance, the Then3 gate bears %then: 3%, which tells that the gate is 1 if the test statement 3 succeeds, %go: 5%, which tells that the same gate starts the statement 5 right away, and %emit: X%, which tells that X is emitted when the gate is 1. The last two pragmas are actually what remains of a gate Go_5_0 that was initially created from Emit statement 5 but swept away since it simply acted as a buffer between the statements 3 and 7. Buffer sweeping carefully propagates pragmas.

Each Pause assembly statement generates a register, while all the other statements generate combinational gates. Generally speaking, the register part comes either from Esterel temporal statements such as pause, "await S", "every S", and "loop ... each S", which define sequential behavior, or from access to previous signal status pre(S) used, for instance, in the rising edge detection sequential expression "S and not pre(S)". The combinational logic is generated by the control and signal propagation statements such as signal emission "emit S", signal presence test "if S then ... else ... end", sequencing ';', parallel '||', etc.

2.4   User-Defined Names of Registers

Generated register names are particularly important since they are fundamental for ECOs and usually preserved by the backend circuit synthesis flow. To make names more readable, one can associate a tag with a register-generating statement in the source Esterel code:

```
await@Wait A;
sustain@Sust Y
```

When setting a special Esterel compiler option -eco, the compiler embeds the tag in the register names, which become PauseReg_Wait_4_0 and PauseReg_Sust_8_0 instead of PauseReg_4_0 and PauseReg_8_0. Furthermore, with this option, the register input gates are not subject to sweeping; they are named `PauseRegIn_Wait_4_0` and `PauseRegIn_Sust_8_0`. Since they are outputs of the combinational part, they are not swept by synthesis backends and easier to find when ECOs are needed.

2.5   Modular Compilation and Traceability

Esterel programs can involve calls to submodules. There are two main modes of HDL generation: *global*, where submodule assembly codes are inlined in the global module code; *modular*, in which submodules are compiled separately into HDL designs and instantiated in the main module HDL. Modular compiling is necessary for large applications, while global compiling makes it possible to deeply optimize modules by analyzing their global behavior. Mixed modes where some modules are inlined and others are separately compiled is also available.

A potential problem with global compiling is gate name instability. Indeed, each gate is named with an instance index and a statement index. Adding one statement to a submodule can modify the numbering of the statements in the other submodules. Using the `-eco` option of the Esterel compiler, we alleviate this problem by naming the gates relative to their position in the submodule instance.

Finally, gates must be sorted according to control and data dependencies before being printed in HDL or C. Little changes in source code can have dramatic effect on the resulting order. To improve code stability for ECOs, we dissociate the gate definitions and the gate instantiation ordering, printing the gate definitions in statement order and their instantiations in causal order. This will not be detailed further.

2.6   Traceability from Graphical State Machines

Esterel supports program design by hierarchical and concurrent safe state machines (SSMs), an evolution of C. André's SyncCharts [1] supporting Mealy and Moore machines. SSMs are translated into textual Esterel source code to be compiled. In SSMs, only terminal states without contents generate control registers; transitions, concurrency, and hierarchical macro-states only generate combinational logic. Terminal states can be named, and the names are propagated to the generated Esterel `pause` statements using the @ tag symbol. Then, when using the `-eco` compiler option discussed in Section 2.5, graphical state names are pushed into HDL register names.

3   Sequential Optimization

The reader may have found that the circuit in Figure 2 is too heavy for the purpose. This is often typical for a circuit generated in syntax-directed translation by high-level synthesis, to which two kinds of optimizations can be applied:

– *Combinational optimizations*, which are classical in synthesis backends. They optimize logic using algebraic and Boolean methods with don't care calculations [18].

– *Sequential optimizations*, which indirectly change how the state is encoded by registers. This step is rarely done by standard synthesis backends, but is found in control compilers such as Esterel or PBS [15].

For sequential optimization, the simplest idea would be to count the number of reachable states of the design, say N, and to allocate $log_2(N)$ registers to hold them. In practice, this fails since the necessary state encoding / decoding circuitry tends to blow up. Finding the right register allocation is difficult even for small designs. Furthermore, even if an optimal allocation is found, the obtained circuit can be quite bad in overall terms because of encoding combinational logic complexity. In practice, it is better to look for less aggressive register reduction schemes that try to ensure a better register / logic compromise by respecting the behavioral structure of the design.

Therefore, for Esterel optimization, we try to respect the initial encoding while removing its redundancies in a controlled way. We use reachable-state based algorithms presented in [19, 16, 17]. Here, we briefly present the three main ones: redundant register elimination, incompatible registers folding, and boot register elimination. We apply these techniques only on the control path of the circuit, because the data path needs to be handled very differently.

3.1   Redundant Register Elimination

We say that a register is *redundant* if it can be replaced by a function of the other registers without altering the sequential behavior of the circuit. For instance, in the circuit of Figure 2, we can replace R8 by "not(Boot or R4)". The newly generated function can be merged with the rest of the combinational logic and simplified with it.

In [5], Madre and Coudert have presented a simple algorithm to check whether a given register r is redundant. Let r be the vector of all registers, and let $\mathcal{R}(r)$ be the characteristic function of the reachable state space of the circuit. Call $\mathcal{R}_r$ and $\mathcal{R}_{\bar{r}}$ the positive and negative cofactors of $\mathcal{R}$ by r, characterized by the Shannon decomposition $\mathcal{R} = r\mathcal{R}_r + \bar{r}\mathcal{R}_{\bar{r}}$. The cofactors are functions of the variables in $r' = r - \{r\}$. Then r is redundant if and only if the conjunction $\mathcal{R}_r(r')\mathcal{R}_{\bar{r}}(r')$ of the cofactors is 0. One can replace r either by the positive cofactor $\mathcal{R}_r(r')$ or by the negation of the negative cofactor $\overline{\mathcal{R}_{\bar{r}}(r')}$, whichever expression is simpler (they are functionally equal).

Of course, deciding whether a redundant register replacement is useful is a very difficult global optimization problem. We use heuristics based on the size of the cofactor supports (active variables), replacing registers only if their support is relatively small. The threshold is user-adjustable.

3.2   Merging Exclusive Register Groups

Consider the following Esterel program:

```
{ await A || await B };
{ await C || await D };
emit X
```

The behavior goes in two phases: waiting for the last of A and B, and waiting for the last of C and D to emit X. Call RA, RB, RC, and RD the 4 registers generated by the 4 `await` statements. Then RA and RB are concurrent and can take any of the possible 4 value pairs, and so are RC and RD. However, the RA-RB and RC-RD groups are dependent: the disjunction predicates $RA \vee RB$ and $RC \vee RD$ are exclusive, i.e. cannot be true together. Therefore, we can safely superpose the register pairs using an auxiliary switch register SW. For instance, we can use two registers RE and RF and set $RA = RE \wedge SW$, $RB = RF \wedge SW$, $RC = RE \wedge \overline{SW}$, and $RD = RF \wedge \overline{SW}$. We are left with 3 registers instead of 4 at the cost of introducing some gates that could possibly be reduced by combinational optimization. The effect would be more pronounced if the sequential components had more registers.

Notice that exclusive register folding can be detected from source code only, without computing reachable states. This is a clear advantage of explicit parallel / sequence temporal structures over the classical HDL division between combinational and sequential processes. Knowing when to effectively apply exclusive register folding is subject to heuristics that are outside the scope of this paper.

3.3   Boot Register Elimination

In the circuit translation from Esterel, the initial instant is always triggered by the single Boot register, all other registers being initialized to 0. It may happen that this initial global state can be suppressed by removing the Boot register and changing the initial value of the other registers. In this case, the new circuit is obviously simpler. This is possible if there exists an initial value allocation to the other registers that leads to the same behavior and the same target states as the initial boot state. Algorithms are presented in [19].

3.4   Reversible and Traceable Sequential Optimization

An important property of the sequential optimizations we have presented is that they are *reversible*: the suppressed registers can be reconstructed from the kept ones. This will be very important for ECOs. In practice, we iteratively chain several optimization algorithms. To be able to reconstruct the old registers in function of the new ones, we could keep the undo information at every optimization step, which would be fairly error-prone. We find it much simpler to use a simpler trick: add the original registers as outputs of the circuit before running the optimization algorithms. The trick has an additional advantage: it makes it possible to use any optimizer and to optimize the circuit as a black box.

Technically speaking, call $\mathcal{C}$ the original circuit, i its input vector, o its output vector, and r its register vector. The circuit is determined by the combinational function $(o, r') = \mathcal{C}(i, r)$, where r' is the new state vector for registers. Keeping the original registers as outputs amounts to considering a circuit $\mathcal{C}_r$ of the form $(o, r', r) = \mathcal{C}_r(i, r)$, where the input-output transformation from r to r is simply the identity function. Sequentially optimizing $\mathcal{C}_r$ yields a new set of registers s and a new circuit $\mathcal{D}$ having type $(o, s', r) = \mathcal{D}(i, s)$. When running $\mathcal{D}$, on an input sequence, the values of the original register vector r of C is directly recovered from $\mathcal{D}$'s outputs.

From $\mathcal{D}$, we can recover two circuits: a circuit $\mathcal{E}$ obtained by dropping the r outputs, and a circuit $\mathcal{D}_r$ obtained by retaining only the r output of C. The latter circuit summarizes all the undo parts of sequential optimizations, since any original register in r can be reconstructed by combinational logic from the final registers in s and the inputs in i, which are the same as for C.

After the removal of the r outputs, we go one step further and apply combinational optimization to $\mathcal{E}$, yielding the final implementation circuit $\mathcal{F}$. Surprisingly, other registers may fall out in this process, if they were used to compute old registers in r but useless for the input/output behavior. Such non-functional registers can be due to state space redundancies, meaning that the original circuit did not implement a minimal state graph. Therefore, they could not be removed by the previous optimizations that preserved the reachable state space. The last combinational step to $\mathcal{F}$ can actually perform some state graph minimization, which was unexpected *a priori*. This step is also reversible: the removed registers can be reconstructed by combinational logic from the remaining ones and from inputs by taking their definition from remaining registers and primary inputs in $\mathcal{D}$. (Register difference between $\mathcal{E}$ and $\mathcal{F}$ might actually exhibit unwanted source code redundancies in the design; we have not explored this yet.)

In the experiments, we ran the algorithms on a number of controllers from real designs, and observed only minor differences between direct optimization and our chain of reversible optimizations, sometimes only after the last step from $\mathcal{E}$ to $\mathcal{F}$. The results are summarized in the table below. Columns "pi" and "po" show the number of inputs and outputs, "org" is the original circuit, "diropt" the one obtained by direct optimization, and $\mathcal{E}$ and $\mathcal{F}$ the ones obtained by the optimization chain described above. For each circuit, the two numbers count registers and sum-of-product literals. For the 4 first circuits, we show two different register / logic compromises, without or with exclusive register merging. All optimizations were sequentially verified.

design	pi	po	org		diropt		$\mathcal{E}$		$\mathcal{F}$	
disk1	38	36	56	548	45	420	45	451	45	425
					13	599	13	725	13	641
disk2	34	35	55	693	38	440	41	449	38	444
					22	601	24	667	22	635
photo	30	150	110	949	99	679	102	763	100	796
					58	866	61	1096	58	881
robot	31	29	86	694	79	472	82	519	80	489
					27	833	27	1000	27	818
bus	19	20	89	445	35	399	37	555	34	441
dma	8	56	47	510	16	265	21	303	16	259
modem	70	152	46	515	14	245	14	275	14	246
mailbox	596	517	41	2359	35	2550	25	2414	25	2272

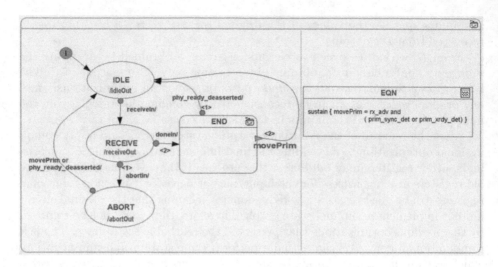

Fig. 3. Original Esterel model

4   ECO Examples in Unoptimized Mode

We present in this section different ECO manipulations. Our assumption is that the fix is easily done in the Esterel model. But the circuit being already signed-off, it is not possible to use the modified model and generate a new layout. Instead, one must identify which changes of the already generated circuit correspond to the change in the Esterel model.

Adding a Term in an Equation. Consider the program of Figure 3. It is made of an explicit hierarchical automaton and of a textual equation in parallel. The END state is a macrostate whose contents will be presented below. Suppose the definition of MovePrim should be modified by adding the prim_pmreq_det signal as follows:

```
sustain{ movePrim = rx_adv and
                  ( prim_sync_det or prim_xrdy_det
                  or prim_pmreq_det)}
```

Let us examine how to modify a VHDL code generated from the original Esterel model and signed-off before the change was done in the specification. In Esterel Studio, by clicking on the sustain statement, we print the list of HDL variables generated by the equation. Then, we read their equations in the HDL code, which are as follows:

```
Go_106_0_L0D0   := Cont_108_0_L0D0 or Boot_0_0
Or_1_107_0_L0D0 := Status_prim_sync_det_S7_0
                   or Status_prim_xrdy_det_S8_0
And_0_107_0_L0D0 := Status_rx_adv_S5_0 and Or_1_107_0
SigExpTrue_107_0_L0D0 := Go_106_0 and And_0_107_0
Status_movePrim_S15_0 := SigExpTrue_107_0
```

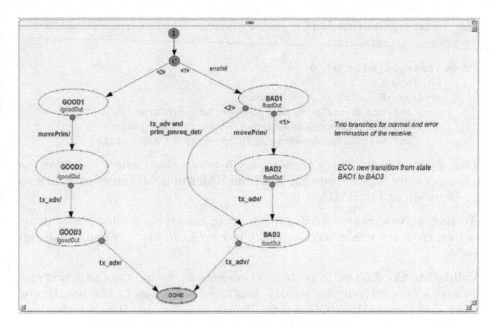

Fig. 4. Adding a transition in a FSM

The signal status gates bear the names of the signals. One can see that `movePrim` is emitted when `Go` is true and the decomposed Boolean expression (from the second and the third equations) is true. Notice that actual IO signals keep their names while local signals generate variables of the form `Status_movePrim`. The ECO simply consists in changing the second equation into

```
Or_1_107_0_LODO  := Status_prim_sync_det_S7_0
                    or Status_prim_xrdy_det_S8_0
                    or prim_pmreq_det
```

Adding a Transition Between Two States. Figure 4 shows the contents of the macro-state labelled `END` in Figure 3. We need to add a transition between `BAD1` and `BAD3`, with trigger "`tx_adv and prim_pm_req_det`". The first step is to find the state registers and their inputs in the HDL code. Here, one can search for the `BAD1` and `BAD2` names, and find registers `PauseReg_BAD1_53_0` and `PauseReg_BAD3_37_0` with respective combinational inputs `PauseRegIn_BAD1_53_0` and `PauseRegIn_BAD3_37_0`. Clicking on the states of the FSM also shows the corresponding registers.

We need to modify the input equations of `BAD1` as emphasized below (new code in italic):

```
PauseRegIn_BAD1_53_0 :=
  Go_51_0_LODO
  and not(PauseReg_BAD1_53_0              -- in BAD1
          and tx_adv and prim_pmreq_det); -- trigger true
```

The change ensures that Bad1 is exited when the trigger is true. For BAD3, the change is more intricate:

```
PauseRegIn_BAD3_37_0  :=
  Go_35_0
  or (PauseReg_BAD1_53_0 -- in BAD1
        and tx_adv and prim_pmreq_det -- trigger true
        and not phy_ready_deasserted -- go to IDLE state
        and not Status_movePrim_S15_0); -- go to BAD2 state
```

The last two negated signals are necessary to ensure that the new transition has a lower priority than the existing ones from BAD1 to IDLE (preemption as seen on Figure 3), and to BAD2.

Adding a New State. Adding a new state consists in adding a new pause register and a new transition equations, which is similar to the example explained above.

Validating the ECOs. To prove ECO correctness, we use the fsm_verify sequential equivalence checker already mentioned in Section 1. The new Esterel program is compiled into blif using the Esterel compiler, and the manually modified HDL program in Verilog or VHDL is compiled into blif using a synthesis tool such as Design Compiler and a blif library. We prove sequential equivalence between both blif designs using the fsm_verify. This technique has proved efficient for relatively large control-dominated designs. Of course, any HDL sequential equivalence technique is usable as well. If the modifications do not alter the register set, a combinational equivalence is sufficient.

5   ECOs on Optimized Designs

Let us perform the ECO of Section 4 after sequential optimization. The direct identification of registers and gates has become impossible. However, if the reversible ECO-friendly optimization is used, it is possible to re-generate the old registers as function of the new ones. A correspondence table is automatically generated as follows:

Original register	Function of new registers
PauseReg_107_0	not eco_31 or not eco_23 or eco_1
Boot_0_0	not eco_1 and eco_23 and eco_31
PauseReg_BAD3_37_0	eco_1 and eco_13
PauseReg_BAD1_53_0	eco_1 and eco_23 and eco_27
PauseReg_BAD2_45_0	eco_1 and eco_23 and eco_31
PauseReg_GOOD3_67_0	not eco_1 and eco_23 and eco_27
PauseReg_GOOD1_83_0	eco_1 and not eco_23 and eco_27
PauseReg_GOOD2_75_0	eco_1 and not eco_23 and eco_31
PauseReg_IDLE_100_0	not eco_1 and not eco_23 and eco_31
PauseReg_ABORT_17_0	not eco_1 and not eco_23 and eco_27
PauseReg_RECEIVE_92_0	not eco_1 and eco_13

Adding Extra Logic to Exit a State. To add the required transitions from
BAD1 it is necessary to modify exit conditions for state BAD1.

```
variable in_BAD1 : std_logic;
variable eco_exit_BAD1 : std_logic;
in_BAD1 := Aux_1_eco_1 and Aux_3_eco_23 and Aux_4_eco_27;
eco_exit_BAD1 := in_BAD1 and tx_adv and prim_pmreq_det;
V7_Aux_1_eco_1_last  <= Aux_73_eco_2 and not eco_exit_BAD1;
V7_Aux_3_eco_23_last <= Aux_76_eco_24 and not eco_exit_BAD1;
V7_Aux_4_eco_27_last <= Aux_79_eco_28 and not eco_exit_BAD1;
```

The equation defining in_BAD1 comes directly from the table above. The
state BAD1 is encoded in the optimized circuit with the three registers eco_1,
eco_23, eco_27 all at '1'. So the next state functions for registers encoding
in_BAD1 should take false value when eco_exit_BAD1 is true.

Adding Extra Logic to Enter a State. New logic is also added to enter
state BAD3: the optimized registers encoding BAD3 are or-ed with the new transition trigger. Here also, one must take care of transitions from BAD1 to IDLE
(triggered by phy_ready_deasserted) and to BAD2 (triggered by movePrim),
which have higher priority. Since Phy_ready_deasserted is a primary input, it
is still present in the optimized circuit. The internal signal movePrim has been
optimized away in the optimized circuit, and we must reconstruct it. The table above indicates that BAD2 is encoded as (eco_1 and eco_23 and eco_31).
Therefore the transition from BAD1 to BAD2 is taken when in_BAD1 and the inputs of eco_1, eco_23 and eco_31 are all at 1. The HDL code is modified to
reflect changes on the inputs of registers encoding BAD3, i.e. eco_1 and eco_13:

```
variable BAD1_to_BAD2 : std_logic;
variable BAD1_to_IDLE : std_logic;
variable exit_BAD1 : std_logic;
BAD1_to_BAD2 := in_BAD1 and Aux_73_eco_2 and Aux_76_eco_24
                          and Aux_83_eco_32;
BAD1_to_IDLE := in_BAD1 and phy_ready_deasserted;
exit_BAD1 := BAD1_to_BAD2 or BAD1_to_IDLE;
V7_Aux_1_eco_1_last  <= (Aux_73_eco_2 and not eco_exit_BAD1)
                          or (eco_exit_BAD1 and not exit_BAD1);
V7_Aux_2_eco_13_last <= Aux_68_eco_14
                          (eco_exit_BAD1 and not exit_BAD1);
```

These new Boolean expressions can be optimized to reduce extra logic.

Adding a New State. Adding a new state in an optimized circuit can be performed by adding a new register, or by using a previously unused encoding of the
existing registers. The first approach is simple and done as already explained in
this paper. The second approach is more difficult because the existing transitions
to and from the states encoded with the reused registers are impacted.

Validating the ECOs. The ECO is validated in the same way as for unoptimized circuits and as explained in Section 4. However, notice that the correspondence table of the original registers and the new ones can be used to simplify
the equivalence checking between the two versions of the same circuit: the unoptimized one and the optimized one. Indeed, one can build a new circuit by

composing the optimized circuit $\mathcal{D}$ with $\mathcal{D}_r$. This new circuit can be verified against the original circuit using a *combinational* equivalence checking, which is much more efficient than sequential equivalence checking.

6   Conclusion

We have shown that ECO is traceable even in the case of heavy sequential optimization of control-dominated designs written in Esterel. The three key ideas are modular synthesis, traceability from source code to circuits and back, and reversible sequential optimization. In particular, we have shown that sequential optimization reversibility makes it possible to transform the sequential ECO problem into the more classical combinational ECO problem by reconstructing the removed registers. After ECO is performed, sequential equivalence techniques are used to verify circuit changes w.r.t. source code changes. The ECO flow we have described is supported by the Esterel Studio tool suite.

Our work was focused on developing a method for handling late design changes in the context of the Esterel flow. We believe however, that it is of a more general value and that a similar method can be applied to any high-level design flow that uses optimization in generating RTL.

Acknowledgements

We thank Chunduri Rama Mohan from Intel for posing the problem and Xavier Fornari and Marc Perreaut from Esterel Technologies for their help during this work.

References

1. C. André. Representation and analysis of reactive behaviors: A synchronous approach. In *Proc. CESA'96, Lille, France*, July 1996.
2. G. Berry. Esterel on hardware. *Philosophical Transactions Royal Society of London A*, 339:87–104, 1992.
3. G. Berry. *The Constructive Semantics of Pure Esterel*. Draft book, available at http://www.esterel.org, version 3, July 1999.
4. D. Brand, A. Drumm, S. Kundu, and PS. Narain. Incremental synthesis. In *Proc. ICCAD*, 1994.
5. O . Coudert C. Berthet, J-C. Madre. New ideas on symbolic manipulation of finite state machines. In *Proc. ICCAD*, 1990.
6. O. Coudert, J-C. Madre, and H. Touati. Tiger 1.0 user manual. Technical report, Digital Equipment Paris Research Lab, 1993.
7. M. Drini and D. Kirovski. Behavioral synthesis via engineering change. In *Proc. DAC*, 2002.
8. S. Hassoun. Fine grain incremental rescheduling via architectural retiming. In *Proc. 11th International Symposium on System Synthesis*, 1998.

9. Shi-Yu Huang, Kwang-Ting Cheng, Kuang-Chien Chen, Forrest Brewer, and Chung-Yang Huang. Aquila: An equivalence checking system for large sequential designs. *IEEE Trans. Comput.*, 49(5):443–464, 2000.
10. M. Sarrafzadeh J. Cong. Incremental physical design. In *Proc. ISPD*, 2000.
11. J.-H R. Jiang and R. K. Brayton. On the verification of sequential equivalence. *IEEE Trans. Computer-Aided Design of Integrated Circuits and Systems*, 22(6):686–697, 2003.
12. D. W. Knapp. Manual rescheduling and incremental repair of register-level datapaths. In *Proc. ICCAD*, 1989.
13. C. Lin, K. Chen, S. Chang, and M. Marek-Sadowska. Logic synthesis for engineering change. In *Proc. DAC*, 1995.
14. S. Singh M. Sheeran and G. Stalmarck. Checking safety properties using induction and a sat-solver. In *Proc. Formal Methods in Computer Aided Design (FMCAD 2000), Springer LNCS*, 2000.
15. Andrew Seawright and Wolfgang Meyer. Partitioning and optimizing controllers synthesized from hierarchical high-level descriptions. In *Proceedings of the 35th annual conference on Design automation conference*, pages 770–775. ACM Press, 1998.
16. E. Sentovich, H. Toma, and G. Berry. Latch optimization in circuits generated from high-level descriptions. In *Proc. International Conf. on Computer-Aided Design (ICCAD)*, 1996.
17. E. Sentovich, H. Toma, and G. Berry. Efficient latch optimization using exclusive sets. In *Proc. Digital Automation Conference (DAC)*, 1997.
18. E.M. Sentovich, K.J. Singh, L. Lavagno, C. Moon, R. Murgai, A. Saldanha, H. Savoj, P.R. Stephan, R.K. Brayton, and A.L. Sangiovanni-Vincentelli. SIS: A system for sequential circuit synthesis. Technical report, University of California at Berkeley, 1992. Memorandum No. UCB/ERL M92/41.
19. H. Touati and G. Berry. Optimized controller synthesis using Esterel. In *Proc. International Workshop on Logic Synthesis IWLS'93, Lake Tahoe*, 1993.
20. C.A.J. van Eijk. Sequential equivalence checking based on structural similarities. *IEEE Trans. Computer-Aided Design of Integrated Circuits and Systems*, 19(7):814–819, 2000.
21. Y. Watanabe and R.K. Brayton. Incremental synthesis for engineering changes. In *Proc. ICCAD*, 1991.

Non-miter-based Combinational Equivalence Checking by Comparing BDDs with Different Variable Orders

In-Ho Moon and Carl Pixley

Synopsys Inc., Hillsboro, OR
{mooni,cpixley}@synopsys.com

Abstract. This paper describes a new method that is useful in combinational equivalence checking with very challenging industrial designs. The method does not build a miter; instead it builds BDDs of reference and implementation circuits independently – so that each BDD can have its best order while building the BDD – then compares the two BDDs directly without transforming one variable order to the other. In the comparison, checking containment of two BDDs is necessary to handle don't cares efficiently. Even though there are polynomial algorithms for checking equality of two BDDs, those algorithms are not extendible to containment checking. Thus we also present an efficient algorithm, of polynomial complexity, to check both equality and containment of two BDDs with different variable orders. Our non-miter-based method was able to verify many hard industrial designs previously infeasible with existing miter-based state-of-the-art techniques. Experimental results show that the non-miter-based method is very efficient for designs that are especially difficult to check due to dissimilarities and don't cares. The current work does not suggest an alternative that replaces conventional equivalence checking algorithms, but rather an approach that augments their capability for designs that are very hard to check.

1 Introduction

The combinational equivalence checking problem is to determine whether two circuits are combinationally equivalent. Typically, the circuits are at different levels of abstraction, with one being a reference design and the other its implementation. Combinational equivalence checking is being used extensively in industrial design and is a mature problem. However, given that equivalence checking is known to be an NP-hard problem, it is naive to believe that the problem is entirely solved. There are still many real designs that current state-of-the-art equivalence checking tools cannot verify. For those hard verifications, users have to perform extra workarounds, such as specifying equivalent nets between two circuits explicitly, changing hierarchical boundaries and so on. To avoid such tedious workarounds, more powerful equivalence checking technology is required.

BDDs(Binary Decision Diagrams [6]) and SAT(Boolean Satisfiability [13, 18]) are two major techniques in equivalence checking. BDD-based equivalence checking is trivial if the BDD size does not grow too large; however, that is not the case in most real designs. Therefore the *cut*-based method [2, 14, 10] has been used to avoid building huge monolithic BDDs. Even though this method has been used successfully, since it

A.J. Hu and A.K. Martin (Eds.): FMCAD 2004, LNCS 3312, pp. 144–158, 2004.

causes *false negative* problem [2], it still suffers from false negative resolutions that are expensive and infeasible in many cases in real designs. To avoid the false negative problem, Moondanos *et al.* presented a method of simplifying a function for a net [17]. In this method, instead of simply introducing a free variable for a net on a cut, the function driving the net is replaced with a simplified function which preserves the range of values on the cut. Later, Moon *et al.* presented an improved method of simplifying functions for multiple nets at once by range computation and parametric representation [16, 12],

All these technologies for combinational equivalence checking are based on the miter [5] (so called *miter-based*). The miter contains a reference circuit and its implementation circuit, and the two circuits are XNORed so that the miter output is *true* when the circuits are equivalent. The miter-based method also implies that both the reference and implementation circuits are put together into a single circuit and equivalence checking is performed on the single circuit.

However, even though the miter-based technologies work quite well in most cases, we have found that mitering contributes to hard verifications, especially for BDD-based techniques when two circuits are very dissimilar. This is because 1) best variable order keeps changing during building BDDs and 2) in the presence of don't cares, the best BDD variable orders for the two circuits could be significantly different for both static ordering and dynamic variable reordering. One example is shown to explain this in Section 2. Also the hard verifications due to dissimilarity come from 1) different levels of abstraction such as RTL-to-Gate verification, 2) don't cares in reference circuit, and 3) different architectures of arithmetic units.

Experimentally, in many hard designs previously infeasible with existing miter-based state-of-the-art techniques, we were able to build BDDs for reference and implementation circuits by building the two BDDs separately in two different BDD managers so that each BDD manager can be free to choose its own BDD variable order optimally. If we could efficiently compare the two BDDs with different variable orders in two different BDD managers, we would have a new way of efficient equivalence checking. This method is called *non-miter-based* equivalence checking since mitering is not required for equivalence checking and the method does not build the two BDDs in one BDD manager.

In this paper, we present a method for non-miter-based equivalence checking and also propose an efficient algorithm for comparing two BDDs with different variable orders. The comparison algorithm handles not only equality but also containment of two BDDs. The containment checking is necessary to handle don't cares efficiently. This is explained in Section 2. Even though there are algorithms with polynomial complexity [8, 4] for checking equality of two Free BDDs, those algorithms are not extendible to containment checking. We can also compare two BDDs with different variable orders by rebuilding a BDD in the BDD manager of the other BDD [3]. However, there is a strong possibility of BDD blow-ups during the rebuilding process.

To our knowledge, the proposed method is the first practical approach in non-miter-based equivalence checking[1], and the algorithm comparing BDDs is also the first in

---

[1] A similar idea was briefly mentioned in [3] by transforming the variable order of one BDD to that of the other. However, that was rather experimental purpose to show the performance of the transforming.

checking containment of two BDDs with different variable orders with polynomial complexity. The non-miter-based equivalence checking does not suggest an alternative that replaces conventional equivalence checkers, but rather an approach that augments their capability for designs that are very hard to check due to dissimilarities and don't cares.

The remainder of this paper is organized as follows. Section 2 presents non-miter-based equivalence checking. Section 3 describes the proposed algorithm to compare two BDDs with different variable orders. Section 4 provides an algorithm to generate counter-examples. Section 5 explains related work. Section 6 analyzes the non-miter-based method. Experimental results are shown in Section 7, and we conclude with Section 8.

2   Non-miter-based Combinational Equivalence Checking

Non-miter-based combinational equivalence checking can be done by building BDDs of reference and implementation circuits separately in two different BDD managers. Therefore, each BDD manager is free to find optimal variable orders for either reference or implementation circuit individually during both static ordering [9] and dynamic variable reorderings [20]. The non-miter-based method also uses the *cut*-based method to avoid building huge monolithic BDDs.

Then we need to compare the two BDDs with different variable orders in different BDD managers, without transforming the variable order of one BDD to that of the other. This is because transforming a BDD with one variable order to another order allows a strong possibility of BDD blow-up. How to compare the two BDDs is described in Section 3.

2.1   Handling Don't Cares

Don't cares come from RTL descriptions where functions are incompletely specified. A function with don't cares is modeled as an interval as in [1, 22].

Let f be the function of reference circuit and g be the function of implementation circuit. In the presence of don't cares in the circuits (for generality, assume both reference and implementation circuits have don't cares), each circuit has an interval of minimum and maximum functions ($[f_{min}, f_{max}]$, $[g_{min}, g_{max}]$). In this case, we can build BDDs of f_{min} and f_{max} in one BDD manager and BDDs of g_{min} and g_{max} in another BDD manager, allowing each manager to have its own BDD variable order. In addition, we could also build each BDD of f_{min} and f_{max} separately in different BDD managers, and the same for g_{min} and g_{max}. Then, equivalence checking can be done by containment checking that tests whether g_{min} and g_{max} reside between f_{min} and f_{max} as below.

$$f_{min} \leq g_{min}$$
$$f_{max} \geq g_{max} .$$

Figure 1 shows Karnaugh maps of reference and implementation functions as an example of equivalence checking with don't cares. The interval functions of f are

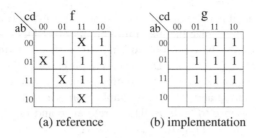

Fig. 1. Equivalence checking with don't cares.

Table 1. Best orders and BDD sizes for each set of functions.

Order	f_{min}	f_{max}	g	f_{min}, f_{max}	f_{min}, f_{max}, g
adbc	**6**	**6**	8	**9**	12
badc	7	7	**5**	11	13
bcda	7	**6**	6	11	15

$f_{min} = a'bd + abc + a'cd'$ and $f_{max} = bc + bd + a'c + a'b + cd$. The function of g is $bc + bd + a'c$. In this case, since g resides between f_{min} and f_{max}, we say the implementation is *equivalent* to the reference, since we are interested in equivalences only inside care sets.

Table 1 shows the number of BDD nodes for each set of functions after BDDs are built, depending on different variable orders. The bold numbers in the table are the optimum BDD sizes including a constant node. The best order for the reference functions in Column 5 is $adbc(a < d < b < c)$, whereas the best order for the implementation in Column 4 is $badc$. Even though the implementation is equivalent to the reference ($f_{min} \leq g \leq f_{max}$), their best orders are quite different due to don't cares. When the implementation is not equivalent, their best orders could be significantly different. In an extreme case, the difference could be exponential in terms of the number of BDD nodes between two orders, and this actually happens in practice (see Section 7). Thus, it is preferable to compare two BDDs directly without transforming one variable order to the other in order to avoid BDD blow-ups.

The numbers in Column 6 are the cases when we build BDDs of a miter. However, the XNOR cell is excluded in the miter for this comparison. We can easily see that the numbers are always bigger than those in the other columns in a given order, as the numbers in Column 5 are always bigger than those in Column 2 and 3. The numbers in Table 1 also imply *difficulty level* to build the BDDs. In other words, the bigger a number is, the more chances of BDD blow-ups exist. In this example, assuming we can get the optimal order, if we build the BDDs of f_{min}, f_{max}, and the BDD of g in one BDD manager, the difficulty level is 12. Whereas, if we build the BDDs of f_{min} and f_{max} in one BDD manager and the BDD of g in another BDD manager, the difficulty level is $Max(9, 5) = 9$. Notice that we take the maximum number for the difficulty level since a BDD blow-up is very likely to happen in the BDD manager with the highest difficulty level, if a BDD blow-up happens. Furthermore, if we build each BDD of f_{min}, f_{max}, and g separately in three different managers, the difficulty level becomes

Max(6, 6, 5) = 6. Thus, it is better to keep the number of functions in a BDD manager as small as possible to minimize the maximum number of BDD nodes. This example explains why the non-miter-based works well in hard verification problems.

Furthermore, since peak sizes of BDD nodes are observed in the middle of building BDDs rather than at the end in general and there are many cases where variable orders we get from static ordering and dynamic variable reorderings are quite far from optimum orders, it makes sense to build BDDs of reference and implementation circuits separately, as shown in the last order($bcda$) in Table 1.

2.2 Cut-Points

Using cut-points in BDD-based equivalence checking is inevitable to deal with industrial designs [14, 10, 19]. To set the cut-points, identifying internal equivalences between reference and implementation designs is required. Due to the nature of this problem, it is easier to do with a miter. Thus, we use the miter partially only to find internal equivalences. Then, we assign a free variable for each internal equivalence on both nets in reference and implementation designs.

2.3 False Negative Resolution

After we introduce free variables on cut-points, if the results are equivalent, the designs are equivalent. If the results are not equivalent, this could be a false negative. Thus we need to justify whether this discrepancy is a true negative or not. Unlike finding the cut-points, false negative resolution can be done in just one BDD manager, either reference or implementation.

The way we justify false negatives is conceptually a combination of the methods in [11, 19]. When we have a false negative, we have a BDD showing the difference between two designs. Then, for each cut-point in the support of the BDD, we compose the variable associated with the cut-point with its function. This function could be in terms of the primary inputs, in which case the process stops, or a function of other cut-points, in which case all new cut variables must be eliminated. The other cut-points are set by moving the current cut-points toward the primary inputs by k topological levels [11]. In the moving process, if there is a hierarchical boundary, we prefer to hold cut-points on the boundaries as much as possible [19]. The process stops when the difference BDD becomes a constant or contains only primary inputs. There are many cases where the difference BDD becomes zero before reaching the primary inputs while composing the cut variables.

3 Comparing Two BDDs with Different Variable Orders

Once two BDDs of reference and implementation circuits are built with different variable orders in different BDD managers, the remaining problem is to perform either one equality checking if there are no don't cares or two containment checkings if there are don't cares. The algorithms proposed in this section handle both equality and containment checkings in a single framework. The algorithms can also generate counter-examples if the two circuits are not equivalent. Generating counter-examples is explained in Section 4. The algorithms are based on BDD minterm counting [6]. Minterm counting on a BDD can be done by traversing each node just one time, meaning linear complexity in terms of the number of BDD nodes [6]. Minterm counting is fast and independent of variable orders, which is very nice.

3.1   Necessary and Sufficient Conditions

Let f and g be the BDDs of the reference and implementation circuits, respectively, in different BDD managers. Let x be the input variables of f and g and n be the number of the variables. $|f|$ represents the number of minterms in f. For equality checking of the two BDDs, the number of minterms on function f and g is necessarily the same. Similarly, for containment checking of the two BDDs, the relation between the number of minterms should be satisfied on function f and g, according to the operator. Formally,

$$f \bigtriangleup g \rightarrow |f| \bigtriangleup |g| \ ,$$

where $\bigtriangleup$ is a *comparison operator* among EQ(=), LEQ($\leq$), or GEQ($\geq$). However, this condition is not sufficient for equality or containment checking. Thus we take cofactors of f and g with respect to a variable x_i, then in order to check $f_{x_i} \bigtriangleup g_{x_i}$ and $f_{\neg x_i} \bigtriangleup g_{\neg x_i}$, we compare the numbers of minterms; $|f_{x_i}|$ against $|g_{x_i}|$ and $|f_{\neg x_i}|$ against $|g_{\neg x_i}|$.

$$f_{x_i} \bigtriangleup g_{x_i} \rightarrow |f_{x_i}| \bigtriangleup |g_{x_i}|$$
$$f_{\neg x_i} \bigtriangleup g_{\neg x_i} \rightarrow |f_{\neg x_i}| \bigtriangleup |g_{\neg x_i}| \ .$$

These are additional necessary conditions. We check these necessary conditions recursively until a cofactored function becomes a constant. On a constant function, the following condition is sufficient for equality or containment checking.

$$f_{\hat{x}_1 \hat{x}_2 ... \hat{x}_m} \bigtriangleup g_{\hat{x}_1 \hat{x}_2 ... \hat{x}_m} \longleftrightarrow |f_{\hat{x}_1 \hat{x}_2 ... \hat{x}_m}| \bigtriangleup |g_{\hat{x}_1 \hat{x}_2 ... \hat{x}_m}| \ ,$$

where each $\hat{x}_i$ is either x_i or $x_{\neg i}$ independently, and $m \leq n$. During checking of the necessary and sufficient conditions, once any violation is found, the two BDDs are not equivalent and we generate counter-examples. Notice that if we take cofactors with respect to all variables in the variable order of either f or g, BDD node creation occurs only in one BDD manager. A naive implementation will have an exponential number of checks. Actually checking only sufficient conditions suffices for equality or containment checking. However, we can have early terminations for failing cases by checking necessary conditions and we can make a linear number of checks in terms of BDD nodes (smaller BDD size of the two BDDs) for equality checking and quadratic number of checks ($bdd\_size(f) * bdd\_size(g)$) for containment checking by having a hash table to store intermediate results to avoid the same computations due to BDD node sharing.

3.2   Algorithm for Comparing Two BDDs

Figure 2 shows the pseudo-code of the algorithm for comparing two BDDs. In Procedure *CheckEquivalence*, f and g are the BDDs of the reference and implementation circuits, respectively. Op represents the comparison operator and can be either EQ,

```
CheckEquivalence(f, g, op, *ce) {
    /* op : {EQ, GEQ, LEQ}; */
    /* *ce : counter-example; */
    path = BDD_ONE;
    PushNode(f, g, op, path);
    while (N = PopNode()) {
        status = CheckNode(N→f, N→g, N→op, N→path, ce);
        if (status == FAIL) return FAIL;
    }
    return PASS;
}


CheckNode(f, g, op, path, *ce) {
    if (FindHash(f, g, op)) return PASS;
    else {
        if (CheckMinterms(f, g, op)) {
            InsertHash(f, g, op);
            if (f or g is a constant) return PASS;
        } else {
            *ce = GenerateCounterExamples(f, g, op, path);
            return FAIL;
        }
    }
    x = top variable in f and g;
    /* top_f = top variable in f; */
    /* top_g = top variable in g; */
    /* π_f is the variable order for f; */
    /* top variable = min(top_f, top_g) in π_f; */
    PushNode(f_x, g_x, op, x ∧ path);
    PushNode(f_¬x, g_¬x, op, ¬x ∧ path);
    return PASS;
}
```

Fig. 2. Algorithm for comparing two BDDs.

LEQ or GEQ. The procedure returns PASS if two circuits are equivalent, or FAIL if not equivalent and generates counter-examples through ce.

The procedure keeps an event queue of virtual nodes N that are sub-problems of checking equivalence. N has four elements: f is a BDD from reference circuit, g is a BDD from implementation circuit, op is a comparison operator, and $path$ is a cube representing a path from the root node to the node N. *PushNode* makes a virtual node N and puts it into the event queue. Initially, the queue contains one event with the two BDDs of the reference and implementation circuits. Then, *PopNode* takes a node N from the event queue with a selection strategy that can be BFS(breadth-first search) or DFS(depth-first search), or any combination of BFS and DFS. With the chosen node, we check equivalence on the node by calling *CheckNode*. We do this until the event queue becomes empty.

CheckNode checks equivalence of two BDDs on a node chosen in *CheckEquivalence*. *FindHash* checks whether it has already been done by searching the hash table. If not, the number of minterms on f and g are computed, and their relation according to *op* is checked in *CheckMinterms*. While computing the number of minterms of a BDD, the BDD manager keeps all the number of minterms of live BDD nodes in a hash table for efficiency. If the relation holds, the result is added to the hash table. Otherwise, counter-examples are generated. In the case of no violation, we generate two more sub-problems into the event queue by cofactoring with respect to the top variable x between f and g, unless f or g is a constant. The recursion with choosing the top variable follows the order in π_f that is the variable order for f. Then the cofactorings on f does not create any new BDD nodes.

3.3   Improved Algorithm by Conflict Checking

Checking equivalence on a node can be improved by conflict checking instead of minterm counting for checking necessary conditions. To prove $f \triangle g$, if we split f and g with respect to x, the necessary conditions are $f_x \triangle g_x$ and $f_{\neg x} \triangle g_{\neg x}$. Figure 3 shows an improved algorithm for checking equivalence on a node via conflict checking. *CheckConflict* tries to find any conflict among all sub-problems (*i.e.* necessary conditions). If there is no conflict, it generates two more sub-problems, (f_1, g_1, op_1) and (f_2, g_2, op_2). *BddRegular* returns the regular BDD node to suppress complemented BDD node. The procedure returns NO_CONFLICT, CONFLICT, or REFINE(a conflict that can be resolved by updating op_1 and op_2 to EQ). Here are some examples on conflict checking.

$$(f, g, EQ) \,\&\, (\neg f, \neg g, EQ) \;\Rightarrow NO\_CONFLICT$$
$$(f, g, EQ) \,\&\, (f, \neg g, EQ) \;\Rightarrow CONFLICT$$
$$(f, g, LEQ) \,\&\, (\neg f, \neg g, GEQ) \Rightarrow NO\_CONFLICT$$
$$(f, g, LEQ) \,\&\, (f, \neg g, LEQ) \;\Rightarrow CONFLICT$$
$$(f, g, LEQ) \,\&\, (f, g, GEQ) \;\;\Rightarrow REFINE \; to \, (f, g, EQ)$$
$$(f, g, LEQ) \,\&\, (f, g, EQ) \;\;\;\Rightarrow REFINE \; to \, (f, g, EQ)$$

For instance, suppose that one sub-problem is $f = g$ and there is another sub-problem, $f = \neg g$. Then, we know that either of them must fail, whereas the two sub-problems are necessary conditions for the original problem comparing two original BDDs. Thus, we can conclude that the two original BDDs are not equivalent. In case of $f \leq g$ and $f \geq g$, either of them must fail unless $f = g$ in which case the two necessary conditions are still satisfied. Thus the two necessary conditions are refined to $f = g$.

Major differences in *CheckNode* from that in Figure 2 are 1) no minterm counting is involved except when generating counter-examples, 2) inserting sub-problems themselves (instead of intermediate results) into the hash table, 3) finding failures by checking conflict of one sub-problem against other sub-problems instead of checking correctness of the sub-problem, and 4) calling *FindHash* with BDD regular nodes and without operator. If *status* is REFINE, we just update $N{\rightarrow}op$ to EQ.

Compared to the algorithm in Figure 2, the algorithm in Figure 3 is much faster, since no minterm counting is involved except when generating counter-examples. But

```
CheckNode(f, g, op, path, *ce) {
    F = BddRegular(f);
    G = BddRegular(g);
    if (N = FindHash(F, G)) {
        status = CheckConflict(f, g, op, N→f, N→g, N→op);
        if (status == NO_CONFLICT) return PASS;
        else if (status == CONFLICT) {
            if (CheckMinterms(f, g, op))
                *ce = GenerateCounterExamples(N→f, N→g, N→op, path);
            if (!(*ce))
                *ce = GenerateCounterExamples(f, g, op, path);
            return FAIL;
        } else { /* REFINE */
            N→op = EQ;
            return PASS;
        }
    } else {
        InsertHash(f, g, op);
        if (f or g is a constant) return PASS;
    }
    x = top variable in f and g;
    PushNode(fx, gx, op, x ∧ path);
    PushNode(f¬x, g¬x, op, ¬x ∧ path);
    return PASS;
}


CheckConflict(f1, g1, op1, f2, g2, op2) {
    F1 = BddRegular(f1);
    G1 = BddRegular(g1);
    F2 = BddRegular(f2);
    G2 = BddRegular(g2);
    if (F1 != F2 || G1 != G2) status = NO_CONFLICT;
    else if (F1 == F2 && G1 == G2) status = NO_CONFLICT;
    else if (F1 != F2 && G1 != G2) {
        if (op1 == op2) {
            if (op1 == EQ) status = NO_CONFLICT;
            else status = REFINE;
        } else {
            if (op1 == EQ || op2 == EQ) status = REFINE;
            else status = NO_CONFLICT;
        }
    } else status = CONFLICT;
    return status;
}
```

Fig. 3. Improved algorithm by conflict checking.

there is a potential drawback that finding a violation could be delayed with more recursions. However, it seems that, in practice, a conflict occurs almost always right on or after the recursion where two BDDs are not equivalent.

4   Generating Counter-Examples

Once any violation is found in the algorithms in Section 3, we generate counter-examples. *GenerateCounterExamples* in Figure 4 takes two BDDs (f and g on a node N where the violation is found with op), and *path* that is a cube representing a path from the root node to the node N. If either f or g is a constant, counter-example ce can be computed trivially. Otherwise, we need to find whether the violation comes from the positive or negative branch by counting the number of minterms. Here notice that there is almost always a difference in the number of minterms in either or both positive or negative cofactors in practice. However, it is possible to have the same number of minterms when we have different functions. Thus, if *CheckMinterms* on the positive branch returns *true* and *GenerateCounterExamples* returns *nil*, we try to find a counter-example on the negative branch.

```
GenerateCounterExamples(f, g, op, path) {
    if (f or g is constant) {
        ce can be computed trivially;
        if (no counter-example is found) return nil;
        return ce ∧ path;
    }
    if (CheckMinterms(f_x, g_x, op)) {
        ce = GenerateCounterExamples(f_¬x, g_¬x, op, ¬x ∧ path);
        if (ce) return ce;
    }
    return GenerateCounterExamples(f_x, g_x, op, x ∧ path);
}
```

Fig. 4. Generating counter-examples.

5   Related Work

There are several techniques to compare two BDDs with different variable orders. One approach is to transform one BDD to match the variable order of the other BDD. This can be done by rebuilding a BDD in the BDD manager of the other BDD [3], or by changing the variable order of one BDD manager to that of the other BDD manager using *sifting* [20]. Both methods introduce a strong possibility of BDD blow-ups. Even though the authors in [3] claimed that the complexity of the method by rebuilding is polynomial, the claim holds only when two BDDs are functionally equivalent. If two BDDs are not functionally equivalent, the worst case complexity of the method is still exponential since the BDD size with the other order is unknown and could be exponential. The experimental results in Section 7 show that this really happens in practice.

A second approach is to find a good common variable order between the two different variable orders. This is known as the multiple variable order problem [7, 21]. However, finding a good common order is not easy in many cases and may not exist in some cases. Furthermore, there is still the possibility of BDD blow-up.

A third approach is to compare the two BDDs directly without changing any variable orders. This was first done by Fortune *et al.* [8]. The authors presented a polynomial time algorithm for equality checking, The algorithm works on two Free BDDs when one of them is fully ordered. The equality checking of the BDDs is done by checking whether their cofactors are equivalent recursively. Later, Blum *et al.* presented an algorithm for testing equality of two Free BDDs [4]. However, the algorithm can give *false positives* with probability of error less than $\frac{1}{2}^k$ by running the algorithm k times. These two algorithms cannot handle containment checking and cannot provide any counter-examples.

The algorithms presented in this paper are conceptually similar to the one described in [8], but our algorithms check necessary conditions at each recursion. The checking of necessary conditions allows early termination for failing cases, and it extends to containment checking that is necessary to handle don't cares. Therefore, our algorithms handle both equality and containment checking in a single framework with polynomial complexity, and also generate counter-examples. Notice that the complexity of both the proposed algorithms and the ones in [8,4] is polynomial for both passing and failing cases.

BDD minterm counting was also used for Boolean function matching in technology mapping [15].

6   Analysis of the Non-miter-based Method

Even though the non-miter-based method can verify many hard verifications that the miter-based methods cannot (see Section 7), there are also many cases that can be verified by miter-based method, but not by the non-miter-based method. This is mainly because those cases can be easily verified by SAT or ATPG, but those are hard for BDD-based method, and vice versa.

There are also many cases where the non-miter-based method takes more time and space than the miter-based methods. Suppose that an implementation circuit is identical to its reference circuit. Then the non-miter-based method takes twice the time and space compared to the miter-based method since the non-miter-based method has to build the BDD of the same circuit twice. Similar degradations also happen for the cases where structural similarity between the reference and implementation designs is very high, and for the cases where verification is reasonably easy.

Furthermore, in the presence of imperfect variable orders we get from both static ordering and dynamic variable reorderings, even when the structural similarity is low, there could be cases where building a BDD of miter is easier than building BDDs of the reference and implementation designs separately especially when dynamic variable reordering is turned on.

Therefore, it is preferable to combine the non-miter-based method with the miter-based methods to improve the overall performance.

7   Experimental Results

We have implemented the non-miter-based method with existing miter-based methods. The miter-based methods have many state-of-the-art engines such as BDD, SAT, ATPG, functional learning, and so on. The strategy for using multiple engines is to switch one engine to another as soon as a given resource limit is reached for the engine. The resource limit is gradually increased for each engine. For the non-miter-based method,

Table 2. Results on hard compare-points.

Circuit	Cpoint	Cell	Input	Similarity	Miter-based		Non-miter-based				
							Rebuild [3]		Proposed		
					Time	Memory	Time	Memory	Time	Memory	Tcomp
Design1	32	4582	356	0.029	Time-out		Time-out		58.7	80.4	9.5
Design2	24	2922	135	0.106	Time-out		Time-out		30.2	80.1	10.23
Design3	11	2656	65	0.032	Time-out		231.9	114.4	15.6	26.1	2.4
Design4	47	6594	320	0.227	Time-out		Time-out		113.2	80.9	7.9
Design5	26	5837	89	0.060	Time-out		Time-out		82.2	48.0	23.1
Design6	24	2843	242	0.269	1050.6	86.9	Memory-out		844.1	80.1	8.2

we use the interleaving algorithm [9] to get static variable orders, and dynamic variable reordering is turned on during building BDDs. We have run all experiments on a 750MHz SUN UltraSPARC-III with 8G-byte memory.

Table 2 compares performance on several hard designs. The first column lists industrial designs which the miter-based methods cannot verify except $Design6$, and the designs have only the compare-points that the miter-based methods were not able to verify. We have tried to verify those hard compare-points by BDD, SAT, and ATPG with unlimited resource limit in the miter-based approach, but none of them were able to verify the cases. The next 4 columns show the number of compare-points to verify, the number of cells in both reference and implementation circuits, the number of inputs, and the similarity number showing how the implementation is similar to the reference in terms of circuit structure. If two circuits are exactly the same, the similarity is 1.0. If two circuits are totally dissimilar, the similarity is 0.0. The similarity was measured by applying 1024 random input patterns, and the similarity is defined by the number of nets having the same signatures divided by the number of total nets.

The next 6 columns compare the overall performance of the proposed method in this paper against the miter-based method, and the Rebuild method in [3]. The times in the table are in seconds and the memory usages are in M bytes. The time-out limit was 10 CPU hours and the memory-out limit was 4G bytes.

Table 2 shows that the non-miter-based method can augment the capability of the miter-based methods, especially on hard verifications. Surprisingly, among the 5 time-out cases with the miter-based method, even though these cases were very hard for BDD, SAT, and ATPG, each of the cases was verified within 2 minutes with less than 280M bytes. We believe this is mainly because the best orders for reference and implementation circuits are significantly different and the differences come from the dissimilarity shown in Column 5. However, the non-miter-based method is virtually independent of the dissimilarity, and the main problem is the difficulty of building BDDs of reference and implementation circuits separately.

We can also easily see that the proposed method outperforms the method in [3]. Among the 5 time-out cases with the miter-based method, 4 cases were still hard for the Rebuild method. This was mainly because there were BDD blow-ups during building BDDs without cut-points. This shows the effectiveness of using cut-points in general.

Especially in $Design6$, the algorithm by rebuilding was not able to finish due to the BDD blow-up during rebuilding even after two BDDs are built. The sizes of the reference and implementation BDDs are 23990 and 1537, respectively, before the BDDs blow up. However, the proposed algorithm completed easily with small memory consumption. This is because once two BDDs are given, the complexity of comparing the two BDDs is still polynomial even when the two BDDs are functionally not equivalent.

The last column in Table 2 shows how much time was spent for comparing BDDs other than building BDDs from the time spent by the proposed method. This shows that the time for comparing BDDs is relatively much smaller than the time for building BDDs. This clearly shows that the proposed algorithm is fast and effective. All designs in the table have don't cares and this implies that a lot of containment checking is involved in comparing BDDs.

Table 3 compares the performance a combined method of the miter-based and non-miter-based methods against when each method used stand-alone. The designs in this table are the same as in Table 2, but the designs contain all compare-points, not only the hard compare-points but also easy ones for the miter-based method. Among the 5 time-out cases with the miter-based method, there are still 3 cases that are hard for the non-miter-based method only. This is again because there were some compare-points verified easily by SAT or ATPG, but those compare-points were too hard for the non-miter-based method.

Table 3. Results on hard designs.

Circuit	Cpoint	Cell	Input	Similarity	Miter-based Only		Non-miter-based Only		Miter-based + Non-miter-based	
					Time	Memory	Time	Memory	Time	Memory
Design1	192	15384	519	0.030	Time-out		Time-out		333.9	98.9
Design2	5754	39675	566	0.107	Time-out		Time-out		293.8	278.1
Design3	272	7609	146	0.039	Time-out		284.4	95.8	80.2	89.0
Design4	91	12566	320	0.235	Time-out		Time-out		706.6	111.8
Design5	441	17569	98	0.173	Time-out		165.9	53.3	934.0	176.7

However, the combined method was able to verify all the cases efficiently. This clearly shows that combining the miter-based and non-miter-based is necessary and the non-miter-based method augments the capability of the miter-based method significantly. In $Design3$, the combined method was 3.5X faster than the non-miter-based method. This was also because some compare-points were much easier to verify by SAT or ATPG. On the other hand, in $Design5$, the combined method was 6X slower than the non-miter-based method. This was mainly because in the multiple engine strategy, there were cases when an engine is dispatched, but the engine does not make any progress. This is a very hard problem to predict which engine is going to be good for certain compare-points.

8   Conclusions

We have demonstrated that building BDDs of reference and implementation circuits independently was easily done for many hard verifications in combinational equivalence checking. This implies that mitering can contribute to hard verifications for BDD solvers. Therefore we have proposed a non-miter-based equivalence checking that builds BDDs of reference and implementation circuits separately in different BDD managers, then compares directly the BDDs with different variable orders without transforming one variable order to the other.

We have also presented efficient algorithms to compare two BDDs with different variable orders, and the algorithms can handle not only equality but also containment checkings with polynomial complexity. This algorithm is the first in checking containment of two BDDs with different variable orders.

We were able to verify many hard verifications with the combined method of the miter-based and non-miter-based equivalence checking, and experimental results show that the non-miter-based method is very efficient especially for very dissimilar circuits that are hard to verify, and complements miter-based methods significantly.

Even though the combined method solved many hard verifications, there are still many designs that neither the miter-based nor the non-miter-based method cannot solve. The main problem is still in building BDDs and in finding good cut-points that make building BDDs easier and that do not cause false negatives. Now we are investigating a method to build BDDs efficiently and to orchestrate multiple engines.

References

1. D. Anastasakis, R. Damiano, H. T. Ma, and T. Stanion. A practical and efficient method for compare-point matching. In *Proceedings of the Design Automation Conference*, pages 305–310, New Orleans, LA, June 2002.
2. C. L. Berman and L. H. Trevillyan. Functional comparison of logic designs for VLSI circuits. In *Proceedings of the International Conference on Computer-Aided Design*, pages 456–459, Santa Clara, CA, November 1989.
3. J. Bern, C. Meinel, and A. Slobodova. Global rebuilding of obdd's avoiding memory requirement maxima. *IEEE Transactions on CAD*, 15(1):131–134, January 1996.
4. M. Blum, A. Chandra, and M. Wegman. Equivalence of free boolean graphs can be decided probabilistically in polynomial time. In *Information Processing Letters*, volume 10, 2, pages 80–82, 1980.
5. D. Brand. Verification of large synthesized designs. In *Proceedings of the International Conference on Computer-Aided Design*, pages 534–537, Santa Clara, CA, November 1993.
6. R. E. Bryant. Graph-based algorithms for Boolean function manipulation. *IEEE Transactions on Computers*, C-35(8):677–691, August 1986.
7. G. Cabodi, S. Quer, C. Meinel, H. Sack, A. Slobodova, and C. Stangier. Binary decision diagrams and the multiple variable order problem. In *International Workshop on Logic Synthesis*, Lake Tahoe, CA, May 1998.
8. S. Fortune, J. Hopcroft, and E. Schmidt. The complexity of equivalence and containment for free single variable program schemes. In *ICALP'78 Automata, Languages and Programming*, pages 227–240, 1978. LNCS 62.
9. H. Fujii, G. Ootomo, and C. Hori. Interleaving based variable ordering methods for ordered binary decision diagrams. In *Proceedings of the International Conference on Computer-Aided Design*, pages 38–41, Santa Clara, CA, November 1993.
10. A. Kuehlmann and F. Krohm. Equivalence checking using cuts and heaps. In *Proceedings of the Design Automation Conference*, pages 263–268, Anaheim, CA, June 1997.

11. A. Kuehlmann, V. Paruthi, F. Krohm, and M. K. Ganai. Robust boolean reasoning for equivalence checking and functional property checking. *IEEE Transactions on CAD*, 21(12):1377–1394, December 2002.
12. H. H. Kwak, I.-H. Moon, J. Kukula, and T. Shiple. Combinational equivalence checking through function transformation. In *Proceedings of the International Conference on Computer-Aided Design*, San Jose, CA, November 2002.
13. J. P. Marques-Silva and K. A. Sakallah. GRASP: A search algorithm for propositional satisfiability. *IEEE Transactions on CAD*, 48(5):506–521, May 1999.
14. Y. Matsunaga. An efficient equivalence checker for combinational circuits. In *Proceedings of the Design Automation Conference*, pages 629–634, June 1996.
15. J. Mohnke and S. Malik. Permutation and phase independent boolean comparison. In *Proceedings of the European Conference on Design Automation*, pages 86–92, Paris, France, February 1993.
16. I.-H. Moon, H. H. Kwak, J. Kukula, T. Shiple, and C. Pixley. Simplifying circuits for formal verification using parametric representation. In *Formal Methods in Computer Aided Design*, pages 52–68. Springer-Verlag, November 2002. LNCS 2517.
17. J. Moondanos, C.-J. H. Seger, Z. Hanna, and D. Kaiss. Clever: Divide and conquer combinational logic equivalence verification with false negative elimination. In B. Berry, H. Comon, and A. Finkel, editors, *13th Conference on Computer Aided Verification (CAV'01)*, pages 131–143. Springer-Verlag, Paris, July 2001. LNCS 2101.
18. M. W. Moskewicz, C. F. Madigan, Y. Zhao, L. Zhang, and S. Malik. Chaff: Engineering an efficient SAT solver. In *Proceedings of the Design Automation Conference*, pages 530–535, June 2001.
19. J. Park, M. Burns, C. Pixley, and H. Cho. An efficient logic checker for industrial circuits. *Journal of Electronic Testing*, 16(1-2):91–106, February 2000.
20. R. Rudell. Dynamic variable ordering for ordered binary decision diagrams. In *Proceedings of the International Conference on Computer-Aided Design*, pages 42–47, Santa Clara, CA, November 1993.
21. C. Scholl, B. Becker, and A. Brogle. Multiple variable order problem for binary decision diagrams: Theory and practical application. In *Proceedings of the Asia and South Pacific Design Automation Conference*, pages 85–90, February 2001.
22. T. Stanion. Circuit synthesis verification method and apparatus. *U.S. Patent 6,056,784*, May 2000.

Scalable Automated Verification
via Expert-System Guided Transformations

Hari Mony[1], Jason Baumgartner[1], Viresh Paruthi[1],
Robert Kanzelman[2], and Andreas Kuehlmann[3]

[1] IBM Systems Group, Austin, TX
[2] IBM Engineering & Technology Services, Rochester, MN
[3] Cadence Berkeley Labs, Berkeley, CA

Abstract. *Transformation-based verification* has been proposed to synergistically leverage various transformations to successively simplify and decompose large problems to ones which may be formally discharged. While powerful, such systems require a fair amount of user sophistication and experimentation to yield greatest benefits – every verification problem is different, hence the most efficient transformation flow differs widely from problem to problem. Finding an efficient proof strategy not only enables exponential reductions in computational resources, it often makes the difference between obtaining a conclusive result or not. In this paper, we propose the use of an *expert system* to automate this proof strategy development process. We discuss the types of rules used by the expert system, and the type of feedback necessary between the algorithms and expert system, all oriented towards yielding a conclusive result with minimal resources. Experimental results are provided to demonstrate that such a system is able to automatically discover efficient proof strategies, even on large and complex problems with more than 100,000 state elements in their respective cones of influence. These results also demonstrate numerous types of algorithmic synergies that are critical to the automation of such complex proofs.

1 Introduction

Despite advances in formal verification technologies, there remains a large gap between the size of many industrial design components and the capacity of fully-automated formal tools. General exhaustive algorithms such as symbolic reachability analysis [1] solve a PSPACE-complete problem and are limited to design slices with significantly fewer than one thousand state elements. Overapproximate proof techniques such as induction [2] solve an NP-complete problem and may be applied to significantly larger designs, though are often prone to inconclusive results in such cases. Consequently, even a piece of an industrial processor execution unit (much less an entire chip) is likely to be too large for a reliable application of automatic proof techniques.

Technologies such as bounded model checking (BMC) [3] and semi-formal verification [4, 5] address the simpler NP-complete problem of exhaustive bounded search, leveraging the bug-finding power of formal algorithms against much larger designs. Though *incomplete*, hence generally unable to provide proofs of correctness, such applications have become prevalent throughout the industry due to their scalability and

A.J. Hu and A.K. Martin (Eds.): FMCAD 2004, LNCS 3312, pp. 159–173, 2004.
© Springer-Verlag Berlin Heidelberg 2004

ability to efficiently flush out most design flaws. Nevertheless, once such approaches exhaust their ability to find bugs, the end-user is often left debating how many resources to expend before giving up and hoping that the lack of falsification ability is as good as a proof.

The concept of *transformation-based verification* (TBV) [6] has been proposed to synergistically apply various transformation algorithms to simplify and decompose large problems into sufficiently small problems that may be formally discharged. While the complexity of a verification problem is not necessarily related to its size, the complexity class of the algorithms indicates an exponential worst-case relationship between these metrics, which is validated by practical experience. By resource-bounding any possibly costly BDD- or SAT-based analysis, it is possible to limit the complexity of most transformations used in a TBV system to polynomial while exploiting their ability to render exponential speedups to the overall verification flow as noted in [6, 7].

The strength of TBV is based upon the availability of a variety of different complementary transformations which are able to successively chip away at the verification problem until it can be handled by a terminal decision procedure. We have found that the power of TBV is often able to yield a proof for large problems which otherwise would be candidates only for falsification techniques. However, in cases, achieving such results requires a fair amount of user sophistication and trial-and-error – every verification problem is different, hence the most efficient transformation flow varies widely from problem to problem. Given a TBV system with a finite number of algorithms, each with a finite number of discretely-valued parameters, there are a countably infinite number of distinct proof strategies that could be attempted. Finding an efficient proof strategy not only entails exponential reductions in overall computational resources, it often makes the difference between obtaining a conclusive result or not.

In this paper, we propose the use of an *expert system* to automatically guide the flow of a transformation-based verification system. We discuss the type of rules used by the expert system to ensure that commonly-useful, low-resource strategies are explored first, then gradually more expensive strategies are attempted. We have found this approach useful for quickly yielding conclusive results for simpler problems, and efficiently obtaining more costly yet conclusive strategies for more difficult problems. We additionally discuss the type of feedback necessary between the TBV system and the expert system, needed to enable the expert system to effectively experiment with proof strategies. Lastly, we discuss the learning procedure used by the expert system to ensure that it leverages the feedback of previous experimentation in its quest for the best-tuned proof strategy for the problem at hand – ultimately seeking a conclusive result. Experimental results are provided to demonstrate that such a system is able to automatically yield proofs of correctness for large designs (with more than 100,000 state elements in their cones of influence) by maximally exploiting the synergy of the transformation and verification algorithms within the system against the problem under consideration.

Mechanizing the application of proof strategies is not a new concept; it is an essential component of most general-purpose theorem provers, e.g., HOL [8], PVS [9], and ACL2 [10]. However, the presented TBV approach is well-tuned for the verification of safety properties of hardware designs, incorporating numerous specialized transformations that are applicable to large systems. Finding a good scheduling and parameter setting for these transformations is non-trivial, though key to full automation.

2 Netlists: Syntax and Semantics

Borrowing the notation of [7], a *netlist* is a tuple $\langle \langle V, E \rangle, G, Z, T \rangle$ comprising a directed graph with vertices V and edges $E \subseteq V \times V$. Function $G : V \mapsto types$ represents a semantic mapping from vertices to gate $types$, including constants, primary inputs (i.e., nondeterministic bits), registers (denoted as the set R), and combinational gates with various functions. Function $Z : R \mapsto V$ is the initial value mapping. At time 0, the value of register r is defined to be the value of gate $Z(r)$; the value of r at time $i + 1$ is defined as the value of the gate sourcing the input edge to r at time i. The *semantics of a netlist* are defined in terms of semantic traces: 0, 1 valuations to gates over time which are consistent with G and Z.

Our verification problem is represented entirely as a netlist, and consists of a set of *targets* $T \subseteq V$ correlating to a set of properties $AG(\neg t), \forall t \in T$. We say that target t is *hittable* if it evaluates to 1 along some trace, and that t is *unreachable* if no trace may hit t. We thus assume that the netlist is a composition of the *design under verification*, its *environment* (encoding *input assumptions*), and its *property automata*[1].

In our experiments, we map all designs onto a netlist representation containing only constants, primary inputs, two-input AND gates, inverters, and registers, using straightforward logic synthesis techniques. Because inverters may be represented implicitly as edge attributes in the netlist representation [12], we assess the result of various transformation flows in terms of only register, primary input, and AND gate counts.

3 Transformation-Based Verification

Transformation-based verification was proposed in [6] as a framework wherein one may synergistically utilize the power of various transformation algorithms to iteratively simplify and decompose complex problems until they become tractable for automated formal verification. All algorithms are encapsulated as *engines*, each interfacing via a common modular API. Each engine receives a verification problem represented as a netlist, then performs some processing on that problem. This processing could include an attempt to solve the problem (e.g., with a bounded model checking or reachability engine) or it could include an attempt to simplify or decompose the verification problem using a transformation (e.g. with a retiming or redundancy removal engine). In the latter case, it is generally desirable to pass the simplified problem to another engine to further process that problem. As verification results are obtained on the simplified problem, those results propagate through the sequence of engines in reverse order, with each transformation engine undoing the effects of the transformations it performed to present its parent engine with results that are consistent with the netlist that its parent transmitted. A particular instance of a TBV system is depicted in Figure 1.

The most useful verification and falsification engines tend to consume exponential resources. In contrast, the applied transformations either require only polynomial resources or are applied in a resource-constrained manner. They may ultimately reduce

---

[1] Due to the ability to synthesize safety properties into automata [11], this invariant-checking model is rarely a practical limitation.

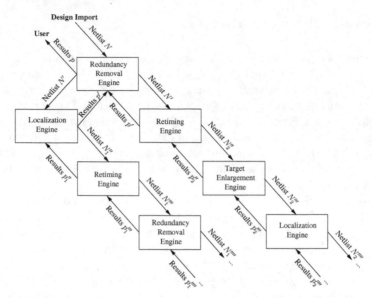

Fig. 1. Example flow of a transformation-based verification system

problem size by orders of magnitude compared to the initial size (even after a simple cone-of-influence reduction and constant propagations). We have found that the impact of such transformations on high-performance gigahertz-class designs is particularly pronounced, effectively automatically *undoing* many of the commonly employed high-performance microarchitecture and design techniques such as pipelining and addition of redundant logic to minimize propagation delays (e.g., replicating a lookup queue in two places in the circuit), which otherwise make the verification task of a given design component more difficult from one design generation to the next. A well-tuned transformation flow can therefore solve a problem with exponentially lesser resources than another, and even enable a conclusive result which otherwise would be infeasible.

3.1   Example Transformation Algorithms

In this section we introduce the transformation and verification engines used in our experiments. Recall that we measure netlist size in terms of register count, primary input count, and AND gate count (after a cone-of-influence reduction with respect to T). Each transformation explicitly attempts to reduce only one or two metrics, and may increase the others. Numerous options are available for each of these engines to bound resources and specify algorithmic parameters.

- **COM:** a redundancy removal engine, which attempts to merge functionally equivalent gates. This engine uses on-the-fly compression techniques as the netlist is received (such as associative hashing to preclude the creation of redundant AND gates) in addition to combinational post-processing techniques such as resource-bounded BDD- and SAT-based analysis (which are NP-complete sub-problems) to identify functionally redundant gates [12]. This engine is guaranteed not to increase any of the three size metrics.

- **EQV:** another redundancy removal engine, similar to that of [13]. This engine uses a variety of heuristics (such as symbolic simulation) to *guess* redundancy candidates, then uses induction to prove and subsequently exploit that redundancy. Its reductions may far exceed those possible with **COM** and eliminate every redundant gate in the netlist; however, this problem is PSPACE-complete, hence often lossy short-cuts must be accepted which trade reduction potential for run-time gains. This engine is guaranteed not to increase any of the three size metrics.
- **RET:** a min-area retiming engine [6, 14], which attempts to reduce the number of registers in the netlist by shifting them across combinational gates. This approach is guaranteed not to increase register count, but in calculation of retimed initial values via structural symbolic simulation, it may increase the other two metrics.
- **BIG:** a structural target enlargement engine [15], which replaces a target by the characteristic function of the set of states which may hit that target within k time-steps, simplified with respect to the set of states which may hit that target in fewer than k time-steps. **BIG** is guaranteed not to increase register count nor primary input count, but may increase AND gate count.
- **CUT:** a range-preserving parametric-reencoding engine [7, 16], which replaces the fanin-side of a *cut* of the netlist graph with a trace-equivalent, yet simpler, piece of logic. **CUT** is guaranteed not to increase primary input count nor register count, but may increase AND gate count.
- **LOC:** a localization engine, which isolates a cut of the netlist local to the targets by replacing internal gates by primary inputs. This is similar to the processing of **CUT**, though in contrast, **LOC** does *not* preserve the range of the cut. This is the only transformation used in our experiments which is not both sound and complete – proofs of correctness on the localized design are valid for the unlocalized design, but counterexamples may be spurious (hence may need to be suppressed). To help guide the cut-selection process, the engine uses a light-weight SAT-based refinement scheme [17] to include only that logic which is deemed necessary. **LOC** is guaranteed not to increase register count nor AND gate count.
- **RCH:** an MLP-based symbolic reachability engine [18]. It is a general-purpose proof-capable engine, solving a PSPACE-complete problem.
- **SCH:** a semi-formal search engine [4,5], which interleaves random simulation (to identify *deep*, interesting states), symbolic simulation (using either BDDs or a structural SAT solver [12]) to branch out from states explored during random simulation, and induction to attempt low-resource proofs of unreachability.

4   Tuning TBV Proof Strategies

Arriving at a well-tuned TBV engine flow with minimal effort is a nontrivial task for several reasons. The first is due to the number of possible proof strategies; given a system with k distinct engines, there exist k^i possible distinct engine sequences of length i. Some engines are significantly more resource-intensive than others. It is therefore rarely an effective strategy to exhaustively attempt all possible engine flows of a certain depth.

Instead, one will often wish to resort to a heuristic approach of partially exploring the *tree* of possible engine flows beginning with lower-cost, often-effective flows. One will then analyze their effectiveness upon the corresponding problem (e.g., their achieved reduction) to decide what to attempt next – whether to pursue appending further transformations onto the end of some of those already-explored flows, or to try some new, possibly more expensive flows in the quest for obtaining a conclusive result. Viewed another way, the user prioritizes among each node of the explored tree based upon the size of the problem at that node and the suspected reduction potential beyond that node (e.g., if a deeper transformation flow is attempted beyond that node), and systematically chooses promising nodes from which to further experiment.

The second difficulty is due to the irreversibility of certain transformations. Several verification-oriented transformations – particularly approximate ones such as localization – alter the netlist in a manner which may not be readily reversible[2]. Thus, applying transformations A then B may yield a different netlist than applying B then A, and performing a certain transformation may destroy the ability to subsequently solve the problem without backtracking out of that transformation. This precludes a simple depth-first search from being an effective proof strategy; some degree of branching and bounding must be performed. To compound this problem, recall that there are three netlist size metrics that we consider; many transformations reduce one or two of these, and may substantially increase the others. Different algorithms are more sensitive to some of these metrics than others – e.g., symbolic reachability analysis is highly sensitive to register count whereas structural SAT solvers are more sensitive to AND gate count. This overall makes it difficult to rate the effectiveness of a given transformation.

Given the amount of experimentation necessary to solve complex verification problems, there exists a strong motivation to attempt to automate this overall process. This automation may save considerable manual effort for expert users, furthermore enabling a much faster time to a conclusive result due to the ability to automatically explore proof strategies in parallel. Additionally, it enables even casual users (for example, a logic designer who is not versed in formal methods) to obtain results that otherwise would not be obtainable, at least until the problem is transferred to an expert user of the tool. Finally, an automated process may well be able to effectively *learn* strategies and algorithmic synergies that may otherwise go unexplored even by an expert user.

5   Automating TBV Proof Strategies via an Expert System

In this section, we describe how to fully automate the process of obtaining efficient proof strategies with a TBV system. The overall architecture of this automated system is depicted in Figure 2. At the center of this system is the TBV core itself. Problems are imported into the TBV system, and the results are reported, via the *User Interface*. The verification process itself is controlled via the *Proof Strategy Interface* which includes the *Engine Control Interface* through which the engine selection process is performed, and the *Engine Feedback Interface* through which feedback is reported to indicate how well the various engines are performing upon the active problem.

---

[2] The process of *reversing a transformation* is often emulated by removing the corresponding engine from a given transformation flow.

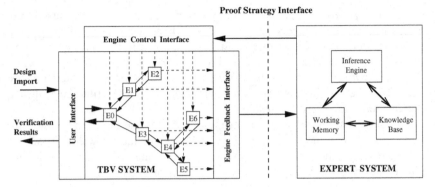

Fig. 2. Integration of an expert system with a TBV system

An example run of the TBV system is depicted in Figure 2. The problem is first processed using the proof strategy of engine E0, then E1, then E2, each selected via the *Engine Control Interface*. Next, assume that, based upon the *Feedback* received from these engines, the controller of the verification process wishes to attempt a different proof strategy. The controller will thus preclude attempting to further transform the problem after E2, and instead instruct the TBV system to pass the transformed problem from E0 to a new engine flow beginning with E3[3].

The control of the TBV process is traditionally carried out by running pre-packaged strategies, which is limited in that a conclusive strategy for a difficult problem may not be previously known. Alternatively, it may be put under the control of a user who will wish to manually tune the flow based upon *Feedback* provided by the system, using the heuristic experimentation process described in Section 4. To achieve full automation of the verification process while retaining the ability to experiment to yield conclusive results on difficult problems, we propose to eliminate the need for user interaction by attaching an *expert system* to the *Proof Strategy Interface*.

5.1   Expert Systems

Feigenbaum [19] defined an expert system as "an intelligent computer program that uses knowledge and inference procedures to solve problems that are difficult enough to require significant human expertise for their solution." Expert systems are often used to solve complex problems with ill-defined domains for which no algorithmic solution is known or which belong to an intractable class of problems. Countless types of expert system applications have been proposed over the past decades.

The three main architectural components of an expert system are the following.

---

[3] It is an implementation-specific detail as to whether the TBV system will retain the branch containing engines E1 and E2 in scope. Retaining engines outside of the active proof path increases overall resource consumption, though facilitates subsequent experimentation along those prior branches without needing to re-run those flows. Note also that the exploration of distinct branches may be performed by multiple machines operating in parallel, possibly transferring *snapshots* of the transformed netlist.

- The *knowledge base*, which contains the domain-specific knowledge used to solve problems. This knowledge can be elicited from human experts, or it can be learned by the system itself. Knowledge is often represented in the form of *rules* which govern the solution strategies employed by the expert system.
- The *working memory*, which refers to task-specific data for the problem under consideration. The working memory is the data that is read and written to as the expert system attempts to solve the problem.
- The *inference engine*, which contains the algorithms used to leverage the rules in the knowledge base in order to solve problems. Once the knowledge base is built and the task-specific data is read into the working memory, the inference engine will begin evaluating rules to attempt to solve the problem.

5.2   Expert System Implementation

In this section we provide an overview of the implementation of an expert system for deriving effective proof strategies for a TBV system. Figure 3 depicts the high-level experimentation algorithm. As the expert system experiments with the problem and partially explores the tree of possible proof strategies, it records data learned from that experimentation in a database called the *Tree of Knowledge* during step 3[4]. As discussed in Section 4, there are two primary decisions involved in the experimentation process: choosing a promising node in an engine flow from which to further experiment (decided during step 1), and selecting the next engine to append onto that chosen node (decided during step 2).

The Tree of Knowledge. The *Tree of Knowledge* is a database of information learned during prior experimentation on the active problem, which may generally comprise results obtained in a parallel-processing environment. Each node in the tree corresponds to the run of a particular engine instance (including its options) and the *Feedback* received from that run. The recorded *Feedback* information may include the following.

1. The transformed netlist size, and information about any solved targets.
2. The resources consumed by that engine run.
3. Dynamically-obtained information on how an engine's options could be improved. This feedback includes two aspects.
   (a) How to initialize the system to a given node with lesser resources. For example, SAT-solvers use various heuristics in their processing; the best heuristic for a given problem may enable dramatic speedups vs. another heuristic. If a SAT-based engine determines during its run that a particular heuristic worked best, it may report that information to be recorded in the *Tree of Knowledge* so that a future run can initialize to this node more quickly.
   (b) *Hints* to yield a superior flow. For example, if a redundancy removal engine sees that it precluded some analysis due to resource limitations, likely hurting its reduction potential, it would provide feedback so that a future run could increase the corresponding type of resources and yield superior reductions.

---

[4] The results of user-guided experimentation may also be recorded in this database.

while (¬solved) {

1. Choose a node from the *Tree of Knowledge* from which to perform further experimentation; initialize the TBV system to that node (call this engine E_i).
2. Choose an engine E_{i+1} to append to the initialized node; instruct engine E_i to pass its transformed problem to E_{i+1}, then run engine E_{i+1}.
3. Extract feedback from the run of E_{i+1}; update the *Tree of Knowledge* with this data.

}

Fig. 3. High-level expert system algorithm

Choosing a Node for Further Experimentation. During step 1 of the algorithm of Figure 3, the expert system chooses a node from the *Tree of Knowledge* from which to perform further experimentation, then initializes the TBV system into the corresponding state. To make this decision, the expert system assigns a *priority* to each node in the *Tree of Knowledge* using a set of rules; it then performs a weighted random selection among the prioritized nodes. Several classes of rules are used to assign priorities.

- **Prefer smaller netlists.** An important set of rules is based upon the size of the netlist at corresponding nodes in the tree – the smaller the problem, the closer to a conclusive result the system tends to be, though this trend is certainly not guaranteed. However, recall that there are three distinct size metrics considered. The size-related priority ascribed to a node is thus varied during the experimentation, from strategies using equal weights among all the metrics, to strategies using brute-force to minimize the number of registers (without regard to other metrics) in the hope of yielding an inductive target or one which is amenable to reachability analysis, to more experimental strategies which prioritize towards nodes which managed to significantly reduce *any* of the metrics in the hope that a subsequent flow may compensate for increases in the other metrics and ultimately yield a proof.
- **Prioritize away from well-explored branches.** Based upon the previous set of rules, the system will tend to perform near-exhaustive exploration of the first explored branch consisting of strictly decreasing size metrics. While this is indeed an advantageous strategy to begin with, it may preclude necessary experimentation along a completely different flow to yield a complex proof. Therefore, a class of rules is needed to prioritize away from nodes in the tree that have been more thoroughly explored – i.e., deeper exploration is no longer yielding significant reductions despite having experimented with most advantageous engine types.
- **Exploit low-cost re-initializations.** Note that there is a computational cost associated with initializing the TBV system to a given node (that is not already in scope), namely that of re-running the desired transformation flow up to the desired node. It is therefore often advantageous to have a set of rules prioritizing towards a fair amount of experimentation from or near the active nodes before re-initialization into completely different branches.
- **Identify the causes of unsuccessful branches.** In cases, the reason that a proof cannot be obtained along a branch may be attributed to a transformation which occurred much earlier in the flow. For example, if an instance of **LOC** subsequently renders a spurious counterexample, it is of no utility to perform further experimen-

tation under that instance. As another example, it may be the case that the problem at a branch is suffering from far too many primary inputs to complete a reachability computation and none of the available algorithms is able to compensate for that metric, and that an earlier instance of **RET** was the cause of a significant increase in input count. Though the **Prioritize away from well-explored branches** class of rules will ultimately bring us out of heavy exploration of such branches, another class of rules is useful to attempt to further leverage information about the *cause* of unsuccessful branches, and to backtrack sufficiently far to circumvent that causal engine, instead of continuing to branch to other points under that causal engine.

Choosing an Engine to Append to the Initialized Node. During step 2 of the algorithm of Figure 3, the expert system must decide what engine type to append to the initialized node. Because any engine type may be run at any given time, rules are again deployed to determine priorities for these possibilities; the expert system then performs a weighted random selection among the prioritized possibilities. The following classes of rules are useful to prioritize among the possible choices.

- **Begin with low-cost flows.** The primary objective is to obtain verification results as quickly as possible, so the initial priorities are set to attempt commonly-effective, low-cost flows first. Whether falsifying or proving, reduction algorithms can yield dramatic improvements in runtimes and enable conclusive results that otherwise may be missed given available resources, so the priorities of low-cost reductions such as **COM** and **RET** are initially high. Additionally, the priorities of low-cost falsification and proof engines such as **SCH** are initially high.
- **Gradually attempt more expensive flows.** As more and more experimentation is performed, the expert system acknowledges that the problem is increasingly more difficult, hence gradually increases the priority of its heavier-weight reduction algorithms such as **EQV**. Additionally, as more and more attempts at falsification render inconclusive results, the priority of proof-capable flows including **LOC** and **RCH** are increased and the priority of falsification engines such as **SCH** are decreased.
- **Exploit known algorithmic synergies.** Known synergies between transformations should be exploited by a set of rules. For example, running a redundancy removal engine after retiming often helps reduce the potential increase in combinational logic caused by that engine, hence priorities should be adjusted accordingly.
- **Explore the potential of unknown algorithmic synergies.** Because every problem is different, it is generally impossible to predict the possible algorithmic synergies that will be key to solving that problem, hence the system should have a set of rules to attempt to prioritize towards such experimentation. It is rarely useful to re-run the same engine type back-to-back, without any intermediate transformations. However, it is often the case that repeated calls of a given transformation engine, interspersed with other transformations, is an effective strategy whereby one transformation synergistically unlocks further reduction potential for another. A generic way to encode this trend is to analyze the extent to which the size metrics changed since the last run of a given engine type, and update the priority for instantiating that engine type accordingly. For example, assume that the current engine flow is **RET**, **COM**, **CUT** where **CUT** performed slight reductions, whereas

COM performed significant reductions. The priority of appending **RET** to this flow is increased since the netlist changed significantly in size since **RET** was last run, whereas the priority of appending **COM** is decreased due to the lack of change in netlist size since that engine last ran. Note that such experimentation may result in the eventual learning of commonly useful known synergies – this has the potential to enable the overall system to grow in effectiveness as it is deployed upon more and more problems, especially as new engine types are added to the system.

- **Leverage the Tree of Knowledge.** The *Tree of Knowledge* contains information about prior experimentation. Because the concept of initializing the system into a previously-explored node is covered by step 1, re-running an already attempted child engine of the initialized node is lowered in priority in this step, particularly if that child did not yield a beneficial reduction. Also, the *hints* recorded from prior runs may be used to attempt to obtain an improved proof strategy.

6   Experimental Results

In this section we provide the experimental results of the integration of an expert system with a TBV system. All experiments were run using a single processor and 4GB main memory on an IBM RS/6000 Model 43P-S85 (850MHz), using the IBM internal verification tool *SixthSense*. In addition to the engines discussed in Section 3.1, we utilized a phase abstraction engine [20] on all IBM designs prior to importing them into the tool.

We had intended to provide a large set of results showing the run-time difference of various proof strategies; however, the majority were easily discharged by a straight-forward proof strategy. For example, we ran the 42 designs of the ISCAS89 testsuite using each primary output as a target[5]. Except for one target of S635, the overall system was able to discharge all 1615 resulting targets using the proof strategy **COM**, **RET**, **COM**, **SCH**, **BIG**, **RCH** in less than 35 cumulative minutes of runtime[6]. We therefore consider these to be easy problems; rather than describing these experiments in more detail, we turn our attention to significantly more difficult problems.

Table 1 comprises some of the most difficult verification problems we have encountered among IBM designs. The first column is a label column, indicating the name of the corresponding design and the metric being tracked in the corresponding row. The second reflects the size of the original, unreduced verification problem. The successive columns indicate the size of the problem *after* the corresponding transformation engine (indicated in the row labeled with the design name) was run. The total run-time, memory consumption, and result of the corresponding proof strategy is also provided.

MFC is a memory flow controller. ERAT is an effective-to-real address translation unit. IOC is an I/O Controller. RING comprises starvation and prioritization correctness properties for network arbitration logic. SQM is an InfiniBand store queue manager. MMU and SMM are different memory management units; we report results for several different types of properties for these. All of these had undergone many months of simulation-based analysis prior to importing into the TBV framework, and weeks

---

[5] Though these may not be meaningful properties to check of these designs, none are otherwise available for them; additionally, these are easily-reproducible experiments.

[6] The target of S635 requires 2^{32} inexpensive image computations to hit.

of analysis using commonly-effective falsification and proof strategies had been performed within the TBV system without conclusive results prior to deploying the expert system. SMM and SQM were the most difficult of these examples, requiring nearly four days of experimentation by the expert system (running one thread). RING was the second most difficult, requiring nearly two days. The others were solved within one day of experimentation. We noted the following trends in our experiments.

- **LOC** performs an overapproximate transformation; the choice of too small of a localized cone may render a spurious counterexample. More generally, localization locks us into a netlist where redundancy removal techniques may be weakened: e.g., gates which are constant in the original netlist may not be constant in the localized netlist. It is thus important to choose a large enough cone not only to prevent spurious counterexamples, but also to prevent weakening other redundancy removal transformations which may ultimately be needed to yield a conclusive result. It therefore came as a surprise to us that the expert system found, after some experimentation, that some of our most difficult problems were efficiently solvable when performing localization after only basic reductions. For these cases, early localization was a successful strategy since it quickly identified a sufficiently large cone that remained unreachable, yielding a significantly smaller netlist against which we could successfully apply more costly reductions. Note that nested localizations intermixed with other transformations often yields increasing reductions[7].
- **RET** often substantially reduces register count, though may significantly increase combinational logic due to the symbolic simulation necessary to compute retimed initial values. While **COM, CUT,** and **EQV** are useful in offsetting this increase, as one adds more **RET** calls, more and more of the registers begin to attain symbolic initial values as reachability data is effectively locked into their initial values. Some of these runs show that the expert system found it effective to resort to a more costly **EQV** coupled with fewer retiming runs accordingly.
- Redundancy removal is almost always a useful transformation. **EQV** may yield dramatic reductions, though tends to be the most expensive transformation discussed if used with sufficiently high resources to yield near-optimal reductions.
- A general characteristic of TBV is that one reduction often enables another, in turn allowing the same transformation to yield increasing reductions when interspersed with other transformations. For example, redundancy removal, parametric re-encoding, and localization are able to break connections which constitute re-timing traps, enabling multiple retiming instances to yield increasing reductions as noted in [6]. Redundancy removal often enables parametric reduction that otherwise could not be obtained [7]. Retiming may enable a gate that acts as a constant only after the first several time-steps of execution to be merged as a constant in a sound and complete fashion [7], enabling further redundancy removal.

For MFC, the flow of **RET** before **LOC** was critical; without the simplification enabled by retiming, the localized cones became hopelessly large. ERAT and IOC com-

---

[7] A similar observation on the utility of nested localizations was noted in [21], applied in an approach which extracts an *unsatisfiable core* from a BMC SAT instance. Our application in a TBV domain yields greater flexibility in its ability to leverage various transformations between the localization instances.

prised a large degree of redundant logic. Both **EQV** and **RET** are required to solve these targets, though the former is much more expensive than the latter – it was found that the combinational gate increase by **RET** caused the best strategy to place that engine after **EQV**. RING.P required multiple retiming passes to render an inductive target. RING.S was an interesting case; our last **EQV** call was a thorough and costly one, requiring nearly five hours of run time. Once reduced, we found a valid counterexample of depth 192 on the resulting design in less than one minute. Without this reduction, we found that we could not complete the localization refinement of the failing time-step within a period of 36 hours, without which the localized cone yielded spurious counterexamples. This illustrates the power of TBV not only to enable complex proofs, but to yield exponential speedups to the bug-finding process. SQM required aggressive redundancy removal to enable a highly-effective retiming and localization step, which in turn enabled the property to be trivialized during a subsequent aggressive redundancy removal step. SMM was a difficult problem for which we have not found a shorter proof-capable strategy, though its overall run-time was quite reasonable. The winning strategy was to iteratively leverage all of the discussed transformations to chip away at the netlist size, even requiring what seemed to be rather poor engine choices (e.g., note that **RET** was instantiated numerous times yielding a reduction of only one register, at the cost of tripling primary input count). Additionally, that strategy chose many low-resource calls to **CUT** which yielded only modest reductions; larger-resource calls yielded much greater primary input reductions, but at the cost of much greater AND gate increases which slowed the overall flow. Ultimately, the synergy between the algorithms rendered a sufficiently small netlist to enable a proof by induction or reachability.

7 Conclusion

In this paper we propose the use of an *expert system* to automate the experimentation necessary to obtain an efficient proof strategy for a *transformation-based verification* system [6]. We discuss details of how to integrate an expert system with a TBV system, and of how to customize the expert system to enable it to yield conclusive verification results with minimal resources. Our experiments demonstrate the utility of such an overall system in automatically yielding complex proofs for large industrial designs with over 100,000 registers in their cone of influence, even after simple redundancy removal. This integration eliminates the need for manual effort or formal expertise to yield conclusive results on such difficult problems. Additionally, this integration enables the exploitation of parallel processing to automatically *learn* algorithmic synergies critical to the solution of such complex problems which otherwise may go undiscovered.

Acknowledgements

The authors would like to thank Geert Janssen, Mark Williams, and Jessie Xu for their contributions to numerous aspects of the TBV system, as well as for insights into the integration of the expert system into this framework.

Table 1. Experimental results of expert-system guided proof strategies; all numbers *after* phase abstraction. COM: a low-cost redundancy removal engine; EQV: a more expensive redundancy removal engine; RET: a min-area retiming engine; LOC: a localization engine (the associated number represents the number of BMC steps used in refinement re-finement); BIG: a target-enlargement engine (the associated number represents the number of enlargement steps performed); CUT: a parametric re-encoding engine (the associated number represents the number of image computations needed to complete reachability); RCH: a reachability engine (the associated number represents the number of SAT-based induction steps performed); SCH: a semi-formal verification engine (the associated number represents the number of SAT-based induction steps performed). P indicates a passing *target unreachable* result, and F refers to a failing *target hit* result; the total run-time and memory consumption of the corresponding proof strategy is also provided

MFC

	Initial	COM	RET	COM	LOC:130	CUT	RCH:104
Registers	146627	119147	100928	100902	132	407	P
ANDs	8570021	721158	726839	705113	407		6957s
Inputs	33096	29022	106020	30337	11	10	1.1GB

ERAT

	Initial	COM	RET	EQV	COM	LOC:50	
Registers	456637	19921	419	337	273	257	F
ANDs	316432	167619	3440	2679	1851	1739	2831s
Inputs	6874	68	63	183	126	126	884MB

IOC

	Initial	COM	EQV	RET	EQV	COM	LOC:70	COM	CUT	COM	RCH:258
Registers	241078	28795	2342	2332	2332	2329	185	185	185	185	P
ANDs	1320354	198278	17566	16743	16606	2540	2540	2536	1938		29026s
Inputs	2044	333	49	578	578	49	348	348	43		3.1GB

RING.S

	Initial	COM	EQV	RET	EQV	CUT	COM	EQV	LOC:192	
Registers	50988	20768	2320	1932	1932	1930	1930	1930	1841	F
ANDs	412804	137588	15434	18114	15691	15086	15467	15086	14194	24028s
Inputs	5313	2730	572	1419	1172	851	850	850	850	2.5GB

RING.P

	Initial	COM	RET	COM	CUT	COM	RET	COM	CUT	COM	SCH:3
Registers	50748	21252	8503	3944	3944	3944	1948	1438	1348	1348	P
ANDs	419937	137261	129113	52140	53883	50790	48170	48077	47327	3504	337s
Inputs	5232	2891	17505	4248	3081	3077	3814	3814	3504	3504	339MB

SQM

	Initial	COM	EQV	CUT	COM	RET	COM	CUT	COM	LOC:30	EQV
Registers	34276	16017	11293	11293	11293	10812	10811	10811	10811	144	P
ANDs	552487	252296	159168	165068	165894	147464	146826	146232	146651	17388	1285363s
Inputs	36220	16071	5119	4266	4255	4354	458	450	450	3311	1.1GB

MMU.0

	Initial	COM	LOC:40	RET	COM	RET	COM	RET	COM	BIG:1	RCH:84
Registers	124297	70193	1766	1766	1766	113	99	97	97	95	P
ANDs	763499	409675	103838	104213	104749	68152	609	1026	430	703	8406s
Inputs	1377	168	16290	16095	15209	12202	621	350	34	41	2.9GB

MMU.4

	Initial	COM	LOC:40	COM	CUT	EQV	LOC:40	EQV	BIG:6	RCH:64
Registers	124297	70193	456	455	455	287	98	78	60	53 P
ANDs	763499	409675	25122	25121	24318	23152	537	906	304	490 8278s
Inputs	1377	168	4325	4325	3904	3786	99	78	22	17 2.8GB

MMU.8

	Initial	COM	LOC:40	COM	RET	COM	RET	COM	CUT	RCH:86
Registers	124297	70193	2681	2681	2681	108	97	95	95	P
ANDs	763499	409675	104749	104737	105096	68152	609	1026	350	8398s
Inputs	1377	168	15390	15209	15209	12202	435	609	350	2.9GB

SMM.2

	Initial	COM	LOC:60	COM	CUT	LOC:50	COM	LOC:50	RET	COM	CUT	RET	COM	CUT	RET	COM	LOC:50	BIG:3	COM	CUT	COM	RCH:73
Registers	363359	33063	968	967	967	967	889	663	648	663	628	647	629	628	629	628	415	351	84	84	79	79 P
ANDs	209745	195258	34321	33523	31795	31692	31428	31024	31017	30257	29398	28927	25394	24639	24755	25092	25394	24639	32123	34281	33981	32959 10471s
Inputs	261	71	7140	7140	6591	6591	6763	6763	6494	6241	6164	6116	6241	6164	4773	4783	4959	4731	4010	4010	4961	4920 47 2.3GB

SMM.3

	Initial	COM	LOC:60	CUT	EQV	CUT	LOC:50	CUT	LOC:50	EQV	CUT	LOC:50	CUT	LOC:50	EQV	CUT	LOC:50	BIG:4	COM	LOC:50	COM	EQV
Registers	363359	33063	968	1317	1316	1188	929	929	929	825	825	825	824	825	825	766	766	628	628	589	284	270
ANDs	209745	195258	74009	72586	72203	52718	52629	52585	34766	34675	34631	34404	35444	34766	34960	32913	32946	33981	34093	31717	9523	9050
Inputs	261	71	7140	11105	10853	10853	7846	7839	7839	4960	4951	4951	18854	4951	4959	4773	4783	4028	4010	3847	859	863

References

1. O. Coudert, C. Berthet, and J. C. Madre, "Verification of synchronous sequential machines based on symbolic execution," in *Int'l Workshop on Automatic Verification Methods for Finite State Systems*, June 1989.
2. M. Sheeran, S. Singh, and G. Stalmarck, "Checking safety properties using induction and a SAT-solver," in *Formal Methods in Computer-Aided Design*, Nov. 2000.
3. A. Biere, A. Cimatti, E. M. Clarke, and Y. Zhu, "Symbolic model checking without BDDs," in *Tools and Algorithms for Construction and Analysis of Systems*, March 1999.
4. M. Ganai, A. Aziz, and A. Kuehlmann, "Enhancing simulation with BDDs and ATPG," in *Design Automation Conference*, June 1999.
5. P.-H. Ho, T. Shiple, K. Harer, J. Kukula, R. Damiano, V. Bertacco, J. Taylor, and J. Long, "Smart simulation using collaborative formal and simulation engines," in *Int'l Conference on Computer-Aided Design*, Nov. 2000.
6. A. Kuehlmann and J. Baumgartner, "Transformation-based verification using generalized retiming," in *Computer-Aided Verification*, July 2001.
7. J. Baumgartner, *Automatic Structural Abstraction Techniques for Enhanced Verification*. PhD thesis, University of Texas, Dec. 2002.
8. M. Gordon, "Mechanizing programming logics in higher order logic," in *Current Trends in Hardware Verification and Automated Theorem Proving*, Springer-Verlag, 1989.
9. M. Srivas, H. Rueß, and D. Cyrluk, "Hardware verification using PVS," in *Formal Hardware Verification: Methods and Systems in Comparison*, Springer-Verlag, 1997.
10. M. Kaufmann, P. Manolios, and J. S. Moore, *Computer-Aided Reasoning: An Approach*. Kluwer Academic Publishers, 2000.
11. E. A. Emerson, "Temporal and modal logic," *Handbook of Theoretical Computer Science*, vol. B, 1990.
12. A. Kuehlmann, V. Paruthi, F. Krohm, and M. Ganai, "Robust Boolean reasoning for equivalence checking and functional property verification," *IEEE Transactions on Computer-Aided Design*, vol. 21, no. 12, 2002.
13. P. Bjesse and K. Claessen, "SAT-based verification without state space traversal," in *Formal Methods in Computer-Aided Design*, November 2000.
14. J. Baumgartner and A. Kuehlmann, "Min-area retiming on flexible circuit structures," in *Int'l Conference on Computer-Aided Design*, Nov. 2001.
15. J. Baumgartner, A. Kuehlmann, and J. Abraham, "Property checking via structural analysis," in *Computer-Aided Verification*, July 2002.
16. I.-H. Moon, H. H. Kwak, J. Kukula, T. Shiple, and C. Pixley, "Simplifying circuits for formal verification using parametric representation," in *Formal Methods in Computer-Aided Design*, Nov. 2002.
17. D. Wang, *SAT based Abstraction Refinement for Hardware Verification*. PhD thesis, Carnegie Mellon University, May 2003.
18. I.-H. Moon, G. D. Hachtel, and F. Somenzi, "Border-block triangular form and conjunction schedule in image computation," in *Formal Methods in Computer-Aided Design*, Nov. 2000.
19. E. A. Feigenbaum, "Themes and case studies of knowledge engineering," in *Expert Systems in the Micro-Electronic Age*, 1979.
20. J. Baumgartner, T. Heyman, V. Singhal, and A. Aziz, "An abstraction algorithm for the verification of level-sensitive latch-based netlists," *Formal Methods in System Design*, no. 23, 2003.
21. A. Gupta, M. Ganai, Z. Yang, and P. Ashar, "Iterative abstraction using SAT-based BMC with proof analysis," in *Int'l Conference on Computer-Aided Design*, Nov. 2003.

Simple Yet Efficient Improvements
of SAT Based Bounded Model Checking

Emmanuel Zarpas

IBM Haifa Research Laboratory
zarpas@il.ibm.com

Abstract. In this paper, we show how proper benchmarking, which matches day-to-day use of formal methods, allows us to assess direct improvements for SAT use for formal methods. Proper uses of our benchmark allowed us to prove that previous results on tuning SAT solver for Bounded Model Checking (BMC) were overly optimistic and that a simpler algorithm was in fact more efficient.

1 Introduction

Over the past decade, verification via model checking has evolved from a theoretical concept to a production-level technique. It is being actively used in chip design projects across the industry, where formal verification engineers can now tackle the verification of large industrial hardware designs.

Assessing theoretical results requires more than simply getting experimental results on some benchmarks. Rather, results must be attained for a wide range of benchmarks, under conditions as close as possible to real-life formal verification. In order to illustrate the significance of proper benchmarking, we demonstrate how applying overly restrictive benchmarking can be misleading. We, then, show how proper benchmarking, which matches day-to-day use of formal methods, allows us to assess direct improvements. We present a method of splitting up the problem, which verification engineers usually meet in day-to-day real-life work. This allows us to distribute the problem in a simple and efficient way. This distribution technique is simple, but we, nevertheless, prove that it is very efficient by benchmarking. In a more general way, our goal is to show how very simple ideas can be proven to have great impact by experimentation.

This paper is organized as follows: Section 2 discusses our work in tuning decision-heuristics for a SAT solver and shows how proper benchmarking proved that the results were too optimistic. Section 3 explains how we assessed the performance of a straightforward distributed SAT Bounded Model Checking algorithm. Section 4 summarizes our conclusions. The benchmark we mainly used in this paper (the IBM Formal Verification Benchmark), is presented in Appendix A.

2 Decision Heuristics for Tuning SAT

This section presents some decision heuristics for tuning the zChaff VSIDS for bounded model checking as in [15]. The experimental results use a predecessor

A.J. Hu and A.K. Martin (Eds.): FMCAD 2004, LNCS 3312, pp. 174–185, 2004.

of the IBM Formal Verification Benchmark. The next section shows how proper use of the IBM Formal Verification (Cf. appendix A). Benchmarking proves the results in this section are too optimistic.

2.1   Bounded Model Checking and SAT Basis

BMC Basis: BMC translates a safety formula from LTL [14] into a propositional formula under bounded semantics. The general structure of a $G(P)$ formula, as generated in BMC [5], is as follows:

$$\phi: \quad I_0 \wedge \bigwedge_{i=0}^{k-1} \rho(i, i+1) \wedge \left(\bigvee_{i=0}^{k} \neg P_i\right)$$

where I_0 is the initial state, $\rho(i, i+1)$ is the transition between cycles i and $i+1$, and P_i is the property in cycle i.

If this propositional formula is proven to be satisfiable, the satisfying assignment provided by the SAT solver is a counterexample to the property $G(P)$. To convert the initial propositional formula into Conjunctive Normal Form (used as the input format by most SAT solvers), extra variables are introduced to avoid combinatory explosion. Usually, these extra variables represent more than 80% of the total number of variables in the CNF formula.

SAT Basis: SAT is the problem of determining the satisfiability of a Boolean formula. The problem was used by Cook to define NP-completeness [6]. Today, many implementations are available for solving the problem, such as Grasp[16] and zChaff [12]. Most of them are based on the complete DPLL algorithm [7], we now describe as in [12]:

```
while(true) {
  if (!decide()) // if no unassigned vars
      return(satisfiable) ;
  while (!bcp()) {
      if (!resolveConflict ())
         return (not satisfiable) ;
} }


bool resolveConflict() {
  d=most recent decision not 'tried both ways' ;
  if (d==null) // no such d was found
      return false ;

  flip the value of d;
  mark d as tried both ways ;
  undo any invalidated implications;
  return true;
}
```

decide() is a function that chooses the next variable according to which branching will occur. There are many heuristics for choosing this next variable, such as DLIS (Dynamic Largest Individual Sum) and VSIDS (Variable State Independent Decaying Sum). zChaff uses VSIDS as its decision heuristic. bcp() returns true when the boolean constraint propagation (bcp) [12] finishes without conflict. Our next subsection focuses on tuning this heuristic for BMC.

2.2   Tuning VSIDS

The original zChaff decision VSIDS strategy is as follows:

1. Each variable in each polarity has a counter, which is initialized to 0.

2. When a clause is added (by learning) to the database, the counter associated with each literal in the clause is incremented.

3. The (unassigned) variables and polarity with the highest counter are chosen at each decision.

4. Periodically, all counters are divided by a constant.

One of Strichman's [17] main ideas is as follows: in the Davis-Putnam decision procedure, the variable of the original propositional formula is used first and in a specific static order. This static order is determined by a breadth first search of the (k-unfolding of the) variable dependency graph; the search starts from the set $\bigcup_{0 \leq i \leq k} \neg P_i$. Roughly speaking the intuition behind this, is that the formula variables are the most critical. We chose to implement several decision heuristics on top of zChaff[1]. We tuned the zChaff VSIDS decision heuristic in several different ways. First, we wanted to reflect the idea of static order (SO) [17]. Second, we wanted to implement a heuristic that gives priority to dominant variables (DV) over any other variables, but otherwise relies on zChaff decisions. This is because it is unclear from [17] whether the improvements were due to the static order or to the priority given to the dominant variables (i.e., the variables from the initial propositional formula before the conversion to CNF, or domain variables). Because zChaff uses the VSIDS decision strategy, which is less time consuming than the decision heuristic used by Strichman with GRASP (i.e., DLIS), it is not clear whether the benefits from a static order would still be realized. Therefore, we also implemented a static order heuristic and dominant variables priority heuristics to act as a tie breaker for the zChaff decision (respectively SB and DVB). The four decision strategies implemented are described in details in [15].

---

[1] We used the zChaff SAT solver because this solver has been stable for a few years and its source code is available for research and academic purposes. Even though zChaff did not win the SAT2003 contest, its results on the IBM benchmarks are comparable to the results achieved by the winning tools. In fact, our own experiment [23] with the IBM CNF benchmark show results slightly better for zChaff than for Berkmin561 [10]. We believe these heuristic results should be re-usable for other modern SAT solvers [10, 13, 8].

Table 1. The results are displayed in seconds, with two significant digits. Timeout was set to 10000 seconds

	VSIDS	DVB	SB	DV	SO	min(DVB,SB, DV,SO)
1_2001	18	12	31	14	170	(DVB) 12
2_2001	1400	620	820	300	1300	(DV) 300
3_2001	43	66	190	240	240	(DVB) 66
4_2001	4000	1000	800	210	120	(SO) 120
5_2001	2400	44	240	170	100	(DVB) 44
6_2001	1000	67	190	3800	250	(DVB) 67
7_2001	340	120	140	8	19	(DV) 8
8_2001	13	10	34	14	4800	(DVB) 10
9_2001	71	44	110	190	900	(DVB)44
10_2001	70	70	110	86	timeout	(DVB) 70
11_2001	4800	4200	6400	timeout	3100	(SO) 3100
12_2001	44	42	73	46	51	(DVB) 42
13_2001	78	6	58	6	52	(DVB) 6
14_2001	32	31	42	18	26	(DV) 18
15_2001	13	13	13	13	13	13
16_2001	timeout	timeout	9200	timeout	180	(SO) 180
17_2001	7600	4000	3100	2400	timeout	(DV) 2400
18_2001	11	85	95	6	3000	(DV) 6
19_2001	timeout	timeout	timeout	1600	8700	(DV) 1600

2.3 Experimental Results

For the experiments described in this paper we used zChaff 2001.2.17 (for a comparaison between performances of zChaff 2001.2.17 and 2004.5.13, see for examples [23]).

In our first experiments, we used a predecessor of the IBM Formal Verification Benchmark. For each model we used only one CNF (see Table 1 contend for experimental results). In Table 2, we computed speedup, taking the VSIDS heuristic as a reference: therefore we did not take into account IBM_16 and IBM_19, for which VSIDS times out. We could also have decided to take the Static Order (SO) heuristic as a reference and not take IBM_10 and IBM_17 into account. However, SO is the only heuristic that times out for IBM_10 and IBM_17, while three out of five heuristics time out for IBM_16 and IBM_19. When we compared min(DVB,SB,DV,SO) with VSIDS for each case, we were impressed: Running four concurrent instances of SAT, each with a different heuristic, should give a theoretical speedup greater than six. Indeed if we could build a tool which would run concurrently SAT instances with DVB, SB, DV and SO heuristics, this would solve SAT problems about six times faster than with VSIDS heuristics[2].

---

[2] Arguably we should have compared it to VSIDS run on six machines concurrently. Anyway we will see in the following that using these six heuristics concurrently gives, in real-life situations, unenthusiastic results.

Table 2. The results are computed without IBM_16 and IBM_19 for which VSIDS times out

	VSIDS	DVB	SB	DV	SO
Total time	21933	10430	12446	> 17521	> 34141
Global speedup (VSIDS total time/total time)		2.10	1.76	< 1.25	< 0.64
Average speedup (average VSIDS time/time)		6.11	2	< 6.26	< 5.15

In order to evaluate this claim, we made some additional experiments, with a different approach. First, we decided to use the IBM Formal Verification Benchmark, which is wider than its predecessors; the fact that it is available online (for academic organizations) allows to reproduce our results. Second, we decided not to run SAT as a stand-alone with one or two CNFs per model, but to run our global bounded model checking tool, as a regular user would, without any prior knowledge of the model. We began with a bound equal to 10, and in the case where no satisfiable assignment is found for the CNF generated by BMC translation, we incremented the bound by 5, and so on. In other words, in order to try to falsify a safety formula, say $G\ (P)$), we usually try to find a satisfiable assignment for

$$\phi_0: \quad I_0 \wedge \bigwedge_{i=0}^{9} \rho(i, i+1) \wedge (\bigvee_{i=0}^{10} \neg P_i)$$

if it fails, we try

$$\phi_1: \quad I_0 \wedge \bigwedge_{i=0}^{14} \rho(i, i+1) \wedge (\bigvee_{i=11}^{15} \neg P_i)$$

and keep incrementing until a satisfiable assignment is found for some ϕ_j, some timeout is reached, or a user defined maximal bound is reached.

This is the most common approach for day-to-day use of BMC. Even when the completeness threshold d (as in [5]) is known, it is very often too big to allow the BMC to finish with $k = d$. Therefore, most of the time, users will try to falsify a formula with BMC, without knowing whether the formula holds or not, or which k would be needed to get a satisfiable ϕ_k.

We ran RuleBase with five concurrent SAT BMC instances (each of them using a different decision heuristic from VSIDS, DV, DVB, SB, SO). Each instance was independent and run on a single workstation with a 867841X Intel(R) Xeon(TM) CPU 2.40GHz with 512 KB first level cache, and 2.5 GB physical memory, running with Red Hat Linux release 7.3. Surprisingly, we got a speedup of only 1.14 (see the following section and Concur 5/5 heuristics results in Table 4). This can be explained by several factors:

- The search includes a SAT search together with pre-processing and BMC translation (translation from the model with a given bound to a CNF). SAT is only a part of the whole process, however the bottom line for formal verification is performance of this global process.

- For each model, several CNFs (from BMC translation with different bounds) are searched for satisfiability. All in all, SAT was run in many more CNFs than for the 2001 benchmark (several CNFs from the 2001 benchmarks are generated from the IBM Benchmark). Running SAT on a benchmark that was too small did not accurately reflect the conditions of day-to-day formal verification. This led us to anticipate overly optimist conclusions.

3   A Simple but Efficient Distributed SAT BMC Algorithm

We conducted several experiments with the IBM Formal Verification Benchmark. In fact, it has become one of our main tools to assess new search engines and algorithms. The experiments we present here were conducted to offer a better assessment of different decision heuristics for zChaff and to assess a straightforward distributed algorithm for bounded model checking. The results provide a good perspective on the importance of the IBM Formal Verification Benchmark.

3.1   Experimental Settings

We ran RuleBase on the IBM benchmark with several configurations on 867841X Intel(R) Xeon(TM) CPU 2.40GHz with 512 KB first level cache, and 2.5 GB physical memory, blade workstations running Red Hat Linux release 7.3. When RuleBase was used with engines distributed on several workstations, they were interconnected with a 1 Gb Ethernet LAN. The different configurations are as follows:

- Sequential: RuleBase runs SAT bounded model checking on a single workstation. The bounds used sequentially include k=0...10, k=11...15,..., k=46...50. As soon as a satisfiable assignment is found, the search is over. If no satisfiable assignment is found for any of the bounds, the result is then unsat with bound 50.
- Concur 7: RuleBase distributes the tasks corresponding to the seven first bounds to seven workstations (i.e., BMC translation and SAT search for k=0...10, k=11...15,..., k=36...40). As soon as a satisfiable assignment is found, the whole search is over. If a task finishes without finding a satisfiable assignment, the next task is then assigned to the now idling workstation (until there are no tasks left, in which case the result is unsat 50).
- Concur 5: This uses the same principle as Concur 7, but distributes tasks in a five by five manner to five workstations.
- Concur 3: This uses the same principle as Concur 7, but distributes tasks in a three by three manner to three workstations.
- Concur 5, 5 heuristics: RuleBase runs five independent SAT BMC instances (similar to sequential). Each of the SAT BMC instances uses a different decision heuristic for zChaff, from VSIDS, SO, SB, DV, DVB.

- Concur 9 2/nodes: RuleBase distributes the nine SAT BMC tasks (corresponding to bounds k=0...10, k=11...15,..., k=46...50) on five bi-processors workstations.

Table 3 presents the experimental results for the rules from the IBM Benchmark. We omitted the rules that ran in under two minutes with Sequential configuration and the rules that timed out (timeout was set at two and a half hours) for every configuration. For this experiment, we used bi-processor workstations with 867841X Intel(R) Xeon(TM) CPUs 2.40GHz with 512 KB first level cache, and 2.5 GB physical memory, running with Red Hat Linux release 7.3. Speedup NA means the search timed out for both configurations (i.e., Sequential and the given configuration).

Table 3. Experimental results with the IBM Formal Verification Benchmark. S stands for Sequential, C7 for Concur 7, C5 for Concur 5, C3 for Concur 3, H5 for Concur 5 with five heuristics, C 9/2 for Concur 9 with two processes per node

	result	S	C7	C5	H5	C9/2	C3
		(hh:mm:ss)	(speedup)	(speedup)	(speedup)	(speedup)	(speedup)
02_1 rule 1	unsat 50	00:06:00	2.0	1.9	1.5	2.0	1.6
02_1 rule 2	unsat 50	00:08:19	2.8	2.7	1.5	2.8	2.2
02_3 rule 2	unsat 50	00:09:02	2.7	2.6	1.4	2.7	2.5
02_3 rule 4	unsat 50	00:09:46	2.4	2.3	1.2	2.4	1.9
02_3 rule 6	unsat 50	00:09:25	2.3	2.2	1.7	2.4	1.8
02_3 rule 7	unsat 50	00:05:18	2.0	1.9	1.1	2.1	1.7
06	sat 31	00:02:25	1.8	1.7	1.1	1.8	1.6
10	unsat 50	00:29:47	2.7	2.6	1.9	2.8	2.0
11 rule 1	sat 31	00:25:26	8.9	8.2	1.3	8.8	7.4
14 rule 1	unsat 50	00:02:10	2.3	2.2	1.0	2.7	1.7
14 rule 2	unsat 50	00:25:43	2.9	2.7	1.0	1.9	2.2
17_1 rule 2	pass	00:05:13	2.5	2.4	1.0	2.1	1.9
18	sat 29	00:38:59	1.4	1.3	1.3	1.1	1.3
19	sat 29	00:02:23	1.4	1.4	1.1	1.2	1.2
20	sat 44	> 02:30:00	1.9	1.8	NA	1.8	1.3
22	unsat 50	> 02:30:00	NA	NA	1.6	NA	NA
23	sat 36	> 02:30:00	6.8	6.8	NA	6.3	5.9
26	unsat 50	00:15:25	3.4	3.1	1.0	3.8	2.3
29	sat 26	> 02:30:00	26.5	26.6	NA	21.8	9.7

3.2   Interpretation of Results

We noticed that Concur 9 2/node performs more poorly than Concur 5. This may seem quite surprising at first. However, we should keep in mind that BMC translation and SAT solving are very memory accesses consuming. Therefore, memory access can be a bottleneck when running two SAT instances on bi-processor workstations.

Heuristic tuning sometimes allows spectacular speedup for SAT solving (the only way we were able to achieve a result for 22). However, the overall improvement for SAT BMC, even when concurrently running several heuristics, is altogether marginal (though this approach could be mixed with the Concur approach).

Concur 7 and Concur 5 produce results that are similar, however, the Concur 3 results are significantly poorer. Therefore, the ideal configuration for our search (incremental bounded model checking with a maximal bound of 50) appears to be Concur 5.

Concur k (*i. e.* Concur 3, Concur 5, Concur 7) configurations may give more than linear[3] speedup (e.g., 11 rule 1 and 29). The difficulty of a SAT BMC search does not necessarily grow with the bound. For some rules, it is far more difficult to prove there are no satisfiable assignment for k-5 than to find a satisfiable assignment for k, when searching concurrently. On the other hand, for some models, if k is the smallest bound for which a satisfiable assignment can be found, it will be easier to find a satisfiable agreement for k+5 than for k. Because k is the length of the shortest counter-examples to the model, it is likely that there will be more counter-examples of a longer length, eg k+5, and so more satisfiable assignments.

In summary, Concur k configurations have the biggest speedup potential for models that fail (in a number of cycles less than the maximal bound). Most such models from our benchmark fail in less than 30 cycles. This explains why Concur 7 displays little improvement when compared to Concur 5. In order to exhibit better performance for Concur k with k greater than or equal to 7, we would have to run the SAT BMC with a greater maximal bound and probably a broader benchmark (with models failing within a greater number of cycles). As can be observed in Table 4, the Concur 5 and Concur 3 results are quite good, especially considering that these two configurations distribute their tasks in a straightforward manner on five and three nodes, respectively.

Table 4. The results are computed without the "NA" cases

	Concur 7	Concur 5	Concur3	5 heuristics
Global speedup (Sequential total time/total time)	> 3.40	> 3.40	> 2.78	> 1.14
Average speedup (average Sequential time/time)	> 4.26	> 4.13	> 2.49	> 1.29

4   Conclusions

We explained how we used the IBM Formal Verification Benchmark to prove that previous results on SAT tuning were too optimistic and to assess the efficiency of a straightforward distribution for day-to-day SAT bounded model checking. We

---

[3] With respect to the number of processors.

noted that a wider benchmark would allow even better and sounder assessments. As a result, we plan to make the IBM Formal Verification Benchmark library a living repository. We will add new design models in the future, to increase the benchmark diversity and keep it relevant in light of new technological advances.

Acknowledgment

The author wishes to thank Fabio Somenzi for his help on the IBM Formal Verification Benchmark translation to BLIF and, Cindy Eisner, Sharon Keidar, and Ofer Strichman for careful reviews and important comments of previous version of this paper.

A   The IBM Formal Verification Benchmark

With the increased use of formal verification, benchmarking new verification algorithms and tools against real-life test-cases is now a must in order to assess performance gains. However, industrial designs are generally highly proprietary; therefore, models generated from these designs are usually not published. This makes difficult to assess the results reported in papers from the industry, as their benchmarks are usually not available and it is not possible to compare the published results with those achieved by other engines. Additionally, formal verification algorithms described in academic papers are often difficult to assess in terms of performance, since they are usually not applied to "real-life" benchmarks.

We want to stress how difficult it is to assess the real practical value of more sophisticate theoretical results without proper benchmarking. In the past, benchmarking enabled significant technology improvements, such as those for BDD packages in [18]. In the same way, many major improvements to boolean satisfiability solvers were proven useful by experimental results [19]. This may appear trivial, however there are many examples in the literature where elaborated and complex algorithms are not evaluated in a satisfactory manner. From the author's experience, the claims of several papers could not be reproduced using the IBM Formal Verification Benchmark.

The IBM Formal Verification Benchmark library encompasses 37 declassified models, from 31 different hardware designs. The IBM Formal Verification benchmark library is available for academic users from the IBM Haifa verification projects web site [21].

The designs presented in the library are industrial designs that were verified by IBM teams. Each of the benchmark's 37 files contains:

- A group of one or more temporal formulas, collectively called "rule". To avoid language compatibility issues related to the specification language, the original PSL/Sugar [3,1] formulas were translated into very simple $G(p)$ formulas (still written in PSL/Sugar), which most model checkers can readily address.

– A design model in PSL/Sugar environment description layer format. Some variables were renamed and some simple reductions were applied to hide the original design intent.

The models presented are of different sizes (Cf. Table 5) and varying degrees of complexity. However, as shown in Table 6 and Table 3, the same problem can sometimes be easily solved by one verification engine and at the same time with difficulty for another engine. For this reason, we tried to use a variety of problems. This benchmark is available in PSL/Sugar [1] and in Sugar1 format [3]. It was also translated to BLIF[20] format. The CNF output of BMC, applied to the benchmark for several bounds, is available from [22]. Some of these CNFs were used for the SAT2003 and SAT2004 contests[11, 26].

Table 5. IBM Formal Verification Benchmark Circuits Details

Name	Variables	Gates	Formulas	Name	Variables	Gates	Formulas
IBM 01	94	3266	1	IBM 17-1	1582	29190	2
IBM 02-1	139	1699	5	IBM 17-2	1581	28807	2
IBM 02-2	135	1671	1	IBM 18	78	4768	1
IBM 02-3	177	1983	7	IBM 19	120	5557	1
IBM 03	109	2656	1	IBM 20	78	4805	1
IBM 04	222	5067	1	IBM 21	78	4768	1
IBM 05	309	8410	1	IBM 22	103	6451	1
IBM 06	132	3375	1	IBM 23	102	6259	1
IBM 07	438	1341	1	IBM 24-1	49048	125896	3
IBM 08	395	84886	1	IBM 24-2	44807	115151	2
IBM 09	232	2000	1	IBM 25	120	4501	1
IBM 10	218	8702	6	IBM 26	1713	9640	1
IBM 11	222	8987	3	IBM 27	42	999	1
IBM 12	224	1055	1	IBM 28	95	3303	1
IBM 13	1506	17459	27	IBM 29	90	2562	1
IBM 14	156	3066	2	IBM 30	180	6654	1
IBM 15	231	4884	1	IBM 31-1	224	2488	3
IBM 16-1	1163	21750	1	IBM 31-2	224	2488	2
IBM 16-2	1162	21674	6				

We present some sample results[4] achieved against this benchmark. To achieve these results, we used the Discovery engine, one of the RuleBase Classic [2] BDD engines. Each rule was run "from scratch" (i.e., without taking advantage of any pre-existing BDD orders). In real-life projects, the Discovery engine runs considerably faster when a good BDD order was found previously. This occurs because RuleBase can take advantage of rules previously run for this design, and get the best BDD order for a new rule. However, since the notion of "good order"

---

[4] These sample results were achieved with the RuleBase version available through the RuleBase University Program [25].

Table 6. Experimental Results – time out: 3 hours

Name	Discovery	Name	Discovery
IBM 01	0:04:29	IBM 17-1	time out
IBM 02-1	0:02:04	IBM 17-2	time out
IBM 02-2	0:00:30	IBM 18	0:02:49
IBM 02-3	0:01:23	IBM 19	0:05:46
IBM 03	0:01:26	IBM 20	0:08:35
IBM 04	0:05:25	IBM 21	0:04:14
IBM 05	0:19:09	IBM 22	1:40:22
IBM 06	0:07:31	IBM 23	0:09:32
IBM 07	0:01:05	IBM 24-1	time out
IBM 08	0:23:38	IBM 24-2	time out
IBM 09	0:00:06	IBM 25	time out
IBM 10	2:48:16	IBM 26	time out
IBM 11	1:32:45	IBM 27	0:00:18
IBM 12	time out	IBM 28	1:34:52
IBM 13	0:03:44	IBM 29	0:15:18
IBM 14	time out	IBM 30	time out
IBM 15	3:08:01	IBM 31-1	time out
IBM 16-1	time out	IBM 31-2	time out
IBM 16-2	0:08:15		

is not very precise, and because an accurate description of such an order would comprise its entire listing, we only present results of runs without pre-existing orders.

In fact, RuleBase includes a set of engines of significantly higher performance than those referenced here.

We used an IBM Cascades PC with a Pentium III 700 MHz microprocessor running Red Hat Linux Advanced Server Release 2.1AS (Pensacola). The results are presented in Table 6 in an hh:mm:ss format.

References

1. Accelera. PSL/Sugar LRM. http://www.eda.org/vfv/
2. I. Beer *et al.* RuleBase: An Industry Oriented Formal Verification Tool. In *33rd Design Automation Conference, DAC 96. ACM/IEEE*, 1996.
3. I. Beer *et al.* The Temporal Logic Sugar. In *Computer Aided Verification, Proceedings of the 13th International Conference, CAV 2001. LNCS 2102*, July 2001.
4. A. Biere *et al.* Symbolic Model Checking Without BDDs. In *Proceedings of the workshop on Tools and Algorithms for Construction and Analysis of Systems (TACAS99)*, 1999.
5. A. Biere et al. Bounded Model Checking. In *Vol. 58 of Advances in Computers. Academic Press (pre-print)*, 2003.
6. S. Cook. The Complexity of Theorem Proving Procedures. In *Proceeding, Third Annual ACM Symp. on the Theory of Computing*, 1971.

7. M. Davis, G. Logemann, and D. Loveland. A machine program for theorem proving. In *Journal of the ACM, 5(7)*, 1962.
8. N. Een, N. Sorensson. An Extensible SAT-solver, SAT 2003.
9. E. Emerson and C. Lei. Modalities for Model Checking: Branching Time Strikes Back. In *Science of Computer Programming, 8:275-306*, 1986.
10. E. Goldberg, Y. Novikov. BerkMin: a Fast and Robust SAT-solver In *Proceedings of the Design, Automation and Test in Europe. DATE'02.*, 2002.
11. D. Le Berre, L. Simon. The essentials of the SAT 2003 competition. In *Proceeding of the Sixth International Confetence on Theory and Applications od Satisfiability Testing (SAT 2003)*, LNCS 2919, pp 468-487, 2003.
12. M. Moskewicz *et al.* Chaff: Engineering an Efficient SAT Solver. In *38th Design Automation Conference, page 530-535. ACM/IEEE*, 2001.
13. A. Nadel. JeruSAT satisfiablility solver. Available on-line. http://www.geocities.com/alikn78/
14. A. Pnueli. A Temporal Logic of Concurrent Programs. In *Theoretical Computer Science*, Vol 13, pp 45-60, 1981.
15. O. Shacham, E. Zarpas, Tuning the VSIDS Decision Heuristic for Bounded Model Checking. In *Proceeding of the 4th International Workshop on Microprocessor, Test and Verification*, IEEE Computer Society, Austin, Mai 2003.
16. J. Silva, K. Sakallah. Grasp - a New Search Algorithm for Satisfiability. In *Technical Report TR-CSE-292996, University of Michigan*, 1996.
17. O. Strichman. Tuning SAT Checkers for Bounded Model Checking. In *Computer-Aided Verification: 12th International Conference*, Lecture Notes in Computer Science, 1855. Springer-Verlag, 2000.
18. B. Yang et al. A Performance Study of BDD-Bases Model Checking. In *Formal Methods in Computer-Aided Design: 2nd International Conference*, Lecture Notes in Computer Science, 1522. Springer-Verlag, 1998.
19. L. Zhang and S. Malik The Quest for Efficient Boolean Satisfiability Solvers, in *Proceedings of 14th Conference on Computer Aided Verification (CAV2002)*, Copenhagen, Denmark, July 2002
20. Berkley Logic Interechange Format (BLIF). University of California, Berkley, 1992. http://www-cad.eecs.berkeley.edu/Respep/Research/vis/usrDoc.html
21. IBM Formal Verification Benchmark Library. http://www.haifa.il.ibm.com/projects/verification/RB_Homepage/ fvbenchmarks.html
22. CNF Benchmarks from IBM Formal Verification Benchmarks Library. http://www.haifa.il.ibm.com/projects/verification/RB_Homepage/ bmcbenchmarks.html
23. IBM CNF Benchmark Illustration. http://www.haifa.il.ibm.com/projects/verification/RB_Homepage/ bmcbenchmarks_illustrations.html
24. Web version of the RuleBase User Manual. http://www.haifa.il.ibm.com/projects/verification/RB_Homepage/
25. RuleBase University Program. http://www.haifa.il.ibm.com/projects/verification/Formal_Methods-Home/university.html
26. SAT2004 contest. http://satlive.org/SATCompetition/2004/

Simple Bounded LTL Model Checking

Timo Latvala[1,*], Armin Biere[2], Keijo Heljanko[1,**], and Tommi Junttila[3,***]

[1] Laboratory for Theoretical Computer Science
Helsinki University of Technology
P.O. Box 5400, FI-02015 HUT, Finland
{Timo.Latvala,Keijo.Heljanko}@hut.fi
[2] ETH Zürich, Computer Systems Institute
CH-8092 Zürich, Switzerland
biere@inf.ethz.ch
[3] ITC-IRST
Via Sommarive 18, 38050 Povo, Trento, Italy
junttila@irst.itc.it

Abstract. We present a new and very simple translation of the bounded model checking problem which is linear both in the size of the formula and the length of the bound. The resulting CNF-formula has a linear number of variables *and* clauses.

Keywords: bounded model checking, LTL, linear translation, NuSMV.

1 Introduction

Bounded model checking [1] (BMC) is a technique for finding bugs in finite state system designs violating properties specified in linear temporal logic (LTL). The method works by mapping a *bounded* model checking problem to the satisfiability problem (SAT). Given a propositional formula encoding a Kripke structure M representing the system, an LTL formula ψ and a bound k, a propositional formula $|[M, \psi, k]|$ is created that is satisfiable if and only if the Kripke structure M contains a counterexample to ψ of length k.

BMC has established itself as a complementary method to symbolic model checking methods based on (ordered) binary decision diagrams (BDDs). The biggest advantage of BMC compared to BDDs is its space efficiency; there are some Boolean functions which cannot be succinctly encoded as a BDD. BMC also produces counterexamples of minimal length, which eases their interpretation and understanding for debugging purposes. However, predicting the cases where BMC is more efficient compared to

---

* Work supported by the Helsinki Graduate School in Computer Science, the Academy of Finland (project 53695), and the Nokia Foundation.

** Work partially supported by FET project ADVANCE contract No IST-1999-29082, EPSRC grant 93346/01 (An Automata Theoretic Approach to Software Model Checking), and the Academy of Finland (project 53695 and grant for research work abroad).

*** This work has been sponsored by the CALCULEMUS! IHP-RTN EC project, contract code HPRN-CT-2000-00102, and has thus benefited of the financial contribution of the Commission through the IHP programme.

A.J. Hu and A.K. Martin (Eds.): FMCAD 2004, LNCS 3312, pp. 186–200, 2004.
© Springer-Verlag Berlin Heidelberg 2004

BDD-based methods is difficult [2]. Furthermore, BMC is an incomplete method unless we can determine a value for the bound k which guarantees that no counterexample has been missed. Several papers [1, 3, 4] have investigated techniques for computing this bound.

The two main ways of improving the performance of BMC is either to improve solver technology or to modify the encoding of the problem to SAT. Improvements of the second kind usually rely on the appealing idea that simpler is better. The intuition is that an encoding which results in fever variables and clauses is usually easier to solve. We present a new simple encoding for the BMC problem which is linear in the bound, the system description (i.e. the size of the transition relation as a propositional formula) and the size of the specification as an LTL formula. The resulting propositional formula has both a *linear number of variables and clauses*.

We have experimentally evaluated our new encoding. Our experiments compare the sizes of the encodings and the required time to solve the instances.

2   Bounded Model Checking

In bounded model checking we consider finite sequences of states in the system, while LTL formulas specify the infinite behaviour of the system. The key observation by Biere et al. [1] was that a finite sequence can still represent an infinite path if it contains a loop. An infinite path $\pi = s_0 s_1 s_2 \ldots$ is a (k, l)-loop if there exists integers l and k such that $s_{l-1} = s_k$ and $\pi = (s_0 s_1 \ldots s_{l-1})(s_l s_{l+1} \ldots s_k)^\omega$ (we also use the term k-loop). A bounded path $s_0 s_1 \ldots s_k$ of length k can either have $k+1$ unique states or represent an infinite path with a (k, l)-loop if $s_k = s_{l-1}$ for some $1 \leq l \leq k$. This can actually be interpreted in two different ways (corresponding to the same infinite path π). Either the back edge of the loop is from s_{k-1} to s_{l-1} (the dashed back edge in Fig. 1) or the back edge is from s_k to s_l (the solid back edge in Fig. 1). The new *loop shape* depicted on the right side of Fig. 1 requires $k > 0$ for k-loops, which we will silently assume for the rest of the paper. This loop shape allows a more compact translation than the one in [1], replacing the $k+1$ copies in the original translation for closing the loop by k comparisons between bit vectors encoding states.

When k is fixed there are $k+1$ different loop possibilities for a bounded path. There are k different (k, l)-loops and it is of course also possible that no loop exists. The basic idea of Biere et al. [1] was to write a formula which is satisfiable iff the path is a model of the negation of the LTL specification, for each of these cases. The complete translation simply joins the cases in one big disjunction.

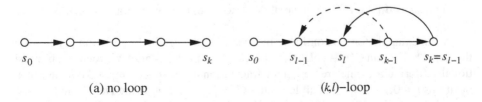

(a) no loop (k, l)-loop

Fig. 1. The two possible cases for a bounded path

Example. Consider a Kripke structure M and the formula $\psi = \mathbf{GF}\neg p$, "infinitely often not p". The negation of the formula is $\mathbf{FG}p$, "eventually always p". We will write a formula which encodes all possible witnesses of length k for the formula $\mathbf{FG}p$. First, we need a formula that captures all paths of length k. Let $T(s,s')$ be the transition relation of M as a propositional formula and $I(s)$ a predicate over the state variables defining the initial states. A path of length k is encoded by the formula:

$$|[M]|_k := I(s_0) \wedge \bigwedge_{i=1}^{k} T(s_{i-1}, s_i). \tag{1}$$

Since the formula we are considering requires an infinite witness we can skip the no loop case. For fixed k and l we use the following rules to build the formula $_l|[\neg\psi]|_k$ for capturing witnesses of $\neg\psi$, adapted from [1] to our new loop shape (the dashed back edge):

$$_l|[\mathbf{F}\phi]|_k^i := \bigvee_{j=min(i,l-1)}^{k-1} {}_l|[\phi]|_k^j \qquad\qquad _l|[\mathbf{G}\phi]|_k^i := \bigwedge_{j=min(i,l-1)}^{k-1} {}_l|[\phi]|_k^j$$

Thus $_l|[\psi]|_k^0 = \bigvee_{i=0}^{k} \bigwedge_{j=min(i,l-1)}^{k-1} p(s_j)$. For each possible (k,l)-loop we must express the condition $L_l := (s_k = s_{l-1})$. Here the states s_i are bit vectors and equality $s_i = s_j$ is defined by $\bigwedge_{m=1}^{n} s_i[m] \Leftrightarrow s_j[m]$, assuming the vectors have n elements and the m:th element is denoted $s_i[m]$. The final formula which is satisfiable iff there exists a counterexample of length $k > 0$ is:

$$|[M]|_k \wedge \left(\bigvee_{l=1}^{k} \left(L_l \wedge {}_l|[\psi]|_k^0 \right) \right) = I(s_0) \wedge \bigwedge_{i=1}^{k} T(s_{i-1}, s_i) \wedge$$

$$\bigvee_{l=1}^{k} \left(L_l \wedge \bigvee_{i=0}^{k-1} \bigwedge_{j=min(i,l-1)}^{k-1} p(s_j) \right)$$

Without sharing the formula is obviously cubic in k. Let us focus on the LTL part, the big underlined disjunction over $l = 1, \ldots, k$. A first level of sharing can be obtained by associating the inner conjunction to the right, resulting in a quadratic DAG representation. Using the same general idea, the inner disjunction can be associated to the left. The overall size becomes linear. As an example see the circuit in Fig. 2 for $k = 4$. It can still be further optimised by applying $a \vee (a \wedge b) \equiv a$, which essentially results in removing the middle column of or-gates. However, as has been noted in [5], using associativity in synthesis is difficult and in general does not avoid the worst case, which is at least cubic.

As an example for the non-linear behaviour of the original translation [1] consider the (E)LTL formula $G(r \to (p\mathbf{U}q))$. In the result of the translation we focus on propositional subformulas, which represent the translation of the inner temporal operator at all positions $i = 0, \ldots, k-1$ and all loop starts $l = 1, \ldots, k$. Following Def. 13 in [1] these formulas are sum of product forms. Each product is a cube of the predicates p and q at various states. In Fig. 3 we list all cubes that occur as subformulas for $k = 4$. Each cube

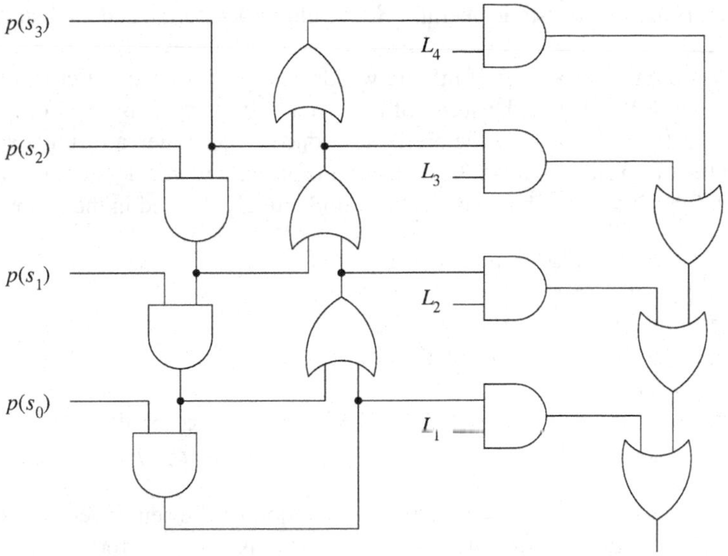

Fig. 2. Circuit encoding for the LTL formula $\mathbf{FG}p$ for $k = 4$

q			
q			p
q		p	p
q	p	p	p

	q		
	q		p
	q	p	p
p	q	p	p
p	q		p
p	q		

		q	
	p	q	
p	p	q	
p	p	q	p
	p	q	p
		q	p

			q
		p	q
	p	p	q
p	p	p	q

Fig. 3. Non-linear number of cubes in the translation of $G(r \rightarrow (p\mathbf{U}q))$ for $k = 4$

is represented by one row of the four matrices in Fig. 3. Each of the matrices collects those cubes where q holds at the same position resp. in the same state.

The number of cubes is at least quadratic in k. For each position j where q holds, the p sequences can be shared. Therefore an upper bound on the overall size is $O(k^3)$ and not $O(k^4)$. The exact size is hard to calculate, but with $\Omega(k^2)$ different cubes in the example, the size has a quadratic lower bound as well.

2.1 LTL

An LTL formula φ is defined over a set of atomic propositions AP. An LTL formula has the following syntax:

1. $\psi \in AP$ is an LTL formula.
2. If ψ and φ are LTL formulae then so are $\neg\psi$, $\mathbf{X}\psi$, $\psi\mathbf{U}\varphi$, $\psi\mathbf{R}\varphi$, $\psi \wedge \varphi$, and $\psi \vee \varphi$.

The operators are the next-time operator $\mathbf{X}$, the until operator $\mathbf{U}$, and its dual the release operator $\mathbf{R}$.

Each formula defines a set of infinite words (models) over 2^{AP}. Let $\pi \in (2^{AP})^\omega$ be an infinite word. We denote the suffix of a word $\pi = \sigma_0\sigma_1\sigma_2\ldots$ by $\pi^i = \sigma_i\sigma_{i+1}\sigma_{i+2}\ldots$ where $\sigma_i \in 2^{AP}$, and π_i denotes the prefix $\pi_i = \sigma_0\sigma_1\ldots\sigma_i$. When a formula ψ defines a word π at time i this is denoted $\pi^i \models \psi$. The set of infinite words defined by a formula ψ is $\{\pi \in (2^{AP})^\omega \mid \pi \models \psi\}$. The relation '$\models$' is inductively defined in the following way.

$$\pi^i \models \psi \quad \Leftrightarrow \psi \in \sigma_i \text{ for } \psi \in AP.$$
$$\pi^i \models \neg\psi \quad \Leftrightarrow \pi \not\models \psi.$$
$$\pi^i \models \psi \vee \varphi \Leftrightarrow \pi^i \models \psi \text{ or } \pi^i \models \varphi.$$
$$\pi^i \models \psi \wedge \varphi \Leftrightarrow \pi^i \models \psi \text{ and } \pi^i \models \varphi.$$
$$\pi^i \models \mathbf{X}\psi \quad \Leftrightarrow \pi^{i+1} \models \psi.$$
$$\pi^i \models \psi\mathbf{U}\varphi \Leftrightarrow \exists n \geq i \text{ such that } \pi^n \models \varphi \text{ and } \pi^j \models \psi \text{ for all } i \leq j < n.$$
$$\pi^i \models \psi\mathbf{R}\varphi \Leftrightarrow \forall n \geq i, \pi^n \models \varphi \text{ or } \pi^j \models \psi \text{ for some } i \leq j < n.$$

If $\pi^0 \models \psi$ we simply write $\pi \models \psi$. This presentation of the semantics is intentionally redundant. The additional operators allow us to transform any formula to a *positive normal form*. Formulas in positive normal form have negations only in front of atomic propositions. Using the dualities $\psi\mathbf{U}\varphi \equiv \neg(\neg\psi\mathbf{R}\neg\varphi)$, $\neg\mathbf{X}\psi \equiv \mathbf{X}\neg\psi$ and De Morgan's law, any formula can be transformed without blowup to positive normal form by pushing in the negations. All formulas considered in this paper are assumed to be in positive normal form. We also make use of the standard abbreviations $\top \equiv p \vee \neg p$ for some arbitrary $p \in AP$, $\bot \equiv \neg\top$, $\mathbf{F}\psi \equiv \top\mathbf{U}\psi$ ('finally'), and $\mathbf{G}\psi \equiv \bot\mathbf{R}\psi \equiv \neg\mathbf{F}\neg\psi$ ('globally').

A formula holds in a Kripke structure if all paths of the Kripke structure are accepted by the formula. Formally, a Kripke structure is a tuple $M = (S, T, s_0, L)$, where S is a set of states, $T \subseteq S \times S$ the transition relation, $s_0 \in S$ the initial state, and $L: S \to 2^{AP}$ a function labelling all states with atomic propositions. We require that the transition relation is total. A path of the Kripke structure is a sequence of states $\xi = s_0s_1s_2\ldots$ where s_0 is the initial state and for all $i \geq 0$ we have that $(s_i, s_{i+1}) \in T$. The corresponding word π of a path $\xi = s_0s_1s_2\ldots$ is $\pi = L(s_0)L(s_1)L(s_2)\ldots$. We write $M \models \psi$, if for all paths $\xi = s_0s_1s_2\ldots$ of M the corresponding word π is defined by ψ, i.e. $\pi \models \psi$.

Bounded model checking uses a *bounded semantics of LTL* which safely under approximates the normal semantics. It allows us to use a bounded prefix $\pi_k = s_0s_1\ldots s_k$ of an infinite path π to check the formula. The semantics does a case split depending on if the infinite π is a k-loop or not. Biere et al. [1] have shown that if a formula ψ is true in the bounded semantics, denoted $\pi \models_k \psi$, this implies that $\pi \models \psi$. The definition below assumes the formula is in positive normal form.

Definition 1. *([1, 6]) Given an infinite path π and bound $k \in \mathbb{N}$, a formula ψ holds in a path π with bound k iff $\pi \models_k^0 \psi$ where*

$$\pi \models_k^i p \qquad \Leftrightarrow p \in s_i \text{ for } p \in AP$$
$$\pi \models_k^i \neg p \qquad \Leftrightarrow p \notin s_i \text{ for } p \in AP$$

$$\pi \models_k^i \psi_1 \wedge \psi_2 \Leftrightarrow \pi \models_k^i \psi_1 \text{ and } \pi \models_k^i \psi_2$$
$$\pi \models_k^i \psi_1 \vee \psi_2 \Leftrightarrow \pi \models_k^i \psi_1 \text{ or } \pi \models_k^i \psi_2$$

$$\pi \models_k^i \mathbf{X}\psi \quad \Leftrightarrow \quad \begin{cases} \pi \models_k^{i+1} \psi & \pi \text{ is a } k\text{-loop} \\ \pi \models_k^{i+1} \psi \wedge (i < k) & \text{otherwise} \end{cases}$$

$$\pi \models_k^i \psi_1 \mathbf{U} \psi_2 \quad \Leftrightarrow \quad \begin{cases} \exists j \geq i : \pi \models_k^j \psi_2 \wedge \forall n, i \leq n < j : \pi \models_k^n \psi_1 & k\text{-loop} \\ \exists j, i \leq j \leq k : \pi \models_k^j \psi_2 \wedge \forall n, i \leq n < j : \pi \models_k^n \psi_1 & \text{otherwise} \end{cases}$$

$$\pi \models_k^i \psi_1 \mathbf{R} \psi_2 \quad \Leftrightarrow \quad \begin{cases} \forall j \geq i : \pi \not\models_k^j \psi_2 \implies \exists n, i \leq n < j : \pi \models_k^n \psi_1 & k\text{-loop} \\ \exists j, i \leq j \leq k : \pi \models_k^j \psi_1 \wedge \forall n, i \leq n \leq j : \pi \models_k^n \psi_2 & \text{otherwise} \end{cases}$$

3 A New Translation

Our new translation takes advantage of the fact that for lasso-shaped Kripke structures the semantics of LTL and CTL coincide [7, 8]. The intuition is that when each state has one successor (i.e. the path is lasso-shaped) the semantics of the path quantifiers **A** and **E** of CTL agree. An LTL formula can therefore be evaluated in a lasso-shaped Kripke structure by a CTL model checker by prefixing each temporal operator by an **E** path quantifier [8], which results in a CTL formula[1]. We can thus use the fixpoint characterisation of CTL model checking as a starting point for our translation. The new translation also separates the concern of if the path has a (k, l)-loop from the semantics to an independent part of the translation.

The intuition behind our translation is the following. Following [1], we generate a propositional formula which generates all paths of length k. A part is added to the translation which makes a choice between the following possibilities. Either (a) there is no loop, or (b) there is a loop, i.e. a state s_{l-1} such that $s_k = s_{l-1}$ for some index $1 \leq l \leq k$. The choice and additional constraints under which the choice can be made are implemented as follows. Fresh variables l_i, which do not depend on the state variables in any way, are introduced with appropriate constraints such that if l_i is true then $s_{i-1} = s_k$. We allow at most one l_i to be true in a satisfying truth assignment. This results in a lasso-shaped Kripke structure or a simple finite path if no l_i is true. Allowing simple finite paths is an optimisation and does not affect correctness, but can in some cases (formulas with safety-counterexamples) result in shorter counterexamples. Model checking is accomplished by generating propositional formulas to evaluate the greatest and least fixpoints as required by the implicit CTL formula.

Let M be the Kripke structure of the system and $T(s, s')$ the symbolic transition relation. We consider an unrolling of states $s_0 s_1 \ldots s_k$. Each s_i is a vector of state variables. The unrolling is obtained by equation (1). We require that the Kripke structure is lasso-shaped or a finite path. The variables l_i can seen as selecting one (or possibly none) of the possible (k, l)-loops. This is accomplished by the following constraints.

$$\|[LoopConstraints]\|_k \Leftrightarrow Loop_k \wedge AtMostOne_k$$

$$Loop_k \Leftrightarrow \bigwedge_{i=1}^k (l_i \Rightarrow (s_{i-1} = s_k))$$

$$AtMostOne_k \Leftrightarrow \bigwedge_{i=1}^k (SmallerExists_i \Rightarrow \neg l_i)$$

$$SmallerExists_1 \Leftrightarrow \bot$$

$$SmallerExists_{i+1} \Leftrightarrow SmallerExists_i \vee l_i, \text{ where } 0 < i \leq k$$

---

[1] Naturally, we could also use the **A** path quantifier.

In contrast to [1], our definitions also allow the no loop case even if the path has a (k,l)-loop.

The until operator $\mathbf{E}(\psi_1 \mathbf{U} \psi_2)$ can be evaluated by computing the least fixed point $\mathbf{E}(\psi_1 \mathbf{U} \psi_2) = \mu Z.\psi_2 \vee (\psi_1 \wedge \mathbf{EX} Z)$ (see e.g. [9]) while the release operator $\mathbf{E}(\psi_1 \mathbf{R} \psi_2)$ can be evaluated by computing the greatest fixpoint $\mathbf{E}(\psi_1 \mathbf{R} \psi_2) = \nu Z.\psi_2 \wedge (\psi_1 \vee \mathbf{EX} Z)$. The fixpoints are evaluated by first computing an approximation $\langle\langle \cdot \rangle\rangle_i$ for each state and subformula. After this the results of the approximation are used to compute the final result $\|[\cdot]\|_i$. We evaluate the fixpoints for s_i where $0 \leq i \leq k+1$. The last case $k+1$ is added to make the connections to fixpoints easier to see from the translation.

:=	$i \leq k$	$i = k+1$
$\|[p]\|_i$	p_i	$\bigvee_{j=1}^{k} (l_j \wedge p_j)$
$\|[\neg p]\|_i$	$\neg p_i$	$\bigvee_{j=1}^{k} (l_j \wedge \neg p_j)$
$\|[\mathbf{X}\psi]\|_i$	$\|[\psi]\|_{i+1}$	$\bigvee_{j=1}^{k} \left(l_j \wedge \|[\psi]\|_{j+1} \right)$
$\|[\psi\mathbf{U}\varphi]\|_i$	$\|[\varphi]\|_i \vee (\|[\psi]\|_i \wedge \|[\psi\mathbf{U}\varphi]\|_{i+1})$	$\bigvee_{j=1}^{k} \left(l_j \wedge \langle\langle \psi\mathbf{U}\varphi \rangle\rangle_j \right)$
$\|[\psi\mathbf{R}\varphi]\|_i$	$\|[\varphi]\|_i \wedge (\|[\psi]\|_i \vee \|[\psi\mathbf{R}\varphi]\|_{i+1})$	$\bigvee_{j=1}^{k} \left(l_j \wedge \langle\langle \psi\mathbf{R}\varphi \rangle\rangle_j \right)$
$\langle\langle \psi\mathbf{U}\varphi \rangle\rangle_i$	$\|[\varphi]\|_i \vee (\|[\psi]\|_i \wedge \langle\langle \psi\mathbf{U}\varphi \rangle\rangle_{i+1})$	$\bot$
$\langle\langle \psi\mathbf{R}\varphi \rangle\rangle_i$	$\|[\varphi]\|_i \wedge (\|[\psi]\|_i \vee \langle\langle \psi\mathbf{R}\varphi \rangle\rangle_{i+1})$	$\top$

The auxiliary translation $\langle\langle \cdot \rangle\rangle$ which computes the approximations for the fixpoints is defined in the last two rows.

Let us consider the case $\psi = \psi_1 \mathbf{R} \psi_2$. We initialise $\langle\langle \psi \rangle\rangle_{k+1}$ to true since we are approximating a greatest fixpoint. When $0 \leq i \leq k$, the auxiliary translation $\langle\langle \psi \rangle\rangle_i$ is the normal fixpoint definition of the release operator. The computed approximation of the fixpoint $\langle\langle \psi \rangle\rangle$ is used to initialise $\|[\psi]\|_{k+1}$ with the value of $\langle\langle \psi \rangle\rangle_l$, the value of the approximation in the successor of s_k, when we are dealing with a (k,l)-loop. Finally, $\|[\psi]\|_i$, where $0 \leq i \leq k$, computes the accurate values for each state s_i, again using the standard fixpoint characterisation of release.

Given a Kripke structure M, an LTL formula ψ, and a bound k, the complete encoding as a propositional formula is given by $\|[M,\psi,k]\|$.

$$\|[M,\psi,k]\| = \|[M]\|_k \wedge \|[LoopConstraints]\|_k \wedge \|[\psi]\|_0$$

Theorem 1. *Given a finite Kripke structure M, a bound $k \in \mathbb{N}$ and an LTL formula ψ, M has a path π with $\pi \models_k \psi$ iff $\|[M,\psi,k]\|$ is satisfiable.*

Proof. The proof sketch follows the argument at the beginning of this Section. For both directions we can assume that π is given and is a path of M. Further assume that π is a (k,l) loop. The other case is obvious from the definitions. The bounded semantics on a (k,l) loop coincides with the unbounded semantics. What remains to be proven is that the LTL part of the translation when partially instantiated with π is satisfiable iff $\pi \models \psi$.

Instead of checking whether ψ holds along π we check the corresponding CTL formula ψ' on π interpreted as a Kripke structure itself. The CTL formula ψ' is obtained from ψ by prefixing every temporal operator with the existential path quantifier

E. The ECTL formula ψ' can be translated into an alternation free formula of the modal mu-calculus, which in turn can be transformed into a set of mutual recursive boolean equations with fixpoint semantics as in [10]. The event-driven linear fix point algorithm of [10] is then reformulated symbolically as a non-recursive boolean equation system, which is equivalent to our definition of $||[\cdot]||$. $\square$

As in Theorem 9 of [1] we can lift our Theorem 1 to the unbounded semantics. An upper bound on k would then be of the order $O(|\psi| \cdot |M| \cdot 2^{|\psi|})$. This is easy to show using the automata-theoretic approach to model checking.However, our main result is the following:

Theorem 2. $||[M, \psi, k]||$ *seen as Boolean circuit is linear in* $|T|$, $|\psi|$, *and* k. *More precisely, it is of the size* $O(|I| + ((|T| + |\psi|) \cdot k))$, *where* $|I|$ *and* $|T|$ *are the sizes of the initial state predicate and the transition relation seen as Boolean circuits, respectively*[2].

Proof. Obviously the translation of $LoopConstraints_k$ is linear w.r.t. k, since both $Loop_k$ and $AtMostOne_k$ loop once over k. We will argue the linearity of $||[\cdot]||$ using the until-case, as it is the most complex. For each $0 \le i \le k$, the translation adds a constant number of constraints. The case $i = k + 1$ adds k constraints that refer to $\langle\langle \mathbf{U} \rangle\rangle_i$. This does not result in a quadratic formula, even though $\langle\langle \mathbf{U} \rangle\rangle_i$ is linear, because $\langle\langle \mathbf{U} \rangle\rangle_i$ can clearly be shared between the constraints. Linearity of $\langle\langle \mathbf{U} \rangle\rangle_i$ is obvious as only a constant number of constraints are added for each $0 \le i \le k + 1$. $\square$

3.1   Optimising the Translation

A simple way to optimise the translation is to introduce special translations for certain derived operators. We have developed special translations for $\mathbf{G}\psi, \mathbf{F}\psi, \mathbf{GF}\psi$ and $\mathbf{FG}\psi$. These formulas have similarities which can also be seen in the way they share translations in the case $i = k + 1$. Note that the translations of $||[\mathbf{GF}\psi]||_i$ and $||[\mathbf{FG}\psi]||_i$ are only dependent on the case $i = k + 1$ since the semantics of the formulas only places requirements on states inside the loop.

:=	$i \le k$	$i = k + 1$
$\|[\mathbf{G}\psi]\|_i$	$\|[\varphi]\|_i \wedge \|[\mathbf{G}\psi]\|_{i+1}$	$\bigvee_{j=1}^{k} \left(l_j \wedge \langle\langle \mathbf{G}\psi \rangle\rangle_j \right)$
$\|[\mathbf{F}\psi]\|_i$	$\|[\varphi]\|_i \vee \|[\mathbf{F}\psi]\|_{i+1}$	$\bigvee_{j=1}^{k} \left(l_j \wedge \langle\langle \mathbf{F}\psi \rangle\rangle_j \right)$
$\|[\mathbf{GF}\psi]\|_i$	$\|[\mathbf{GF}\psi]\|_{k+1}$	$\bigvee_{j=1}^{k} \left(l_j \wedge \langle\langle \mathbf{F}\psi \rangle\rangle_j \right)$
$\|[\mathbf{FG}\psi]\|_i$	$\|[\mathbf{FG}\psi]\|_{k+1}$	$\bigvee_{j=1}^{k} \left(l_j \wedge \langle\langle \mathbf{G}\psi \rangle\rangle_j \right)$
$\langle\langle \mathbf{G}\psi \rangle\rangle_i$	$\|[\varphi]\|_i \wedge \langle\langle \mathbf{G}\psi \rangle\rangle_{i+1}$	$\top$
$\langle\langle \mathbf{F}\psi \rangle\rangle_i$	$\|[\varphi]\|_i \vee \langle\langle \mathbf{F}\psi \rangle\rangle_{i+1}$	$\bot$

The translations for the above derived operators can be further optimised at the cost of introducing $k + 1$ additional variables. However, the new variables are functionally dependent on the variables l_i and are shared by all subformulas using them. The variables

---

[2] This bound applies to both to the number of gates and the number of wire connections between the gates of the Boolean circuit in question.

InLoop$_j$, where $0 < j \le k$, express the fact that the state s_j is in the loop selected by the l_i variables. Additionally, we introduce the variable *LoopExists* which is true iff the path $s_0 s_1 \ldots s_k$ has a (k,l)-loop. In other words, *LoopExists* is false iff π_k is treated as a simple path without a loop. This is encoded by the following definitions.

$$InLoop_{i+1} \Leftrightarrow InLoop_i \vee l_{i+1} \text{ for } 0 < i < k$$

$$InLoop_1 \Leftrightarrow l_1$$

$$LoopExists \Leftrightarrow InLoop_k$$

With the *InLoop$_i$* variables we can eliminate the need for the auxiliary translation $\langle\langle\cdot\rangle\rangle$ for the derived operators. This simplifies the translation in most cases. The change in the translation is small as only the case $i = k + 1$ changes. Sharing also occurs between the translation for different operators as the translations for $\mathbf{G}\psi$ and $\mathbf{FG}\psi$, and for $\mathbf{F}\psi$ and $\mathbf{GF}\psi$ are the same.

$$|[\mathbf{G}\psi]|_{k+1} = |[\mathbf{FG}\psi]|_{k+1} = LoopExists \wedge \bigwedge_{i=1}^{k} \left(\neg InLoop_i \vee |[\psi]|_i\right)$$

$$|[\mathbf{F}\psi]|_{k+1} = |[\mathbf{GF}\psi]|_{k+1} = \bigvee_{i=1}^{k} \left(InLoop_i \wedge |[\psi]|_i\right)$$

3.2   Fairness

In many cases we wish to restrict the possible executions of the system to disallow executions which are unrealistic or impossible in the physical system. The standard way is to add fairness constraints to the model in order to only obtain interesting counterexamples.

There are a few well-known notions of fairness. *Justice* (weak fairness) requires that certain conditions are true infinitely often. *Compassion* (strong fairness) requires that if certain conditions are true infinitely often then certain other conditions must also hold infinitely often.

Let $\{J_1, \ldots, J_j\}$ be a set of Boolean predicates over the state variables which define the conditions that should be true infinitely often. Justice can then be expressed as the LTL formula

$$\mathcal{J} = \bigwedge_{i=1}^{j} \mathbf{GF} J_i.$$

Similarly, compassion can be expressed as an LTL formula. A set of pairs of Boolean predicates $\{(L_1, U_1), \ldots, (L_c, U_c)\}$ over the state variables define the compassion sets. Compassion is defined by the formula

$$C = \bigwedge_{i=1}^{c} \left(\mathbf{GF} L_i \Rightarrow \mathbf{GF} U_i\right).$$

We include the fairness constraints in the specification. Thus, instead of model checking the formula ψ, we check the formula $\mathcal{J} \wedge C \rightarrow \psi$. Since our propositional encoding of LTL formulas is linear, our overhead for handling fairness is linear in the number of fairness constraints.

4   Related Work

This work can be seen as a continuation of the work done in [11]. There the bounded model checking problem for LTL is translated into the problem of finding a stable model of a normal logic program (another NP-complete problem, see references in [11]) of essentially (modulo a constant) the same size as the translation presented here. The main differences to that work are the following. (i) The translation of [11] uses the close correspondence between the stable model semantics with the notion of a least fixpoint of a set of Boolean equations. The "formula variable dependency graphs" of the translation of [11] are in fact cyclic, while in this work they are acyclic. Seeing the translation of [11] as a propositional formula would result in a translation which is *not* sound. By using the correspondence between least fixpoints and stable models the translation for until and release formulas in [11] do not require the auxiliary translations $\langle\langle\cdot\rangle\rangle$. Thus the translation of [11] had to be significantly changed in order to use SAT. Additionally, the best known automatic translation of the stable model problem to SAT is non-linear [12]. (ii) The translation in [11] employs a different system modelling formalism, which allows for partial order semantics based optimisations. (iii) Moreover, the translation in [11] also allows for deadlocking systems with LTL interpreted over finite paths in the case of a deadlock, a feature left for further work in this paper. (iv) Finally, the implementation presented in this work is new, and based on the NuSMV2 [13] system.

Others have also considered the problem of improving the BMC encoding [5, 6, 4]. Cimatti et al. [5] analyse the original encoding [1] and suggest several optimisa- tions. For instance, they propose a linear encoding for formulas of the form **GF**p. Their translation is, however, not linear in general. Frisch et al. [6] approach the translation problem by using a normal form of LTL and take advantage of the properties of the normal form. Their procedure modifies the original model and is similar to symbolic tableau-style approaches for LTL model checking. According to their experiments their approach produces smaller encodings than [5]. However, their encoding is also non- linear in the general case. The non-linearity occurs at least in those cases when model checking a formula ψ such that after converting $\neg\psi$ to positive normal form it contains until or finally operators. Closest to their method is the so called *semantic* translation for BMC [14, 4]. The method follows closely the standard automata theoretic approach to model checking and creates a product system $M \times B_{\neg\psi}$, where $B_{\neg\psi}$ is a Büchi au- tomaton representing the negation of the property. The existence of a counterexample is demonstrated by finding a fair loop in the product system. Since only fair loops are accepted the method does not find counterexamples without a loop. This is the main drawback of the method, and is something which could be improved upon in the future. The greatest advantage of the method is that it can leverage the significant amount of research which has been invested in improving the efficiency of LTL to Büchi automata translators. The translation results in a linear number of variables but a quadratic num- ber clauses because of the way fairness is handled. Naturally, the semantic translation could also be improved to linear by e.g. using the translation presented in this work or that of [5]. Furthermore, the approach used in the experiments of [4] results in a translation which is exponential in the LTL formula length as the Wring system used produces explicit state Büchi automata instead of symbolic ones. Related to the seman- tic translation is the work of [15], which uses a similar product construction. Although

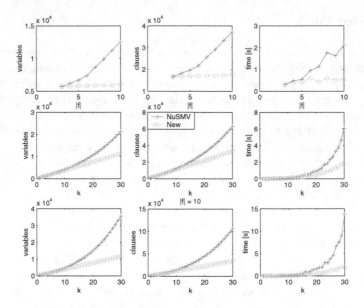

Fig. 4. Plots for NuSMV and New, averages over random formulae

the method is linear in general, the number of state bits in the model is doubled. This blowup does not occur with our method.

Many researchers have also investigated improving SAT solver efficiency. Strichman [2] uses the special properties of the formula **G**p to improve solver efficiency of BMC problems. As most safety properties can be reduced to checking invariants, the methods introduced are applicable for safety properties in general. Gupta et al. [16] use BDD model checking runs for training the solvers to achieve better performance.

5   Experiments

The translation has been straightforwardly implemented as a recursive procedure which does case analysis based on the translation. Implementation simplicity is, in our opinion, one of the main strengths of the new translation. The only implementation optimisation used was a simple cache, implemented as a lookup table, for the values of $|[\cdot]|_i$ and $\langle\langle\cdot\rangle\rangle_i$. This avoids a blow up in run time for certain formulas and speeds up the generation of the Boolean formula. All encoding optimisations mentioned in Sect. 3.1 have of course been implemented.

In order to evaluate the practical impact of our new linear translation we have performed two series of experiments. The first series of experiments evaluates the performance of the encoding on random formulae in small random Kripke structures, while the second series of experiments benchmarks the performance on real-life examples. Our implementation is compared against two bounded LTL model checking algorithms. Firstly we compare against the standard NuSMV encoding [13], which includes many of the optimisations of [5]. We also compare against the encoding of [6] which we will call Fixpoint. We do not compare against the SNF encoding also available in [6] since generally the Fixpoint encoding performs better than SNF. In order to make all other

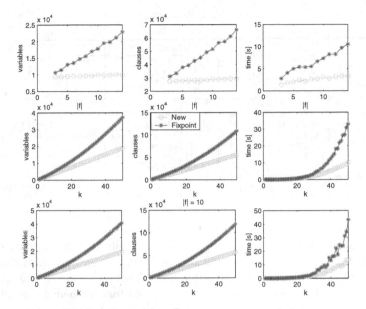

Fig. 5. Plots for Fixpoint and New, averages over random formulae

implementation differences as small as possible, all of the encodings were benchmarked on top of the NuSMV version of D. Sheridan [6] (obtained from his homepage on 18th of March 2004) which contains several BMC related optimisations not included in the standard NuSMV 2.1 distribution. We expect that benchmarking the implementations on top of NuSMV 2.1 would result in larger running times for all the implementations in question at least in the random Kripke structures benchmark. It should be noted that the compact CNF conversion [17] option of the tool was disabled.

In the first series of experiments we generated small random Kripke structures and random formulae using techniques from [8]. The experiments give us some sense of how the implementations scale when the bound or the size of the formula is increased. To demonstrate the cases where the non-linearity of the Fixpoint translation occurs we generated formulas ¬ψ which in positive normal form contains a larger percentage of finally and until operators than other temporal operators. For each formula size we generate 40 formulas, which we then model check by forcing the model checker to look for counterexamples which are of exactly the length specified by the bound. The random Kripke structures we use contain 30 states and one weak fairness constraint which holds in two randomly selected states. We measure the time used to solve the SAT instance and the number clauses and variables in the instance.

When benchmarking against NuSMV default translation we varied the size of the formula from 3 to 10. For each formula size we let the bound grow up to $k = 30$. When benchmarking against Fixpoint translation we were able to increase both the bounds used and the formula sizes to better demonstrate the differences between the two translations. We varied the size of the formula from 3 to 14. For each formula size we let the bound grow up to $k = 50$.

Table 1. Benchmarks

Model	k	NuSMV			Fixpoint			New		
		vars	clauses	time	vars	clauses	time	vars	clauses	time
abp	16	19,476	57,373	32.3	18,643	54,637	43.7	18,024	52,969	7.4
brp	10	7,599	21,811	1.3	8,550	24,256	1.2	7,471	21,397	1.5
	15	11,494	33,226	18.7	13,150	37,636	22.0	11,116	32,047	17.9
	20	15,514	45,016	471	18,050	51,916	351	14,761	42,697	484
dme	10	53,400	141,438	2.0	54,407	144,022	0.9	53,293	141,087	2.6
	20	104,885	283,733	180	107,527	290,902	263	104,173	281,537	471
	30	156,870	427,528	1,199	161,847	441,382	1,855	155,053	421,987	1,544
pci	10	56,414	167,753	58.3	56,232	167,042	56.6	55,911	166,214	51.5
	15	85,359	254,133	568	84,372	250,947	370	83,756	249,279	382
	20	115,204	343,213	5,921	112,612	335,152	2,216	111,601	332,344	2,102
srg16	20	N/A	N/A	N/A	10,540	28,786	2.3	5,196	14,921	2.7
	40	N/A	N/A	N/A	25,600	71,686	16.6	10,336	29,841	22.3
	60	N/A	N/A	N/A	45,460	128,986	105	15,476	44,761	83.0

In Figures 4 and 5 there are nine plots in each figure which depict the results from tests with random formulae of the new translation against NuSMV and Fixpoint, respectively. The three top plots show the average time, average number of clauses, and average number of variables for each formula size over all bounds. In the second row we have computed the same measures when averaged for each bound over all formula sizes. The last row shows the averages when the size of formula is fixed at ten. The plots clearly show the non-linearity of the competing translations [5, 6] with respect to the bound. Something the plots do not show is time for generating the problems. Our experience is that the new implementation and Fixpoint generated the Boolean formulas almost instantaneously while for the NuSMV encoding there were cases where generation time dominated. In fact, a couple of NuSMV data points had to be omitted from the averages due to the fact that the generation of the SAT instance took several hours.

In the second series of experiments we used real-life examples. As specifications we favoured longer formulas since all implementations can translate simple formulas linearly. The models we used were a model of the alternating bit protocol (abp), a distributed mutual exclusion algorithm (dme), a bounded resource protocol (brp), a model of a pci bus (pci), and a model of a 16-bit shift register (srg16). The results for the real-life examples are summarised in Table 1. We measured the number of variables, cumulative number of clauses and the time used to verify formulas for the reported maximum bound. For the real-life examples, Fixpoint or the new translation are usually the fastest. Our new translation is the most compact one in all cases. However, the differences are small as the model part of the translation dominates the translation size. The shift register example (srg16) shows the strength of a linear translation. NuSMV could not manage $k = 20$ in a reasonable time while Fixpoint displays non-linear growth with respect to k.

All experiments were performed on a computer with an AMD Athlon XP 2000+ processor and 1 GiB of RAM using the SAT solver zChaff [18], version 2003.12.04.

6   Conclusions

We have presented a translation of the bounded LTL model checking problem to SAT which is linear in the bound and the size of the formula. The translation produces a linear number of variables and clauses in the resulting CNF.

Our benchmarks show that our new translation scales better both in size of the bound and the size of the formula than previous implementations [5, 6]. The translation remains linear in all cases. However, in some cases either the size of the formula or the bound must be made large before the benefit shows. One avenue of future work is to include some of the optimisations presented in [5] in order to the improve the performance of our translation for short formulas and small bounds.

Other avenues of future work also exist. One fairly straightforward generalisation of our translation is the ability to handle deadlocking executions. This could probably be done in a manner similar to [11]. Another interesting topic is generalising our translation to include past temporal logic as the translation of [19]. The presented translation could also benefit from specific SAT solver optimisations. When the translation is seen as producing Boolean circuits, all of the circuits are monotonic if the *InLoop* variables and state variables (and their negated versions) are given as inputs. A solver (also CNF-based) could be optimised to take advantage of this.

Acknowledgements

We would like to thank D. Sheridan for sharing his NuSMV implementation with us.

References

1. Biere, A., Cimatti, A., Clarke, E., Zhu, Y.: Symbolic model checking without BDDs. In: Tools and Algorithms for the Constructions and Analysis of Systems (TACAS'99). Volume 1579 of LNCS., Springer (1999) 193–207
2. Strichman, O.: Accelerating bounded model checking of safety properties. Formal Methods in System Design **24** (2004) 5–24
3. Kroenig, D., Strichman, O.: Efficient computation of recurrence diameters. In: Verification, Model Checking, and Abstract Interpretation (VMCAI'2003). Volume 2575 of LNCS., Springer (2003) 298–309
4. Clarke, E., Kroenig, D., Oukanine, J., Strichman, O.: Completeness and complexity of bounded model checking. In: Verification, Model Checking, and Abstract Interpretation (VMCAI'2004). Volume 2937 of LNCS., Springer (2004) 85–96
5. Cimatti, A., Pistore, M., Roveri, M., Sebastiani, R.: Improving the encoding of LTL model checking into SAT. In: Verification, Model Checking, and Abstract Interpretation (VMCAI'2002). Volume 2294 of LNCS., Springer (2002) 196–207
6. Frisch, A., Sheridan, D., Walsh, T.: A fixpoint encoding for bounded model checking. In: Formal Methods in Computer-Aided Design (FMCAD'2002). Volume 2517 of LNCS., Springer (2002) 238–255
7. Kupferman, O., Vardi, M.: Model checking of safety properties. Formal Methods in System Design **19** (2001) 291–314
8. Tauriainen, H., Heljanko, K.: Testing LTL formula translation into Büchi automata. STTT - International Journal on Software Tools for Technology Transfer **4** (2002) 57–70
9. Clarke, E., Grumberg, O., Peled, D.: Model Checking. The MIT Press (1999)
10. Cleaveland, R., Steffen, B.: A linear-time model-checking algorithm for the alternation-free modal mu-calculus. Formal Methods in System Desing **2** (1993) 121–147
11. Heljanko, K., Niemelä, I.: Bounded LTL model checking with stable models. Theory and Practice of Logic Programming **3** (2003) 519–550

12. Janhunen, T.: A counter-based approach to translating logic programs into set of clauses. In: Proceedings of the 2nd International Workshop on Answer Set Programming (ASP'03). Volume 78., Sun SITE Central Europe (CEUR) (2003) 166–180

13. Cimatti, A., Clarke, E., Giunchiglia, E., Giunchiglia, F., Pistore, M., Roveri, M., Sebastiani, R., Tacchella, A.: NuSMV 2: An opensource tool for symbolic model checking. In: Computer Aided Verification (CAV'2002). Volume 2404 of LNCS., Springer (2002) 359–364

14. de Moura, L., Rueß, H., Sorea, M.: Lazy theorem proving for bounded model checking. In: Conference on Automated Deduction (CADE'02). Volume 2392 of LNCS., Springer (2002) 438–455

15. Schuppan, V., Biere, A.: Efficient reduction of finite state model checking to reachability analysis. Software Tools for Technology Transfer (STTT) **5** (2004)

16. Gupta, A., Ganai, M., Wang, C., Yang, Z., Ashar, P.: Learning from BDDs in SAT-based bounded model checking. In: Proceedings of the 40th Conference on Design Automation, IEEE (2003) 824–829

17. Jackson, P., Sheridan, D.: The optimality of a fast CNF conversion and its use with SAT. Technical Report APES-82-2004, APES Research Group (2004) Available from http://www.dcs.st-and.ac.uk/ apes/apesreports.html.

18. Moskewicz, M., Madigan, C., Zhao, Y., L.Zhang, Malik, S.: Chaff: Engineering an efficient SAT solver. In: Proceedings of the 38th Design Automation Conference. (2001)

19. Benedetti, M., Cimatti, A.: Bounded model checking for past LTL. In: Tools and Algorithms for Construction and Analysis of Systems (TACAS'2003). Volume 2619 of LNCS., Springer (2003) 18–33

QUBE++: An Efficient QBF Solver

Enrico Giunchiglia, Massimo Narizzano, and Armando Tacchella*

DIST, Università di Genova, Viale Causa, 13 – 16145 Genova, Italy
{enrico,mox,tac}@dist.unige.it

Abstract. In this paper we describe QUBE++, an efficient solver for Quantified Boolean Formulas (QBFs). To the extent of our knowledge, QUBE++ is the first QBF reasoning engine that uses lazy data structures both for unit clauses propagation and for pure literals detection. QUBE++ also features non-chronological backtracking and a branching heuristic that leverages the information gathered during the backtracking phase. Owing to such techniques and to a careful implementation, QUBE++ turns out to be an efficient and robust solver, whose performances exceed those of other state-of-the-art QBF engines, and are comparable with the best engines currently available on SAT instances.

1 Introduction

The implementation of efficient reasoning tools for deciding the satisfiability of Quantified Boolean Formulas (QBFs) is an important issue in several research fields, including Verification [1, 2], Planning (Synthesis) [3, 4], and Reasoning about Knowledge [5]. Focusing on computer-aided design, both formal property verification (FPV) and formal circuit equivalence verification (FCEV) represent demanding and, at the same time, very promising application areas for QBF-based techniques. For instance, in FPV based on bounded model checking (BMC) [6] counterexamples of lengths limited by a given bound are sought. BMC techniques showed to be excellent for bug finding (see, e.g., [7]), but, unless the bound corresponds to the diameter of the system, BMC tools cannot fully verify the system, i.e., certify it as bug-free. One possible solution, in the words of [6], is: "New techniques are needed to determine the diameter of the system. In particular it would be interesting to study efficient decision procedures for QBF". Still in the FPV arena, it is well known that symbolic model checking of safety properties amounts to solving a symbolic reachability problem (see, e.g., [8]): symbolic reachability can be translated efficiently to the satisfiability of a QBF, while corresponding SAT encodings do not have the same property. In the FCEV arena, a possible application of QBF reasoning is checking equivalence for partial implementations [1]: as in the case of diameter calculation and symbolic reachability, this application requires the expressive power of QBFs in order to be translated efficiently to an equivalent automated reasoning task.

In the recent years, QBF tools have known a fast and steady development. Witnessing the vitality of the field, the 2003 evaluation of QBF solvers [9] hosted eleven

---

* The authors wish to thank MIUR, ASI and the Intel Corporation for their financial support, and the reviewers who helped to improve the original manuscript.

A.J. Hu and A.K. Martin (Eds.): FMCAD 2004, LNCS 3312, pp. 201–213, 2004.

solvers that were run on 1720 benchmarks, about half of which coming from randomly generated instances, and the other half coming from encoding of problems into QBF (so called *real-world* instances). The encodings obtained considering Verification and Synthesis problems [1–4] represented about 50% of the total share of real-world instances. The evaluation showed that research in QBF reasoning reached a decent level of maturity, but also that there is still a lot of room for improvement. For instance, although QBF solvers are close relatives of the SAT solvers routinely used in FPV and FCEV applications, they are still lagging behind SAT solvers in terms of efficiency and sophistication.

In this paper we describe QUBE++, a QBF reasoning engine which using lazy data structures both for unit clauses propagation and for pure literals detection. QUBE++ also features a specifically tailored non-chronological backtracking method and a branching heuristic that leverages the information gathered during the backtracking phase. To the extent of our knowledge, QUBE++ is the first solver that combines all the above features in a single tool. Like most current state-of-the-art QBF solvers, QUBE++ is based on the Davis, Putnam, Logemann, Loveland procedure (DPLL) [10, 11]. As such, QUBE++ explores an implicit AND-OR search tree alternating three phases: simplification of the formula (lookahead), choice of a branching literal when no further simplification is possible (heuristic), and backtracking when a contradiction or a satisfying assignment is found (lookback). Each of these phases has been optimized in QUBE++. As for lookahead, we implemented an extension of the lazy data structures described in [12] which enable an efficient detection of unit and monotone literals. Lookback is based on learning as introduced in [13], with improvements generalizing those first used in SAT by GRASP [14]. The heuristic is designed to exploit information gleaned from the input formula initially, and then to leverage the information extracted during lookback. It is worth pointing out that the innovation in QUBE++ comes from the above techniques, as well as from the effort of combining them. Despite their apparent orthogonality, the specific algorithms that we have conceived (e.g., lookback-based heuristic), the nature of the problems that we have faced (e.g., pure literal detection in presence of learned clauses), and the quest for efficiency, posed nontrivial issues that turned the engineering of QUBE++ into a challenging research task.

Since QUBE++ has been designed to perform at its best on real-world QBF instances and to bridge the gap with SAT solvers, we have compared it with other state-of-the-art QBF solvers using verification and synthesis benchmarks from the 2003 QBF evaluation [9], and with the solver ZCHAFF [15] using the test set of challenging real-world SAT benchmarks presented in [16]. Owing to the techniques that we describe and to their careful implementation, QUBE++ turns out to be faster than QUBEREL, QUBEBJ and SEMPROP, i.e., the best solvers on non-random instances according to [9], and also faster and more robust than YQUAFFLE, a new and re-engineered version of QUAFFLE [17]. On the SAT benchmarks, QUBE++ bridges the gap with SAT solvers by conquering about 90% of the instances and losing, in a median-to-median comparison of the run times, only a factor of two from ZCHAFF, while QUBEREL, the best among the QBF solvers that we tried on real-world QBF instances, conquers only 50% of the problems and it is, in a median-to-median comparison of the run times, one order of magnitude slower than ZCHAFF.

The paper is structured as follows. We first review the logic of QBFs. Then we present the basic algorithm of QuBE++ and its three main features: optimized lookahead, UIP-based lookback, and lookback-based heuristic. We comment the results of the experiments outlining the efficiency of QuBE++, and then we conclude with related work and some final remarks.

2   Basics

Consider a set P of propositional letters. An *atom* is an element of P. A *literal* is an atom or the negation thereof. Given a literal l, $|l|$ denotes the atom of l, and $\bar{l}$ denotes the *complement* of l, i.e., if $l = a$ then $\bar{l} = \neg a$, and if $l = \neg a$ then $\bar{l} = a$, while $|l| = a$ in both cases. A *propositional formula* is a combination of atoms using the k-ary ($k \geq 0$) connectives $\wedge$, $\vee$ and the unary connective $\neg$. In the following, we use $\top$ and $\bot$ as abbreviations for the empty conjunction and the empty disjunction respectively. A *QBF* is an expression of the form

$$\varphi = Q_1 x_1 Q_2 x_2 \ldots Q_n x_n \Phi \qquad (n \geq 0) \tag{1}$$

where every Q_i ($1 \leq i \leq n$) is a quantifier, either existential $\exists$, or universal $\forall$; $x_1 \ldots x_n$ are distinct atoms in P, and Φ is a propositional formula. $Q_1 x_1 Q_2 x_2 \ldots Q_n x_n$ is the *prefix* and Φ is the *matrix* of (1). A literal l is *existential*, if $\exists |l|$ is in the prefix, and *universal* otherwise. We say that (1) is in *Conjunctive Normal Form* (CNF) when Φ is a conjunction of *clauses*, where each clause is a disjunction of literals in $x_1 \ldots x_n$; we say that (1) is in *Disjunctive Normal Form* (DNF) when Φ is a disjunction of *terms*, where each term is a conjunction of literals in $x_1 \ldots x_n$. We use the term *constraints* when we refer to clauses and terms indistinctly. The semantics of a QBF φ can be defined recursively as follows. If the prefix is empty, then φ's satisfiability is defined according to the truth tables of propositional logic. If φ is $\exists x \psi$ (resp. $\forall x \psi$), φ is satisfiable if and only if φ_x or (resp. and) $\varphi_{\neg x}$ are satisfiable. If $\varphi = Qx\psi$ is a QBF and l is a literal, φ_l is the QBF obtained from ψ by substituting l with $\top$ and $\bar{l}$ with $\bot$.

3   QuBE++

In Figure 1 we present the pseudo-code of SOLVE, the basic search algorithm of QuBE++. SOLVE generalizes standard backtrack algorithms for QBFs by allowing instances of the kind $Q_1 x_1 \ldots Q_n x_n \Phi$, where $\Phi = \Psi \vee \Theta$, Ψ is a conjunction of clauses, and Θ is a disjunction of terms: initially Ψ contains the matrix of the input QBF and Θ is $\bot$. Under these assumptions, clauses (resp. terms) are added to Ψ (resp. Θ) during the learning process as shown in [13]. SOLVE returns TRUE if the input QBF is satisfiable and FALSE otherwise. In Figure 1, one can see that SOLVE takes four parameters: Q is the prefix, i.e., the list $Q_1 x_1, \ldots, Q_n x_n$, Σ is the set of clauses corresponding to Ψ, Π is the set of terms corresponding to Θ, and S is a set of literals called *assignment* (initially $\Pi = \emptyset$ and $S = \emptyset$). In the following, as customary in search algorithms, we deal with constraints as if they were *sets* of literals. SOLVE works in four steps (line numbers refer to Figure 1):

bool SOLVE(Q, Σ, Π, S)
  1 **do**
  2   $\langle Q', \Sigma', \Pi', S' \rangle \leftarrow \langle Q, \Sigma, \Pi, S \rangle$
  3   $\langle Q, \Sigma, \Pi, S \rangle \leftarrow$ SIMPLIFY(Q', Σ', Π', S')
  4 **while** $\langle Q, \Sigma, \Pi, S \rangle \neq \langle Q', \Sigma', \Pi', S' \rangle$
  5 **if** $\Sigma = \emptyset$ **or** $\emptyset_\forall \in \Pi$ **then return** TRUE
  6 **if** $\emptyset_\exists \in \Sigma$ **and** $\Pi = \emptyset$ **then return** FALSE
  7 $l \leftarrow$ CHOOSE-LITERAL(Q, Σ, Π)
  8 **if** l is existential **then**
  9   **return** SOLVE$(Q, \Sigma \cup \{l\}, \Pi, S)$ **or**
         SOLVE$(Q, \Sigma \cup \{\bar{l}\}, \Pi, S)$
10 **else**
11   **return** SOLVE$(Q, \Sigma, \Pi \cup \{\bar{l}\}, S)$ **and**
        SOLVE$(Q, \Sigma, \Pi \cup \{l\}, S)$

set SIMPLIFY(Q, Σ, Π, S)
12 **while** $\{l\}_\exists \in \Sigma$ **or** $\{\bar{l}\}_\forall \in \Pi$ **do**
13   $S \leftarrow S \cup \{l\}$
14   $Q \leftarrow$ REMOVE$(Q, |l|)$
15   **for each** $c \in \Sigma$ s.t. $l \in c$ **do**
16     $\Sigma \leftarrow \Sigma \setminus \{c\}$
17   **for each** $t \in \Pi$ s.t. $\bar{l} \in t$ **do**
18     $\Pi \leftarrow \Pi \setminus \{t\}$
19   **for each** $c \in \Sigma$ s.t. $\bar{l} \in c$ **do**
20     $\Sigma \leftarrow (\Sigma \setminus \{c\}) \cup \{c \setminus \{\bar{l}\}\}$
21   **for each** $t \in \Pi$ s.t. $l \in t$ **do**
22     $\Pi \leftarrow (\Pi \setminus \{t\}) \cup \{t \setminus \{l\}\}$
23 **for each** l s.t. $\bar{l} \notin k$ for all $k \in (\Sigma \cup \Pi)$ **do**
24   **if** l is existential **then** $\Sigma \leftarrow \Sigma \cup \{l\}$
25   **else** $\Pi \leftarrow \Pi \cup \{l\}$
26 **return** $\langle Q, \Sigma, \Pi, S \rangle$

Fig. 1. Basic search algorithm of QUBE++.

1. Simplify the input instance with SIMPLIFY (lines 1–4): SIMPLIFY is iterated until no further simplification is possible.
2. Check if the *termination condition* is met, i.e., if we are done with the current search path and backtracking is needed (lines 5–6): if the test in line 5 is true, then S is a *solution*, while if the test in line 6 is true, then S is a *conflict*; $\emptyset_\exists$ (resp. $\emptyset_\forall$) stands for the *empty clause* (resp. *empty term*), i.e., a constraint comprised of universal (resp. existential) literals only.
3. Choose heuristically a literal l (line 7) such that (i) $|l|$ is in Q, and (ii) there is no other literal l' such that (i) $|l'|$ is in Q and (ii) $|l'|$ is quantified differently from $|l|$ and it occurs before $|l|$ in the prefix; the literal returned by CHOOSE-LITERAL is called *branching literal*.
4. Branch on the chosen literal: if the literal is existential, then an *OR node* is explored (line 9), otherwise an *AND node* is explored (line 11).

Consider an instance $\langle Q, \Sigma, \Pi \rangle$. In the following we say that a literal l is:

- *open* if $|l|$ is in Q, and *assigned* otherwise;
- *unit* if there exists a clause $c \in \Sigma$ (resp. a term $t \in \Pi$) such that l is the only existential in c (resp. universal in t) and there is no universal (resp. existential) literal $l' \in c$ (resp. $l' \in t$) such that $|l'|$ is before $|l|$ in the prefix;
- *monotone* if for all constraints $k \in (\Sigma \cup \Pi)$, $\bar{l} \notin k$.

Now consider the simplification routine SIMPLIFY in Figure 1: $\{l\}_\exists$ (resp. $\{l\}_\forall$) denotes a constraint which is unit in l, and REMOVE(Q, x_i) returns the prefix obtained from Q by removing $Q_i x_i$. The function SIMPLIFY has the task of finding and assigning all unit and monotone literals at every node of the search tree. SIMPLIFY loops while either Σ or Π contains a unit literal (line 12). Each unit literal l is added to the current assignment (line 13), removed from Q (line 14), and then it is assigned by:

- removing all the clauses (resp. terms) to which l (resp. $\bar{l}$) pertains (lines 15-18), and
- removing $\bar{l}$ (resp. l) from all the clauses (resp. terms) to which $\bar{l}$ (resp. l) pertains (lines 19-22).

We say that an assigned literal l (i) *eliminates* a clause (resp. a term) when l (resp. $\bar{l}$) is in the constraint, and (ii) *simplifies* a clause (resp. a term) when $\bar{l}$ (resp. l) is in the constraint. After assigning all unit literals, SIMPLIFY checks and propagates any monotone literal.

For the sake of clarity we have presented QUBE++ with recursive chronological backtracking. To avoid the expensive copying of data structures that would be needed to save Σ and Π at each node, QUBE++ features a non-recursive implementation of the lookback procedure. The implementation is based on an explicit search stack and on data structures that can assign a literal during lookahead and then retract the assignment during lookback, i.e., restore Σ and Π to the configuration before the assignment was made.

4   Optimized Lookahead Algorithm

As reported by [15] in the case of SAT instances, a major portion of the runtime of the solver is spent in the lookahead process. Running a profiler on a DPLL-based QBF solver like QUBE++ confirms this result: on all the instances that we have tried, lookahead always amounted to more than 70% of the total runtime. The need for a fast lookahead procedure is accentuated by the use of smart lookback techniques such as learning [13], where the solver augments the initial set of constraints with other ones discovered during the search. With learning, possibly large amounts of lengthy constraints have to be processed quickly, otherwise the overhead will dwarf the benefits of learning itself.

The implementation of lookahead in QUBE++ is based on an extension of the three literal watching (3LW) and the clause watching (CW) lazy data structures presented in [12] to detect, respectively, unit and monotone literals. The description of CW and 3LW in [12] considers only the case where $\Pi = \emptyset$, but it is sufficient to understand CW implementation in QUBE++. As for 3LW, in QUBE++ it is organized as follows. For each constraint, QUBE++ has to watch three literals w_1, w_2 and w_3: if the constraint is a clause, then w_1, w_2 are existential and w_3 is universal; otherwise, w_1, w_2 are universal and w_3 is existential. Dummy values are used to handle the cases when a clause (resp. a term) does not contain at least two existential (resp. universal) literals and one universal (resp. existential) literal. 3LW for clauses works in the same way as described in [12], while for terms it works as follows. Each time a literal l is assigned, the terms where l is watched are examined. For each such term:

- If l is universal then, assuming $l = w_1$:
  - if w_2 or w_3 eliminate the term then stop;
  - if w_2 is open, then check the universal literals to see if there exists $l_\forall$ such that $l_\forall \neq w_2$ and $l_\forall$ is either open, or it eliminates the term; if so, let $w_1 \leftarrow l_\forall$ and stop, otherwise check the existential literals to see if there exists $l_\exists$ such that either $l_\exists$ eliminates the term or $l_\exists$ is before w_2 in the prefix; if so, let $w_3 \leftarrow l_\exists$ and stop, otherwise a unit literal (w_2) is found;

- finally, if w_2 is assigned (i.e., w_2 simplified the term) then check the existential literals to see if there exists $l_\exists$ such that $l_\exists$ eliminates the term; if so, let $w_3 \leftarrow l_\exists$ and stop, otherwise an empty term is found.
- If l is existential then, if both w_1 and w_2 are open, or if w_1 or w_2 are eliminating the term, then stop; if either w_1 or w_2 is open (say it is w_2) then check the existential literals to see if there exists $l_\exists$ such that either $l_\exists$ eliminates the term or $l_\exists$ is before w_2 in the prefix; if so, let $w_3 \leftarrow l_\exists$ and stop, otherwise a unit literal (w_2) is found.

By keeping separate account of existential and universal literals in the constraints, 3LW always performs less operations than the other lazy data structures described in [12]. The 3LW algorithm is sound and complete in the sense that it correctly identifies unit and empty constraints, and that it detects all such constraints when they arise at a given node of the search tree. The same can be stated for CW (as described in [12]) and monotone literals. The use of 3LW and CW speeds up the lookahead process by examining fewer constraints, and the search process as a whole, by avoiding the bookkeeping work needed by non-lazy data structures when assignments are retracted during backtracking.

Lazy data structures do not provide up-to-date information about the status of the formula, e.g, how many constraints have been eliminated, or how many binary, ternary, etc. constraints are left. Therefore, they have an impact on the implementation of QuBE++ and, in particular, on the termination condition (when are all the clauses in Σ eliminated?) and on the search heuristic (how to score literals?). The first issue is solved having QuBE++ try to assign all the literals: if no empty constraint is detected and all the literals have been assigned, then a solution is found. As for the heuristic, the issue is more complicated and we have dedicated a separate section to it. Despite these apparent limitations, we have run experiments using the real-world instances from the QBF evaluation that confirm the efficiency of lazy data structures vs. a non-lazy counterpart. We compared QuBE++ vs. an early version of the system using a non-lazy data structure; both versions featured chronological backtracking so that no advantage for fast exploration of large constraints sets is expected for lazy data structures. Moreover, the version using non-lazy data structures keeps track of eliminated clauses, and therefore identifies solutions as soon as they arise. Even in this unfavorable setting, lazy data structures are, on average, 25% faster then their non-lazy counterpart. Considering the ratio of literal assignments vs. CPU time, lazy data structures perform, on average, two times more assignments per second than a non-lazy data structure.

5 UIP-Based Lookback Algorithm

Only a minority of state-of-the-art QBF solvers uses standard chronological backtracking (CB) as lookback algorithm (see [9]). This is not by chance, since CB may lead to the fruitless exploration of possibly large subtrees where all the leaves are either conflicts (in the case of subtrees rooted at OR nodes) or solutions (in the case of subtrees rooted at AND nodes). This is indeed the case when the conflicts/solutions are caused by some choice done way up in the search tree. To solve this problem [18] introduced conflict backjumping and solution backjumping (CBJ, SBJ) for QBFs. Using CBJ (resp. SBJ) the lookback procedure jumps over the choices that do not belong to the reason of the conflict (resp. solution) that triggered backtracking. Intuitively, given a QBF instance $\langle Q, \Sigma, \Pi \rangle$, if S is a conflict (resp. a solution), then a reason R is a subset of S such that $\langle Q, \Sigma \cup \{l : \bar{l} \in R\}, \Pi \rangle$ (resp. $\langle Q, \Sigma, \Pi \cup \{R\} \rangle$) is logically equivalent to $\langle Q, \Sigma, \Pi \rangle$. Reasons are initialized when a conflict or a solution is detected, and they are updated while backtracking. For details regarding this process, see [13]. With CBJ/SBJ reasons are discarded while backtracking over the nodes that caused the conflict or the solution, and this may lead to a subsequent redundant exploration. With learning as introduced for QBFs by [13], the reasons computed may be stored as constraints to avoid repeating the same search.

The fundamental problem with learning is that unconstrained storage of clauses (resp. terms) obtained by the reasons of conflicts (resp. solutions) may lead to an exponential memory blow up. In practice, it is necessary to introduce criteria (i) for limiting the constraints that have to be learned, and/or (ii) for unlearning some of them. The implementation of learning in QUBE++ works as follows. Assume that we are backtracking on a literal l assigned at decision level n, where the *decision level* of a literal is the number of nodes before l. The constraint corresponding to the reason for the current conflict (resp. solution) is learned only if:

1. l is existential (resp. universal),
2. all the assigned literals in the reason except l, are at a decision level strictly smaller than n, and
3. there are no open universal (resp. existential) literals in the reason that are before l in the prefix.

Once QUBE++ has learned the constraint, it backjumps to the node at the maximum decision level among the literals in the reason, excluding l. We say that l is a *Unique Implication Point* (UIP) and therefore the lookback in QUBE++ is *UIP-based*. Notice that our definition of UIP generalizes to QBF the concepts first described by [14] and used in the SAT solver GRASP. On a SAT instance, QUBE++ lookback scheme behaves similarly to the "1-UIP-learning" scheme used in ZCHAFF and described in [19]. Even if QUBE++ is guaranteed to learn at most one clause (resp. term) per each conflict (resp. solution), still the number of the learned constraints may blow up, as the number of backtracks is not guaranteed to be polynomial. To stop this course, QUBE++ scans periodically the set of learned constraints in search of those that became *irrelevant*, i.e., clauses (resp. terms) where the number of open literals exceeds a given parameter r. The method, called *relevance bounded learning* and introduced for SAT solvers by [20], ensures that the number of learned clauses and terms is $O(m^r)$, where m is the number of distinct atoms in the input formula.

6 Lookback-Based Heuristic

The report by [9] lists the development of an effective heuristic for QBF solvers among the challenges for future research. To understand the nature of such a challenge, consider QBFs having the form

$$\exists X_1 \forall X_2 \exists X_3 ... \forall X_{n-1} \exists X_n \Phi \qquad (2)$$

where each $X_i = x_{i1}, \ldots x_{im_i}$, and $Q_i X_i$ stands for $Q_i x_{i1} \ldots Q_i x_{im_i}$. Running a heuristic on (2) amounts to choosing an open literal among a set X_i, with the proviso that all the atoms in the sets X_j with $j < i$ must be assigned before we can choose atoms from the set X_i. Varying n and each of the m_i's, we can range from formulas like

$$\exists x_1 \forall x_2 \exists x_3 \ldots \forall x_{n-1} \exists x_n \Phi \tag{3}$$

where $m_i = 1$ for every i, to formulas like

$$\exists x_1 \exists x_2 \ldots \exists x_m \Phi \tag{4}$$

where $n = 1$, i.e., (4) is a SAT instance. If we consider QBFs of the sort (3) then it is likely that the heuristic is almost useless: unless an atom $|l|$ is removed from the prefix because l is either unit or monotone, the atom to pick at each node is fixed. On the other hand, considering QBFs of the sort (4), we know from the SAT literature that nontrivial heuristics are essential to reduce the search space. In practice, QBF instances lay between the extremes marked by (3) and (4), and instances like (3) are fairly uncommon, particularly in real-world problems. For this reason, it does make sense to try to devise a heuristic for QuBE++, but to make it efficient, we must also minimize its overhead. This task is complicated further by the fact that QuBE++ uses lazy data structures, and therefore the heuristic cannot efficiently extract complete and up-to-date information about the formula.

Given all these considerations, we designed CHOOSE-LITERAL in QuBE++ to use the information gleaned from the input formula at the beginning of the search, and then to exploit the information gathered during the learning process. This can be done with a minimum overhead, and yet enable QuBE++ to make informed decisions at each node. The heuristic is implemented as follows. To each literal we associate two counters, initially set to 0: the number of clauses c such that $l \in c$, and the number of terms t such that $l \in t$. Each time a constraint is added, either because it is an input clause or a learned constraint, the counters are incremented; when a learned constraint is removed, the counters are decremented. This generates a tiny overhead since constraints are examined anyways during the learning/unlearning process. In order to choose a suitable branching literal, we arrange literals in a priority queue according to (i) the prefix level of the corresponding atom, (ii) the score and (iii) the numeric ID. In this way, atoms at prefix level i are always before atoms at prefix levels $j > i$, no matter the score; among atoms that have the same prefix level, the open literal with the highest score comes first; ties are broken preferring low numeric IDs. Choosing a branching literal is thus inexpensive, since it amounts to picking the first literal in the priority queue. Periodically, we rearrange the priority queue by updating the score of each literal l: this is done by halving the old score and summing to it the variation in the number of constraints k such that $l \in k$, if l is existential, or the variation in the number of constraints k such that $\bar{l} \in k$, if l is universal. The variations are measured with respect to the last update. Rearranging the priority queue is an expensive operation, and therefore QuBE++ does it only at multiples of a fixed threshold in the number of nodes. In this way, the overhead of the update is amortized over as many nodes as the threshold value. Clearly, a higher threshold implies less overhead per node, but also a less accurate choice of the branching literal.

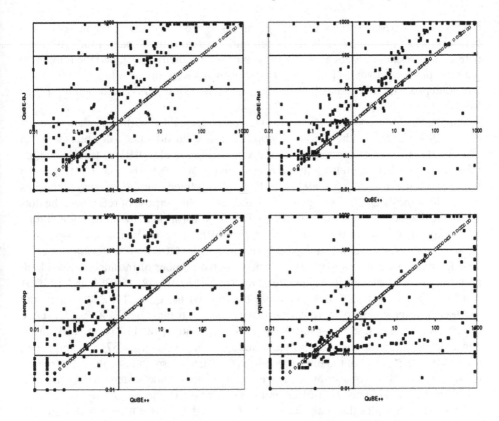

Fig. 2. Correlation plots of QuBE++ vs. state-of-the-art QBF solvers.

The intuition behind the heuristic is to favor existential literals which eliminate a lot of clauses and simplify a lot of terms, thereby incrementing the chances of finding a solution; conversely, the heuristic favors universal literals which simplify a lot of clauses and eliminate a lot of terms, thereby incrementing the chances of finding a conflict. The fact that the scores are periodically slashed helps the solver to keep focus on more recent learned constraints (a similar technique is employed by ZCHAFF [15] for SAT instances).

7   Experimental Results

In order to validate QuBE++ and tune its performances we have run several experiments using real-world instances extracted from those available at QBFLIB [21]. Here we show the results of a comparison between QuBE++ and the state-of-the-art QBF solvers that were reported as best on non-random instances by [9]. In particular, we selected the three top performers on this kind of instances: SEMPROP [22], QuBEbj [18], and QuBErel [13]. Since at the time of the evaluation the performances of QUAFFLE could not be fairly assessed because of a parser problem, we decided to include also its new version YQUAFFLE in our analysis. For all the solvers considered, we report the results of their most recent versions available at the time this paper was submitted for review (April 2004). To run the comparison, we have used the same set of 450 verification and planning (synthesis) benchmarks that constituted part of the QBF evaluation: 25% of these instances are from verification problems [1, 2], and the remaining are from planning domains [3, 4]. All the experiments were run on a farm of PCs, each one equipped with a Pentium IV 2.4GHz processor, 1GB of RAM, and running Linux RedHat 7.2.

In Figure 2 we compare the performances of QUBE++ with the other state-of-the-art QBF solvers. In the plots of Figure 2, each solid-fill square dot represents an instance, QUBE++ solving time is on the x-axis (log scale), QUBEBJ (top-left), QU-BEREL (top-right), SEMPROP (bottom-left) and YQUAFFLE (bottom-right) solving times are on the y-axes (log scale). The diagonal (outlined diamond boxes) represents the solving time of QUBE++ against itself and serves the purpose of reference: the dots above the diagonal are instances where QUBE++ performs better than its competitors, while the dots below are the instances where QUBE++ performances are worse than the other solvers. By looking at Figure 2 we can see that QUBE++ performances compare favorably with its competitors. Considering the number of instances solved both by QUBE++ and each of its competitors, on 268/342, 301/342, 259/308 and 198/301 instances QUBE++ is as fast as, or faster than QUBEBJ, QUBEREL, SEMPROP and YQUAFFLE respectively. A more detailed analysis reveals that QUBE++ is at least one order of magnitude faster than QUBEBJ (resp. SEMPROP) on 112 (resp. 163) problems, and it is at least one order of magnitude slower on 36 (resp. 37) problems, i.e., about 44% (resp. 60%) of the instances where QUBEBJ (resp. SEMPROP) is faster than QUBE++. QUBE++ is also at least one order of magnitude faster than QUBEREL on 79 instances, and one order of magnitude slower on 15 instances only. In the case of YQUAFFLE the plot thickens, since QUBE++ and YQUAFFLE results disagree on 54 instances. Noticeably, (i) for each one of these instances the satisfiability result of QUBE++ is independently confirmed by at least one solver among QUBEBJ, QU-BEREL and SEMPROP, and (ii) some of the instances where YQUAFFLE reports a satisfiability (resp. unsatisfiability) result have been declared as unsatisfiable (resp. satisfiable) by the benchmark author. However, since a certificate of satisfiability (or unsatisfiability) in QBF is not as easy to produce and to check as it is in SAT, none of the solvers that we have tried produces a witness that can be used to check its result. Therefore we must rely on a majority argument to declare YQUAFFLE "wrong", and to consider its 54 mismatching answers as if the solver failed to complete within the time limit. With this proviso, on the remaining 396 instances (of which 360 solved both by QUBE++ and YQUAFFLE) QUBE++ is strictly faster than YQUAFFLE on 212 instances, and on 115 of them it is at least one order of magnitude faster. On the other hand, YQUAFFLE is at least one order of magnitude faster than QUBE++ on 56 instances only. In conclusion, it is fair to say that QUBE++ is more robust and also faster than YQUAFFLE, since the above extrapolated data correspond to the best-case scenario in which YQUAFFLE results agree with all the other solvers, and fixing it did not hurt its performances.

In Figure 3 (left) we compare the runtime distribution of QUBEREL, QUBEBJ and SEMPROP[1] with respect to QUBE++: the x-axis is an ordinal in the range (1-375), and

---

[1] We have discarded YQUAFFLE from this analysis because we cannot fully rely on its answers and, consequently, on its solving times.

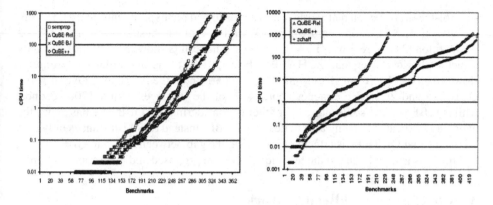

Fig. 3. Runtime distributions of QUBE++ vs. state-of-the-art QBF solvers (left) and on SAT instances (right).

the y-axis is CPU seconds on a logarithmic scale. The plot in Figure 3 is obtained by ordering the results of each solver independently and in ascending order. We show only the part of the plot where at least one of the solvers completed within the time limit of 900 seconds. By looking at Figure 3 (left) it is evident that QUBE++ advances considerably the state of the art in the solution of real-world QBF instances. Within the time limit, QUBE++ solves 22, 33, and 61 more instances than QUBEREL, QUBEBJ, and SEMPROP, respectively. A quantitative analysis on the data shown in Figure 3 (left) is obtained by comparing QUBE++ with the *SOTA solver*, i.e., SEMPROP, QUBEBJ and QUBEREL running in parallel on three different processors. Focusing on a subset of 273 nontrivial benchmarks, i.e., those where the run time of either QUBE++ or the SOTA solver exceeds 10^{-1} seconds, we see that:

- On 215 instances, QUBE++ is as fast as, or faster than, the SOTA solver and, in a median-to-median comparison of run times, QUBE++ is about five times faster; on 49 of these instances the gap is more than one order of magnitude.
- On 58 instances, QUBE++ is slower than the SOTA solver: on 18 of these instances, QUBE++ (and QUBEREL) run time exceeds the time limit, while SEMPROP and QUBEBJ manage to solve 8 and 11 instances, respectively; on the remaining 40, QUBE++ is a factor of 7.5 slower than the SOTA solver, but, individually, it is only a factor of 1.9, 4.8 and 1.5 slower than SEMPROP, QUBEBJ and QUBEREL, respectively (all the factors obtained comparing median run times).

On the remaining 177 trivial instances, all the solvers perform equally well. Summing up, QUBE++ performances are individually much better than SEMPROP, QUBEBJ and QUBEREL, and are even better than the SOTA solver obtained by combining all the three of them.

As we said in the introduction, [9] reports that QBF solvers are still lagging behind SAT solvers in terms of efficiency and sophistication. In Figure 3 (right) we checked the standing of QUBE++ with respect to this issue using a set of 483 challenging real-world SAT instances (described in [16]). We compared QUBE++, QUBEREL, the best state-of-the-art solver on real-world QBFs according to our experiments, and ZCHAFF, the winner of SAT 2002 competition [23] and one of the best solvers in SAT 2003 competition [24] on real-world SAT instances. The results show that QUBE++ is only a factor of two slower than ZCHAFF, while QUBEREL is one order of magnitude slower than ZCHAFF (median-to-median comparison on the run times). Overall, both QUBE++ and ZCHAFF conquer about 90% of the instances within 1200 seconds, while QUBEREL can solve only 50% of them. Considering that QUBE++ has to pay the overhead associated to being able to deal with QBFs instead of SAT instances only, it is fair to say that QUBE++ is effectively bridging the gap between SAT and QBF solvers, and that this is mainly due to the techniques that we proposed and their combination.

8   Conclusions and Related Work

In this paper we have described QUBE++, an efficient QBF solver QBF instances. QUBE++ owes its efficiency to the propagation scheme based on lazy data structures tied with the UIP-based learning method and a lookback-based search heuristic. To the extent of our knowledge, QUBE++ is the first QBF solver to feature such a powerful combination of techniques. On real-world QBF instances, QUBE++ shows order-of-magnitude improvements with respect to SEMPROP, QUBEBJ, QUBEREL, and YQUAF-FLE. On a test set of challenging real-world SAT benchmarks, QUBE++ bridged the gap with SAT solvers as it was comparable to ZCHAFF, while QUBEREL lagged severely behind both ZCHAFF and QUBE++.

Considering other state-of-the-art QBF solvers adopting some form of smart lookback scheme, we have SEMPROP [22] that features a different form of learning, non-lazy data structures and a different heuristic; QUBEBJ [18] and QUBEREL [13] that feature non-lazy data structures, a different heuristic and lookback methods on which those of QUBE++ are based, but with different implementations; QUAFFLE [17] restricted learning to conflicts, and featured a non-lazy data structure; as for YQUAFFLE, no detailed description of its relevant features is available to the extent of our knowledge; finally, WATCHEDCSBJ (see, e.g., [12] for a description of its implementation) features lazy data structures restricted to clauses, and CBJ/SBJ without learning. We did not report about QUAFFLE and WATCHEDCSBJ, since QUAFFLE has been replaced by YQUAF-FLE, while WATCHEDCSBJ turned out to be slower than SEMPROP on real-world QBF instances according to our experiments.

References

1. C. Scholl and B. Becker. Checking equivalence for partial implementations. In *38th Design Automation Conference (DAC'01)*, 2001.
2. Abdelwaheb Ayari and David Basin. Bounded model construction for monadic second-order logics. In *12th International Conference on Computer-Aided Verification (CAV'00)*, number 1855 in LNCS, pages 99–113. Springer-Verlag, 2000.
3. J. Rintanen. Constructing conditional plans by a theorem prover. *Journal of Artificial Intelligence Research*, 10:323–352, 1999.
4. C. Castellini, E. Giunchiglia, and A. Tacchella. Sat-based planning in complex domains: Concurrency, constraints and nondeterminism. *Artificial Intelligence*, 147(1):85–117, 2003.

5. Guoqiang Pan and Moshe Y. Vardi. Optimizing a BDD-based modal solver. In *Proceedings of the 19th International Conference on Automated Deduction*, 2003.
6. A. Biere, A. Cimatti, E. Clarke, and Y. Zhu. Symbolic Model Checking without BDDs. In *Proceedings of TACAS*, volume 1579 of *LNCS*, pages 193–207. Springer-Verlag, 1999.
7. F. Copty, L. Fix, Ranan Fraer, E. Giunchiglia, G. Kamhi, A. Tacchella, and M. Y. Vardi. Benefits of Bounded Model Checking at an Industrial Setting. In *Proc. of CAV*, LNCS. Springer-Verlag, 2001.
8. P. A. Abdulla, P. Bjesse, and N. Eén. Symbolic Reachability Analisys Based on SAT-Solvers. In *Proceedings of TACAS*, volume 1785 of *LNCS*, pages 411–425. Springer-Verlag, 2000.
9. D. Le Berre, L. Simon, and A. Tacchella. Challenges in the QBF arena: the SAT'03 evaluation of QBF solvers. In *Sixth International Conference on Theory and Applications of Satisfiability Testing (SAT 2003)*, volume 2919 of *Lecture Notes in Computer Science*. Springer Verlag, 2003.
10. M. Davis and H. Putnam. A computing procedure for quantification theory. *Journal of the ACM*, 7(3):201–215, 1960.
11. M. Davis, G. Logemann, and D. Loveland. A machine program for theorem proving. *Communications of the ACM*, 5(7):394–397, 1962.
12. I. Gent, E. Giunchiglia, M. Narizzano, A. Rowley, and A. Tachella. Watched data structures for QBF solvers. In *Sixth International Conference on Theory and Applications of Satisfiability Testing (SAT'03)*, pages 348–355, 2003. Extended Abstract.
13. E. Giunchiglia, M. Narizzano, and A. Tacchella. Learning for quantified boolean logic satisfiability. In *Eighteenth National Conference on Artificial Intelligence (AAAI'02)*. AAAI Press/MIT Press, 2002.
14. J. P. Marques-Silva and K. A. Sakallah. GRASP - A New Search Algorithm for Satisfiability. In *Proceedings of IEEE/ACM International Conference on Computer-Aided Design*, pages 220–227, November 1996.
15. M. W. Moskewicz, C. F. Madigan, Y. Zhao, L. Zhang, and S. Malik. Chaff: Engineering an efficient SAT solver. In *Proceedings of the 38th Design Automation Conference (DAC'01)*, pages 530–535, 2001.
16. E. Giunchiglia, M. Maratea, and A. Tacchella. (In)Effectiveness of Look-Ahead Techniques in a Modern SAT Solver. In *9th Conference on Principles and Practice of Constraint Programming (CP 2003)*, volume 2833 of *Lecture Notes in Computer Science*. Springer Verlag, 2003.
17. L. Zhang and S. Malik. Conflict driven learning in a quantified boolean satisfiability solver. In *Proceedings of International Conference on Computer Aided Design (ICCAD'02)*, 2002.
18. E. Giunchiglia, M. Narizzano, and A. Tacchella. Backjumping for Quantified Boolean Logic Satisfiability. In *Seventeenth International Joint Conference on Artificial Intelligence (IJCAI 2001)*. Morgan Kaufmann, 2001.
19. L. Zhang, C. F. Madigan, M. W. Moskewicz, and S. Malik. Efficient conflict driven learning in a Boolean satisfiability solver. In *International Conference on Computer-Aided Design (ICCAD'01)*, pages 279–285, 2001.
20. R. J. Bayardo, Jr. and R. C. Schrag. Using CSP Look-Back Techniques to Solve Real-World SAT instances. In *Proc. of AAAI*, pages 203–208. AAAI Press, 1997.
21. E. Giunchiglia, M. Narizzano, and A. Tacchella. Quantified Boolean Formulas satisfiability library (QBFLIB), 2001. www.qbflib.org.
22. R. Letz. Lemma and model caching in decision procedures for quantified boolean formulas. In *Proceedings of Tableaux 2002*, LNAI 2381, pages 160–175. Springer, 2002.
23. L. Simon, D. Le Berre, and E. A. Hirsch. The SAT2002 Competition, 2002.
24. L. Simon and D. Le Berre. The essentials of SAT 2003 Competition. In *Sixth International Conference on Theory and Applications of Satisfiability Testing (SAT 2003)*, volume 2919 of *Lecture Notes in Computer Science*. Springer Verlag, 2003.

Bounded Probabilistic Model Checking
with the Murφ Verifier

Giuseppe Della Penna[1], Benedetto Intrigila[1], Igor Melatti[1,*],
Enrico Tronci[2], and Marisa Venturini Zilli[2]

[1] Dip. di Informatica, Università di L'Aquila, Coppito 67100, L'Aquila, Italy
{dellapenna,intrigila,melatti}@di.univaq.it
[2] Dip. di Informatica Università di Roma "La Sapienza"
Via Salaria 113, 00198 Roma, Italy
{tronci,zilli}@dsi.uniroma1.it

Abstract. In this paper we present an explicit verification algorithm for Probabilistic Systems defining *discrete time/finite state* Markov Chains. We restrict ourselves to verification of *Bounded* PCTL formulas (BPCTL), that is, PCTL formulas in which all *Until* operators are bounded, possibly with different bounds. This means that we consider only paths (system runs) of bounded length. Given a Markov Chain $\mathcal{M}$ and a BPCTL formula Φ, our algorithm checks if Φ is satisfied in $\mathcal{M}$. This allows to verify important properties, such as reliability in *Discrete Time Hybrid Systems*.

We present an implementation of our algorithm within a suitable extension of the Murφ verifier. We call FHP-Murφ (*Finite Horizon Probabilistic* Murφ) such extension of the Murφ verifier.

We give experimental results comparing FHP-Murφ with (a finite horizon subset of) PRISM, a state-of-the-art symbolic model checker for Markov Chains. Our experimental results show that FHP-Murφ can effectively handle verification of BPCTL formulas for systems that are out of reach for PRISM, namely those involving arithmetic operations on the state variables (e.g. hybrid systems).

1 Introduction

Model checking techniques [5, 12, 19, 18, 25, 32] are widely used to verify correctness of digital hardware, embedded software and protocols by modeling such systems as *Nondeterministic Finite State Systems* (NFSSs).

However, there are many reactive systems that exhibit uncertainty in their behavior, i.e. which are stochastic systems. Examples of such systems are: fault tolerant systems, randomized distributed protocols and communication protocols. Typically, stochastic systems cannot be conveniently modeled using NFSSs. However, they can often be modeled by *Markov Chains* [2, 15]. Roughly speaking, a Markov Chain can be seen as an automaton labeled with (outgoing) probabilities on its transitions.

---

* Corresponding Author: Igor Melatti. Tel: +39 0862 43 3189 Fax: +39 0862 43 3057.

A.J. Hu and A.K. Martin (Eds.): FMCAD 2004, LNCS 3312, pp. 214–229, 2004.
© Springer-Verlag Berlin Heidelberg 2004

For stochastic systems correctness can only be stated using a probabilistic approach, e.g. using a *Probabilistic Logic* (e.g. [33, 8, 14]). This motivates the development of *Probabilistic Model Checkers* [9, 1, 20], i.e. of model checking algorithms and tools whose goal is to automatically verify (probabilistic) properties of stochastic systems (typically Markov Chains). For example, a probabilistic model checker may automatically verify a system property like "the probability that a message is not delivered after 0.1 seconds is less than 0.80". Note that, following [20, 21], we are using the expression "probabilistic model checking" to mean model checking of probabilistic systems.

Many methods have been proposed for probabilistic model checking, e.g. [11, 3, 8, 14–16, 22, 31, 33].

To the best of our knowledge, currently, the state-of-the-art probabilistic model checker is PRISM [30, 1, 21]. PRISM overcomes the limitations due to the use of linear algebra packages in Markov Chain analysis by using *Multi Terminal Binary Decision Diagrams* (MTBDDs) [7], a generalization of *Ordered Binary Decision Diagrams* (OBDDs) [4] allowing real numbers in the interval $[0, 1]$ on terminal nodes. Roughly speaking, PRISM can use three approaches to Markov Chain analysis. Namely: a sparse matrix based approach (based on linear algebra packages), a symbolic approach (based on the CUDD package [10]) and a hybrid approach, which uses MTBDDs to represent the system transition matrix and sparse matrix algorithms to carry out the (quantitative) probabilistic analysis [21]. As shown in [21], PRISM hybrid approach is faster than probabilistic model checkers based only on MTBDDs (e.g., ProbVerus [34]) and avoids the state explosion problem of probabilistic model checkers based only on sparse matrices (e.g., ETMCC [17] or the algorithms in [14, 15]).

Here we are mainly interested in automatic analysis of *discrete time/finite state* Markov Chains modeling *Discrete Time Hybrid Systems*. Such Markov Chains can in principle be analyzed using PRISM. However, our experience is that, using PRISM on our systems, quite soon we run into a *state explosion* problem, i.e. we run out of memory because of the huge OBDDs built during the model checking process. This is due to the fact that hybrid systems dynamics typically entails many arithmetical operations on the state variables. This makes life very hard for OBDDs, thus making usage of a symbolic probabilistic model checker (e.g. like PRISM) on such systems rather problematic.

To this end in [27] is presented an explicit disk based algorithm for automatic *Finite Horizon* safety analysis of Markov Chains. The algorithm in [27] has been implemented in the probabilistic model checker FHP-Murφ (Finite Horizon Probabilistic Murφ) [6].

The experimental results in [27] show that FHP-Murφ outperforms PRISM on (discrete time) hybrid systems verification. Note however that PRISM can handle all PCTL [14] logic, whereas FHP-Murφ only handles *finite horizon safety properties* (e.g. like "the probability of reaching an error state in k steps is less than a given threshold"). Moreover, in [28] it is shown that FHP-Murφ input language is more natural than the PRISM one in order to specify many Stochastic Systems.

Unfortunately there are many interesting (finite horizon) properties that cannot be expressed as safety properties. For example reliability and robustness properties like: *"the probability of reaching within k_1 steps an undesired state, which will not be left with high probability within k_2 steps, is low"* cannot be verified using the algorithm given in [27]. By an *undesired state* we mean a state in which the system should *not* be, e.g. a state in which the system cannot stay for a too long time, otherwise a damage occurs. Of course such properties can also be handled by PRISM, however then we hit the state explosion barrier quite soon when handling hybrid systems (our goal here).

The above considerations suggest extending FHP-Murφ capabilities so as to handle all *Bounded PCTL* (BPCTL) properties. That is, PCTL properties in which all *Until* operators are bounded, possibly with different bounds. In other words, we consider only paths (system runs) of bounded length. Clearly BPCTL allows us to define reliability properties and, indeed, much more. Our results can be summarized as follows.

– We present (Section 3) a new explicit verification algorithm for *finite state/ discrete time* Markov Chains. Our present algorithm can handle *all* BPCTL formulas, whereas the one presented in [27] can only handle safety properties. Moreover, our present algorithm *is not a simple extension of the one in* [27], since, to handle the reliability properties we are interested in, which result in BPCTL properties with nested *Untils*, we had to completely re-engineer it. Namely, the BF (*Breadth First*) visit of the state transition graph in [27] has been changed into a DF (*Depth First*) visit (see Section 3), with an *ad-hoc* caching strategy that allows to better handle BPCTL properties with nested *Untils*. Finally, our algorithm is *disk based*, therefore, because of the large size of modern hard disks, memory is hardly a problem for us. Computation time instead is our bottleneck. However, our algorithm can trade RAM with computation time, i.e. the more RAM available the faster our computation (see Section 3.1). To the best of our knowledge, this is the first time that such an algorithm for probabilistic model checking is proposed.
– We present (Section 3.2) an implementation of our algorithm within the FHP-Murφ verifier.
– We present (Section 4.1) experimental results comparing our *BPCTL enhanced* FHP-Murφ with PRISM on the two probabilistic dining philosophers protocols included in the PRISM distribution, and also on the two modified version of the same protocols presented in [27]. Our experimental results show that BPCTL enhanced FHP-Murφ can handle systems that are out of reach for PRISM. However, as long as PRISM does not hit state explosion, PRISM is faster than our FHP-Murφ (as to be expected).
– We present (Section 4.2) experimental results on using BPCTL enhanced FHP-Murφ for a probabilistic analysis of a "real world" hybrid system, namely the Turbogas Control System of the Co-generative power plant described in [26]. Because of the arithmetic operations involved in the definition of system dynamics, this hybrid system is out of reach for OBDDs (and thus for PRISM), whereas FHP-Murφ can complete verification of interesting reliability properties within a reasonable amount of time.

2   Basic Notation

2.1   Markov Chains

Let S be a finite set. We regard functions from S to the real interval $[0, 1]$ and functions from $S \times S$ to $[0, 1]$ as row vectors and as matrices, respectively. If $\mathbf{x}$ is a vector and $s \in S$ we also write $\mathbf{x}_s$ or $(\mathbf{x})_s$ for $\mathbf{x}(s)$. If $\mathbf{P}$ is a matrix and $s, t \in S$ we also write $\mathbf{P}_{s,t}$ or $(\mathbf{P})_{s,t}$ for $\mathbf{P}(s,t)$.

On vectors and matrices we use the standard matrix operations. Namely: $\mathbf{xP}$ is the row vector $\mathbf{y}$ s.t. $\mathbf{y}_s = \sum_{j \in S} \mathbf{x}_j \mathbf{P}_{j,s}$ and $\mathbf{AB}$ is the matrix $\mathbf{C}$ s.t. $\mathbf{C}_{s,t} = \sum_{j \in S} \mathbf{A}_{s,j} \mathbf{B}_{j,t}$.

We define $\mathbf{A}^n$ in the usual way, i.e.: $\mathbf{A}^0 = \mathbf{I}$, $\mathbf{A}^{n+1} = \mathbf{A}^n \mathbf{A}$, where $\mathbf{I}$ (*the identity matrix*) is the matrix defined as follows: $\mathbf{I}(s, j) = \mathbf{if}\ (s = j)\ \mathbf{then}\ 1\ \mathbf{else}\ 0$.

We denote with $\mathcal{B}$ the set $\{0, 1\}$ of boolean values. As usual 0 stands for *false* and 1 stands for *true*.

We give some basic definitions on Markov Chains. For further details see, e.g. [2].

A *distribution* on S is a function $\mathbf{x} : S \to [0, 1]$ s.t. $\sum_{i \in S} \mathbf{x}(i) = 1$. Thus a distribution on S can be regarded as a $|S|$-dimensional row vector $\mathbf{x}$. A distribution $\mathbf{x}$ represents *state $j \in S$* iff $\mathbf{x}(j) = 1$ (thus $\mathbf{x}(i) = 0$ when $i \neq j$).

If distribution $\mathbf{x}$ represents $s \in S$, by abuse of language we also write $\mathbf{x} \in S$ to mean that distribution $\mathbf{x}$ represents a state and we use $\mathbf{x}$ in place of the element of S represented by $\mathbf{x}$.

In the following we often represent states using distributions. This allows us to use matrix notation to define our computations.

Definition 1. *1. A Discrete Time Markov Chain (just Markov Chain in the following) is a triple $\mathcal{M} = (S, \mathbf{P}, q)$ where: S is a finite set (of states), $q \in S$ and $\mathbf{P} : S \times S \to [0, 1]$ is a transition matrix, i.e. for all $s \in S$, $\sum_{t \in S} \mathbf{P}(s, t) = 1$. (We included the initial state q in the Markov Chain definition since in our context this will often shorten our notation.)*

2. An execution sequence (or path) in the Markov Chain $\mathcal{M} = (S, \mathbf{P}, q)$ is a nonempty (finite or infinite) sequence $\pi = s_0 s_1 s_2 \ldots$ where s_i are states and $\mathbf{P}(s_i, s_{i+1}) > 0$, $i = 0, 1, \ldots$. If $\pi = s_0 s_1 s_2 \ldots$ we write $\pi(k)$ for s_k. The length of a finite path $\pi = s_0 s_1 s_2 \ldots s_k$ is k (number of transitions), whereas the length of an infinite path is ω. We denote with $|\pi|$ the length of π. We denote with $Path(\mathcal{M}, s)$ the set of infinite paths π in $\mathcal{M}$ s.t. $\pi(0) = s$, whereas $Path_k(\mathcal{M}, s)$ is set of paths π in $\mathcal{M}$ s.t. $\pi(0) = s$ and $|\pi| = k$. If $\mathcal{M} = (S, \mathbf{P}, q)$ we write also $Path(\mathcal{M})$ for $Path(\mathcal{M}, q)$. Moreover, we say that a state $s \in S$ is reachable in k steps when it exists a path $\pi \in Path_k(\mathcal{M})$ such that $\pi(k) = s$.

3. For $s \in S$ we denote with $\sum(s)$ the smallest σ-algebra on $Path(\mathcal{M}, s)$ which, for any finite path ρ starting at s, contains the basic cylinders $\{\ \pi \in Path(\mathcal{M}, s) \mid \rho$ is a prefix of $\pi\ \}$. The probability measure Prob on $\sum(s)$ is the unique measure with $Prob(\{\pi \in Path(\mathcal{M}, s) | \rho$ is a prefix of $\pi\}) = \mathbf{P}(\rho)$

$$= \prod_{i=0}^{k-1} \mathbf{P}(\rho(i), \rho(i+1)) = \mathbf{P}(\rho(0), \rho(1))\mathbf{P}(\rho(1), \rho(2)) \cdots \mathbf{P}(\rho(k-1), \rho(k)),$$

where $k = |\rho|$.

E.g. given a distribution $\mathbf{x}$, the distribution $\mathbf{y}$ obtained by one execution step of Markov Chain $\mathcal{M} = (S, \mathbf{P}, q)$ is computed as: $\mathbf{y} = \mathbf{xP}$. In particular if $\mathbf{y} = \mathbf{xP}$ and $\mathbf{x}(s) = 1$ we have that $\forall t[\mathbf{y}(t) = (\mathbf{P})_{s,t}]$.

The Markov Chain definition in Definition 1 is appropriate to study mathematical properties of Markov Chains. However Markov Chains arising from probabilistic concurrent systems are usually defined using a suitable programming language rather than a stochastic matrix. As a matter of fact the (huge) size of the stochastic matrix of concurrent systems is one of the main obstructions to overcome in probabilistic model checking.

Thus a Markov Chain is presented to a model checker by defining (using a suitable programming language) a *next state* function that returns the needed information about the immediate successors of a given state. The following definition formalizes this notion.

Definition 2. *A* Probabilistic Finite State System *(PFSS) $\mathcal{S}$ is a 4-tuple $(S, q, \mathcal{A}, \mathbf{next})$, where S is a finite set (of states), $q \in S$, $\mathcal{A}$ is a finite set of labels and* $\mathbf{next}$ *is a function taking a state s as argument and returning a set $\mathbf{next}(s)$ of triplets $(t, a, p) \in S \times \mathcal{A} \times [0, 1]$ s.t. $\sum_{(t,a,p) \in \mathbf{next}(s)} p = 1$.*

We can associate a Markov Chain to a PFSS in a unique way.

Definition 3. *Let $\mathcal{S} = (S, q, \mathcal{A}, \mathbf{next})$ be a PFSS. The Markov Chain associated to $\mathcal{S}$ is $\mathcal{S}^{mc} = (S, \mathbf{P}, q)$, where $\mathbf{P}(s, t) = \sum_{(t,a,p) \in \mathbf{next}(s)} p$.*

Moreover, a state sequence $\pi = s_0 s_1 s_2 \ldots$ is a path in $\mathcal{S}$ iff it is a path in $\mathcal{S}^{mc}$.

2.2　BPCTL

In this Section we give syntax (Definition 4) and semantics (Definition 5) for BPCTL (*Bounded PCTL*). BPCTL formulas only consider PCTL formulas in which all *Until* operators are bounded, possibly with different bounds. This means that we consider only paths (system runs) of bounded length.

Definition 4. *Let AP be a finite set of atomic propositions, i.e. of functions $p : S \to \{0, 1\}$. The BPCTL language $\mathcal{L}_{BPCTL}$ is the language generated by the following grammar:*

$$\Phi ::= tt \mid p \mid \Phi_1 \wedge \Phi_2 \mid \neg\Phi \mid [\mathbf{X}\Phi]_{\sqsupseteq\alpha} \mid [\Phi_1 \mathbf{U}^{\leq k} \Phi_2]_{\sqsupseteq\alpha}$$

where $\alpha \in [0, 1]$ and $k \in \mathbb{N}$ and the symbol $\sqsupseteq$ is one of the symbols $>, \geq$.

Definition 5. *Let $\mathcal{M} = (S, \mathbf{P}, q)$ be a Markov Chain. Then, the satisfaction relation $\models \subseteq S \times \mathcal{L}_{BPCTL}$ is defined, for all $s \in S$, as follows:*

- $s \models tt$;
- $s \models p$ *iff* $p(s) = 1$;
- $s \models \Phi_1 \wedge \Phi_2$ *iff* $s \models \Phi_1$ *and* $s \models \Phi_2$;
- $s \models \neg\Phi$ *iff* $s \not\models \Phi$;
- $s \models [\mathbf{X}\Phi]_{\sqsupseteq\alpha}$ *iff* $Prob\{\pi \in Path(\mathcal{M}, s) \mid \pi(1) \models \Phi\} \sqsupseteq \alpha$;
- $s \models [\Phi_1 \ \mathbf{U}^{\leq k} \ \Phi_2]_{\sqsupseteq\alpha}$ *iff* $Prob\{\pi \in Path(\mathcal{M}, s) \mid \exists h \leq k \ s. \ t. \ [\pi(h) \models \Phi_2 \ and \ \forall i < h \ \pi(i) \models \Phi_1]\} \sqsupseteq \alpha$.

Moreover, let F be a BPCTL formula. Then, $\mathcal{M} \models F$ iff $q \models F$.

Finally, let $\mathcal{S}$ be a PFSS. Then, $\mathcal{S} \models F$ iff $\mathcal{S}^{mc} \models F$.

Finally, we give two definitions that will be useful in the following.

Definition 6. *Let $\mathcal{M} = (S, \mathbf{P}, q)$ be a Markov Chain, Φ, Ψ be BPCTL formulas, $k \in \mathbb{N}$ and $s \in S$. Then we write $P_s[\Phi \ \mathbf{U}^{\leq k} \ \Psi]$ for $Prob\{\pi \in Path(\mathcal{M}, s) \mid \pi \models \Phi \ \mathbf{U}^{\leq k} \ \Psi\}$.*

Definition 7. *A BPCTL formula Φ is said to be a $\mathbf{U}$-formula iff there are BPCTL formulas Φ_1, Φ_2 s.t. $\Phi \equiv [\Phi_1 \ \mathbf{U}^{\leq k} \ \Phi_2]_{\sqsupseteq\alpha}$.*

Remark 1. From Definition 5, we can intuitively see that the truth value for $s \models \Phi$ can be evaluated by taking into account only paths of finite length k, provided that k is large enough and computing, when needed, $Prob\{\pi \in Path_k(\mathcal{M}, s) \mid \mathcal{P}(\pi)\}$ (for some path property $\mathcal{P}$) as $\sum_{\pi \ s.t. \ \mathcal{P}(\pi)} \mathbf{P}(\pi)$.

If we denote with $s \models_k \Phi$ the semantics that considers only paths of length k, then we have the following theorem.

Theorem 1. *Let $\mathcal{M} = (S, \mathbf{P}, q)$ be a Markov Chain and Φ be a BPCTL formula. Then, there exists a k such that, for all $s \in S$ and for all $h \geq k$, $s \models \Phi$ iff $s \models_h \Phi$.*

The reader is referred, for the mathematical details, to the online appendices of the present paper [13] (Appendix A).

3   Explicit BPCTL Model Checking

In this Section we present an explicit algorithm to verify if a PFSS $\mathcal{S} = (S, q, \mathcal{A}, next)$ satisfies a given BPCTL formula F ($\mathcal{S} \models F$).

By Definition 5, it is clear that the most difficult case in the verification of F is to compute the truth value of a $\mathbf{U}$-formula. In [27], we solved this problem by implementing a BF (*Breadth First*) visit of the $\mathcal{S}$ state space. However, a BF visit it is not effective when dealing with nested $\mathbf{U}$-formulas, which are exactly the kind of formulas defining the robustness and reliability properties we are interested in.

In fact, suppose that $F \equiv [tt \ \mathbf{U}^{\leq k_1} \ \Phi_1]_{\sqsupseteq\alpha}$, with $\Phi_1 \equiv [tt \ \mathbf{U}^{\leq k_2} \ \phi]_{\sqsupseteq\beta}$, being ϕ and atomic proposition. To determine if a state s is such that $s \models F$, we have to check, for all states t that are reachable from s in at most k_1 steps, if $t \models \Phi_1$; that is, we have to start, for all t, a nested BF visit. However, it is possible to avoid some of these nested visits. Now we will show how, using a DF visit and a cache, we reach this goal.

Our idea is that, using a DF visit, it is possible to compute, for all states r reached during the computation of $P_t[tt\ \mathbf{U}^{\leq k_2}\ \phi]$ (needed to check if $t \models \Phi_1$), the value $P_r[tt\ \mathbf{U}^{\leq k_2 - h}\ \phi]$, being h the number of transitions steps leading from t to r; this comes from the recursiveness of the DF visit itself. So, if we save in a cache slot r, Φ_1, h and $P_r[tt\ \mathbf{U}^{\leq k_2 - h}\ \phi]$, then this latter value may be used to avoid a nested DF visit when r is possibly reached again.

Note that the BF visit proposed in [27] is only able to say if the state s from which we start the visit is such that $s \models F$ (or $s \models \Phi_1$), so it is hard to apply such a caching strategy to the algorithm proposed in [27].

The rest of this Section is organized as follows. In Sect. 3.1 we give a formal description of our algorithm, explaining it also by means of a simple running example; in Section 3.2 we explain how we implemented the algorithm in the Murφ verifier.

3.1   Explicit Verification of BPCTL Formulas

In this Section we give a formal description of the algorithm, verifying a generic BPCTL formula. Let $\mathcal{S} = (S, q, \mathcal{A}, \texttt{next})$ be a PFSS and F be a BPCTL formula. We want to check if $\mathcal{S} \models F$ (see Definition 5) holds.

The main function BPCTL, taking $\mathcal{S}$ and F and returning true iff $\mathcal{S} \models \Phi$, is in Figure 1. This function uses, as auxiliary functions, the following ones:

BPCTL_rec (also in Figure 1), is a recursive function that calls itself or the other auxiliary functions, as needed by the syntactical structure of the given BPCTL formula;

```
/* the main function */
bool BPCTL(PFSS S, formula F) {
 return BPCTL_rec(S, q, F); } /* BPCTL() */

bool BPCTL_rec(PFSS S, state s, formula F) {
 if (F ≡ 1) return true;
 else if (F is an atomic proposition p) return p(s) = 1;
 else if (F ≡ ¬F₁) return !BPCTL_rec(S, s, F₁);
 else if (F ≡ F₁ ∧ F₂)
  return BPCTL_rec(S, s, F₁) && BPCTL_rec(S, s, F₂);
 else if (F ≡ [X Φ]⊒α) return evalX(S, s, F);
 else if (F ≡ [Φ U Ψ]⊒α) return evalU(S, s, F); } /* BPCTL_rec() */


bool evalX(PFSS S, state s, formula F) {
 Let F ≡ [X Φ]⊒α;
 sum = 0; /* accumulates the probability to see Φ in 1 step from s */
 for each (s_next, a, p_next) in next(s) {
  if (BPCTL_rec(S, s_next, Φ)) sum = sum + p_next;
 } /* for */
 return (sum ⊒ α); } /* evalX() */
```

Fig. 1. Functions BPCTL, BPCTL_rec and evalX

```
cache C;

bool evalU(PFSS S, state s, formula F){
  Let F ≡ [Φ U≤k Ψ]⊒α;
  {valid, result} = try_to_evaluate(C, s, F);
  if (valid)
    /* this means that function try_to_evaluate has been able to
       evaluate if s ⊨ F by using only the cache */
    return result;
  else {
    prob = DF_Search(S, s, F, 0);
    return prob ⊒ α; } /* else */ } /* evalU */

double DF_Search(PFSS S, state s, formula F, int horizon) {
  if (BPCTL_rec(S, s, Ψ)) prob = 1.0;
  else if (!BPCTL_rec(S, s, Φ)) prob = 0.0;
  else { prob = 0.0;
    if (horizon < k) {
      for all (s_next, a, p_next) in next(s){
        prob_tmp = present_cache(C, s, F, k - horizon));
        if (prob_tmp == -1) /* value not found */
          prob = prob + p_next*DF_Search(S, s_next, F, horizon + 1);
        else
          prob = prob + p_next*prob_tmp;
    } /* for */ } /* if */ } /* else */
    /* s exploration ended, the computed value can be inserted in C */
    insert_cache(C, s, F, k, prob);
    return prob; } /* DF_Search */
```

Fig. 2. Functions evalU and DF_Search

evalX (also in Figure 1), is dedicated to the evaluation of formulas of form
$[\mathbf{X}\ \Phi]_{\sqsupseteq\alpha}$;

evalU (Figure 2), is dedicated to the evaluation of formulas of form
$[\Phi\ \mathbf{U}^{\leq k}\ \Psi]_{\sqsupseteq\alpha}$;

DF_Search (also in Figure 2), is a recursive auxiliary function for evalU, computing a finite horizon DF visit of the PFSS S.

Correctness of the Algorithm. The reader is referred, for the proof of the algorithm correctness, to the online appendices of the present paper [13] (Appendix B).

We illustrate how our algorithm works by means of the simple PFSS S shown in Figure 3. Given the BPCTL formula $F \equiv [tt\ \mathbf{U}^{\leq 2}\ \phi]_{\geq 0.5}$, where ϕ is an atomic proposition such that $\phi(s_1) = \phi(s_4) = \phi(s_7) = 1$ and is 0 on the other states (as shown in Figure 3), we want to verify if $s_0 \models F$.

Then, from BPCTL(S, F), going through BPCTL_rec and evalU, DF_Search$(S, s_0, F, 0)$ is called, and the DF visit of S begins. Supposing that $\mathtt{prob}_{s_i}$ is the value for the variable prob when DF_Search is called on the state s_i, we have that $\mathtt{prob}_{s_0} = 0$, and a recursive call to s_1 is made. Here, $\mathtt{prob}_{s_1} = 1$ (since $\phi(s_1) = 1$), and no recursive call is made; on the return to the previous call (on s_0), we have $\mathtt{prob}_{s_0} = \frac{1}{3} \times 1$. Then, a recursive call on s_2 is made, from which other two recursive calls are made, first on s_3 and then on s_4. None of these two calls makes other recursive calls: s_3 because is called with $\mathtt{horizon} = 2$, s_4 because $\phi(s_4) = 1$. This latter call will set $\mathtt{prob}_{s_4} = 1$ and then $\mathtt{prob}_{s_2} = \frac{1}{2}$.

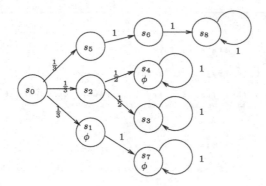

Fig. 3. A PFSS simple example

Now, we return in the visit to s_0, and now $\mathbf{prob}_{s_0} = \frac{1}{3} + \frac{1}{3}\mathbf{prob}_{s_2} = \frac{1}{3} + \frac{1}{3}\frac{1}{2} = 0.5$. Then, other two nested calls on s_5 and s_6 are made but, since none of the two satisfies ϕ, $\mathbf{prob}_{s_0}$ does not change. So, the final result is that $s_0 \models F$, since $0.5 \geq 0.5$. Note that s_7 and s_8 are never reached: the former because is only reachable from s_1, that is not expanded since $\phi(s_1) = 1$, the latter because is beyond the F horizon, i.e. it is not reached in at most 2 steps from s_0.

For what concerns the cache, it is organized as follows. Each cache slot contains a state s (C[h].state in Figure 4) together with a U-formula $F \equiv [\Phi \ \mathbf{U}^{\leq h} \ \Psi]_{\exists \alpha}$ (C[h].form), an integer h (C[h].horizon) and the respective $P_s[\Phi \ \mathbf{U}^{\leq h} \ \Psi]$ (C[h].prob). In this way, we exploit the recursiveness of the DF visit, which allows us to compute, for every state t reached during the computation of $s \models F$, the number $P_t[\Phi \ \mathbf{U}^{\leq h} \ \Psi]$, where h is the number of steps that t needs to reach the horizon (i.e. $h = k - j$, being j the number of steps from s to t). In this way, we avoid to perform already done computations, so saving time with a fixed amount of memory.

This saving may take place in two ways:

- when evalU calls try_to_evaluate (see Figure 4), to attempt to avoid a call to DF_Search. This function is based on the fact that $P_s[\Phi \ \mathbf{U}^{\leq h_1} \ \Psi] \leq P_s[\Phi \ \mathbf{U}^{\leq h_2} \ \Psi]$ for all $s \in S$, BPCTL formulas Φ, Ψ and $h_1 \leq h_2$. This implies that, even if the searched pair (state, formula) is not present in the cache with the required horizon, we can say if $s \models F$: as an example, this happens if the horizon stored in the cache is less than the required one, but the stored probability is already greater than α;
- when DF_Search calls present_cache, to attempt to avoid a recursive call. In this case, the recursive call can be avoided only if we find in the cache the exact entry for the state, the formula and the horizon, since here we need the exact probability value. To exemplify this, consider again Figure 3, and suppose that there were two transitions from s_0 to s_2, both with probability $\frac{1}{6}$. Then, the second recursive call on s_2 is avoided, since the first call has put on the cache the value $P_{s_2}[tt \ \mathbf{U}^{\leq 1} \ \phi]$, which is returned by function present_cache.

```
{bool, bool} try_to_evaluate(cache C, state s, formula F) {
 Let F ≡ [Φ U≤ᵏ Ψ]⊒α;
 /* The 4 fields of each cache slot h have the following meaning: let
   C[h].form=[Φ₁ U≤ⁱ Φ₂]⊒β; then, C[h].prob = P_{C[h].state}[Φ₁ U≤C[h].horizonΦ₂]
 */
 if (<s, F> is not in C) return {false, _};
 else {
  for all j such that (C[j].state == s && C[j].form == F) {
   if (C[j].horizon == k) return {true, C[j].prob ⊒ α};
   else if (C[j].horizon > k && !(C[j].prob ⊒ α))
    return {true, false};
   else if (C[j].horizon < k && C[j].prob ⊒ α)
    return {true, true};
  } /* for */
  return {false, _}; } /* else */ } /* try_to_evaluate */
```

Fig. 4. Function try_to_evaluate

```
int M = max length of the open addressing cache collision chain;

void insert_cache(cache C, state s, formula F, int hor, double prob) {
 h = hash(s);
 while (C[h] is not empty) {
  h = hash(s);
  if (more than M times in this while) break;
 } /* while */
 if (C[h] is empty) return C[h].prob;
 if (the previous while has been broken too many often w.r.t. the
  number of calls to insert_cache) M = M*2;
 if (C[h] contains s and F && C[h].horizon < hor)
  overwrite C[h] with {s, F, hor, prob} } /* insert_cache */
```

Fig. 5. Function insert_cache

Finally, function insert_cache, being slightly different from the usual implementation, is in Figure 5. In this function, when a free cache slot has not been found, a slot is overwritten only if it refers to the same pair (state, formula), and has minor horizon. In this way, we overwrite only information obtained with less computation resources. Moreover, the hash collision chain due to open addressing is dynamically extended when too many insertions fail. It is so clear that our algorithm trades memory with time: if we are given more memory, we will have a larger cache, which will be able to store more probabilities, thus avoiding more recursive calls to the DF visit.

3.2   Implementation Within the Murφ Verifier

We implemented the algorithm given in Section 3 within the Murφ verifier. We started from FHP-Murφ [27], a probabilistic version of Murφ in which only a subset of BPCTL formulas can be verified.

Since FHP-Murφ already allows specification of PFSSs, the input language has been modified only to allow definition of BPCTL formulas.

On the other hand, the verification algorithm has been implemented along the lines shown in Figure 1, 2 and 4. The only adjustment is in function evalU, that cannot be implemented using standard C recursion. So, a stack has been implemented to explicitly handle the recursive calls. Since we are in a bounded framework, the stack size is limited, and is given by the following definition.

Definition 8. *Let stack_size:* $\mathcal{L}_{BPCTL} \to \mathbb{N}$ *be the function returning the stack size that is needed to verify a BPCTL formula* Φ. *Then stack_size is defined as follows:*

- *stack_size(tt) = stack_size(p) = 0*
- *stack_size(*$\Phi_1 \wedge \Phi_2$*) =* max{*stack_size(*Φ_1*), stack_size(*Φ_2*)*}
- *stack_size(*$[\mathbf{X}\Phi]_{\sqsupseteq\alpha}$*) = stack_size(*$\neg\Phi$*) = stack_size(*$\Phi$*);*
- *stack_size(*$[\Phi_1 \mathbf{U}^{\leq k}\Phi_2]_{\sqsupseteq\alpha}$*) = k +* max{*stack_size(*Φ_1*), stack_size(*Φ_2*)*}

Hence, the amount of memory needed by the verification task is fixed, so we have that our real bottleneck is time, and not memory. However, to handle the case in which we need more memory than the available one, we implemented the swap-to-disk mechanism *stack cycling*, which is also implemented in the DF-based verifier SPIN [19]. With this technique, only a part of the stack is maintained in RAM: when there is a push or a pop operation outside of the stack part in RAM, then a disk block (containing a certain number of states) is used to store or retrieve the desired states. This mechanism avoids too frequent disk accesses due to repetition of push-pop operations.

In this way, we use the RAM to store part of the DF stack and of our cache. Our experiments show that typically we can take the RAM size for the DF stack as inversely proportional to the number of nested **U**-formulas, since, in this case, it is important to have a large cache in order to speed up the verification process.

4   Experimental Results

To show the effectiveness of our approach we run two kinds of experiments.

First, in Section 4.1, we compare verifications of BPCTL formulas done with FHP-Murφ with verifications of the same models done with the probabilistic model checker PRISM [30].

Second, in Section 4.2, we run FHP-Murφ to verify a robustness property on a quite large probabilistic hybrid systems. Since our main goal is to use FHP-Murφ to prove hybrid systems robustness properties, this second kind of evaluation is very interesting for us.

4.1   Probabilistic Dining Philosophers

In this Section we give our experimental results on using FHP-Murφ on the probabilistic protocols included in PRISM distribution [30]. We do not consider the protocols that lead to Markov Decision Processes or to Continuous Time Markov Chains, since FHP-Murφ cannot deal with them. Hence we only consider

NPHIL	Result	Murφ Mem (MB)	PRISM Mem (MB)	Murφ Time (s)	PRISM Time (s)
5	false	5.0e+2	1.701300e+00	3.41117000e+03	1.318000e+00
6	false	5.0e+2	1.430420e+01	>3.0000000e+05	1.260300e+01

Fig. 6. Results for the Pnueli-Zuck protocol as it is.found in the PRISM distribution. We use a machine with 2 processors (both INTEL Pentium III 500Mhz) and 2GB of RAM. Murφ options: -m500 (use exactly 500MB of RAM). PRISM options: default options

NPHIL	Result	Murφ Mem (MB)	PRISM Mem (MB)	Murφ Time (s)	PRISM Time (s)
3	true	5.0e+2	1.419900e+00	1.79230000e+03	2.018000e+00
4	true	5.0e+2	2.355610e+01	1.42337890e+05	1.034140e+02

Fig. 7. Results for the Lehmann-Rabin protocol as it is found in the PRISM distribution.The fields have the same meaning of Fig. 6

NPHIL	MAX_WAIT	Result	Murφ Mem (MB)	PRISM Mem (MB)	Murφ Time (s)	PRISM Time (s)
5	3	false	5.0e+2	9.168246e+02	1.28381900e+04	1.196793e+03
5	4	false	5.0e+2	N/A	1.27377300e+04	N/A

Fig. 8. Results for the Pnueli-Zuck protocol as it was modified in [27]. The fields have the same meaning of Fig. 6. N/A means that PRISM was unable to complete the verification; in this case, also the -m and -s (totally MTBDD and algebraic verification algorithm respectively) have been used, with the same result

NPHIL	MAX_WAIT	Result	Murφ Mem (MB)	PRISM Mem (MB)	Murφ Time (s)	PRISM Time (s)
3	4	true	5.0e+2	7.014830e+01	5.00634000e+03	5.359870e+02
4	3	true	5.0e+2	N/A	1.11480680e+05	N/A

Fig. 9. Results for the Lehmann-Rabin protocol as it was modified in [27]. The fields have the same meaning of Fig. 6

Pnueli-Zuck [29] and Lehmann-Rabin [23, 24] probabilistic dining philosophers protocols. For both of these protocols, we use two versions: the one which can be found in the PRISM distribution, and the modified version allowing *quality of service* properties verifications, as it is described in [27].

For what concerns the BPCTL properties to be verified, we proceed as follows. For the models in the PRISM distribution, we choose one of the relative BPCTL properties and we modify it so as to obtain an equivalent BPCTL property. In fact, the PRISM BPCTL properties about these protocols are of the type $\phi_P \equiv p \rightarrow [tt \ \mathbf{U}^{\leq k} \ q]_{\geq \alpha}$, where p and q are atomic propositions. However, these formulas are not evaluated on the initial state (which is the standard PCTL semantics), but on all reachable states. To obtain a comparable result with FHP-Murφ, we verify the property $\Phi_M \equiv [tt \ \mathbf{U}^{\leq d} \ (p \wedge \neg [tt \ \mathbf{U}^{\leq k} B]_{\geq \alpha})]_{\leq 0}$, where d is the diameter of the protocol state space, i.e. the length of maximum path between two states. In this way, we have that $q \models \Phi_M$ iff, for all reachable states s, $s \models \Phi_P$.

Our results are in Figure 6 and 7 (with $k = 20$). Note that, in these set of experiments, which do not involve mathematical operations, PRISM works better, while FHP-Murφ take too much time to complete the verifications.

For the modified models, we verify a reliability property. In fact, in this models, there is a set of error states, i.e. those satisfying a special atomic proposition ϕ_{err} (informally, *"a philosopher does not eat for a too long time, and dies for starvation"*). To define our reliability property, we introduce a new atomic proposition ϕ_{und}, which is a weaker version of ϕ_{err} in the sense that, for all states s, if s satisfies ϕ_{err}, then it satisfies also ϕ_{und} (informally, *"a philosopher does not eat for a long time, and he is in danger"*). So, our undesired states are those satisfying ϕ_{und}. The reader is referred, for a detailed description of ϕ_{err} and ϕ_{und}, to the online appendices of the present paper [13] (Appendix C).

Now, we want to say that, when an undesired state s is reached, then the system almost always reaches, from s and in a few steps, a non-error state. Then, our property states that there is a low probability that if we reach in k_1 steps a state s such that $\phi_{und}(s)$ holds, and there is not a high probability of reaching, from s and in $k_2 = \frac{k_1}{10}$ steps, a state t such that $\neg\phi_{err}(t)$. The corresponding BPCTL formula is $[tt\ \mathbf{U}^{\leq k_1}\ (\phi_{und} \wedge \neg[tt\ \mathbf{U}^{\leq k_2} \neg\phi_{err}]_{\geq 1})]_{\leq 0}$. We give this BPCTL formula both to PRISM and FHP-Murφ.

Our results are in Figures 8 and 9 (with $k_1 = 20$). We can observe that, requiring these protocols some mathematical operations, there are cases (i.e., the last rows in Figures 8 and 9) in which no PRISM strategy (i.e., MTBDD based, sparse matrix based, hybrid approach) is able to complete the verification task, while FHP-Murφ does.

4.2   Analysis of a Probabilistic Hybrid System with FHP-Murφ

In this section we show our experimental results on using FHP-Murφ for the analysis of a *real world* hybrid system. Namely, the *Control System* for the *Gas Turbine* of a 2MW *Electric Co-generative Power Plant* (ICARO) in operation at the ENEA Research Center of Casaccia (Italy).

Our control system (*Turbogas Control System*, TCS, in the following) is the heart of ICARO and is indeed the most critical subsystem in ICARO. Unfortunately TCS is also the largest ICARO subsystem, thus making the use of model checking for such hybrid system a challenge.

In [26] it is shown that by adding finite precision real numbers to Murφ, we can use Murφ to automatically verify TCS. In particular in [26] it has been shown the following. If the the speed of variation of the user demand for electric power (MAX_D_U in the following) is greater than or equal to 25 (kW/sec), TCS fails in maintaining ICARO parameters within the required safety ranges. A TCS state in which one of ICARO parameters is outside its given safety range is of course considered an *error state*. On the other hand, a state is considered a *undesired state* when it is outside a larger safety range (the system will crash if it stays in such a state for a too long time).

In [27] FHP-Murφ has been used to verify finite horizon probabilistic safety properties of TCS.

Here we show that by using BPCTL enhanced FHP-Murφ we can verify robustness properties of TCS. Here is an example: *"if the system reaches an undesired state, it is able to return to a non-undesired state with a high prob-*

MAX_D_U	Visited States	Rules Fired	k_1	CPU Time (s)	Probability
35	1.159160e+05	3.477480e+05	800	3.702400e+03	4.104681e-03
45	4.098000e+04	1.229400e+05	700	1.313900e+03	1.792883e-02
50	4.067700e+04	1.220310e+05	700	1.307850e+03	3.825000e-02

Fig. 10. Results on a machine with 2 processors (both INTEL Pentium III 500Mhz) and 2GB of RAM. Murφ options used: -m500 (use 500 MB of RAM)

ability". Our robustness property is so equivalent to say that there is a low probability of reaching an undesired state s, such that there is not an high probability of reaching a non-undesired state from s. The relative BPCTL formula is $[tt\ \mathbf{U}^{\leq k_1}\ (\neg\phi \wedge \neg[tt\ \mathbf{U}^{\leq k_2}\phi]_{\geq 1})]_{\leq 0}$, where ϕ defines the undesired states. The two constants k_1 and k_2 are chosen in such a way that k_1 is sufficient to reach an undesired state (if the first undesired state is reached in d steps, then $k_1 = \lceil \frac{d}{100} \rceil 100$), and k_2 is not too high (in our experiments, we took $k_2 = \frac{k_1}{100}$).

Our results are in Figure 10, where we show, in the field "Probability" the value $P_q[tt\ \mathbf{U}^{\leq k_1}\ (\neg\phi \wedge \neg[tt\ \mathbf{U}^{\leq k_2}\phi]_{\geq 1})]$, being q the system initial state.

5 Conclusions

We presented (Section 3) an *explicit* verification algorithm for Probabilistic Systems defining *discrete time/finite state* Markov Chains. Given a Markov Chain $\mathcal{M}$ and Bounded PCTL formula Φ our algorithm checks if $\mathcal{M} \models \Phi$.

We presented (Section 3.2) an implementation of our algorithm within a suitable extension of the Murφ verifier that we call FHP-Murφ (*Finite Horizon Probabilistic*-Murφ).

We presented (Section 4) experimental results comparing FHP-Murφ with (a finite horizon subset of) PRISM, a state-of-the-art symbolic model checker for Markov Chains. Our experimental results show that FHP-Murφ can handle systems that are out of reach for PRISM, namely those involving arithmetic operations on the state variables (e.g. hybrid systems).

PRISM handles Continuous Time Markov Chains (CTMC) using a symbolic approach. This works well as long as the system dynamics does not involve heavy arithmetical computations. To enlarge the class of automatically verifiable probabilistic systems, future work includes extending our explicit approach to CTMCs. Another possible research direction is to extend Murφ so as to handle *unbounded until* PCTL formulas.

References

1. C. Baier, E. M. Clarke, V. Hartonas-Garmhausen, M. Kwiatkowska, and M. Ryan. Symbolic model checking for probabilistic processes. In Pierpaolo Degano, Roberto Gorrieri, and Alberto Marchetti-Spaccamela, editors, *ICALP'97, Proceedings*, volume 1256 of *LNCS*, pages 430–440. Springer, 1997.
2. E. Behrends. *Introduction to Markov Chains*. Vieweg, 2000.

3. Bianco and de Alfaro. Model checking of probabilistic and nondeterministic systems. In P. S. Thiagarajan, editor, *Foundations of Software Technology and Theoretical Computer Science, 15th Conference, Bangalore, India, December 18-20, 1995, Proceedings*, volume 1026 of *LNCS*, pages 499–513. Springer, 1995.
4. R. Bryant. Graph-based algorithms for boolean function manipulation. *IEEE Trans. on Computers*, C-35(8):677–691, Aug 1986.
5. J. R. Burch, E. M. Clarke, K. L. McMillan, D. L. Dill, and L. J. Hwang. Symbolic model checking: 10^{20} states and beyond. *Inf. Comput.*, 98(2):142–170, 1992.
6. Cached murphi web page: http://www.dsi.uniroma1.it/~tronci/cached.murphi.html.
7. E. M. Clarke, K. L. McMillan, X Zhao, M. Fujita, and J. Yang. Spectral transforms for large boolean functions with applications to technology mapping. In *Proceedings of the 30th international on Design automation conference*, pages 54–60. ACM Press, 1993.
8. C. Courcoubetis and M. Yannakakis. Verifying temporal properties of finite-state probabilistic programs. In *Proceedings of the IEEE Conference on Decision and Control*, pages 338–345, Piscataway, NJ, 1988. IEEE Press.
9. Costas Courcoubetis and Mihalis Yannakakis. The complexity of probabilistic verification. *J. ACM*, 42(4):857–907, 1995.
10. Cudd web page: http://vlsi.colorado.edu/~fabio/.
11. L. de Alfaro. Formal verification of performance and reliability of real-time systems. Technical Report STAN-CS-TR-96-1571, Stanford University, 1996.
12. David L. Dill, Andreas J. Drexler, Alan J. Hu, and C. Han Yang. Protocol verification as a hardware design aid. In *Proceedings of the 1991 IEEE International Conference on Computer Design on VLSI in Computer & Processors*, pages 522–525. IEEE Computer Society, 1992.
13. Online appendices: http://www.di.univaq.it/melatti/FMCAD04/.
14. B. Jonsson H. Hansson. A logic for reasoning about time and probability. *Formal Aspects of Computing*, 6(5):512–535, 1994.
15. H. Hansson. *Time and Probability in Formal Design of Distributed Systems*. Elsevier, 1994.
16. Sergiu Hart and Micha Sharir. Probabilistic temporal logics for finite and bounded models. In *Proceedings of the sixteenth annual ACM symposium on Theory of computing*, pages 1–13. ACM Press, 1984.
17. H. Hermanns, J.-P. Katoen, J. Meyer-Kayser, and M. Siegle. A tool for model-checking markov chains. *Software Tools for Technology Transfer*, 4(2):153–172, Feb 2003.
18. G. J. Holzmann. *Design and Validation of Computer Protocols*. Prentice Hall, New Jersey, 1991.
19. G. J. Holzmann. The spin model checker. *IEEE Trans. on Software Engineering*, 23(5):279–295, May 1997.
20. M. Kwiatkowska, G. Norman, and D. Parker. PRISM: Probabilistic symbolic model checker. In Tony Field, Peter G. Harrison, Jeremy T. Bradley, and Uli Harder, editors, *TOOLS 2002, Proceedings*, volume 2324 of *LNCS*, pages 200–204. Springer, 2002.
21. M. Kwiatkowska, G. Norman, and D. Parker. Probabilistic symbolic model checking with PRISM: A hybrid approach. In Joost-Pieter Katoen and Perdita Stevens, editors, *TACAS 2002, Held as Part of ETAPS 2002, Proceedings*, volume 2280 of *LNCS*, pages 52–66. Springer, 2002.
22. Kim G. Larsen and Arne Skou. Bisimulation through probabilistic testing. *Inf. Comput.*, 94(1):1–28, 1991.

23. D. Lehmann and M. Rabin. On the advantages of free choice: A symmetric fully distributed solution to the dining philosophers problem (extended abstract). In *Proc. 8th Symposium on Principles of Programming Languages*, pages 133–138, 1981.

24. N. Lynch, I. Saias, and R. Segala. Proving time bounds for randomized distributed algorithms. In *Proceedings of the thirteenth annual ACM symposium on Principles of distributed computing*, pages 314–323. ACM Press, 1994.

25. Murphi web page: http://sprout.stanford.edu/dill/murphi.html.

26. G. Della Penna, B. Intrigila, I. Melatti, M. Minichino, E. Ciancamerla, A. Parisse, E. Tronci, and M. V. Zilli. Automatic verification of a turbogas control system with the murφ verifier. In Oded Maler and Amir Pnueli, editors, *HSCC 2003 Proceedings*, volume 2623 of *LNCS*, pages 141–155. Springer, 2003.

27. G. Della Penna, B. Intrigila, I. Melatti, E. Tronci, and M. V. Zilli. Finite horizon analysis of markov chains with the murφ verifier. In Daniel Geist and Enrico Tronci, editors, *CHARME 2003, Proceedings*, volume 2860 of *LNCS*, pages 394–409. Springer, 2003.

28. G. Della Penna, B. Intrigila, I. Melatti, E. Tronci, and M. V. Zilli. Finite horizon analysis of stochastic systems with the murφ verifier. In Carlo Blundo and Cosimo Laneve, editors, *ICTCS 2003, Proceedings*, volume 2841 of *LNCS*, pages 58–71. Springer, 2003.

29. A. Pnueli and L. Zuck. Verification of multiprocess probabilistic protocols. *Distrib. Comput.*, 1(1):53–72, 1986.

30. Prism web page: http://www.cs.bham.ac.uk/~dxp/prism/.

31. R. Segala and N. Lynch. Probabilistic simulations for probabilistic processes. In Bengt Jonsson and Joachim Parrow, editors, *CONCUR '94, Proceedings*, volume 836 of *LNCS*, pages 481–496. Springer, 1994.

32. Spin web page: http://spinroot.com.

33. M. Vardi. Automatic verification of probabilistic concurrent finite-state programs. In *26th Annual Symposium on Foundations of Computer Science*, pages 327–338, Portland, Oregon, Oct 1985. IEEE CS Press.

34. E. M. Clarke V. Hartonas-Garmhausen, S. V. Aguiar Campos. Probverus: Probabilistic symbolic model checking. In Joost-Pieter Katoen, editor, *ARTS'99, Proceedings*, volume 1601 of *LNCS*, pages 96–110. Springer, 1999.

Increasing the Robustness of Bounded Model Checking by Computing Lower Bounds on the Reachable States

Mohammad Awedh and Fabio Somenzi

University of Colorado at Boulder
{awedh,fabio}@colorado.edu

Abstract. Most symbolic model checkers are based on either Binary Decision Diagrams (BDDs), which may grow exponentially large, or Satisfiability (SAT) solvers, whose time requirements rapidly increase with the sequential depth of the circuit. We investigate the integration of BDD-based methods with SAT to speed up the verification of safety properties of the form $G f$, where f is either propositional or contains only the next-time temporal operator X. We use BDD-based reachability analysis to find lower bounds on the reachable states and the states that reach the bad states. Then, we use these lower bounds to shorten the counterexample or reduce the depth of the induction step (termination depth). We present experimental results that compare our method to a pure BDD-based method and a pure SAT-based method. Our method can prove properties that are hard for both the BDD-based and the SAT-based methods.

1 Introduction

BDD-based symbolic model checking [11] is widely used in formal verification of hardware and software systems. Recently, however, this technique has been challenged by the use of propositional satisfiability (SAT) with the introduction of Bounded Model Checking (BMC) [2]. BMC has been able to refute LTL formulae for models that have proved too hard for BDD-based methods. The disadvantages of this technique are that it is not complete in practice because a tight bound of the maximum length of a counterexample is often not available; and that its time requirements rapidly increase as the depth of the search increases.

The issue of completeness is addressed in [16] and [8], which add an induction proof to BMC so that both verification and falsification of safety properties becomes possible. In [12], the same problem is solved by the use of interpolants. The induction proof of [16] concludes that an invariant holds if all states of all paths of length k starting from the initial states satisfy the invariant, and, moreover, there is no simple path of length $k + 1$ starting at an initial state or leading to a state that violates the property. The disadvantage of this method is that the number and sizes of the SAT instances increase. In addition, the induction proof depends on the longest simple paths between two states, which may be much longer than the shortest paths between them.

In a simple path each state differs form all the others. This condition can be easily expressed with a number of clauses that is quadratic in the length of the path k. Recent work [10] reduces the number of additional clauses to $O(k \log^2 k)$: A bitonic sorting network is used to obtain an ordered permutation of the states in the path. A path

A.J. Hu and A.K. Martin (Eds.): FMCAD 2004, LNCS 3312, pp. 230–244, 2004.

contains two equal states if and only if its corresponding ordered (sorted) permutation contains two equal adjacent states.

The interpolation method [12] uses the refutation proofs generated by the SAT solver to compute an *interpolant*. An interpolant can be used to compute an over-approximation of the reachable states.

Reachability analysis computes a set of states that are reachable from a given set of states; it may prove that an invariant holds at all states that are reachable from the initial states (forward reachability); or it may prove that no initial state has a path to a state that violates the invariant (backward reachability). The success of using reachability analysis to check invariants owes much to the use of the canonical Binary Decision Diagrams (BDDs) [4] to represent Boolean functions. However, for large systems, BDDs may grow too large. Several techniques have been proposed to overcome this limitation. Among them, High Density reachability analysis [15] attempts to reduce the size of the BDD representation of the reached states, while reaching as many states as possible. At each iteration, a subset of the newly reached states is chosen such that its BDD represents many states with few nodes. Hence, the high-density approach computes an under-approximation of the reachable states.

A combination of over-approximated forward reachability and exact backward reachability is described in [5]; however, this technique is limited by the exact backward traversal step which may become very expensive.

Target enlargement is used in [1] to prove reachability. The authors use SAT-based bounded model checking to check for the reachability of the current enlarged target. If reachability can not be proved, then they perform composition-based pre-image computations until the size of the BDD that represents the enlarged target exceeds a given limit. If the property is not proved, a simpler enlarged target is constructed and added to the netlist of the model for a subsequent verification flow. The enlargement of the target states is bounded by an over-approximation of the diameter of the circuit that can be computed by analyzing the netlist representing the model. This requires a model to have special structure; hence, this bound is not always useful.

In this paper, we present a new technique for symbolic model checking that integrates BDD-based reachability analysis and BMC augmented with induction. We use SAT to check for the existence of a counterexample of length k or to find the termination depth, which is bounded by the recurrence diameter [2]. The path of length k does not necessarily connect initial states to target states as in traditional BMC; instead, BDD-based reachability analysis reduces the gap between the initial states and the target states. Since for large systems, reachability analysis is very expensive, we aggressively under-approximate.

We compute a subset of the states that are reachable from the initial states; this subset includes all the initial states. Then, we compute all the successors of the states in this subset. Similarly, we compute a subset of the states from which the target states can be reached; this subset includes all the target states. Then, we compute all the predecessors of the states in this subset. Finally, we look for a path connecting these two subsets of states or try to prove that no such path exists.

Our method differs form the method of [1] in that we control the size of the intermediate BDDs by under-approximation rather than applying early quantification of primary input variables. Our approach has the advantage that it goes deeper in the reachable states, and hence has more chances to reduce the counterexample and the termination depth. Another important difference is that we use the SAT-based method after we compute the under-approximation of the enlarged target and initial states, whereas the method of [1] alternates between using SAT to check for the reachability of the enlarged target states and BDDs to compute the enlarged target states.

BDD-based method and SAT-based method have been combined in the context of abstraction refinement [7, 13]. In [7, 13], the SAT-based method is used to check whether a counterexample found in the abstract model is a true counterexample in the concrete model. If the SAT instance is unsatisfiable, [13] uses the proofs of unsatisfiability derived from the SAT-based method as a guide to refine the abstract model.

Integrating BDD-based methods with SAT-based methods helps one to check properties that are hard for both approaches. Specifically, our method simplifies the SAT instances, while using BDDs only for manageable subsets of the reachable states.

We present an experimental comparison of our new method with the methods implemented in VIS [3]. For invariants, we compare our method to the BDD-based invariant checking in VIS, and to VIS's BMC. For safety properties that contain only the next-time temporal operator X, we compare our method to the BDD-based LTL model checking in VIS and to VIS's BMC.

In Section 2, we review background material. In Section 3, we present our approach, while in Section 4 we explain how to generate a counterexample for failing properties. We present experimental results In Section 5 and conclude in Section 6.

2   Background

We model the systems to be verified as *Kripke structures* and we specify properties in Linear-time Temporal Logic (LTL).

Definition 1. *A* Kripke structure M *over a set of atomic propositions* AP *is a 4-tuple* $M = \langle S, I, \Delta, L \rangle$ *where:*

- S *is a finite set of states.*
- $I \subseteq S$ *is a set of initial states.*
- $\Delta \subseteq S \times S$ *is a transition relation that is total: For every state* $s \in S$ *there is a state* $t \in S$ *such that* $\Delta(s, t)$.
- $L : S \to 2^{AP}$ *is a function that labels each state with a set of atomic propositions that are true in that state. For* $p \in AP$, *we write the predicate* $p(s)$ *to indicate* $p \in L(s)$.

Each state is a valuation of the *state variables*. Current state $s \in S$ is defined over the state variables $V_s = \{s_1, \ldots, s_n\}$. Next state $t \in S$ is defined over the state variables $V_t = \{t_1, \ldots, t_n\}$. The state at time i is written s^i.

Definition 2. *A path* π *in Kripke structure* M *is an infinite sequence of states* $s^0, s^1, \ldots$ *such that for any two consecutive states* s^i *and* s^{i+1} *in* π $\Delta(s^i, s^{i+1})$ *holds. We define* $\pi^i = (s^i, s^{i+1}, \ldots)$.

Definition 3. *An* LTL *formula is defined as follows*

- *An atomic proposition* $p \in AP$, true, *and* false *are LTL formulae.*
- *If* f *and* g *are LTL formulae, then so are* $\neg f$, $f \wedge g$, $f \vee g$, $X f$, *and* $f \cup g$.

A propositional formula *is an LTL formula that does not contain the temporal operators* $(X$ *and* $U)$. *We define* $f \mathrel{R} g = \neg(\neg f \cup \neg g)$, $F f = \text{true} \cup f$, *and* $G f = \text{false} \mathrel{R} g$.

The semantic of LTL formulae are defined over infinite paths. An atomic proposition p holds along a path π if $p(s^0)$ holds. Satisfaction for true, false, and the Boolean connectives is defined in the obvious way; $\pi \models X f$ iff $\pi^1 \models f$; and $\pi \models f \cup g$ iff there exists $i \geq 0$ such that $\pi^i \models g$, and for $j < i$, $\pi^j \models f$.

A *safety* property states that something bad will never happen. Sistla [17] provides a syntactic characterization of LTL safety formulae: Every propositional formula is a safety formula, and if f and g are safety formulae, then so are $f \vee g$, $f \wedge g$, $X f$, $G f$, and $f \mathrel{R} g$. Not all safety properties are captured by this definition. The violation of safety property $G f$ is witnessed by a path starting from an initial state and leading to a state that violates f. We call the set of states that violate f *target states*, and we denote them by T.

Our method works on LTL safety properties of the form $G f$, where f is either a propositional formula, or a path formula that contains only the temporal operator X (e.g., $G(p \to X q)$). For these properties, we use BDD operations to find the states satisfying $\neg f$. Since no fixpoint computations are required, these BDD operations seldom result in unwieldy BDDs[1].

Image computation is the process of computing the successors $P(t)$ of a set of states $Q(s)$ in the state transition graph described by $\Delta(s, t)$, and is defined by:

$$P(t) = \exists s \,.\, Q(s) \wedge \Delta(s, t) \;. \tag{1}$$

Pre-image computation is the process of computing the predecessors $P(s)$ of a set of states $Q(t)$ in the state transition graph described by $\Delta(s, t)$, and is defined by:

$$P(s) = \exists t \,.\, Q(t) \wedge \Delta(s, t) \;. \tag{2}$$

A set of states $\{s^0, s^1, \ldots, s^n\}$ forms a *path* of length n if it satisfies:

$$path_n = \bigwedge_{0 \leq i < n} \Delta(s^i, s^{i+1}) \;.$$

A *simple path* is a *path* along which all states are unique. It satisfies:

$$simplePath_n = path_n \wedge \bigwedge_{0 \leq i < j \leq n} (s^i \neq s^j) \;.$$

Invariants are safety properties of the form $G f$, where f is a propositional formula. If f holds in all reachable states, the invariant is called an inductive invariant. Reachability analysis can be used to check the validity of invariants. It may compute all the

---

[1] We explain in Sect. 6 how to generalize our method to verify all safety properties.

states reachable from the initial states and prove that f holds at all of them (forward reachability); or, it may compute all the states from which a state that violates f may be reached, and prove that no initial state is included in them (backward reachability). The success of this technique often depends on the use of the canonical Binary Decision Diagrams (BDD) [4] for representing Boolean functions. However, in some cases, BDDs grow too large and make reachability analysis too expensive. High Density reachability analysis [15] was introduced to contain the size of BDDs.

High Density reachability analysis mixes breadth-first and depth-first searches in computing the reachable states. A BDD is used to represent the reachable states, but its size is controlled by dropping states that decrease its density. The density of a BDD is the ratio of the number of states it represents to the number of its nodes. By controlling the density of the BDD that represents the reachable state, one obtains a BDD that represents an under-approximation of the reachable states.

Boolean Satisfiability (SAT) is a well-known NP-complete problem. It consists of determining a satisfying variable assignment of a given propositional formula or determining that no such assignment exists. Many SAT solvers assume that the propositional formula is represented in conjunctive normal form (CNF). A CNF formula is a conjunction of clauses. Each clause is a disjunction of literals. A literal is a variable or its complement.

Bounded Model Checking (BMC) [2] is a SAT-based model checking approach for linear time properties. BMC reduces the search for a counterexample to propositional satisfiability. Given a model M, an LTL formula φ, and a bound k, BMC tries to falsify $M \models \varphi$ by proving the existence of a witness of length k for the negation of the LTL formula.

BMC generates a propositional formula $[\![M, \neg\varphi]\!]_k$ that is satisfiable if and only if a counterexample to φ of length k exists; $[\![M, \neg\varphi]\!]_k$ is defined as follows:

$$[\![M, \neg\varphi]\!]_k = [\![M]\!]_k \wedge [\![\neg\varphi]\!]_k \ , \tag{3}$$

where $[\![M]\!]_k$ is a propositional formula describing a path of length k that starts at the initial states:

$$[\![M]\!]_k = I \wedge path_k \ , \tag{4}$$

and $[\![\neg\varphi]\!]_k$ expresses the satisfaction of $\neg\varphi$ along that path. For a safety property $\varphi = G f$, we are looking for a state that violates f. Hence, $[\![\neg\varphi]\!]_k$ is defined as:

$$[\![\neg\varphi]\!]_k = \bigvee_{0 \le i \le k} \neg f_i \ . \tag{5}$$

In [16], the authors use induction to verify invariants. An invariant $G f$ holds if all states of every path of length k starting from an initial state satisfy f; and if f holds in all the states of some simple path of length k (not necessarily starting from the initial states), then it also holds in all the successors of the last state of the path. We refer to k as the *termination depth*.

SAT can be used to prove the induction in two steps. First, one calls the SAT solver on a propositional formula that describes an initialized path of length k to a target state. If the SAT solver returns *unsatisfiable*, then one calls the SAT solver on a propositional formula that describes a simple path of length k to a target state, such that no other state along the path is a target state. If the SAT solver returns *unsatisfiable*, then the formula passes. Likewise, one can check for the existence of a simple path such that the first state, and no other state, is initial.

3   The Algorithm

We verify a safety property $G f$, where f is either propositional or contains only the next-time temporal operator X, by attempting to prove or disprove the reachability of $\neg f$ from the initial states I. We integrate the BDD-based under-approximation reachability analysis with the SAT-based method in procedure bdd_sat. As illustrated in Fig. 1, first we compute the *outer boundary* of a subset of the states reachable from the initial states I by calling the function $ComputeReach(I, T, Fwd)$. If we cannot conclude, that is, if no target state has been reached, we find the outer boundary of a subset of the states that reach the target states T by calling the function $ComputeReach(T, I, Bwd)$. If we could not reach any conclusion because the results of the two reachability analyses do not intersect, then we invoke the SAT solver to find a path between the new sets of states, or to prove that such a path does not exist and the property holds. We call the newly computed subsets the *boundary states*. Figure 2 depicts our new technique.

```
bdd_sat(I, T) {
    (status, newI) = ComputeReach(I, T, Fwd);
    if (status == undecided ) {
        (status, newT) = ComputeReach(T, newI, Bwd);
        if (status == undecided ) {
            status = Check(newI, newT);
        }
    }
    return status;
}
```

Fig. 1. The bdd_sat algorithm

Figure 4 shows the algorithm *ComputeReach(S, E, dir)* that returns either a forward or a backward under-approximation of the reachable states. In this algorithm, R at the i-th iteration of the *while* loop denotes the set of states proved reachable in i or fewer iterations. New_i denotes the set of new states at iteration i. We store New_i for later use in the generation of a counterexample in case the property fails. The frontier F denotes the set of states in the interval between the newly reached states New_i and the reached states R. We control the size of the BDD of the approximate reachable states by computing partial images of the frontier set, and we stop computing the reachable states when no new states are reached, when the size of the BDD of the approximate reachable states exceeds a certain threshold, or when a counterexample is found, whichever comes first.

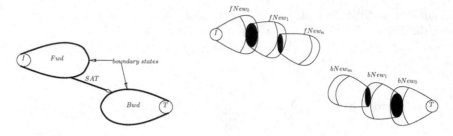

Fig. 2. bdd_sat technique

Fig. 3. Forward and Backward under-approximation reachability analysis

To compute approximate forward reachability, we call the function *Compute-Reach(I, T, Fwd)*. Initially, the frontier F is equal to the initial states I. At each iteration, we compute a set of states that can be reached in one time frame by calling *computeImage(F, Fwd)*. The iteration is terminated if the set of newly reached states, New_i, is empty. Then, we check if New_i intersects the target states. If it does, the property fails otherwise, we compute the new frontier F by calling the BDD operation *BddBetween(New_i, R)*, where *BddBetween* picks a set of states between New_i and R such that its BDD size is not larger than the BDD size of either. The set of reachable states R is the collection of all new reachable states and the initial states I.

In order to deal with the possible explosion of BDD sizes, the new frontier F is calculated by computing an under-approximation of the BDD that represents the states in *BddBetween(New_i, R)*. If the size of the resulting BDD exceeds a certain limit (500 BDD nodes in our experiments), we compute a subset of the frontier by extracting a cube that is closest to the target states by calling *ComputeCloseCube*. This function extracts an implicant of F that is at minimum Hamming distance from T, thus selecting states expected to be closer to the target. Figure 3 illustrates the above algorithm graphically.

Finally, we compute the outer boundary of the under-approximation of the reachable states R (boundary states):

$$S_i = image(R) - R \ .$$

S_i is the set of states that are reachable in one step from R but are not in R. Hence, we reduce the size of the BDD that represents the *boundary states*. In consequence we reduce the number of generated clauses when using the SAT-based method. Similarly, we use approximate backward reachability, *ComputeReach(T, I, Bwd)*, to compute the outer boundary S_t of the subset of the states that reach the target states.

If the set of boundary states S_i is empty, then R contains the complete reachable states. So, if R intersects T, then the property fails, otherwise the property passes. Similarly, if S_t is the empty set, a null intersection of R with $newI$ indicates that the property passes; otherwise the property fails. Finally, if S_i and S_t do not intersect, then we use BMC to find a path between S_i and S_t, or use the induction proof to prove that there is no path between S_i and S_t and hence the property holds.

Both S_i and S_t are represented by BDDs. So, we need to generate a propositional formula in CNF from a BDD when using the SAT-based method. We follow the method

```
ComputeReach(S, E, dir) {
    status = undecided;
    if(S ∩ E ≠ ∅) return(fail, ∅);
    R = New₀ = F = S;
    while (size(R) ≤ threshold₁ ) {
        To = computeImage(F, dir);
        Newᵢ = To - R;
        if (Newᵢ == ∅) break;
        if(Newᵢ ∩ E ≠ ∅) return(fail, ∅);
        R = R ∪ Newᵢ;
        F = BddBetween(Newᵢ, R);
        F = BddUnderApprox(F);
        if(size(F) > threshold₂)
            F = ComputeCloseCube(F, T);
    }
    B = computeImage(R, dir) - R
    if(B == ∅) {
        B = R;
        if(R ∩ E ≠ ∅) status = fail;
        else status = pass;
    }
    return(status, B)
}
```

Fig. 4. Compute under-approximate reachable states R starting from set of states S and heading toward set of states E. Based on dir, $computeImage(R, dir)$ performs either forward image computation, or backward image computation

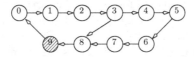

Fig. 5. Induction proofs can be sped up by reachability lower bounds

that is presented in [6], which decomposes the BDD into sub-BDDs and introduces an auxiliary variable for each sub-BDD. The CNF is generated for each sub-BDD F by expressing $\neg F$ in disjunctive normal form (DNF), and generating a clause for each disjunct in the DNF.

We use Fig. 5, which shows a fragment of a Kripke structure, to illustrate how our method reduces the termination depth. States $0, \ldots, 9$ are unreachable from the initial states (which are not shown) and state 9 is a bad state – one that violates f. The longest simple path reaching this state is of length 9. When we apply backward reachability for two steps, states 8, 3, and 7 are added to the target states. As a result, the length of the longest simple paths to a target state that does not go through another target state decreases to 3.

4   Counterexample Generation

If a property fails, we generate a counterexample to help debugging. This counterexample may not be a shortest counterexample due to the approximation of forward and backward reachability. In our method, we prove that a property fails in three ways: Using only forward approximate reachability analysis; using both forward and backward approximate reachability analyses; and using both reachability analyses and SAT.

If we initially set $S_t = T$, then we combine the above three cases into two situations. If the boundary states S_i and S_t do not overlap, we use the variable assignment returned by the SAT solver to construct a path which starts from state $s^n \in S_i$ and ends at state $s^m \in S_t$. If $s^n \notin I$, we generate a path from $s^i \in I$ to s^n. Similarly, we generate a path form s^m to $s^t \in T$ when $s^m \notin T$. If the boundary states S_i and S_t overlap, then $s^n \in S_i \cap S_t$ and $s^m = s^n$.

In summary, if there exists a counterexample in M between I and T, then this counterexample can be constructed from the following three paths, each of which may be empty:

- A path from $s^i \in I$ to $s^n \in S_i$ when $s^n \notin I$.
- A path from $s^m \in S_t$ to $s^t \in T$ when $s^m \notin T$.
- A path from s^n to s^m when $S_i \cap S_t = \emptyset$.

5   Experimental Results

We have implemented our new method in VIS [3, 18]. We implemented both the basic BMC algorithm of [2] and the induction proof as in [16]. We use zChaff [14] to check for the satisfiability of propositional formulae. The experiments were performed on an IBM IntelliStation with a 1.7 GHz Pentium IV CPU and 2 GB of RAM running Linux. The datasize limit was set to 1.5 GB.

The results presented in the following tables are for models that are either from industry or from the VIS Verification Benchmark set [19]. For each model, we count each safety property G f, where f is either propositional or contains only the next-time temporal operator X, as a separate experiment. We exclude experiments such that all the methods that we compare finish in less than 60 seconds. For all experiments, we increase the value of the bound k by 1 every time, and we check for termination at each step.

In our experiments, the threshold value that we use to control the size of the BDD of the approximate reachable states is 10000. We have chosen this value so that all models of different sizes use our method efficiently. If the size of this threshold is too small, larger models will not benefit from using approximate reachability. However, a larger value of this threshold causes a large number of clauses to be generated when applying the SAT-based method, and hence a slower model checking.

Table 1 shows the results of using our method for the invariants G f, where f is a propositional formula. We compare the performance of our method *bdd_sat* to the pure SAT-based method *bmc* and the pure BDD-based method *check invariant*, both in VIS. The first column in this table is the name of the model, the second is the number of state variables, and the third, labeled #, is the property number. The remaining columns are

Table 1. Comparison of bdd_sat, bmc, and ci on invariants

Model	state vars	#	bdd_sat					bmc			ci	
			img	pre	st	k	t (s)	st	k	t (s)	st	t (s)
am2910	99	1	0	0	P	$I(0)$	**0.1**	P	$I(0)$[1]	**0.1**		TO[2]
b12	115	1	21	0	F	2	**4.29**	F	14	137.49	F	5.7
b12abs	49	1	9	0	F	4	**4.04**	F	13	62.83	F	147.8
ball	85	1	0	0	P	$I(0)$	**0.07**	P	$I(0)$	0.1		TO
		2	8	5	U	20	89.93	U	20	**18.76**		TO
black jack	102	1	7	18			TO			TO		TO
		2	7	16	F	8	247.45	F	13	**19.13**		TO
bpb	36	1	25	0	F	-	**15.32**	F	9	193.45	F	40.00
D4	230	1	19	3	F	14	971.46	F	24	**23.12**	F	77.3
		2	19	3			TO	U	20	**90.7**	P	238.6
D14	96	1	9	2	F	9	208.49	F	14	**65.88**		TO
		2	0	0	P	$I(0)$	0.12	P	$I(0)$	**0.1**		TO
D16	531	1	5	3	F	-	**2.27**	F	8	8.38		TO
		2	0	0	P	$I(0)$	0.5	P	$I(0)$	**0.4**		TO
D18	506	1	12	5	F	10	247.11	F	23	**83.78**	F	129.34
D24	238	1	8	0	F	-	**0.65**	F	9	2.29		TO
		2	15	10	P	$I(6)$	58.19	P	$I(10)$	**9.39**		TO
		3	11	2	P	-	**10.0**	U	20	75.55		TO
daio_receiver_b	53	1	11	0	U	20	373.67	U	20	9.08	F	**1.7**
dekker	6	1	13	0	P	-	0.01	P	18	303.03	P	**0.0**
IBM01	141	1	15	3	F	-	**0.73**	F	14	70.96	F	4.4
IBM02_1	157	1	37	4	U	20	1310.51	U	20	81.12	P	**4.9**
nd3	100	1	0	0	P	$I(0)$	**0.3**	P	$I(0)$	**0.3**		TO
palu	37	1	6	4	F	1	**575.22**			TO		TO
peterson	6	1	10	0	P	-	0.01	U	20	126.94	P	**0.0**
ppprod	140	1	7	0	P	-	**0.2**	P	$I(6)$	66.6	P	9.3
s1269b	37	1	0	0	P	$I(0)$	0.1	P	$I(0)$	**0.0**		TO
		2	14	1	P	$I(0)$	19.52	P	$I(1)$	**0.79**		TO
s1423	74	1	3	0	P	-	**0.0**	P	$I(4)$	0.06		TO
		2	13	4	P	-	**0.68**	U	20	19.36		TO
		3	10	9	P	$I(48)$	**1720.22**			TO		TO
		4	9	324	F	-	**5.98**	F	61	161.98		TO
		5	10	22	F	12	97.18	F	35	**9.52**		TO
soap	140	1	0	0	P	$I(0)$	**0.1**	P	$I(0)$	**0.1**	P	60.21
Tom_P3	254	1	8	3	F	-	**4.41**	F	16	397.45	F	10.3
Tom_P4	254	1	8	2	F	-	**0.83**	F	11	75.30	F	3.3
UsbPhy	87	1	0	0	P	AT[3]	**0.0**	P	AT	**0.0**	P	88.7
		2	6	6	F	28	777.46	F	36	88.57	F	**8.5**
viper	215	1	4	1	F	-	260.77	F	4	**20.66**	F	623.4
		2	4	2	F	0	312.84	F	5	**36.17**	F	1620.3
vsaR	66	1	86	2	P	-	4.43	P	$I(2)$	**1.09**		TO
		2	165	8	F	5	35.8	F	23	**33.13**		TO
		3	15	2	P	-	**2.52**	U	30	120.02		TO

[1] Inductive proof (termination depth).

[2] Time Out.

[3] Always True.

Table 2. Comparison of bdd_sat, bmc, and ltl on safety properties containing X

Model	state vars	#	bdd_sat img	pre	st	k	t (s)	bmc st	k	t (s)	ltl st	t (s)
am2910	99	1	0	1	P	AT	**6.8**	U	50	534.33		TO
		2	3	2	P	-	1535.82	U	50	**510.34**		TO
bpb	36	1	5	1	P	-	**0.0**	U	30	TO	P	4.1
		2	9	1	P	-	**0.05**	U	32	TO	P	93.2
fabric	85	1	26	2	P	$I(2)$	37.71	U	50	90.43	P	**1.5**
heap	22	1	1	2	P	-	**0.1**	U	50	131.29	P	0.3
		2	0	1	P	AT	**0.1**	U	50	133.09	P	0.3
3proc	48	1	0	1	P	AT	**0.0**	U	50	213.36	P	8.3
		2	50	2	F	-	**0.16**	F	14	7.37	F	1124.2
PPC60X_bus	47	1	1	1	F	-	**0.51**	F	4	1.11	F	1.0
		2	1	1	F	-	**0.4**	F	3	0.63	F	7.0
		3	0	1	P	AT	6.3	U	50	215.54	P	**1.1**
		4	2	1	F	-	**0.0**	F	5	1.6	F	2.1
viper	215	1	2	2	P	-	**25.31**	U	42	TO		TO

divided into three groups: *bdd_sat*, *bmc*, and *ci*, respectively. The column labeled *st* in each group indicates whether each property passes (*P*), fails (*F*), or remains undecided (*U*); if a property fails, the number in the column labeled *k* is the length of the coun-terexample. The columns labeled *t* give the times in second for each method; a *TO* in this column indicates a time greater than 1800 s. The columns labeled *img* and *pre* give the number of image and pre-image computations respectively.

The column labeled *k* in each group may provide additional information. If the entry in this column is a dash, it indicates that the *bdd_sat* method proves the property without using the SAT-based part. A $I(n)$ in this column, indicates that the method proves that the property passes using the induction proof with termination depth of n. If n equals 0 the property is an *inductive invariant*.

Table 2 shows the results of using our method for safety properties G f, where f is not propositional, but contains only the temporal operator X. It is organized similarly to Table 1, except that we use the pure BDD-based method *ltl*, which checks for language emptiness, instead of *check invariant*. Passing properties of this form cannot be proved by *bmc* because the induction proof is restricted to invariants in our implementation.

From both tables one sees that our new method could prove properties that are hard for both the BDD-based and the SAT-based methods. In Table 1, our method fails to decide 5 out of 43 properties, whereas *bmc* fails to decide 11 and *ci* fails to decide 24. In Table 2, *bdd_sat* decides all the 14 properties, whereas *bmc* fails to decide 10 of them and *ltl* fails to decide 3 of them. For example, in Table 1 *bdd_sat* refutes the property for the model *palu* in less than ten minutes, while *bmc* and *ci* time out. In addition, for the model *viper* in Table 2, *bdd_sat* proves the property true in 25.31 seconds, while *ltl* and *bmc* do not reach a decision in 1800s.

Our new method decreases the length of the paths to be found by SAT and reduces the termination depth. For model *b12* in Table 1, *bdd_sat* finds a counterexample in 2 steps, while *bmc* finds the counterexample in 14 steps. In model *D24* in Table 1, second

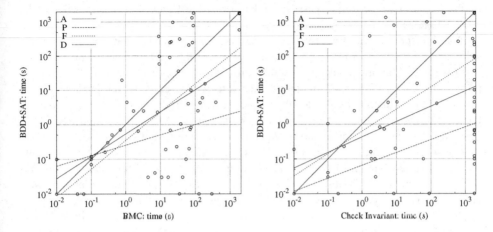

Fig. 6. Run times of bdd_sat against other methods

property, *bdd_sat* proves the property with termination depth 6; *bmc* proves the same property with termination depth 10. For model *fabric* in Table 2, *bdd_sat* proves the property with termination depth 2; *bmc* can not reach a decision in 1800s.

For a given value of k, our method explores longer paths than *BMC*. So, our method has more chances to conclude for the same value of k. For the second property of the *ball* model in Table 1, *bdd_sat* computes 8 images and 5 preimages; hence, *bdd_sat* actually explores paths of length up to 33.

Our method can go much deeper than *BMC* within the same amount of memory. For the *IBM02_1* model, *bdd_sat* computes 37 images and 4 pre-images before calling the SAT solver. For the same example, if we run *bmc* for $k = 36$, zChaff runs out of memory. The search of a larger fraction of the state space explains the longer time reported in Table 1 for *bdd_sat* in this experiment.

For inductive invariants, whose termination depth is 0, both *bdd_sat* and *bmc* perform better than *ci*. For instance, for model *nd3* in Table 1, *bdd_sat* and *bmc* prove the property in 0.3 seconds, while *ci* times out.

By only using the BDD-based part of our method, we have successfully proved properties that are hard for the pure BDD-based method. For the model *vsaR* in Table 1, we have proved the properties in a short amount of time while *ci* times out. Similarly, *ltl* times out for the model *viper* in Table 2.

Our method has a major advantage over *ci* because it combines forward and backward searches. For examples like the inductive invariants, backward reachability may be much more efficient than forward reachability. For model *s1269b* in Table 1, *bdd_sat* proves the second property with termination depth of 0, while *ci* times out. Backward reachability proves that all bad states are unreachable in one step, while approximate forward reachability does not take as much time as *ci*.

In addition, our method can decide that a formula passes or fails by checking if the formula is equivalent to either true or false before using either the BDD-based or the SAT-based method. The first property of model *UsbPhy* in Table 1 and *am2910* in Table 2 are both proved to pass by showing that the BDD of both properties is the constant one.

Varying the degree of approximation in *bdd_sat* obviously produces different results, and no specific setting works uniformly well for all examples. One should spend less time in reachability analysis, or even skip it altogether, for those models for which pure BMC is fast. Our implementation uses a fixed approach, which leads to mixed results. This is illustrated in Table 1 by the second property of model *blackjack* and by the only property of model *bpb*. Comparing to the pure SAT-based method, the BDD-based under-approximation method of *bdd_sat* significantly slows down verification for *blackjack*. In contrast, it significantly reduces the verification time of *bpb*. In both cases, *bdd_sat* is faster than *ci*. More importantly, aggressive approximation causes the fraction of time spent in reachability analysis to decrease as the size of the model increases. Hence, our mixed approach is more robust than one based exclusively on SAT.

Occasionally, *bdd_sat* fails to decide properties that *ci* successfully verifies. This is because SAT-based methods are not uniformly superior to BDD-based methods. Indeed, for all the experiments in which *bdd_sat* fails to decide the properties, *bmc* also fails.

In Fig. 6, we plot the performance of *bdd_sat* against the performance of *bmc* (left graph) and *check invariant* (right graph) methods. The vertical axes give the times in seconds taken by the *bdd_sat* method. The horizontal axes give the times in seconds taken by the other methods. Each point represents one model checking run. Points below the diagonal, labeled D, indicate a faster run time for the *bdd_sat* method. In the direct comparison over 59 experiments, our method performs better than *bmc* in 30 of them, and ties with *bmc* in 9 of them. Our method outperforms *ci* in 45 experiments, and ties with *ci* in 5 experiments, *ci* times out in 23 experiments.

We also plot $y = a \cdot x^b$ in Fig. 6, where a and b are obtained by least-square fitting of the experiment data. The line labeled A is for all properties, the line labeled P is for the passing properties, and the one labeled F is for the failing properties. Using Student's t test, we can infer that the improvement by our method is statistically significant. However, the improvement for the passing properties is statistically more significant than the improvement of the failing properties.

6   Conclusions

We have presented a new symbolic model checking method that integrates SAT-based BMC with BDD-based approaches. Our method reduces the lengths of the paths to be examined by the SAT solver to find a counterexample or to prove termination. As a result, our new method can prove properties that are hard for both the BDD-based and the SAT-based methods. Since forward and backward under-approximations contain all the initial states and all the bad states, respectively, then given enough resources, our method is correct and complete.

We have tested our method on safety property $G f$ (f is either a propositional formula or a path formula that contains only the temporal operator X). However, our method could be used to verify other safety properties. For instance, a counterexample to the safety property $G(p \rightarrow q R p)$ is an initialized path that starts at a state that satisfies $p \wedge \neg q$, goes through states that satisfy $\neg q$, and ends at a state that satisfies

$\neg p$. The BDD-based methods can be used to enlarge the initial and target states, and the SAT-based method is used to look for a path between the two enlarged sets of states along which $\neg q$ is true.

In our method, we use BDDs to improve the SAT-based method. We may do the opposite by letting SAT help the BDD-based methods. One way to do so is to use the SAT solver to get an over-approximation of the reachable states. In [12], when the SAT solver finds the formula unsatisfiable, an *interpolant* is derived from a proof of unsatisfiability. This interpolant is an over-approximation of the reachable states. This information could be used to reduce the size of BDDs in the BDD-based method. In addition, we may analyze the proof of unsatisfiability produced by the SAT solver, to extract hints for BDD-based guided search, or variable orders for the BDDs.

Because the search for a counterexample and the induction proof are growing incrementally, our technique should benefit from the use of an *incremental* SAT solver [20, 9].

References

1. J. Baumgartner, A. Kuehlmann, and J. Abraham. Property checking via structural analysis. In E. Brinksma and K. G. Larsen, editors, *Fourteenth Conference on Computer Aided Verification (CAV'02)*, pages 151–165. Springer-Verlag, Berlin, July 2002. LNCS 2404.
2. A. Biere, A. Cimatti, E. Clarke, and Y. Zhu. Symbolic model checking without BDDs. In *Fifth International Conference on Tools and Algorithms for Construction and Analysis of Systems (TACAS'99)*, pages 193–207, Amsterdam, The Netherlands, Mar. 1999. LNCS 1579.
3. R. K. Brayton et al. VIS: A system for verification and synthesis. In T. Henzinger and R. Alur, editors, *Eighth Conference on Computer Aided Verification (CAV'96)*, pages 428–432. Springer-Verlag, Rutgers University, 1996. LNCS 1102.
4. R. E. Bryant. Graph-based algorithms for Boolean function manipulation. *IEEE Transactions on Computers*, C-35(8):677–691, Aug. 1986.
5. G. Cabodi, P. Camurati, and S. Quer. Symbolic exploration of large circuits with enhanced forward/backward traversals. In *Proceedings of the Conference on European Design Automation*, pages 22–27, Grenoble, France, Sept. 1994.
6. G. Cabodi, S. Nocco, and S. Quer. Improving SAT-based bounded model checking by means of BDD-based approximate traversal. In *Proceedings of the Conference on Design, Automation and Test in Europe*, pages 898–905, Munich, Germany, Mar. 2003.
7. E. Clarke, A. Gupta, J. Kukula, and O. Strichman. SAT based abstraction-refinement using ILP and machine learning. In E. Brinksma and K. G. Larsen, editors, *Fourteenth Conference on Computer Aided Verification (CAV 2002)*, pages 265–279. Springer-Verlag, July 2002. LNCS 2404.
8. L. de Moura, H. Rueß, and M. Sorea. Bounded model checking and induction: From refutation to verification. In W. A. Hunt, Jr. and F. Somenzi, editors, *Fifteenth Conference on Computer Aided Verification (CAV'03)*, pages 1–13. Springer-Verlag, Boulder, CO, July 2003. LNCS 2725.
9. N. Eén and N. Sörensson. Temporal induction by incremental SAT solving. *Electronic Notes in Theoretical Computer Science*, 89(4), 2003. First International Workshop on Bounded Model Checking. http://www.elsevier.nl/locate/entcs/.
10. D. Kröning and O. Strichman. Efficient computation of recurrence diameters. In *Verification, Model Checking, and Abstract Interpretation*, pages 298–309, New York, NY, Jan. 2003. Springer. LNCS 2575.

11. K. L. McMillan. *Symbolic Model Checking*. Kluwer Academic Publishers, Boston, MA, 1994.
12. K. L. McMillan. Interpolation and SAT-based model checking. In W. A. Hunt, Jr. and F. Somenzi, editors, *Fifteenth Conference on Computer Aided Verification (CAV'03)*, pages 1–13. Springer-Verlag, Berlin, July 2003. LNCS 2725.
13. K. L. McMillan and N. Amla. Automatic abstraction without counterexamples. In *International Conference on Tools and Algorithms for Construction and Analysis of Systems (TACAS'03)*, pages 2–17, Warsaw, Poland, Apr. 2003. LNCS 2619.
14. M. Moskewicz, C. F. Madigan, Y. Zhao, L. Zhang, and S. Malik. Chaff: Engineering an efficient SAT solver. In *Proceedings of the Design Automation Conference*, pages 530–535, Las Vegas, NV, June 2001.
15. K. Ravi and F. Somenzi. High-density reachability analysis. In *Proceedings of the International Conference on Computer-Aided Design*, pages 154–158, San Jose, CA, Nov. 1995.
16. M. Sheeran, S. Singh, and G. Stålmarck. Checking safety properties using induction and a SAT-solver. In W. A. Hunt, Jr. and S. D. Johnson, editors, *Formal Methods in Computer Aided Design*, pages 108–125. Springer-Verlag, Nov. 2000. LNCS 1954.
17. A. P. Sistla. Safety, liveness and fairness in temporal logic. *Formal Aspects in Computing*, 6:495–511, 1994.
18. URL: http://vlsi.colorado.edu/~vis.
19. Vis verification benchmarks. http://vlsi.colorado.edu/~vis.
20. J. Whittemore, J. Kim, and K. Sakallah. SATIRE: A new incremental satisfiability engine. In *Proceedings of the Design Automation Conference*, pages 542–545, Las Vegas, NV, June 2001.

Bounded Verification of Past LTL[*]

Alessandro Cimatti[1], Marco Roveri[1], and Daniel Sheridan[2]

[1] Istituto per la Ricerca Scientifica e Tecnologica (IRST)
Via Sommarive 18, 38050 Povo, Trento, Italy
{cimatti,roveri}@irst.itc.it
[2] School of Informatics, The University of Edinburgh
Kings Buildings, Mayfield Road, Edinburgh EH9 3JZ, UK
d.j.sheridan@sms.ed.ac.uk

Abstract. Temporal logics with past operators are gaining increasing importance in several areas of formal verification for their ability to concisely express useful properties. In this paper we propose a new approach to bounded verification of PLTL, the linear time temporal logic extended with past temporal operators. Our approach is based on the transformation of PLTL into Separated Normal Form, which in turn is amenable for reduction to propositional satisfiability. An experimental evaluation shows that our approach induces encodings which are significantly smaller and more easily solved than previous approaches, in the cases of both model checking and satisfiability problems.

1 Introduction

Temporal logics with past operators are being devoted increasing interest in a number of application areas (e.g. formal verification [12, 5, 10], requirement engineering [13, 17], and automated task planning [2]). In the widely-used setting of Linear Temporal Logics (LTL), past operators do not add expressive power with respect to pure-future: any LTL formula with past operators can be rewritten by only using future-time operators [11]. On the other hand, past operators are very useful in practice, since they help to keep specifications compact, simple, and easy to understand. This practical consideration has a formal counterpart in the fact that LTL with past operators is exponentially more succinct than LTL with pure-future operators [14].

In this paper we tackle the problem of lifting SAT-based verification techniques, which are becoming a prominent technology in many application areas, to deal with past operators. We focus on *bounded* verification for PLTL, where the analysis is limited to behaviors of a fixed number of time steps.

---

[*] This work is partially sponsored by the PROSYD EC project, contract number IST-2003-507219, and the CALCULEMUS! IHP-RTN EC project, contract code HPRN-CT-2000-00102, and has thus benefited of the financial contribution of the Commission through the IHP programme. We thank Paul Jackson, Roberto Sebastiani and Simone Semprini for their useful comments and feedback.

Our interpretation of bounded verification encompasses both Bounded Model Checking and Bounded Satisfiability. *Bounded Model Checking* [4] focuses on design verification: given a model M (typically representing a design) and a formula φ (typically representing a desired property), checking the existence of a counterexample (a behavior of M which violates φ) over k steps is reduced to a purely propositional satisfiability problem, and solved with an efficient SAT solver.

Bounded Satisfiability is more directed to the analysis of requirements, which is gaining a significant practical interest. In fact, we are witnessing the take off of property-based design paradigms (e.g. with the acceptance of the PSL/Sugar language [1] as a IEEE standard language for property specification). This highlights the increased recognition of the importance of properties that are intended to specify the design intent, rather than the design itself. The object of the verification is now a set of requirements, represented as a set of PLTL formulae Γ. Different forms of analysis can be envisaged: for instance, we may be interested in checking whether Γ is *k-satisfiable*, that is, if it admits a model which can be presented within k steps; checking whether a certain formula φ is *k-possible* with respect to Γ, corresponding to $\Gamma \wedge \varphi$ being k-satisfiable; and checking whether a certain formula φ is a necessary consequence (an assertion) for Γ, corresponding to $\Gamma \wedge \neg\varphi$ not being k-satisfiable. These problems can be easily reduced to checking the (bounded) satisfiability of a generic set of formulae (or, equivalently, of their conjunction). They can also be seen as a bounded model checking problem where the model is completely unspecified; compared to model checking, however, we notice that a model might not even be available at an early stage of the development process. This shift in focus makes the problems significantly different from a pragmatic point of view.

In this paper, we propose a new encoding of PLTL into propositional logic, based on the use of Separated Normal Form (SNF) for PLTL [8]. The main idea underlying the SNF reduction is the introduction of additional variables (subsequently referred to as 'SNF variables') to take into account the truth value of sub-formulae. The evolution of SNF variables is constrained by rules that can be seen as defining a transition relation of an observer automaton. The encoding can be enhanced further by considering that, in the bounded case, eventualities can be expressed with a fix-point construction. Our approach generalizes the construction of Frisch et al. [9], that shows significant improvements over the original construction presented in [4]. We carried out an experimental evaluation, where the SNF-based approach proposed in this paper is compared with the direct extension of BMC to past from [3]. The results show that the SNF approach results in a much more efficient implementation, yielding encodings that are smaller (in terms of clauses) and that are solved much more easily by the propositional solver.

This paper is structured as follows. Section 2 covers the syntax and semantics of PLTL. In Section 3 we introduce the Separated Normal Form for PLTL. In Section 4 we discuss how to generate efficient encodings for bounded model checking of PLTL. Section 5 provides an experimental evaluation of our technique, and we draw some conclusions in Section 6.

2   Linear Temporal Logic with Past Operators

In this paper we consider PLTL, i.e. the Linear Temporal Logic (LTL) augmented with past operators. The starting point is standard LTL, the formulae of which are constructed from propositional atoms by applying the future temporal operators $\mathbf{X}$ (next), $\mathbf{F}$ (future), $\mathbf{G}$ (globally), $\mathbf{U}$ (until), and $\mathbf{R}$ (releases), in addition to the usual Boolean connectives. PLTL extends LTL by introducing the past operators $\mathbf{Y}$, $\mathbf{Z}$, $\mathbf{O}$, $\mathbf{H}$, $\mathbf{S}$, and $\mathbf{T}$, which are the temporal duals of the future operators and allow us to express statements on the past time instants. The $\mathbf{Y}$ (for "**Y**esterday") operator is the temporal dual of $\mathbf{X}$ and refers to the *previous* time instant. At any non-initial time, $\mathbf{Y}\varphi$ is true if and only if φ holds at the previous time instant. The $\mathbf{Z}$ operator is similar to the $\mathbf{Y}$ operator, and it only differs in the way the initial time instant is dealt with: at time zero, $\mathbf{Y}\varphi$ is false, while $\mathbf{Z}\varphi$ is true.

The $\mathbf{O}$ (for "**O**nce") operator is the temporal dual of $\mathbf{F}$ (sometimes in the future), so $\mathbf{O}\varphi$ is true iff φ is true at some past time instant (including the present time). Likewise, $\mathbf{H}$ (for "**H**istorically") is the past-time version of $\mathbf{G}$ (always in the future), so that $\mathbf{H}\varphi$ is true iff φ is always true in the past. The $\mathbf{S}$ (for "**S**ince") operator is the temporal dual of $\mathbf{U}$ (until), so that $\varphi \mathbf{S}\psi$ is true iff ψ holds somewhere in the past and φ is true from then up to now. Finally, we have $\varphi \mathbf{T}\psi = \neg(\neg\varphi \mathbf{S}\neg\psi)$ ($\mathbf{T}$ is called the "**T**rigger" operator), exactly as in the future case we have $\varphi \mathbf{R}\psi = \neg(\neg\varphi \mathbf{U}\neg\psi)$.

The syntax of PLTL is formally defined as follows:

Definition 1 (Syntax of PLTL). *The grammar for PLTL formulae is*

$$PLTL \ni \varphi, \psi \doteq p \mid \neg\varphi \mid \varphi \circ^{\mathbf{B}} \psi \mid \circ_1^{\mathbf{F}} \varphi \mid \varphi \circ_2^{\mathbf{F}} \psi \mid \circ_1^{\mathbf{P}} \varphi \mid \varphi \circ_2^{\mathbf{P}} \psi$$

where $p \in \mathcal{A}$ and $\mathcal{A}$ is a finite set of atomic propositions, $\circ^{\mathbf{B}} \in \{\wedge, \vee\}$ stands for a Boolean connective, $\circ_1^{\mathbf{F}} \in \{\mathbf{X}, \mathbf{F}, \mathbf{G}\}$ and $\circ_2^{\mathbf{F}} \in \{\mathbf{R}, \mathbf{U}\}$ are future temporal operators (unary and binary, respectively), and $\circ_1^{\mathbf{P}} \in \{\mathbf{Y}, \mathbf{Z}, \mathbf{O}, \mathbf{H}\}$ and $\circ_2^{\mathbf{P}} \in \{\mathbf{T}, \mathbf{S}\}$ are past temporal operators (unary and binary).

In the following, we use φ and ψ to denote PLTL formulae, and p to denote propositions in $\mathcal{A}$. We write $\varphi \rightarrow \psi$ for $\neg\varphi \vee \psi$, and $\varphi \leftrightarrow \psi$ for $(\varphi \rightarrow \psi) \wedge (\psi \rightarrow \varphi)$. As usual, PLTL formulae are interpreted over (linear) structures, that are basically infinite sequences of assignments to the propositions.

Definition 2 (Semantics of PLTL). *A linear structure π over a finite set of propositions $\mathcal{A}$ is a function $\pi : \mathbb{N} \rightarrow 2^{\mathcal{A}}$.*

Let π be a linear structure over $\mathcal{A}$, let φ and ψ be PLTL formulae, and let $i, j, k \in \mathbb{N}$. Then φ holds in π at time i, written $(\pi, i) \models \varphi$, is inductively defined in Figure 1. φ is true in π, written $\pi \models \varphi$, iff $(\pi, 0) \models \varphi$.

Although the use of past operators in LTL does not introduce expressive power, it may allow to express temporal properties in an exponentially more succinct manner [14]. On an informal (but very important) level, past operators allow us to formalize properties more naturally. For instance, *if a problem is*

$$(\pi, i) \models p \qquad \text{iff} \quad p \in \pi(i)$$
$$(\pi, i) \models \neg\varphi \qquad \text{iff} \quad (\pi, i) \not\models \varphi$$
$$(\pi, i) \models \varphi \vee \psi \qquad \text{iff} \quad (\pi, i) \models \varphi \text{ or } (\pi, i) \models \psi$$
$$(\pi, i) \models \varphi \wedge \psi \qquad \text{iff} \quad (\pi, i) \models \varphi \text{ and } (\pi, i) \models \psi$$

$$(\pi, i) \models \mathbf{X}\varphi \qquad \text{iff} \quad (\pi, i+1) \models \varphi$$
$$(\pi, i) \models \mathbf{F}\varphi \qquad \text{iff} \quad \exists j \geq i.\, (\pi, j) \models \varphi$$
$$(\pi, i) \models \mathbf{G}\varphi \qquad \text{iff} \quad \forall j \geq i.\, (\pi, j) \models \varphi$$
$$(\pi, i) \models \varphi \mathbf{U}\psi \qquad \text{iff} \quad \exists j \geq i.\, ((\pi, j) \models \psi \text{ and } \forall k : i \leq k < j.\, (\pi, k) \models \varphi)$$
$$(\pi, i) \models \varphi \mathbf{R}\psi \qquad \text{iff} \quad \forall j \geq i.\, ((\pi, j) \models \psi \text{ or } \exists k : i \leq k < j.\, (\pi, k) \models \varphi)$$

$$(\pi, i) \models \mathbf{Y}\varphi \qquad \text{iff} \quad i > 0 \text{ and } (\pi, i-1) \models \varphi$$
$$(\pi, i) \models \mathbf{Z}\varphi \qquad \text{iff} \quad i = 0 \text{ or } (\pi, i-1) \models \varphi$$
$$(\pi, i) \models \mathbf{O}\varphi \qquad \text{iff} \quad \exists j \leq i.\, (\pi, j) \models \varphi$$
$$(\pi, i) \models \mathbf{H}\varphi \qquad \text{iff} \quad \forall j \leq i.\, (\pi, j) \models \varphi$$
$$(\pi, i) \models \varphi \mathbf{S}\psi \qquad \text{iff} \quad \exists j \leq i.\, ((\pi, j) \models \psi \text{ and } \forall k : j < k \leq i.\, (\pi, k) \models \varphi)$$
$$(\pi, i) \models \varphi \mathbf{T}\psi \qquad \text{iff} \quad \forall j \leq i.\, ((\pi, j) \models \psi \text{ or } \exists k : j < k \leq i.\, (\pi, k) \models \varphi)$$

Fig. 1. The semantics of PLTL

diagnosed, then a failure must have previously occurred, can be represented in PLTL as

$$\mathbf{G}(problem \rightarrow \mathbf{O}\ failure)$$

that is more natural than its pure-future counterpart $\neg(\neg failure\ \mathbf{U}\ problem)$. Similarly, the property *grants are issued only upon requests* can be easily specified as

$$\mathbf{G}(grant \rightarrow \mathbf{Y}(\neg grant\ \mathbf{S}\ request))$$

compared to the corresponding pure-future translation

$$(request\ \mathbf{R}\ \neg grant)\ \wedge\ \mathbf{G}(grant \rightarrow (request \vee (\mathbf{X}(request\ \mathbf{R}\ \neg grant)))).$$

As for the pure future case, any formula in PLTL can be reduced to *Negation Normal Form* (NNF), where negation only occurs in front of atomic propositions. This linear time transformation is obtained by pushing the negation towards the leaves of the syntactic tree of the formula, and exploiting the dualities between conjunction and disjunction, $\mathbf{F}$ and $\mathbf{G}$, $\mathbf{U}$ and $\mathbf{R}$, $\mathbf{O}$ and $\mathbf{H}$, and $\mathbf{S}$ and $\mathbf{T}$. Notice that, in the case of previous time we have to rely on the two properties $\neg\mathbf{Y}\varphi \equiv \mathbf{Z}\neg\varphi$ and $\neg\mathbf{Z}\varphi \equiv \mathbf{Y}\neg\varphi$, which extend the single future-case rule $\neg\mathbf{X}\varphi \equiv \mathbf{X}\neg\varphi$ (we have both $\neg\mathbf{Y}\varphi \not\equiv \mathbf{Y}\neg\varphi$ and $\neg\mathbf{Z}\varphi \not\equiv \mathbf{Z}\neg\varphi$, because of their semantics at the initial time point). We write the transformation to NNF of a formula φ as $\text{NNF}(\varphi)$.

3   Separated Normal Form for PLTL

The Separated Normal Form (SNF) [7] is a clause-like normal form for temporal logic, based on the Separation Theorem [11]. A formula in SNF has the general form

$$\mathbf{G}\left(\bigwedge_i (P_i \rightarrow F_i)\right)$$

where each implication $P_i \rightarrow F_i$, also referred to as a *rule*, relates some past time formula P_i to some future time formula F_i. Each rule has one of the following forms:

$$\mathbf{start} \rightarrow \bigvee_j l_j \qquad \bigwedge_i l_i \rightarrow \bigvee_j l_j \qquad \bigwedge_i l_i \rightarrow \mathbf{X} \bigvee_j l_j \qquad \bigwedge_i l_i \rightarrow \mathbf{F} \bigvee_j l_j$$

where l_i, l_j are literals (i.e. either atomic propositions or negations of atomic propositions), and **start** is an abbreviation for $\mathbf{Z} \perp$. In the following, the rules are referred to as start, invariant, next, and eventuality rules, respectively.

Every PLTL formula can be mapped onto a formula in SNF which is equi-satisfiable [8]. With respect to [8], we generalize the form of the rules to permit general propositional formulae in place of $\bigwedge_i l_i$ and $\bigvee_j l_j$. A further slight difference is that we adopt a non-strict semantics for time operators, so that all temporal operators other than $\mathbf{X}$, $\mathbf{Y}$ and $\mathbf{Z}$ take into account the present time instant. In order to reduce to SNF a generic PLTL formula γ, we define a transformation that manipulates sets of formulae. We start from the singleton set $\{\mathbf{start} \rightarrow \mathrm{NNF}(\gamma)\}$, which intuitively states that γ has to hold in the initial state of any satisfying structure. Then, the conversion is carried out by the function $\mathrm{SNF}(\cdot)$, which takes in input a set of formulae, and applies some transformation to a member of the set. The function is applied repeatedly until a set of rules is obtained. Intuitively, the transformations are devoted to eliminating occurrences of "complex" temporal operators by reducing them to more basic ones (i.e. $\mathbf{X}$ and $\mathbf{F}$). To this end, each transformation can introduce new SNF variables, one for each temporal sub-formula being eliminated. In order to highlight their intuitive meaning, SNF variables are denoted as underlined temporal formulae (e.g. $\underline{\mathbf{XG}\varphi}$).

The transformations defining $\mathrm{SNF}(\cdot)$ are reported in Figures 2 and 3. We write Γ for the subset of formulae which are not affected by the transformation, φ and ψ for PLTL formulae in NNF, and f and g for propositional formulae. In the rule being transformed, φ is the sub-formula that is not affected. We also write $\psi(\mathbf{G}f)$ to say that $\mathbf{G}f$ occurs in ψ, while $\psi(g)$ stands for the formula obtained by substituting every occurrence of $\mathbf{G}f$ with g in ψ. The same notation is used for the other temporal operators. The first four transformations in Figure 2, $\mathrm{SNF}_{[\mathbf{X}]}$, $\mathrm{SNF}_{[\mathbf{F}]}$, $\mathrm{SNF}_{[\mathbf{Y}]}$ and $\mathrm{SNF}_{[\mathbf{Z}]}$ are used to rename sub-formulae. The others have an intuitive interpretation, based on the fix-point characterizations of temporal operators. Consider the simple case of a $\mathbf{G}f$ formula: the corresponding set of rules is $\{\mathbf{start} \rightarrow f \wedge \underline{\mathbf{XG}f}, \underline{\mathbf{XG}f} \rightarrow \mathbf{X}(f \wedge \underline{\mathbf{XG}f})\}$. The intuitive interpretation for the SNF variable $\underline{\mathbf{XG}f}$ is that $\mathbf{G}f$ holds in the next state. Similarly, consider

$$\text{SNF}_{[\mathbf{X}]}(\{\varphi \to \psi(\mathbf{X}\,f)\} \cup \Gamma) \doteq \left\{ \begin{array}{c} \varphi \to \psi(\mathbf{X}\,f) \\ \hline \mathbf{X}\,f \to \mathbf{X}\,f \end{array} \right\} \cup \Gamma$$

$$\text{SNF}_{[\mathbf{F}]}(\{\varphi \to \psi(\mathbf{F}\,f)\} \cup \Gamma) \doteq \left\{ \begin{array}{c} \varphi \to \psi(\mathbf{F}\,f) \\ \hline \mathbf{F}\,f \to \mathbf{F}\,f \end{array} \right\} \cup \Gamma$$

$$\text{SNF}_{[\mathbf{Y}]}(\{\psi(\mathbf{Y}\,f) \to \varphi\} \cup \Gamma) \doteq \left\{ \begin{array}{c} \psi(\mathbf{Y}\,f) \to \varphi \\ \hline \mathbf{Y}\,f \to \mathbf{Y}\,f \end{array} \right\} \cup \Gamma$$

$$\text{SNF}_{[\mathbf{Z}]}(\{\psi(\mathbf{Z}\,f) \to \varphi\} \cup \Gamma) \doteq \left\{ \begin{array}{c} \psi(\mathbf{Z}\,f) \to \varphi \\ \hline \mathbf{Z}\,f \to \mathbf{Z}\,f \end{array} \right\} \cup \Gamma$$

$$\text{SNF}_{[\mathbf{G}]}(\{\varphi \to \psi(\mathbf{G}\,f)\} \cup \Gamma) \doteq \left\{ \begin{array}{c} \varphi \to \psi(f \wedge \mathbf{X}(\mathbf{G}\,f)) \\ \hline \mathbf{X}(\mathbf{G}\,f) \to \mathbf{X}(\overline{f \wedge \mathbf{X}(\mathbf{G}\,f)}) \end{array} \right\} \cup \Gamma$$

$$\text{SNF}_{[\mathbf{U}]}(\{\varphi \to \psi(f \,\mathbf{U}\,g)\} \cup \Gamma) \doteq \left\{ \begin{array}{c} \varphi \to \psi(g \vee (f \wedge \mathbf{X}(f \,\mathbf{U}\,g))) \\ \mathbf{X}(f \,\mathbf{U}\,g) \to \mathbf{X}(g \vee (\overline{f \wedge \mathbf{X}(f \,\mathbf{U}\,g)})) \\ \varphi \to \mathbf{F}\,g \end{array} \right\} \cup \Gamma$$

$$\text{SNF}_{[\mathbf{R}]}(\{\varphi \to \psi(f \,\mathbf{R}\,g)\} \cup \Gamma) \doteq \left\{ \begin{array}{c} \varphi \to \psi(g \wedge (f \vee \mathbf{X}(f \,\mathbf{R}\,g))) \\ \mathbf{X}(f \,\mathbf{R}\,g) \to \mathbf{X}(g \wedge (\overline{f \vee \mathbf{X}(f \,\mathbf{R}\,g)})) \end{array} \right\} \cup \Gamma$$

$$\text{SNF}_{[\mathbf{O}]}(\{\psi(\mathbf{O}\,f) \to \varphi\} \cup \Gamma) \doteq \left\{ \begin{array}{c} \psi(f \vee \mathbf{Y}(\mathbf{O}\,f)) \to \varphi \\ \mathbf{Y}(f \vee \mathbf{Y}(\overline{\mathbf{O}\,f})) \to \mathbf{Y}(\mathbf{O}\,f) \end{array} \right\} \cup \Gamma$$

$$\text{SNF}_{[\mathbf{H}]}(\{\psi(\mathbf{H}\,f) \to \varphi\} \cup \Gamma) \doteq \left\{ \begin{array}{c} \psi(f \wedge \mathbf{Z}(\mathbf{H}\,f)) \to \varphi \\ \mathbf{Z}(f \wedge \mathbf{Z}(\overline{\mathbf{H}\,f})) \to \mathbf{Z}(\mathbf{H}\,f) \end{array} \right\} \cup \Gamma$$

$$\text{SNF}_{[\mathbf{S}]}(\{\psi(f \,\mathbf{S}\,g) \to \varphi\} \cup \Gamma) \doteq \left\{ \begin{array}{c} \psi(g \vee (f \wedge \mathbf{Z}(f \,\mathbf{S}\,g))) \to \varphi \\ \mathbf{Z}(g \vee (f \wedge \mathbf{Z}(\overline{f \,\mathbf{S}\,g}))) \to \mathbf{Z}(f \,\mathbf{S}\,g) \end{array} \right\} \cup \Gamma$$

$$\text{SNF}_{[\mathbf{T}]}(\{\psi(f \,\mathbf{T}\,g) \to \varphi\} \cup \Gamma) \doteq \left\{ \begin{array}{c} \psi(g \wedge (f \vee \mathbf{Z}(f \,\mathbf{T}\,g))) \to \varphi \\ \mathbf{Z}(g \wedge (f \vee \mathbf{Z}(\overline{f \,\mathbf{T}\,g}))) \to \mathbf{Z}(f \,\mathbf{T}\,g) \end{array} \right\} \cup \Gamma$$

$$\text{SNF}_{[\mathbf{Y2X}]}(\{\mathbf{Y}\,f \to \varphi\} \cup \Gamma) \doteq \{f \to \mathbf{X}\,\varphi\} \cup \Gamma$$

$$\text{SNF}_{[\mathbf{Z2X}]}(\{\mathbf{Z}\,f \to \varphi\} \cup \Gamma) \doteq \left\{ \begin{array}{c} \mathbf{start} \to \varphi \\ f \to \mathbf{X}\,\varphi \end{array} \right\} \cup \Gamma$$

Fig. 2. Part of the transformation function for SNF

the rule $\mathbf{O}(f) \to g$: the corresponding set of rules is $\{f \vee \mathbf{Y}\mathbf{O}f \to g,\ f \vee \mathbf{Y}\mathbf{O}f \to \mathbf{X}\,\mathbf{Y}\mathbf{O}f\}$. The intuition here is that the SNF variable $\mathbf{Y}\mathbf{O}f$ will hold in the next state if f holds in the current state, or it held in some previous state. It is easy to see that the above transformations only introduce SNF variables, and $\mathbf{F}, \mathbf{X}, \mathbf{Y}$ and $\mathbf{Z}$ operators; together, $\text{SNF}_{[\mathbf{Y2X}]}$ and $\text{SNF}_{[\mathbf{Z2X}]}$ replace previous operators with next operators, so that the only remaining operators are $\mathbf{F}$ and $\mathbf{X}$.

The transformations in Figure 2 rely on past operators appearing on the left side of rules and future operators on the right. The transformations $\text{SNF}_{[\text{p2p}]}$ and $\text{SNF}_{[\text{f2f}]}$, reported Figure 3, are used to move operators onto the appropriate side (we use φ_P to denote a PLTL formula with at least an occurrence of a past

$$\mathrm{SNF}_{[\mathrm{p2p}]}(\{\mathbf{start} \to \varphi_P\} \cup \varGamma) \doteq \{\mathrm{NNF}(\neg\varphi_P) \to \neg\mathbf{start}\} \cup \varGamma$$

$$\mathrm{SNF}_{[\mathrm{f2f}]}(\{\psi_{\neg P} \to \neg\mathbf{start}\} \cup \varGamma) \doteq \{\mathbf{start} \to \mathrm{NNF}(\neg\psi_{\neg P})\} \cup \varGamma$$

$$\mathrm{SNF}_{[\mathbf{start}\mathbf{Y}]}(\{\mathbf{start} \to \mathbf{Y}\,\varphi\} \cup \varGamma) \doteq \{\mathbf{start} \to \bot\} \cup \varGamma$$

$$\mathrm{SNF}_{[\mathbf{start}\mathbf{Z}]}(\{\mathbf{start} \to \mathbf{Z}\,\varphi\} \cup \varGamma) \doteq \{\mathbf{start} \to \top\} \cup \varGamma$$

Fig. 3. The transformation functions to deal with combining past and future

temporal operator applied to a purely propositional formula, and $\varphi_{\neg P}$ to denote a formula with no such occurrences). The other transformations in Figure 3 avoid renaming $\mathbf{Y}$ and $\mathbf{Z}$ operators in trivial cases.

In order to guarantee the termination of the transformation described above, some syntactic restrictions need to be enforced. The application of $\mathrm{SNF}_{[\mathbf{F}]}$ is forbidden in cases where the $\mathbf{F}$ operator is the main connective of the conclusion, i.e. when the transformed rule has the form $\psi \to \mathbf{F}g$; similar restrictions apply to $\mathrm{SNF}_{[\mathbf{X}]}$, $\mathrm{SNF}_{[\mathbf{Y}]}$, and $\mathrm{SNF}_{[\mathbf{Z}]}$. Furthermore, transformations $\mathrm{SNF}_{[\mathbf{Y2X}]}$ and $\mathrm{SNF}_{[\mathbf{Z2X}]}$ must not be used while the right hand side is $\neg\mathbf{start}$.

4   Encoding Bounded Verification of PLTL into SAT

Traditionally, temporal logics are used to express requirements over designs, represented as Kripke structures.

Definition 3. *A (Boolean) Kripke structure over $\mathcal{A}$ is a tuple $M = \langle S, I, T \rangle$, where $S = 2^{\mathcal{A}}$ is a finite set of states, $I \subseteq S$ is the set of initial states, $T \subseteq S \times S$ is a transition relation between states. A path in M is an infinite sequence of states $s_0, s_1, \ldots$ such that $s_0 \in I$ and, for all i, $T(s_i, s_{i+1})$. Given a path $s_0, s_1, \ldots$, the corresponding linear structure maps i to s_i, for every i. A formula φ is existentially valid in M ($M \models \mathbf{E}\varphi$) iff it is true in the linear structure associated to some path π in M. Conversely, φ is universally valid in M ($M \models \mathbf{A}\varphi$) iff it is true in every linear structure associated to a path in M.*

Clearly, there is a duality between the existential and the universal versions of the model checking problem, i.e. $M \models \mathbf{A}\varphi$ iff $M \not\models \mathbf{E}\neg\varphi$. The universal model checking problem can be intuitively interpreted as checking if all the behaviors in the system represented by M comply with the requirement φ; the existential version is often interpreted as the problem of finding a witness to a violation of a required property. In the following, we assume that a Kripke structure M is given, and do not distinguish between a path in M and the corresponding linear structure. The satisfiability problem for φ can be seen as a model checking problem $M \models \varphi$, where M is a completely unconstrained Kripke structure of the form $\langle S, S, S \times S \rangle$, with $S = 2^{\mathcal{A}}$, and $\mathcal{A}$ is the set of atomic propositions in φ.

Bounded Verification. The idea underlying bounded verification is to look for linear structures that can be presented with a number of steps (i.e. transitions) which is fixed a priori. We assume that the number of steps, also called the bound, is denoted k and given. While completeness may be lost, the exploitation of the bound often enables the use of alternate search techniques. The idea of Bounded Model Checking [4] is to reduce an existential model checking problem $M \models \varphi$ with bound k to the problem of checking the satisfiability of a propositional formula $[\![M \models_k \varphi]\!]$: this is satisfiable iff there exists a path in M which can be presented with k transitions and satisfies φ. The encoding is structured as a conjunction $\text{PATH}_k \wedge [\![\varphi]\!]_k$, where the (propositional) models of the first conjunct correspond to finitely-expressible paths in M, while the second component encodes the requirements induced by φ. In the following, we assume that $\mathcal{A}$ is the set of atomic propositions occurring in M and in φ. We do not address the construction for PATH_k, which is standard. The case of bounded satisfiability simply reduces to the case of bounded model checking by simply dropping the PATH_k component from the encoding.

The problem of bounded satisfiability for φ is reduced to a propositional satisfiability problem as follows. The language of the propositional theory is defined by introducing, for each atomic proposition p in $\mathcal{A}$, $k + 1$ propositional variables of the form $p(i)$, with i ranging from 0 to k. When the propositional variable $p(i)$ is assigned to true [false, respectively], the intuitive meaning is that p holds [does not hold] in the i-th state of the linear structure. In addition, the language of the propositional theory contains, for each SNF variable associated to $\text{SNF}(\varphi)$, $k + 1$ propositional variables.

Intuitively, with bounded verification, it is possible to encode two different kinds of linear structures for φ: without loops, and with loops. When no loop is required, the propositional model corresponds to a whole class of linear structures sharing the same finite prefix, and which is sufficient to show the satisfiability of the formula φ. Intuitively, this is the case of violations to safety properties, which require that nothing bad ever happens – and it is therefore sufficient to show a finite path leading to a bad situation. When a loop is required, the propositional model corresponds to a lasso-shaped linear structure, which is made up of a finite prefix u followed by a portion v repeated infinitely many times. Intuitively, this is the case of violations to liveness properties, which requires that something good should happen. In this case, the structure reaches a point where only bad states keep repeating. While the case of a "finite" prefix requires no additional constraints, in order to find a looping behavior we enforce that the k-th state be equal to same preceding state. In the propositional theory, a loop-back from k to l, with $l < k$, is captured by stating that, for each atomic proposition $p \in \mathcal{A}$, the corresponding propositional variables at k and l are assigned the same truth values, i.e. $_lL_k \doteq \bigwedge_{p \in \mathcal{A}} (p(l) \leftrightarrow p(k))$.

Encoding the SNF Rules. The problem of k-satisfiability for a PLTL formula φ is obtained by encoding each rule in $\text{SNF}(\varphi)$ over the $k + 1$ time instants, depending on the existence of a loop. The encoding is structured as follows:

$$\bigwedge_{i=0}^{k} \bigwedge_{\rho \in \text{SNF}(\varphi)} -[\![\rho]\!]_k^i \quad \vee \quad \bigvee_{l=0}^{k-1} \left({}_lL_k \wedge \bigwedge_{i=0}^{k} \bigwedge_{\rho \in \text{SNF}(\varphi)} {}_l[\![\rho]\!]_k^i \right)$$

where $\iota[\![\cdot]\!]_i^k$ stands for the encoding operator over a path of k steps, at step i, with loop-back at l. We use $l \in \mathbb{N}$ to denote the loop-back point, while $l = -$ denotes the absence of a loop. The rules are encoded as follows:

$$\iota[\![\textbf{start} \rightarrow f]\!]_k^i \doteq \begin{cases} \iota[\![f]\!]_k^i & \text{if } i = 0 \\ \top & \text{otherwise} \end{cases}$$

$$\iota[\![f \rightarrow g]\!]_k^i \doteq \iota[\![f]\!]_k^i \rightarrow \iota[\![g]\!]_k^i$$

$$\iota[\![f \rightarrow \mathbf{X} g]\!]_k^i \doteq \begin{cases} \iota[\![f]\!]_k^i \rightarrow \iota[\![g]\!]_k^{i+1} & \text{if } i < k \\ \iota[\![f]\!]_k^i \rightarrow \iota[\![g]\!]_k^{l+1} & \text{if } i = k \text{ and } l \in \mathbb{N} \\ \iota[\![f]\!]_k^i \rightarrow \bot & \text{if } i = k \text{ and } l = - \end{cases}$$

$$\iota[\![f \rightarrow \mathbf{F} g]\!]_k^i \doteq \begin{cases} \begin{aligned} &-[\![f]\!]_k^i \rightarrow -[\![g \vee \mathbf{XF}g]\!]_k^i \quad \wedge \\ &-[\![\underline{\mathbf{XF}g} \rightarrow \mathbf{X}(g \vee \underline{\mathbf{XF}g})]\!]_k^i \end{aligned} & \text{if } l = - \\ \begin{aligned} &-[\![f]\!]_k^i \rightarrow -[\![g \vee \underline{\mathbf{XF}g}]\!]_k^{min(i,l)} \quad \wedge \\ &\iota[\![\underline{\mathbf{XF}g} \rightarrow \mathbf{X}(g \vee \underline{\mathbf{XF}g})]\!]_k^i \end{aligned} & \text{if } l \in \mathbb{N} \end{cases}$$

Intuitively, the rules are expanded as follows. The start rules express constraints only on the initial situation, and therefore have no effect on the subsequent time points. The invariant rules equally affect all of the time instants. The next rules are encoded in three different ways, depending on k, i, and l. Before the last state, the expansion is independent of l and k: the premise f is codified at state i, and the matrix of the conclusion g at $i+1$. At the last state, the premise is codified at k, while the matrix of the conclusion is either expanded at $l+1$, when a loop exists, or reduces to false, in case of no loop-back. The expansion of the eventuality rule requires the preliminary creation of an SNF variable, $\mathbf{XF}g$, representing the fact that the eventuality is to be fulfilled at next state. Then, in the case of no loop-back, the expansion basically performs a renaming, generating an invariant rule, and a next rule describing the dynamics together with the enforcement of the eventuality before the end of the path. This description expresses the loop optimization obtained in [9] with the introduction of the bound operator. The loop case is reduced to the case without a loop at $min(i,l)$: this encompasses both the possibility of $i \geq l$, i.e. i is in the loop, and of $i < l$, i.e. l is before the loop.

The expansion of purely propositional formulae is straightforward. Notice however that their conversion may impact the way in which the corresponding CNF is obtained, and therefore on the efficiency of the SAT solver. For lack of space we do not address these issues here (see e.g. [16]).

The number of propositional variables in the encoding is $O((|\mathcal{A}| + n) \cdot k)$, where n is the number of occurrences of temporal operators in φ. In fact, each transformation introduces one new SNF variable, and each temporal operator can result in the introduction of up to two new variables. The worst case is the $\mathbf{U}$ operator, that requires the application of $\text{SNF}_{[\mathbf{U}]}$, with the encoding for $\mathbf{F}$ introducing a second variable. We also notice that the number of rules in $\text{SNF}(\varphi)$ is linear in n: for each occurrence of a temporal operator, SNF applies exactly one transformation, which can in turn require the application of another transformation. The worst case is again associated with the expansion of $\mathbf{U}$. The number of rule instances in the above encoding is $O(n \cdot k^2)$, because of the different loop-back points.

Loop Independence Optimization. In order to overcome the quadratic dependence on k, we further develop the encoding, arriving at a formulation with a number of rule instances that is $O(n \cdot k)$. We exploit the fact that the encoding for most of the rules can be written to be the same in both the loop and non-loop cases, and we explicitly factor it out. This is obtained by rewriting the rules in a way that is independent of the actual existence and position of a loop-back, and by factoring them out of the big disjunction over the possible loop-back points. The encoding is structured as follows:

$$\bigwedge_{i=0}^{k-1} \bigwedge_{\rho \in \mathrm{SNF}(\varphi)} {}^{\mathrm{LI}}[\![\rho]\!]_k^i \ \wedge\ \left(\bigwedge_{\rho \in \mathrm{SNF}(\varphi)} {}^{\mathrm{LD}}_{-}[\![\rho]\!]_k^k \ \vee\ \bigvee_{l=0}^{k-1} \left({}_l L_k \wedge \bigwedge_{\rho \in \mathrm{SNF}(\varphi)} {}^{\mathrm{LD}}_{l}[\![\rho]\!]_k^k \right) \right)$$

where ${}^{\mathrm{LI}}[\![\cdot]\!]_k^i$ and ${}^{\mathrm{LD}}[\![\cdot]\!]_k^i$ denote the *loop-independent* encoding and the *loop-dependent* encoding operators. The definition of ${}^{\mathrm{LI}}[\![\cdot]\!]_k^i$ for the start, invariant and next rules coincides with ${}_{-}[\![\cdot]\!]_k^i$. For the eventuality rule $f \to \mathbf{F}g$, we first notice that the dependence on l in $min(i,l)$, in the loop case, can be eliminated with a disjunction of the encodings at i and at l. That is, ${}_l[\![\mathbf{F}\,g]\!]_k^i$ is replaced by ${}_l[\![\mathbf{F}\,g]\!]_k^i \vee {}_l[\![\mathbf{F}\,g]\!]_k^l$. The factorization is completed by renaming every occurrence of ${}_l[\![\mathbf{F}\,g]\!]_k^l$ with a newly introduced variable $\mathrm{ATL}(\mathbf{F}g)$. The same variable is disjuncted to ${}_{-}[\![\mathbf{F}\,g]\!]_k^i$ in the case without a loop. The encoding thus becomes, regardless of the loop-back point,

$$ {}^{\mathrm{LI}}[\![f \to \mathbf{F}\,g]\!]_k^i \ \dot{=}\ \begin{cases} {}_{-}[\![f]\!]_k^i \to ({}_{-}[\![g \vee \underline{\mathbf{XF}g}]\!]_k^i \vee \mathrm{ATL}(\mathbf{F}g)) & \wedge \\ {}_{-}[\![\underline{\mathbf{XF}g} \to \mathbf{X}(g \vee \underline{\mathbf{XF}g})]\!]_k^i \end{cases} $$

The encoding of the loop-dependent part for the start, invariant and next rules coincides with the encoding operator defined in previous section. (For the sake of clarity, we do not make explicit the fact that the invariant rules are independent of the loop, and could therefore be factored out; this fact is however exploited in the implementation.) The case of eventuality is encoded as follows.

$$ {}^{\mathrm{LD}}_{l}[\![f \to \mathbf{F}\,g]\!]_k^k \ \dot{=}\ \begin{cases} {}_{-}[\![f]\!]_k^k \to \neg\mathrm{ATL}(\mathbf{F}g) & \wedge \\ \quad {}_{-}[\![\underline{\mathbf{XF}g} \to \mathbf{X}(g \vee \underline{\mathbf{XF}g})]\!]_k^i & \text{if } l = - \\ ({}_{-}[\![f]\!]_k^k \wedge \mathrm{ATL}(\mathbf{F}g)) \to {}_{-}[\![g \vee \underline{\mathbf{XF}g}]\!]_k^l & \wedge \\ \quad {}_l[\![\underline{\mathbf{XF}g} \to \mathbf{X}(g \vee \underline{\mathbf{XF}g})]\!]_k^k & \text{if } l \in \mathbb{N} \end{cases} $$

We remark that "ATL" variables are untimed: unlike the variables in φ and from the SNF variables, they are not replicated $k+1$ times. We achieve independence from the loop since different characterising clauses are activated, depending on the particular value of l.

5   Experimental Analysis

In this section, we compare the SNF approach with the method for bounded model checking for PLTL proposed in [3], hereafter referred to as the *direct encoding*, that is a generalisation of the encoding for LTL [4]. The direct encoding is defined by recursively descending the structure of the formula being encoded, and distinguishing between the case without a loop and the case with a loop. In the case without a loop, the truth of a PLTL formula only depends on the finite prefix, and the interpretation of past operators always progresses towards the points closer to the origin (i.e., from i to 0). In the case of the loop, the problem is significantly more complicated: in fact, when interpreting a PLTL formula within the loop, the interpretation of going into the past may correspond either to going into the prefix before the loop-back point, or back to the future. The problem is solved by introducing the notion of past temporal horizon of a formula, that is then used as an upper bound to the number of virtual unrolls needed when generating the encoding for the formula. Similar to the pure-future case, the direct encoding does not introduce additional variables, so that witnesses of the form $\alpha \cdot \beta^k \cdot \beta^\omega$ can be reached with $k = |\alpha| \cdot |\beta|$ steps.

Both methods were implemented in NuSMV [6]. For each problem instance, and for each method, we report the total time required by NuSMV (on a Pentium 4, 1.8GHz processor with 1Gb RAM) to build and solve the encodings up to the reported bound, using zChaff [15] as the SAT solver; the reported bound corresponds to the first satisfiable instance, or to the largest unsatisfiable instance solved within the time limit.

We first ran the test from [3] involving past operators, i.e. the Alternating Bit Protocol (from the NuSMV distribution) with a property of the form

$$\mathbf{G}(\texttt{sender.state} = \texttt{waitForAck} \rightarrow \mathbf{Y}\,\mathbf{H}\,\texttt{sender.state} \neq \texttt{waitForAck})$$

The direct encoding required 87.2 secs. to generate the encoding and solve the problem, while the SNF-based encoding requires only 56.2 secs. Both methods find a counterexample at depth 17.

In order to stress the ability of the two methods to process past operators and to find short counterexamples, we conceived the Counter(N) problem set: a counter starts at 0, progresses up to N, and then loops back at $N/2$. We evaluate a set of parameterized properties, of the form

$$P(i) \doteq \neg\mathbf{F}(\mathbf{O}((c = N/2) \wedge \mathbf{O}((c = N/2 + 1)\ldots \wedge \mathbf{O}(c = N/2 + i)\ldots)))$$

The value of i is a measure of the nesting of past operators, while the structure of the property requires that the loop (of length $N/2$) must be traversed backwards several times in order to reach a counterexample.

The results are reported in Table 1, where T.O. indicates a runtime exceeding 1800 secs. The direct encoding suffers from the nesting of the property, which influences the past temporal horizon and therefore requires a larger number of virtual unrolls. Most of the time is in fact spent in the generation of the

Table 1. The results for Counter(N)

	Counter(16)		Counter(32)		Counter(64)	
	Direct	SNF	Direct	SNF	Direct	SNF
$P(0)$	0.07 8	0.06 8	0.5 16	0.19 16	8.10 32	0.96 32
$P(1)$	8.43 17	0.27 17	680.94 33	1.50 33	T.O. 37	11.20 65
$P(2)$	256.99 17	1.03 26	T.O. 21	7.33 50		68.60 98
$P(3)$	T.O. 13	3.27 35		27.73 67		282.01 131
$P(4)$		8.89 44		81.59 84		966.92 164

encodings. On the contrary, the encodings are generated efficiently by the SNF-based method, and the time required by the SAT solver is also very limited. SNF-based encodings seem to yield a significant speed up, even if longer paths need to be explored in order to find a counterexample. Notice however that in this problem set the component related to the model is not very significant. Although the ability to construct counterexamples with virtual unroll of the past might be a win, there is clearly a tradeoff between the time that is saved in searching shortened counterexamples compared to the time that is invested in generating more complex encodings.

As a further step, we compared the SNF and the direct encodings on a test set from the domain of requirement engineering for software systems. The starting point is a description of a real-world scenario written in Formal Tropos [10], a language for the description of early requirements. The test set is obtained by conversion from the Formal Tropos model, parameterized in the number of instances for each class in the model, to a set of (ground) PLTL formulae. The parameterization sets the number of instances with which each class in the description is populated. Different kinds of checks are performed, ranging from feasibility of built-in or domain-specific properties (EXISTS and POSS), for which witnesses are sought, and assertion violations (ASS), for which counterexamples are sought[1].

The results are reported in Table 2. We tackle problems for three degrees of instantiation: Size 1 corresponds to one object per class; Size 1.5 corresponds to the instantiation of one object for some classes and two objects for the remaining ones; in Size 2, each class is instantiated twice. The first column identifies the problem; three sets of columns follow, one for each size instantiation. T.O. indicates that the run-time exceeded 1800 secs. The maximum bound was set to 20. The instances which reached the maximal bound or timed out are unsatisfiable. The reported bound represents the length of the witness (for POSS and EXISTS), or of the counterexample (for ASS); or, in case of a timeout, the depth of the largest k for which the analysis was completed.

The results show that, on this class of problems, the direct encoding is somewhat superior on easier instances which are satisfiable with a small bound. However, on the harder instances, often requiring the exploration to higher bounds,

---

[1] More details on the Formal Tropos problem set can be found at
http://sra.itc.it/tools/t-tool/experiments/cm/

Table 2. The results on the examples from [10]

PropType	Size 1		Size 1.5		Size 2	
	Direct	SNF	Direct	SNF	Direct	SNF
EXISTS	0.10 1	0.46 1	1.00 1	2.69 1	32.57 1	45.92 1
POSS_1	0.09 2	0.52 2	1.59 2	3.12 2	42.62 2	53.02 2
POSS_2	0.08 2	0.52 2	1.55 2	3.19 2	43.20 2	52.88 2
POSS_3	0.13 3	0.62 3	2.94 3	3.85 3	64.67 3	63.00 3
POSS_4	0.10 2	0.54 2	1.47 2	3.15 2	42.72 2	53.29 2
POSS_5	0.12 3	0.60 3	2.95 3	3.95 3	66.11 3	63.87 3
POSS_6	18.61 20	7.77 20	1.50 2	3.19 2	41.80 2	52.69 2
POSS_7	18.78 20	8.10 20	0.91 20	2.66 20	32.39 20	45.88 20
POSS_8	19.36 20	7.86 20	1.92 2	3.28 2	43.23 2	53.80 2
POSS_9	0.11 2	0.52 2	1.58 2	3.14 2	41.92 2	53.97 2
POSS_10	21.55 20	10.69 20	2.96 3	3.83 3	64.11 3	63.76 3
POSS_11	0.16 3	0.60 3	2.98 3	3.83 3	66.01 3	63.03 3
POSS_12	22.21 20	8.34 20	T.O. 16	559.50 20	T.O. 9	T.O. 13
ASS_1	21.36 20	9.22 20	T.O. 16	851.10 20	T.O. 9	T.O. 12
ASS_2	21.44 20	9.04 20	T.O. 16	217.08 20	T.O. 9	T.O. 18
ASS_3	22.44 20	9.71 20	T.O. 16	192.77 20	42.31 2	52.98 2
ASS_4	21.72 20	10.70 20	1.54 2	3.12 2	44.38 2	56.29 2
ASS_5	20.59 20	8.80 20	T.O. 16	217.87 20	T.O. 9	T.O. 17
ASS_6	17.91 20	7.89 20	T.O. 16	173.54 20	T.O. 9	1730.54 20
ASS_7	17.52 20	7.81 20	T.O. 16	197.76 20	T.O. 9	T.O. 16
ASS_8	21.70 20	8.62 20	T.O. 16	504.25 20	T.O. 9	T.O. 13
ASS_9	21.12 20	10.69 20	T.O. 16	363.21 20	T.O. 9	T.O. 14
ASS_10	21.51 20	9.50 20	T.O 16	840.48 20	T.O. 9	T.O. 12
ASS_11	20.77 20	11.42 20	T.O. 16	114.16 20	T.O. 9	T.O. 15
ASS_12	21.81 20	10.75 20	T.O. 16	142.81 20	T.O. 9	1779.20 20

the gain obtained by means of the SNF encoding with respect to the direct encoding is uniform. For the hardest problem instances, the speed up becomes very significant, sometimes bigger than an order of magnitude. The use of SNF also allows problems to be tackled that were previously out of reach within the time limit; when both methods time out, SNF is uniformly able to cover problem instances with higher length.

6   Conclusions and Future Work

In this paper, we have proposed the use of Separated Normal Form for the generation of encodings for bounded verification of Linear Temporal Logic with Past. We have shown the effectiveness of the approach by an experimental comparison with the previously available direct method [3], where our SNF-based approach is able to gain up to one order of magnitude.

The SNF transformation appears to bring the benefits of a pure future encoding without the usual exponential blowup associated with past to future transformations; this is believed to be a result of the bounded nature of the encoding, and future work will examine fully the theoretical implications of this. For the experimental work, the similarity between SNF and alternating automata calls for a comparison with this, and other, automata techniques.

Broadening the scope of the work, we expect that the techniques presented will be amenable to SAT-based induction in order to achieve completeness. Similarly, the SNF encoding is particularly suitable for use with incremental SAT solvers. These systems have proved useful for bounded model checking to reduce the amount of work involved in iterating up to a bound; for requirements verification the amount of repeated work currently necessary when testing multiple formulae with respect to a set of requirements will be reduced. Finally, we plan to extend the work to make use of non-Boolean SAT solvers to avoid the Booleanization of the data paths.

References

1. Accellera. *Accelera Property Specification Language: Reference Manual – Version 1.0.*
2. F. Bacchus and F. Kabanza. Control strategies in planning. In *Proceedings of the AAAI Spring Symposium Series on Extending Theories of Action: Formal Theory and Practical Applications*, pages 5–10, Stanford University, CA, USA, March 1995.
3. M. Benedetti and A. Cimatti. Bounded model checking for past LTL. In *Tools and Algorithms for the Construction and Analysis of Systems, 9th International Conference, TACAS'03*, Lecture Notes in Computer Science, Warsaw, Poland, April 2003. Springer-Verlag.
4. A. Biere, A. Cimatti, E. M. Clarke, and Y. Zhu. Symbolic model checking without BDDs. In W.R. Cleaveland, editor, *Tools and Algorithms for the Construction and Analysis of Systems. 5th International Conference, TACAS'99*, volume 1579 of *Lecture Notes in Computer Science*, pages 193–207. Springer-Verlag, July 1999.
5. J. Castro, M. Kolp, and J. Mylopoulos. A requirements-driven development methodology. In *Proceedings of the 13th International Conference on Advanced Information Systems Engineering*, 2001.
6. A. Cimatti, E.M. Clarke, F. Giunchiglia, and M. Roveri. NuSMV: a new Symbolic Model Verifier. In N. Halbwachs and D. Peled, editors, *Proceedings of the Eleventh Conference on Computer-Aided Verification (CAV'99)*, number 1633 in Lecture Notes in Computer Science, pages 495–499, Trento, Italy, July 1999. Springer-Verlag.
7. M. Fisher. A resolution method for temporal logic. In *Proceedings of the Twelfth International Joint Conference on Artificial Intelligence (IJCAI)*. Morgan Kaufmann, August 1991.
8. M. Fisher and P. Noël. Transformation and synthesis in METATEM Part I: Propositional METATEM. Technical Report UMCS-92-2-1, Department of Computer Science, University of Manchester, Manchester M13 9PL, England, February 1992.
9. A. Frisch, D. Sheridan, and T. Walsh. A fixpoint based encoding for bounded model checking. In M D Aagaard and J W O'Leary, editors, *Formal Methods in Computer-Aided Design; 4th International Conference, FMCAD 2002*, volume 2517 of *Lecture Notes in Computer Science*, pages 238–254, Portland, OR, USA, November 2002. Springer-Verlag.

10. A. Fuxman, L. Liu, M. Pistore, M. Roveri, and J. Mylopoulos. Specifying and analyzing early requirements in Tropos: Some experimental results. In *Proceedings of the* 11th *IEEE International Requirements Engineering Conference*, Monterey Bay, California USA, September 2003. ACM-Press.

11. D. Gabbay. The declarative past and imperative future. In H. Barringer, editor, *Proccedings of the Colloquium on Temporal Logic and Specifications*, volume 398 of *Lecture Notes in Computer Science*, pages 409–448. Springer-Verlag, 1989.

12. S. Gnesi, D. Latella, and G. Lenzini. Formal verification of cryptographic protocols using history dependent automata. In *Proceedings of the of the 4th Workshop on Sistemi Distribuiti: Algoritmi, Architetture e Linguaggi*, 1999.

13. O. Kupferman, N. Piterman, and M. Vardi. Extended temporal logic revisited. In *Proceedings of the 12th International Conference on Concurrency Theory*, number 2154 in Lecture Notes in Computer Science, pages 519–534. Springer Verlag, 2001.

14. F. Laroussinie, N. Markey, and Ph. Schnoebelen. Temporal logic with forgettable past. In *Proceedings of the 17th IEEE Symp. Logic in Computer Science (LICS'2002)*, pages 383–392, Copenhagen, Denmark, July 2002. IEEE Comp. Soc. Press.

15. M. Moskewicz, C. Madigan, Y. Zhao, L. Zhang, and S. Malik. Chaff: Engineering an efficient SAT solver. In *39th Design Automation Conference*, Las Vegas, June 2001.

16. D. Sheridan. The optimality of a fast CNF conversion and its use with SAT. Technical Report APES-82-2002, APES Research Group, March 2004. Available from `http://www.dcs.st-and.ac.uk/~apes/apesreports.html`.

17. A. van Lamsweerde. Goal-oriented requirements engineering: A guided tour. In *Proceedings of the 5th IEEE International Symposium on Requirements Engineering*, pages 249–263, 2001.

A Hybrid of Counterexample-Based and Proof-Based Abstraction

Nina Amla and Ken L. McMillan

Cadence Design Systems

Abstract. Counterexample- and proof-based refinement are complementary approaches to iterative abstraction. In the former case, a single abstract counterexample is eliminated by each refinement step, while in the latter case, all counterexamples of a given length are eliminated. In counterexample-based abstraction, the concretization and refinement problems are relatively easy, but the number of iterations tends to be large. Proof-based abstraction, on the other hand, puts a greater burden on the refinement step, which can then become the performance bottleneck. In this paper, we show that counterexample- and proof-based refinement are extremes of a continuum, and propose a hybrid approach that balances the cost and quality of refinement. In a study of a large number of industrial verification problems, we find that there is a strong relation between the effort applied in the refinement phase and the number of refinement iterations. For this reason, proof-based abstraction is substantially more efficient than counterexample-based abstraction. However, a judicious application of the hybrid approach can lessen the refinement effort without unduly increasing the number of iterations, yielding a method that is somewhat more robust overall.

1 Introduction

Abstraction is a necessary element of any approach to applying model checking to large scale systems. Abstraction means, in effect, removing information about a system which is not relevant to a property we wish to verify. Although there are many kinds of abstraction available, one simple approach that works well in verifying large hardware designs is to simply throw away those parts of the circuit that are not deemed relevant to the property. This is known as a *localization* abstraction. In effect, we view the system as a large collection of constraints, and abstraction as removing irrelevant constraints. The goal in this case is not so much to eliminate constraints *per se*, as to eliminate state variables that occur only in the irrelevant constraints, and thereby to reduce the size of the state space. A reduction of the state space in turn increases the efficiency of model checking, which is based on exhaustive state space exploration.

The first attempt to automate this simple kind of abstraction is due to Kurshan [10], and is known as *counterexample guided abstraction refinement*. This method begins with an empty set of constraints (or a seed set provided by the user), and applies model checking to attempt to verify the property. If a counterexample is found, it is analyzed to find a set of constraints whose addition

A.J. Hu and A.K. Martin (Eds.): FMCAD 2004, LNCS 3312, pp. 260–274, 2004.

to the system will rule out the counterexample. The process is then repeated until the property is found to be true, or until a concrete counterexample is produced. To produce a concrete counterexample, we must find a valuation for the unconstrained variables, such that all the original constraints are satisfied.

A number of variations on this basic technique have appeared [1, 4, 7, 17]. Some of the recent methods pose the concretization problem (construction of a concrete counterexample) as a Boolean satisfiability (SAT) problem and apply modern SAT methods [12] to this problem. Another approach [5] also applies ILP and machine learning techniques to the refinement problem (choosing which constraints to add to rule out an abstract counterexample). Yet another method [3] uses a SAT solver for both concretization and refinement, deriving a refinement from a refutation proof generated by the SAT solver in the concretization step.

An alternative to this counterexample-driven refinement loop is called proof-based abstraction [11]. In this approach, a SAT solver or other decision procedure is used to generate a proof that there is no counterexample of k steps. The set of constraints used in this proof becomes the abstraction. The advantage of this approach is that all counterexamples of length k are ruled out at once, whereas the counterexample-driven approach may require many refinement iterations to accomplish this. Moreover, choosing an abstraction refinement based on a single abstract counterexample is risky, since there may be many ways to eliminate one specific counterexample that are not relevant to the property being proved. In the proof-based approach, the choice of abstraction is based only on the property and the system being verified, so this problem is eliminated. The main disadvantage of the proof-based approach, however, is that it may be much more costly to prove that there are no counterexamples of length k than to refute a single abstract counterexample. Thus, the refinement step becomes the bottleneck in the verification process.

In this paper, we show that counterexample- and proof-based refinement are extremes of a continuum, and propose a hybrid approach that balances the cost and quality of refinement. That is, instead of attempting to refute all counterexamples of a given length, we use a SAT solver to refute as large a class of counterexamples as possible within a given time bound. This is done in such a way that the one abstract counterexample found by the model checker is always refuted. Thus, as the time bound increases, we approach proof-based abstraction, while as the time bound goes to zero we approach counterexample-based abstraction. We set the time bound in such a way that the times spent on the refinement and model checking phases of the procedures are balanced. In the case when the SAT solver terminates quickly, we gain the advantages of proof-based abstraction. On the other hand, if the SAT solver is slow, the procedure sacrifices some quality in the refinement for speed. Conversely, if the model checker is running quickly we spend little time on refinement, but if it runs slowly, we spend more time on refinement in the hope of producing a better abstraction.

We tested these three approaches on over one thousand industrial circuit verification problems, being careful to obtain an "apples to apples" comparison. The main conclusions from this study are:

- The number of refinement iterations is strongly related to the effort expended in the SAT solver in the refinement step, with greater effort resulting in fewer iterations.
- Because of this, the overall performance of proof-based abstraction is substantially better than counterexample-based abstraction for this benchmark set.
- Any attempt to reduce the refinement effort must be carefully tuned so as not to unduly increase the number of iterations. By a conservative application of the hybrid approach, we obtained a method that, overall, is more somewhat more robust than proof-based abstraction, reducing the number of unsolved problems by approximately 6%.

1.1   Related Work

In [8], proof-based and counterexample-based abstraction are used in different phases of an iterative abstraction refinement process. Here, by contrast, we use a single abstraction phase that is intermediate between the proof-based and counterexample-based approach, in such a way that the effort applied in abstraction and model checking can be balanced. Other methods have been proposed that attempt to mitigate the problems associated with refinement based on a single counterexample. These are based on generalizing the abstract counterexample is some way, in the hope of preventing the refinement procedure from refuting the counterexample based on irrelevant facts. For example, in [6], the abstract counterexample is generalized by removing valuations of variables that do not affect the truth value of the property in the given counterexample. In [16], the generalized counterexample is derived from the sequence of reachable states approximations computed by the model checker (the so-called "onion rings"). In these approaches there is no means of balancing the computational effort spend on refinement and model checking. In the present work, by contrast, we let the refinement procedure itself determine the generality of the refinement. The greater the run time bound, the more general will be the result. In the limit, the class of refuted counterexamples becomes, in effect, all counterexamples of the same length as the abstract counterexample. By adjusting the time bound appropriately, we can prevent the refinement step from becoming a bottleneck.

1.2   Outline

We begin in the next section with some relevant background on SAT techniques. Then, in section 3, we introduce the hybrid abstraction method. Finally, in section 4, we present the test results.

2   Extracting Proofs from SAT Solvers

The Boolean satisfiability problem (SAT) is to determine if a given Boolean formula has a satisfying assignment. Most solvers assume that the formula is given in conjunctive normal form (CNF), that is, as a set of clauses. This is not a significant restriction since, using a standard construction, we can transform an arbitrary formula into a satisfiability-equivalent CNF formula in linear time. Given a CNF formula, a SAT solver can then produce a satisfying assignment if one exists.

If the formula is unsatisfiable, it is also possible to produce a *refutation*, that is, a proof that the formula is inconsistent, typically using resolution steps. Most modern SAT solvers, such as CHAFF [12], or GRASP [14] can be modified to do this. Refutations are a key element of the refinement algorithm presented here. To understand the hybrid refinement algorithm, we need to understand at least at an abstract level, how the solver works and how refutations are produced.

2.1   Refutations

To begin at the beginning, a *clause* is a disjunction of zero or more *literals*, each being either a Boolean variable or its negation. We assume that clauses are *non-tautological*, that is, no clause contains a variable and its negation. A clause set is *satisfiable* when there is a truth assignment to the Boolean variables that makes all clauses in the set true.

Given two clauses of the form $c_1 = v \lor A$ and $c_2 = \neg v \lor B$, we say that the *resolvent* of c_1 and c_2 is the clause $A \lor B$, provided $A \lor B$ is non-tautological. For example, the resolvent of $a \lor b$ and $\neg a \lor \neg c$ is $b \lor \neg c$, while $a \lor b$ and $\neg a \lor \neg b$ have no resolvent, since $b \lor \neg b$ is tautological. It is easy to see that any two clauses have at most one resolvent. The resolvent of c_1 and c_2 (if it exists) is a clause that is implied by $c_1 \land c_2$ (in fact, it is exactly $(\exists v)(c_1 \land c_2)$). We will say that a *refutation* P for a set of clauses C is a derivation of the empty clause (false) from the clauses in C using resolution steps.

2.2   Basic SAT Algorithm

The main loop of a typical DPLL-style SAT solver is represented in pseudo-code in figure 1. While searching for a satisfying assignment A, the solver makes *decisions*, or arbitrary truth assignments to variables, and generates from these an *implication graph*. This is a directed acyclic graph whose vertices are truth assignments to variables, where each node is implied by its predecessors in the graph together with single clause.

As an example, suppose that our clause set is $\{(\neg a \lor b), (\neg b \lor c \lor d)\}$ and we have already decided the assignments $\{a, \neg c\}$. A possible implication graph is shown below:

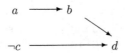

The literal b is implied by node a and the clause $(\neg a \lor b)$, while d is implied by the nodes b, $\neg c$, and clause $(\neg b \lor c \lor d)$.

```
procedure solve
    repeat
        update the implication graph
        while some clause c in conflict
            infer conflict clause c' from c by resolution
            backtrack: undo decisions until c' not in conflict
            update the implication graph
        end while
        if empty clause is present, return UNSAT
        if assignment A is total, return SAT
        decide: assign a value to some unassigned variable in A
    end repeat
```

Fig. 1. Basic DPLL SAT procedure

A clause is said to be in *conflict* when the negations of all its literals appear in the implication graph. When a conflict occurs, the SAT solver generates a *conflict clause* – a new clause that is implied by the existing clauses in the set. This is usually explained in terms of finding a cut in the implication graph, but from our point of view it is better understood as a process of resolving the "clause in conflict" with clauses in the implication graph to generate a new clause (that is also in conflict). We can also think of each resolution step as applying an implication from the implication graph in the contrapositive.

A crucial point about conflict clauses for present purposes is that a conflict clause contradicts some subset of the current decisions. To be specific, this is the set of decisions which derive the negations of its literals in the implication graph. Thus, in effect, the conflict clause rules out a space of possible assignments. We will use this fact later in our refinement procedure to eliminate classes of possible counterexamples.

In order to generate a refutation in the unsatisfiable case, we have only to record, for each generated conflict clause, the sequence of clauses that were resolved to infer that clause. The SAT solver produces an "unsatisfiable" answer when it generates the empty clause as a conflict clause (and thus rules out all possible assignments). At this point, we can produce a proof of unsatisfiability by, for example, a depth-first search starting from the empty clause, recursively deducing each clause in terms of the sequence of clauses that originally produced it. Note that, in general, not all conflict clauses generated during the SAT procedure will actually be needed to derive the empty clause.

3   A Hybrid Approach to Abstraction Refinement

We now consider how a proof-generating SAT solver can be used in the concretization and refinement steps of the iterative abstraction process. As mentioned above, we think of a system as a set of constraints and a localization abstraction as simply a subset of these constraints that is sufficient to prove a given property.

The properties we wish to verify are linear-time temporal properties expressed, for example, in the logic LTL. This problem can be reduced, however, to the simpler problem of existence of an accepting run of a finite automaton. This transformation has been extensively studied [13, 15, 2], and will not be described here. To further simplify matters, we will consider only the problem of finding finite counterexamples to safety properties. We assume that the problem of safety property verification is given in terms of a one-letter automaton on finite words, such that the property is false exactly when the automaton has an accepting run. Such a construction can be found, for example, in [9].

As in symbolic model checking, the automaton itself will be represented implicitly by Boolean formulas. The state space of the automaton is defined by a set V of Boolean variables. We will denote by V^k, for any $k \geq 0$, the set consisting of a distinct variable v_i, for every $v \in V$ and $0 \leq i \leq k$. A valuation of V^k can be thought of as a sequence of $k+1$ states of the automaton. A *state predicate* P is a Boolean formula over V. We will denote by P_i the predicate P with variable v_i substituted for every $v \in V$. The predicate P_i can be thought of as "P at time i". To represent transition relations, we introduce a set of "next state" variables V', consisting of a distinct variable v' for each $v \in V$. A *state relation* C is a Boolean formula over $V \cup V'$. We will denote by C_i the formula C with v_i substituted for v and v_{i+1} substituted for v', for each $v \in V$.

We will define a (one-letter) *automaton* as a triple $M = (I, C, F)$, where the initial constraint I and final constraint F are state predicates, and the transition constraint C is a state relation. Typically, F represents the set of states that violate some safety property. A *run* of M, of length k, is a truth assignment to V^k satisfying $I_0 \wedge \bigwedge_{i=0..k-1} C_i \wedge F_k$. That is, the initial constraint must hold in the first state, the transition constraint must hold in all consecutive pairs of states, and the final condition must hold in the last state. We will refer to the above formula as the k-step reachability formula, and denote it $R_k(M)$.

In our framework, a run of the automaton corresponds to a counterexample to the safety property. Thus, to verify the property we need to prove that $R_k(M)$ is unsatisfiable for any $k \geq 0$. This can be done using standard symbolic model checking methods [2], for example by iteratively computing the states reachable from I and checking whether the intersection of this set with F is empty.

3.1   Localization Abstraction

To allow localization abstraction, we assume that the formulas I, C and F are each formed as the conjunction of a set of component constraints. A component constraint may represent, for example, the behavior of a single gate in a circuit, or some larger aggregate, such as the "fanin cone" of a register. A *localization* of an automaton $M = (I, C, F)$, is an automaton $\bar{M} = (\bar{I}, \bar{C}, \bar{F})$, such that $\bar{I} \subseteq I$, $\bar{C} \subseteq C$ and $\bar{F} \subseteq F$ (where we take the liberty of confusing a set of constraints with its conjunction). In other words, localization abstraction means just taking a subset of the available constraints. If the constraints represent gates and registers in a circuit, this means in effect removing some gates and registers, leaving their outputs as free variables. It is immediate that if $\bar{M}$ does not admit a run, then M also does not admit a run. The advantage of this from a practical point of view is that $\bar{M}$ may refer to fewer variables than M, and hence may be easier to verify, owing to the smaller set of states that must be considered.

Of course the difficulty is how to choose which constraints to include in $\bar{M}$. The iterative approach, introduced by Kurshan [10], starts with a small "seed" localization $\bar{M}$ (which could be empty). Suppose the model checker finds a run $\bar{A}$ of $\bar{M}$. We will refer to $\bar{A}$ as an *abstract counterexample*. We then attempt to *concretize* the abstract counterexample by filling in the values of those variables not present in $\bar{M}$, so as to obtain a run of M. If the concretization succeeds we have obtained a concrete counterexample and we are done. Otherwise, we *refine* the abstraction by adding a sufficient set of constraints to $\bar{M}$ to rule out the abstract counterexample $\bar{A}$. The procedure is then repeated using the new $\bar{M}$. This continues until either $\bar{M}$ proves the property or concretization of an abstract counterexample succeeds. This general procedure is known as counterexample guided abstraction refinement.

Now let us consider the problems of concretization and refinement in a little more detail. Let $\bar{V}$ be the "support" of $\bar{M}$, that is, the set of variables v such that either v or v' occurs in $\bar{M}$. Suppose now that we have a run $\bar{A}$ of the localization $\bar{M}$. That is, $\bar{A}$ is a truth assignment to V^k satisfying $R_k(\bar{M})$. The problem of concretization is to find a run of M that agrees with $\bar{A}$ over $\bar{V}^k$. This is easily stated as a SAT problem. A concretization of $\bar{A}$ is a satisfying assignment to the following *concretization formula*:

$$R_k(M) \wedge \bigwedge_{v \in \bar{V}^k} (v \leftrightarrow \bar{A}(v))$$

Thus, a SAT solver can be used find a concretization if one exists. On the other hand, if the concretization formula is unsatisfiable, then the SAT solver can produce a refutation proof. As observed in [3], we can use this proof to induce a refinement (that is, a set of constraints that rule out the abstract counterexample). We will assume that all the component constraints in M have been expressed in conjunctive normal form, as sets of clauses. Now suppose that P is a refutation of the concretization formula. The *extension* of constraint set Q induced by P is defined as:

$$E_P(Q) = \{\phi \in Q \mid \text{for some clause } c \in \phi, \text{ for some } 0 \leq i \leq k, c_i \text{ occurs in } P\}$$

In other words, $E_P(Q)$ is the set of constraints in Q that have at least one clause occurring in the proof, at some time. If we refine our localization $\bar{M}$ by adding the constraints occurring in the proof, we are guaranteed that the abstract counterexample cannot be concretized in the new $\bar{M}$. To be more precise, let

$$\bar{M}' = (\bar{I} \cup E_P(I), \bar{C} \cup E_P(C), \bar{F} \cup E_P(F))$$

Since $\bar{M}'$ contains all the constraints used in proof P, it follows that P is also a proof that abstract counterexample $\bar{A}$ cannot be concretized in $\bar{M}'$. Thus, $\bar{M}'$ is a suitable refinement of $\bar{M}$ with respect to the abstract counterexample $\bar{A}$.

3.2   Proof-Based Abstraction

An alternative approach introduced in [11] is called *proof-based* abstraction. The idea is that instead of eliminating one abstract counterexample at a time, we disregard the content of the abstract counterexample and eliminate all counterexamples of length k at once. One way of looking at this is that we let $\bar{V} = \emptyset$. Thus the concretization formula reduces to simply $R_k(M)$. A concretization is thus defined as any run of the concrete automaton M that has the same length as the abstract counterexample. Moreover, if the concretization formula is unsatisfiable, the extension induced by its refutation is sufficient to rule out *all* counterexamples of length k.

This approach has two potential advantages. First, because a large class of abstract counterexamples is eliminated in one iteration, the number of iterations of the refinement loop may be dramatically reduced. Second, it may be possible to refute a specific abstract counterexample for many reasons that are unrelated to the actual property being proved. Thus the counterexample based approach runs the risk of adding irrelevant constraints due to accidents in the choice of the abstract counterexample. The proof based approach, since it is based on only the circuit and the property should in principle be less prone to this pitfall.

A potential disadvantage of the proof-based approach is that the SAT solver is given a much less constrained problem to solve, since the abstract counterexample values are not applied as constraints. In most cases it is substantially more time consuming to refute all counterexamples of a given length than to refute one specific counterexample. In fact, in [11] it was observed that in most cases the majority of run time was taken by the concretization phase rather than the model checking phase.

3.3   A Hybrid Approach

To avoid this latter difficulty, we propose here a hybrid approach. That is, we attempt a full refutation of all counterexamples of length k. However, if the run time of the SAT solver becomes excessive, we terminate the solver and settle for a refutation of some smaller space of counterexamples, as represented by a conflict clause. This is done in such a way that, in the worst case, at least the abstract counterexample $\bar{A}$ is refuted. Thus at one extreme, as the SAT solver run time is allowed to increase without bounds, we have proof-based abstraction, while at the other, as the SAT solver run time limit tends to zero, we have counterexample-based abstraction. In practice, we balance the run time of the SAT solver and model checker, so that neither one becomes a bottleneck.

In order to do this we need to solve the following problem. The concretization formula contains a set of constraints of the form $v \leftrightarrow \bar{A}(v)$, for each $v \in \bar{V}^k$. These correspond to the values in the abstract counterexample. We would like to refute the concretization formula using as few of these constraints as possible, within an allotted time. The fewer constraints we use in the refutation, the larger the class of counterexamples we will eliminate from the localization. To do this we take the following heuristic approach. We begin with the formula $R_k(M)$, as in proof-based refinement. We then "warm up" the SAT solver by making an initial series of decisions that correspond to the valuation $\bar{A}$. We allow the SAT solver to run for a limited amount of time. If the solver does not terminate within this time, we then add the constraints $v \leftrightarrow \bar{A}(v)$, and continue until the solver terminates. If, during the warm-up phase, the solver backtracks out of any of the initial decisions, it will infer a conflict clause that contradicts some subset of the abstract counterexample valuations. This corresponds to a class of abstract counterexamples. The longer we allow the warm-up phase to run, the larger this class will become. After we apply the constraints from $\bar{A}$, this conflict clause will cause the solver to terminate immediately, without making any decisions. The smaller the subset of $\bar{A}$ that is contradicted in the warm-up phase, the smaller will be the set of constraints used in the refutation, and hence the larger will be the space of counterexamples refuted. If we run the warm-up phase long enough the empty clause will be inferred, and no constraints from $\bar{A}$ will be used in the refutation.

Figure 3.3 gives a pseudo-code representation of the hybrid concretization procedure. It takes as parameters the concrete model M, the abstract counterexample $\bar{A}$, the support $\bar{V}$ of the localization, and a time limit. It returns either a concrete counterexample A, or an extension that rules out $\bar{A}$. The procedure "solve" in the figure executes the main loop of the SAT solver until termination, or until the given time limit is reached. In our implementation, time is measured by the number of implications made in the implication graph, since this correlates well with actual run time and is deterministic. Our SAT solver is *incremental*, in the sense that we can add new clauses and restart the solver, while maintaining all previously inferred conflict clauses.

Lines 3–6 represent the warm-up phase. We ignore any result produced by this phase. The only information preserved from the warm-up phase is the set of inferred conflict clauses. Note that if lines 3–6 are removed, we revert to a fully counterexample based procedure. On the other hand, if the time limit is ∞, we have a fully proof-based procedure. In practice,we set the limit so that the run time of the SAT solver is proportional to the run time of the model checker in generating $\bar{A}$, thus balancing the effort used for model checking and concretization.

3.4   Optimizations

A number of optimizations can be used to make the above procedure more efficient. First, it is impractical to use the entire support of the localization in $\bar{V}$. The concretization problem in this case is too constrained, resulting in very small refinements and a large number of iterations. Instead we let $\bar{V}$ be just the set of state-holding variables occurring in the localization $\bar{M}$. In hardware designs, these are the outputs of the registers.

Second, the localization reduction tends to introduce a large number of free variables, corresponding to the outputs of gates and registers that have been eliminated. This slows down the BDD-based model checker substantially. For this reason, we use a technique described in [11] that uses the refutation P as a guide in replacing free variables with a constant "don't care" value in a sound and complete manner.

procedure concretize($M = (I, C, F)$, $\bar{A}$, $\bar{V}$, limit)
1   initialize solver
2   add $I_0 \wedge \bigwedge_{i=0..k-1} C_i \wedge F_k$ to clause set
3   for $i = 0 \ldots k$
4   for $v \in \bar{V}$
5   decide $v_i = \bar{A}(v_i)$
6   solve(limit)
7   for $i = 0 \ldots k$
8   for $v \in \bar{V}$
9   if $\bar{A}(v_i) = 1$ add (v_i) to clause set else add $(\neg v_i)$
10   solve(∞)
11   if UNSAT (with refutation P)
12   return $(E_P(I), E_P(C), E_P(F))$
13   else return satisfying assignment A

Third, we use constraints to represent the behavior of individual gates rather than than the "fanin cones" of the registers as done in the other methods of localization abstraction cited here. This also tends to substantially reduce the number of free variables in some cases, resulting in better performance of the model checker.

Fourth, with the proof-based approach, another optimization is possible. That is, when a new value of k is encountered, we discard the previous localization. Heuristically speaking, when we rule out all counterexamples of length exactly k, we also tend to rule out all counterexamples of length less than k. Thus in most cases the previously obtained localization is redundant and can be discarded. In some cases this may cause us to redo previous work in refuting shorter counterexamples, but in most cases the result is a net performance gain. We will call this the "non-cumulative" optimization.

Finally, we should note that the counterexample-based refinement procedure described in [3] uses refutations to induce a refinement, but is somewhat more complex than the simple approach described above. It considers the prefixes of the abstract counterexample in order of increasing length. When concretization fails for some prefix of length k, it uses as the extension only those constraints occurring in the proof at time $k - 1$. The apparent motivation for this is that these constraints are in some sense the ones responsible for separating the reachable abstract counterexample state at time $k - 1$ from the unreachable one at time k. This approach is not guaranteed to rule out the abstract counterexample, since the entire proof is not used. It does however guarantee the length of the shortest unconcretizable prefix of the abstract counterexample is reduced, so that eventually the counterexample must be eliminated. In this paper, we *do not* use this technique, though in principle it can be applied to all three refinement approaches: the counterexample-based method, the proof-based method and the hybrid approach. The reason is that it would tend to increase the number of refinement iterations, which we found to be the most important factor in performance. For the same reason, we do not attempt to improve the localizations by detecting and eliminating unnecessary constraints, as this would introduce overhead, and also potentially increase the number of iterations.

Table 1. Robustness of refinement methods on three benchmark sets

Benchmark	Probs.	Resolved	Proof-based unresolved		Hybrid unresolved		Cex-based unresolved	
			true	false	true	false	true	false
comm1	86	61	8	2	2	6	15	10
comm2	333	234	12	7	29	20	66	18
comm3	630	524	13	4	12	37	54	41

Table 2. Iteration data for the methods on benchmark sets

Benchmark	Probs.	Proof-based				Hybrid				Cex-based			
		iter	depth	size	ratio	iter	depth	size	ratio	iter	depth	size	ratio
comm1	61	4	21	43	0.8	17	20	51	2.5	46	20	50	20.8
comm2	234	5	33	29	13.9	12	25	33	15.8	42	15	25	74.1
comm3	524	3	10	18	2.8	8	8	19	4.8	19	8	19	13.4

4 Practical Experience

We now compare the practical performance of the three refinement approaches, using a large set of hardware verification problems as benchmarks. The purpose here is to provide an "apples to apples" comparison, between the approaches. Thus, all three methods use the same basic loop and the same SAT solver. The primary difference between them is that the proof-based approach puts no limit on the warm-up time, the counterexample-based approach uses no warm-up, and the hybrid approach approximately balances the warm-up time with the model checker run time. As mentioned in the previous section, the proof-based method also uses the "non-cumulative" optimization.

The results presented here do not provide direct comparison with the many counterexample guided abstraction refinement techniques in the literature, which use various methods of localization, counterexample generalization, and localization improvement. Rather, we are attempting to quantify the tradeoff of effort in the refinement step *vs.* the number of refinement iterations, as represented by the counterexample- and proof-based approaches.

We apply the methods to three benchmark sets. These are collections of hardware verification problems developed by users of formal verification tools on commercial hardware designs. For each benchmark set, we set an upper time limit for verification, and measure the number of problems that can be resolved within this time. The time limit, which is chosen automatically based on a user defined effort limit, is 3600 seconds for the first set, 1000 seconds for second set and 100 seconds for the last benchmark set.

Table 1 shows, for each benchmark, the number of problems, the number of problems that can be resolved by all three methods and the number of unresolved problems for each method. The method with the fewest unresolved problems is in some sense the most robust. We have divided the problems into true properties and false properties. The conclusion we can draw from the table is that the proof-based method is the most robust.

Table 3. Robustness of refinement methods with the proviso on three benchmark sets

Benchmark	Probs.	Resolved	Proof-based unresolved		Hybrid unresolved		Cex-based unresolved	
			true	false	true	false	true	false
comm1	86	61	8	2	0	0	2	2
comm2	333	234	12	7	12	8	33	7
comm3	630	524	13	4	7	3	15	12

Table 4. Iteration data for the methods with the proviso on benchmark sets

Benchmark	Probs.	Proof-based				Hybrid				Cex-based			
		iter	depth	size	ratio	iter	depth	size	ratio	iter	depth	size	ratio
comm1	61	4	21	43	0.8	9	20	48	1.5	13	20	44	2.9
comm2	234	5	33	29	13.0	7	28	33	15.3	13	25	33	28.4
comm3	524	3	10	18	2.8	6	8	18	3.3	9	8	18	5.2

The results can be explained by considering the number of refinement iterations required for each method. Table 2 shows, for each method, the average number of refinement iterations, the last bounded model checking depth and the average size of the final abstraction, for problems that completed. As might be expected, the counterexample-based method requires a considerably larger number of iterations than the proof-based method, with the hybrid method falling somewhere in between. We also observe that the proof-based method goes deeper than the other two methods on average and yields smaller abstractions. The ratio column in Table 2 is the ratio of the time spent in the model checker to the time spent in the SAT solver, Note that this number does not take into account the time spent in constructing the bounded model checking problem which in many cases was not trivial. Not surprisingly, we see that the hybrid and counterexample-based techniques spend more time in the model checking phase than the proof-based technique. Clearly, whatever time is saved in each individual refinement step by considering only one counterexample is being offset by the larger number of iterations. The hybrid approach, while reducing the number of iterations somewhat, still requires too many iterations to make it competitive with the proof-based approach.

To remedy this problem, we then effected the following proviso: if two successive refinement iterations produce abstract counterexamples of the same length, the next iteration is always proof-based (without restriction on SAT solver effort). That is, if the single-counterexample or the hybrid refinement approach happens to rule out all counterexamples of a given length, then we benefit from a shorter run time in the SAT solver. If not, we do not allow continued iteration at a given counterexample length, but instead use a full proof step to force the counterexample length to increase.

Tables 3 and 4 show the robustness and iteration data for the three methods with the proviso (the numbers for proof-based abstraction are, of course, unchanged). With this approach, the number of iterations for counterexample-

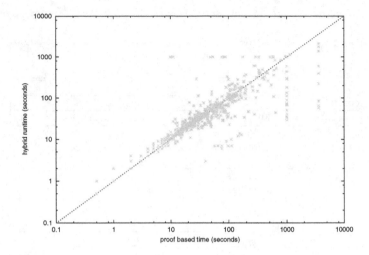

Fig. 2. Run time of Proof-based method versus Hybrid method with the proviso

based and hybrid are reduced. We find that the most robust method overall is the hybrid method, which reduces the number of unsolved problems by about 6%. Figures 2 and 3, which plot run time in seconds, show that the three methods are highly correlated in general. The hybrid method with the proviso appears to be slightly slower than the proof-based method but dominates the counterexample method with the proviso.

We now consider the quality of refinement for the hybrid and proof-based methods. Both methods do bounded model checking at the same depth 690 times, and the average size of the resulting abstractions at these depths is approximately 19% smaller with the proof-based method. However, it appears that smaller abstractions may not always be better, since the hybrid method seems to benefit from getting larger abstractions at a lower depth. For instance, on the 27 properties that were unresolved by the proof-based method but were resolved by the hybrid method, we found that the proof-based method needed to go deeper on average because it gets a smaller abstraction, and this appears to be a contributing factor in not resolving these problems.

5   Conclusion

We have seen that counterexample- and proof-based refinement form two extremes of a continuum in refinement effort, and that between these two, a hybrid approach is possible that balances the cost and quality of refinement. Rather than refuting a single abstract counterexample, or attempting to refute all counterexamples of a given length, we can use an incremental SAT solver to attempt to refute as large a space of counterexamples as possible within a given time bound. Our approach involves "warming up" the SAT solver using the abstract counterexample to provide the initial decisions.

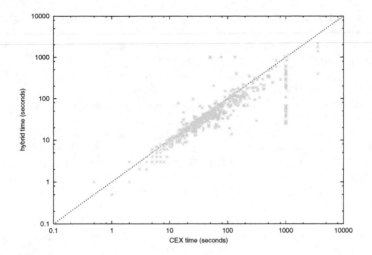

Fig. 3. Run time of Counterexample-based versus Hybrid methods with the proviso

Tests on industrial circuit verification problems show that the refinement effort strongly effects the number of refinement iterations, to the extent that reductions in refinement effort are more than offset by the resulting increase in the number of iterations. However, by applying the hybrid approach conservatively, we can obtain an abstraction mechanism that is more robust than either a purely counterexample- or proof-based approach.

For future work, it would be useful to develop more sophisticated approaches to the problem of "strongest proof within a time bound". This could in turn lead to techniques to reduce the number of system constraints used in the proof, and hence improve the quality of the abstraction, within resource limits.

References

1. F. Balarin and A. Sangiovanni-Vincentelli. An iterative approach to language containment. In *Computer Aided Verification (CAV'93)*, pages 29–40, 1993.
2. J. R. Burch, E. M. Clarke, K. L. McMillan, D. L. Dill, and J. Hwang. Symbolic model checking: 10^{20} states and beyond. In *LICS*, June 1990.
3. P. Chauhan, E. Clarke, J. Kukula, S. Sapra, H. Veith, and D. Wang. Automated abstraction refinement for model checking large state spaces using sat based conflict analysis. In *FMCAD*, November 2002.
4. E. M. Clarke, O. Grumberg, S. Jha, Y. Lu, and H. Veith. Counterexample-guided abstraction refinement. In *Computer Aided Verification*, pages 154–169, 2000.
5. E. M. Clarke, A. Gupta, J. Kukula, and O. Strichman. SAT based abstraction-refinement using ILP and machine learning techniques. In *CAV*, 2002.
6. M. Glusman, G. Kamhi, S. Mador-Haim, R. Fraer, and M. Y. Vardi. Multiple-counterexample guided iterative abstraction refinement. In *TACAS*, 2003.
7. S. G. Govindaraju and D. L. Dill. Counterexample-Guided choice of projections in approximate symbolic model checking. In *ICCAD*, 2000.

8. A. Gupta, M. Ganai, Z. Yang, and P. Ashar. Iterative abstraction using sat-based bmc with proof analysis. In *ICCAD*, 2003.
9. O. Kupferman and M. Y. Vardi. Model checking of safety properties. *Formal Methods in System Design*, 19(3):291–314, 2001.
10. R. P. Kurshan. *Computer-Aided-Verification of Coordinating Processes*. Princeton University Press, 1994.
11. K. L. McMillan and N. Amla. Automatic abstraction without counterexamples. In *TACAS*, 2003.
12. M. W. Moskewicz, C. F. Madigan, Y. Z., L. Z., and S. Malik. Chaff: Engineering an efficient SAT solver. In *Design Automation Conference*, pages 530–535, 2001.
13. A. Pnueli O. Lichtenstein. Checking that finite state concurrent programs satisfy their linear specification. In *POPL*, 1985.
14. J. P. M. Silva and K. A. Sakallah. GRASP–a new search algorithm for satisfiability. In *ICCAD*, 1996.
15. M.Y. Vardi and P. Wolper. An automata-theoretic approach to automatic program verification. In *Logic in Computer Science (LICS '86)*, pages 322–331, 1986.
16. C. Wang, B. Li, H. Jin, G. Hachtel, and F. Somenzi. Improving ariadne's bundle by following multiple threads in abstraction refinement. In *ICCAD*, 2003.
17. D. Wang, P. Ho, J. Long, J. H. Kukula, Y. Zhu, H. Tony Ma, and R. Damiano. Formal property verification by abstraction refinement with formal, simulation and hybrid engines. In *Design Automation Conference*, pages 35–40, 2001.

Memory Efficient All-Solutions SAT Solver and Its Application for Reachability Analysis

Orna Grumberg, Assaf Schuster, and Avi Yadgar

Computer Science Department, Technion, Haifa, Israel

Abstract. This work presents a *memory-efficient All-SAT engine* which, given a propositional formula over sets of *important* and *non-important* variables, returns the set of all the assignments to the *important* variables, which can be extended to solutions (satisfying assignments) to the formula. The engine is built using elements of modern SAT solvers, including a scheme for learning conflict clauses and non-chronological backtracking. Re-discovering solutions that were already found is avoided by the search algorithm itself, rather than by adding blocking clauses. As a result, the space requirements of a solved instance do not increase when solutions are found. Finding the next solution is as efficient as finding the first one, making it possible to solve instances for which the number of solutions is larger than the size of the main memory.
We show how to exploit our All-SAT engine for performing *image computation* and use it as a basic block in achieving full reachability which is purely SAT-based (no BDDs involved).
We implemented our All-SAT solver and reachability algorithm using the state-of-the-art SAT solver Chaff [19] as a code base. The results show that our new scheme significantly outperforms All-SAT algorithms that use blocking clauses, as measured by the execution time, the memory requirement, and the number of steps performed by the reachability analysis.

1 Introduction

This work presents a *memory-efficient All-SAT engine* which, given a propositional formula over sets of *important* and *non-important* variables, returns the set of all the assignments to the *important* variables, which can be extended to solutions (satisfying assignments) to the formula. The All-SAT problem has numerous applications in AI [21] and logic minimization [22]. Moreover, many applications require the ability to instantiate all the solutions of a formula, which differ in the assignment to only a subset of the variables. In [14] such a procedure is used for predicate abstraction. In [7] it is used for re-parameterization in symbolic simulation. In [18, 6] it is used for reachability analysis, and in [13] it is used for pre-image computation. Also, solving QBF is actually solving such a problem, as shown in [15].

Most modern SAT solvers implement the DPLL[9, 8] backtrack search. These solvers add clauses to the formula in order to block searching in subspaces that are known to contain no solution. All-SAT engines that are built on top of modern SAT solvers tend to extend this method by using additional clauses, called *blocking clauses*, to block solutions that were already found [18, 6, 13, 14, 7, 20]. However, while the addition of

A.J. Hu and A.K. Martin (Eds.): FMCAD 2004, LNCS 3312, pp. 275–289, 2004.

blocking clauses prevents repetitions in solution creation, it also significantly inflates the size of the solved formula. Thus, the engine slows down corresponding to the number of solutions that were already found. Eventually, if too many solutions exist, the engine may saturate the available memory and come to a stop.

In [6] an optimization is employed to the above method. The number of blocking clauses and the run time are reduced significantly by inferring from a newly found solution a set of related solutions, and blocking them all with a single clause. This, however, is insufficient when larger instances are considered. Moreover, the optimization is applicable only for formulae which originated from a model.

In this work we propose an efficient All-SAT engine which does not use blocking clauses. Given a propositional formula and sets of important and non-important variables, our engine returns the set of all the assignments to the important variables, which can be extended to solutions to the formula. Setting the non-important variables set to be empty, yields all the solutions to the formula. Similar to previous works, our All-SAT solver is also built on top of a SAT solver. However, in order to block known solutions, it manipulates the backtracking scheme and the representation of the implication graph. As a result, the size of the solved formula does not increase when solutions are found. Moreover, since found solutions are not needed in the solver, they can be stored in external memory (disk or the memory of another computer), processed and even deleted. This saving in memory is a great advantage and enables us to handle very large instances with huge number of solutions. The memory reduction also implies time speedup, since the solver handles much less clauses. In spite of the changes we impose on backtracking and the implication graph, we manage to apply many of the operations that made modern SAT solvers so efficient. We derive conflict clauses based on conflict analysis, apply non-chronological backtracking to skip subspaces which contain no solutions, and apply conflict driven backtracking under some restrictions.

We show how to exploit our All-SAT engine for reachability analysis, which is an important component of model checking. Reachability analysis is often used as a preprocessing step before checking. Moreover, model checking of most safety temporal properties can be reduced to reachability analysis [1]. BDD-based algorithms for reachability are efficient when the BDDs representing the transition relation and the set of model states can be stored in memory [4, 5]. However, BDDs are quite unpredictable and tend to explode on intermediate results of image computation. When using BDDs, a great effort is invested in finding the optimal variables order. SAT-based algorithms, on the other hand, can handle models with larger number of variables. However, they are mainly used for Bounded Model Checking (BMC) [2].

Pure SAT-based methods for reachability [18, 6] and model checking of safety properties [13, 20] are based on All-SAT engines, which return the set of all the solutions to a given formula. The All-SAT engine receives as input a propositional formula describing the application of a transition relation T to a set of states S. The resulting set of solutions represents the image of S (the set of all successors for states in S). Repeating this step, starting from the initial states, results in the set of all reachable states.

Similar to [18, 6], we exploit our All-SAT procedure for computing an image for a set of states, and then use it iteratively for obtaining full reachability. Several optimizations are applied at that stage. Their goals are to reduce the number of found solutions by avoiding repetitions between images; to hold the found solutions compactly; and to keep the solved formula small.

An important observation is that for image computation, the solved formula is defined over variables describing current states $\overline{x}$, inputs $\overline{I}$, next states $\overline{x'}$, and some auxiliary variables that are added while transforming the formula to CNF. However, many solutions to the formula are not needed: the only useful ones are those which give different values to $\overline{x'}$. This set of solutions is efficiently instantiated by our algorithm by defining $\overline{x'}$ as the important variables. Since the variables in $\overline{x'}$ typically constitute just 10% of all the variables in the formula [23], the number of solutions we search for, produce, and store, is reduced dramatically. This was also done in [18, 6, 13, 20].

Other works also applied optimizations within a single image [6] and between images [18, 6]. These have similar strength to the optimization we apply between images. However, *within* an image computation we gain significant reductions in memory and time due to our new All-SAT procedure, and the ability to process the solutions outside the engine before the completion of the search. This gain is extended to the reachability computation as well, as demonstrated by our experimental results.

In [11], a hybrid of SAT and BDD methods is proposed for image computation. This implementation of an All-SAT solver does not use blocking clauses. The known solutions are kept in a BDD which is used to restrict the search space of the All-SAT engine. While this representation might be more compact than blocking clauses, the All-SAT engine still depends on the set of known solutions when searching for new ones. Moreover, since our algorithm does not impose restrictions on learning, we believe it can be used to enhance the performance of such hybrid methods as well.

In [3, 12] all the solutions of a given propositional formula are found by repeatedly choosing a value to one variable, and splitting the formula accordingly, until all the clauses are satisfied. However, in this method, all the solutions of the formula are found, while many of them represent the same next state. Therefore, it can not be efficiently applied for quantifier elimination and image computation.

We have built an All-SAT solver based on the state-of-the-art SAT solver Chaff [19]. Experimental results show that our All-SAT algorithm outperforms All-SAT algorithms based on blocking clauses. Even when discovering a huge number of solutions, our solver does not run out of memory, and does not slow down. Similarly, our All-SAT reachability algorithm also achieves significant speedups over blocking clauses-based All-SAT reachability, and succeeds to perform more image steps.

The rest of the paper is organized as follows. Section 2 gives the background needed for this work. Sections 3 and 4 describe our algorithm and its implementation. Section 5 describes the utilization of our algorithm for reachability analysis. Section 6 shows our experimental results, and Section 7 includes conclusions.

2 Background

2.1 The SAT Problem

The *Boolean satisfiability problem* (SAT) is the problem of finding an assignment A to a set of Boolean variables V such that a Boolean formula $\phi(V)$ will have the value 'true' under this assignment. A is called a *satisfying assignment*, or a *solution*, for ϕ.

We shall discuss formulae presented in the conjunctive normal form (CNF). That is, ϕ is a conjunction of clauses, while each clause is a disjunction of literals over V. A literal l is an instance of a variable or its negation: $l \in \{v, \neg v \mid v \in V\}$. We shall consider a clause as a set of literals, and a formula as a set of clauses.

A clause cl is satisfied under an assignment A iff $\exists l \in cl, A(l) = true$. For a formula ϕ given in CNF, an assignment satisfies ϕ iff it satisfies all of its clauses. Hence, if, under an assignment A (or a partial assignment), all of the literals of some clause in ϕ are false, than A does not satisfy ϕ. We call this situation a *conflict*.

2.2   Davis-Putnam-Logemann-Loveland Backtrack Search (DPLL)

We begin by describing the *Boolean Constraint Propagation* (*bcp()*) procedure. Given a partial assignment A and a clause cl, if there is one literal $l \in cl$ with no value, while the rest of the literals are all false, then in order to avoid a conflict, A must be extended such that $A(l) = true$. cl is called a *unit clause* or an *asserting clause*, and the assignment to l is called an *implication*. The *bcp()* procedure finds all the implications at a given moment. This procedure is efficiently implemented in [19, 10, 26, 17, 16].

The DPLL algorithm [9, 8] walks the binary tree that describes the variables space. At each step, a *decision* is made. That is, a value to one of the variables is chosen, thus reaching deeper in the tree. Each decision is assigned with a new *decision level*. After a decision is made, the algorithm uses the *bcp()* procedure to compute all its implications. All the implications are assigned with the corresponding decision level. If a conflict is reached, the algorithm backtracks in the tree, and chooses a new value to the most recent variable not yet tried both ways. The algorithm terminates if one of the leaves is reached with no conflict, describing a satisfying assignment, or if the whole tree was searched and no satisfying assignment was found, meaning ϕ is unsatisfiable.

2.3   Optimizations

Current state of the art SAT solvers use Conflict Analysis, Learning, and *Conflict Driven Backtracking* to optimize the DPLL algorithm [27, 17]. Upon an occurrence of a conflict, the solver creates a *conflict clause* which implies the reverse assignment to some variable in the highest level. This clause is added to the formula to prune the search tree [27, 17]. In order to emphasize the recently gained knowledge, the solver uses *conflict driven backtracking*: Let l be the highest level of an assigned variable in the conflict clause. The solver discards some of its work by invalidating all the assignments above l. The implication of the conflict clause is then added to l [27]. This implies a new order of the variables in the search tree. Note that the other variables for which the assignments were invalidated, may still assume their original values, and lead to a solution.

Next we describe the *implication graph*, which is used to create conflict clauses. An *Implication Graph* represents the current partial assignment during the solving process, and the reason for the assignment to each variable. For a given assignment, the implication graph is not unique, and depends on the decisions and the order used by the *bcp()*. We denote the asserting clause that implied the value of l by $ante(l)$, and refer to it as the antecedent of l. If l is a decision, $ante(l) = NULL$. Given a partial assignment A:

- The implication graph is a directed acyclic graph $G(L, E)$.
- The vertices are the literals of the current partial assignment: $\forall l \in L, l \in \{v, \neg v \mid v \in V \land A(l) = true\}$.
- The edges are the reasons for the assignments: $E = \{(l_i, l_j) \mid l_i, l_j \in L, l_i \in ante(l_j)\}$. That is, for each vertex l, the incident edges represent the clause $ante(l)$. A decision vertex has no incident edge.
- Each vertex is also assigned with the decision level of the corresponding variable.

When a conflict occurs, there are both true and false vertices of some variable, denoted *conflicting variable*. A *Unique Implication Point* (UIP) in an implication graph is a vertex of the current decision level, through which all the paths from the decision vertex of this level to the conflict pass. There may be more than one UIP, and we order them starting from the conflict. The decision variable of a level is always a UIP. When conflict driven backtracking is used, the conflict analysis creates a conflict clause which is a unit clause. This clause implies the reverse assignment to one of the UIPs. After backtracking, the opposite value of the UIP becomes an implication, and the conflict clause is its antecedent [27]. Figure 1(a,b) shows an implication graph with a conflict and two UIPs, and the pruning of the search tree by a conflict clause.

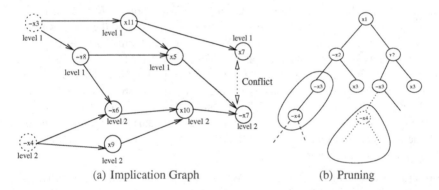

(a) Implication Graph   (b) Pruning

Fig. 1. (a) An implication graph describing a conflict. The roots are decisions. $\neg x_4$ and x_{10} are UIPs. (b) Adding the clause (x_3, x_4) prunes the search tree of the subspace defined by $\neg x_3 \land \neg x_4$.

2.4   The All-SAT Problem

Given a Boolean formula presented in CNF, we would like to find all of its solutions as defined in the SAT problem.

The Blocking Clauses Method: A straight forward method to find all of the formula's solutions is to modify the DPLL SAT solving algorithm such that when a solution is found, a blocking clause describing its negation is added to the solver, thus preventing the solver from reaching the same solution again. The last decision is then invalidated, and the search is continued normally. Once all of the solutions are found, there will be no satisfying assignment to the current formula, and the algorithm will terminate.

This algorithm suffers from exponential space growth as it adds a clause at the size of V for each solution found. Another problem is that the increasing number of clauses in the system will slow down the *bcp()* procedure which will have to look for implications in an increasing number of clauses.

3 Memory Efficient All-SAT Algorithm

3.1 Conventions

Assume we are given a partition of the variables to important and non-important variables. Two solutions to the problem which differ in the non-important variables only are considered the same solution. Thus, a solution is defined by a subset of the variables.

A *subspace* of assignments, defined by a partial assignment σ, is the set of all assignments which agree with σ on its assigned variables. A subspace is called *exhausted* if all of the satisfying assignments in it (if any) were already found. At any given moment, the current partial assignment defines the subspace which is now being investigated.

We now present our All-SAT algorithm. A proof of its correctness is given in [25].

3.2 The All-SAT Algorithm

Our algorithm walks the search tree of the important variables. We call this tree the *important space*. Each leaf of this tree represents an assignment to the important variables which does not conflict with the formula. When reaching such a leaf, the algorithm tries to extend the assignment over the non-important variables. Hence, it looks for a solution within the subspace defined by the important variables. Note that the walk over the *important space* should be exhaustive, while only one solution for the non-important variables should be found. This search is illustrated in Figure 2(a).

We incorporate these two behaviors into one procedure by modifying the decision and backtracking procedures of a conflict driven backtrack search, and the representation of the implication graph.

Important First Decision Procedure: We create a new decision procedure which looks for an unassigned variable from within the important variables. If no such variable is found, the usual decision procedure is used to choose a variable from the non-important set. This way, at any given time, the decision variables are a sequence of important variables, followed by a sequence of non important variables. At any given time, the *important decision level* is the maximal level in which an important variable is a decision. An example is given in Figure 2(a).

Exhaustive Walk of the Important Space: An exhaustive walk of the *important space* is performed by extending the original DPLL algorithm with the following procedures: Chronological backtracking after a leaf of the *important space* is handled; Learning a conflict clause and chronological backtracking upon an occurrence of a conflict; Non-chronological backtracking when a subspace of the problem is proved to be *exhausted*.

Chronological backtracking, as in DPLL, is done by flipping the highest important decision variable not yet flipped. This means that under the previous decisions, the last decision variable *must* assume the reverse assignment. Hence, its new value is an implication of the previous decisions. Therefore, in order to perform a chronological backtrack, we flip the highest decision and assign it with the level below. This way,

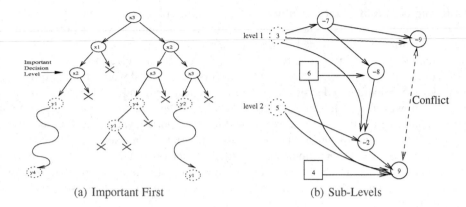

(a) Important First   (b) Sub-Levels

Fig. 2. (a) Important First Decision. x variables are important and y are non-important. (b) An implication graph in the presence of flipped decisions. 6 and 4 define new sub-levels.

the highest decision is always the highest decision not yet flipped. Higher decisions which were already flipped are regarded as its implications. Note, though, that there is no clause implying the values of the flipped decisions. Therefore, a new definition for the implication graph is required.

We change the definition of the implication graph as follows: Root vertices in the graph still represent the decisions, but also decisions flipped because of previous chronological backtracking. Thus, for conflict analysis purposes, a flipped decision is considered as defining a new decision sub-level. The result is a graph in which the nodes represent actual assignments to the variables, and the edges represent real clauses, making it a valid implication graph. This graph describes the current assignment, though not the current decisions. An example for such a graph is given in Figure 2(b).

Given the modified graph, the regular conflict analysis is performed, and leads to a UIP in the newly defined sub-level. The generated conflict clause is added to the formula to prune the search tree, as for solving the SAT problem. Modifying the implication graph and introducing the new sub-levels may cause the conflict clause not to be asserting. However, since we do not use conflict driven backtracking in the *important space*, our solver does not require that the conflict clauses will be asserting.

We now consider the case in which a conflict clause is asserting. In this case, we extend the current assignment according to it. Let c_1 be a conflict clause, and lit its implication. Adding lit to the current assignment may cause a second conflict, for which lit is the reason. Therefore, we are able to perform conflict analysis again, using lit as a UIP. The result is a second conflict clause, c_2 which implies $\neg lit$. It is obvious now that neither of the assignments to lit will resolve the current conflict. The conclusion is that the reason for this situation lies in a lower decision level, and that a larger subspace is *exhausted*. We calculate $c_3 \leftarrow resolution(c_1, c_2)$ [9] and resolve the conflict by backtracking to the decision level preceding the highest level of a variable in c_3, which is the level below the highest decision level of a variable in c_1 or c_2. Note that backtracking to any level higher than that would not resolve the conflict as both c_1 and c_2 would imply lit and $\neg lit$ respectively. Therefore, by this non-chronological backtracking, we skip a large *exhausted* subspace.

Assigning Non-important Variables: After reaching a leaf in the *important space*, we have to extend the assignment to the non important variables. At this point, all the important variables are assigned with some value. Note, that since we only need one extension, we actually have to solve the SAT problem for the given formula with the current partial assignment. This is done by allowing the normal work of the optimized SAT algorithm, including decisions, conflict clause learning, and conflict driven back-tracking. However, we allow backtracking down to the *important decision level* but not below it, in order not to change the assignment to the important variables. If no solution is found, the current assignment to the important variables can not be extended to a solution for the formula, and should be discarded. On the other hand, if a solution to the formula is found, its projection over the important variables is a valid output. In both cases, we backtrack to the *important decision level* and continue the exhaustive walk of the *important space*.

4 Implementation

We implemented our All-SAT engine using zChaff [19] as a base code. This SAT solver uses the VSIDS decision heuristic [19], an efficient *bcp()* procedure, conflict clause learning, and conflict driven backtracking. We modified the decision procedure to match our important-first decision procedure, and added a mechanism for chronological back-tracking. We implemented the exhaustive walk over the *important space* using chrono-logical backtracking, and by allowing non-chronological backtracking when subspaces without solutions are detected. We used the original optimized SAT solving procedures above the *important decision level*, where it had to solve a SAT problem. Next, we describe the modifications imposed on the solver in the *important space*.

The original SAT engine represents the current implication graph by means of an *assignment stack*, hereafter referred to as *stack*. The *stack* consists of levels of assignments. The first assignment in each level is the decision, and the rest of the assignments in the level are its implications. Each implication is in the lowest level where it is implied. Thus, an implication is implied by some of the assignments prior to it, out of which at least one is of the same level. For each assigned variable, the *stack* holds its value and its antecedent, where the antecedent of a decision variable is NULL.

In the following discussion, *backtrack to level i* refers to the following procedure: a) Flipping the decision in level $i + 1$. b) Invalidation of all the assignments in levels $i + 1$ and above, by popping them out of the *stack*. c) Pushing the flipped decision at the end of level i, with NULL antecedent. d) Executing *bcp()* to calculate the implications of the flipped decision.

We perform *chronological backtracking* from level j within the *important space* by backtracking to level $j - 1$. This way, the flipped decisions appear as implications of prior ones, and the highest decision not yet flipped is always the highest in the *stack*. The assignments with NULL antecedents, which represent *exhausted* subspaces, remain in the *stack* until a whole subspace which includes them is *exhausted*. An example for this procedure is given in Figure 3(a,b).

Our *stack* now includes decision variables, implications, and flipped decisions, which appear as implications but with no antecedents. Using this *stack* we can con-

```
   1  6          1  6          1  6           1   6              1  6
  -5  4         -5  4         -5  4          -5   4            -5 4
  -2  7    8    -2  7    8    -2  7    8     -2   7    8       -2 7 8 -3
   3 -10 -9      3 -10 -9      3 -10 -9       3  -10  -9
  11 -15        11 -15        11 -15 -12     11  -15  -12
  12            12 16   14 -6                -14 18   -13 -4
 -16 -6  -14
  (a) A leaf    (b) Conflict  (c)            (d) Implication   (e) Backtrack
                              Chronological
                              Backtrack
```

Fig. 3. *Important Space* Resolve Conflict (a) Reaching a leaf of the *important space*. '-10' has NULL antecedent (b) Chronological backtrack which causes a conflict. '16' has NULL antecedent, clause $c_1 = (-1, 2, -14)$ is generated. (c) Chronological backtrack. (d) '-14', the implication of clause c_1, is pushed into the *stack*, and leads to a conflict. Clause $c_2 = (-4, 2, -3, 14)$ is generated. $c_3 \leftarrow resolution(c_1, c_2) = (-1, 2, -3, -4)$. (e) Backtracking to the highest level in c_3.

struct the implication graph according to the new definition given in section 3.2. Thus we can derive a conflict clause whenever a conflict occurs.

Decisions about *exhausted* subspaces are made during the process of resolving a conflict, as described next. We define a *generated clauses stack*, which is used to temporarily store clauses that are generated during conflict analysis[1]. In the following explanation, refer to Figure 3(b-e). (b) When a conflict occurs, we analyze it and learn a new conflict clause according to the 1UIP scheme [27]. This clause is added to the solver to prune the search tree, and is also pushed into the *generated clauses stack* to be used later. (c) We perform a chronological backtrack. A pseudo code for this procedure is shown in Figure 4('chronological backtrack'). If this caused another conflict, we start the resolving process again. Otherwise, we start calculating the implications of the clauses in the *generated clauses stack*.

(d) Let c_1 be a clause popped out of the *generated clauses stack*. If c_1 is not asserting, we ignore it. If it implies *lit*, we push *lit* into the *stack* and run *bcp()*. For simplicity of presentation, *lit* is pushed to a new level in the *stack*. If a new conflict is found, we follow the procedure described in Section 3.2 to decide about *exhausted* subspaces. We create a new conflict clause, c_2, with *lit* as the UIP. c_1 and c_2 imply *lit* and $\neg lit$ respectively. We calculate $c_3 \leftarrow resolution(c_1, c_2)$ [9]. (e) We backtrack to the level preceding the highest level of an assigned variable in c_3. Thus, we backtrack higher, skipping a large *exhausted* subspace. A pseudo code of this procedure is given in Figure 4.

5 Reachability and Model Checking Using All Solution Solver

5.1 Reachability

We now present one application of our All-SAT algorithm. Given the set of initial states of a model, and the transition relation, we would like to find the set of all the states

---

[1] We still refer to the decision stack as *stack*.

```
Important_Space_resolve_conflict() {
   while (conflict ∨ generated_clauses.size > 0) {
      if (conflict) {
```

chronological backtrack	if (current level == 0) return FALSE $cl \leftarrow$ generate conflict clause with 1UIP generated_clauses.push(cl) backtrack one level

```
      } else {
```

Implicate Conflict Clauses	$cl_1 \leftarrow$ generated_clauses.pop() if (cl_1 is asserting) { $lit \leftarrow$ unit literal in cl_1 push lit into the *stack*

Non-Chronological Backtracking	if (*bcp()* = CONFLICT) {
	    $cl_2 \leftarrow$ generate conflict clause with lit as UIP
	    $cl_3 \leftarrow resolution\ of\ (cl_1, cl_2)$
	    $generated\_clauses.push(cl_3)$
	    backtrack to the level preceding the highest level in cl_3
	}
	}

```
      }
   }
   return TRUE
}
```

Fig. 4. *Important Space* resolve conflict.

reachable from the initial states. We denote by $\overline{x}$ the vector of the model state variables, and by $S_i(\overline{x})$ the set of states at distance i from the initial states. The transition relation is given by $T(\overline{x}, \overline{I}, \overline{x'})$ where $\overline{x}$ represents the current state, $\overline{I}$ represents the input and $\overline{x'}$ represents the next state. For a given set of states $S(\overline{x})$, the set of reachable states from them at distance 1 (i.e., their successors), denoted $Image(S(\overline{x}))$, is

$$Image(S(\overline{x})) = \{\overline{x'} \mid \exists \overline{x}, \exists \overline{I}, S(\overline{x}) \wedge T(\overline{x}, \overline{I}, \overline{x'})\} \tag{1}$$

Given S_0, the set of initial states, calculating the reachable states is done by iteratively calculating S_i, and adding them to the reachable set S^*, until S_i contains no new states. The rechability algorithm is shown in Figure 5(a).

5.2   Image Computation Using All-SAT

We would like to use our All-SAT algorithm in order to implement line 5 in the reachability algorithm (Figure 5(a)). In order to do that, we have to find all of the solutions for the following formula:

$$S(\overline{x}) \wedge T(\overline{x}, \overline{I}, \overline{x'}) \wedge \neg S^*(\overline{x'}) \tag{2}$$

Each solution to (2) represents a valid transition from one of the states in the set $S(\overline{x})$ to a new state $\overline{x'}$, which is not in $S^*(\overline{x'})$. Including $\neg S^*(\overline{x'})$ in the image computation was also done in [6, 18].

We now have to construct a CNF representation for Formula 2. We represent each state $\overline{x}$ as the conjunction of its literals. Therefore, $S^*(\overline{x'})$ is in DNF, and $\neg S^*(\overline{x'})$ is in CNF. Creating the CNF representation for S is done by introducing auxiliary variables. The translations of both sets are linear in the size of the sets. Representing T as a CNF is also possible by introducing auxiliary variables [2].

Each solution is an assignment to all of the variables in the CNF, and its projection over $\overline{x'}$ defines the new state. We avoid repetitive finding of the same $\overline{x'}$ by setting $\overline{x'}$ to be the important variables in our All-SAT solver. A state is found once, regardless of its predecessors, input, or the assignment to the auxiliary variables added during the CNF construction. Making the decisions from within the model variables proved to be efficient when solving SAT problems for BMC [23].

5.3 Minimization

Boolean Minimization: A major drawback of the implementation described above is the growth of S^* between iterations of the algorithm, and of S during the image computation. This poses a problem even when the solutions are held outside the solver. Representing each state by a conjunction of literals is pricey when their number increases. Therefore we need a way to minimize this representation. We exploit the fact that a set of states is actually a DNF formula and apply Boolean minimization methods to find a minimal representation for this formula. For example, the solutions represented by $(x_0 \wedge x_1) \vee (x_0 \wedge \neg x_1)$, can be represented by (x_0).

In our tool, we use Berkeley's 'Espresso'[24], which receives as an input a set of DNF clauses and returns their minimized DNF representation. Our experimental results show a reduction of up to 3 orders of magnitude in the number of clauses required to represent the sets of solutions when using this tool.

On-the-Fly Minimization: Finding all the solutions for Formula (2), and then minimizing them, is not feasible for large problems since their number would be too large to store and for the minimizer to handle. Therefore, during the solving process, whenever a preset number of solutions is found, the solver work is suspended, and we use the minimizer to combine them with the current S and S^*. The output, then, is stored again in S and S^* respectively, to be processed with the next batch of solutions found by the All-SAT solver. This way, we keep S^*, S and the input to the minimizer small. Note, also, that each batch of solutions includes new states only, due to the structure of Formula 2. Employing logical minimization on-the-fly, before finding all the solutions, is possible since previous solutions are not required when searching for the next ones, and the work of the minimizer is independent of the All-SAT solver. Moreover, the minimization and the computation of the next batch of solutions can be performed concurrently. However, this is not implemented in our tool. Note, that this minimization does not effect the performance of the All-SAT solver.

We now have a slightly modified reachability algorithm as shown in Figure 5(b).

6 Experimental Results

As the code base for our work, we use the zChaff SAT solver [19] which is one of the fastest available state of the art solvers. zChaff implements conflict analysis with

$\overline{Reachability(S_0(\overline{x}))}$
0) $S \leftarrow S_0$
1) $S^* \leftarrow S_0$

$\overline{Reachability(S_0)}$
1) $S^* \leftarrow S_0$
2) $S \leftarrow S_0$
3) $while \ (S \neq \phi) \ \{$
4) $S^* \leftarrow S^* \cup S$
5) $S \leftarrow Image(S) \setminus S^*$
6) $\}$
7) $return S^*$

(a) Reachability

3) $while(S \neq \phi)\{$
4) $P \leftarrow createCNF \ (S(\overline{x}) \wedge T'(\overline{x},\overline{I},\overline{x'}) \wedge \neg S^*(\overline{x'}))$
5) $S \leftarrow \phi$
5) $repeat\{$
6) $temp \leftarrow find \ next \ batch \ of \ solutions \ for \ (P)$
7) $S \leftarrow S \cup temp$
8) $minimize(S)$
9) $S^* \leftarrow S^* \cup temp$
10) $minimize(S^*)$
11) $\} \ while((temp \neq \phi)$
12) $\}$
13) $return \ \ S^*$

(b) New Reachability

Fig. 5. Reachability Algorithms. (a) Regular reachability algorithm. (b) Reachability using out All-SAT solver. Lines 5-11 are the implementation of the on-the-fly minimization.

conflict driven backtrack, and uses efficient data structures. Since zChaff is open source, we were able to modify the code according to our method.

For comparison, we used the same code base to implement the blocking clauses method. In order to avoid repetition of the same assignments to the important variables, we constructed the blocking clauses from the important variables only. We improved the blocking clauses by using the decision method described in Section 3.2. This way, the blocking clauses can be constructed from only the subset of the important variables which are decision variables, since the rest of the assignments are implied by them. This improvement reduced space requirements as well as solution times of the blocking clauses method substantially.

All experiments use dedicated computers with 1.7Ghz Intel Xeon cpu and 1GB RAM, running Linux. The problem instances are from the ISCAS'89 benchmark.

6.1   All-SAT Solver

Figure 6 shows the performance of our new All-SAT solver. The problems are CNF representations of the transition relations of the models in the benchmark. In cases where a model name is followed by '*', the instance consists of multiple transitions and initial conditions of a model. The important variables were arbitrarily chosen.

The table clearly shows a significant speedup for all problems that the blocking clauses method could solve. Smaller number of clauses shortens the time of the *bcp()* procedure, and also allows more work to be performed in higher levels of the memory hierarchy (main memory and cache). The speedup increases with the hardness of the problem and the computation time.

Our solver is capable of solving larger instances, for which the blocking clauses method runs out of memory. The number of solutions for these instances is simply

name	Clauses	Vars	Sol	T1 (s)	T2 (s)	S.U.
s510	964	280	64	0.00	0.00	1.00
s1488	983	286	64	0.00	0.00	1.00
s1494	19153	4919	12	0.00	0.00	1.00
s15850	166	48	2	0.00	0.00	1.00
s208.1	47	22	11	0.00	0.00	1.00
s23	303	97	5	0.00	0.00	1.00
s298	437	137	8	0.00	0.00	1.00
s382	462	140	8	0.00	0.00	1.00
s400	462	96	2	0.00	0.00	1.00
s420.1	498	153	5	0.00	0.00	1.00
s444	1620	129	2	0.00	0.00	1.00
s499	561	161	5	0.00	0.00	1.00
s526	1528	192	3	0.00	0.00	1.00
s635	1438	192	2	0.00	0.00	1.00
s838.1	1406	191	2	0.00	0.00	1.00
s938	558	160	5	0.00	0.00	1.00
s526n	479	138	36	0.00	0.00	0.50
s208.1*	160	50	512	0.01	0.01	1.00
s713	158	48	512	0.01	0.02	2.20
s208.1*	190	61	512	0.01	0.02	2.67
s832	454	136	183	0.01	0.02	1.29
s820	404	129	344	0.01	0.03	3.11
s208.1*	585	161	480	0.03	0.05	1.77
s208.1*	610	167	960	0.06	0.10	1.64

name	Clauses	Vars	Solutions	T1 (s)	T2(s)	S.U.
s641	10064	2338	224	0.03	0.16	5.81
s953	1279	271	1188	0.07	0.24	3.52
s1238	49699	13476	80	0.06	0.48	8.39
s9234.1	239	77	640	0.35	0.55	1.57
s967	959	277	6504	0.14	0.59	4.35
s38584	1302	299	2272	0.13	0.81	6.31
s1423	1884	560	28590	0.45	29.9	66.44
s1269	2191	679	32768	0.82	50	60.75
s13207	18993	3890	24576	4.40	459	104.39
s3271	4426	1349	6.70E+07	1191	M.O.	-
s9234.1	10007	2317	3.50E+07	3411	M.O.	-
s1512	2320	657	1.30E+08	4601.5	M.O.	-
s3330	2496	775	1.50E+08	4891	M.O.	-
s38417	48783	13261	8.30E+06	11379	M.O.	-
s5378	1072	4031	5.00E+08	26493	M.O.	-
s635*	1496	192	> 4E+09	107644	M.O.	-
s6669	11963	3639	> 4E+09	172800	M.O.	-
s13207.1	18774	3847	> 1E+09	T.O.	M.O.	-
s15850.1	18957	4850	> 1.2E+09	T.O.	M.O.	-
s3384	5073	1784	> 4E+09	T.O.	M.O.	-
s35932	55173	20155	> 7.5E+07	T.O.	M.O.	-
s38584.1	49735	13449	> 2E+08	T.O.	M.O.	-
s4863	10470	3001	> 1.3E+09	T.O.	M.O.	-
s991	1635	560	> 5.5E+08	T.O.	M.O.	-

Fig. 6. All-SAT solving time. Vars: The number of variables in the problem. About half the variables are important. Sol: The number of solutions found. T1: The time required for our new All-SAT solver, T2: The time required for the blocking clauses-based algorithm. M.O.: Memory Out. S.U.: Speedup - the ratio T2/T1. The timeout was set to 48 hours.

too high to store in main memory as clauses. In contrast, using our new method, the solutions can be stored on the disk or in the memory of neighboring machines.

The last seven rows in the table show instances for which our solver timed out. In none of these cases, despite the huge number of solutions found (much larger than the size of the main memory in the machine employed), did the solver run out of memory.

6.2 Reachability

Figure 7 shows the performance of our reachability analysis tool, calculating reachability for the benchmark models. Since [6] and [18] are the only reachability analysis algorithms that, as far as we know, depend solely on SAT procedures, the table shows a comparison with the performance reported in [6]. Figure 8 shows the instances for which the reachability analysis did not complete. Here, again, a comparison to [6] is shown. The tables show significant speedup for the completed problems, and deeper steps for those not completed.

7   Conclusions

In this work we presented an All-SAT engine which efficiently finds all the assignments to a subset of the variables, which can be extended to solutions to a given propositional

Model	# FLOPS	# steps	# states	T1 (sec)	T2 (sec)	Speedup
s386	6	8	13	0.1	0.21	2.10
s298	14	19	218	0.2	0.33	1.65
s832	5	11	25	0.1	0.47	4.70
s510	6	47	47	0.1	0.47	4.70
s820	5	11	25	0.2	0.48	2.40
s208.1	8	256	256	0.1	0.56	5.60
s1488	6	22	48	0.3	0.87	2.90
s1494	6	22	48	0.1	0.87	8.70
s499	22	22	22	0.3	1.74	5.80
s953	29	10	504	0.1	2.01	20.10
s641	19	7	1544	0.2	2.24	11.20
s713	19	7	1544	1	2.53	2.53
s967	29	10	549	0.2	3.12	15.60
s1196	18	3	2615	0.3	6.79	22.63
s1238	18	3	2615	0.2	7.26	36.30
s382	21	151	8865	4	7.7	1.93
s400	21	151	8865	4	7.8	1.95
s444	21	151	8865	4	8	2.00
s526n	21	151	8868	5	9.21	1.84
s526	21	151	8868	5	9.35	1.87
s349	15	7	2625	3	14.8	4.93
s344	15	7	2625	3	15.3	5.10

Fig. 7. Reachability Analysis Performance. #FLOPS is the number of flip-flops in the model. #states is the total number of reachable states. T1 is the time required for our tool. T2 is the time as given in [6] using 1.5Ghz dual AMD Athlon cpu with 3GB RAM.

Model	#FLOPS	Depth 1 (1000 sec')	Time to reach Depth 1 (sec)	Max depth Completed	Actual time for max depth (sec)
S1269	37	1	10	1	10
S1423	74	3	28	4	615
S13207	669	2	8	3	140
S1512	57	4	70	23	31761
S9234	228	8	314	111	251764
S15850	597	5	192	7	8467
S38584	1452	2	1	4	2134

Fig. 8. Reachability Analysis Performance. 'Depth 1' is the maximal depth reached in [6] with timeout of 1000 seconds. 'Time to reach Depth 1' is the time required for our tool to complete the same depth. The 'Max depth' and the 'Actual time for max depth' are the maximal steps successfully completed by our tool, and the time required for it. The Timeout is generally 3600 seconds (1 hour), with longer timeouts for s1512, s9234 and s15850.

formula. We achieve this goal by incorporating a backtrack search and a conflict driven search into one complete engine. Our engine's memory requirements are independent of the number of solutions. This implies that, during the computation, the number of solutions already found does not become a parameter of complexity in finding further solutions. It also implies that the size of the instance being solved fits in smaller and faster levels of the memory hierarchy. As a result, our method is faster than blocking clause-based methods, and can solve instances that produce solution sets too large to fit in memory. We have demonstrated how to use our All-SAT engine for memory-efficient reachability computation.

References

1. I. Beer, S. Ben-David, and A. Landver. On-the-fly model checking of RCTL formulas. In *10th Computer Aided Verification*, pages 184–194, 1998.
2. A. Biere, A. Cimatti, E. M. Clarke, M. Fujita, and Y. Zhu. Symbolic model checking using SAT procedures instead of BDDs. In *DAC*. IEEE Computer Society Press, June 1999.
3. Elazar Birnbaum and Eliezer L. Lozinskii. The good old davis-putnam procedure helps counting models. *Journal of Artificial Intelligence Research*, 10:457–477, 1999.
4. R. E. Bryant. Graph-based algorithms for boolean function manipulation. *IEEE transactions on Computers*, C-35(8):677–691, 1986.
5. J. R. Burch, E. M. Clarke, K. L. McMillan, D. L. Dill, and L. J. Hwang. Symbolic model checking: 10^{20} states and beyond. *Information and Computation*, 98(2):142–170, June 1992.
6. P. Chauhan, E. M. Clarke, and D. Kroening. Using SAT based image computation for reachability analysis. Technical Report CMU-CS-03-151, Carnegie Mellon University, 2003.
7. P. P. Chauhan, E. M. Clarke, and D. Kroening. A SAT-based algorithm for reparameterization in symbolic simulation. In *DAC*, 2004.
8. M. Davis, G. Logemann, and D. Loveland. A machine program for theorem proving. *CACM*, 5(7), July 1962.
9. M. Davis and H. Putnam. A computing procedure for quantification theory. *JACM*, 7(3):201–215, July 1960.
10. E. Goldberg and Y. Novikov. Berkmin: A fast and robust SAT-solver. In *DATE*, 2002.
11. Aarti Gupta, Zijiang Yang, Pranav Ashar, and Anubhav Gupta. SAT-based image computation with application in reachability analysis. In *FMCAD*, LNCS 1954, 2000.
12. Roberto J. Bayardo Jr. and Joseph Daniel Pehoushek. Counting models using connected components. In *AAAI/IAAI*, pages 157–162, 2000.
13. H. J. Kang and I. C. Park. SAT-based unbounded symbolic model checking. In *DAC*, 2003.
14. S. K. Lahiri, R. E. Bryant, and B. Cook. A symbolic approach to predicate abstraction. In *CAV*. LLNCS 2725, July 2003.
15. R. Letz. Advances in decision procedures for quantified boolean formulas. In *IJCAR*, 2001.
16. Chu Min Li and Anbulagan. Heuristics based on unit propagation for satisfiability problems. In *IJCAI (1)*, pages 366–371, 1997.
17. J.P. Marques-Silva and K.A. Sakallah. Conflict analysis in search algorithms for propositional satisfiability. In *IEEE ICTAI*, 1996.
18. Ken L. McMillan. Applying SAT methods in unbounded symbolic model checking. In *Computer Aided Verification*, 2002.
19. M.W. Moskewicz, C.F. Madigan, Y. Zhao, L. Zhang, and S. Malik. Chaff: engineering an efficient SAT solver. In *39th Design Aotomation Conference (DAC'01)*, 2001.
20. D. Plaisted. Method for design verification of hardware and non-hardware systems. United States Patents, 6,131, 078, October 2000.
21. D. Roth. On the hardness of approximate reasoning. *Artificial Intelligence*, 82(1-2), 1996.
22. S. Sapra, M. Theobald, and E. M. Clarke. SAT-based algorithms for logic minimization. In *ICCD*, 2003.
23. Ofer Shtrichman. Tuning SAT checkers for bounded model checking. In *CAV*, 2000.
24. Berkeley University of California. Espresso, two level boolean minimizer, 1990.
25. A. Yadgar. Solving All-SAT problem for reachability analysis. M.Sc. thesis, Technion, Israel Institute of Technology, Department of Computer Schience, 2004.
26. H. Zhang. SATO: An efficient propositional prover. In *(CADE)*, 1997.
27. L. Zhang, C. F. Madigan, M. W. Moskewicz, and S. Malik. Efficient conflict driven learning in boolean satisfiability solver. In *ICCAD*, 2001.

Approximate Symbolic Model Checking
for Incomplete Designs

Tobias Nopper and Christoph Scholl

Institute of Computer Science
Albert-Ludwigs-University Freiburg
D-79110 Freiburg im Breisgau, Germany

Abstract. We consider the problem of checking whether an incomplete design can still be extended to a complete design satisfying a given CTL formula and whether the property is satisfied for all possible extensions. Motivated by the fact that well-known model checkers like SMV or VIS produce incorrect results when handling unknowns by using the programs' non-deterministic signals, we present a series of approximate, yet sound algorithms to process incomplete designs with increasing quality and computational resources. Finally we give a series of experimental results demonstrating the effectiveness and feasibility of the presented methods.

1   Introduction

Deciding the question whether a circuit implementation fulfills its specification is an essential problem in computer-aided design of VLSI circuits. Growing interest in universities and industry has led to new results and significant advances concerning topics like property checking, state space traversal and combinational equivalence checking.

For proving properties of sequential circuits, Clarke, Emerson, and Sistla presented model checking for the temporal logic CTL [1]. Burch, Clarke, and McMillan et al. improved the technique by using symbolic methods based on binary decision diagrams [2] for both state set representation and state traversal in [3, 4].

In this paper we will consider how to perform model checking of *incomplete* circuits, i.e. circuits which contain unknown parts. These unknown parts are combined into so-called Black Boxes. In doing so, we will approach two potentially interesting questions, whether it is still possible to replace the Black Boxes by circuit implementations, so that a given model checking property is satisfied ('realizability') and whether the property is satisfied for any possible replacement ('validity').

There are three major benefits symbolic model checking for incomplete circuits can provide: First, instead of forcing the verification runs to the end of the design process where the design is completed, it rather allows model checking in early stages of design, where parts may not yet be finished, so that errors can be detected earlier. Second, complex parts of a design can be replaced by Black Boxes, simplifying the design, while many properties of the design still can

A.J. Hu and A.K. Martin (Eds.): FMCAD 2004, LNCS 3312, pp. 290–305, 2004.

be proven, yet in shorter time. Third, the location of design errors in circuits not satisfying a model checking property can be narrowed down by iteratively masking potentially erroneous parts of the circuit.

Some well-known model checking tools like SMV [4] (resp. NuSMV [5]) and VIS [6] provide the definition of non-deterministic signals (see [7–9]). At first sight, signals coming from unknown areas can be handled as non-deterministic signals, but we will show that modeling by non-deterministic signals is not capable of answering the questions of realizability ('is there a replacement of the Black Boxes so that the overall implementation satisfies a given property?') or validity ('is a given property satisfied for all Black Box replacements?'). This approach is even not able to provide approximate solutions for realizability or validity.

Whereas an *exact* solution to the realizability problem for incomplete designs with several Black Boxes (potentially containing an unrestricted amount of memory) is undecidable in general [10], we will present *approximate* solutions to symbolic model checking for incomplete designs. Our algorithms will not give a definite answer in every case, but they are guaranteed to be sound in the sense that they will never give an incorrect answer. First experimental results given in Sect. 5 prove effectiveness and feasibility of these approximate methods.

Our methods are based on symbolic representations of incomplete combinational circuits [11]. Using these representations we provide different methods for approximating the sets of states satisfying a given property φ. During one run of symbolic model checking we compute both underapproximations and overapproximations of the states satisfying φ and we will use them to provide approximate answers for realizability and validity.

The work of Huth et al. [12], which introduced Kripke Modal Transition Systems (KMTSs), comes closest to our approach. Whereas our simplest algorithm can be modeled by using KMTSs, KMTSs are not able to model the fact that the Black Box outputs can not take different values at the same time, a constraint that will be considered in our most advanced algorithm.

Black Boxes in incomplete designs may be seen as Uninterpreted Functions (UIFs) in some sense. UIFs have been used for the verification of pipelined microprocessors [13], where a validity problem is solved under the assumption that both specification and implementation contain the same Uninterpreted Functions. Whereas in [13–16] a dedicated class of problems for pipelined microprocessors is solved (which is basically reduced to a combinational problem using an inductive argument), we will deal here with arbitrary incomplete sequential circuits and properties given in the full temporal logic CTL.

The paper is structured as follows: After giving a brief review of symbolic model checking and of representations for incomplete designs in Sect. 2, we will discuss the results of the method handling Black Boxes using non-deterministic signal definitions as provided by SMV and VIS, together with the arising problems in Sect. 3. In Sect. 4, we will introduce several algorithms capable of performing sound and approximate symbolic model checking for incomplete circuits. Finally we give a series of experimental results demonstrating the effectiveness and feasibility of the presented methods in Sect. 5 and conclude the paper in Sect. 6.

2   Preliminaries

2.1   Symbolic Model Checking for Complete Designs

Before we introduce symbolic model checking for incomplete designs we will give a brief review of the well-known symbolic model checking for complete designs [3].

Symbolic model checking is applied to Kripke structures which may be derived from sequential circuits on the one hand and to a formula of a temporal logic (in our case CTL (Computation Tree Logic)) on the other hand.

We assume a (complete) sequential circuit to be given by a Mealy automaton $M := (\mathbb{B}^{|\vec{q}|}, \mathbb{B}^{|\vec{x}|}, \mathbb{B}^{|\vec{y}|}, \delta, \lambda, \vec{q}^{\,0})$ with state set $\mathbb{B}^{|\vec{q}|}$, the set of inputs $\mathbb{B}^{|\vec{x}|}$, the set of outputs $\mathbb{B}^{|\vec{y}|}$, transition function $\delta : \mathbb{B}^{|\vec{q}|} \times \mathbb{B}^{|\vec{x}|} \to \mathbb{B}^{|\vec{q}|}$, output function $\lambda : \mathbb{B}^{|\vec{q}|} \times \mathbb{B}^{|\vec{x}|} \to \mathbb{B}^{|\vec{y}|}$ and initial state $\vec{q}^{\,0} \in \mathbb{B}^{|\vec{q}|}$. In the following we will use $\vec{x} = (x_0, \dots, x_{n-1})$ $(n = |\vec{x}|)$ for vectors of input variables, $\vec{y}$ for vectors of output variables, $\vec{q}$ for current state variables and $\vec{q}^{\,\prime}$ for next state variables.

The states of the corresponding Kripke structure are defined as a combination of states and inputs of M. The resulting Kripke structure for M is given by $struct(M) := (S, R, L)$ with:

$$S := \mathbb{B}^{|\vec{q}|} \times \mathbb{B}^{|\vec{x}|}$$

$$R := \left\{ ((\vec{q}, \vec{x}), (\vec{q}^{\,\prime}, \vec{x}^{\,\prime})), \,|\, \vec{q}, \vec{q}^{\,\prime} \in \mathbb{B}^{|\vec{q}|}, \, \vec{x}, \vec{x}^{\,\prime} \in \mathbb{B}^{|\vec{x}|}, \, \delta(\vec{q}, \vec{x}) = \vec{q}^{\,\prime} \right\}$$

$$L((\vec{q}, \vec{\epsilon})) := \left\{ x_i \,|\, \epsilon_i = 1 \right\} \cup \left\{ y_i \,|\, \lambda_i(\vec{q}, \vec{\epsilon}) = 1 \right\}.$$

As usual we write $struct(M), s \models \varphi$ if φ is a CTL formula that is satisfied in state $s = (\vec{q}, \vec{x}) \in S$ of $struct(M)$. If it is clear from the context which Kripke structure is used, we simply write $s \models \varphi$ instead of $struct(M), s \models \varphi$. $\models$ is defined recursively:

$s \models \varphi; \; \varphi \in V \iff \varphi \in L(s)$ $(V = $ set of atomic propositions$)$

$s \models \neg\varphi \iff s \not\models \varphi$

$s \models (\varphi_1 \vee \varphi_2) \iff s \models \varphi_1$ or $s \models \varphi_2$

$s \models EX\varphi \iff \exists s' \in S : R(s, s')$ and $s' \models \varphi$

$s \models EG\varphi \iff s \models \varphi$ and $\exists s' \in S : R(s, s')$ and $s' \models EG\varphi$

$s \models E\varphi_1 U\varphi_2 \iff s \models \varphi_2$ or $(\exists s' \in S : R(s, s')$ and $s \models \varphi_1$ and $s' \models E\varphi_1 U\varphi_2)$

The remaining CTL operations $\wedge$, EF, AX, AU, AG and AF can be expressed by using $\neg$, $\vee$, EX, EU and EG [4].

In symbolic model checking, sets of states are represented by characteristic functions, which are in turn represented by BDDs. Let $Sat(\varphi)$ be the set of states of $struct(M)$ which satisfy formula φ and let $\chi_{Sat(\varphi)}$ be its characteristic function, then $\chi_{Sat(\varphi)}$ can be computed recursively based on the characteristic function $\chi_R(\vec{q}, \vec{x}, \vec{q}^{\,\prime}) := \prod_{i=0}^{|\vec{q}|-1} \left(\delta_i(\vec{q}, \vec{x}) \equiv q_i' \right)$ of the transition relation R:

$$\chi_{Sat(x_i)}(\vec{q}, \vec{x}) := x_i$$

$$\chi_{Sat(y_i)}(\vec{q}, \vec{x}) := \lambda_i(\vec{q}, \vec{x})$$

```
χEG(χX) {                          χEU(χX, χY) {
  old := 1;                          old := 0;
  new := χX;                         new := χY;
  while (old ≠ new) {                while (old ≠ new) {
    old := new;                        old := new;
    new := χX · χEX(old);              new := χY + (χX · χEX(old));
  }                                  }
  return new;                        return new;
}                                  }
```

Fig. 1. Fixed point iteration algorithms

$$\chi_{Sat(\neg\varphi)}(\vec{q}, \vec{x}) \quad := \overline{\chi_{Sat(\varphi)}}(\vec{q}, \vec{x})$$

$$\chi_{Sat((\varphi_1 \vee \varphi_2))}(\vec{q}, \vec{x}) := \chi_{Sat(\varphi_1)}(\vec{q}, \vec{x}) + \chi_{Sat(\varphi_2)}(\vec{q}, \vec{x})$$

$$\chi_{Sat(EX\varphi)}(\vec{q}, \vec{x}) \quad := \chi_{EX}(\chi_{Sat(\varphi)})(\vec{q}, \vec{x})$$

$$\chi_{Sat(EG\varphi)}(\vec{q}, \vec{x}) \quad := \chi_{EG}(\chi_{Sat(\varphi)})(\vec{q}, \vec{x})$$

$$\chi_{Sat(E\varphi_1 U\varphi_2)}(\vec{q}, \vec{x}) := \chi_{EU}(\chi_{Sat(\varphi_1)}, \chi_{Sat(\varphi_2)})(\vec{q}, \vec{x})$$

$$\text{with} \quad \chi_{EX}(\chi_X)(\vec{q}, \vec{x}) \quad := \exists \vec{q}' \exists \vec{x}'(\chi_R(\vec{q}, \vec{x}, \vec{q}') \cdot (\chi_X|_{\substack{\vec{q} \leftarrow \vec{q}' \\ \vec{x} \leftarrow \vec{x}'}})(\vec{q}', \vec{x}'))$$

χ_{EG} and χ_{EU} can be evaluated by the fixed point iteration algorithms shown in Fig. 1.

A Mealy automaton satisfies a formula φ iff φ is satisfied in all the states of the corresponding Kripke structure which are derived from the initial state $\vec{q}^0$ of M:

$$M \models \varphi \iff \forall \vec{x} \in \mathbb{B}^{|\vec{x}|} : struct(M), (\vec{q}^0, \vec{x}) \models \varphi$$

$$\iff \forall \vec{x}(\chi_{Sat(\varphi)}|_{\vec{q}=\vec{q}^0}) = 1$$

2.2   Incomplete Designs

Representing Incomplete Designs: If parts of a circuit are not yet known or cut off, we have to handle *incomplete designs*. In this section we briefly review symbolic representations of incomplete designs which we will need in Sect. 4.

Unknown parts of the design are combined into so-called 'Black Boxes' (see Fig. 2a for a combinational example with one Black Box).

For simulating the circuit wrt. some input vector we can make use of the ternary $(0, 1, X)$-logic [17,11]: We assign a value X to each output of the Black Box (since the Black Box outputs are unknown) and we perform a conventional $(0, 1, X)$-simulation [18] (see Fig. 2b). If the value of some primary output is X, we do not know the value due to the unknown behavior of the Black Boxes.

For a symbolic representation of the incomplete circuit we model the additional value X by a new variable Z as in [19,11]. For each output g_i of the incomplete design with primary input variables $x_1, \ldots, x_n$ we obtain a BDD representation of g_i by using a slightly modified version of symbolic simulation with

$$g_i|_{\substack{x_1=\epsilon_1 \\ x_n=\epsilon_n}} = \begin{cases} 1, & \text{if the (0,1,X)-simulation with input } (\epsilon_1, \ldots, \epsilon_n) \text{ produces } 1 \\ 0, & \text{if the (0,1,X)-simulation with input } (\epsilon_1, \ldots, \epsilon_n) \text{ produces } 0 \\ Z, & \text{if the (0,1,X)-simulation with input } (\epsilon_1, \ldots, \epsilon_n) \text{ produces } X \end{cases}$$

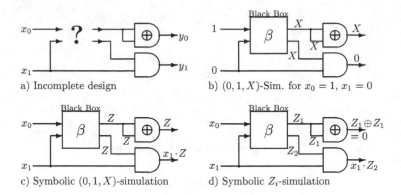

Fig. 2. Incomplete design

This modified version of symbolic simulation is called *symbolic (0,1,X)-simulation*, see Fig. 2c for an example.

Since $(0, 1, X)$-simulation can not distinguish between unknown values at different Black Box outputs, some information is lost in symbolic $(0, 1, X)$-simulation. This problem can be solved at the cost of additional variables: Instead of using the same variable Z for all Black Box outputs, we introduce a new variable Z_i for each Black Box output and perform a (conventional) symbolic simulation. This approach was called symbolic Z_i-simulation in [11]. Fig. 2d shows an example for symbolic Z_i-simulation. (Note that the first output can now be shown to be constant 0.)

In Sect. 4 we will use symbolic $(0, 1, X)$-simulation and symbolic Z_i-simulation to approximate transition functions and output functions of incomplete sequential circuits.

Please note that in contrast to [11], we will consider Black Boxes that can be replaced not only by combinational, but also by sequential circuits, so that for two states in a computation path that generate the same Black Box input, the Black Box may answer with different outputs.

Realizability and Validity: In Sect. 4 we will present methods realizing approximate symbolic model checking for incomplete designs. We will consider two types of questions:

1. Is there a replacement of the Black Boxes in the incomplete design, so that the resulting circuit satisfies a given CTL formula φ? If this is true, then the property φ is called *realizable* for the incomplete design. The corresponding decision problem is called *realizability* problem.

2. Is a CTL formula φ satisfied for all possible replacements of the Black Boxes? If this is the case, then φ is *valid* for the incomplete design; the corresponding decision problem is denoted as *validity* problem.

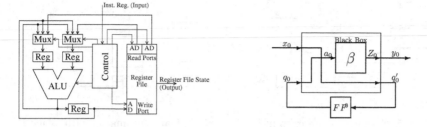

Fig. 3. Pipelined ALU   **Fig. 4.** First Counterexample

3 Model Checking for Incomplete Designs Using Non-deterministic Signals

Well-known CTL model checkers such as SMV and VIS provide so-called 'non-deterministic assignments' resp. 'non-deterministic signals' to model non-determinism [7–9]. At first sight it appears to be advisable using non-deterministic signals for handling Black Box outputs, since the functionality of Black Boxes is not known. In this section we motivate our approach by the observation that non-deterministic signals lead to incorrect results when used for model checking of incomplete designs. We will show that they even can not be used to obtain approximate results by analyzing two small examples.

Before doing so, we will report on a larger and more familiar example showing the same problems. Interestingly, incorrect results of SMV (resp. VIS) due to non-deterministic signals can be observed for the well-known pipelined ALU circuit from [3] (see Fig. 3). In [3], Burch et al. showed by symbolic model checking that (among other CTL formulas) the following formulas are satisfied for the pipelined ALU[1]:

$$AG\big((EX)^2\mathbf{R} \equiv (AX)^2\mathbf{R}\big) \tag{1}$$

$$AG\big((EX)^3\mathbf{R} \equiv (AX)^3\mathbf{R}\big) \tag{2}$$

Now we assume that the ALU's adder has not yet been implemented and it is replaced by a Black Box. The outputs of the Black Box are modeled by non-deterministic signals. In this situation SMV provides the result that (2) is not satisfied[2]. However, it is clear that there is at least one replacement of the Black Box which satisfies the CTL formula (a replacement by an adder, of course). Moreover, it is not hard to see, that the formula is even true *for all* possible replacements of the Black Box by any (combinational or sequential) circuit, so one would expect SMV to provide a positive answer both for (1) and (2).

Obviously, the usage of non-deterministic signals leads to non-exact results. Yet, one might consider that although the results are not exact, they might be

---

[1] The formulas essentially say that the content of the register file $\mathbf{R}$ two (resp. three) clock cycles in the future is uniquely determined by the current state of the system.

[2] Using VIS, the verification already fails for (1) – this is due to a slightly different modeling of automata by Kripke structures in VIS and SMV.

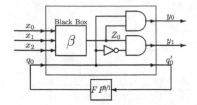   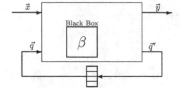

Fig. 5. Second Counterexample   **Fig. 6.** Mealy automaton with Black Box

approximate in some way. We will disprove this by analyzing two small exemplary circuits with SMV (similar considerations can be done for VIS as well).

Hypothesis 1: A Negative Result of SMV Means That a Property Is Not Valid.

Figure 4 shows a counterexample for this hypothesis: If we substitute the Black Box output by a non-deterministic signal, SMV provides the result that $\varphi_1 = AG(AXy_0 \vee AX\neg y_0)$ is *not* satisfied. Now consider two finite primary input sequences which differ only in the last element. Since the Black Box input does not depend on the primary input, but only on the state of the flip flop, these two primary input sequences produce the same input sequence at the Black Box input. Thus, the primary output (which is the same as the Black Box output) will be the same for both input sequences. This means that the CTL formula φ_1 is satisfied for all possible Black Box substitutions, thus it is valid. So we observe that a negative result of SMV does *not* mean that a property is not valid.

Hypothesis 2: A Negative Result of SMV Means That a Property Is Not Realizable.

We consider the circuit shown in Fig. 5 and the CTL formula $\varphi_2 = EX(EGy_0 \vee AGy_1)$. We assume that the flip flop is initialized by 0. If we replace the Black Box output by a non-deterministic signal, SMV provides the result that φ_2 is *not* satisfied. However, it is easy to see that the formula is satisfied if the Black Box is substituted with the constant **1** function; so the property is realizable. Thus, a negative result of SMV does *not* mean that a property is not realizable.

Hypothesis 3: A Positive Result of SMV Means That a Property Is Valid.

Again, we consider the example shown in Fig. 5 and the CTL formula $\varphi_2 = EX(EGy_0 \vee AGy_1)$, yet this time we assume that the flip flop is initialized by 1. If we substitute the Black Box output by a non-deterministic signal, SMV provides the result that φ_2 *is* satisfied. Though, it is easy to see that the formula is not satisfied if the Black Box is substituted with the constant **0** function; so the property not valid. Thus, a positive result of SMV does *not* mean that a property is valid.

Hypothesis 4: A Positive Result of SMV Means That a Property Is Realizable.

Finally, we reconsider the circuit shown in Fig. 4 in combination with $\varphi_3 = \neg\varphi_1 = \neg AG(AXy_0 \vee AX\neg y_0)$. Again, we assume the Black Box output to be a non-deterministic signal and we verify the circuit using SMV, which

provides the result that φ_3 *is* satisfied. However, since property φ_3 is the negation of property φ_1 which has been proven to be valid when considering the first
hypothesis, it is quite obvious that φ_3 is not realizable. Thus, a positive result
of SMV does *not* mean that a property is realizable.

Conclusion. Using non-deterministic signals for Black Box outputs is obviously
not capable of performing correct Model Checking for incomplete designs – the
approach is even not able to provide an approximate algorithm for realizability
or validity[3].

    This motivates our work presented in the next section: we will define approx-
imate methods for proving validity and for falsifying realizability of Black Box
implementations. The results are not complete, but they are sound, i.e. depending on the formula and the incomplete design they may fail to prove validity or
falsify realizability, but they will never return incorrect results.

4   Symbolic Model Checking for Incomplete Designs

4.1   Basic Principle

Symbolic model checking computes the set $Sat(\varphi)$ of all states satisfying a CTL
formula φ and then checks whether all initial states are included in this set. If
so, the circuit satisfies φ.

    The situation becomes more complex if we consider incomplete circuits, since
for each replacement of the Black Boxes we may have different state sets satisfying φ. In contrast to conventional model checking we will consider two sets
instead of $Sat(\varphi)$: The first set is called $Sat_E^{ex}(\varphi)$ and it contains all states, for
which *there is* at least one Black Box replacement so that φ is satisfied. To obtain $Sat_E^{ex}(\varphi)$ we could *conceptually* consider all possible replacements R of the
Black Boxes, compute $Sat^R(\varphi)$ for each such replacement by conventional model
checking and determine $Sat_E^{ex}(\varphi)$ as the union of all these sets $Sat^R(\varphi)$. The
second set is called $Sat_A^{ex}(\varphi)$ and it contains all states, for which φ is satisfied
for *all* Black Box replacements. Conceptually, $Sat_A^{ex}(\varphi)$ could be computed as an
intersection of all sets $Sat^R(\varphi)$ obtained for all possible replacements R of the
Black Boxes.

    Given $Sat_E^{ex}(\varphi)$ and $Sat_A^{ex}(\varphi)$, it is easy to prove validity and to falsify real-
izability for the incomplete circuit: If all initial states are included in $Sat_A^{ex}(\varphi)$,
then all initial states are included in $Sat^R(\varphi)$ for each replacement R of the
Black Boxes and thus, φ is satisfied for all replacements of the Black Boxes
("φ is valid"). If there is at least one initial state not belonging to $Sat_E^{ex}(\varphi)$,

---

[3] Yet, there are subclasses of CTL, for which VIS and SMV can provide correct results: Considering $ACTL$ (type A temporal operators only, negation only allowed for
atomic propositions), a positive result of SMV/VIS means that the property is valid.
Considering $ECTL$ (analogously for E operators), a negative result of VIS means
that the property is not realizable; this is not true for SMV due to its universal
abstraction of the primary inputs at the end of the evaluation.

then this initial state is not included in $Sat^R(\varphi)$ for all replacements R of the Black Boxes and thus, there is no replacement of the Black Boxes so that φ is satisfied for the resulting complete circuit ("φ is not realizable").

4.2   Approximations

For reasons of efficiency we will not compute exact sets $Sat_E^{ex}(\varphi)$ and $Sat_A^{ex}(\varphi)$. Instead we will compute *approximations* $Sat_E(\varphi)$ and $Sat_A(\varphi)$ of these sets. To be more precise we will compute overapproximations $Sat_E(\varphi) \supseteq Sat_E^{ex}(\varphi)$ of $Sat_E^{ex}(\varphi)$ and underapproximations $Sat_A(\varphi) \subseteq Sat_A^{ex}(\varphi)$ of $Sat_A^{ex}(\varphi)$.

Because of $Sat_E(\varphi) \supseteq Sat_E^{ex}(\varphi) \supseteq Sat^R(\varphi)$ for arbitrary replacements R of the Black Boxes we can also guarantee for $Sat_E(\varphi)$ that φ is not realizable if some initial state is not included in $Sat_E(\varphi)$. Analogously we can guarantee that φ is valid if all initial states are included in $Sat_A(\varphi)$ (since $Sat_A(\varphi) \subseteq Sat_A^{ex}(\varphi) \subseteq Sat^R(\varphi)$).

Approximations of $Sat_E(\varphi)$ and $Sat_A(\varphi)$ will be computed based on an approximate transition relation and on approximate output functions for the corresponding Mealy automaton M. In incomplete designs we have Black Boxes in the functional block defining the transition function δ and the output function λ (see Fig. 6). For this reason there are two types of transitions for the automaton: We have

- transitions which exist independently from the replacement of the Black Boxes, i.e. for all possible replacements of the Black Boxes (we will call them 'fixed transitions') and
- transitions which may or may not exist in a complete version of the design – depending on the implementation for the Black Boxes (we will call them 'possible transitions').

We will work with two types of approximations of the transition relation $\chi_R(\vec{q}, \vec{x}, \vec{q}')$: An underapproximation $\chi_{R_A}(\vec{q}, \vec{x}, \vec{q}')$ will only contain fixed transitions and an overapproximation $\chi_{R_E}(\vec{q}, \vec{x}, \vec{q}')$ will contain at least all possible transitions (of course, this includes all fixed transitions).

In the same manner we will approximate the sets of states $Sat(y_i)$ in which the output value y_i of λ_i is true:

- an underapproximation $Sat_A(y_i)$ contains only states in which y_i is true independently from the replacements of the Black Boxes and
- an overapproximation $Sat_E(y_i)$ contains at least all states in which y_i may be true for some replacement of the Black Boxes.

Based on these approximations χ_{R_A}, χ_{R_E}, $Sat_A(y_i)$, and $Sat_E(y_i)$ we will compute the underapproximations $Sat_A(\varphi)$ and overapproximations $Sat_E(\varphi)$ mentioned above for arbitrary CTL formulas φ.

In the following we will present different approximate methods which will (among other things) differ from the accuracy of approximating transition relation and output functions. More exact methods will identify more fixed transitions and less possible transitions. We will make use of symbolic $(0, 1, X)$-simulation and symbolic Z_i-simulation for computing δ and λ as described in Sect. 2.

Symbolic Z-Model Checking: We apply symbolic $(0, 1, X)$-simulation (see Sect. 2) for computing δ and λ. Thus, we introduce a new variable Z, which is assigned to each output of a Black Box and symbolic $(0, 1, X)$-simulation provides symbolic representations of functions $\lambda_i(\vec{q}, \vec{x}, Z)$ and $\delta_j(\vec{q}, \vec{x}, Z)$.

Output Functions: If $\lambda_i|_{\vec{q}=\vec{q}^{\text{fix}}, \vec{x}=\vec{x}^{\text{fix}}} = 1$ for some state $(\vec{q}^{\text{fix}}, \vec{x}^{\text{fix}}) \in \mathbb{B}^{|\vec{q}| \times |\vec{x}|}$, we know that λ_i is 1 in this state independently from the replacement of the Black Boxes, so we include $(\vec{q}^{\text{fix}}, \vec{x}^{\text{fix}})$ into $Sat_A(y_i)$ and $Sat_E(y_i)$. If $\lambda_i|_{\vec{q}=\vec{q}^{\text{fix}}, \vec{x}=\vec{x}^{\text{fix}}} = Z$, then the output λ_i may or may not be equal to 1 and thus, we include $(\vec{q}^{\text{fix}}, \vec{x}^{\text{fix}})$ into $Sat_E(y_i)$, but not into $Sat_A(y_i)$. This leads to the following symbolic representations:

$$\chi_{Sat_A(y_i)}(\vec{q}, \vec{x}) = \forall Z\big(\lambda_i(\vec{q}, \vec{x}, Z)\big), \qquad \chi_{Sat_E(y_i)}(\vec{q}, \vec{x}) = \exists Z\big(\lambda_i(\vec{q}, \vec{x}, Z)\big).$$

Transition Functions: An analogous argumentation leads to fixed transitions and possible transitions of χ_R, since the outputs of the transition functions may be definitely 1 or 0 (independently from the Black Boxes) or they may be unknown: For χ_{R_A}, representing only fixed transitions we obtain

$$\chi_{R_A}(\vec{q}, \vec{x}, \vec{q}') = \left(\prod_{i=0}^{|\vec{q}|-1} \forall Z\big(\delta_i(\vec{q}, \vec{x}, Z) \equiv q_i'\big)\right) \tag{3}$$

and for χ_{R_E} representing at least all possible transitions we obtain

$$\chi_{R_E}(\vec{q}, \vec{x}, \vec{q}') = \left(\prod_{i=0}^{|\vec{q}|-1} \exists Z\big(\delta_i(\vec{q}, \vec{x}, Z) \equiv q_i'\big)\right). \tag{4}$$

Note that χ_{R_A} defined in this way underapproximates the set of all fixed transitions due to well-known deficiencies of $(0, 1, X)$-simulation [11] and χ_{R_E} overapproximates the set of all possible transitions (the same is true for $\chi_{Sat_A(y_i)}$ and $\chi_{Sat_E(y_i)}$, respectively).

In order to compute $Sat_A(\varphi)$ and $Sat_E(\varphi)$ recursively for arbitrary CTL formulas we need rules to evaluate operators EX, $\neg$, $\lor$, EG and EU.

Computing $Sat_A(EX\psi)$ and $Sat_E(EX\psi)$: Given $Sat_A(\psi)$, the set of states which definitely satisfy ψ for all Black Box replacements, we include into $Sat_A(EX\psi)$ all states with a fixed transition to a state in $Sat_A(\psi)$. It is easy to see that these states definitely satisfy $EX\psi$, independently from the replacement of the Black Boxes. Likewise, we include all the states into $Sat_E(EX\psi)$ which have a possible transition to a state in $Sat_E(\psi)$. Fig. 7 illustrates the sets. Thus, we have

$$\chi_{Sat_A(EX\psi)}(\vec{q}, \vec{x}) = \exists \vec{q}' \exists \vec{x}' \big(\chi_{R_A}(\vec{q}, \vec{x}, \vec{q}') \cdot \big(\chi_{Sat_A(\psi)}|_{\substack{\vec{q}\leftarrow\vec{q}'\\\vec{x}\leftarrow\vec{x}'}}\big)(\vec{q}', \vec{x}')\big)$$

and $\quad \chi_{Sat_E(EX\psi)}(\vec{q}, \vec{x}) = \exists \vec{q}' \exists \vec{x}' \big(\chi_{R_E}(\vec{q}, \vec{x}, \vec{q}') \cdot \big(\chi_{Sat_E(\psi)}|_{\substack{\vec{q}\leftarrow\vec{q}'\\\vec{x}\leftarrow\vec{x}'}}\big)(\vec{q}', \vec{x}')\big).$

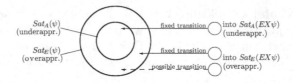

Fig. 7. Evaluation of $Sat_A(EX\psi)$ and $Sat_E(EX\psi)$

Computing $Sat_A(\neg\psi)$ and $Sat_E(\neg\psi)$: $Sat_E(\psi)$ is an overapproximation of all states in which ψ *may be* satisfied for some Black Box replacement. Thus, we do know that for an arbitrary state in $\mathbb{B}^{|\vec{q}|} \times \mathbb{B}^{|\vec{x}|} \setminus Sat_E(\psi)$ there is no Black Box replacement so that ψ is satisfied in this state or, equivalently, $\neg\psi$ is definitely satisfied in this state for all Black Box replacements. This means that we can use $\mathbb{B}^{|\vec{q}|} \times \mathbb{B}^{|\vec{x}|} \setminus Sat_E(\psi)$ as an underapproximation $Sat_A(\neg\psi)$. Since an analogous argument holds for $Sat_A(\psi)$ and $Sat_E(\neg\psi)$ we define

$$\chi_{Sat_A(\neg\psi)}(\vec{q},\vec{x}) = \overline{\chi_{Sat_E(\psi)}(\vec{q},\vec{x})} \qquad \text{and} \qquad \chi_{Sat_E(\neg\psi)}(\vec{q},\vec{x}) = \overline{\chi_{Sat_A(\psi)}(\vec{q},\vec{x})}.$$

Evaluating $\vee$, EG and EU: It is easy to see that $\chi_{Sat_A(\varphi_1\vee\varphi_2)} = \chi_{Sat_A(\varphi_1)} \vee \chi_{Sat_A(\varphi_2)}$ and $\chi_{Sat_E(\varphi_1\vee\varphi_2)} = \chi_{Sat_E(\varphi_1)} \vee \chi_{Sat_E(\varphi_2)}$. Moreover, $\varphi = EG\psi$ and $\varphi = E\psi_1 U\psi_2$ can be evaluated by standard fixed point iterations according to Figures 1a and 1b based on the evaluation of EX defined above (two separate fixed point iterations for Sat_A and Sat_E).

Altogether we obtain an algorithm to compute approximations for $Sat_A(\varphi)$ and $Sat_E(\varphi)$. According to the arguments given at the beginning of this section we need just $Sat_E(\varphi)$ to falsify realizability and we need just $Sat_A(\varphi)$ to prove validity. However, evaluation of negation shows that it is advisable to compute both $Sat_A(\varphi)$ and $Sat_E(\varphi)$ in parallel, since we need $Sat_A(\psi)$ to compute $Sat_E(\neg\psi)$ and we need $Sat_E(\psi)$ to compute $Sat_A(\neg\psi)$. Note that we do not need to perform two separate model checking runs to compute $Sat_E(\varphi)$ and $Sat_A(\varphi)$. By using an additional encoding variable e and defining $\chi_R = \chi_{R_A} + e \cdot \chi_{R_E}$, we can easily combine the two computations of $\chi_{Sat_A(\varphi)}$ and $\chi_{Sat_E(\varphi)}$ into one computation for $\chi_{Sat(\varphi)} = \chi_{Sat_A(\varphi)} + e \cdot \chi_{Sat_E(\varphi)}$. More details can be found in [20].

Example: Again, we consider the incomplete circuit shown in Fig. 4. It is quite obvious that in every state at least one of the two primary outputs y_0 and y_1 has to be 0 independently from the Black Box implementation. This is expressed by the CTL formula $\varphi := AG(\neg y_0 \vee \neg y_1)$. By recursively evaluating the subformulas using the approximate algorithm described above, we obtain $\chi_{Sat_A(\varphi)} = \chi_{Sat_E(\varphi)} = 1$ and thus we can prove that the formula is satisfied for all possible replacements of the Black Box.

Symbolic Z_i-Model Checking. We obtain a second and more accurate approximation algorithm by replacing symbolic $(0, 1, X)$-simulation by symbolic Z_i-simulation. In symbolic Z_i-simulation we introduce a new variable Z_i for each output of a Black Box. The output functions $\lambda_i(\vec{q}, \vec{x}, \vec{Z})$ and transition functions $\delta_j(\vec{q}, \vec{x}, \vec{Z})$ will now depend on a vector $\vec{Z}$ of additional variables. As in the previous section, we include a state $(\vec{q}^{\text{fix}}, \vec{x}^{\text{fix}}) \in \mathbb{B}^{|\vec{q}| \times |\vec{x}|}$ into $Sat_A(y_i)$ iff $\lambda_i|_{\vec{q}=\vec{q}^{\text{fix}}, \vec{x}=\vec{x}^{\text{fix}}} = 1$ and we include it into $Sat_E(y_i)$ iff $\lambda_i|_{\vec{q}=\vec{q}^{\text{fix}}, \vec{x}=\vec{x}^{\text{fix}}} = 1$ or $\lambda_i|_{\vec{q}=\vec{q}^{\text{fix}}, \vec{x}=\vec{x}^{\text{fix}}}$ depends on the variables $\vec{Z}$. The transition relation is computed accordingly. The advantage of symbolic Z_i-simulation lies in the fact that the cofactors mentioned above may be 1 or 0 whereas the corresponding cofactors of $(0, 1, X)$-simulation are equal to Z. In general this leads to smaller overapproximations $Sat_E(\varphi)$ and larger underapproximations $Sat_A(\varphi)$. The formulas for a recursive evaluation of a CTL formula are similar to the previous section (just replace Z by $\vec{Z}$).

An additional improvement of approximations can be obtained by replacing equation (4) by $\chi_{R_E}(\vec{q}, \vec{x}, \vec{q}') = \exists \vec{Z} \left(\prod_{i=0}^{|\vec{q}|-1} \left(\delta_i(\vec{q}, \vec{x}, \vec{Z}) \equiv q_i' \right) \right)$.

Symbolic Output Consistent Z_i-Model Checking. In this section we will further improve the accuracy of the approximations presented in the last section. Again, we will use the incomplete circuit in Fig. 4 (with flip flop initialized to 0) to motivate the need for an improvement. Consider the CTL formula $EF(y_1 \wedge \neg y_1)$. It is easy to see that the algorithm given in the last section is neither able to prove validity nor falsify realizability for the given incomplete design and the given formula, since the output y_1 will be 0 or 1 depending on the output of the Black Box. However, it is clear that there will be no time during the computation when y_1 is both true and false. This problem can only be solved if we change our state space by including the Black Box outputs into the states of the Kripke structure, i.e. the state space is extended from $(\vec{q}, \vec{x})$ to $(\vec{q}, \vec{x}, \vec{Z})$. In this way the Black Box output values $\vec{Z}$ are constant within each single state and therefore in our example y_1 will have a fixed value for each state.

Detailed information on modifications which have to be made for this version of the model checking procedure is omitted due to lack of space. It can be found in [20].

5   Experimental Results

To demonstrate the feasibility and effectiveness of the presented methods we implemented a prototype model checker called MIND (Model Checker for Incomplete Designs) based on the BDD package CUDD 2.3.1 [21]. MIND uses 'Lazy Group Sifting' [22], a reordering technique particularly suited for model checking, and partitioned transition functions [23].

For a given incomplete circuit and a CTL formula, MIND first tries to gain information by using symbolic Z-model checking. In the case that no result can yet be obtained, MIND moves on to symbolic Z_i-model checking and later – if necessary – to symbolic output consistent Z_i-model checking.

For our experiments we used a class of simple synchronous pipelined ALUs similar to the ones presented in [3] (see also Sect. 3, Fig. 3). In contrast to [3], our pipelined ALU contains a combinational multiplier. Since combinational multipliers show exponential size regarding to their width if represented by BDDs

Table 1. Faulty pipelined ALU with 16 registers: Falsifying the realizability of $\varphi_1 = AG(''\mathrm{R}_2 := \mathrm{R}_0 \oplus \mathrm{R}_1'' \to ((AX)^2\mathrm{R}_0 \oplus (AX)^2\mathrm{R}_1 \equiv (AX)^3\mathrm{R}_2))$ using symb. Z-model checking

word width	No Black Boxes					Adder and multiplier replaced by Black Boxes					Adder, multiplier and 12 registers replaced by Black Boxes				
	BDD vars	memory used	BDD nodes	RO time	time	BDD vars	memory used	BDD nodes	RO time	time	BDD vars	memory used	BDD nodes	RO time	time
2	115	15648180	144681	16.54	18.95	117	8875028	88166	7.29	8.84	69	7691172	48443	1.68	2.44
4	191	47698020	268028	128.12	199.09	193	43750260	429830	215.66	274.99	97	14688292	105926	22.92	30.45
8	343	63229572	2233159	1804.83	2286.06	345	28912788	118064	54.92	61.97	153	39908148	107613	18.24	48.87
10						421	47499956	305772	243.77	319.97	181	37586452	139006	26.38	68.68
16			more than 12.000 sec.			649	47498820	169453	96.69	161.03	265	48107812	104683	30.42	110.65
32						1257	50710356	220204	563.31	763.83	489	51717572	171161	95.52	523.28
48						1865	65334916	242826	692.58	3603.20	713	64384116	169745	159.66	2132.44
64								more than 12.000 sec.			937	102258804	296314	308.78	4148.28

[2], symbolic model checking for the complete design can only be performed up to a moderate bit width of the ALU.

In the following we compare a series of complete pipelined ALUs with 16 registers in the register file and varying word width to two incomplete pendants: For the first, the adder and the multiplier are substituted by Black Boxes and for the second, 12 of the 16 registers in the register file are masked out as well.

All experiments were performed on an Intel Pentium4 2.6GHz with 1GB RAM and with a limited runtime of 12.000 seconds.

In a first experiment we inserted an error to the implementation of the XOR operation, so it produced incorrect results. We then checked the CTL formula $\varphi_1 = AG(''\mathrm{R}_2 := \mathrm{R}_0 \oplus \mathrm{R}_1'' \to ((AX)^2\mathrm{R}_0 \oplus (AX)^2\mathrm{R}_1 \equiv (AX)^3\mathrm{R}_2))$ which corresponds to formula (1) in [3]. It says that whenever the instruction $\mathrm{R}_2 := \mathrm{R}_0 \oplus \mathrm{R}_1$ is given at the inputs, the values in R_2 three clock cycles in the future will be identical to the exclusive-or of R_0 and R_1 in the state two clock cycles in the future (R_0, R_1 and R_2 are the respective first, second and third register in the register file). This property is false for our complete, but *faulty* design, independently of how the adder and multiplier function are implemented. Due to that, φ_1 is satisfied for no possible Black Box replacement in the incomplete pipelined ALUs, thus not realizable. Note that the Black Boxes lie *inside* the cone of influence for this CTL formula.

In Tab. 1 we give the results for both complete and incomplete pipelined ALUs with varying word width tested with φ_1. For each word width and each pipelined ALU, the table shows the number of BDD variables ('BDD vars'), the peak memory usage, the peak number of BDD nodes, the time spent while reordering the BDD variables ('RO time') and the overall time in CPU seconds.

As mentioned above, a multiplier has a large impact on BDD size and thus on computation time. On account of this, the model checking procedure for complete pipelined ALUs with multipliers of word width beyond 8 bit exceeds the time limit. In contrast to that, the incomplete pipelined ALUs without adder and multiplier can still be verified (using symbolic Z-model checking) and φ_1 can be proven to be unrealizable up to a word width of 48 bit.

The results for the incomplete pipelined ALU, in which most of the register file has been replaced by Black Boxes as well, show a further speedup compared to the complete pipelined ALU, making it possible to prove the unrealizability of φ_1 up to a word width of 64 bit. This is mainly due to the decrease of needed

Table 2. Correct pipelined ALU with 16 registers: Proving the validity of $\varphi_1 = AG\big(''R_2 := R_0 \oplus R_1'' \to \big((AX)^2 \mathbf{R}_0 \oplus (AX)^2 \mathbf{R}_1 \equiv (AX)^3 \mathbf{R}_2\big)\big)$ using symbolic output consistent Z_i-model checking

word width	No Black Boxes					Adder and multiplier replaced by Black Boxes					Adder, multiplier and 12 registers replaced by Black Boxes				
	BDD vars	memory used	BDD nodes	R O time	time	BDD vars	memory used	BDD nodes	R O time	time	BDD vars	memory used	BDD nodes	R O time	time
2	115	14293796	167732	24.80	27.07	120	18539828	78710	29.68	35.45	96	6289428	40067	3.37	3.99
4	191	44312916	260432	136.43	209.52	200	32040036	280644	141.86	164.02	152	16982804	107882	32.54	42.98
8	343	70257572	2062505	1734.78	3149.34	360	48240820	266458	250.10	358.87	264	43916036	184957	87.71	210.44
10						440	50132196	334578	381.38	534.24	320	35504804	125120	90.69	162.18
16		more than 12.000 sec.				680	56091444	403086	770.80	1529.96	488	46152532	138276	88.95	297.70
32						1320	69133684	641417	2939.57	7539.18	936	51112436	174608	264.92	1224.07
48						1960	79099060	234256	1462.76	9458.99	1384	54541588	212548	422.95	3270.27
64								more than 12.000 sec.			1832	50217764	299242	827.25	2599.73

BDD variables, caused by the reduction of many q_i and q_i' variables to a single Z variable and the simplification of the transition function, which does no longer depend on the input functions of the registers that have been masked out.

Thus, we are able to mask out the most complex parts of the pipelined ALU – the multiplier and the adder – and most of the register file without losing any significance of the result.

In a second experiment we considered the same CTL formula as above, yet this time we used a *correct* implementation of the XOR operation. In this case, φ_1 is satisfied for the complete and valid for the incomplete pipelined ALUs.

In Tab. 2 we give the results for both complete and incomplete pipelined ALUs tested with φ_1. In this example, symbolic Z-model checking and symbolic Z_i-model checking were not able to prove the validity of φ_1. However, in all cases the formula could be proved by output consistent Z_i-model checking, which extends the state variables by the Z_i variables. So the values given in Tab. 2 are the overall values for Z-model checking, Z_i-model checking and output consistent Z_i-model checking, since the implementation considers the methods one after the other until one is able to provide a definite result. Table 2 clearly shows that our method outperforms the conventional model checking of the complete version – for the same reasons as given above.

We also checked $\varphi_2 = AG\big((EX)^2\mathbf{R} \equiv (AX)^2\mathbf{R}\big)$ from [3], which is true for the complete design and valid for the incomplete designs, as already mentioned in Sect. 3. This can be proven by using output consistent Z_i-model checking. Since the results are similar to the ones given above, detailed information on the results is omitted due to lack of space and can be found in [20].

Taken together, the results show that by masking out expensive parts of the pipelined ALU we are still able to provide correct (i.e. sound) and useful results, yet at shorter time and with fewer memory consumption.

6   Conclusions and Future Work

We introduced three approximate methods to realize symbolic model checking for incomplete designs. Our methods are able to provide sound results for falsifying realizability and for proving validity of incomplete designs (even if the Black Boxes lie inside the cone of influence for the considered CTL formula).

Experimental results using our prototype implementation MIND proved that the need for computational resources (memory and time) could be substantially decreased by masking complex parts of a design and by using model checking for the resulting incomplete design. The increase in efficiency was obtained while still providing sound and useful results.

At the moment we are working on further improvements concerning the accuracy of our approximate symbolic model checking methods. Starting from a concept for exact symbolic model checking of incomplete designs (containing several Black Boxes with bounded memory) we develop appropriate approximations trading off accuracy and computational resources.

References

1. E.M. Clarke, E.A. Emerson, and A.P. Sistla. Automatic verification of finite–state concurrent systems using temporal logic specifications. *ACM Trans. on Programming Languages and Systems*, 8(2):244–263, 1986.
2. R.E. Bryant. Graph - based algorithms for Boolean function manipulation. *IEEE Trans. on Comp.*, 35(8):677–691, 1986.
3. J.R. Burch, E.M. Clarke, K.L. McMillan, D.L. Dill, and L.J. Hwang. Symbolic model checking: 10^{20} states and beyond. *Information and Computation*, 98(2):142–170, 1992.
4. K.L. McMillan. *Symbolic Model Checking*. Kluwer Academic Publisher, 1993.
5. A. Cimatti, E.M. Clarke, F. Giunchiglia, and M. Roveri. NuSMV: a new Symbolic Model Verifier. In N. Halbwachs and D. Peled, editors, *Proceedings Eleventh Conference on Computer-Aided Verification (CAV'99)*, number 1633 in Lecture Notes in Computer Science, pages 495–499, Trento, Italy, July 1999. Springer.
6. The VIS Group. VIS: A system for verification and synthesis. In *Computer Aided Verification*, volume 1102 of *LNCS*, pages 428–432. Springer Verlag, 1996.
7. K.L. McMillan. *The SMV system - for SMV version 2.5.4*. Carnegie Mellon University, Nov. 2000.
8. K. L. McMillan. *The SMV language*. Cadence Berkeley Labs.
9. T. Villa, G. Swamy, and T. Shiple. *VIS User's Manual*. Electronics Research Laboratory, University of Colorado at Boulder.
10. A. Pnueli and R. Rosner. Distributed systems are hard to synthesize. In *31th IEEE Symp. Found. of Comp. Science*, pages 746–757, 1990.
11. C. Scholl and B. Becker. Checking equivalence for partial implementations. In *Design Automation Conf.*, pages 238–243, 2001.
12. Michael Huth, Radha Jagadeesan, and David Schmidt. Modal transition systems: A foundation for three-valued program analysis. In Sands D., editor, *Proceedings of European Symposium on Programming*, number 2028 in Lecture Notes in Computer Science, pages 155+. Springer, April 2001.
13. J.R. Burch and D.L. Dill. Automatic verification of microprocessor control. In *Computer Aided Verification*, volume 818 of *LNCS*, pages 68–80. Springer Verlag, 1994.
14. K. Sajid, A. Goel, H. Zhou, A. Aziz, and V. Singhal. BDD-based procedures for a theory of equality with uninterpreted functions. In *Computer Aided Verification*, volume 1447 of *LNCS*, pages 244–255. Springer Verlag, 1998.

15. S. Berezin, A. Biere, E.M. Clarke, and Y. Zhu. Combining symbolic model checking with uninterpreted functions for out-of-order processor verification. In *Int'l Conf. on Formal Methods in CAD*, pages 369–386, 1998.

16. R.E. Bryant, S. German, and M.N. Velev. Processor verification using efficient reductions of the logic of uninterpreted functions to propositional logic. *ACM Transactions on Computational Logic*, 2(1):1–41, 2001.

17. A. Jain, V. Boppana, R. Mukherjee, J. Jain, M. Fujita, and M. Hsiao. Testing, verification, and diagnosis in the presence of unknowns. In *VLSI Test Symp.*, pages 263–269, 2000.

18. M. Abramovici, M.A. Breuer, and A.D. Friedman. *Digital Systems Testing and Testable Design*. Computer Science Press, 1990.

19. C. Scholl and B. Becker. Checking equivalence for partial implementations. Technical Report 145, Albert-Ludwigs-University, Freiburg, October 2000.

20. T. Nopper and C. Scholl. Symbolic model checking for incomplete designs. Technical report, Albert-Ludwigs-University, Freiburg, March 2004.

21. F. Somenzi. *CUDD: CU Decision Diagram Package Release 2.3.1*. University of Colorado at Boulder, 2001.

22. H. Higuchi and F. Somenzi. Lazy group sifting for efficient symbolic state traversal of FSMs. In *Int'l Conf. on CAD*, pages 45–49, 1999.

23. R. Hojati, S.C. Krishnan, and R.K. Brayton. Early quantification and partitioned transition relations. In *Int'l Conf. on Comp. Design*, pages 12–19, 1996.

Extending Extended Vacuity

Arie Gurfinkel and Marsha Chechik

Department of Computer Science, University of Toronto
Toronto, ON M5S 3G4, Canada
{arie,chechik}@cs.toronto.edu

Abstract. There has been a growing interest in detecting whether a logic specification holds in the system *vacuously*. For example, a specification "every request is eventually followed by an acknowledgment" holds vacuously on those systems that never generate requests. In a recent paper, Armoni et al. have argued against previous definitions of vacuity, defined as sensitivity with respect to syntactic perturbation. They suggested that vacuity should be *robust*, i.e., insensitive to trivial changes in the logic and in the model, and is better described as sensitivity with respect to semantic perturbation, represented by universal propositional quantification. In this paper, we extend the above suggestion by giving a formal definition of robust vacuity that allows us to define and detect vacuous satisfaction and vacuous failure for arbitrary CTL* properties, even with respect to multiple occurrences of subformulas. We discuss complexity of our approaches and study the relationship between vacuity and abstraction.

1 Introduction

Model-checking gained wide popularity as an automated technique for effective analysis of software and hardware systems. Yet a major problem in practical applications of model-checking is that a successful run of the model-checker does not necessarily guarantee that the intended requirement is satisfied by the system [3]. For example, the property "every request must be followed by an acknowledgment" holds vacuously in a system that is known to never produce a request. Industrial researchers at the IBM Haifa Research Laboratory observed that vacuity is a serious problem [3] and that "... typically 20% of specifications pass vacuously during the first formal verification runs of a new hardware design, and that vacuous passes always point to a real problem in either the design, or its specification, or the environment" [3]. Further justification is given by case studies conducted by Purandare and Somenzi [21].

A recent paper by Armoni et al. [1] provides an excellent summary of the work on vacuity detection. We summarize only a few aspects of this work here. Vacuity detection research progressed along two separate axes. One [4, 3, 18, 15] aims at increasing the scope of applicability of vacuity detection algorithms. This research deals with deciding vacuity for temporal logics, from subsets of CTL and LTL to CTL*, looking at formulas with one occurrence or several occurrences [1] of a subformula, looking at vacuous satisfaction and vacuous failure of formulas, and generating witnesses for non-vacuity. Most of this work assumes a *syntactic* definition of vacuity, provided by Beer et al. [4]: φ is vacuous in a subformula ψ if ψ can be replaced by any temporal logic formula.

A.J. Hu and A.K. Martin (Eds.): FMCAD 2004, LNCS 3312, pp. 306–321, 2004.

An orthogonal line of research, initiated by Armoni et al. [1], is to examine the *meaning* of vacuity. The authors specified vacuity via universal quantification, formally defining it as satisfying the expression $\forall x \cdot \varphi[\psi \leftarrow x]$. With this definition, several different interpretations of the domain of x yield different notions of vacuity. When x ranges over temporal logic formulas, this corresponds to syntactic vacuity of [3], called *formula* vacuity in [1]. When checking vacuity of LTL properties, as is the goal of [1], x can also range over the set of computations, resulting in *trace* vacuity. Alternatively, x can range over boolean functions over the statespace, resulting in *structure* vacuity.

Armed with these definitions, the authors faced the task of choosing the most desirable one, both in terms of computational tractability, but more importantly, in terms of its correspondence to the intuitive notion of vacuity. Such a notion should be *robust*, i.e., insensitive to changes in the design that do not relate to the formula. For example, a property "if p is true now, it will remain true in the next state" should not be affected by adding a proposition q to the model. Robustness also includes insensitivity to the specification language: a formula passing vacuously, e.g., in a language with only negation and conjunction, should not pass nonvacuously once the specification language is extended, e.g., by adding implication. Armoni at al. exemplify that neither structure nor formula vacuity are robust. Structure vacuity depends too much on the model, and is sensitive to trivial modifications that do not correspond to changes in the design. Formula vacuity depends on the syntax of the underlying logic. For example, [1] presents an LTL formula that can be considered both vacuous in the model, and non-vacuous when past operators are allowed. The authors argue that trace vacuity is robust, but since robustness is specified only informally, it is not clear whether that argument is correct. Armoni et al. also prove that the decision procedure for checking vacuous *satisfaction* for LTL formulas over trace vacuity is tractable, making it the most desirable definition.

What is the "right" definition of vacuity? Does it change as we transition from LTL properties to CTL^* and from vacuous satisfaction (i.e., checking formulas that are known to hold in the system) to vacuous failure? Is vacuity detection under this robust definition tractable? We address these questions in this paper. In particular, we formalize the notion of robust vacuity and use the quantified temporal logic formulation of Armoni et. al to extend semantic vacuity to branching temporal logics such as CTL^*. Like [1], our definition is applicable to subformulas of both pure and mixed polarity. Note that our extension is not trivial when we move from linear-time to branching-time logic, i.e., from traces to trees. Although quantification over trees has been studied by Kupferman [17], neither of the interpretations suggested in her paper are robust enough, and a different interpretation is needed.

We further show that in general, vacuity detection for CTL^* is expensive, but identify several important fragments of CTL^* for which vacuity detection, or at least detecting vacuous satisfaction, is no harder than model-checking. One of such fragments is checking vacuous satisfaction of $ACTL^*$, which subsumes results of [1].

Verification of even medium-size models is impossible without abstraction. Since vacuity checking should supplement every verification activity, what happens with vacuity under abstraction? In this paper, we prove that vacuity is preserved by abstraction. Further, we show a surprising fact: vacuity detection algorithm is *more precise* than traditional abstract model-checking, that is, it is sometimes possible to determine that a formula is vacuously satisfied by an abstract model, even if the result of abstract model-checking is inconclusive!

The rest of paper is organized as follows: after providing the necessary background in Section 2, we define robust vacuity in Section 3 and study the complexity of vacuity detection. In Section 4, we discuss how vacuity detection can be reduced to 3-valued model-checking and how various semantics for 3-valued model-checking [5, 6] correspond to different notions of vacuity. Section 5 studies the relationship between vacuity and abstraction. Section 6 concludes the paper.

2   Background

In this section, we fix the notation and give the necessary background on model-checking and quantified temporal logics.

Models. We denote the set of boolean values {true, false} by $\mathbf{2}$. A model is a Kripke structure $K = (S, R, S_0, AP, I)$, where S is a finite set of states, $R : S \times S \to \mathbf{2}$ is a total transition relation, $S_0 \subseteq S$ is a set of initial states, AP is a set of atomic propositions, and $I : S \times AP \to \mathbf{2}$ is a labeling function, assigning a value to each atomic proposition $a \in AP$ in each state. A path π of K is an infinite sequence of states in which every consecutive pair of states is related by the transition relation. We denote a path starting at state s by π_s, and the set of all such paths by Π_s.

Temporal Logic. Computation Tree Logic CTL* is a branching-time temporal logic constructed from propositional connectives, temporal operators X (next), U (until), F (future), and G (globally), and path quantifiers A (forall) and E (exists). CTL* denotes the set of all state formulas $\varphi = c \mid \varphi \wedge \varphi \mid \varphi \vee \varphi \mid \neg\varphi \mid A\psi \mid E\psi$, where c is an atomic proposition, and $\psi = \varphi \mid X\psi \mid \psi\ U\ \psi \mid F\psi \mid G\psi$ is a path formula. The formal semantics of CTL* is available in [8]. We write $||\psi||^K(\pi) = \text{true}$, or $||\psi||^K(\pi)$, to mean that ψ is satisfied by a path π of K. For state formulas, $||\varphi||^K(s)$ denotes the value of φ in state s of K, and is defined as follows:

$$||A\psi||^K(s) \triangleq \bigwedge\nolimits_{\pi_s \in \Pi_s} ||\psi||^K(\pi_s) \qquad\qquad ||E\psi||^K(s) \triangleq \bigvee\nolimits_{\pi_s \in \Pi_s} ||\psi||^K(\pi_s)$$

φ holds in K, denoted $||\varphi||^K$, iff it holds in every initial state: $\bigwedge\nolimits_{s_0 \in S_0} ||\varphi||^K(s_0)$.

We write $\varphi[x]$ to indicate that the formula φ may contain an occurrence of x, in which case x is *positive* (or of *positive polarity*) if it occurs under the scope of an even number of negations, and *negative* otherwise. A subformula x is *pure* in φ if all of its occurrences have the same polarity. We write $\varphi[x \leftarrow y]$ for a formula obtained from φ by replacing x by y. A formula φ is *universal* (or in ACTL*) if all of its temporal path quantifiers are universal, and is *existential* (or in ECTL*) if they are existential. In both cases, negation is only allowed at the level of atomic propositions.

The fragment of CTL* in which all formulas are of the form $A\psi$, where ψ is a path formula, is called the Linear Temporal Logic (LTL). The fragment in which every occurrence of a path quantifier is immediately followed by a temporal operator is called Computation Tree Logic (CTL).

Quantified Temporal Logic. Quantified Temporal Logic QCTL* is an extension of CTL* with universal and existential quantification over atomic propositions [17]. In this paper, we consider a fragment $\{\varphi, \forall x \cdot \varphi, \exists x \cdot \varphi \mid \varphi \in \text{CTL}^*\}$, still referring to it as QCTL^*.

The syntax of QCTL^* does not restrict the domain of quantifiers. Thus, there are several different definitions of QCTL^* semantics with respect to a Kripke structure; we consider three of these: *structure* [17], *tree* [17], and *amorphous* [9].

Structure Semantics. Under this semantics, each free variable x is interpreted as a boolean function over the statespace, i.e., $x \in [S \rightarrow \mathbf{2}]$. For example, $\forall x \cdot \varphi$ is true in K under structure semantics if replacing x by an arbitrary boolean function results in a formula that is true in K. Formally, the semantics of a quantifier $Q \in \{\forall, \exists\}$ is:

$$||Qx \cdot \varphi||_s^K \triangleq Qx \in [S \rightarrow \mathbf{2}] \cdot ||\varphi[x]||^K \quad \text{(structure semantics)}$$

Alternatively, structure semantics can be understood as follows. For an atomic proposition x in K, let K_{-x} denote the result of removing x from K, i.e., $AP_{-x} = AP \setminus \{x\}$. We say that K' is an $\{x\}$-*variant* of K if K'_{-x} and K are isomorphic. A formula $\forall x \cdot \varphi[x]$ is satisfied by K under structure semantics iff $\varphi[x]$ holds in all $\{x\}$-variants of K.

Tree Semantics. Tree semantics of QCTL^* is defined on the computation tree $T(K)$ obtained by unrolling K from its initial state. Formally,

$$||Qx \cdot \varphi||_T^K \triangleq Qx \cdot ||\varphi[x]||_s^{T(K)} \quad \text{(tree semantics)}$$

That is, a formula $\forall x \cdot \varphi[x]$ is satisfied by K under tree semantics iff it is satisfied by every $\{x\}$-variant of the computation tree of K.

Amorphous Semantics. We start by revisiting the notions of simulation and bisimulation.

Definition 1. *[20] Let K and K' be Kripke structures with identical sets of atomic propositions AP. A relation $\rho \subseteq S \times S'$ is a simulation relation iff $\rho(s, s')$ implies that*

1. $\forall p \in AP \cdot I'(s', p) \Leftrightarrow I(s, p)$, *and*
2. $\forall t' \in S' \cdot R'(s', t') \Rightarrow \exists t \in S \cdot R(s, t) \wedge \rho(t, t')$

A state s *simulates* a state s' if $(s, s') \in \rho$. A Kripke structure K simulates K' iff every initial state of K' is simulated by an initial state of K. Simulation between K and K' preserves ACTL^*: for any $\varphi \in \text{ACTL}^*$, $||\varphi||^K \Rightarrow ||\varphi||^{K'}$. K and K' are *bisimilar* iff there exists a simulation relation ρ between K and K' such that ρ^{-1} is a simulation between K' and K. The set of all structures bisimilar to K is denoted by $\mathcal{B}(K)$. Bisimulation preserves CTL^*: $\forall \varphi \in \text{CTL}^* \cdot \forall K' \in \mathcal{B}(K) \cdot ||\varphi||^K \Leftrightarrow ||\varphi||^{K'}$.

Let K and K' be Kripke structures such that the set of atomic propositions of K' is $AP \cup \{x\}$. Then, K and K' are $\{x\}$-*bisimilar* iff K and K'_{-x} are bisimilar. The set of all $\{x\}$-bisimilar structures to K is denoted by $\mathcal{B}_x(K)$.

Amorphous semantics of QCTL^* is defined as follows:

$$||Qx \cdot \varphi[x]||_a^K \triangleq QK' \in \mathcal{B}_x(K) \cdot ||\varphi[x]||^{K'} \quad \text{(amorphous semantics)}$$

That is, a formula $\forall x \cdot \varphi[x]$ is satisfied by K under amorphous semantics iff $\varphi[x]$ is satisfied by every $\{x\}$-bisimulation of K.

For universally quantified formulas, amorphous semantics imply tree semantics, and tree semantics imply structure semantics; further, the implication is strict [9].

3 Extended Vacuity

In this section, we construct a "robust" definition of vacuity for temporal logic and study complexity of vacuity detection.

3.1 Defining Vacuity

As argued by Armoni et al. [1], vacuity is robust if (a) it is independent of the details of the logic used to formalize the property, e.g., if φ is deemed to be vacuous as a propositional formula, it must remain so in logics that subsume propositional logic, such as CTL; and (b) it is independent of a particular modeling of the system, i.e., the vacuity cannot be "fixed" by changing the model to an equivalent one.

We start our exploration of vacuity with propositional logic. A model of a propositional formula φ is simply a valuation of all atomic propositions of φ, and the value of each propositional formula is either true or false. Thus, we can check the dependence of φ on a subformula ψ by checking whether replacing ψ by true and false affects the value of φ.

Definition 2. *A propositional formula φ is vacuous in a subformula ψ, or simply ψ-vacuous, in a model K iff replacing ψ by* true *and* false *does not affect the value of φ:* $||\varphi[\psi \leftarrow \text{true}]||^K = ||\varphi[\psi \leftarrow \text{false}]||^K$.

Vacuity of a propositional formula in a model K can be expressed as validity of a quantified boolean formula in K; that is, φ is ψ-vacuous iff $\forall x \in \mathbf{2} \cdot ||\varphi[\psi \leftarrow x]||^K$ or $\forall x \in \mathbf{2} \cdot ||\neg\varphi[\psi \leftarrow x]||^K$. Note that this definition ensures that vacuity of a formula φ in a model K does not change if we extend K with new atomic propositions, or allow for new logical connectives, such as implication.

It may seem that Definition 2 describes robust vacuity for temporal logic as well, but it is not the case. For example, consider the formula $\varphi = (AXp) \vee (AX\neg p)$ that formalizes the property "p changes deterministically". According to our intuition, φ expresses a "reasonable" requirement and is not vacuous in any model. Yet in any model both $(AX\text{true}) \vee (AX\neg\text{true})$ and $(AX\text{false}) \vee (AX\neg\text{false})$ evaluate to true, which makes φ vacuous according to Definition 2.

The problem is that the interpretation of a temporal formula in a model is its value in *every* state of the model. Therefore, replacing a subformula by true and false is not sufficient for identifying whether the subformula is important. Following this, we extend the definition of vacuity to account for all boolean functions over the statespace of the model, i.e., $S \to \mathbf{2}$. The resulting definition was introduced in [1] as *structure vacuity*.

Definition 3. *[1] A temporal logic formula φ is structure ψ-vacuous in a model K iff* $\forall x \in [S \to \mathbf{2}] \cdot ||\varphi[\psi \leftarrow x]||^K$ *or* $\forall x \in [S \to \mathbf{2}] \cdot ||\neg\varphi[\psi \leftarrow x]||^K$.

Once again, Definition 3 is not strong enough to capture our intuition, because it makes vacuity dependent on a particular model of the system. For example, consider the two models in Figure 1, both describing a system in which p holds along every execution. According to Definition 3, the formula $\varphi = (AXp) \vee (AX\neg p)$ is p-vacuous in the model in Figure 1(a), but is not p-vacuous in the model in Figure 1(b).

As indicated by the example, it is not sufficient to define vacuity with respect to a *particular* model K. Instead, it should also consider any model that is equivalent to K.

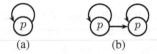

(a)   (b)

Fig. 1. Two models of a system in which p holds along every execution.

For temporal logic, two models are considered to be equivalent iff they are bisimilar, which leads us to the final definition of vacuity.

Definition 4. *A temporal logic formula φ is ψ-vacuous in a Kripke structure K iff it is structure ψ-vacuous in K and is ψ-vacuous in any Kripke structure K' that is bisimilar to K. That is, $\forall K' \in \mathcal{B}(K) \cdot \forall x \in [S' \rightarrow \mathbf{2}] \cdot ||\varphi[\psi \leftarrow x]||^{K'}$, or $\forall K' \in \mathcal{B}(K) \cdot \forall x \in [S' \rightarrow \mathbf{2}] \cdot ||\neg\varphi[\psi \leftarrow x]||^{K'}$.*

Here, S' is the statespace of K'. Definition 4 closely matches the amorphous semantics for quantified temporal logic [9]. Thus, checking vacuity can be reduced to checking validity of a quantified temporal logic formula: φ is ψ-vacuous in a Kripke structure K iff $||\forall x \cdot \varphi[\psi \leftarrow x]||_a^K$ or $||\forall x \cdot \neg\varphi[\psi \leftarrow x]||_a^K$. That is, $\varphi[\psi \leftarrow x]$ is either satisfied or violated in every model that is $\{x\}$-bisimilar to K. This definition is independent of any particular logic. For example, a propositional formula is propositionally vacuous iff it is vacuous by Definition 4; a CTL formula is vacuous iff it is vacuous as a CTL* formula, etc. Note that Definition 4 is bisimulation-closed, and is therefore insensitive to different encodings of the model.

We conclude this section by summarizing some of the key properties of vacuity.

Theorem 1. *Let φ be a temporal logic formula, ψ be any non-constant proper subformula of φ, and K be a Kripke structure. Then,*

1. *if φ is valid or unsatisfiable, then φ is vacuous in any model;*
2. *if ψ is valid or unsatisfiable, then φ is ψ-vacuous in any model;*
3. *if φ is ψ-vacuous in K, and K' is bisimilar to K, then φ is ψ-vacuous in K';*
4. *if φ is ψ-vacuous in K, and K' is an arbitrary Kripke structure, then φ is ψ-vacuous in $K||K'$ (synchronous parallel composition of K and K').*

3.2   Complexity of Vacuity Detection

In this section, we study the complexity of detecting vacuity for temporal logics CTL and CTL*.

In general, detecting vacuity for CTL and CTL* is in the same complexity class as the satisfiability problem for these logics.

Theorem 2. *The complexity of detecting whether a formula φ is ψ-vacuous is EXPTIME-complete for CTL, and 2EXPTIME-complete for CTL*.*

The proof of this and most other theorems in this paper is available in the Appendix.

Although vacuity detection for an arbitrary CTL* formula is computationally expensive, we identify several important fragments for which vacuity detection is in the same complexity class as model-checking.

Syntactically Monotone Formulas. A formula φ is *monotonically increasing* in a subformula ψ iff $(x \Rightarrow y) \Rightarrow (\varphi[\psi \leftarrow x] \Rightarrow \varphi[\psi \leftarrow y])$, and is *monotonically decreasing* if $(x \Rightarrow y) \Rightarrow (\varphi[\psi \leftarrow x] \Leftarrow \varphi[\psi \leftarrow y])$; furthermore, φ is said to be *monotone* in ψ iff it is either monotonically increasing or decreasing. A formula φ is *syntactically monotone* in ψ iff ψ occurs with pure polarity in φ. The complexity of detecting whether a formula φ, monotone in ψ, is also ψ-vacuous is the same as the complexity of model-checking φ:

Theorem 3. *If a temporal logic formula φ is monotone in a subformula ψ, then the complexity of detecting whether φ is ψ-vacuous in a Kripke structure K is $2 \times MC(\varphi)$, where $MC(\varphi)$ is the complexity of model-checking φ in K.*

Unfortunately, deciding whether a formula is monotone in a subformula is as hard as detecting vacuity.

Theorem 4. *The complexity of deciding whether a formula φ is monotone in a subformula ψ is EXPTIME-hard for CTL, and 2EXPTIME-hard for CTL*.*

Although deciding whether a formula is monotone is expensive, syntactic monotonicity is easy to establish, and it guarantees monotonicity.

Theorem 5. *If φ is a CTL* formula that is syntactically monotone in ψ, then φ is also monotone in ψ.*

Thus, deciding vacuity for a CTL* formula in a subformula of pure polarity, and therefore syntactically monotone, is of the same complexity as model-checking.

True ACTL* Formulas and False ECTL* Formulas. Here, we show that for ACTL* formulas that are known to be true in a given model, vacuity detection is as cheap as model-checking. Dually, the complexity of detecting vacuity of ECTL* formulas that are known to be violated by the model is also as cheap as model-checking.

For a given Kripke structure K, we define $K_x = (AP_x, S \times \{0,1\}, S_0 \times \{0,1\}, R_x, I_x)$, where $AP_x = AP \cup \{x\}$; $I_x(\langle s,i \rangle, p) = I(s,p)$; $I_x(\langle s,i \rangle, x) = \text{true} \Leftrightarrow i = 1$; and $R_x(\langle s,i \rangle, \langle t,j \rangle) \Leftrightarrow R(s,t)$. K_x is a synchronous parallel composition of K with a Kripke structure containing a single non-deterministic atomic proposition x. Note that K_x is $\{x\}$-bisimilar to K, where the bisimulation is given by $\rho_x = \{(s, \langle s,i \rangle) \mid i \in \{0,1\}\}$. Moreover, any K' that is $\{x\}$-bisimilar to K is simulated by K_x.

Theorem 6. *Let K be a Kripke structure, and K_x be as described above. Then, if K' is $\{x\}$-bisimilar to K, then it is simulated by K_x.*

Since simulation preserves ACTL*, vacuity detection for an arbitrary ACTL* formula is reducible to model-checking over K_x. Note that this also proves that our definition of vacuity for LTL is equivalent to trace vacuity of Armoni et al [1].

Theorem 7. *Let φ be an ACTL* formula, ψ be a subformula of φ, and K be a Kripke structure. If φ is known to be satisfied by K, then complexity of detecting vacuity of φ in ψ is $2 \times MC(\varphi)$.*

Note that the statespace of K_x is double of K. However, K_x does not impose any restrictions on the atomic proposition x; therefore, the symbolic representation of the transition relation of K_x is identical to that of K!

Reducing CTL* Formulas. For a fixed model K, any temporal formula φ is logically equivalent to a propositional formula over the atomic propositions of K, denoted $Prop(\varphi, K)$. If ψ is a state subformula of φ, then replacing ψ by its propositional equivalent $Prop(\psi, K)$ does not affect the value of φ in K, and any model bisimilar to K. That is,

$$\forall K' \in \mathcal{B}(K) \cdot ||\varphi||^{K'} = ||\varphi[\psi \leftarrow Prop(\varphi, K')]||^{K'} \quad \text{(propositional substitution)}$$

For example, if ψ is true in a state s iff the propositional formula $p \wedge q$ is true in s, then $Prop(\psi, K) = p \wedge q$, and every occurrence of ψ can be replaced by $p \wedge q$.

Propositional substitution preserves vacuity, in the sense that a formula φ is ψ-vacuous iff a formula φ', obtained by replacing all subformulas that do not contain ψ with their propositional equivalents, is ψ-vacuous.

Theorem 8. *Let $\varphi[x, \psi]$ be an CTL* formula, with a subformula x and a state subformula ψ, and K be a Kripke structure. Then, φ is x-vacuous iff $\varphi[x, \psi \leftarrow Prop(\psi, K)]$ is x-vacuous.*

This theorem can be used to reduce some CTL* formulas to ACTL*, thus reducing the complexity of vacuity detection for them. In particular, if a subformula ψ of φ occurs in the scope of only universal path quantifiers, replacing all other state subformulas of φ reduces φ to an ACTL* formula.

Theorem 9. *Let φ be a CTL* formula, ψ be a subformula of φ that occurs in the scope of only universal path quantifiers. Then, if a Kripke structure K satisfies φ, the complexity of detecting vacuity of φ in ψ is $2 \times MC(\varphi)$.*

4   Vacuity Detection via 3-Valued Model Checking

In this section, we show that 3-valued model-checking provides a uniform framework for studying vacuity detection.

4.1   3-Valued Model-Checking

A 3-valued Kleene logic **3** [16] is an extension of a classical two-valued logic of true and false, with an additional value maybe, representing uncertainty. Propositional operators in this logic, called Kleene operators, are defined via the *truth* ordering $\sqsubseteq$, where false $\sqsubseteq$ maybe $\sqsubseteq$ true. Intuitively, $a \sqsubseteq b$ indicates that a is *less true* than b. Conjunction and disjunction are given by meet (minimum) and join (maximum) operators of the truth ordering, respectively. Negation is defined as: $\neg$true $=$ false, $\neg$false $=$ true, and $\neg$maybe $=$ maybe. Kleene logic preserves most of the laws of classical logic, such as De Morgan laws ($\neg(a \wedge b) = \neg a \vee \neg b$), and an involution of negation ($\neg\neg a = a$), but not the laws of excluded middle ($a \vee \neg a =$ true) and non-contradiction ($\neg a \wedge a =$ false). The values of Kleene logic can also be ordered according to the *information* ordering $\preceq$, where maybe $\preceq$ true and maybe $\preceq$ false. That is, maybe contains the least amount of information, whereas true and false are incomparable.

Model-checking is extended to the 3-valued logic by allowing models with uncertain information, represented by atomic propositions with value maybe. Formally, a model is a 3-valued Kripke structure $K = (AP, S, S_0, R, I)$, where AP, S, S_0, and R are classical, and I is a function $S \times A \to \mathbf{3}$. Any classical Kripke structure is simply a 3-valued Kripke structure that does not make use of maybe values. Adding 3-valued transitions to 3-valued Kripke structures does not increase their expressive power [12].

The semantics of CTL^* is extended to 3-valued models by reinterpreting propositional operators. For example, $||EXp||(s) = \bigvee_{t \in S} R(s,t) \wedge ||p||(t)$, where $\bigvee$ and $\wedge$ are Kleene. In classical models, the 3-valued and two-valued semantics of CTL^* coincide. In what follows, we refer to this semantics as *compositional*.

The information ordering $\preceq$ is extended to 3-valued Kripke structures providing a completeness preorder that connects classical and 3-valued Kripke structures. Intuitively, a 3-valued Kripke structure K is more complete than K', written $K' \preceq K$, if the information contained in K' is less certain than that in K. In this case, K is a *refinement* of K'.

Definition 5. *[5] A relation $\rho \subseteq S \times S'$ is a refinement between 3-valued Kripke structures K and K' iff $\rho(s, s')$ implies*

1. $\forall p \in AP \cdot I(s, p) \preceq I'(s', p)$
2. $\forall t \in S \cdot R(s, t) \Rightarrow \exists t' \in S' \cdot R'(s', t') \wedge \rho(t, t')$
3. $\forall t' \in S' \cdot R'(s', t') \Rightarrow \exists t \in S \cdot R(s, t) \wedge \rho(t, t')$

A state s is refined by a state s' ($s \preceq s'$) if there exists a refinement ρ containing (s, s'). A Kripke structures K is refined by K' ($K \preceq K'$) if there exists a refinement ρ relating their initial states: $\forall s \in S_0 \cdot \exists s' \in S_0' \cdot \rho(s, s')$ and $\forall s' \in S_0' \cdot \exists s \in S_0 \cdot \rho(s, s')$. Intuitively, K refines K' if K is bisimilar to K', provided we ignore the uncertain (**maybe**) atomic propositions of K'. In particular, bisimulation and refinement coincide on classical structures.

Theorem 10. *[5] For 3-valued Kripke structures K and K' and a CTL^* formula φ, $K \preceq K'$ implies $||\varphi||^K \preceq ||\varphi||^{K'}$, i.e., refinement preserves 3-valued CTL^*.*

The refinement relation relates 3-valued and classical models. For a 3-valued Kripke structure K, let $\mathcal{C}(K)$ denote the set of *completions* of K – the set of all classical Kripke structures that refine K. For any completion $K' \in \mathcal{C}(K)$, the structure K can be seen as less precise than K' in the sense that any CTL^* formula that evaluates to a definite value (either **true** or **false**) in K, evaluates to the same value in K'. That is, for any $K' \in \mathcal{C}(K)$ and any CTL^* formula φ, $(||\varphi||^K = \text{true}) \Rightarrow (||\varphi||^{K'} = \text{true})$ and $(||\varphi||^K = \text{false}) \Rightarrow (||\varphi||^{K'} = \text{false})$. The converse, however, does not hold is in general. For example, the formula $p \vee \neg p$ is true in any classical model, yet its value is **maybe** in any state of a 3-valued model that assigns **maybe** to p (i.e., $p \vee \neg p = \text{maybe} \vee \neg\text{maybe} = \text{maybe} \vee \text{maybe} = \text{maybe}$).

To address this imprecision of compositional semantics, Bruns and Godefroid [6] have introduced an alternative semantics, calling it *thorough*.

Definition 6. *[6] Let K be a 3-valued Kripke structure, and φ a CTL^* formula. The value of φ in K under thorough semantics $||\varphi||_t^K$ is:* **true** *iff φ holds in every completion of K,* **false** *if it is* **false** *in every completion, and* **maybe** *otherwise.*

Thorough semantics always produces more exact answers than compositional, i.e., for any 3-valued Kripke structure K and a CTL^* formula φ, $||\varphi||^K \preceq ||\varphi||_t^K$. This additional precision comes at a price of complexity: model-checking a given branching temporal logic formula under compositional semantics is in the same complexity class as classical model-checking; however, its model-checking complexity under thorough semantics is as hard as satisfiability [6].

4.2   Vacuity Detection via 3-Valued Model-Checking

In this section, we show that vacuity detection is closely related to 3-valued model-checking under thorough semantics.

Let K be a Kripke structure, and let K_x be a 3-valued Kripke structure obtained from K by: (a) adding to K a new atomic proposition x, and (b) setting the value of x to maybe in every state. The set $\mathcal{C}(K_x)$ of completions of K_x is equivalent to the set of Kripke structures which are $\{x\}$-bisimilar to K.

Theorem 11. *Let K be a Kripke structure, and K_x be as described above. Then, $K' \in \mathcal{C}(K_x)$ iff K' is $\{x\}$-bisimilar to K.*

This theorem suggests the following reduction from vacuity detection to 3-valued model-checking:

To check whether a formula φ is ψ-vacuous in K:
> Construct a 3-valued Kripke structure K_x.
> Model-check $\varphi[\psi \leftarrow x]$ in K_x under thorough semantics.
> **if** $||\varphi[\psi \leftarrow x]||_t^{K_x} \in \{\text{true}, \text{false}\}$
> > **then return** "φ is ψ-vacuous"
> > **else return** "φ is not ψ-vacuous".

The reduction in the other direction, i.e., from 3-valued model-checking to vacuity detection, is also possible, but is outside the scope of this paper.

As the result of this reduction, any advance in 3-valued model-checking is also applicable to vacuity detection. For example, the complexity of thorough semantics model-checking for CTL and CTL* is known to be EXPTIME- and 2EXPTIME-complete [6], respectively, which provides an alternative proof of the first part of Theorem 2. For another notable example, consider ACTL* persistence properties [19], i.e., properties of the form $AFGp$. These correspond to co-Büchi automata, and the complexity of model-checking these properties under thorough semantics is linear in the size of the model [11]. Thus, for such properties, the complexity of vacuity detection is the same as that of model-checking.

Note that since thorough semantics is more precise than compositional, model-checking $\varphi[\psi \leftarrow x]$ in K_x under compositional semantics yields a sound approximation to vacuity detection. If $||\varphi[\psi \leftarrow x]||^{K_x}$ is either true or false, then φ is ψ-vacuous; otherwise, the result of the model-checking is maybe, which gives no information about vacuity. Moreover, our previous work [14] showed that if ψ occurs in φ with pure polarity, then compositional semantics reduces to checking whether $||\varphi[\psi \leftarrow \text{true}]||^K = ||\varphi[\psi \leftarrow \text{false}]||^K$. Thus, by Theorems 3 and 5, compositional semantics provides a sound and complete algorithm for vacuity detection in subformulas of pure polarity.

An additional benefit of the reduction enables the use of 3-valued model-checkers, which are arguably necessary for combining model-checking and abstraction [11, 22], to solve the vacuity detection problem. Moreover, witnesses and counterexamples, produced by such model-checkers, can be used to explain why a given formula is deemed to be (non-)vacuous. To our knowledge, a 3-valued model-checker with thorough semantics has not been implemented. Further, we are not aware of an algorithm for generating witnesses and counterexamples in this case, but it appears to be equivalent to logic synthesis and thus very expensive. However, compositional 3-valued model-checkers, such as XChek [7], have been implemented, and their witnesses and counterexamples have a natural correspondence to witnesses for non-vacuity [4]. This connection has been explored in our previous work [15].

Finally, reducing vacuity detection to 3-valued model-checking makes it easier to explore the combination of vacuity detection with various abstraction techniques, as we explore in the next section.

5   Vacuity and Abstraction

One of the biggest obstacles in the use of model-checking is the statespace explosion problem – the size of the model doubles with addition of each new atomic proposition. Abstraction appears to be the most effective technique to combat this problem. In this section, we show how vacuity detection can be combined with abstraction techniques for model-checking.

5.1   Abstraction and 3-Valued Model-Checking

The key idea of abstraction is that instead of model-checking a property φ on a (concrete) model K_c, one first constructs an abstraction K_α of K_c, for example, by removing some atomic propositions of K_c, and then checks φ in K_α.

An abstraction is *sound* with respect to a set of properties Φ, if a definite value for any property $\varphi \in \Phi$ in an abstract model K_α, means that φ has the same value in the corresponding concrete model K_c. For example, if φ is true in K_α, it is true in K_c. An abstraction is called *exact* if it is sound with respect to CTL*, and the result of model-checking any φ on the abstract model is always definite. For example, cone of influence and symmetry reductions are exact [8]. Note that if K_α is an exact abstraction of K_c, then K_α and K_c are bisimilar.

3-valued models provide a natural representation for abstract models. A 3-valued (or possibly classical) Kripke structure K_α is an abstraction of K_c iff K_c refines K_α, i.e., $K_\alpha \preceq K_c$. Model-checking a property φ in K_c can be done by model-checking φ in K_α under compositional semantics. If the value of φ in K_α is maybe, then nothing is known about its value in the concrete model. However, by Theorem 10, if φ evaluates to either true or false in K_α, then it has the same value in K_c. This guarantees that the abstraction is sound with respect to CTL*. Common abstraction techniques, such as predicate [13] and Cartesian [2] abstractions, can be cast as 3-valued model-checking problems [10].

In the next section, we extend our definition of vacuity, as well as algorithms for its detection, to 3-valued models, which illustrates how vacuity detection can be combined with most common abstraction techniques.

5.2   Combining Vacuity Detection and Abstraction

Let K_α be a 3-valued Kripke structure. A definition of vacuity in an abstract model should be sound with respect to the abstraction used. That is, if a formula φ is vacuous in K_α, then it must be vacuous in all concretizations of K_α. Note that the set of concretizations of K_α is the same as the set $\mathcal{C}(K_\alpha)$ of its completions. This leads us to the following definition of abstract vacuity:

Definition 7. *A formula φ is ψ-vacuous in an abstract Kripke structure K_α iff it is ψ-vacuous in all concretizations of K_α. Formally,*

- $\forall K \in C(K_\alpha) \cdot \forall K' \in B(K) \cdot \forall x \in [S' \rightarrow \mathbf{2}] \cdot ||\varphi[\psi \leftarrow x]||^{K'}$, *or*
- $\forall K \in C(K_\alpha) \cdot \forall K' \in B(K) \cdot \forall x \in [S' \rightarrow \mathbf{2}] \cdot ||\neg\varphi[\psi \leftarrow x]||^{K'}$

Vacuity of Abstract Models. An exact abstraction K_α is always representable by a classical model, and its set of concretizations $C(K_\alpha)$ is identical to the set $B(K_\alpha)$ of structures bisimilar to K_α. Thus, vacuity given by Definition 4 also satisfies the conditions of Definition 7. As a consequence, an exact abstraction does not affect vacuity.

If K_α is not exact, the reduction from vacuity detection to 3-valued model-checking, as described in Section 4.2, provides us with a vacuity detection algorithm. Recall that K_x denotes a Kripke structure constructed from K by adding a new proposition x and letting it be maybe in every state of K.

Theorem 12. *A formula φ is ψ-vacuous in an abstract model K_α iff $\varphi[\psi \leftarrow x]$ evaluates to* true *or* false *in $(K_\alpha)_x$, under thorough semantics.*

In general, a non-exact abstraction can affect vacuity. A formula vacuous in a concrete Kripke structure K_c can be deemed non-vacuous in its abstraction. Thus, the result "non-vacuous" on an abstract system must be interpreted as "there is not enough information to decide whether the formula is vacuous".

Precision of Vacuity Detection. Recall that abstract model-checking is based on compositional semantics, while vacuity detection algorithm described above is based on thorough. Therefore, it is possible for vacuity detection to provide a more conclusive answer than abstract model-checking! A trivial example is a tautology, e.g., $AXp \lor EX\neg p$, which is true independently of the model and is vacuously true in p. However, in models where p is maybe, this formula is maybe under compositional semantics (used by abstract model-checking) but true under thorough. Thus, an answer that a formula is vacuously true in this case provides more information than results of abstract model-checking the same formula.

Approximating Vacuity Detection. Compositional semantics can also approximate vacuity detection in abstract models: if a formula $\varphi[\psi \leftarrow x]$ is true or false, then φ is ψ-vacuous. Of course, a maybe answer might need to be followed by a more expensive thorough semantics check.

6 Conclusion

In this paper, we give a uniform view of vacuity detection that is applicable to both branching- and linear-time temporal logics and yet enjoys all of the advantages of trace vacuity defined for LTL by Armoni et al [1]. This definition is *robust*, i.e., independent of logic embedding, and closed under bisimulation and thus independent of trivial changes to the model. Unfortunately, general vacuity detection is exponentially more expensive than model-checking. We show that for many useful fragments of temporal logic, vacuity detection is no more expensive than model-checking!

Furthermore, we identify a close connection between 3-valued model-checking and vacuity detection and note that the search for different definitions of vacuity corresponds to the search for different semantics for 3-valued model-checking. This connection suggests that there exists a natural relationship between the mature field of abstraction (not necessarily 3-valued) and the emerging field of vacuity detection. In particular, vacuity can be thought of as abstracting the formula instead of the model. In this paper, we started exploring this relationship by identifying what happens with vacuity under abstraction. Clearly, a much more thorough exploration is necessary; we leave it for future work.

References

1. R. Armoni, L. Fix, A. Flaisher, O. Grumberg, N. Piterman, A. Tiemeyer, and M. Vardi. "Enhanced Vacuity Detection in Linear Temporal Logic ". In *Proceedings of CAV'03*, volume 2725 of *LNCS*, pages 368–380, 2003.
2. T. Ball, A. Podelski, and S. Rajamani. "Boolean and Cartesian Abstraction for Model Checking C Programs". In *Proceedings of TACAS'01*, volume 2031 of *LNCS*, pages 268–283, 2001.
3. I. Beer, S. Ben-David, C. Eisner, and Y. Rodeh. "Efficient Detection of Vacuity in ACTL Formulas". In *Proceedings of CAV'97*, volume 1254 of *LNCS*, pages 279–290, 1997.
4. I. Beer, S. Ben-David, C. Eisner, and Y. Rodeh. "Efficient Detection of Vacuity in Temporal Model Checking". *Formal Methods in System Design*, 18(2):141–163, March 2001.
5. G. Bruns and P. Godefroid. "Model Checking Partial State Spaces with 3-Valued Temporal Logics". In *Proceedings of CAV'99*, volume 1633 of *LNCS*, pages 274–287, 1999.
6. G. Bruns and P. Godefroid. "Generalized Model Checking: Reasoning about Partial State Spaces". In *Proceedings of CONCUR'00*, volume 1877 of *LNCS*, pages 168–182, 2000.
7. M. Chechik, B. Devereux, and A. Gurfinkel. "XChek: A Multi-Valued Model-Checker". In *Proceedings of CAV'02*, volume 2404 of *LNCS*, pages 505–509, 2002.
8. E. Clarke, O. Grumberg, and D. Peled. *Model Checking*. MIT Press, 1999.
9. T. French. "Decidability of Quantifed Propositional Branching Time Logics". In *Proceedings of AI 2001*, volume 2256 of *LNCS*, pages 165–176, 2001.
10. P. Godefroid, M. Huth, and R. Jagadeesan. "Abstraction-based Model Checking using Modal Transition Systems". In *Proceedings of CONCUR'01*, volume 2154 of *LNCS*, pages 426–440, 2001.
11. P. Godefroid and R. Jagadeesan. "Automatic Abstraction Using Generalized Model-Checking". In *Proceedings of CAV'02*, volume 2404 of *LNCS*, pages 137–150, 2002.
12. P. Godefroid and R. Jagadeesan. "On the Expressiveness of 3-Valued Models". In *Proceedings of VMCAI'03*, volume 2575 of *LNCS*, pages 206–222, 2003.
13. S. Graf and H. Saidi. "Construction of Abstract State Graphs with PVS". In *Proceedings of CAV'97*, volume 1254 of *LNCS*, pages 72–83, 1997.
14. A. Gurfinkel and M. Chechik. "Multi-Valued Model-Checking via Classical Model-Checking". In *Proceedings of CONCUR'03*, volume 2761 of *LNCS*, pages 263–277, 2003.
15. A. Gurfinkel and M. Chechik. "How Vacuous Is Vacuous?". In *Proceedings of TACAS'04*, volume 2988 of *LNCS*, pages 451–466, March 2004.
16. S. C. Kleene. *Introduction to Metamathematics*. New York: Van Nostrand, 1952.
17. O. Kupferman. "Augmenting Branching Temporal Logics with Existential Quantification over Atomic Propositions". *Journal of Logic and Computation*, 7:1–14, 1997.
18. O. Kupferman and M. Vardi. "Vacuity Detection in Temporal Model Checking". *STTT*, 4(2):224–233, 2003.
19. Z. Manna and A. Pnueli. *The Temporal Logic of Reactive and Concurrent Systems*. Springer-Verlag, 1992.
20. R. Milner. "An Algebraic Definition of Simulation between Programs". In *Proceedings of IJCAI'91*, pages 481–489, 1971.

21. M. Purandare and F. Somenzi. "Vacuum Cleaning CTL Formulae". In *Proceedings of CAV'02*, volume 2404 of *LNCS*, pages 485–499, 2002.
22. S. Shoham and O. Grumberg. "A Game-Based Framework for CTL Counter-Examples and 3-Valued Abstraction-Refinement". In *Proceedings of CAV'03*, volume 2725 of *LNCS*, pages 275–287, 2003.

A   Proofs of Select Theorems

Theorem 2. *The complexity of detecting whether a formula φ is ψ-vacuous is EXPTIME-complete for CTL, and 2EXPTIME-complete for* CTL*.

Proof:
In Section 3.1, we have shown that vacuity detection is reducible to the model-checking problem for quantified temporal logic with a single quantifier, under amorphous se mantics. The membership follows from the fact that model-checking for this logic is reducible to model-checking it under tree semantics of Kupferman [17]. This yields a vacuity detection algorithm that is quadratic in the size of the model, and exponential in the size of the formula for CTL, and double-exponential for CTL*.

Completeness follows from reducing satisfiability problem for CTL and CTL* to QTL model-checking under amorphous semantics. The reduction is similar to the one used in the proof of Theorem 4.5 in [17].   □

Theorem 3. *If a temporal logic formula φ is monotone in its subformula ψ, then the complexity of detecting whether φ is ψ-vacuous in a Kripke structure K is $2 \times MC(\varphi)$, where $MC(\varphi)$ is the complexity of model-checking φ in K.*

Proof:
We show that if φ is monotone in ψ, it is ψ-vacuous iff replacing ψ by both true and false does not affect the value of φ: $||\varphi[\psi \leftarrow \text{true}]||^K = ||\varphi[\psi \leftarrow \text{false}]||^K$. Since true and false are simply nullary functions from S to $\mathbf{2}$, the ($\Leftarrow$) direction follows trivially. Note that for any Kripke structure K' bisimilar to K, $\forall c \in \mathbf{2} \cdot ||\varphi[\psi \leftarrow c]||^K = ||\varphi[\psi \leftarrow c]||^{K'}$; thus, we only need to show that

$$(||\varphi[\psi \leftarrow \text{true}]||^K = ||\varphi[\psi \leftarrow \text{false}]||^K) \Rightarrow \forall x \in [S \rightarrow \mathbf{2}] \cdot ||\varphi[\psi \leftarrow x]||^K$$

which follows by monotonicity of φ.   □

Theorem 4. *The complexity of deciding whether a formula φ is monotone in a subformula ψ is EXPTIME-hard for CTL, and 2EXPTIME-hard for* CTL*.

Proof:
We show that the validity problem for CTL is reducible to deciding monotonicity of a CTL formula. Consider the formula $(p \wedge q) \Rightarrow AX(p \wedge q)$ which is not monotone in $p \wedge q$. Let φ be an arbitrary CTL formula that does not contain atomic propositions p and q. Then, the formula $(p \wedge q \Rightarrow AX(p \wedge q)) \vee \varphi$ is monotone iff φ is valid. The proof for CTL* is identical.   □

Theorem 5. *If φ is a* CTL* *formula that is syntactically monotone in ψ, then φ is also monotone in ψ.*

Proof:
The proof follows from the monotonicity of CTL* operators.   □

Theorem 6. *Let K be a Kripke structure, and K_x as described in Section 3.2. Then, if K' is $\{x\}$-bisimilar to K, then it is simulated by K_x.*

Proof:
Let $\rho \subseteq S \times S'$ be the $\{x\}$-bisimulation relation between K and K'. We claim that $\rho' = \{(\langle s,i\rangle, t) \mid \rho(s,t) \wedge I'(\langle s,i\rangle, x) = I_x(t,x)\}$ is a simulation between K_x and K'.

From the definition of ρ', we get $\rho(\langle s,i\rangle, t) \Leftrightarrow (I_x(\langle s,i\rangle) = I(t))$, thus, it satisfies the first condition of a simulation. The proof of the second condition is given below.

$$\rho'(\langle s,i\rangle, t) \wedge R'(t,t')$$
$$\Rightarrow \text{(since } K' \text{ is } \{x\}\text{-bisimilar to } K)$$
$$\exists s' \in S \cdot \rho(s', t') \wedge R(s,s')$$
$$\Rightarrow \text{(by definition of } K_x)$$
$$\exists s' \in S \cdot \forall j \in \{0,1\} \cdot R_x(\langle s,i\rangle, \langle s',j\rangle) \wedge \rho(s',t')$$
$$\Rightarrow \text{(since } I'(t', x) \in \mathbf{2})$$
$$\exists s' \in S \cdot \exists j \in \{0,1\} \cdot R_x(\langle s,i\rangle, \langle s',j\rangle) \wedge \rho(s',t') \wedge I_x(\langle s',j\rangle) = I'(t')$$
$$\Rightarrow \text{(by definition of } \rho')$$
$$\exists s' \in S \cdot \exists k \in \{0,1\} \cdot R_x(\langle s,i\rangle, \langle s',j\rangle) \wedge \rho'(\langle s',j\rangle, t')$$

Finally, if t is an initial state of K', then there exists an $i \in \{0,1\}$ such that $\rho(\langle s,i\rangle, t)$ holds, which establishes that ρ is a simulation between K_x and K'.   □

Theorem 7. *Let φ be an ACTL* formula, ψ be a subformula of φ, and K be a Kripke structure. If φ is known to be satisfied by K, then the complexity of detecting vacuity of φ in ψ is $2 \times MC(\varphi)$.*

Proof:
We show that a formula φ satisfied by K is ψ-vacuous iff the formula $\varphi[\psi \leftarrow x]$ is satisfied by K_x. Since K_x is $\{x\}$-bisimilar to K, the proof of ($\Rightarrow$) direction is trivial. For ($\Leftarrow$) direction, if $\varphi[\psi \leftarrow x]$ holds in K_x, then by Theorem 6 $\varphi[\psi \leftarrow x]$ it holds in every $\{x\}$-bisimulation of K.   □

Theorem 8. *Let $\varphi[x, \psi]$ be an CTL* formula, with a subformula x and a state subformula ψ, and let K be a Kripke structure. Then, φ is x-vacuous iff $\varphi[x, \psi \leftarrow Prop(\psi, K)]$ is x-vacuous.*

Proof:

$$\forall K' \in \mathcal{B}(K) \cdot \forall x \in [S' \rightarrow \mathbf{2}] \cdot ||\varphi[x, \psi]||^{K'}$$
$$\Rightarrow \text{(by propositional substitution)}$$
$$\forall K' \in \mathcal{B}(K) \cdot \forall x \in [S' \rightarrow \mathbf{2}] \cdot ||\varphi[x, \psi \leftarrow Prop(\psi, K')]||^{K'}$$
$$\Rightarrow \text{(since } K' \text{ is bisimilar to } K)$$
$$\forall K' \in \mathcal{B}(K) \cdot \forall x \in [S' \rightarrow \mathbf{2}] \cdot ||\varphi[x, \psi \leftarrow Prop(\psi, K)]||^{K'}$$

□

Theorem 11. *Let K be a Kripke structure, and K_x be as described in the beginning of Section 4.2. Then, $K' \in C(K_x)$ iff K' is $\{x\}$-bisimilar to K.*

Proof:
The proof follows trivially from the definitions of $\{x\}$-bisimilarity and refinement.   □

Theorem 12. *A formula φ is ψ-vacuous in an abstract model K_α iff $\varphi[\psi \leftarrow x]$ does not evaluate to* maybe *in $(K_\alpha)_x$, under thorough semantics.*

Proof:
For an atomic proposition x of K, let K_{-x} denote a Kripke structure constructed from K by *removing* x from K; that is, $K = (K_x)_{-x}$. Note that both K and K_{-x} are defined over an identical set of states S. Furthermore, $(K_{-x})_x \preceq K$ under the identity relation $id = \{(s, s) \mid s \in S\}$.

Refinements of K_x are related to refinements of K: $K_x \preceq K' \Leftrightarrow K \preceq (K')_{-x}$ because x is maybe in every state of K_x, and the statespaces of K_x and K are identical. Thus, the set of concretizations of K_x is equivalent to a set obtained by: (a) concretizing K, (b) adding the atomic proposition x, and (c) taking the concretization of the result, i.e. $C(K_x) = C((C(K))_x)$.

Finally, we prove the theorem.

$$||\varphi[\psi \leftarrow x]||_t^{(K_\alpha)_x} = \textsf{true}$$
$$\Leftrightarrow \text{(by Definition 6)}$$
$$\forall K \in C((K_\alpha)_x) \cdot ||\varphi[\psi \leftarrow x]||^K = \textsf{true}$$
$$\Leftrightarrow \text{(since } C(K_x) = C((C(K))_x))$$
$$\forall K \in C(C((K_\alpha))_x) \cdot ||\varphi[\psi \leftarrow x]||^K = \textsf{true}$$
$$\Leftrightarrow \text{(by Definition 6)}$$
$$\forall K \in C(K_\alpha) \cdot ||\varphi[\psi \leftarrow x]||_t^{K_x} = \textsf{true}$$

The proof of the second case is similar.   □

Parameterized Vacuity*

Marko Samer[1] and Helmut Veith[2]

[1] Institute of Information Systems (DBAI)
Vienna University of Technology, Austria
samer@dbai.tuwien.ac.at
[2] Institut für Informatik (I7)
Technische Universität München, Germany
veith@in.tum.de

Abstract. In model checking, a specification is vacuously true, if some subformula can be modified without affecting the truth value of the specification. Intuitively, this means that the property expressed in this subformula is satisfied for a trivial reason, and likely not the intended one. It has been shown by Kupferman and Vardi that vacuity detection can be reduced to model checking of simplified specifications where the subformulas of interest are replaced by constant truth values.

In this paper, we argue that the common definition describes extreme cases of vacuity where the subformula indeed collapses to a constant truth value. We suggest a refined notion of vacuity (weak vacuity) which is parameterized by a user-defined class of *vacuity causes*. Under this notion, a specification is vacuously true, if a subformula collapses to a vacuity cause. Our analysis exhibits a close relationship between vacuity detection and temporal logic query solving. We exploit this relationship to obtain vacuity detection algorithms in symbolic, automata-theoretic, and multi-valued frameworks.

1 Introduction

When a model checker detects that a specification φ is violated, it will output a counterexample. If the specification is satisfied however, there is usually no feedback from the model checker; in particular, the user does not know whether φ is satisfied *vacuously*, i.e., due to a trivial reason. One of the simplest examples of vacuous satisfaction is antecedent failure [2], i.e., the situation when the antecedent φ of an implication $\varphi \Rightarrow \psi$ is not satisfiable in the model, resulting in the vacuous truth of $\varphi \Rightarrow \psi$. Since experience shows that vacuous satisfaction often hints at an error either in the model or in the specification, vacuity detection has gained much interest in the last years from both industry and academia. To cite Beer et al. from IBM Haifa [3]: "Our experience has shown that typically 20% of formulas pass vacuously during the first formal verification runs of a new hardware design, and that vacuous passes always point to a real problem in either the design or its specification or environment."

---

* This work was supported by the European Community Research Training Network "Games and Automata for Synthesis and Validation" (GAMES), the EU Project ECRYPT, and by the Austrian Science Fund Project Z29-N04. The results presented in this paper have been developed as part of [18].

A.J. Hu and A.K. Martin (Eds.): FMCAD 2004, LNCS 3312, pp. 322–336, 2004.

Intuitively, vacuity means that the truth value of a formula φ is independent of the truth value of a subformula, i.e., the subformula can be replaced by any other formula without changing the truth value of φ. Thus, a naive approach for detecting vacuity would be to check the truth value of a formula for all possible substitutions of all sub-formulas. However, this is obviously infeasible in practice. Therefore, Kupferman and Vardi have shown in their seminal paper [15], that in the case of CTL*, vacuity detection can be reduced to model checking if the subformulas occur with pure polarity (i.e., under an even or an odd number of negations, but not mixed). In particular, they have shown that a formula φ is vacuously satisfied with respect to a subformula ψ iff the truth value of φ remains unchanged when replacing ψ by the constant truth values $\top$ (*true*) resp. $\bot$ (*false*) depending on the polarity of ψ. Thereafter, Beer et al. [4] generalized this result to any logic with polarity.

Example 1 (Classical vacuity). The specification $\mathbf{AX}(p \vee \mathbf{AX}\, q)$ is trivially satisfied in every model where the stronger formula $\mathbf{AX}\, p$ holds (since $\mathbf{AX}\, p \Rightarrow \mathbf{AX}(p \vee \mathbf{AX}\, q)$). In this case, the subformula $\mathbf{AX}\, q$ can be replaced by $\bot$, that is $\mathbf{AX}(p \vee \bot) = \mathbf{AX}\, p$, without affecting the truth value. Hence, $\mathbf{AX}(p \vee \mathbf{AX}\, q)$ is vacuously satisfied.

The main motivation for the work in this paper is the observation (already mentioned in [4]) that the common notion of vacuity described above does not suffice to capture the intuitive range of "trivial" satisfaction.

Example 2 (Limits of classical vacuity). The specification $\mathbf{AX}\,\mathbf{AF}\, p$ is trivially satisfied in every model where the stronger formula $\mathbf{AX}\, p$ holds (since $\mathbf{AX}\, p \Rightarrow \mathbf{AX}\,\mathbf{AF}\, p$). This form of trivial satisfaction however, does not fall under the common notion of vacuity since neither p nor $\mathbf{AF}\, p$ can be replaced by $\bot$ without affecting the truth value. A similar example due to Pnueli [17] will be described later in more detail.

In this example, the simplicity of $\mathbf{AX}\, p$ in comparison to the specification $\mathbf{AX}\,\mathbf{AF}\, p$ makes one wonder whether $\mathbf{AX}\,\mathbf{AF}\, p$ was indeed satisfied for the right reasons. The question however, if satisfaction of $\mathbf{AX}\, p$ already can act as a cause for vacuity, depends heavily on the application and on the application knowledge of the engineer. It would therefore be useful to let the verification engineer determine which formulas can be rightfully regarded as vacuity causes – e.g., all propositional formulas, or all formulas which depend only on immediately adjacent system states. By varying a set $\mathcal{K}$ of vacuity causes, we can thus obtain a more fine-grained notion of vacuity which is parameterized by $\mathcal{K}$. In this setting, classical vacuity amounts to the special case where $\mathcal{K}$ consists of the constant truth values $\bot$ and $\top$. When $\mathcal{K}$ is different from $\{\bot, \top\}$, we shall speak of *weak vacuity*.

Example 3. Let $\mathcal{K} = \{\bot, \top, p\}$ be the set of vacuity causes. Then the subformula $\mathbf{AX}\, q$ in Example 1 can be replaced by $\bot \in \mathcal{K}$ without affecting the truth value. Hence, the specification is vacuously satisfied in the classical sense. Moreover, in Example 2, the subformula $\mathbf{AF}\, p$ can be replaced by the stronger formula $p \in \mathcal{K}$ without affecting the truth value. Hence, the specification is vacuously satisfied in our weaker sense.

In this paper, we systematically investigate the notion of parameterized vacuity. In particular, this paper makes the following technical and methodological contributions:

- We define the notion of weak vacuity, and argue that it extends the common notion of vacuity in a natural and important way.
- We establish a close relationship between weak vacuity detection and temporal logic query solving (reviewed in Sections 2 and 3) which gives rise to a systematic framework for weak vacuity detection. In particular, the connection to temporal logic query solving enables us to compute the strongest vacuity causes in $\mathcal{K}$.
- We show how to extend existing query solving algorithms as to work with different sets of vacuity causes $\mathcal{K}$. Besides the application in vacuity detection, our observations also extend the range of existing query solving algorithms per se. Not surprisingly, the vacuity detection capabilities of our approach strongly depend on the set $\mathcal{K}$ of vacuity causes.
- The notion of vacuity has also been used to compute interesting witnesses and counterexamples, i.e., witnesses and counterexamples which exhibit the semantical possibilities inherent in the specification to a possibly large extent. We extend this work to our notion of weak vacuity.

This paper is organized as follows: In Section 2, we recall some basic definitions and results on vacuity detection and temporal logic queries. Then we present our generalization of vacuity in Section 3 consisting of three subsections. Section 3.1 shows how the classical vacuity notion can be embedded into temporal logic queries. The most important part of this paper is then presented in Section 3.2, where we introduce our generalization to *weak vacuity*. Afterwards, in Section 3.3, we show how to construct vacuity witnesses for weak vacuity. Existing query solving algorithms and modifications for vacuity detection are presented in Section 4. In Section 5, we give a short overview of related work. Finally, we conclude in Section 6.

2   Background on Vacuity Detection and Temporal Logic Queries

In this section, we present the background on vacuity detection and temporal logic queries. Since our results do not depend on the syntax of the underlying logic, we do not need to restrict our considerations to a particular temporal logic. We say *temporal logic formula* to denote formulas of some underlying temporal logic.

2.1   Vacuity Detection

Since most of the definitions and results concerning vacuity use the substitution of subformulas of a given formula, Kupferman and Vardi [15] introduced the notation $\varphi[\psi \leftarrow \theta]$ to denote the result of substituting the subformula ψ (i.e., all occurrences of ψ) of φ by θ. This allows us to formulate the following two definitions which are adapted from [3].

Definition 1   (Affect). *The subformula ψ of φ affects φ in $\mathfrak{M}$ iff there is a formula θ such that the truth values of φ and $\varphi[\psi \leftarrow \theta]$ are different in $\mathfrak{M}$.*

With this definition at hand, we are able to define what we mean by vacuity.

Definition 2 (Vacuity). *The model $\mathfrak{M}$ satisfies φ vacuously iff $\mathfrak{M} \models \varphi$ and there is some subformula ψ of φ such that ψ does not affect φ in $\mathfrak{M}$.*

Note that according to this definition, all subformulas have to be checked in order to detect non-vacuity. For practical reasons, this can be easily modified in such a way that vacuity is checked with respect to user-selected subformulas which are considered to be relevant. Therefore, a special kind of vacuity was introduced by Beer et al. [4], namely ψ-vacuity. We slightly adapt their definition in order to preserve a consistent terminology.

Definition 3 (ψ-Vacuity). *Let ψ be a subformula of formula φ. The model $\mathfrak{M}$ satisfies φ ψ-vacuously iff $\mathfrak{M} \models \varphi$ and ψ does not affect φ in $\mathfrak{M}$.*

It is easy to see that a formula is vacuously satisfied iff it is ψ-vacuously satisfied for some subformula ψ. Kupferman and Vardi [15] have shown that if there exist multiple occurrences of ψ in φ, then vacuity detection is much harder because one occurrence of the subformula may be positive (i.e., under an even number of negations) and another occurrence of the same subformula may be negative (i.e., under an odd number of negations). Therefore, they required that every subformula occurs only once, which guarantees that the substituted subformula occurs with pure polarity (i.e., either positive or negative) which, on the other hand, guarantees some kind of monotonicity. Under this assumption, they have shown that checking ψ-vacuity of a satisfied formula φ can be reduced to model checking $\varphi[\psi \leftarrow \bot]$ (if ψ occurs positive) respectively $\varphi[\psi \leftarrow \top]$ (if ψ occurs negative).

2.2 Temporal Logic Queries

Our aim in this paper is to bring vacuity detection and temporal logic queries together. Therefore, in the following we summarize some basics of temporal logic queries which we will need afterwards.

Definition 4 (Query). *A temporal logic query is a temporal logic formula where some subformula is replaced by a special symbol ?, called placeholder.*

We say a query is *positive* iff all occurrences of the placeholder are under an even number of negations, a query is *negative* iff all occurrences of the placeholder are under an odd number of negations, a query is of *pure polarity* iff it is positive or negative, and a query is of *mixed polarity* iff it is neither positive nor negative.

Definition 5 (Solution). *Let γ be a query, $\mathfrak{M}$ be a model, and φ be a formula. We write $\gamma[\varphi]$ to denote the result of substituting all occurrences of the placeholder in γ by φ. If $\mathfrak{M} \models \gamma[\varphi]$, then we say that φ is a solution to γ in $\mathfrak{M}$. We denote the set of all solutions to γ in $\mathfrak{M}$ by $sol(\mathfrak{M}, \gamma) = \{\varphi \mid \mathfrak{M} \models \gamma[\varphi]\}$.*

To obtain the maximum information a query provides, it is necessary to consider *all* solutions. However, since the number of solutions is likely to be very large, it is desirable to have strongest solutions that subsume all other solutions. We assume in the following that the set of solutions to a query always forms a partially ordered set with minimal and maximal elements (with respect to logical implication). Note that this does not need to be the case in general because there may exist infinite implication chains such as $\mathbf{F}\,p \Leftarrow \mathbf{XF}\,p \Leftarrow \mathbf{XXF}\,p \Leftarrow \mathbf{XXXF}\,p \Leftarrow \cdots$ if p holds in a cycle. To overcome this problem, we can simply restrict the set of potential solutions to a set of user-selected formulas (e.g., propositional formulas). Then the minimal elements of the solutions in this set are the strongest solutions we are interested in.

Definition 6 (Minimal solutions). *A set of solutions S to a query γ in a model $\mathfrak{M}$ is the set of* minimal solutions *iff for all $\mu_1, \mu_2 \in S$ it holds that $\mu_1 \Rightarrow \mu_2$ implies $\mu_1 = \mu_2$, and for every solution $\varphi \in \mathrm{sol}(\mathfrak{M}, \gamma)$ it holds that there exists a $\mu \in S$ such that $\mu \Rightarrow \varphi$. If the set of minimal solutions contains only one element, then this element is called the* least *solution.*

A query γ can be seen as a function $\gamma : \varphi \mapsto \gamma[\varphi]$ that maps formulas to formulas. Thus, an important and natural property is monotonicity; in particular, queries for which the corresponding function is monotonically increasing.

Definition 7 (Monotonic query). *A query γ is* monotonic *iff $\varphi \Rightarrow \psi$ implies $\gamma[\varphi] \Rightarrow \gamma[\psi]$ for all formulas φ and ψ.*

The following lemma presents two special solutions to monotonic queries. Its proof is a simple generalization of the proof in [7] on CTL queries.

Lemma 1. *Let γ be a monotonic query and $\mathfrak{M}$ be a model.*

- *The query γ has a solution in $\mathfrak{M}$ iff $\mathfrak{M} \models \gamma[\top]$.*
- *Every formula is a solution to γ in $\mathfrak{M}$ iff $\mathfrak{M} \models \gamma[\bot]$.*

3   From Vacuity to Parameterized Vacuity

In this section, we show that temporal logic queries can be seen as a uniform framework for vacuity detection and how the conventional concept of vacuity can be nicely generalized by using terms of temporal logic queries. To this aim, consider the query $\gamma = \varphi[\psi \leftarrow ?]$, which we obtain by replacing subformula ψ by the placeholder. Obviously, it holds that $\gamma[\theta] = \varphi[\psi \leftarrow \theta]$, which indicates how to use temporal logic queries for vacuity detection.

Definition 8 (Annotation). *A query γ* annotates *a formula φ iff $\gamma[\psi] = \varphi$ for some subformula ψ of φ.*

This definition enables us to encode selected occurrences of a subformula ψ in φ into a query γ. Then checking if ψ affects φ can be done by determining the solutions to γ. Hence, checking vacuity can be reduced to query solving. In order to do this, we need another definition.

Definition 9 (Equivalence). *A query γ is* equivalent *to a formula φ in a model $\mathfrak{M}$, in symbols $\gamma \equiv_{\mathfrak{M}} \varphi$, iff for all formulas θ it holds that $\gamma[\theta] \Leftrightarrow \varphi$ in $\mathfrak{M}$.*

3.1 Strong Vacuity

Now, we are able to define vacuity by temporal logic queries. We call it *strong* vacuity because later we will also define a more general and therefore weaker form of vacuity.

Definition 10 (Strong vacuity). *Let φ be a formula annotated by a query γ. Then the model $\mathfrak{M}$ satisfies φ strong γ-vacuously iff $\mathfrak{M} \models \varphi$ and $\gamma \equiv_{\mathfrak{M}} \varphi$.*

Obviously, a comparison between vacuity and strong vacuity makes only sense when the set of annotating queries which we take into account for strong vacuity detection contains only those queries where all occurrences of a subformula are simultaneously replaced by the placeholder. More formally, the annotating queries are given by $\{\varphi[\psi \leftarrow ?] \mid \psi$ is some subformula of $\varphi\}$. Then it is easy to see that vacuity and strong vacuity coincide. This is not surprising because so far we have essentially reformulated the notation concerning vacuity in terms of temporal logic queries. However, as we will see later, temporal logic queries provide us with another point of view of vacuity which will be crucial to weak vacuity.

Recall that Kupferman and Vardi [15] investigated vacuity of CTL* formulas with respect to subformulas with pure polarity (i.e., either positive or negative). Beer et al. [4] have shown that this approach can be generalized to any logic with polarity. In terms of temporal logic queries, this can be further generalized by considering arbitrary monotonic queries. Note that pure polarity implies monotonicity but not vice versa.

The following lemma is our first step towards a generalization. Its proof is similar to the proof of Theorem 1 in [15]. The main difference is the use of Lemma 1, which is based on the purely semantical property of monotonicity in contrast to Lemma 1 in [15], which is based on the syntactic (and therefore more specific) property of pure polarity. Note that it is sufficient to consider only queries that are monotonically increasing; the case for queries that are monotonically decreasing is symmetric.

Lemma 2. *Let φ be a formula annotated by a monotonic query γ. Then $\gamma \equiv_{\mathfrak{M}} \varphi$ iff $\gamma[\top] \Leftrightarrow \gamma[\bot]$ in $\mathfrak{M}$.*

The following theorem can be proven by using Lemma 1 and Lemma 2. In clear analogy to [15], it allows us to reduce vacuity detection with respect to *monotonic* queries to a single model checking call.

Theorem 1. *Let φ be a formula annotated by a monotonic query γ. Then the model $\mathfrak{M}$ satisfies φ strong γ-vacuously iff $\mathfrak{M} \models \gamma[\bot]$.*

The key observation in this theorem is that checking the formula $\gamma[\bot]$ in $\mathfrak{M}$ can also be seen as computing the strongest solutions to the query γ in $\mathfrak{M}$. If there is a single strongest solution equivalent to $\bot$, then $\mathfrak{M}$ satisfies φ strong γ-vacuously. Hence, we have reduced vacuity detection to query solving. But what can we say if the strongest solutions to γ in $\mathfrak{M}$ are not equivalent to $\bot$? We will answer this question by a generalization of strong vacuity below.

3.2 Weak Vacuity

Recall that a subformula ψ does not affect the truth value of φ in $\mathfrak{M}$ iff ψ can be replaced by *any* other formula without changing the truth value of the resulting formula in $\mathfrak{M}$. However, as mentioned by Beer et al. [4], this definition of vacuity is sometimes "missing the point". We demonstrate this by an example proposed by Pnueli:

Example 4 (Pnueli [17]). Consider the formula $\mathbf{AG\,AF}\,p$ and let $\mathfrak{M}$ be a model such that $\mathfrak{M} \models \mathbf{AG}\,p$. Then it trivially holds that $\mathfrak{M} \models \mathbf{AG\,AF}\,p$. Since it cannot be the case that $\mathfrak{M} \models \mathbf{AG}\,\bot$, we know that $\mathbf{AF}\,p$ affects the truth value of $\mathbf{AG\,AF}\,p$ in $\mathfrak{M}$, i.e., $\mathfrak{M}$ does not satisfy $\mathbf{AG\,AF}\,p$ strong γ-vacuously, where $\gamma = \mathbf{AG}\,?$. However, our intuition tells us that $\mathfrak{M}$ satisfies $\mathbf{AG\,AF}\,p$ vacuously since it holds due to a trivial reason, namely because the stronger formula $\mathbf{AG}\,p$ holds in $\mathfrak{M}$. In terms of temporal logic queries, this means that $\mathfrak{M} \models \gamma[\mathbf{AF}\,p]$ holds vacuously because (i) $\mathfrak{M} \models \gamma[p]$, (ii) γ is monotonic, and (iii) $p \Rightarrow \mathbf{AF}\,p$.

The approach proposed by Beer et al. [4] for solving this problem is to refine the standard definition of vacuity in such a way that formulas as in the example above are identified as vacuously satisfied: "Instead of checking whether a subformula can be replaced by *any* other subformula, we will check whether it can be replaced by *some* 'simpler' formula." They did not give a formal definition of the term "simpler" but they presented some examples: p is simpler than $\mathbf{AF}\,p$, $\mathbf{AG}\,p$ is simpler than $\mathbf{AF}\,p$, and $(\mathbf{AG}\,p) \wedge (\mathbf{AF}\,q)$ is simpler than $\mathbf{A}(p\,\mathbf{U}\,q)$.

From these examples it is easy to see, especially with the knowledge of temporal logic queries in mind, that "simpler" means stronger with respect to logical implication, i.e., $p \Rightarrow \mathbf{AF}\,p$, $\mathbf{AG}\,p \Rightarrow \mathbf{AF}\,p$, and $(\mathbf{AG}\,p) \wedge (\mathbf{AF}\,q) \Rightarrow \mathbf{A}(p\,\mathbf{U}\,q)$.

The intuition to refine vacuity is therefore to define a formula to be vacuously satisfied if there is a subformula that can be replaced by a stronger formula without affecting the truth value. Finding such stronger formulas can be done by solving temporal logic queries. In fact, we will show that it suffices to compute the minimal solutions to a query. However, as already mentioned in Section 2.2, such minimal solutions do not need to exist in general. Moreover, when computing some stronger formulas (not necessarily minimal) they may not be interesting in the sense that they do not justify the truth value of the original formula by a *trivial* reason. Therefore, we have to restrict the set of potential solutions to a set of user-selected formulas which are considered to be interesting for detecting vacuity – we call the elements of this set *vacuity causes*.

Definition 11 (Vacuity causes). *A set of* vacuity causes $\mathcal{K}$ *is a partially ordered set with respect to logical implication of formulas in a given logic such that every subset of $\mathcal{K}$ has a finite number of minimal and maximal elements.*

In the following, we will implicitly assume that $\{\bot, \top\} \subseteq \mathcal{K}$ in order to guarantee that strong vacuity is a special case of our generalization to weak vacuity. It is now easy to see that our definition of weak vacuity will be *parameterized* by a set of vacuity causes. Important natural examples of vacuity causes are:

- **Classical vacuity causes** $\{\bot, \top\}$, which yields strong vacuity.
- **Propositional vacuity causes** (e.g., $p \Rightarrow \mathbf{AF}\,p$)
- **Bounded vacuity causes**, i.e., formulas with a maximum nesting depth of temporal operators. In particular:
  - **Local vacuity causes**, where the next operator is the only allowed temporal operator (e.g., $\mathbf{AX}(p \vee \mathbf{AX}\,p) \Rightarrow \mathbf{AF}\,p$).
  - **Invariants** (e.g., $\mathbf{AG}\,p \Rightarrow p$)

The following definition formalizes our generalization by weakening the requirement $\mathfrak{M} \models \gamma[\bot]$ in Theorem 1 accordingly.

Definition 12 (Weak vacuity). *Let φ be a formula annotated by a monotonic query γ such that $\varphi = \gamma[\psi]$ and $\mathcal{K}$ be a set of vacuity causes. Then the model $\mathfrak{M}$ satisfies φ weak γ-vacuously with vacuity causes in $\mathcal{K}$ iff*

1. *$\mathfrak{M} \models \varphi$ and $\psi \Leftrightarrow \bot$ or*
2. *there exists a formula $\theta \in \mathcal{K}$ such that $\mathfrak{M} \models \gamma[\theta]$ and $\theta \Rightarrow \psi$ but $\psi \not\Rightarrow \theta$.*

Remark 1. Note that the definition of weak vacuity makes only sense for monotonic queries. Moreover, note that if (1) holds true, no solution strictly weaker than ψ can exist, since $\theta \Rightarrow \bot$ is true only for $\theta \Leftrightarrow \bot$.

A naive algorithm for detecting weak vacuity according to Definition 12 can be formulated as follows:

Algorithm 1 Detecting weak vacuity
---
1.   Select a subformula ψ of φ.
2.   Define γ such that $\varphi = \gamma[\psi]$.   // Encode selected occurrences of ψ in γ.
3.   **if** $\mathfrak{M} \models \varphi$ **and** $\psi \Leftrightarrow \bot$ **then**   // Special case of strong vacuity.
4.   **output** $\bot$;   // Output vacuity cause.
5.   **else**
6.   **for all** $\theta \in \mathrm{sol}(\mathfrak{M}, \gamma) \cap \mathcal{K}$ **do**   // Compute solutions to γ in $\mathfrak{M}$.
7.   **if** $\theta \Rightarrow \psi$ **and** $\psi \not\Rightarrow \theta$ **then**   // Weak vacuity conditions.
8.   **output** θ ;   // Output vacuity cause.

However, in order to detect weak vacuity, it suffices to compute the strongest resp. minimal solutions to γ in $\mathfrak{M}$ which is stated in the following theorem. The restriction to minimal solutions does not only reduce the computation effort but also provides more compact information on the causes of weak vacuity.

Theorem 2. *Let φ be a formula annotated by a monotonic query γ and $\mathcal{K}$ be a set of vacuity causes. Further, let S be the set of minimal solutions to γ in a model $\mathfrak{M}$ restricted to elements in $\mathcal{K}$. Then $\mathfrak{M}$ satisfies φ weak γ-vacuously with vacuity causes in $\mathcal{K}$ iff $\mathfrak{M}$ satisfies φ weak γ-vacuously with vacuity causes in S.*

Corollary 1. *Line 6 in Algorithm 1 can be replaced by*

$$\textbf{for all } \theta \in \min_{\Rightarrow}(\mathrm{sol}(\mathfrak{M}, \gamma) \cap \mathcal{K}) \textbf{ do.}$$

Remark 2. It is easy to see that the computation of solutions according to Line 6 in our algorithm can be optimized in such a way that the computation of solutions by $\mathrm{sol}(\mathfrak{M}, \gamma)$ directly computes the set of minimal solutions in $\mathcal{K}$. Moreover, note that only those solutions computed in Line 6 are relevant which meet the requirements of Line 7. Hence, formula ψ can also be used to reduce the search space during the computation in Line 6.

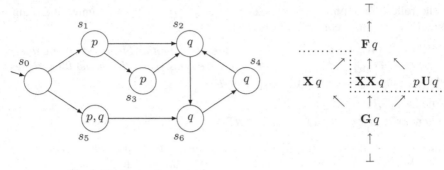

Fig. 1. Weak vacuity example

Fig. 2. Poset of vacuity causes

Example 5. Consider the Kripke structure $\mathfrak{M}$ shown in Figure 1 and the poset $\mathcal{K}$ of vacuity causes shown in Figure 2. Further, let $\varphi = \mathbf{AXF}\,q$ be the LTL formula for which we want to check vacuity with respect to the subformula $\psi = \mathbf{F}\,q$ in $\mathfrak{M}$. Thus, we define $\gamma = \mathbf{AX}\,?$. It is easy to see that $\mathfrak{M} \models \varphi$ and that φ does not hold strong γ-vacuously in $\mathfrak{M}$ since $\mathfrak{M} \not\models \gamma[\bot]$ (cf. Theorem 1).

In order to check weak vacuity, let us consider the solutions to γ in $\mathfrak{M}$. It is easy to see that $\mathrm{sol}(\mathfrak{M}, \gamma) \cap \mathcal{K} = \{\mathbf{XX}\,q, p\,\mathbf{U}\,q, \mathbf{F}\,q, \top\}$, which are the elements above the dotted line in Figure 2. This is also the set computed in Line 6 in Algorithm 1. According to Theorem 2, however, it suffices to consider the set $\min_{\Rightarrow}(\mathrm{sol}(\mathfrak{M}, \gamma) \cap \mathcal{K}) = \{\mathbf{XX}\,q, p\,\mathbf{U}\,q\}$. Thus, it remains to check the weak vacuity conditions of Line 7 in Algorithm 1, which are satisfied by both formulas. Hence, the two vacuity causes $\mathbf{XX}\,q$ and $p\,\mathbf{U}\,q$ indeed cause weak γ-vacuity of $\mathbf{AXF}\,q$ in $\mathfrak{M}$.

Finally, it remains to show how to extend the construction of non-vacuity witnesses concerning weak vacuity.

3.3   Witness Construction

If a formula is not satisfied by the model, the model checker returns a counterexample that helps the user to correct the error in the model or the specification. On the other hand, if the formula is satisfied by the model, standard model checkers do not return a witness, which would also be helpful for the user to verify that the specification holds in a way as intended. In particular, after the vacuity detection process, where all errors causing vacuous satisfaction should have been corrected, a witness would prove that the specification holds indeed non-vacuously. The generation of vacuity witnesses is discussed in [3, 15, 4, 11]. Since the generation of witnesses concerning strong vacuity can be easily reformulated in terms of temporal logic queries, we will concentrate on the generation of witnesses concerning weak vacuity in the following.

At first we recall the relevant definitions of Beer et al. [4]. One of the main difficulties in witness construction is to construct an *interesting* witness, i.e., a witness that is as small as possible. To this aim, a pre-order on models resp. witnesses is necessary.

Definition 13 (Pre-order on models). *Given a logic $\mathcal{L}$, we define the natural pre-order $\prec_{\mathcal{L}}$ of $\mathcal{L}$ on the set of models: $\mathfrak{M}' \prec_{\mathcal{L}} \mathfrak{M}$ iff for all $\varphi \in \mathcal{L}$ we have that $\mathfrak{M} \models \varphi \Rightarrow \mathfrak{M}' \models \varphi$.*

Natural pre-orders on models of the temporal logics LTL, CTL, CTL*, ACTL, and ACTL* can be found in [4]. Since it is clear now that such a pre-order on models depends on the logic under consideration, for simplicity we will omit the subscript for the logic and simply write $\prec$ in the following.

Now, we are able to define what we understand by an interesting witness. Note that we consider the more general concept of witnesses with respect to a set of queries and not with respect to a single query. This is because a witness that proves non-vacuity with respect to a set of queries simultaneously contains much more information than the witnesses with respect to each single query in this set. The following definition is a straight forward adaption of Beer et al. [4].

Definition 14 (Interesting witness[1]). *Let φ be a formula and Γ be a set of queries that annotate φ. Further, let $\mathfrak{M}$ be a model and $\mathcal{K}$ be a set of vacuity causes. Then the model $\mathfrak{C} \prec \mathfrak{M}$ is an* interesting strong (weak) Γ-vacuity witness *of φ in $\mathfrak{M}$ with vacuity causes in $\mathcal{K}$ iff $\mathfrak{C}$ is a minimal model with respect to $\prec$ such that for all $\gamma \in \Gamma$, $\mathfrak{C}$ does not satisfy φ strong (weak) γ-vacuously with vacuity causes in $\mathcal{K}$.*

Note that there exists an interesting γ-vacuity witness of a formula φ in a model $\mathfrak{M}$ iff φ does not hold γ-vacuously in $\mathfrak{M}$ [4]. However, note further that a single interesting witness with respect to a set of queries does not need to exist [4]. Hence, if a single witness with respect to a set of queries does not exist, we have to split the set and construct a witness for each subset.

Kupferman and Vardi [15] defined a witness formula in order to generate an interesting witness. It is easy to see that their construction works also for interesting strong vacuity witnesses based on our approach of temporal logic queries. Now, we define a generalization of their witness formula in order to generate an interesting vacuity witness concerning weak vacuity.

Definition 15 (Witness formula). *Let φ be a formula and Γ be a set of monotonic queries that annotate φ. Further, let $\mathcal{K}$ be a set of vacuity causes. Then the* weak Γ-vacuity witness formula *of φ with vacuity causes in $\mathcal{K}$ is given by*

$$witness_{weak}(\varphi, \Gamma, \mathcal{K}) \;=\; \varphi \wedge \bigwedge_{\substack{\gamma \in \Gamma, \varphi = \gamma[\psi] \\ \nu \in \max_{\Rightarrow}(\{\theta \in \mathcal{K}\,|\,\theta \Rightarrow \psi, \psi \not\Rightarrow \theta\})}} \neg\gamma[\nu].$$

The witness formula consists of a conjunction of the formula φ itself, because φ must be true on the witness, and of formulas that must not be true on the witness, namely formulas where the relevant subformulas ψ have been replaced by some stronger vacuity causes. The following theorem is an analogous result to Theorem 7 in [15].

---

[1] A restricted definition of an interesting witness is presented in [15] where only paths are considered to be simple enough to be interesting. However, there may exist simple witnesses (cf. tree-like counterexamples [9]) in cases where no path witnesses exist.

Theorem 3. *Let φ be a formula and Γ be a set of monotonic queries that annotate φ. Further, let $\mathcal{K}$ be a set of vacuity causes. Then a minimal (wrt. the pre-order on the models) counterexample of $\neg witness_{weak}(\varphi, \Gamma, \mathcal{K})$ in a model $\mathfrak{M}$ is an interesting weak Γ-vacuity witness of φ in $\mathfrak{M}$ with vacuity causes in $\mathcal{K}$.*

Example 6. Consider the Kripke structure $\mathfrak{M}$ shown in Figure 1 and the poset $\mathcal{K}$ of vacuity causes shown in Figure 2. In order to compare strong and weak vacuity witnesses, we need a formula that simultaneously does not hold strong and not weak vacuously in $\mathfrak{M}$ with vacuity causes in $\mathcal{K}$. From Example 5, we know that, e.g., $\mathbf{AXXX}\,q$ does not hold weak γ-vacuously (where $\gamma = \mathbf{AX}\,?$) and therefore not strong γ-vacuously. Thus, let $\varphi = \mathbf{AXXX}\,q$ be the formula for which we want to construct vacuity witnesses. Since we consider LTL formulas, counterexamples and vacuity witnesses are paths (cf. Beer et al. [4]). There exist three paths in $\mathfrak{M}$: $\pi_1 = s_0, s_1, s_2, s_6, s_4, \ldots$, $\pi_2 = s_0, s_1, s_3, s_2, s_6, s_4, \ldots$, and $\pi_3 = s_0, s_5, s_6, s_4, s_2, \ldots$. It is easy to see that all three paths are interesting strong γ-vacuity witnesses of φ in $\mathfrak{M}$, i.e., all three paths are minimal and $\pi_i \not\models \gamma[\bot]$ for all $1 \leq i \leq 3$. However, π_3 cannot be a weak γ-vacuity witness because $\pi_3 \models \gamma[\mathbf{G}\,q]$, i.e., there exists a formula stronger than $\mathbf{XX}\,q$ in $\mathcal{K}$ that is a solution to γ on π_3. More formally, π_3 does not be a counterexample to $\neg witness_{weak}(\varphi, \gamma, \mathcal{K})$ in $\mathfrak{M}$ (cf. Theorem 3), where $witness_{weak}(\varphi, \gamma, \mathcal{K}) = \varphi \wedge \neg \gamma[\mathbf{G}\,q]$. On the other hand, it is easy to see that π_1 and π_2 are interesting weak γ-vacuity witnesses of φ in $\mathfrak{M}$ with vacuity causes in $\mathcal{K}$.

The remaining question now is how to compute the set of minimal solutions or at least one minimal solution that satisfies the conditions of Theorem 2. Finding an appropriate solution (if it exists) in the set of minimal solutions is much simpler if there exists only one minimal solution, i.e., the least solution. Monotonic temporal logic queries that always have a least solution, are investigated in [7, 20, 21].

Although there exist algorithms in the literature for computing propositional solutions to temporal logic queries, to our knowledge there have been no investigations for finding arbitrary solutions because this is much harder. Note, however, that there are two aspects of query solving for vacuity detection which reduces its complexity: First, the set of solutions is restricted to formulas that are identified as vacuity causes, i.e., that are elements of $\mathcal{K}$. Second, it suffices to find a (minimal) solution that is *stronger than a given formula*. This constraints restrict the search space and therefore we believe that computing solutions for vacuity detection can be done more efficiently.

4   Query Solving Algorithms for Vacuity Detection

There exist several algorithms in the literature for computing propositional solutions to temporal logic queries. In this section, we review the different approaches and indicate how to extend them in order to get non-propositional solutions. For simplicity, we will focus on the case of local solutions, i.e., formulas with bounded nesting depth where the next operator is the only allowed temporal operator. It is then easy to see how extensions for arbitrary non-propositional solutions can be obtained. Note that throughout this section, we assume that the reader is somewhat familiar with the existing algorithms. For a detailed account, we refer to the corresponding papers in the literature.

The common basic principle of the query solving algorithms is to evaluate the query recursively on its syntactic structure. Thus, for our purposes it is sufficient to redefine the case for the placeholder. Let us first introduce some notation. Since local solutions consist of nested **AX** and **EX** operators, we define $\gamma_A = $ **AX**? and $\gamma_E = $ **EX**?. Moreover, for every query γ and every set of formulas Φ, we define $\gamma \circ \Phi = \bigwedge \{\gamma[\varphi] \mid \varphi \in \Phi\}$. For example, if $\gamma = $ **AX EX**? and $\Phi = \{p \wedge \neg q, $ **AF** $q\}$, then $\gamma \circ \Phi = \{$**AX EX** $(p \wedge \neg q) \wedge $ **AX EX AF** $q\}$.

Chan [7] investigated queries that always have a least solution, called *valid* queries[2]. He proved that deciding whether a given CTL query is valid is ExpTime-complete. Therefore, he presented a syntactic fragment of valid CTL queries and, based on the properties of these queries, he defined a symbolic mixed forward and backward traversal algorithm to solve them. The solution computed by this algorithm is a unique set of states in the model whose characteristic function is the least solution to the query.

Chan's symbolic algorithm does not lend itself naturally to the case of **EX**. Local solutions in his approach are therefore restricted to the operator **AX**. Chan's algorithm *solve* is modified in such a way that we add the maximum nesting depth n of local solutions as third argument. This number remains unchanged for all recursive calls except the case for the placeholder, which is redefined in the following way:

$$
\text{solve}(?, \mathcal{S}, n) = \begin{cases} \{\mathcal{S}\} & : \quad n - 0 \\ \text{solve}(?, \mathcal{S}, 0) \cup (\gamma_A \circ \text{solve}(\gamma_A, \mathcal{S}, n - 1)) & : \quad n > 0 \end{cases}
$$

Bruns and Godefroid [5] have shown how to solve queries of any temporal logic having a translation to alternating automata. The key idea of their approach is to generalize the transition function of alternating automata in such a way that disjunction and conjunction are replaced by special meet and join operations of a Boolean lattice of propositional formulas resp. solutions:

$$
\mathcal{A} \underline{\wedge} \mathcal{B} = \min_{\Rightarrow}(\{a \vee b \mid a \in \mathcal{A}, b \in \mathcal{B}\}) \quad \text{and} \quad \mathcal{A} \underline{\vee} \mathcal{B} = \min_{\Rightarrow}(\mathcal{A} \cup \mathcal{B})
$$

The resulting automata are called *extended alternating automata (EAA)*. To solve a query γ in a model $\mathfrak{M}$, the query has to be translated into an EAA $\mathfrak{A}_\gamma$ and the product automaton of $\mathfrak{A}_\gamma$ and $\mathfrak{M}$ has to be built. Each node of an accepting run of the product automaton is labeled with an element of the underlying lattice (i.e., a set of propositional formulas). It is shown that the maximum value labeling the root of an accepting run of the product automaton is the set of minimal solutions to γ in $\mathfrak{M}$. This maximum value is computed by simultaneously checking non-emptiness for every value of the underlying lattice.

For an extension to compute local solutions, the transition function has to be modified in such a way that we add the maximum nesting depth n of local solutions as fourth argument. Similar to Chan's algorithm, this number remains unchanged for all recursive calls except the case for the placeholder, which is redefined in the following way:

---

[2] Note that Chan's fragment was erroneous and has been corrected in [19, 20].

$$\rho(?, \mathcal{P}, k, n) = \left\{ \begin{array}{ll} \{\bigwedge\{p \mid p \in \mathcal{P}\} \wedge \bigwedge\{\neg p \mid p \in \mathcal{A} \setminus \mathcal{P}\}\} & : \quad n = 0 \\ \rho(?, \mathcal{P}, k, 0) \vee & \\ (\gamma_A \circ \rho(\gamma_A, \mathcal{P}, k, n-1)) \vee & : \quad n > 0 \\ (\gamma_E \circ \rho(\gamma_E, \mathcal{P}, k, n-1)) & \end{array} \right\}$$

Chechik, Devereux, and Gurfinkel [13, 8, 12] investigated CTL query solving by using their multi-valued model checker $\mathcal{X}$Chek. Multi-valued CTL model checking is based on two extensions of standard model checking: (1) The labeling function of Kripke structures allows a variable not only to be true or false at a particular state but to have a value of an underlying lattice. (2) The temporal logic CTL is extended to $\mathcal{X}$CTL in order to refer to such values within the formula. In the case of query solving, the lattice underlying the multi-valued model checking framework is based on propositional formulas. Query solving is then reduced to multi-valued model checking by translating a given query into a $\mathcal{X}$CTL formula such that the value of this formula in the model is the set of solutions to the query. In addition, this approach also allows to solve queries with multiple placeholders and mixed polarity.

In order to obtain more general solutions by modifying their algorithm, we need the set of all characteristic functions over the set of atomic propositions $\mathcal{A}$ defined by $\Phi = \{\bigwedge\{p \mid p \in \mathcal{P}\} \wedge \bigwedge\{\neg p \mid p \in \mathcal{A} \setminus \mathcal{P}\} \mid \mathcal{P} \subseteq \mathcal{A}\}$. Now, the semantics of queries has to be modified in such a way that we add the maximum nesting depth n of local solutions as argument. This number remains unchanged for all recursive definitions of the semantics except the case of the placeholder, which is redefined in the following way:

$$[\![?]\!]_n(s) = \left\{ \begin{array}{ll} \{\bigsqcup_{\varphi \in \Phi}([\![\varphi]\!](s) \sqcap \uparrow\{\varphi\})\} & : \quad n = 0 \\ [\![?]\!]_0(s) \sqcup (\gamma_A \circ [\![\gamma_A]\!]_{n-1}(s)) \sqcup (\gamma_E \circ [\![\gamma_E]\!]_{n-1}(s)) & : \quad n > 0 \end{array} \right.$$

Hornus and Schnoebelen [14] dealt with query solving for arbitrary fragments of CTL*. They have shown that deciding whether there exists a single minimal solution in a *fixed* model and computing this solution can be reduced to a linear number (in the size of the model) of model checking calls. Moreover, they have shown that a second minimal solution can be reduced to a quadratic number, a third minimal solution to a cubic number, etc. of model checking calls. Concerning the number of minimal solutions to CTL queries, they proved that deciding whether there exist at least k (in unary) minimal solutions is NP-complete and counting the number of minimal solutions is $\sharp$P-complete.

In short, in order to compute the set of minimal solutions to a query γ, they define a formula φ and check whether $\gamma[\varphi]$ holds in the model. Then φ is modified and $\gamma[\varphi]$ is checked again. This procedure is repeated until φ is identified to be a new minimal solution. Although their approach can also be extended in order to compute non-propositional solutions, we will not describe such an extension due to space restrictions.

5   Related Work

To our best knowledge the first paper in which automatic vacuity detection has been investigated was Beer et al. [3]. They restricted their considerations to the syntactic class w-ACTL of witnessable ACTL formulas. In addition to vacuity detection, they have shown how to generate non-vacuity witnesses for w-ACTL.

Kupferman and Vardi [15] noticed that every occurrence of a subformula of a CTL* formula φ occurs either positive (i.e., under an even number of negations) or negative (i.e., under an odd number of negations) in φ. Together with their restriction to detect vacuity with respect to *occurrences* of subformulas, this allowed them to reduce vacuity detection to model checking. They have also shown how to generate non-vacuity witnesses if the formula is linear witnessable. Beer et al. [4] generalized this approach to vacuity detection in any logic with polarity (i.e., every subformula occurs either positive or negative) and to witness construction in any logic with a pre-order on the models. Several kinds of vacuity semantics (formula semantics, structure semantics, trace semantics) have been investigated by Armoni et al. [1]. It is shown that these semantics are equivalent for vacuity with respect to subformulas of pure (i.e., either positive or negative) polarity. Gurfinkel and Chechik [11] dealt with four-valued vacuity (vacuously true, non-vacuously true, non-vacuously false, vacuously false) and with mutual influence of subformulas when checking vacuity with respect several subformulas simultaneously ("mutual vacuity"). Moreover, in [10] they studied generalizations of the vacuity semantics of Armoni et al. [1]. Recently, Bustan et al. [6] investigated acuity detection in the logic RELTL, an extension of LTL by a regular layer. They defined a formula to be regularly vacuous if there exists a regular subexpression e such that the resulting formula after replacing e by a universal quantified second order interval variable remains true. Analogous to [15], if the subexpression has pure polarity, then regular vacuity detection can be reduced to regular model checking.

6 Conclusion

In this paper we have introduced the notion of weak vacuity which is parameterized by a class of vacuity causes. Based on a close connection to temporal logic queries, we have shown how existing query solving algorithms can be extended and applied for vacuity detection. The extended algorithms are of course not only applicable in the context of vacuity detection. As the current work has focused on methodological and algorithmic questions involving vacuity, this work is naturally continued by practical experiments.

References

1. Roy Armoni, Limor Fix, Alon Flaisher, Orna Grumberg, Nir Piterman, Andreas Tiemeyer, and Moshe Y. Vardi. Enhanced vacuity detection in linear temporal logic. In *Proceedings of the 15th International Conference on Computer Aided Verification (CAV)*, volume 2725 of *Lecture Notes in Computer Science*, pages 368–380. Springer-Verlag, 2003.
2. Derek L. Beatty and Randal E. Bryant. Formally verifying a microprocessor using a simulation methodology. In *Proceedings of the 31st Annual ACM/IEEE Design Automation Conference (DAC)*, pages 596–602. ACM Press, 1994.
3. Ilan Beer, Shoham Ben-David, Cindy Eisner, and Yoav Rodeh. Efficient detection of vacuity in ACTL formulas. In *Proceedings of the 9th International Conference on Computer Aided Verification (CAV)*, volume 1254 of *Lecture Notes in Computer Science*, pages 279–290. Springer-Verlag, 1997.

4. Ilan Beer, Shoham Ben-David, Cindy Eisner, and Yoav Rodeh. Efficient detection of vacuity in temporal model checking. *Formal Methods in System Design*, 18(2):141–163, 2001.
5. Glenn Bruns and Patrice Godefroid. Temporal logic query checking. In *Proceedings of the 16th Annual IEEE Symposium on Logic in Computer Science (LICS)*, pages 409–417. IEEE Computer Society, 2001.
6. Doron Bustan, Alon Flaisher, Orna Grumberg, Orna Kupferman, and Moshe Y. Vardi. Regular vacuity. Submitted for publication.
7. William Chan. Temporal-logic queries. In *Proceedings of the 12th International Conference on Computer Aided Verification (CAV)*, volume 1855 of *Lecture Notes in Computer Science*, pages 450–463. Springer-Verlag, 2000.
8. Marsha Chechik and Arie Gurfinkel. TLQSolver: A temporal logic query checker. In *Proceedings of the 15th International Conference on Computer Aided Verification (CAV)*, volume 2725 of *Lecture Notes in Computer Science*, pages 210–214. Springer-Verlag, 2003.
9. Edmund M. Clarke, Somesh Jha, Yuan Lu, and Helmut Veith. Tree-like counterexamples in model checking. In *Proceedings of the 17th Annual IEEE Symposium on Logic in Computer Science (LICS)*, pages 19–29. IEEE Computer Society, 2002.
10. Arie Gurfinkel and Marsha Chechik. Extending extended vacuity. In *Proceedings of the 5th International Conference on Formal Methods in Computer-Aided Design (FMCAD)*, Lecture Notes in Computer Science. Springer-Verlag, 2004. To appear.
11. Arie Gurfinkel and Marsha Chechik. How vacuous is vacuous? In *Proceedings of the 10th International Conference on Tools and Algorithms for the Construction and Analysis of Systems (TACAS)*, volume 2988 of *Lecture Notes in Computer Science*, pages 451–466. Springer-Verlag, 2004.
12. Arie Gurfinkel, Marsha Chechik, and Benet Devereux. Temporal logic query checking: A tool for model exploration. *IEEE Transactions on Software Engineering*, 29(10):898–914, 2003.
13. Arie Gurfinkel, Benet Devereux, and Marsha Chechik. Model exploration with temporal logic query checking. In *Proceedings of the 10th ACM SIGSOFT Symposium on Foundations of Software Engineering (FSE)*, pages 139–148. ACM Press, 2002.
14. Samuel Hornus and Philippe Schnoebelen. On solving temporal logic queries. In *Proceedings of the 9th International Conference on Algebraic Methodology and Software Technology (AMAST)*, volume 2422 of *Lecture Notes in Computer Science*, pages 163–177. Springer-Verlag, 2002.
15. Orna Kupferman and Moshe Y. Vardi. Vacuity detection in temporal model checking. In *Proceedings of the 10th Advanced Research Working Conference on Correct Hardware Design and Verification Methods (CHARME)*, volume 1703 of *Lecture Notes in Computer Science*, pages 82–96. Springer-Verlag, 1999. Journal version available as [16].
16. Orna Kupferman and Moshe Y. Vardi. Vacuity detection in temporal model checking. *International Journal on Software Tools for Technology Transfer (STTT)*, 4(2):224–233, 2003.
17. Amir Pnueli. 9th International Conference on Computer Aided Verification (CAV), 1997. Question from the audience (cited from [4]).
18. Marko Samer. PhD thesis, Vienna University of Technology. In preparation.
19. Marko Samer. Temporal logic queries in model checking. Master's thesis, Vienna University of Technology, May 2002.
20. Marko Samer and Helmut Veith. Validity of CTL queries revisited. In *Proceedings of the 12th Annual Conference of the European Association for Computer Science Logic (CSL)*, volume 2803 of *Lecture Notes in Computer Science*, pages 470–483. Springer-Verlag, 2003.
21. Marko Samer and Helmut Veith. A syntactic characterization of distributive LTL queries. In *Proceedings of the 31st International Colloquium on Automata, Languages and Programming (ICALP)*, volume 3142 of *Lecture Notes in Computer Science*, pages 1099–1110. Springer-Verlag, 2004.

An Operational Semantics for Weak PSL

Koen Claessen[1] and Johan Mårtensson[2]

[1] Chalmers University of Technology
koen@cs.chalmers.se
[2] Safelogic AB and Göteborg University
johan@safelogic.se

Abstract. Extending linear temporal logic by adding regular expressions increases its expressiveness. However, as for example, problems in recent versions of Accellera's Property Specification Language (PSL) as well as in OpenVera's ForSpec and other property languages show, it is a non-trivial task to give a formal denotational semantics with desirable properties to the resulting logic. In this paper, we argue that specifying an *operational semantics* may be helpful in guiding this work, and as a bonus leads to an implementation of the logic for free. We give a concrete operational semantics for *Weak PSL*, which is the safety property subset of PSL. We also propose a denotational semantics which we show to be equivalent to the operational one. This semantics is inspired by a new denotational semantics proposed in recent related work.

1 Introduction

Accellera and PSL. Accellera [1] is an organization supported by major actors in the electronic design industry with the objective to promote the use of standards in this industry. In spring 2003, a standard property specification language for hardware designs was agreed upon, PSL 1.0 [2]. The standard defines the syntax and semantics of PSL formally. A new version of the language, PSL 1.1 [3] was finalized in spring 2004.

The logical core of PSL consists of standard Linear Temporal Logic (LTL) constructs augmented with regular expressions and aborts. Thus, PSL contains the notion of *formula*, which is an entity of extended LTL that can be satisfied by an infinite sequence of letters, and the notion of *expression*, which is a regular expression that can only be satisfied by a finite sequence of letters. A letter simply defines the values of all variables at one point in time.

Expressions can be converted into formulas, by using, for example, the *weak embedding* of an expression r, written $\{r\}$ in PSL 1.1 syntax. In both PSL 1.0 and 1.1, a sequence s of letters makes $\{r\}$ true, if there is a finite prefix of s that satisfies r or all finite prefixes of s can be extended to satisfy r. However, the nature of this extension is different in the two PSL versions, which accounts for differences mentioned below.

Further, the semantics of PSL has to cope with the fact that properties are supposed to be used both in *static verification* – checking that a property

A.J. Hu and A.K. Martin (Eds.): FMCAD 2004, LNCS 3312, pp. 337–351, 2004.

holds solely by analyzing the design – and in *dynamic verification* – checking that a property holds for a concrete and finite trace of the design. To deal with dynamic verification, satisfiability is extended to finite (*truncated*) sequences even for formulas [7, 8].

Anomalies. The semantics of both PSL 1.0 and 1.1 are given by means of denotational semantics. One problem with this approach is that for some constructs it may be far from obvious what definition should be chosen. Making a seemingly intuitively correct decision can lead to undesirable properties of the resulting logic.

For example in PSL 1.0 the formula[1] $\{[*]; a\}$, which is the weak embedding of an expression that is satisfied by any sequence ending with the atom a, is satisfied by any sequence that makes a always false. However, the formula $\{[*]; F\}$ (where we have simply replaced a by the false constant F) is not satisfied by any sequence. Thus, $\{[*]; F\}$ is not satisfied even if it is aborted at the first time instance. This issue is discussed in for example [7, 4].

In response to this, Accellera has developed a different semantical paradigm that is used in the current iteration, PSL 1.1. In this semantics, the notion of model is changed by introducing a new semantical concept; a special letter $\top$ that can satisfy any one-letter expression, regardless if it is contradictory or not. Unfortunately, PSL 1.1 suffers from a similar anomaly: F and $\{a\&\&\{a; a\}\}$ (a so-called *structural contradiction*) are equivalent in an intuitive sense (neither can be satisfied on actual runs of a system), but are not interchangeable in formulas. Thus $\{[*]; F\}$ is satisfied if it is aborted at the first time instance whereas $\{[*]; \{a\&\&\{a; a\}\}\}$ is not. This peculiarity is not specific to PSL; it is for example also present in ForSpec's reset semantics.

There is work underway within Accellera to deal with this anomaly either by discouraging the use of particular "degenerate formulas" (e.g. those containing structural contradictions), thus excluding the ones that are not well-behaved in this respect, or by extending the model concept further to include models on which structural contradictions are satisfied.

Operational Semantics. The company Safelogic develops tools for static and dynamic verification of PSL properties of hardware designs. When implementing our tools, we faced two problems. Firstly, particular simplification rules we expected to hold in the logic actually did not hold and could thus not be used. Secondly, in the denotational semantics definitions there is no indication as how to implement checkers and verifiers for PSL properties.

Our approach was to define a *structural operational semantics* for the subset of PSL we considered. This subset is precisely the subset of PSL in which safety properties can be expressed. The operational semantics is a small-step letter-by-letter semantics with judgments of the form $\phi \overset{\ell}{\to} \psi$. The intention is that in order to check if a sequence s starting with the letter ℓ satisfies ϕ, we simply check that the tail of s (without ℓ) satisfies ψ, and so on.

---

[1] In PSL 1.0 weak embedding does occur but not in the form of independent formulas. This difference to PSL 1.1 is irrelevant to the present point, so we ignore it for the sake of simplicity of presentation.

There are two advantages of this approach. (1) The operational semantics can directly be used for implementing dynamic verification of properties, and also forms the basis of the implementation of our static verification engine. (2) When specifying a structural operational semantics, there are far less choices to be made than in a denotational semantics, so there is less room for mistakes.

In a recent related work a new denotational semantics for LTL with regular expressions on truncated words has been investigated [8]. This semantics can be extended to a full PSL semantics that fixes the anomalies in the semantics of PSL 1.0 and 1.1 [10]. We have shown that our operational semantics is sound and complete on the weak fragment of PSL with respect to such an extension of this denotational semantics to full PSL. Hopefully, the next iteration of PSL will adopt a denotational semantics with this property!

This Paper. The rest of this paper is organized as follows. In Section 2, we specify a safety property subset of PSL. In Section 3, we define a structural operational semantics for this language. In Section 4, we present a denotational semantics for our subset of PSL, corresponding to [8, 10]. In Section 5, we show lemmas relating the two semantics, and state soundness and completeness of our operational semantics. Section 6 concludes.

2   Weak Property Language

In this section, we identify a subset of PSL, called Weak Property Language (WPL). This subset can only be used to write safety properties. As is done in the PSL Language Reference Manuals [2, 3], we start by assuming a non-empty set P of *atomic propositions*, and a set of boolean expressions B over P. We assume two designated boolean expressions **true**, **false** belonging to B.

We start by defining regular expressions, which then provide the base case in the definition of full WPL.

Definition 1 (RE). *If $b \in B$, the language of regular expressions (REs) r has the following grammar:*

$$r ::= \perp \mid \varepsilon \mid b \mid r_1; r_2 \mid r_1|r_2 \mid r_1 \&\& r_2 \mid r^*.$$

The expression $\perp$ denotes the expression with the empty language, ε is the expression that only contains the empty word (see Section 4.4 for an explanation of why those expressions not present in [2, 3] were introduced), $r_1; r_2$ stands for sequential composition between r_1 and r_2, $r_1|r_2$ stands for choice, $r_1 \&\& r_2$ stands for intersection, r^* is the Kleene star.

Now we are in a position to define full WPL.

Definition 2 (WPL). *If r, r_1 and r_2 are REs, and b a boolean expression, the language of WPL formulas ϕ and ψ has the following grammar:*

$$\phi, \psi ::= \{r\} \mid \phi_1 \wedge \phi_2 \mid \phi_1 \vee \phi_2 \mid X\phi \mid \phi_1 W \phi_2 \mid r \mapsto \phi \mid \phi \, \mathbf{abort} \, b.$$

The formula $\{r\}$ is the weak embedding of the expression r, $\phi_1 \wedge \phi_2$ is formula conjunction, $\phi_1 \vee \phi_2$ is formula disjunction, $X\phi$ is the next operator, $\phi_1 W \phi_2$ is the weak until operator, $r \mapsto \phi$ is suffix implication, and $\phi \, \mathbf{abort} \, b$ is the abort operator. The logical negation operator $\neg$ only appears at the boolean level, and not at the formula level, because that would enable the creation of non-safety formulas.

Suffix implication $r \mapsto \phi$ is satisfied by a word if whenever r accepts a prefix of the word, the formula ϕ holds on the rest of that word. The formula $\phi \, \mathbf{abort} \, b$ is satisfied by a word if ϕ is not made false by that word before b holds. A formal definition of these constructs is given in Section 3 by means of an operational semantics, and in Section 4 by means of a denotational semantics.

For reasons of simplicity we have omitted the treatment of the overlapping operators : and $\mapsto$. The semantic definitions for those operators (See [6, 10]) are very similar to those for ; and $\mapsto$.

3 A Structural Operational Semantics for WPL

It is customary to give semantics to temporal logics using sequences of states, where each state contains information about the truth-values of all atoms. In the PSL formal semantics [2, 3], a state is called a *letter*, written ℓ, and sequences of states are called *words*. The set of all letters is written Σ. The details of letters are not important here. However, we assume that there is a satisfaction relation $\Vdash$ between states Σ and boolean expressions B, such that for all letters $\ell \in \Sigma$, $\ell \Vdash \mathbf{true}$ and $\ell \nVdash \mathbf{false}$.

In this section, we present a structural operational semantics for WPL. Our operational semantics is inspired by Brzozowski's derivatives of regular expressions [5]. We use judgments of the form

$$\phi \xrightarrow{\ell} \psi.$$

The intuition behind such a judgment is that in order to check if a word starting with the letter ℓ satisfies ϕ, one can just as well check that ψ is satisfied by the word without the first letter. So, for a finite word $w = (\ell_0, \ell_2, \ldots, \ell_n)$, we can check if w satisfies ϕ by finding $\phi_0 \ldots \phi_n$ such that

$$\phi \xrightarrow{\ell_0} \phi_0 \xrightarrow{\ell_1} \phi_1 \ldots \xrightarrow{\ell_n} \phi_n,$$

and check that none of ϕ_i is false. We will be more formal about this later.

3.1 Letters and Words

We define the following preliminaries. A *word* is a finite or infinite sequence of letters from Σ. We use ϵ to denote the empty word. We use juxtaposition to denote concatenation, i.e. if $w = (\ell_0, \ldots, \ell_n)$ and $v = (\ell'_0, \ldots (, \ell'_n))$ then $wv = (\ell_0, \ldots, \ell_n, \ell'_0, \ldots (, \ell'_n))$. If w is infinite then wv is w. We observe that concatenation is associative, i.e. $w(vu) = (wv)u$ for all w, v and u, and ϵ is the identity, i.e. $\epsilon w = w\epsilon = w$ for all w. We will use ℓ both for denoting the letter ℓ and the word consisting of the single letter ℓ.

Word indexing is defined as follows. If $i < |w|$ then w^i is the $i + 1^{st}$ letter of w and $w^{i\cdots}$ is the suffix of w starting at i. If $i \geq |w|$ then $w^{i\cdots} = \epsilon$. If $k \leq j < |w|$, then $w^{k\cdots j}$ means $(w^k, \ldots, w^j)$. If $j < k < |w|$, then $w^{k\cdots j}$ is ϵ.

We use $v \leq w$ and 'v is a *prefix* of w' to say that there is a u such that $vu = w$ and $v < w$ to say that $v \leq w$ and $v \neq w$.

3.2   Operational Rules for RE

We start by giving rules for the basic REs. A boolean expression b accepts a letter ℓ only if ℓ satisfies b. In that case, the remaining expression is the empty word. Falsity and the empty word accept no letters.

$$\text{(Bool)} \qquad b \xrightarrow{\ell} \begin{cases} \varepsilon & \text{if } \ell \Vdash b \\ \bot & \text{otherwise} \end{cases}$$

$$\text{(Bot)} \qquad \bot \xrightarrow{\ell} \bot$$

$$\text{(Empty)} \qquad \varepsilon \xrightarrow{\ell} \bot$$

For sequential composition $r_1; r_2$, we use two rules. If r_1 cannot accept the empty word, r_2 will not be touched. However, if r_1 can accept the empty word, we need to consider the case that r_2 accepts ℓ as well. Thus, we need a function em that calculates if a given RE can accept the empty word or not.

Definition 3. *We define (inductively) for REs:*

$$\text{em}(\bot) = \textbf{false}$$
$$\text{em}(\varepsilon) = \textbf{true}$$
$$\text{em}(b) = \textbf{false}$$
$$\text{em}(r_1; r_2) = \text{em}(r_1) \textbf{ and } \text{em}(r_2)$$
$$\text{em}(r_1 | r_2) = \text{em}(r_1) \textbf{ or } \text{em}(r_2)$$
$$\text{em}(r_1 \&\& r_2) = \text{em}(r_1) \textbf{ and } \text{em}(r_2)$$
$$\text{em}(r^*) = \textbf{true}$$

The rules for sequential composition then look as follows.

$$\text{(Seq1)} \qquad \frac{r_1 \xrightarrow{\ell} r_1'}{r_1; r_2 \xrightarrow{\ell} r_1'; r_2} \quad \text{not em}(r_1)$$

$$\text{(Seq2)} \qquad \frac{r_1 \xrightarrow{\ell} r_1' \quad r_2 \xrightarrow{\ell} r_2'}{r_1; r_2 \xrightarrow{\ell} (r_1'; r_2) | r_2'} \quad \text{em}(r_1)$$

The rules for choice and intersection simply apply the rules to both of the operands.

$$(\textsc{ReOr}) \qquad \frac{r_1 \xrightarrow{\ell} r_1' \quad r_2 \xrightarrow{\ell} r_2'}{r_1 | r_2 \xrightarrow{\ell} r_1' | r_2'}$$

$$(\textsc{ReAnd}) \qquad \frac{r_1 \xrightarrow{\ell} r_1' \quad r_2 \xrightarrow{\ell} r_2'}{r_1 \&\& r_2 \xrightarrow{\ell} r_1' \&\& r_2'}$$

And finally, for a Kleene star r^* to accept a letter, the expression r must be able to accept the letter.

$$(\textsc{Star}) \qquad \frac{r \xrightarrow{\ell} r'}{r^* \xrightarrow{\ell} r'; r^*}$$

3.3   Operational Rules for WPL

Weak embedding of expressions simply parses the ℓ through the expression until what is left of the expression can accept the empty word.

$$(\textsc{Re}1) \qquad \frac{r \xrightarrow{\ell} r'}{\{r\} \xrightarrow{\ell} \{r'\}} \quad \text{not } \mathsf{em}(r)$$

$$(\textsc{Re}2) \qquad \{r\} \xrightarrow{\ell} \{\mathbf{true}^*\} \quad \mathsf{em}(r)$$

Here, we use the formula $\{\mathbf{true}^*\}$ since it accepts every word.

Formula disjunction and conjunction are identical to their regular expression counterparts.

$$(\textsc{WplOr}) \qquad \frac{\phi_1 \xrightarrow{\ell} \phi_1' \quad \phi_2 \xrightarrow{\ell} \phi_2'}{\phi_1 \vee \phi_2 \xrightarrow{\ell} \phi_1' \vee \phi_2'}$$

$$(\textsc{WplAnd}) \qquad \frac{\phi_1 \xrightarrow{\ell} \phi_1' \quad \phi_2 \xrightarrow{\ell} \phi_2'}{\phi_1 \wedge \phi_2 \xrightarrow{\ell} \phi_1' \wedge \phi_2'}$$

The rule for next simply drops the next operator.

$$(\textsc{Next}) \qquad X\phi \xrightarrow{\ell} \phi$$

The rule for weak until is directly derived from the fact that weak until is a solution of the following equation: $\phi_1 W \phi_2 = \phi_2 \vee (\phi_1 \wedge X(\phi_1 W \phi_2))$.

$$(\textsc{Until}) \qquad \frac{\phi_1 \xrightarrow{\ell} \phi_1' \quad \phi_2 \xrightarrow{\ell} \phi_2'}{\phi_1 W \phi_2 \xrightarrow{\ell} \phi_2' \vee (\phi_1' \wedge (\phi_1 W \phi_2))}$$

For suffix implication, there are two rules: one that triggers the formula ϕ to be true when r accepts the empty word, and one that does not trigger ϕ. One can see these rules as dual to the rules for sequential composition.

$$(\text{S\textsc{i}1}) \qquad \frac{r \xrightarrow{\ell} r'}{r \Mapsto \phi \xrightarrow{\ell} r' \Mapsto \phi} \quad \text{not } em(r)$$

$$(\text{S\textsc{i}2}) \qquad \frac{r \xrightarrow{\ell} r' \quad \phi \xrightarrow{\ell} \phi'}{r \Mapsto \phi \xrightarrow{\ell} (r' \Mapsto \phi) \wedge \phi'} \quad em(r)$$

Finally, an abort checks its formula until the boolean becomes true. So, when checking $\phi\,\textbf{abort}\,b$ with respect to ℓ we first check whether ϕ is already contradicted. If not and b is satisfied by ℓ then we abort the checking of $\phi\,\textbf{abort}\,b$ by accepting. If b is not satisfied by ℓ or ϕ is contradicted already then we do not abort.

$$(\text{A\textsc{bort}1}) \qquad \frac{\phi \xrightarrow{\ell} \phi'}{\phi\,\textbf{abort}\,b \xrightarrow{\ell} \phi'\,\textbf{abort}\,b} \quad \text{not } ok(\phi) \text{ or } \ell \not\Vdash b$$

$$(\text{A\textsc{bort}2}) \qquad \phi\,\textbf{abort}\,b \xrightarrow{\ell} \{\textbf{true}^*\} \quad ok(\phi) \text{ and } \ell \Vdash b$$

In order to calculate if a regular expression or formula has been contradicted, we use the function ok, which is to be defined in the next section.

This concludes the operational rules for WPL. As standard, we define $\rightarrow$ to be the least relation satisfying the above operational rules. However, it is easy to see that $\rightarrow$ actually is a total function from formulas and letters to formulas.

3.4 Not Yet Contradicted

Here, we define the function ok that calculates whether a given regular expression or formula has been contradicted yet, w.r.t. the sequence of letters that has already been visited. An expression or formula is said to be ok when it has not yet been contradicted in this sense. For basic regular expressions, only $\perp$ is not ok. For composite expressions and formulas, this information is simply propagated.

Definition 4. *We define (inductively) for REs and WPLs:*

$$\begin{aligned}
ok(\perp) &= \textbf{false} & ok(\{r\}) &= ok(r) \\
ok(\varepsilon) &= \textbf{true} & ok(\phi_1 \wedge \phi_2) &= ok(\phi_1) \textbf{ and } ok(\phi_2) \\
ok(b) &= \textbf{true} & ok(\phi_1 \vee \phi_2) &= ok(\phi_1) \textbf{ or } ok(\phi_2) \\
ok(r_1; r_2) &= ok(r_1) & ok(X\phi) &= \textbf{true} \\
ok(r_1 | r_2) &= ok(r_1) \textbf{ or } ok(r_2) & ok(\phi_1 W \phi_2) &= ok(\phi_1) \textbf{ or } ok(\phi_2) \\
ok(r_1 \&\& r_2) &= ok(r_1) \textbf{ and } ok(r_2) & ok(r \Mapsto \phi) &= \textbf{true} \\
ok(r^*) &= \textbf{true} & ok(\phi\,\textbf{abort}\,b) &= ok(\phi)
\end{aligned}$$

Finally, we make the following observation, which is that any regular expression accepting the empty string is an ok expression.

Lemma 1 (Empty is OK). *For all REs r,* $\mathsf{em}(r) \Rightarrow \mathsf{ok}(r)$.

The function ok is used in the operational rules for **abort**, but also in the definition of the operational semantics.

3.5   The Operational Semantics

As we have seen in the informal explanation of the operational rules, we are interested in the result of applying the rules above iteratively to formulas with respect to words from the alphabet Σ. This is possible to do since the rules presented above are deterministic; given a formula ϕ and a letter ℓ, there is a unique formula ϕ' such that $\phi \xrightarrow{\ell} \phi'$. Thus, the relation $\xrightarrow{\ell}$ is a total function.

Iteratively applying the operational rules on a formula ϕ over the letters of a word w is written $\phi\langle w \rangle$:

Definition 5 (After a Word). *For a RE or WPL p and a finite word w, we (inductively) define* $p\langle w \rangle$ *as follows:*

$$p\langle \epsilon \rangle = p,$$
$$p\langle \ell w \rangle = p'\langle w \rangle, \ where \ p \xrightarrow{\ell} p'.$$

Now we are ready to define what it means for a formula to be true according to the operational semantics, denoted by $\vdash$.

Definition 6 (The Operational Semantics). *For all WPLs and REs p, and all words w we define*

$$w \vdash p \ \Leftrightarrow \ for \ all \ finite \ v \ such \ that \ v \le w, \mathsf{ok}(p\langle v \rangle).$$

Intuitively, this means that a word w makes a formula ϕ true if and only if iteratively applying the operational semantics on ϕ using w only produces ok formulas.

We observe the following useful lemma, which says that if an expression of formula is not ok, it will stay not ok even after applying it to a word.

Lemma 2 (Conservation of Misery). *For all WPLs and REs p, we have*

$$\neg\,\mathsf{ok}(p) \Rightarrow \ for \ all \ finite \ u, \ \neg\,\mathsf{ok}(p\langle u \rangle).$$

It immediately follows, that for finite words w, in order to decide if $w \vdash p$, it suffices to check the final result $p\langle w \rangle$.

Lemma 3. *For all WPLs and REs p, if w is finite*

$$w \vdash p \ \Leftrightarrow \ \mathsf{ok}(p\langle w \rangle).$$

Since all functions involved in the above are computable, this gives us a simple procedure for checking if a finite word satisfies a formula according to the operational semantics.

Note that the operational semantics presented above does not have the anomaly described in the introduction. For example, we have, for all words w, that $w \vdash \{\mathbf{true}^*; (a\&\&(a; a))\}$. To see this, observe that, for any ℓ, $\{\mathbf{true}^*; (a\&\&(a; a))\} \overset{\ell}{\to} \{(\mathbf{true}^*; (a\&\&(a; a)))|r\}$, for some r. Thus, the ok-ness of the formula is not affected by accepting any finite word.

3.6   Properties of the Operational Semantics

We observe the following interesting properties of the operational semantics and iterated application of the operational rules. These lemmas are key steps in the correctness proofs for the completeness and soundness theorems in Sections 5.2 and 5.3. Apart from this, the details of this section are not important for the remainder of the paper.

We start with some observations related to applying an expression or formula to a word.

Lemma 4. *For all REs and WPLs p, all letters ℓ, and all finite words w and v, we have*

$$p\langle w \rangle \langle v \rangle = p\langle wv \rangle,$$

$$p \overset{\ell}{\to} p\langle \ell \rangle,$$

$$p\langle w \rangle \overset{\ell}{\to} p\langle w\ell \rangle.$$

The second observation we make is that applying a word preserves disjunctions and conjunctions.

Lemma 5 (Preservation of Disjuncts and Conjuncts). *For all finite words w, for WPLs ϕ and ψ, and for REs r_1 and r_2,*

$$(\phi \vee \psi)\langle w \rangle = \phi\langle w \rangle \vee \psi\langle w \rangle$$
$$(\phi \wedge \psi)\langle w \rangle = \phi\langle w \rangle \wedge \psi\langle w \rangle$$
$$(r_1|r_2)\langle w \rangle = r_1\langle w \rangle \mid r_2\langle w \rangle$$
$$(r_1\&\&r_2)\langle w \rangle = r_1\langle w \rangle \ \&\& \ r_2\langle w \rangle$$

Finally, a direct consequence of the above lemma and Lemma 2 is that disjunction and conjunction are compositional w.r.t. the operational semantics.

Lemma 6 (Operational Compositionality). *For all finite words w, for WPLs ϕ and ψ, and for REs r_1 and r_2,*

$$w \vdash \phi \vee \psi \Leftrightarrow w \vdash \phi \ or \ w \vdash \psi$$
$$w \vdash \phi \wedge \psi \Leftrightarrow w \vdash \phi \ and \ w \vdash \psi$$
$$w \vdash r_1|r_2 \Leftrightarrow w \vdash r_1 \ or \ w \vdash r_2$$
$$w \vdash r_1\&\&r_2 \Leftrightarrow w \vdash r_1 \ and \ w \vdash r_2$$

4 Denotational Semantics

Alternatively, we can define a denotational semantics for WPL. The following definitions are inspired by a related not yet published work [8]. In Section 4.4 we briefly describe the relation between this semantics and the official PSL 1.1 one.

4.1 Weak and Neutral Words

We have noted that for all finite w and all REs r, $w \vdash \mathbf{true}*; r$. It doesn't matter whether r is satisfiable or not. We want the denotational semantics to mirror this. So our definition must provide a kind of partial matching where the word w is only required to match "the beginning" of the RE r, mirroring the way in which an RE is true according to the operational semantics if it is not yet contradicted when the word finishes.

To accomplish this we introduce in addition to the usual *neutral* words also *weak* words.

Let N denote the set of finite and infinite words over Σ, and $N^f \subset N$ the set of finite words over Σ. The elements of N are called *neutral words*. Let $W = \{u^- | u \in N^f\}$. We assume that W and N are disjunct and that the mapping $(-)^-$ is injective. Whenever the notation u^- is used, it is understood that $u \in N^f$. The elements of W are called *weak words*. Note in particular that $\epsilon^- \in W$.

Let $A = N \cup W$, and define concatenation in A as follows. For all $u, v \in N$, uv is equal to the concatenation in N, and if u is finite then $u(v^-) = (uv)^-$. For all $u, v \in A$, if u is infinite or $u \in W$ then $uv = u$. With this definition concatenation in A is associative and ϵ is the unique identity element. Define the length of an element w in N as the number of letters in w if w is finite and ω otherwise, and in A according to $|u^-| = |u|$ for all $u \in N^f$.

Word indexing in A is defined as follows. For $i < |w|$, $(w^-)^i = w^i$. We let $(w^-)^{i\cdots} = (w^{i\cdots})^-$. We also let $(w^-)^{k\cdots j} = w^{k\cdots j}$ for $j, k < |w|$.

4.2 Tight Satisfaction

We start by giving a definition of *tight satisfaction* $\models$. Tight satisfaction relates finite words from A to REs. A finite neutral word intuitively tightly satisfies a regular expression if the word completely matches the expression. A finite weak word intuitively tightly satisfies a regular expression if the process of matching the word (from left to right) does not contradict the expression.

Definition 7. *Let r, r_1 and r_2 denote REs, b a boolean, and $w, w_1, \ldots, w_j$ words in A. We define inductively:*

$$w \not\models \bot$$

$$w \models b \qquad\qquad \Leftrightarrow either\ w = \epsilon^-,\ or\ |w| = 1\ and\ w^0 \Vdash b$$

$$w \models r_1; r_2 \qquad \Leftrightarrow there\ are\ w_1, w_2\ such\ that\ w = w_1 w_2\ and\ w_1 \models r_1\ and\ w_2 \models r_2$$

$$w \models r_1 | r_2 \qquad \Leftrightarrow w \models r_1\ or\ w \models r_2$$

$$w \models r_1 \&\& r_2 \Leftrightarrow w \models r_1\ and\ w \models r_2$$

$$w \models r^* \qquad\qquad \Leftrightarrow either\ w = \epsilon,\ or$$
$$there\ exists\ w_1, w_2, \ldots, w_j\ such\ that\ w = w_1 w_2 \cdots w_j$$
$$and\ for\ all\ i\ such\ that\ 1 \le i \le j, w_i \models r$$

$$w \models \varepsilon \qquad\qquad \Leftrightarrow w \models \mathbf{false}^*$$

We note the following lemmas.

Lemma 7. *For all REs r that do not syntactically contain $\bot$ as a subexpression, we have that $\epsilon^- \models r$.*

Lemma 8. *For all REs r and $v, w \in A$ such that $v \le w$, we have that $w \models r \Rightarrow v\epsilon^- \models r$.*

4.3   Formula Satisfaction

We now define *formula satisfaction* $\models$. Formula satisfaction relates words from N to WPLs, and defines when a finite or infinite word satisfies a formula. A word intuitively satisfies a formula if the process of accepting the word does not contradict the formula.

Definition 8. *Let ϕ and ψ denote WPLs, b a boolean, r an RE, and w, u, v etc. words in N. We define inductively:*

$$w \models \{r\} \qquad \Leftrightarrow for\ all\ finite\ v \le w\ there\ is\ u \le v^-,\ such\ that\ u \models r$$

$$w \models \phi \wedge \psi \qquad \Leftrightarrow w \models \phi\ and\ w \models \psi$$

$$w \models \phi \vee \psi \qquad \Leftrightarrow w \models \phi\ or\ w \models \psi$$

$$w \models X\phi \qquad\quad \Leftrightarrow if\ |w| \ge 1\ then\ w^{1\cdots} \models \phi$$

$$w \models \phi W \psi \qquad \Leftrightarrow for\ all\ k\ such\ that\ w^{k\cdots} \not\models \phi\ there\ is\ j \le k\ such\ that\ w^{j\cdots} \models \psi$$

$$w \models r \mapsto \phi \quad \Leftrightarrow for\ all\ u, v\ such\ that\ uv = w\ if\ u \models r\ then\ v \models \phi$$

$$w \models \phi\,\mathbf{abort}\,b \Leftrightarrow either\ w \models \phi,\ or$$
$$there\ is\ k < |w|\ such\ that\ w^k \Vdash b\ and\ (w^{0\cdots k-1}) \models \phi$$

The following lemma follows by structural induction from Lemma 7:

Lemma 9. *For all WPLs ϕ that do not syntactically contain $\bot$ as a subexpression, we have that $\epsilon \models \phi$.*

Note that the denotational semantics presented above does not have the anomaly described in the introduction. For example, we have, for all words w, that $w \models \{\mathbf{true}^*; (a\&\&(a; a))\}$. To see this, take any finite prefix v of w. Then we have $v \models \mathbf{true}^*$ and $\epsilon^- \models a\&\&(a; a)$. It follows that $v\epsilon^- \models \mathbf{true}^*; (a\&\&(a; a))$.

4.4   Relations to PSL Semantics

An investigation into the relation between the semantics of Section 4 and the official PSL semantics is outside the scope of this article. We have however investigated this relation thoroughly. We have provided a refined criterion of degeneracy and a denotational relation of satisfaction for the entire unclocked PSL language on weak, neutral and strong words, and showed that ours is equivalent to the official PSL 1.1 one on formulas that are non-degenerate in this sense. For details of this see [10].

The semantics in Section 4 is a simplified version of the semantics of [10]. It is simplified in three ways:

1. It only covers the weak fragment of PSL.
2. It omits certain operators like : and $\mapsto$, as explained in Section 2.
3. It omits a requirement of non-emptiness present in the case for $\{r\}$.

This last omission was made for the sake of simplicity of presentation. A consequence of the PSL 1.1. semantics is that if $|w| > 0$ then $w \not\vDash \{\varepsilon\}$. It is perhaps not impossible to define operational rules that mirror this requirement, but it seems to require more complicated rules than the ones we present.

We also introduced the RE symbols $\bot$ and ε that are not present in [2, 3]. It was necessary to differentiate falsity that is already visited ($\bot$ which should be false on ϵ^-) from falsity that is not already visited (**false** which should be true on ϵ^-) in the operational rules to get Lemma 10. It was also convenient for defining the operational rules in a succinct way to introduce a symbol ε that is only tightly satisfied by empty words.

5   Relations Between the Semantics

In this section we show that the operational semantics and denotational semantics are tightly coupled. The proofs are merely outlines; for more details see [6].

5.1   The Stepping Lemmas

We can show the following two basic lemmas, which confirms our intuition about the operational judgments $r \xrightarrow{\ell} r'$ and $\phi \xrightarrow{\ell} \phi'$.

Lemma 10 (RE Stepping). *For REs r and r', if $r \xrightarrow{\ell} r'$, then for all $w \in A$*

$$\ell w \mathrel{\vDash\!\!\!\mid} r \Leftrightarrow w \mathrel{\vDash\!\!\!\mid} r'.$$

Using Lemma 10 we can prove the following.

Lemma 11 (WPL Stepping). *For WPLs ϕ and ψ, if $\phi \xrightarrow{\ell} \phi'$, then for all $w \in N$*

$$\ell w \vDash \phi \Leftrightarrow w \vDash \phi'.$$

The above lemmas are key steps in the completeness and soundness proofs.

5.2   Completeness

In order to show completeness of the operational semantics with respect to the denotational semantics, we first observe the following. If a words satisfies an RE, then that RE is ok.

Lemma 12 (Tight True is Ok). *For any RE r, and for $w \in A$*

$$w \!\models\!\equiv r \Rightarrow \mathsf{ok}(r).$$

We can lift that observation to the level of WPLs.

Lemma 13 (True is Ok). *For any WPL ϕ, and for $w \in A$*

$$w \models \phi \Rightarrow \mathsf{ok}(\phi).$$

Lemmas 11 and 4 can be be used to show the following generalization of Lemma 11 which shows the tight relationship between the denotational semantics $\models$ and applying a formula to a word.

Lemma 14. *For any WPL ϕ, and for $w \in N$*

$$w \models \phi \Leftrightarrow \text{ for every finite } v \text{ such that } vu = w, u \models \phi\langle v \rangle.$$

Finally, we use Lemmas 14 and 13 to show completeness.

Theorem 1 (Completeness). *For any WPL ϕ, and for $w \in N$*

$$w \models \phi \Rightarrow w \vdash \phi.$$

5.3   Soundness

In order to show soundness of the operational semantics with respect to the denotational semantics, we use Lemmas 1, 5 to show a tight relationship between the denotational semantics $\models\!\equiv$ and applying an expression to a word.

Lemma 15 (Empty is Tight). *For any RE r, and for all finite $v \in N$*

$$\mathsf{em}(r\langle v \rangle) \Leftrightarrow v \!\models\!\equiv r.$$

Lemmas 5 and 15 can be used to show that the operational semantics is compositional w.r.t. sequential composition.

Lemma 16 (Seq is Sound). *For any two REs r_1 and r_2, and for all words w*

$w \vdash r_1; r_2 \Rightarrow$

  either $w \vdash r_1$ or there are v, u such that $vu = w$ and $v \!\models\!\equiv r_1$ and $u \vdash r_2$.

We use Lemma 16, 10, 7, 6 to show the following very strong lemma.

Lemma 17 (Tight Soundness). *For any RE r, and for all finite $w \in N$*

$$w \vdash r \Rightarrow w^- \!\models\!\equiv r.$$

Finally, we use Lemma 17, 11, 6 to show soundness.

Theorem 2 (Soundness). *For any WPL ϕ, and for $w \in N$*

$$w \vdash \phi \Rightarrow w \models \phi.$$

6   Conclusions and Future Work

We have defined an operational semantics for the weak fragment of PSL, and proved it sound and complete with respect to a new denotational semantics. This denotational semantics is a straightforward extension of earlier work [8], but it is not equivalent to either the official PSL 1.0 or PSL 1.1 semantics. Since our goal was to fix the anomalies in these semantics, it is not surprising that we end up with a different semantics.

However, there is work underway within Accellera to introduce the concept of a "degenerated formula", which is a formula that contains a structural contradiction (such as $a\&\&(a;a)$). The idea is that users of PSL are discouraged to use these degenerated formulas since they are the cause of the anomalies in the official semantics. We have created a formal definition of 'degenerate', and shown that (a variant of) our semantics agrees with the PSL 1.1 semantics for all non-degenerate formulas. The details of this however are beyond the scope of this paper (but see [10]).

Defining an operational semantics can help in guiding the work of defining a denotational one, but it also gives a direct way of implementing dynamic property checking. We also use the operational semantics as a basis of an algorithm for static property checking. It is far from clear how the denotational semantics could guide an implementation.

For space reasons, we have not included all weak PSL operators in our language WPL. Some of these operators, such as the clock operators, are actually expressible in terms of the operators presented here. Others, such as the overlapping versions of sequential composition (written :) and suffix implication (written $\mapsto$), are not expressible in terms of our operators. In any case, for reasons of clarity and efficiency, it is often a good idea to introduce dedicated operational rules for new operators. The actual operational rules for the overlapping operators : and $\mapsto$ are very similar to their non-overlapping counterparts. Dedicated clock rules require some more work; we believe that annotating the $\to$ operator with extra clock information may be the right way to do this.

We are collaborating with Mike Gordon of Cambridge University in encoding our denotational semantics for full PSL [10] in the HOL higher order logic formalism with the purpose of proving relevant properties[2]. Earlier Gordon encoded the official PSL 1.0 and 1.1 semantics in HOL but experienced problems relating to the anomalies when trying to derive observers from those formal specifications [9]. We hope that these problems will be overcome using our semantics.

Currently, we are also working on extending our operational semantics to also deal with non-safety properties. The next step would then be to relate that semantics to the strong satisfiability described in [10].

---

[2] This ongoing work is documented at http://cvs.sourceforge.net/viewcvs.py/hol/ hol98/examples/PSL/experimental-semantics/.

Acknowledgments

We thank the referees, Cindy Eisner and John Havlicek for useful comments on this paper. The second author would also like to thank the two last mentioned and Dana Fisman for good collaboration in developing the weak/strong words semantics for LTL with regular expressions [8], which did inspire the denotational semantics of this paper.

References

1. Accellera. www.accellera.org.
2. Accellera, 1370 Trancas Street, #163, Napa, CA 94558. *Property Specification Language, Reference Manual*, April 2003. www.accellera.org/pslv101.pdf.
3. Accellera, 1370 Trancas Street, #163, Napa, CA 94558. *Property Specification Language, Reference Manual*, 2004. www.eda.org/vfv/docs/PSL-v1.1.pdf.
4. R. Armoni, D. Bustan, O. Kupferman, and M. Vardi. Resets vs. aborts in linear temporal logic. In *Tools and Algorithms for the Construction and Analysis of Systems, TACAS03*, pages 65–80. LNCS 2619, April 2003.
5. J. A. Brzozowski. Derivatives of regular expressions. *Journal of the ACM*, 11(4):481–494, October 1964.
6. K. Claessen and J. Mårtensson. Relating operational and denotational semantics for WPL. Tech. Rep. Available on request from the authors.
7. C. Eisner, D. Fisman, J. Havlicek, Y. Lustig, A. McIsaac, and D. van Campenhout. Reasoning with temporal logic on truncated paths. In *Computer Aided Verification, CAV03*, pages 27–39. LNCS 2725, July 2003.
8. C. Eisner, D. Fisman, J. Havlicek, and J. Mårtensson. Truncating regular expressions. Unpublished.
9. M. Gordon, J. Hurd, and K. Slind. Executing the formal semantics of the Accellera property specification language by mechanised theorem proving. In *Correct Hardware Design and Verification Methods, CHARME03*, pages 200–215. LNCS 2860, October 2003.
10. J. Mårtensson. A weak/strong words semantics for PSL. Tech. Rep. Available on request from the author.

Accepting Predecessors Are Better than Back Edges in Distributed LTL Model-Checking*

Luboš Brim, Ivana Černá, Pavel Moravec, and Jiří Šimša

Department of Computer Science, Faculty of Informatics
Masaryk University Brno, Czech Republic

Abstract. We present a new distributed-memory algorithm for enumerative LTL model-checking that is designed to be run on a cluster of workstations communicating via MPI. The detection of accepting cycles is based on computing maximal accepting predecessors and the subsequent decomposition of the graph into independent predecessor subgraphs induced by maximal accepting predecessors. Several optimizations of the basic algorithm are presented and the influence of the ordering on the algorithm performance is discussed. Experimental implementation of the algorithm shows promising results.

1 Introduction

Model-checking has become a very practical technique for automated verification of computer systems due to its push-button character and has been applied fairly successfully for verification of quite a few real-life systems. Its applicability to a wider class of practical systems has been hampered by the state explosion problem (i.e. the enormous increase in the size of the state space).

The use of distributed and/or parallel processing to combat the state explosion problem gained interest in recent years (see e.g. [4, 5, 10–12, 15]). For large industrial models, the state space does not completely fit into the main memory of a single computer and hence model-checking algorithm becomes very slow as soon as the memory is exhausted and system starts swapping. A typical approach to dealing with these practical limitations is to increase the computational power (especially random-access memory) by building a powerful parallel computer as a network (cluster) of workstations. Individual workstations communicate through message-passing-interface such as MPI. From outside a cluster appears as a single parallel computer with high computing power and huge amount of memory.

In this paper we present a novel approach to distributed explicit-state (enumerative) model-checking for linear temporal logic LTL. LTL is a major logic used in formal verification known for very efficient sequential solution based on automata [16] and successful implementation within several verification tools. The basic idea is to associate a Büchi automaton with the verified LTL formula so that the automaton accepts exactly all the computations of the given model

---

* This work has been partially supported by the Grant Agency of Czech Republic grants No. 201/03/0509.

A.J. Hu and A.K. Martin (Eds.): FMCAD 2004, LNCS 3312, pp. 352–366, 2004.

satisfying the formula. This makes possible to reduce the model-checking problem to the emptiness problem for Büchi automaton. A Büchi automaton accepts a word if and only if there is an *accepting state* reachable from the initial state and from itself.

Courcoubetis et al. [9] proposed an elegant way to find accepting states that are reachable from themselves (to compute *accepting cycles*) by employing a *nested depth first search*. The first search is used to search for reachable accepting states while the second one (*nested*) tries to detect accepting cycles. Our aim is to solve the LTL model-checking problem by distribution, i.e. by utilizing several interconnected workstations. The standard sequential solution as described above is based on the depth-first search (DFS), in particular the *postorder* as computed by DFS is crucial for cycle detection. However, when exploring the state space in parallel, the DFS postorder is not generally maintained any more due to different speeds of involved workstations and communication overhead.

The extremely high effectiveness of the DFS based model-checking procedure in the sequential case is due to a simple and easily computable criterion characterizing the existence of a cycle in a graph: a graph contains a cycle if and only if there is a *back-edge*. A distributed solution requires other appropriate criteria to be used as the DFS based ones do not have the same power in the distributed setting. E.g. in [1] the authors proposed to use *back-level edges* as computed by breadth first search (BFS) as a necessary condition for a path to form a cycle. The reason, why such a criterion works well in a distributed environment is that BFS search can be (unlike DFS) reasonably parallelized. In [7] the used criterion is that each state on an accepting cycle is reachable from an accepting state. Every state can be tested for this criterion independently and thus the algorithm is well distributable. Another example of a necessary condition suitable for distribution and used in [3] employs the fact that the graph to be checked is a product of two graphs and it can contain a cycle only if one of the component graphs has a cycle.

The main idea of our new approach to distributed-memory LTL model-checking has born from a simple observation that all states on a cycle have exactly the same predecessors. Hence, having the same set of predecessors is a necessary condition for two states to belong to the same cycle and the membership in its own set of predecessors is a necessary condition for a state to belong to a cycle. In particular, in case of accepting cycles we can restrict ourselves to accepting predecessors only. Even more, it is not necessary to compute and store the entire set of accepting predecessors for each state, it is sufficient to choose a suitable representative of the set of all accepting predecessors of a given state instead. It is crucial that the cycle-check becomes significantly cheaper if representatives are used. We consider an ordering of states and we choose as a representative of a set of accepting predecessors the accepting predecessor which is maximal with respect to this ordering, called *maximal accepting predecessor*. A necessary condition for a graph to contain an accepting cycle is that there is an accepting state with itself as maximal accepting predecessor. However, this is not a sufficient condition as there can exist an accepting cycle with "its" maximal accepting predecessor lying outside of it. For this reason we systematically re-classify those accepting vertices which do not lie on any cycle as non-accepting and re-compute the maximal accepting predecessors.

The main technical problem is how to compute maximal accepting predecessors in a distributed environment. Our algorithm repeatedly improves the maximal accepting predecessor for a state as more states are considered. This requires propagating a new value to successor states each time the maximum has changed. In this way the procedure resembles the relaxation procedure as used in the single source shortest path problem. The main advantage of such an approach is that relaxations can be performed in an arbitrary order in a BFS manner, hence in parallel. There is even another source of parallelism in our algorithm. Maximal accepting predecessors define independent subgraphs induced by vertices with the same maximal accepting predecessor. These subgraphs can be explored simultaneously and again in an arbitrary order. In both cases a re-distribution of the graph among the workstations involved in the distributed computing might be necessary to optimize the performance of the algorithm.

Another distinguished feature of the algorithm is that due to the breadth-first exploration of the state space the counter-examples produced by the algorithm tend to be short, which is very important for debugging.

There are several known approaches to distribution and/or parallelization of the explicit-state LTL model-checking problem and we relate our algorithm to other work in Section 6.

2 Model-Checking and Accepting Cycles

In the automata-based approach to LTL model-checking [16], one constructs a Büchi automaton $\mathcal{A}_{\neg\Psi}$ for the negation of the property Ψ one wishes to verify and takes its product with the Büchi automaton modeling the given system S. The system (more exactly the model) is correct with respect to the given property if and only if the product automaton recognizes an empty language, i.e. no computation of S violates Ψ. The size of the product automaton is linear with respect to the size of the model and exponential with respect to the size of Ψ.

The model-checking problem is thus reduced to the *emptiness* problem for automata. It can be reduced even further to a graph problem [8]. Let $\mathcal{A} = (\Sigma, S, \delta, s, Acc)$ be a Büchi automaton where Σ is an input alphabet, S is a finite set of states, $\delta : S \times \Sigma \to 2^S$ is a transition relation, s is an initial state and $Acc \subseteq V$ is a set of accepting states. The automaton $\mathcal{A}$ can be identified with a directed graph $G_{\mathcal{A}} = (V, E, s, A)$, called *automaton graph*, where $V \subseteq S$ is a set of vertices corresponding to all *reachable states* of the automaton $\mathcal{A}$, $E = \{(u, v) \mid u, v \in V$ and $v \in \delta(u, a)$ for some $a \in \Sigma\}$, $s \in V$ is a distinguished initial vertex corresponding to the initial state of $\mathcal{A}$ and A is a distinguished set of accepting vertices corresponding to reachable accepting states of $\mathcal{A}$.

Definition 1. *Let* $G = (V, E, s, A)$ *be an automaton graph. The* reachability *relation* $\rightsquigarrow^+ \subseteq V \times V$ *is defined as* $u \rightsquigarrow^+ v$ *iff there is a directed path* $< u_0, u_1, \ldots, u_k >$ *where* $u_0 = u$, $u_k = v$ *and* $k > 0$.

A directed path $< u_0, u_1, \ldots, u_k >$ forms a cycle *if $u_0 = u_k$ and the path contains at least one edge. A cycle is* accepting *if at least one vertex on the path $< u_0, u_1, \ldots, u_k >$ belongs to the set of accepting vertices A.*

Note that according our definition every cycle in an automaton graph is reachable from the initial vertex.

Theorem 1. [8] *Let $\mathcal{A}$ be a Büchi automaton and $G_{\mathcal{A}}$ its corresponding automaton graph. Then $\mathcal{A}$ recognizes a nonempty language iff $G_{\mathcal{A}}$ contains an accepting cycle.*

In this way the original LTL model-checking problem is reduced to the accepting cycle detection problem for automaton graphs and we formulate our model-checking algorithm as a distributed algorithm for accepting cycle detection problem. The algorithm is based on the notion of predecessors. Intuitively, an automaton graph contains an accepting cycle iff some accepting vertex is a predecessor of itself.

To avoid computing of all predecessors for each vertex we introduce a concept of *maximal accepting predecessor*, denoted by *map*. We presuppose a linear ordering of the set of vertices given e.g. by their numbering. Other possible orderings are discussed in Section 4. From now on we therefore assume that for any two vertices u, v we can decide which one is greater. Furthermore, we extend the ordering to the set $V \cup \{null\}$ ($null \notin V$) and put $null < v$ for all $v \in V$.

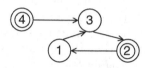

Fig. 1. Undiscovered cycle

Definition 2. *Let $G = (V, E, s, A)$ be an automaton graph. A maximal accepting predecessor function of the graph G, $map_G : V \to (V \cup \{null\})$, is defined as*

$$map_G(v) = \begin{cases} \max\{u \in A \mid u \leadsto^+ v\} & if\ \{u \in A \mid u \leadsto^+ v\} \neq \emptyset \\ null & otherwise \end{cases}$$

Corollary 1. *For any two vertices $u, v \in V$, the vertices cannot lie on the same cycle whenever $map_G(u) \neq map_G(v)$.*

The definition of the maximal accepting predecessor function *map* gives the sufficient condition characterizing the existence of an accepting cycle in the automaton graph.

Lemma 1. *Let $G = (V, E, s, A)$ be an automaton graph. If there is a vertex $v \in V$ such that $map_G(v) = v$ then the graph G contains an accepting cycle.*

The opposite implication is not generally true, for a counterexample see the graph in Figure 1. The accepting cycle $2 \leadsto^+ 2$ is not revealed due to the greater accepting predecessor 4 outside the cycle. However, as the state 4 the does not lie on *any* cycle, it can be safely deleted from the set of accepting states and the accepting cycle will still be discovered in the resulting graph. This idea is formalized in the notion of a *deleting transformation*. Whenever the deleting transformation is applied to an automaton graph G with $map_G(v) \neq v$ for all $v \in V$, it shrinks the set of accepting vertices by deleting those ones which evidently do not lie on any cycle.

Definition 3. *Let $G = (V, E, s, A)$ be an automaton graph and map_G its maximal accepting predecessor function. A deleting transformation, del, is defined as $del(G) = (V, E, s, \overline{A})$, where $\overline{A} = A \setminus \{u \in A \mid \exists v \in V.map_G(v) = u\})$.*

Directly from the definition we have the following result.

Lemma 2. *Let G be an automaton graph and v an accepting vertex in G such that $map(v) \neq v$. Then v is an accepting vertex in $del(G)$.*

Note that the application of the deleting transformation can result in a different *map* function. For the graph G given in Figure 1, $del(G)$ has state 2 as its only accepting state, hence $map_{del(G)}(2) = 2$ (and the existence of the accepting cycle is certified by the new function).

The next Lemma states formally the invariance property just exemplified, namely that the application of the deleting transformation to a graph with an accepting cycle results in a graph having an accepting cycle as well.

Lemma 3. *Let $G = (V, E, s, A)$ be an automaton graph containing an accepting cycle and such that $map(v) \neq v$ for every $v \in A$. Then the graph $del(G)$ contains an accepting cycle.*

Proof: Let C be an accepting cycle in G and $v \in C$ be an accepting vertex. For every successor u of v we have $map(u) \geq map(v) > v$. Therefore the vertex v is accepting in $del(G)$. The transformation does not change the set of vertices and edges and the conclusion follows. $\square$

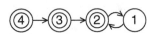

Fig. 2. Deleting transformation

It can happen that even in the transformed graph $del(G)$ there is no vertex such that its *map* value would certify the existence of an accepting cycle. This situation is depicted in Figure 2. However, after a finite number of applications of the deleting transformation an accepting cycle will be certified.

Definition 4. *Let G be an automaton graph. For $i \in \mathbb{N}$ a graph G^i is defined inductively as $G^0 = G$ and $G^{i+1} = del(G^i)$. The set of accepting vertices of G^i is denoted A^i.*

Lemma 4. *Let $G = (V, E, s, A)$ be an automaton graph containing an accepting cycle. Then there is a natural number $i \in \mathbb{N}$ and a vertex $v \in V$ such that $map_{G^i}(v) = v$.*

Proof: Let C be an accepting cycle in G and $u \in A$ be the maximal accepting vertex on C. For any $j \in \mathbb{N}$ let R^j be a set of accepting predecessors of u in G^j, $R^j = \{v \in A^j \mid v \leadsto^+ u\}$. If $map_{G^j}(u) > u$, then obviously $|R^j| > |R^{j+1}|$. Since R^0 is finite, there is an index i for which $|R^{i+1}| = |R^i|$ and $map_{G^i}(u) = u$. In other words, after at most $|R^0| - 1$ applications of the deleting transformation on G the map value of u changes to u. □

Putting together Lemma 1 and Lemma 4 we can state the main theorem justifying the correctness of our algorithm.

Theorem 2. *Let $G = (V, E, s, A)$ be an automaton graph. The graph G contains an accepting cycle if and only if there is a natural $i \in \mathbb{N}$ and a vertex $v \in V$ such that $map_{G^i}(v) = v$.*

Note that for an automaton graph without accepting cycles the repetitive application of the deleting transformation results in an automaton graph with an empty set of accepting states.

3   Distributed Detection of Accepting Cycles

It is now apparent how to make use of the map function and the deleting transformation to build an algorithm which detects accepting cycles. We first present a straightforward approach with the aim to introduce clearly the essence of our distributed algorithm (Subsection 3.1). The distributed-memory algorithm which employs several additional optimizations is presented in Subsection 3.2 and finally, the correctness and complexity of the algorithm is discussed in Subsection 3.3. We do not explicitly describe the actual distribution of the algorithm as this is quite direct and follows the standard technique used e.g. in [1, 6].

3.1   The Algorithmic Essence

The code is rather self-explanatory, we add a few additional comments only. The *MAP* procedure always starts by initializing the *map* value of the initial vertex to *null*, all the other vertices are assigned the undefined initial *map* value, denoted by $\perp$. Every time a vertex receives a new (greater) *map* value, the vertex is pushed into a *waiting* queue and the new *map* value is propagated to all its successors. If an accepting vertex is reached for the first time (line 15) the vertex is inserted into the set *shrinkA* of vertices to be removed from A by the deleting transformation. However, if the accepting vertex is reached from a greater accepting vertex (lines 16 and 17) this value will be propagated to all its successors and the vertex is removed from the set *shrinkA* (Lemma 2).

```
1 proc Main(G)   //G = (V, E, s, A)
2    while A ≠ ∅ do
3        MAP(G)
4        A := A \ shrinkA
5    od
6    report (NO ACCEPTING CYCLE exists)
7 end
```

```
 8 proc MAP(G)
 9    foreach u ∈ V do map(u) := ⊥ od
10    map(s) := null
11    waiting.push(s)
13    while waiting ≠ ∅ do
14          u := waiting.pop()
15          if u ∈ A then if map(u) < u then propagate := u; shrinkA.add(u)
16                                      else propagate := map(u);
17                                           shrinkA.remove(u)
18                        fi
19                  else propagate := map(u)
20          fi
21          foreach (u, v) ∈ E do
22              if propagate = v then report (ACCEPTING CYCLE found) fi
23              if propagate > map(v) then map(v) := propagate
24                                         waiting.push(v) fi
25          od
27    od
28 end
```

3.2   Distributed Algorithm

To build up an effective distributed algorithm we consider two optimizations of the above given basic algorithm. The first one comes out from the fact that every time the set of accepting states has been shrunk and a new *map* function is going to be computed, the algorithm from 3.1 needs to traverse the whole graph, update the flags for vertices removed from the set of accepting vertices, and re-initialize the *map* values to ⊥.

The second improvement is more important with respect to the distribution and it is a consequence of Corollary 1. An accepting cycle in G can be formed from vertices with the same maximal accepting predecessor only. A graph induced by the set of vertices having the same maximal accepting predecessor will be called *predecessor subgraph*. It is clear that every strongly connected component (hence every cycle) in the graph is completely included in one of the predecessor subgraphs. Therefore, after applying the deleting transformation the new *map* function can be computed separately and independently for every predecessor subgraph. This allows for speeding up the computation (values are not propagated to vertices in different subgraphs) and for an efficient distribution of the computation.

In the distributed algorithm *CycleDetection* (see Figure 3) we first compute in parallel the *map* function on the given input graph G (line 2). If no accepting cycle is detected and the set *shrinkA* of vertices to be removed from the set of accepting vertices is nonempty, then the vertices from *shrinkA* define predecessor subgraphs. Every predecessor subgraph is identified through the accepting vertex (*seed*) which is the common maximal accepting predecessor for all vertices in the subgraph. Seeds are stored in the *waitingseed* queue and are used as a parameter when calling the *DistributedMAP* procedure. After the *map* function is computed

```
1   proc CycleDetection(G)   //G = (V, E, s, A)
2     MAP(G)
3     waitingseed := shrinkA
4     shrinkA := ∅
5     while waitingseed ≠ ∅ do
6           while waitingseed ≠ ∅ do
7                 seed := waitingseed.pop()
8                 DistributedMAP(G, seed)
9           od
10          waitingseed := shrinkA
11          shrinkA := ∅
12    od
13    report (NO ACCEPTING CYCLE exists)
15  end

16  proc DistributedMAP(G, seed)
17    oldmap(seed) := seed
18    map(seed) := null
19    waiting.push(seed)
20    while waiting ≠ ∅ do
21          u := waiting.pop()
22          if (u ∈ A) ∧ (u ≠ oldmap(u))
23            then if map(u) < u then propagate := u
24                                     shrinkA.add(u)
25                                else propagate := map(u)
26                                     shrinkA.remove(u) fi
27            else propagate := map(u)
28          fi
29          foreach (u, v) ∈ E do
30            if propagate = v then report (ACCEPTING CYCLE found) fi
31            if map(v) = oldmap(u)
32              then oldmap(v) := oldmap(u)
33                   map(v) := propagate
34                   waiting.push(v)
35              else if (propagate > map(v)) ∧ (oldmap(v) = oldmap(u))
36                     then map(v) := propagate
37                          waiting.push(v)
38                   fi
39            fi
40          od
41    od
42  end
```

Fig. 3. Distributed Cycle Detection Algorithm

for every predecessor subgraph, the vertices that should be deleted from the set of accepting vertices form a new content of the *waitingseed* queue.

Vertices from the same predecessor subgraph are identified with the help of the *oldmap* value. For every vertex v, $oldmap(v)$ maintains the value of $map(v)$

from the previous iteration. When a vertex v with $map(v) = seed$ (line 31) is reached the value of $oldmap(v)$ is set to $seed$. Accepting predecessors are propagated only to successors identified to be in the same predecessor subgraph through the variable $oldmap$ (line 35). Sets $waiting$ and $shrinkA$ are maintained in the same way as in the basic algorithm presented in Subsection 3.1.

For the distributed computation we assume a network of collaborating workstations with no global memory. Communication between workstations is realized by sending messages only. In the distributed computation the input graph is divided into parts, one part per each workstation.

In the $CycleDetection$ algorithm every workstation has local data structures $waitingseed$, $waiting$ and $shrinkA$ and computes the values of the map function for its part of the graph. Workstations have to be synchronized every time the computation of the map function is finished and the set of accepting vertices is to be shrunk.

An important characteristic of the distributed algorithm is that the map values for different predecessor subgraphs can be computed in parallel, i.e. the procedure $DistributedMAP$ can be called for different values of $seed$ in parallel.

Another distinguished feature of our distributed algorithm is the possibility to make use of dynamic re-partitioning, i.e. of a new assignment of vertices to workstations after each iteration. The map function induces a decomposition of the graph into predecessor subgraphs. After a new map function is computed the graph can be re-partitioned so that the new partition function respects predecessor subgraphs as much as possible which can result in significant reduction in the communication among the workstations as well as in speed-up of the entire computation.

In the case the given graph contains an accepting cycle an output reporting such a cycle is required. The proposed algorithm can be simply extended to report an accepting cycle. Let v be a vertex certifying the existence of an accepting cycle ($v = propagate$). Then two distributed searches are initiated. The first one finds a path from the initial vertex s to v and the second one a path from v to itself. In the second search the predecessor subgraph of v is searched-through only.

3.3   Correctness and Complexity

Theorem 3. *The CycleDetection algorithm terminates and correctly detects an accepting cycle in an automaton graph.*

Proof: Every time a vertex is pushed into the $waiting$ queue in both the MAP and the $DistributedMAP$ procedure, its map value is strictly increased. Thus a vertex can be pushed and popped from the $waiting$ queue a finite number of times only and both procedures terminate. As accepting vertices are pushed to the $waitingseed$ queue in $CycleDetection$ only and whenever a vertex is pushed to the $waitingseed$ queue it is deleted from the set of accepting vertices the algorithm terminates.

For the second half it is sufficient to note that the algorithm reports cycle whenever a vertex which is its own maximal accepting predecessor is reached (line 30). The correctness follows from Lemma 1. The other direction follows from Lemma 4 and from the observation that in the procedures *DistributedMAP* and *MAP* the *map* function is correctly computed for all vertices in the actual predecessor subgraph.   □

Theorem 4. *The time complexity of the CycleDetection algorithm is $\mathcal{O}(a^2 \cdot m)$, where m is the number of edges and a is the number of accepting vertices in the input (automaton) graph.*

Proof: The cycle in the *CycleDetection* procedure is repeated at most a times. Every vertex is pushed to the *waiting* queue in the procedures *DistributedMAP* and *MAP* at most a times and all successors of a vertex popped from the *waiting* queue are tested. The overall complexity of both *MAP* and *DistributedMAP* is $\mathcal{O}(a \cdot m)$.   □

   Experiments with model-checking graphs (see Section 5) demonstrate that the actual complexity is typically significantly lower.

4   Ordering of Vertices

One of the key aspects influencing the overall performance of our distributed algorithm is the underlying ordering of the vertices used by the algorithm. The direct way to order the vertices is to use the enumeration order as it is computed in the enumerative on-the-fly model-checking. The first possibility is to order the vertices by the time they have been reached (sooner visited vertices receive smaller values). In this case the algorithm tends to return short counterexamples and generally detects the accepting cycles very quickly. Moreover, since the graph is splitted into "as many" subgraphs "as possible", less iterations are performed. On the other hand, the running time of each iteration increases, because the vertices with small values will be usually updated several times. Alternatively, we can employ the reverse ordering (sooner visited vertices receive larger values). The behavior of the algorithm is now completely different. Both the size of subgraphs and the number of iterations increase, while the number of the subgraphs as well as the running time of each iteration decrease. As a third possibility we can consider a combination of these two orderings, which can result in fast computation with small number of iterations.

   Another set of heuristics can be based on different graph traversal algorithms (e.g. depth-first search or breadth-first search). Finally, yet another simple heuristic is to compare the bit-vector representations of vertices.

   In the future we plan to implement, compare and systematically evaluate all the orderings of vertices mentioned above.

   In our implementation each vertex is identified by a vector of three numbers – the workstation identifier, the row number in the hash table, and the column number in the row. The ordering of vertices is given by the lexicographical ordering of these triples. Note that there are six possible lexicographical orderings and by reversing these orderings one gets another six possibilities. This gives us a range of twelve possible orderings. We have implemented and compared six of them. The results we obtained show that there is no real difference among these six approaches, which in some sense demonstrate the robustness of an ordering with respect to the random partitioning of the graph among the workstations.

5   Experiments

We have implemented the distributed algorithm described in Section 3.2. The implementation has been done in C++ and the experiments have been performed on a network of thirteen Intel Pentium 4 2.6 GHz workstations with 1 GB of RAM each interconnected with a fast 100Mbps Ethernet and using tools provided by our own distributed verification environment – DiVinE.

The vertices have been partitioned among the workstations using random hash function and no re-partitioning was implemented.

We performed several sets of tests on different instances of the model-checking problem with the primary aim to evaluate the scalability of our algorithm. Here we report results for a variant of the *Mutual exclusion protocol* problem based on a token ring and parametrized by the number n of processes (denoted by $TR(n)$) and the *Producer-consumer protocol* problem parametrized by the number n of messages which can be lost in a row (denoted by $PC(n)$). For each parametrized model we report the results for one LTL property. The property being checked over the TR class was $GF(P_0.CS)$, i.e. the process P_0 enter its critical section infinitely many times. The property being checked over the PC class was $GF(Consumer.consume_0 \vee Consumer.consume_1)$, i.e. the consumer will consume some value infinitely many times. Both properties have been satisfied by the respective models.

The results of the experiments are presented in Figure 4 and all the results are taken as an average of 5 executions of the distributed algorithm. Because of the size of state graphs (from 500.000 to 1.5 millions vertices and the amount of memory needed to store a vertex description), we did not get results when running the algorithm on less than 3 workstations due to memory restrictions. Therefore, the shown speedups are calculated relative to 3 workstations instead of one. We found that we gain a linear speedup for reasonably large graphs.

The second set of tests was designed to evaluate the actual performance of the algorithm. We have implemented an experimental version of the *token-based distributed-memory nested depth-first search algorithm* (*Nested DFS*) and compared the running time of both algorithms. The comparison of our algorithm (*DACD*) and the Nested DFS algorithm (*NDFS*) is given in Table 1 for various numbers of workstations (*NW*) involved in the distributed computation. The results shown are running times in seconds. It can be seen that our algorithm outperforms the Nested DFS algorithm even when the number of workstation is small.

We have compared the sequential version of our algorithm to the sequential Nested DFS algorithm as well. As expected, the sequential version of our algorithm performs slightly worse. However, the experiments have demonstrated comparability of both approaches. Our algorithm needs, on average, around 30% more time and memory than Nested DFS algorithm.

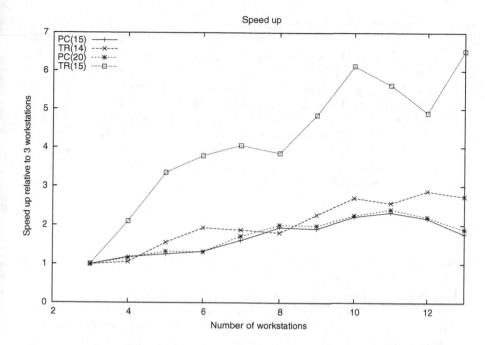

Fig. 4. Scalability of the distributed algorithm

Table 1. Nested DFS vs. DACD on PC(20)

NW	NDFS	DACD	Speedup	NW	NDFS	DACD	Speedup
3	1251	846	1.5	7	1904	208	9.2
4	1801	402	4.5	8	2132	219	9.7
5	1610	252	6.4	9	2166	174	12.4
6	1958	223	8.8	10	2306	137	16.8

We have also considered verification problems on models with an error (e.g. *Dining philosophers*, various models of an elevator, and some communication protocols). Since our algorithm is entirely based on the breadth-first search, the counterexamples were much more shorter than counterexamples provided by the Nested DFS algorithm. Moreover, in all cases the accepting cycle was detected very early by our algorithm (within tens of seconds), while the Nested DFS algorithm was incomparably slower. For the parametrized models where the size of the state space was larger than the size of the (distributed) memory (e.g. for forty dining philosophers), our algorithm detected a counterexample, while the Nested DFS algorithm failed due to memory limitations. These results were almost independent on the ordering of vertices chosen and on the number of workstations involved.

In the erroneous version of the general *Peterson algorithm* for 4 processes, where the error is very "deep" (according to the breadth-first search level). In this case the Nested DFS algorithm detected the counterexample very early, since the depth-first search tends to follow the erroneous path, while our algorithm failed. In several other examples with similar characteristics our algorithm was able to detect the error as well, but later than the Nested DFS algorithm. However, the "depth of an error" is typically small, hence our distributed algorithm will outperform the Nested DFS algorithm in most cases.

The last interesting conclusion we would like to point out is that the number of iterations in all models without an error was up to 20. On the other hand, an error was already detected during the first iteration in all performed tests. As a consequence the algorithm is usually able to detect the faulty behavior without exploring the entire graph (state space).

6   Conclusions

In this paper, we have presented a new distributed-memory algorithm for enumerative LTL model-checking.

We plan to implement two improvements of our algorithm. Both use additional conditions characterizing the existence of an accepting cycle in an automaton graph augmented with the maximal accepting predecessors information.

Suppose that the graph contains an accepting cycle such that the maximal accepting predecessor of this cycle is outside of it. Then there must exist a vertex on the cycle with the in-degree at least two. One of the incoming edges comes from the cycle, a different one comes from the maximal accepting predecessor. Therefore, we do not need to explore a predecessors subgraph which does not fulfill this condition.

For the second condition suppose again that the graph contains an accepting cycle such that the maximal accepting predecessor of this cycle is outside of it. Then the graph must contain at least one another accepting vertex (besides the maximal accepting predecessor). It is possible to combine these two methods. An effective way to check the conditions requires a more sophisticated techniques for computing the set *shrinkA* in the distributed environment.

There are several already known approaches to distributed-memory LTL model-checking. In [14] a distributed implementation of the SPIN model checker, restricted to perform model-checking of safety properties only is described. In [2], the authors build on the safety model-checking work of [14] to create a distributed-memory version of SPIN that does full LTL model-checking. The disadvantage of this algorithm is that it performs only one nested search at a time. Recently, in [7] another algorithm for distributed enumerative LTL model checking has been proposed. The algorithm implements the enumerative version of the symbolic "One-Way-Catch-Them-Young" algorithm [13]. The algorithm shows in many situations a linear behavior, however it is not on-the-fly, hence the whole state space has to be generated. Our algorithm is in some sense similar to [7], although their original ideas are different. Both algorithms work in iterations started from a set of accepting vertices. In general, the time complexity of [7] is better ($\mathcal{O}(n \cdot m)$ in comparison to $\mathcal{O}(a^2 \cdot m)$), but our algorithm has three advantages. It is adjustable according to the input problem by setting some special ordering of vertices, it can guess the counterexample very quickly before the whole graph is traversed and it has one instead of two synchronizations during the iteration cycle. Since the number of iterations is very similar, on the larger and slower nets this can be a significant factor. Similar arguments are valid if comparing our algorithm to another recently proposed algorithm [1]. This algorithm uses back-level edges to discover cycles, works on-the-fly and is effective in finding bugs. All these three algorithms could be meant not to replace but to complement each other.

In [6], the problem of LTL model checking is reduced to detecting negative cycles in a weighted directed graph. Since the basic method (edge relaxation) is the same, the behavior of both algorithms will be generally similar. The algorithm in [6] suffers by clumsy cycle detection, our approach needs costly synchronization and many searches are often redundantly called.

For each of the above mentioned distributed-memory algorithm for the enumerative LTL model-checking there will most likely exist a set of input problems on which it is superior to the others. Our future work will be focused on systematic, mainly experimental, comparison of these algorithms.

References

1. J. Barnat, L. Brim, and J. Chaloupka. Parallel Breadth-First Search LTL Model-Checking. In *18th IEEE International Conference on Automated Software Engineering (ASE'03)*, pages 106–115. IEEE Computer Society, Oct. 2003.
2. J. Barnat, L. Brim, and J. Stříbrná. Distributed LTL Model-Checking in SPIN. In Matthew B. Dwyer, editor, *Proceedings of the 8th International SPIN Workshop on Model Checking of Software (SPIN'01)*, volume 2057 of *LNCS*, pages 200–216. Springer, 2001.
3. J. Barnat, L. Brim, and I. Černá. Property Driven Distribution of Nested DFS. In *Proceedinfs of the 3rd International Workshop on Verification and Computational Logic (VCL'02 – held at the PLI 2002 Symposium)*, pages 1–10. University of Southampton, UK, Technical Report DSSE-TR-2002-5 in DSSE, 2002.
4. S. Blom and S. Orzan. Distributed branching bisimulation reduction of state spaces. In L. Brim and O. Grumberg, editors, *Electronic Notes in Theoretical Computer Science*, volume 89.1. Elsevier, 2003.
5. B. Bollig, M. Leucker, and M. Weber. Local parallel model checking for the alternation-free mu-calculus. In *Proceedings of the 9th International SPIN Workshop on Model checking of Software (SPIN'02)*, volume 2318 of *LNCS*, pages 128–147. Springer, 2002.
6. L. Brim, I. Černá, P. Krčál, and R. Pelánek. Distributed LTL model checking based on negative cycle detection. In Ramesh Hariharan, Madhavan Mukund, and V. Vinay, editors, *Proceedings of Foundations of Software Technology and Theoretical Computer Science (FST–TCS'01)*, volume 2245 of *LNCS*, pages 96–107. Springer, 2001.
7. I. Černá and R. Pelánek. Distributed explicit fair cycle detection. In Thomas Ball and Sriram K. Rajamani, editors, *Model Checking Software, 10th International SPIN Workshop*, volume 2648 of *LNCS*, pages 49–73. Springer, 2003.

8. E. M. Clarke, O. Grumberg, and D. A. Peled. *Model Checking*. MIT Press, Cambridge, Massachusetts, 1999.
9. C. Courcoubetis, M. Vardi, P. Wolper, and M. Yannakakis. Memory-Efficient Algorithms for the Verification of Temporal Properties. *Formal Methods in System Design*, 1:275–288, 1992.
10. H. Garavel, R. Mateescu, and I.M Smarandache. Parallel State Space Construction for Model-Checking. In Matthew B. Dwyer, editor, *Proceedings of the 8th International SPIN Workshop on Model Checking of Software (SPIN'01)*, volume 2057 of *LNCS*, pages 200–216. Springer, 2001.
11. B. R. Haverkort, A. Bell, and H. C. Bohnenkamp. On the efficient sequential and distributed generation of very large Markov chains from stochastic Petri nets. In *Proceedings of the 8th International Workshop on Petri Nets and Performance Models (PNPM'99)*, pages 12–21. IEEE Computer Society Press, 1999.
12. T. Heyman, O. Grumberg, and A. Schuster. A work-efficient distributed algorithm for reachability analysis. In Warren A. Hunt Jr. and Fabio Somenzi, editors, *15th International Conference (CAV'03)*, volume 2725 of *LNCS*, pages 54–66. Springer, 2003.
13. R. Hojati, H. Touati, R. P. Kurshan, and R. K. Brayton. Efficient omega-regular language containment. In G. von Bochmann and D. K. Probst, editors, *Proc. of the Fourth International Workshop CAV'92*, pages 396–409. Springer, 1993.
14. F. Lerda and R. Sisto. Distributed-memory model checking with SPIN. In *Proceedings of the 6th International SPIN Workshop on Model Checking of Software (SPIN'99)*, volume 1680 of *LNCS*, pages 22–39, Berlin, 1999. Springer.
15. R. Palmer and Ganesh Gopalakrishnan. A distributed partial order reduction algorithm. In D. Peled and M. Y. Vardi, editors, *Formal Techniques for Networked and Distributed Systems - FORTE 2002, 22nd IFIP WG 6.1 International Conference Houston, Texas, USA, November 11-14, 2002, Proceedings*, volume 2529 of *LNCS*, page 370. Springer, 2002.
16. M. Y. Vardi and P. Wolper. An automata-theoretic approach to automatic program verification. In *Proc. 1st Symp. on Logic in Computer Science (LICS'86)*, pages 332–344. Computer Society Press, 1986.

Bloom Filters in Probabilistic Verification

Peter C. Dillinger and Panagiotis Manolios

Georgia Institute of Technology
College of Computing, CERCS
801 Atlantic Drive
Atlanta, GA 30332-0280
{peterd,manolios}@cc.gatech.edu

Abstract. Probabilistic techniques for verification of finite-state transition systems offer huge memory savings over deterministic techniques. The two leading probabilistic schemes are hash compaction and the bitstate method, which stores states in a Bloom filter. Bloom filters have been criticized for being slow, inaccurate, and memory-inefficient, but in this paper, we show how to obtain Bloom filters that are simultaneously fast, accurate, memory-efficient, scalable, and flexible. The idea is that we can introduce large dependences among the hash functions of a Bloom filter with almost no observable effect on accuracy, and because computation of independent hash functions was the dominant computational cost of accurate Bloom filters and model checkers based on them, our savings are tremendous. We present a mathematical analysis of Bloom filters in verification in unprecedented detail, which enables us to give a fresh comparison between hash compaction and Bloom filters. Finally, we validate our work and analyses with extensive testing using 3SPIN, a model checker we developed by extending SPIN.

1 Introduction

Despite its simplicity, explicit-state model checking has proved to be an effective verification technique and has led to numerous tools, including SPIN [14], Murφ [18], TLC [23], Java PathFinder [20], etc. The *state explosion problem* is especially acute in explicit-state model checking because the amount of memory required depends linearly on the number of reachable states, which is often too large to enumerate in main memory. Disk can be utilized intelligently [17,23], but such algorithms will probably continue to be outperformed by algorithms that take advantage of the fast random access time of main memory. Storing states more compactly in memory, therefore, is very desirable, and because of the huge memory savings available, storing states in a probabilistic data structure has become a popular approach and the topic of significant research.

Virtually all of the proposed probabilistic verification approaches utilize one of two data structures: a Bloom filter [14] or a compacted hash table [18]. The Bloom filter, dating back to 1970 [1], is the data structure underlying "supertrace" [12], "multihashing" [21], and "bitstate hashing" [13]. Compacted hash tables are utilized by "hashcompact" [21] and the first version of "hash compaction" [18], but the technique was not perfected until [19].

A.J. Hu and A.K. Martin (Eds.): FMCAD 2004, LNCS 3312, pp. 367–381, 2004.
© Springer-Verlag Berlin Heidelberg 2004

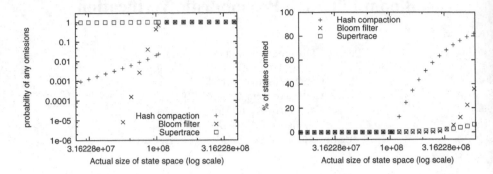

Fig. 1. These graphs show the accuracy of three probabilistic verification techniques/ configurations for various state space sizes. In both graphs, lower is better. The data points for "Hash compaction" and "Bloom filter" are obtained with data structures optimized for a state space size of 10^8, using 400MB of memory. The graphs show the accuracy of the data structures as the size of the state space varies. The left graph shows the probability that even a single omission occurs, while the right graphs shows the expected percentage of states omitted. The "Bloom filter" ($k = 24$) and "Supertrace" ($k = 2$) accuracies are computed using the analyses in Section 3. To compute the "Hash compaction" values we need to know the number of expected collisions in the table for the verifier run represented by each data point [18]. We determine this experimentally by counting the number of collisions in 3SPIN's ordered, compacted table implementation, which in this case uses 32 bits per state and has a maximum visitable size of 104857589.

The literature contains explanations on both sides of the Bloom filter vs. hash compaction debate as to why each data structure is the best. We have found that neither is best, but that there are scenarios under which each is the best choice. More specifically, we identify three probabilistic verification techniques (based on the two data structures), each of which we believe is the best choice for some level of knowledge of the state space size.

When the state space size is completely unknown, Holzmann's supertrace method, which uses a Bloom filter with two hash functions, is the best choice because of its high expected coverage over a wide range of state space sizes (Figure 1, right graph). Supertrace is fast but starts omitting states for state spaces much smaller than other approaches (see Figure 1, left graph). Nevertheless, we can estimate actual state space sizes rather accurately with supertrace (see Section 3.3).

When we know the size of the state space rather accurately – if we have an estimate that we are reasonably certain is within about 15% of the actual size – the best choice is a compacted hash table configured with slightly more cells than the maximum estimated state space size. This technique gives exceptionally high accuracy within this narrow range of state space sizes (Figure 1, left graph), and its speed is similar to supertrace's. If, however, the data structure overflows (right graph) or is underpopulated (left graph), a Bloom filter configured for the same estimate would have been a better choice.

When we have a rough estimate of the state space size, a Bloom filter configured for that estimate can tolerate much more deviation from the estimate than hash compaction can, and is likely to be much more accurate than supertrace. Such a configuration remains a respectable choice even if the estimate is off by a factor of five or more.

This last technique usually calls for a Bloom filter with many more hash functions than supertrace's two, but until our improvements to Bloom filters, introduced in [5], such configurations were unreasonably slow and not considered a good choice: "In a well-tuned model checker, the run-time requirements of the search depend linearly on [the number of hash functions]: computing hash functions is the single most expensive operation a model checker must perform" [14]. "[C]omputing 20 hash functions is quite expensive and will substantially slow down the search. Hash compaction is also superior in this regard, requiring only one 96-bit signature to be calculated" [22]. Our improvements, which require only a 2-3 word signature to be computed on the state descriptor, nullify these claims and make the configured Bloom filter technique a good choice for the rough estimate case.

If supertrace provides an estimate of state space size sufficient for configuring hash compaction, when do we have a only a rough estimate of the state space size? One will have a rough estimate at many times during the development and verification of a model. First of all, small changes to a model during development can easily modify the size of a state space by more than 15%. Secondly, most models are parameterized and the state space sizes of larger instances can only be predicted roughly with respect to smaller instances. Because of its reasonable handling of a wide range of state space sizes, the Bloom filter is preferable in these cases.

Version 2.0 of 3SPIN, our modified version of the SPIN model checker, is designed around the three probabilistic verification modes described above. Whenever 3SPIN finishes a verification run that revealed no errors in the model, it outputs detailed information on the expected accuracy of the run, uses this information to output an estimate of the actual state space size, and recommends bitstate or hashcompact configurations for future runs. We used various versions and configurations of 3SPIN for the experimental results in this paper, but 3SPIN always seeds its hash functions based on the current time, resulting in virtually independent functions among executions. Unless otherwise specified, timings are taken on a 2.2Ghz non-Xeon Pentium4 (Dell Precision 340), with 512MB PC800 RDRAM running Red Hat Linux 9 with the 2.4.20 kernel. We used version 3.1.1 of the GNU C compiler with the following arguments: -O3 -march=pentium3 -mcpu=pentium4.

One category of related work is state space caching and the t-limited scheme of hash compaction [19]. This approach offers more flexibility to hash-compacted tables and might be a reasonable choice if memory is so constrained that a hash-compacted table of the whole state space is too inaccurate, but we don't see this scheme as a viable replacement for the Bloom filter. Unlike state space caching, supertrace is able to explore a huge number of states with no redundant work, allowing it to find errors quickly. Another problem with state-space caching is that it does not give an indication of the size of the state space. This is acceptable in cases where state-space caching is a good choice for the problem size, but trying state-space caching is not a good way to test whether it is a good solution, because it is difficult to distinguish a process that is about to finish from one that will do many times more work than a Bloom filter.

Another category of related work is reductions that can play their own role in tackling state explosion. Both symmetry [3, 7, 6] and partial-order reductions [9, 11] are compatible with the probabilistic techniques discussed. 3SPIN preserves SPIN's partial-order compatibility, but we have disabled it in our tests in order to more accurately measure accuracy and to work with larger state spaces.

This paper examines Bloom filters for verification in unprecedented detail and gives analytical and empirical validation of the speed and accuracy of our improved Bloom filters. Section 2 introduces Bloom filters and reviews basic analyses that, until now, have not been fully utilized by the verification community. Section 3 extends these analyses by presenting two accuracy metrics for evaluating the performance of Bloom filters as visited lists. Section 4 details the effects of sacrificing hash function independence. Section 5 describes replacements for independent hash functions that represent various tradeoffs in efficiency and accuracy, though all our techniques provide huge speed benefits at virtually unobservable accuracy costs. Section 6 gives the results of many tests with modified versions of the SPIN model checker. The results validate our analytical accuracy claims. We end by concisely restating our contributions in Section 7.

2 Bloom Filters

A Bloom filter is used to represent subsets of some universe U. A Bloom filter is implemented as an array of m bits, uses k *index functions* mapping elements in U to $[0..m)$, and supports two basic operations: *add* and *query*. The index functions are traditionally assumed to be hash functions with the standard assumptions that they are random, uniform, and independent, though these assumptions can be replaced with universal hashing arguments. Initially, all bits in the Bloom filter are set to 0. To *add* $u \in U$ to a Bloom filter, the index functions are used to generate k indices into the array and the corresponding bits are set to 1. A *query* is positive iff all k referenced bits are 1. A negative *query* clearly indicates that the element is not in the Bloom filter, but a positive *query* may be due to a *false positive*, the case in which the queried element was not added to the Bloom filter, but all k queried bits are 1 (due to other additions).

We now analyze the probability of a single query of an unadded element returning a false positive (taken from [2]). Note that if p is the probability that a random bit of the Bloom filter is 1, then the probability of a false positive is p^k, the probability that all k index functions map to a 1. If we let i be the number of elements that have been added to the Bloom filter, then $p = 1 - (1 - \frac{1}{m})^{ik}$, as ik bits were randomly selected, with probability $\frac{1}{m}$, in the process of *add*ing i elements. We use $f_{m,k,i}^{\mathrm{BF}}$ to denote the probability that the $(i+1)$st addition causes a false positive.

This construction of the false positive probability is far more accurate than the analyses of bitstate hashing that appear in verification literature [21, 13, 22]. These analyses assumed that every addition to the data structure flips k 0's to 1's. This assumption is far from reasonable, *e.g.*, when the data structure contains half 1's and half 0's, the expected number of 0's that are flipped by an addition is $\frac{k}{2}$. This property is crucial to the flexibility of Bloom filters and is necessary for accurate analysis.

The false positive probability is obviously an important metric, and with some work one can show that it is minimized exactly when $k = (i \log_2 \frac{m}{m-1})^{-1}$. In [2], the term $(1 - \frac{1}{m})^{ik}$ is approximated by $e^{-\frac{ik}{m}}$, and the claim is made that, modulo this approximation, the probability of false positives is minimized when $k = \frac{m}{i} \ln 2$, where ln is $\log_e$. One can show that this last formula is an upper approximation.

3   Bloom Filters in Verification

Although perfect for some applications [16, 8], the false positive rate is insufficient as a metric for evaluating the accuracy of Bloom filters in probabilistic explicit-state model checking. More appropriate metrics are based on the number of states that are omitted from the search, which tells us how much uncertainty there is in the model checking result. The first way to estimate this uncertainty is by computing the expected number of omissions, which could be used to estimate "coverage" as in [13]. The second metric is the probability that one or more omissions occur, as done for hash compaction in [18].

3.1   A Simplified Problem

We start with a simplified problem: given n unique states, add each one to a Bloom filter, but before each addition, query the element against the same Bloom filter to see if it returns a false positive. Each false positive is due to a <u>filter collision</u>, in which all bits indexed were set to one by previous additions. We will designate the number of (Bloom) filter collisions with c^{BF}.

To compute the probability of no filter collisions at all, we start by noting that in a Bloom filter containing i elements, the probability that adding a new element does *not* lead to an omission is just 1 minus the probability of a false positive. The probability of there not being an omission at all is approximately the product of there not being an omission as i ranges from 0 to $n-1$: $P(c^{BF} = 0) = \prod_{i=0}^{n-1} \left(1 - f_{m,k,i}^{BF}\right)$ [1]. The probability that there are one or more filter collisions, $P(c^{BF} > 0) = 1 - P(c^{BF} = 0)$.

To compute the expected number of filter collisions when querying and adding n distinct states, we must compute how much each state is expected to contribute. At run time, each new state contributes 1 filter collision with probability $f_{m,k,i}^{BF}$. Adding all n of these up, we get the expected number of filter collisions:

$$E(c^{BF}) = \sum_{i=0}^{n-1} f_{m,k,i}^{BF} \tag{1}$$

3.2   The General Problem

We now generalize our simplified problem to address the issues in explicit-state model checking, and tailor our analyses accordingly. The results apply more generally to any scenario in which a Bloom filter is used to represent the visited set in a graph search algorithm.

If we assume that the model checker reaches every state, we can apply the analysis given for our simplified problem [2]. This assumption, however, is unsafe because omis-

---

[1] To be more precise, one must assume the n additions are non-colliding. For brevity, we present the very close approximation that ignores this assumption.

[2] In [13], Holzmann points out that SPIN is written so that states are checked for errors each time they are reached (queried against visited list). Analysis in [19] also assumes this technique is employed. This might not be a reasonable choice in all cases, so our analysis is conservative in assuming this technique is not employed.

sions can cause other states never to be reached, and never to be queried against the Bloom filter. We distinguish between two types of omissions:

Definition 1 A *hash omission* is a state omitted from a search because a query of the visited set resulted in a false positive.

Definition 2 A *transitive omission* is a reachable state omitted from a search because none of its predecessors were expanded; thus, the state was never queried against the visited set.

We use o^H to represent the number of hash omissions in a verifier run. The correspondence with the simplified problem tells us that $E(o^H) = E(c^{BF})$ [3] and $P(o^H = 0) = P(c^{BF} = 0)$.

We use o^T to represent the number of transitive omissions in a verifier run, and o to represent the total omissions: $o = o^H + o^T$. An obvious, but useful, lemma is that if there are no hash omissions, then there are no transitive omissions. Consequently, $P(o = 0) = P(o^H = 0)$.

Lemma 1 *(Probability of No Omission)* $o^H = 0$ *implies* $o = 0$

In the presence of hash omissions, the number of transitive omissions can vary wildly – even for the same model and same number of expected hash omissions (see Section 6). Nevertheless, Holzmann has observed that the number of hash omissions is a useful approximation of the total number of transitive omissions [13], meaning we could estimate the total number of omissions as follows (though Holzmann's formulas for $E(o)$ and $E(o^H)$ are different):

$$E(o) \approx 2E(o^H) \tag{2}$$

This estimation is very rough and heavily dependent on the connectivity of the model being checked, but it is consistent with our results in Figure 2. One curve shows the computed values for $E(o^H)$ under the experimental configuration. Very close to that curve is a curve that shows how many filter collisions (false positives) occurred when querying and adding all reachable states to the Bloom filter, just like the simplified problem of Section 3.1. This method gives us an empirical estimate of hash omissions. The last curve shows average total omissions from actual verifier runs.

Another lesson to take from Figure 2 is that getting close to the right k can result in orders of magnitude fewer omissions than using supertrace ($k = 2$).

Finally, the expected number of omissions can be used to estimate the percentage of states covered by a bitstate search, as Holzmann did with less precision in [13]. Our coverage estimate is just $(n - E(o))/n \cdot 100\%$ (see Equation 2).

3.3   Maximizing Accuracy

So far our accuracy analyses have been summative; that is, we can evaluate the accuracy of a search given m, n, and k. However, as discussed in the introduction, we would like

---

[3] To be more precise, n would have to the number of reached states, which would have to account for transitive omissions, which are virtually impossible to predict precisely.

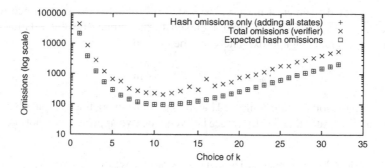

Fig. 2. We show the expected and observed omissions out of a 606,211-state instance of PFTP using 1MB for the Bloom filter, as k is varied. The theoretical optimum value for k is 11. Except for those that are directly computed, each point represents the average of 100 iterations.

to be able to determine what configuration is the best choice given some rough estimate of the state space size, n. The m parameter is easy to choose, however, because it should be as big as possible without the verifier spilling into swap space. Larger Bloom filters (and compacted hash tables) are always more accurate, and thus, this section focuses on the more interesting parameter, k.

k is a complicated factor for accuracy because too many *or* too few index functions hurt accuracy. In fact, for a given m and n there is one k that is the best choice according to our expected omission metric – a consequence of the curve always being concave up with respect to k (see Figure 2). The best k happens to be virtually the same for our probability of omissions metric, which we partially verified by computing virtually the same values found in Table 1 for this other metric. For all practical purposes, optimizing for one of these metrics gives the same result as optimizing for the other.

One approach to minimizing the expected hash omissions is to differentiate Equation 1 with respect to k and set it equal to 0 to find the global minimum. This method gives us the non-discrete choice of k that minimizes the expected omissions, but Bloom filters must use a discrete number of index functions. Rounding to the nearest integer is a reasonable fix but does not always result in the best discrete k.

The large m and n values we encounter in practice mean that the best choice of k depends only on the ratio of m to n. Below we show that if k minimizes the expected omissions for m and n, then k minimizes the expected omissions for cm and cn, because the expect omission curve is the same except for a constant factor of c. To see this, note that $E(o^H) \approx \int_0^n f^{BF}_{m,k,i}\,di$. Using some calculus, we have:

$$E(o^H_{cm,k,cn}) \approx \int_0^{cn} \left(1 - e^{-ki/cm}\right)^k di = c \int_0^n \left(1 - e^{-ki/m}\right)^k di \approx c\,E(o^H_{m,k,n})$$

We can now use Equation 1 to calculate, for any given positive integer value of k, the range of m/n values for which it is the best choice. We do this by picking a large m and computing a barrier value b such that if $m/n < b$, then using k hash functions is better than using $k+1$, and if $m/n > b$, then using $k+1$ hash functions is better than using k. This takes O(m) time. For example, at $m/n \approx 7.73819$, $k = 6$ and $k = 7$ give the same expected number of hash omissions. $k = 7$ remains the best choice for m/n values up to about 9.13545. We derive a closed-form estimate for this relationship by generating a formula that approximately fits the computed values:

$$k_{m/n} = \lceil 3.8^{\left(\frac{m}{n} + 4.2\right)^{-1}} \frac{m}{n} \ln 2 \rceil \qquad (3)$$

Table 1 compares some of the computed barriers with those obtained by our closed-form estimate and illustrates that the difference between the two approaches is not significant.

Table 1. This table shows the m/n barriers that define the ranges for which specific values of k are best. The table compares the values computed using Equation 1 with those taken from the inverse of the estimation formula above (Equation 3). Computing the m/n barriers for the probability of any omissions metric results in virtually the same values.

Barrier between	1 and 2	2 and 3	3 and 4	5 and 6	10 and 11	50 and 51	100 and 101
Computed m/n	1.1346	2.3481	3.6441	6.3529	13.370	70.849	142.95
Closed-form estimate	1.1227	2.3536	3.6513	6.3566	13.372	70.863	142.97

One of the big advantages of Bloom filters is that they can be used to estimate the total size of the state space with high accuracy. 3SPIN uses some tricks beyond the scope of this paper for this purpose, but here is another technique that is just as valid. Let N be the number of states identified as unique by the Bloom filter during the verification and let p be the proportion of 0's in the Bloom filter after verification. From our analysis in Section 2, $p = (1 - \frac{1}{m})^{ik}$, where i is the number of distinct states we attempted to add (note that $i \geq N$ because of false positives). Solving for i, we have $i = \frac{1}{k} \log_{\left(\frac{m-1}{m}\right)} p$. From equation 2, we have that $E(o) \approx 2(i - N)$, thus n (the size of the state space) $\approx i + 2(i - N)$.

Notice one last thing about Bloom filters in verification, if m is several gigabytes or less and m/n calls for more than about 32 index functions, the accuracy is going to be so high that there is not much reason to use more than 32 – for the next several years at least. In response to this, 3SPIN currently limits the user to $k = 32$. The point of this observation is that we do not have to worry about the runtime cost of k being on the order of 64 or 100, because those choices do not really buy us anything over 32.

4   Fingerprinting Bloom Filter

As Section 3.3 demonstrates, getting the highest accuracy for available m and estimated n can require the use of many index functions. In this section we introduce a strategy that can greatly reduce the cost of computing many index functions and analyze how to make its effect on accuracy negligible.

A regular Bloom filter operation applies the state descriptor (δ) to each of k independent hash functions to compute the bit vector indices associated with that state, yielding a time complexity of $k \times |\delta|$. A fingerprinting Bloom filter first applies the state descriptor to a hash function to compute that state's hash fingerprint, φ, and then applies that fingerprint to a set of k functions to get the indices for the state, yielding a complexity of $(|\varphi| \times |\delta|) + (k \times |\varphi|)$.

Let us consider a concrete example, like that used below in Figure 3. Let $k = 24$; let $|\varphi| = 2$ words; and let the state descriptor be $|\delta| = 16$ words, though a complex system could easily require 100 or more words. Thus, using independent hash functions requires 384 units of time for each Bloom filter operation, whereas using fingerprinting requires about 80 units. This is a very significant difference, as hash function computation tends to dominate the time cost of probabilistic model checking [14].

In order to quantify the accuracy impact of fingerprinting, we describe how its operation impacts how Bloom filters can omit states from models.

Definition 3 *A fingerprint collision is a state that is falsely presumed as previously added because a state that hashed to the same fingerprint was added previously.*

Definition 4 *A filter collision is a state that is not a fingerprint collision but is falsely presumed as previously added because all of the bits indexed were set to 1 by previous additions.*

The probability of an addition resulting in a fingerprint collision depends on the size of the fingerprint. If each fingerprint can take a value from 0 to $s - 1$, the probability of the $(i + 1)$st addition causing a fingerprint collision, clearly, is $f^{\text{FP}}_{s,i} = 1 - \left(1 - \frac{1}{s}\right)^i$.

The probability of a false positive in a fingerprinting Bloom filter is the probability of it having a fingerprint collision *or* having a filter collision, which is: $f^{\text{FPBF}}_{m,k,s,i} = 1 - (1 - f^{\text{FP}}_{s,i})(1 - f^{\text{BF}}_{m,k,i})$. A simple overestimate for $f^{\text{FPBF}}_{m,k,s,i}$ is $f^{\text{FP}}_{s,i} + f^{\text{BF}}_{m,k,i}$.

We can use this false positive probability for a fingerprinting Bloom filter ($f^{\text{FPBF}}_{m,k,s,i}$) to compute expected omissions from a search using a fingerprinting Bloom filter, and that is as simple as replacing $f^{\text{BF}}_{m,k,i}$ in Equation 1 with $f^{\text{FPBF}}_{m,k,s,i}$. For brevity, we have omitted the analysis for probability of omissions in a fingerprinting Bloom filter, but when much smaller than 1, the probability of any omissions is virtually the same as the expected hash omissions, because $1 - \prod(1 - x) \approx \sum x$ when $x \ll 1$.

Figure 3 plots the expected hash omissions for a 384MB Bloom filter using 24 index functions and a 64-bit fingerprint, which is about the size of two indices into the Bloom filter. The graph also has a curve for the contribution of filter collisions and for the contribution of fingerprint collisions. The "filter collision" curve shows what we would expect without using fingerprinting, and the "total" curve shows what we would expect from the fingerprinting Bloom filter. Note that the Y-axis for each graph uses a logarithmic scale, and once the accuracy of a fingerprinting Bloom filter is worse than some threshold, fingerprinting has virtually no effect on that accuracy. However, fingerprinting tends to limit how accurate a Bloom filter can get when below that same threshold. This accuracy threshold is determined mostly by the fingerprint size, accommodating higher Bloom filter accuracies if the fingerprint is larger.

5   Implementing Index Functions

Fingerprinting is the first key to enhancing the speed of Bloom filters with more than just a couple index functions, and the second key is to use an effective and efficient

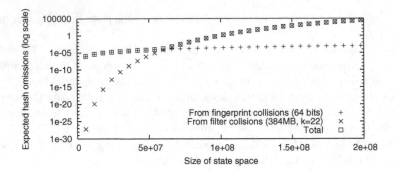

Fig. 3. This graph shows the expected hash omissions contributed by different types of collisions over a range of state space sizes ($0 \leq n \leq 2 \times 10^8$). 384MBytes are allocated to the Bloom filter ($m = 3 \times 2^{30}$) and 24 index functions are used ($k = 24$), the optimal choice for $n = 1 \times 10^8$. The fingerprint size is 64 bits ($s = 2^{64}$).

scheme for computing indices based on the fingerprint. This section describes two techniques introduced in previous work [5], points to some shortcomings in these techniques, and introduces a new technique that overcomes these shortcomings (as validated by results in Section 6).

5.1   Double and Triple Hashing

It is no coincidence that we analyzed fingerprinting Bloom filters in terms of a fingerprint the size of two indices. Our double and triple hashing techniques for Bloom filters employ two and three indices (respectively) to derive all k index values [5]. Double hashing is a well-known method of collision resolution in open-addressed hash tables [4, 15, 10], but we were the first to apply the concept to Bloom filters.

These approaches are easy to understand simply by looking at pseudocode:

Algorithm 1 *This algorithm computes index values for a Bloom filter by using double or **triple** hashing, by excluding or including (respectively) the lines in boldface. The indices for the Bloom filter to probe in its bit vector are stored into the array* f. *The fingerprint can be thought of as the results of the hash functions* a, b, *and (optionally)* c, *which operate on the state descriptor,* δ, *and return values from 0 to* $m - 1$ *(subject to restrictions in text).*

```
x, y := a(δ), b(δ)
z := c(δ)
f[0] := x
for i := 1 .. k-1
        x := (x + y) MOD m
        y := (y + z) MOD m
        f[i] := x
```

The algorithm describes how the values are computed on a sequential machine, and shows the simplicity of such computation. We can also define double and triple hashing mathematically:

$$f[i] = a(\delta) + ib(\delta) \quad (\bmod\ m) \qquad\qquad \text{(Double)} \qquad (4)$$

$$f[i] = a(\delta) + ib(\delta) + \frac{(i)(i-1)}{2}c(\delta) \quad (\bmod\ m) \qquad \text{(Triple)} \qquad (5)$$

Not present in either description are restrictions that must be placed on b to ensure all (or almost all) k indices are unique. In the case of double hashing, if $b(\delta)$ is zero, all indices will be the same, which is very bad for the collision probability. Similarly, if $b(\delta)$ divides m, the number of indices probed will be the minimum of k and $m/b(\delta)$, which could be as small as two. To avoid these cases, $b(\delta)$ should be made non-zero and relatively prime to m. When m is a power of 2, simply make $b(\delta)$ odd. If m is not a power of 2, we recommend making m the largest prime not greater than the requested m, and $b(\delta)$ must merely range from 1 to $m - 1$.

Triple hashing is less prone to the problems described for double hashing, because $b(\delta)$ and $c(\delta)$ must collaborate in generating redundant indices. Applying the same restrictions on $b(\delta)$ as we do for double hashing alleviates any problems. Although this does not guarantee all indices are unique, neither do independent hash functions, and in both cases a significant number of redundant indices for a single state is highly unlikely.

As empirical results in our companion SPIN paper show [5], double hashing imposes an observable accuracy limitation on a Bloom filter. In fact, a double hashing Bloom filter behaves much like a fingerprinting Bloom filter using a fingerprint a little smaller than two indices; that is, the accuracy threshold at which the choice of double hashing causes a noticeable loss of accuracy is worse than we would expect for a two-index fingerprint. In our SPIN implementation we went straight to triple hashing because our hash function produced enough data after a single run to support triple hashing.

For the general case, in which computing a three-index fingerprint could be 50% more costly than computing a two-index fingerprint, great would be a technique that preserves the theoretical accuracy of a two-index fingerprinting Bloom filter but has a per-k cost similar to double hashing.

5.2   Enhanced Double Hashing

A scheme we call "enhanced double hashing" comes much closer to the theoretical accuracy of two-index fingerprinting and has a per-k cost similar to double hashing. Here is the algorithm:

Algorithm 2 *This algorithm computes index values for a Bloom filter using our enhanced double hashing scheme. The indices for the Bloom filter to probe in its bit vector are stored into the array* f. *The two indices of the fingerprint are the results of the hash functions* a *and* b, *which operate on the state descriptor,* δ, *and return values from 0 to* $m - 1$

```
x, y := a(δ) MOD m, b(δ) MOD m
f[0] := x
for i := 1 .. k-1
        x := (x + y) MOD m
        y := (y + i) MOD m
        f[i] := x
```

We can also define enhanced double hashing mathematically:

$$\mathtt{f}\,[i] = a(\delta) + ib(\delta) + \frac{i^3 - i}{6} \quad (\mathrm{mod}\,m) \tag{6}$$

The first way this new scheme improves over double hashing is that $\mathtt{b}$ is no more restricted than $\mathtt{a}$; both of them can be arbitrary indices. Double hashing must make $\mathtt{b}(\delta)$ odd if m is a power of two, effectively reducing the fingerprint size by one bit, which approximately doubles the probability of a fingerprint collision.

The second problem with double hashing is more subtle, because the collisions the problem contributes to are not pure fingerprint collisions. Double hashing suffers from what we call the "approximate fingerprint collision" problem.

Definition 5 *An approximate fingerprint collision is a filter collision whose probability is exacerbated by two or more indices colliding with those of a single previous addition with a related fingerprint.*

What constitutes a relationship between fingerprints depends on the implementation of the index functions. The simplest example for double hashing is when $\mathtt{b}(\delta) = \mathtt{b}(\delta')$ and $\mathtt{a}(\delta) = \mathtt{a}(\delta') - \mathtt{b}(\delta)$ $(\mathrm{mod}\,m)$. If δ has already been added, all but one of the indices for δ' are already set to 1, which does not guarantee a collision (the other index might still be 0), but greatly increases the probability. Another example for double hashing is when $\mathtt{a}(\delta) = \mathtt{a}(\delta')$ and $\mathtt{b}(\delta) = 2\mathtt{b}(\delta')$ $(\mathrm{mod}\,m)$. If δ has already been added, every other index for δ' will collide with the first half the indices for δ.

In fact, the set of indices can be exactly the same if $\mathtt{a}(\delta) = \mathtt{a}(\delta') + (k-1)\mathtt{b}(\delta')$ $(\mathrm{mod}\,m)$ and $\mathtt{b}(\delta) = -\mathtt{b}(\delta')$ $(\mathrm{mod}\,m)$. According to this relationship, any set of indices producible by double hashing can be produced by two pairs of values: one going "forward" and the other going "backward". This would not happen if we made sure $\mathtt{b}(\delta)$ did not reach or exceed $m/2$, effectively reducing the fingerprint size by a bit, but the overall collision probability stays the same in either case.

Because enhanced double hashing does not suffer the drawbacks of double hashing, it preserves the theoretically expected accuracy of a two-index fingerprinting Bloom filter, as our empirical results show in the next section.

6   Empirical Validation

We start this section with results that demonstrate that our implementations and our techniques generalize to arbitrary models of arbitrary size (Table 2).

Table 3 shows that the various implementations of index functions match almost exactly the expected accuracies from our analyses. For example, double hashing performs worse than enhanced double even if two bits of information are removed from the fingerprint in the enhanced double implementation. This is consistent with the shortcomings we described for double hashing.

All of the "theoretical" values in Table 3 are computed from our fingerprinting analysis (Section 4), which assumes independent hash functions are applied to the fingerprint. In this case, the effect of a two-index fingerprint is (barely) observable and enhanced double hashing seems to do as well as we would expect using independent hash functions on the fingerprint.

Table 2. Validation of our approaches various models of various sizes. All these models are included in the SPIN distribution.

Model	Algorithm	States	m	k	% runs full	Expected	Iterations
Peterson4	Triple	7,308,888	32MB	25	99.11%	99.15%	336
Leader7	Triple	723,035	3MB	8	77.34%	75.69%	331
Sort9	Triple	2,509,313	8MB	20	59.88%	63.38%	329
PFTP1,3	Double	104,251,768	400MB	24	35%	30.89%	20
PFTP1,3	Triple	104,251,768	400MB	24	35%	30.89%	20

Table 3. We show the percentage of runs with full coverage when verifying a 914,859-state instance of PFTP using 4MB for the Bloom filter, 27 index functions, and the specified implementation of those index functions (see text). Each data point represents 100,000 iterations.

Implementation	Double	Enh. Double minus 2 bits	Enh. Double minus 1 bit	Enhanced Double	Triple	Independent & no FP
Observed	99.529%	99.740%	99.826%	99.880%	99.898%	99.898%
Theoretical		99.746%	99.820%	99.857%	99.894%	99.894%

The probability of a fingerprint collision with a three-index fingerprint is so low that we would need nine significant digits to notice its effects in the "theoretical expectation" calculations. The empirical results of using triple hashing are consistent with this expectation.

The left component of Figure 4 reminds us that the various index function algorithms only have observably different accuracies when the accuracy is really high. The same figure also shows that the various algorithms follow the same curve and, thus, the best choice for k applies to all of them. In this case, theory says the best choice is $k = 14$, which is consistent with the graph. Also notice that the graph has several outliers. These are not due to flaws in the algorithm, but to the unpredictability of transitive omissions.

The right component of Figure 4 shows execution times for various implementations of the index functions. The small per-k cost of our techniques make them much more efficient when many index functions are used. For example, $k = 28$ for enhanced double hashing is faster (per state explored) than $k = 5$ for independent hash functions, and five times faster than $k = 28$ for independent hash functions.

Our last test (not graphed) estimates how much of the per-k cost of additional index functions under enhanced double hashing is due to main memory latency. When the Bloom filter was sized much larger than the processor cache, $k = 27$ was 44% slower than $k = 10$. However, when the Bloom filter and the code were able to fit in cache, $k = 27$ was only 26% slower. For this machine at least (Katmai Pentium III Xeon, 2MB cache), we can conclude that main memory latency is at least 40% of the per-k cost, which suggests the per-k overhead of our Bloom filters is about is small as possible.

7   Conclusions

We have shown how to obtain Bloom filters that are simultaneously fast, accurate, memory-efficient, scalable, and flexible. As a result, Bloom filters tuned for particular

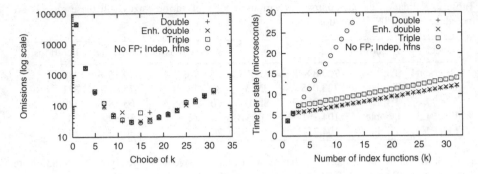

Fig. 4. The left graph shows the number of omissions for various algorithms and choices of k using a 2MB Bloom filter (no consistent difference intended; see text). Each point is an average of 1000 iterations. The graph on the right shows the time per state visited for various index function implementations and choices of k. 8MB was allocated for the Bloom filter, and each data point is the average time per state over 5 verifier runs. Both experiments used a 914,859-state instance of PFTP with 192-byte (48-word) descriptors.

state space size estimates run at speeds approaching a supertrace Bloom filter (two hash functions). When only a rough estimate of the state space size is available, *e.g.*, after a model has been modified, such properly-tuned Bloom filters have a sizable advantage over both supertrace and hash compaction. Supertrace does not take into account any information about estimated state space sizes and, thus, incurs a significant accuracy cost; at the other extreme, hash compaction can offer the highest accuracy of the approaches we have considered, but easily becomes a bad choice if our estimate is off by about 15%. For these reasons, our Bloom filters have an important role to play in the modern practice of model checking and verification.

References

1. B. H. Bloom. Space/time trade-offs in hash coding with allowable errors. *Communications of the ACM*, 13(7):422–426, July 1970.
2. A. Broder and M. Mitzenmacher. Network applications of Bloom filters: A survey. In *Proc. of the 40th Annual Allerton Conference on Communication, Control, and Computing*, pages 636–646, 2002.
3. C.N. Ip and D.L. Dill. Better verification through symmetry. In *Computer Hardware Description Languages and their Applications*, pages 87–100, Ottawa, Canada, 1993. Elsevier Science Publishers B.V., Amsterdam, Netherland.
4. T. H. Cormen, C. Stein, R. L. Rivest, and C. E. Leiserson. *Introduction to Algorithms*. McGraw-Hill Higher Education, 2001.
5. P. C. Dillinger and P. Manolios. Fast *and* accurate bitstate verification for SPIN. In *11th SPIN Workshop*, Barcelona, Spain, April 2004.
6. E.M. Clarke, T. Filkorn, and S. Jha. Exploiting symmetry in temporal logic model checking. In *CAV '93*, pages 450–461, June 1993.
7. F. A. Emerson and A. P. Sistla. Symmetry and model checking. *Formal Methods in System Design: An International Journal*, 9(1/2):105–131, August 1996.

8. L. Fan, P. Cao, J. Almeida, and A. Z. Broder. Summary cache: a scalable wide-area Web cache sharing protocol. *IEEE/ACM Transactions on Networking*, 8(3):281–293, 2000.
9. P. Godefroid and P. Wolper. A partial approach to model checking. In *Logic in Computer Science*, pages 406–415, 1991.
10. G. H. Gonnet. *Handbook of Algorithms and Data Structures*. Addison-Wesley, 1984.
11. G. Holzmann and D. Peled. Partial order reduction of the state space. In *First SPIN Workshop*, Montrèal, Quebec, 1995.
12. G. J. Holzmann. *Design and Validation of Computer Protocols*. Prentice Hall, 1991.
13. G. J. Holzmann. An analysis of bitstate hashing. In *Proc. 15th Int. Conf on Protocol Specification, Testing, and Verification, INWG/IFIP*, pages 301–314, Warsaw, Poland, 1995. Chapman & Hall.
14. G. J. Holzmann. *The Spin Model Checker: Primer and Reference Manual*. Addison-Wesley, Boston, Massachusetts, 2003.
15. D. E. Knuth. *The Art of Computer Programming*, volume 3: Sorting and Searching. Addison Wesley Longman Publishing Co., Inc., 2nd edition, 1997.
16. M. Mitzenmacher. Compressed Bloom filters. In *Proc. of the 20th Annual ACM Symposium on Principles of Distributed Computing*, IEEE/ACM Trans. on Net., pages 144–150, 2001.
17. G. Penna, B. Intrigila, E. Tronci, and M. Zilli. Exploiting transition locality in the disk based Murphi verifier. In *4th International Conference on Formal Methods in Computer Aided Verification*, pages 202–219, 2002.
18. U. Stern and D. L. Dill. Improved probabilistic verification by hash compaction. In P. Camurati and H. Eveking, editors, *Correct Hardware Design and Verification Methods, IFIP WG 10.5 Advanced Research Working Conference, CHARME '95*, volume 987 of *LNCS*, pages 206–224. Springer-Verlag, 1995.
19. U. Stern and D. L. Dill. A new scheme for memory-efficient probabilistic verification. In *IFIP TC6/WG6.1 Joint International Conference on Formal Description Techniques for Distributed Systems and Communication Protocols, and Protocol Specification, Testing, and Verification*, pages 333–348, 1996. Kaiserslautern Germany, October 8-11.
20. W. Visser, K. Havelund, G. Brat, and S. Park. Model checking programs. In *International Conference on Automated Software Engineering*, Sept. 2000.
21. P. Wolper and D. Leroy. Reliable hashing without collision detection. In *5th International Conference on Computer Aided Verification*, pages 59–70, 1993.
22. P. Wolper, U. Stern, D. Leroy, and D. Dill. Reliable probabilistic verification using hash compaction, Unpublished.
23. Y. Yu, P. Manolios, and L. Lamport. Model checking TLA+ specifications. In L. Pierre and T. Kropf, editors, *Correct Hardware Design and Verification Methods, CHARME '99*, volume 1703 of *LNCS*, pages 54–66. Springer-Verlag, 1999.

A Simple Method for Parameterized Verification of Cache Coherence Protocols

Ching-Tsun Chou*, Phanindra K. Mannava, and Seungjoon Park

Intel Corporation
3600 Juliette Lane, SC12-322
Santa Clara, CA 95054, USA
ching-tsun.chou@intel.com

Abstract. We present a simple method for verifying the safety properties of cache coherence protocols with arbitrarily many nodes. Our presentation begins with two examples. The first example describes in intuitive terms how the German protocol with arbitrarily many nodes can be verified using a combination of Murphi model checking and apparently circular reasoning. The second example outlines a similar proof of the FLASH protocol. These are followed by a simple theory based on the classical notion of simulation proofs that justifies the apparently circular reasoning. We conclude the paper by discussing what remains to be done and by comparing our method with other approaches to the parameterized verification of cache coherence protocols, such as compositional model checking, machine-assisted theorem proving, predicate abstraction, invisible invariants, and cut-off theorems.

1 Introduction

The by-now standard method in industry for debugging a cache coherence protocol is to build a formal model of the protocol at the algorithmic level and then do an exhaustive reachability analysis of the model for a small configuration size (typically 3 or 4 nodes) using either explicit-state or symbolic model checking. While this method does offer a much higher degree of confidence in the correctness of the protocol than informal reasoning and simulation can, and protocol designers often have intuitions about why 3 or 4 nodes suffice to exercise all "interesting" scenarios, it is still very desirable to actually have a *proof* that the protocol model is correct for *any* number of nodes.

Proving a protocol correct for any number of nodes (or some other configuration parameters) is called *parameterized verification*. Unfortunately, parameterized verification is in general an undecidable problem [1]. While this result may not be directly applicable to a specific protocol or even a restricted class of protocols, it does suggest that parameterized verification of real-world protocols will likely require a certain amount of human intervention. So our goal here is to figure out how to minimize human intervention and maximize the work done by

---

* Main contact.

A.J. Hu and A.K. Martin (Eds.): FMCAD 2004, LNCS 3312, pp. 382–398, 2004.
© Springer-Verlag Berlin Heidelberg 2004

automatic tools (such as model checkers). Most importantly, we would like the automatic tools to extract the necessary information from the protocol that can guide the human prover to come up with the crucial lemmas that will enable the automatic tools to finish the proof unaided.

Inspired by McMillan's work on compositional model checking [10] and its application to the FLASH cache coherence protocol [12], we present in this paper a simple method for the parameterized verification of cache coherence protocols that meet the above desiderata. Our method has several advantages:

1. It can be used with any model checker. The freedom to choose model checkers is important in practice, as experience shows that for cache coherence protocols explicit-state model checkers are more robust and often more powerful than symbolic model checkers[1]. In this paper we use Murphi [5, 8].
2. It has a clearly spelled-out and, we hope, easy-to-understand theory justifying the soundness of the apparent circularity in its reasoning. The theory is based on the classical notion of *simulation proofs* [15].
3. The invariants, called *noninterference lemmas*, that the human prover has to provide for the proof to go through fall far short of a full-fledged inductive invariant, which are very hard to construct for any nontrivial protocol. This is especially true for more complex protocols such as FLASH.
4. The capability of model checkers to do reachability analysis completely automates the reasoning about the states of individual nodes and is used to discover crucial interactions *between* nodes, which then guide the human prover to formulate the right noninterference lemmas.
5. Having applied our method to the German and FLASH cache coherence protocols successfully, we believe that it is quite applicable to many industrial cache coherence protocols, though certain automation will make it easier and more reliable to use.

The rest of this paper is organized as follows. Sections 2 and 3 explain our method in intuitive terms using as examples the German and FLASH cache coherence protocols. In addition to demonstrating the feasibility of our method, these examples give a flavor of the hardest human task in applying our method: the formulation of noninterference lemmas using insights gained from counterexamples. Once all the counterexamples are removed, the theory developed in Section 4 based on the classical notion of simulation proofs can be used to justify the

---

[1] There are several possible reasons for this. First, the speed and space requirement of explicit executions do not vary a lot with the details of data structures used in the protocol, while BDD performance can be very sensitive to the precise nature of data structures (e.g., FIFO queues tend to be bad for BDDs). Second, explicit-state model checking can take advantage of symmetry reduction [8] in each run, while symmetry reduction only reduces the number of cases to prove, not the complexity of each proof, in symbolic model checking [10]. Third, explicit-state model checkers lend themselves better than symbolic ones to disk-based techniques [4], which can trade time for capacity. SAT-based symbolic model checkers are not known to outperform BDD-based ones on cache coherence protocols [13].

apparently circular reasoning needed in our proofs. Section 5 discusses what remains to be done, in particular how the many tedious tasks performed by hand in the German and FLASH proofs can and should be mechanized. Section 6 compares our method with other approaches to the parameterized verification of cache coherence protocols.

2   Parameterized Verification of the German Protocol

The German protocol [7] is a simple cache coherence protocol devised by Steven German in 2000 as a challenge problem to the formal verification community[2]. Since then it has become a common example in papers on parameterized verification [2, 6, 9, 17]. The Murphi code of the German protocol we will use is shown in Figure 1 and should be self-explanatory. It is essentially the same as the one in [17] except that we have shortened identifier names and added data paths to make it more interesting. The state variable AuxData is an auxiliary variable for tracking the latest value of the cache line and does not affect the execution of the protocol in any way; its sole purpose is to allow us to state the property (DataProp) about the correct data values in memory and caches.

Now let us try to prove that the invariants CtrlProp and DataProp are true in the German protocol (abbreviated as GERMAN below) for an arbitrary number of caching nodes. The basic idea behind our method is as follows. Consider an instance of GERMAN with a large number of caching nodes. Choose any 2 of the caching nodes (the reason for the number 2 will become clear later) and observe the behaviors of them plus the home node (whose data structures are not indexed by NODE). Note that since all caching nodes are symmetric [8] with respect to one another, it does not matter which 2 nodes we choose. We will try to construct an abstract model ABSGERMAN containing the home node plus the 2 chosen nodes with the following properties:

P1. ABSGERMAN permits all possible behaviors that the home node plus the 2 chosen nodes can engage in, including what those nodes that are *not* chosen can do to them.

P2. The behaviors of ABSGERMAN are sufficiently constrained that interesting properties (including CtrlProp and DataProp) can be proved about them.

If we can achieve both P1 and P2, then we can deduce the truth of CtrlProp and DataProp in GERMAN from their truth in ABSGERMAN. But there is clearly a tension between P1 and P2 and it is not obvious how to meet them both. Our strategy is to start with an ABSGERMAN that obviously satisfies P1 but violates P2 and then refine ABSGERMAN over several steps until P2 is satisfied, while maintaining P1 all the time.

We begin with a naive abstraction of GERMAN shown in Figure 2 that is obtained by making the following changes to the model in Figure 1:

---

[2] German's challenge was to verify the protocol fully automatically, which is *not* our goal. But his protocol, being short, is a good medium for presenting our method.

```
const  ---- Configuration parameters ----

  NODE_NUM : 4;
  DATA_NUM : 2;

type  ---- Type declarations ----

  NODE : scalarset(NODE_NUM);
  DATA : scalarset(DATA_NUM);

  CACHE_STATE : enum {I, S, E};
  CACHE : record State : CACHE_STATE; Data : DATA; end;

  MSG_CMD : enum {Empty, ReqS, ReqE, Inv, InvAck, GntS, GntE};
  MSG : record Cmd : MSG_CMD; Data : DATA; end;

var  ---- State variables ----

  Cache : array [NODE] of CACHE;      -- Caches
  Chan1 : array [NODE] of MSG;        -- Channels for Req*
  Chan2 : array [NODE] of MSG;        -- Channels for Gnt* and Inv
  Chan3 : array [NODE] of MSG;        -- Channels for InvAck
  InvSet : array [NODE] of boolean;   -- Nodes to be invalidated
  ShrSet : array [NODE] of boolean;   -- Nodes having S or E copies
  ExGntd : boolean;                   -- E copy has been granted
  CurCmd : MSG_CMD;                   -- Current request command
  CurPtr : NODE;                      -- Current request node
  MemData : DATA;                     -- Memory data
  AuxData : DATA;                     -- Latest value of cache line

  ---- Initial states ----

ruleset d : DATA do startstate "Init"
  for i : NODE do
    Chan1[i].Cmd := Empty; Chan2[i].Cmd := Empty; Chan3[i].Cmd := Empty;
    Cache[i].State := I; InvSet[i] := false; ShrSet[i] := false;
  end;
  ExGntd := false; CurCmd := Empty; MemData := d; AuxData := d;
end end;

  ---- State transitions ----

ruleset i : NODE do rule "SendReqS"
  Chan1[i].Cmd = Empty & Cache[i].State = I
==>
  Chan1[i].Cmd := ReqS;
end end;

ruleset i : NODE do rule "SendReqE"
  Chan1[i].Cmd = Empty & (Cache[i].State = I | Cache[i].State = S)
==>
  Chan1[i].Cmd := ReqE;
end end;

ruleset i : NODE do rule "RecvReqS"
  CurCmd = Empty & Chan1[i].Cmd = ReqS
==>
  CurCmd := ReqS; CurPtr := i; Chan1[i].Cmd := Empty;
  for j : NODE do InvSet[j] := ShrSet[j] end;
end end;

ruleset i : NODE do rule "RecvReqE"
  CurCmd = Empty & Chan1[i].Cmd = ReqE
==>
  CurCmd := ReqE; CurPtr := i; Chan1[i].Cmd := Empty;
  for j : NODE do InvSet[j] := ShrSet[j] end;
end end;
```

```
ruleset i : NODE do rule "SendInv"
  Chan2[i].Cmd = Empty & InvSet[i] = true &
  ( CurCmd = ReqE | CurCmd = ReqS & ExGntd = true )
==>
  Chan2[i].Cmd := Inv; InvSet[i] := false;
end end;

ruleset i : NODE do rule "SendInvAck"
  Chan2[i].Cmd = Inv & Chan3[i].Cmd = Empty
==>
  Chan2[i].Cmd := Empty; Chan3[i].Cmd := InvAck;
  if (Cache[i].State = E) then Chan3[i].Data := Cache[i].Data end;
  Cache[i].State := I; undefine Cache[i].Data;
end end;

ruleset i : NODE do rule "RecvInvAck"
  Chan3[i].Cmd = InvAck & CurCmd != Empty
==>
  Chan3[i].Cmd := Empty; ShrSet[i] := false;
  if (ExGntd = true)
  then ExGntd := false; MemData := Chan3[i].Data; undefine Chan3[i].Data; end;
end end;

ruleset i : NODE do rule "SendGntS"
  CurCmd = ReqS & CurPtr = i & Chan2[i].Cmd = Empty & ExGntd = false
==>
  Chan2[i].Cmd := GntS; Chan2[i].Data := MemData; ShrSet[i] := true;
  CurCmd := Empty; undefine CurPtr;
end end;

ruleset i : NODE do rule "SendGntE"
  CurCmd = ReqE & CurPtr = i & Chan2[i].Cmd = Empty & ExGntd = false &
  forall j : NODE do ShrSet[j] = false end
==>
  Chan2[i].Cmd := GntE; Chan2[i].Data := MemData; ShrSet[i] := true;
  ExGntd := true; CurCmd := Empty; undefine CurPtr;
end end;

ruleset i : NODE do rule "RecvGntS"
  Chan2[i].Cmd = GntS
==>
  Cache[i].State := S; Cache[i].Data := Chan2[i].Data;
  Chan2[i].Cmd := Empty; undefine Chan2[i].Data;
end end;

ruleset i : NODE do rule "RecvGntE"
  Chan2[i].Cmd = GntE
==>
  Cache[i].State := E; Cache[i].Data := Chan2[i].Data;
  Chan2[i].Cmd := Empty; undefine Chan2[i].Data;
end end;

ruleset i : NODE; d : DATA do rule "Store"
  Cache[i].State = E
==>
  Cache[i].Data := d; AuxData := d;
end end;

  ---- Invariant properties ----

invariant "CtrlProp"
  forall i : NODE do forall j : NODE do
    i != j -> (Cache[i].State = E -> Cache[j].State = I) &
              (Cache[i].State = S -> Cache[j].State = I | Cache[j].State = S)
  end end;

invariant "DataProp"
  ( ExGntd = false -> MemData = AuxData ) &
  forall i : NODE do Cache[i].State != I -> Cache[i].Data = AuxData end;
```

Fig. 1. The German cache coherence protocol

1. Set NODE_NUM to 2, which has the effect of changing the type NODE to containing only the 2 nodes chosen for observation.

2. Add a new type declaration: "ABS_NODE : union {NODE, enum{Other}}", which contains the 2 chosen nodes plus a special value Other representing all those nodes that are *not* chosen.

3. If a state variable (including array entries) has type NODE, change it to ABS_NODE, because in the abstract model a node pointer can still point to a node that is not being observed (i.e., an Other). In GERMAN, there is only one variable whose type is so changed: "CurPtr : ABS_NODE".

4. But the occurrences of NODE as array index types are *not* changed, because we are observing only the nodes in NODE (plus the home node, which is not indexed) and have discarded the part of the state corresponding to the nodes represented by Other.

```
const
  NODE_NUM : 2

type
  NODE : scalarset(NODE_NUM);
  ABS_NODE : union {NODE, enum{Other}};

var
  CurPtr : ABS_NODE;

-- Include the original German protocol model
-- here, but with the above changes/additions.

rule "ABS_Skip" end;

rule "ABS_RecvReqS"
  CurCmd = Empty
==>
  CurCmd := ReqS; CurPtr := Other;
  for j : NODE do InvSet[j] := ShrSet[j] end;
end;

rule "ABS_RecvReqE"
  CurCmd = Empty
==>
  CurCmd := ReqE; CurPtr := Other;
  for j : NODE do InvSet[j] := ShrSet[j] end;
end;
```

```
rule "ABS_RecvInvAck"
  CurCmd != Empty & ExGntd = true
==>
  ExGntd := false; undefine MemData;
end;

rule "ABS_SendGntS"
  CurCmd = ReqS & CurPtr = Other & ExGntd = false
==>
  CurCmd := Empty; undefine CurPtr;
end;

rule "ABS_SendGntE"
  CurCmd = ReqE & CurPtr = Other & ExGntd = false &
  forall j : NODE do ShrSet[j] = false end
==>
  ExGntd := true; CurCmd := Empty; undefine CurPtr;
end;

ruleset d : DATA do rule "ABS_Store"
  true
==>
  AuxData := d;
end end;
```

Fig. 2. Abstract German protocol: First version

5. There is nothing to be done about abstracting the state initialization routine `Init`, since no node pointer is initialized to a specific node (`CurPtr` is initialized to undefined).

6. We now consider how to abstract the state transition rulesets, each of which has a node parameter i. There are two cases to consider:

   (a) When i is one of the 2 chosen nodes: This is taken care of by keeping a copy of the original ruleset, since now the type `NODE` contains precisely those 2 nodes. There is one subtlety, though: note that the precondition of ruleset `SendGntE` contains a universal quantification over `NODE`, which is weakened by the "shrinking" of `NODE` to only the 2 chosen nodes. But since the universal quantification occurs positively, this weakening only makes the rule more permissive, which is what we want (recall P1 above).

   (b) When i is an `Other`: We create an abstract version of each ruleset for this case, as shown in Figure 2. The goal is to satisfy P1 without making the abstract rulesets too permissive. Our method is summarized below:

       i. All occurrences of i in the original rulesets are replaced by `Other`.

       ii. All references to the part of the state indexed by `Other` that occur positively in the preconditions are replaced by `true`, since the abstract model does not track that part of the state and hence cannot know the truth values of such references. By substituting `true` for such references, the rules are made more permissive (indeed, often *too* permissive, which we will fix later).

       iii. Similarly, all changes to the part of the state indexed by `Other` are discarded, since they have no effects on the part of the state that the abstract model keeps. As a consequence, the rulesets `SendReq*`,

SendInv, SendInvAck, and RecvGnt* are all abstracted by a single
no-op rule ABS_Skip. Furthermore, since the statement part of ruleset ABS_RecvInvAck now contains only a single "if c then s end",
we move the condition c into the guard of the ruleset.

iv. If a part of the state indexed by Other is assigned to a state variable in the abstract model, we undefine that variable to represent
the fact that the value being assigned is unknown. This happens to
MemData in ruleset ABS_RecvInvAck.

v. The argument about the universal quantification in the precondition
of the ruleset ABS_SendGntE is the same as before.

Clearly, the above abstraction steps are *conservative* in the sense that the ABS-
GERMAN thus obtained permit all possible behaviors of the home node plus any
2 caching nodes in GERMAN. It is, however, *too* conservative: if we model-check
the abstract model in Figure 2, we will get a counterexample. In the rest of this
section we explain how ABSGERMAN can be "fixed" to remove all counterexamples. But before we do that, let us comment out the property DataProp, because
for cache coherence protocols it is generally a good idea to prove all control logic
properties before working on any data path properties, as the latter depends on
the former but not vice versa.

We now do the model checking, which produces the following counterexample
to CtrlProp: node n_1 sends a ReqE to home; home receives the ReqE and sends
a GntE to node n_1; node n_1 receives the GntE and changes its cache state to E;
node n_2 sends a ReqS to home; home receives the ReqS and is about to send
an Inv to node n_1; but suddenly home receives a bogus InvAck from Other
(via ABS_RecvInvAck), which causes home to reset ExGntd and send a GntS
to node n_2; node n_2 receives the GntS and changes its cache state to S, which
violates CtrlProp because node n_1 is still in E. The bogus InvAck from Other
is clearly where things start to go wrong: if there is a node in E, home should
not receive InvAck from any other node. We can capture this desired property
as a *noninterference lemma*:

```
invariant "Lemma_1"
  forall i : NODE do
    Chan3[i].Cmd = InvAck & CurCmd != Empty & ExGntd = true ->
    forall j : NODE do
      j != i -> Cache[j].State != E & Chan2[j].Cmd != GntE
  end end;
```

which says that if home is ready to receive an InvAck from node i (note that
the antecedent is simply the precondition of RecvInvAck plus the condition
ExGntd = true, which is the only case when the InvAck is to have any effect
in ABS_RecvInvAck), then every other node j must not have cache state E or a
GntE in transit to it. (We are looking ahead a bit here: if the part about GntE
is omitted from Lemma_1, the next counterexample will compel us to add it.)
If Lemma_1 is indeed true in GERMAN, then we will be justified to *refine* the
offending abstract ruleset ABS_RecvInvAck as follows:

```
rule "ABS_RecvInvAck"
  CurCmd != Empty & ExGntd = true &
  forall j : NODE do
    Cache[j].State != E & Chan2[j].Cmd != GntE
  end
==> ... end;
```

where we have strengthened the precondition by instantiating Lemma_1 with i = Other. (Note that since Other is distinct from any j in NODE in the abstract model, there is no need to test for the inequality.) Why is this strengthening justified? Because Lemma_1 says that when RecvInvAck with i = Other is enabled, the conjunct we add to the precondition of ABS_RecvInvAck is true anyway, so adding that conjunct does *not* make ABS_RecvInvAck any less permissive.

But how do we prove that Lemma_1 is true in GERMAN? The surprising answer is that we can prove it in the same abstract model where we have used it to refine one of the abstract ruleset! Is there any circularity in our argument? The answer is *no*, and we will develop a theory in Section 4 to justify this claim.

So we can refine ABS_RecvInvAck as shown above and add Lemma_1 as an additional invariant to prove in the abstract model. But this is not yet sufficient for removing all counterexamples. More noninterference lemmas and ruleset refinements are needed for that and the model checker will guide us to discovering them via the counterexamples. The final result of this process is shown in Figure 3, where the step numbers refer to the following sequence of steps:

Step 1: This is the discussion above.

Step 2: A rather long counterexample to Lemma_1 shows the following. Node n_1 acquires an E copy, which is invalidated by a ReqS from Other. But before the InvAck reaches home, home receives a bogus InvAck from Other, which makes home think that there is no E copy outstanding and hence sends GntS to Other. Now node n_2 sends ReqE to home, which receives the stale InvAck from node n_1 and sends GntE to node n_2. But the Inv that home sends to n_1 on behalf of n_2 is still in the network, which now reaches node n_1 and generates a InvAck. So now we have both a InvAck from node n_1 and a GntE to node n_2 in the network, which violates Lemma_1 once Other sends a ReqE to home. The fix to this problem is to outlaw the bogus InvAck from Other by refining ABS_RecvInvAck using a strengthened Lemma_1 asserting that there can be at most one InvAck if it is from an E copy. After this step, CtrlProp is proved[3], so we bring DataProp back by uncommenting it.

Step 3: A trivial counterexample to the first clause of DataProp shows Other doing a store when ExGntd is false. The fix is to refine ABS_Store using a new noninterference lemma Lemma_2 that outlaws this.

---

[3] The fact that CtrlProp is proved for any number of nodes after only two steps and four more steps are needed to prove DataProp, suggests that there are interesting properties about the control logic that are not needed to prove the former but needed for the latter. Interestingly, none of the research papers on verifying GERMAN [2, 6, 9, 17] considered adding the data paths.

```
-- Everything up to rule "ABS_SendGntE"          -- Noninterference lemmas:
-- is exactly the same as in Figure 2.
                                                 invariant "Lemma_1"
rule "ABS_RecvInvAck"                               forall i : NODE do
  CurCmd != Empty & ExGntd = true &                  Chan3[i].Cmd = InvAck & CurCmd != Empty &
  forall j : NODE do                                 ExGntd = true ->
    Cache[j].State != E &      -- Step 1            Chan3[i].Data = AuxData &          -- Step 4
    Chan2[j].Cmd != GntE &     -- Step 1            forall j : NODE do
    Chan3[j].Cmd != InvAck     -- Step 2             j != i -> Cache[j].State != E &   -- Step 1
  end                                                            Chan2[j].Cmd != GntE & -- Step 1
==>                                                             Chan3[j].Cmd != InvAck -- Step 2
  ExGntd := false;                                 end end;
  MemData := AuxData;          -- Step 4
end;                                             invariant "Lemma_2"
                                                   forall i : NODE do
ruleset d : DATA do rule "ABS_Store"                 Cache[i].State = E ->
  ExGntd = true &              -- Step 3            ExGntd = true &                    -- Step 3
  forall j : NODE do                               forall j : NODE do
    Cache[j].State = I &       -- Step 5            j != i -> Cache[j].State = I &     -- Step 5
    Chan2[j].Cmd != GntS &     -- Step 5                        Chan2[j].Cmd != GntS & -- Step 5
    Chan2[j].Cmd != GntE &     -- Step 5                        Chan2[j].Cmd != GntE & -- Step 5
    Chan3[j].Cmd != InvAck     -- Step 6                        Chan3[j].Cmd != InvAck -- Step 6
  end                                              end end;
==>
  AuxData := d;
end end;
```

Fig. 3. Abstract German protocol: Final version

Step 4: A short counterexample to the first clause of `DataProp` shows that `Other` acquires an `E` and then messes up `MemData` by writing back undefined data. The fix is to refine `ABS_RecvInvAck` using a strengthened `Lemma_1` asserting that the written back data must be `AuxData`.

Step 5: A short counterexample to the second clause of `DataProp` shows that a node acquires an `E` copy and then suddenly `Other` does a store that changes `AuxData`. The fix is to refine `ABS_Store` using a strengthened `Lemma_2` asserting that if any node i is in state `E`, then any other node j cannot be in `E` as well. Looking ahead, j should also be required not to be in `S` or about to become `E` or `S`, for similar counterexamples can arise without these additional properties. Again, the model checker will lead us to these additional requirements even if we have not thought of them.

Step 6: A counterexample to `Lemma_1` shows the following. Node n_1 acquires an `E` copy, which is invalidated by a `ReqE` from `Other`. But before the `InvAck` reaches home, `Other` does a store that changes `AuxData` to violate its equality to the data carried by the `InvAck` (which is added to `Lemma_1` in Step 4). The fix is to refine `ABS_Store` using a strengthened `Lemma_2` asserting that if any node has cache state `E`, then any other node cannot have an `InvAck` in transit to home.

After Step 6, all counterexamples disappear. According to the theory developed in Section 4, this means that `CtrlProp` and `DataProp` (plus the noninterference lemmas) have been proved for GERMAN with arbitrarily many nodes.

Now we come to the question of why the abstract model is set up to have 2 nodes. This is because none of the universally quantified formulas in the desired properties (`CtrlProp` and `DataProp`), the noninterference lemmas (`Lemma_1` and

Lemma_2), and the rulesets has more than 2 nested quantifiers over nodes. So a 2-node abstract model suffices to give a "maximally diverse" interpretation to the quantified formulas (i.e., an interpretation in which different quantified variables are not forced to take on the same values due to the small size of the universe of the interpretation).

A related question is why, unlikely McMillan in [10, 12], we have been able to dispense with a three-valued logic in the abstraction and reasoning process. The reason for this is that we have imposed the following syntactic constraints on our models and properties: (1) a state variable (or array entry) of type NODE is never compared with another state variable (or array entry) of the same type, and (2) an array over NODE is never indexed into directly by a state variable (or array entry). For instance, in the rulesets SendGnt* in Figure 1, instead of using CurPtr to index into arrays directly (as is done in [17]), we introduce a bound variable i ranging over NODE, test CurPtr = i in the precondition, and use i to index into arrays. Under these syntactic constraints, the abstraction process outlined above becomes feasible[4] and every logic formula is either true or false in the abstract model, where Other is a possible value of a node-valued state variable (or array entry). Our experience suggests that all practical cache coherence protocols can be modeled and their properties stated under these syntactic constraints. Also note that these constraints make it impossible for a formula to implicitly say that "there are K nodes" (e.g., by stating that K node-valued state variables are pairwise unequal) without a corresponding number of quantifiers over nodes[5].

3   Parameterized Verification of the FLASH Protocol

The Murphi code of FLASH we use is translated from McMillan's SMV code [12], which in turn is translated from Park's PVS code [16]. To be precise, this is a model of the "eager mode" of the FLASH protocol[6].

FLASH is much more complex and realistic than GERMAN. Their numbers of reachable states (after symmetry reduction) are an indication of this: GERMAN has 852, 5235, 28088 states and FLASH has 6336, 1083603, 67540392 states at 2, 3, 4 nodes, respectively. So, with brute-force model checking, FLASH is at best barely verifiable at 5 nodes and definitely not verifiable at 6 nodes. (SMV does not perform any better than Murphi on FLASH.) FLASH is a good test for any proposed method of parameterized verification: if the method works on FLASH, then there is a good chance that it will also work on many real-world cache coherence protocols.

---

[4] Existentially quantified formulas that occur positively in rule preconditions will still cause problems, but in practice they rarely occur and can always be replaced by auxiliary variables that supply explicit witnesses.

[5] We are grateful to Steven German for pointing out this issue to us.

[6] In the *eager mode* of FLASH, the home is allowed to grant an exclusive copy before all shared copies have been invalidated. In contrast, in the *delayed mode* of FLASH, the home must invalidate all shared copies before granting an exclusive copy.

```
invariant "Lemma_1"
    forall h : NODE do forall i : NODE do
    h = Home & Proc[i].CacheState = CACHE_E ->
    Dir.Dirty & WbMsg.Cmd != WB_Wb & ShWbMsg.Cmd != SHWB_ShWb & UniMsg[h].Cmd != UNI_Put &
    forall j : NODE do UniMsg[j].Cmd != UNI_PutX end &
    forall j : NODE do j != i -> Proc[j].CacheState != CACHE_E end
    end end;

invariant "Lemma_2"
    forall h : NODE do forall i : NODE do forall j : NODE do
    h = Home & i != j & j != h & UniMsg[i].Cmd = UNI_Get & UniMsg[i].Proc = j ->
    Dir.Pending & !Dir.Local & PendReqSrc = i & FwdCmd = UNI_Get
    end end end;

invariant "Lemma_3"
    forall h : NODE do forall i : NODE do forall j : NODE do
    h = Home & i != j & j != h & UniMsg[i].Cmd = UNI_GetX & UniMsg[i].Proc = j ->
    Dir.Pending & !Dir.Local & PendReqSrc = i & FwdCmd = UNI_GetX
    end end end;

invariant "Lemma_4"
    forall h : NODE do forall i : NODE do
    h = Home & i != h & InvMsg[i].Cmd = INV_InvAck ->
    Dir.Pending & Collecting & NakcMsg.Cmd = NAKC_None & ShWbMsg.Cmd = SHWB_None &
    forall j : NODE do
        ( UniMsg[j].Cmd = UNI_Get | UniMsg[j].Cmd = UNI_GetX -> UniMsg[j].Proc = h ) &
        ( UniMsg[j].Cmd = UNI_PutX -> UniMsg[j].Proc = h & PendReqSrc = j )
    end end end;

invariant "Lemma_5"
    forall i : NODE do Proc[i].CacheState = CACHE_E -> Proc[i].CacheData = CurrData end;
```

Fig. 4. Noninterference lemmas for FLASH

We have done a proof of the safety properties of FLASH for any number of nodes (which is available upon request) using the same method as described in Section 2. Due to space limitations, we cannot give full details here. Below we only list the main differences between this proof and the proof of GERMAN:

1. The number of nodes in the abstract model is 3 (instead of 2). For, in FLASH, the request processing flow is such that it is convenient to make the home node data structures also indexed by NODE. This has the effect of making some noninterference lemmas contain 3 nested quantifers over nodes.

2. In FLASH there are node-indexed arrays whose entries are node-valued, which is a type of data structures that GERMAN does not have. In the abstract model those node-valued array entries must be allowed to have the value Other, just like node-valued state variables.

3. In FLASH a ruleset may have up to 2 node parameters. A typical example is a node n_1 with the exclusive copy receiving a forwarded request from the home, in which case n_1 sends the copy directly to the requesting node n_2 without going through the home. To abstract such a ruleset, we have to consider four cases: when n_1 and n_2 are both in the abstract model, when n_1 is in but n_2 is Other, when n_2 is in but n_1 is Other, and when n_1 and n_2 are both Other. So a single ruleset in FLASH may be split into up to four rulesets in the abstract model.

Despite these differences and the complexity of FLASH, we find that we need to introduce only five noninterference lemmas (shown in Figure 4) to get the proof to work for both control logic and data path properties. As can be seen, the conjunction of these lemmas fall far short of an inductive invariant. Perhaps more importantly, the total amount of efforts required for the proof is modest: 1 day to translate the SMV code into Murphi code, 0.5 day to flush out translation errors using conventional model checking (up to 4 nodes), 0.5 day to manually abstract the model, and 1 day to iteratively find the noninterference lemmas from counterexamples and to finish the proof. One interesting observation is that the abstract FLASH model has 21411411 reachable states (after symmetry reduction), so its complexity is roughly between 3-node and 4-node FLASH, which makes perfect sense.

4   A Theory Justifying Apparently Circular Reasoning

When the proof in Section 2 or 3 is completed, a small (2- or 3-node) abstract model has been constructed and the model checker has proved several invariants (desired properties and noninterference lemmas) about the abstract model. Why are we then justified in concluding that the desired properties are in fact true for the original parameterized model with any number of nodes? We have made some informal arguments, but they appear alarmingly circular. In particular, why is it sound to prove the noninterference lemmas in the abstract model which have been argued to be more permissive than the original model *using the very same lemmas*? In this section we first develop a theory based on the classical notion of simulation proofs [15] that justifies such apparently circular reasoning, and then shows how it is applied in the GERMAN and FLASH proofs.

4.1   Simulation Proofs

We will use standard set-theoretic notations. For any function $f \in A \to B$ and $C \subseteq A$ and $D \subseteq B$, the **image** of C under f is $f(C) = \{f(a) \in B : a \in C\}$ and the **inverse image** of D under f is $f^{-1}(D) = \{a \in A : f(a) \in D\}$. A useful fact to know is that $f(C) \subseteq D \Leftrightarrow C \subseteq f^{-1}(D) \Leftrightarrow \forall a \in C : f(a) \in D$. We also generalize f to operate on $A \times A$: $f(a, a') = (f(a), f(a'))$. Let V be a set of indices. If B is the (cartesian) **product** of an indexed family of sets, $B = \prod_{v \in V} B_v$, then f naturally induces a family of functions, $f_v \in A \to B_v$ for $v \in V$, such that $f(a) = \langle f_v(a) : v \in V \rangle$.

We will model protocols and their abstractions as state transition systems. Formally, a **state transition system** (STS) $M = (S, I, T)$ consists of a set S of states, a set $I \subseteq S$ of initial states, and a transition relation $T \subseteq S \times S$. An **execution** $(s_0, s_1, \ldots)$ of M is a finite or infinite sequence of states of M such that $s_0 \in I$ and $(s_i, s_{i+1}) \in T$ for all $i \geq 0$. A state s of M is **reachable** iff s is the last state of a finite execution of M; the set of reachable states of M is denoted by $\mathcal{R}(M)$. For an indexed family of STSs, $M_v = (S_v, I_v, T_v)$ for $v \in V$, the **product** STS is $\prod_{v \in V} M_v = (\prod_{v \in V} S_v, \prod_{v \in V} I_v, \prod_{v \in V} T_v)$. Clearly, we have $\mathcal{R}(\prod_{v \in V} M_v) = \prod_{v \in V} \mathcal{R}(M_v)$.

A set of states $P \subseteq S$ is an ***invariant*** of M iff $\mathcal{R}(M) \subseteq P$. A set of states $Q \subseteq S$ is ***inductive*** in M iff $\forall s \in I : s \in Q$ and $\forall (s, s') \in T : s \in Q \Rightarrow s' \in Q$. Clearly, an inductive set of states of M is always an invariant of M, and the set of reachable states of M, $\mathcal{R}(M)$, is the strongest invariant of M and is always inductive. All safety properties of M can be reduced to invariant properties provided that a sufficient amount of history information is recorded in the state, which can always be achieved by adding auxiliary variables.

Milner [15] introduced the notion of *simulation*. The following definition is not the most general possible, but rather is tailored to our needs. Let $M = (S, I, T)$ be a *concrete* STS and $\widetilde{M} = (\widetilde{S}, \widetilde{I}, \widetilde{T})$ an *abstract* STS.

Definition 1. *A **simulation** (P, f) from M to $\widetilde{M}$ consists of an **inductive invariant** $P \subseteq S$ and an **abstraction function** $f \in S \to \widetilde{S}$ such that:*

(1) $\forall s \in I : s \in P \wedge f(s) \in \widetilde{I}$

(2) $\forall (s, s') \in T : s \in P \Rightarrow s' \in P \wedge f(s, s') \in \widetilde{T}$

The notion of simulation is useful because it allows one to infer invariant properties of the concrete system from those of the abstract system.

Theorem 1. *If (P, f) is a simulation from M to $\widetilde{M}$, then:*

(3) $\forall s \in \mathcal{R}(M) : s \in P \wedge f(s) \in \mathcal{R}(\widetilde{M})$

Proof. By induction over the lengths of executions of M.   □

Formula (3) says that each reachable state s of M not only satisfies the inductive invariant P, but also inherits all invariant properties of $\widetilde{M}$ via f^{-1}.

In practice, the main difficulty in using simulation to infer properties of the concrete system from those of the abstract system lies in coming up with a suitable inductive invariant, which is very hard for any nontrivial system. But, fortunately, the following theorem says that there is at least one invariant that always works:

Theorem 2. *For any function $f \in S \to \widetilde{S}$, if:*

(4) $\forall s \in I : f(s) \in \widetilde{I}$

(5) $\forall (s, s') \in T : f(s) \in \mathcal{R}(\widetilde{M}) \Rightarrow f(s, s') \in \widetilde{T}$

then $(f^{-1}(\mathcal{R}(\widetilde{M})), f)$ is a simulation from M to $\widetilde{M}$ and:

(6) $\forall s \in \mathcal{R}(M) : f(s) \in \mathcal{R}(\widetilde{M})$

Proof. Let $P = f^{-1}(\mathcal{R}(\widetilde{M}))$. Since $\mathcal{R}(\widetilde{M})$ is inductive in $\widetilde{M}$, (4) and (5) imply (1) and (2), respectively. So (P, f) is a simulation from M to $\widetilde{M}$. Furthermore, (6) and (3) are equivalent in this case.   □

Theorem 2 is the ultimate source of apparent circularity in our proof method, in the following sense. On the one hand, (6) says that the invariant property that

M inherits from $\widetilde{M}$ is $f^{-1}(\mathcal{R}(\widetilde{M}))$. On the other hand, (5) says that $f^{-1}(\mathcal{R}(\widetilde{M}))$ can also be used as an *assumption* in the inductive step of the simulation proof.

For reasoning about a parameterized concrete system, the abstract system we will use is a product of many small systems, each of which captures a partial *view* of the concrete system. What views are will become clear shortly; here we just want to point out that a view is *not* a node in a cache coherence protocol.

Theorem 3. *Suppose the abstract system is a product STS,* $\widetilde{M} = \prod_{v \in V} \widetilde{M}_v$, *where* $\widetilde{M}_v = (\widetilde{S}_v, \widetilde{I}_v, \widetilde{T}_v)$ *for* $v \in V$. *If for each* $v \in V$:

(7) $\forall s \in I : f_v(s) \in \widetilde{I}_v$

(8) $\forall (s, s') \in T : (\forall u \in V : f_u(s) \in \mathcal{R}(\widetilde{M}_u)) \Rightarrow f_v(s, s') \in \widetilde{T}_v$

then $(f^{-1}(\mathcal{R}(\widetilde{M})), f)$ *is a simulation from* M *to* $\widetilde{M}$ *and:*

(9) $\forall s \in \mathcal{R}(M) : (\forall v \in V : f_v(s) \in \mathcal{R}(\widetilde{M}_v))$

Proof. Theorem 3 is simply a re-statement of Theorem 2 using the following facts: $\widetilde{I} = \prod_{v \in V} \widetilde{I}_v$, $\widetilde{T} = \prod_{v \in V} \widetilde{T}_v$, and $\mathcal{R}(\widetilde{M}) = \prod_{v \in V} \mathcal{R}(\widetilde{M}_v)$.   □

Theorem 3 enables one to break a simulation proof into small subproofs, one for each view v as represented by the abstract system $\widetilde{M}_v$ (see the antecedent of the theorem). Furthermore, (8) says that the conjunction of *all* inherited invariants can be used as an inductive hypothesis in *every* subproof.

4.2   Applying the Theory

We now show how Theorem 3 is used. Let M be GERMAN or FLASH with a large number of nodes.

First, note that the states of M are valuations of a finite number of **state variables** each of which is in one of the following forms:

- A boolean variable, x : B.
- A (node) pointer variable, y : N.
- An array of booleans, z : array $[N]$ of B.
- An array of (node) pointers, w : array $[N]$ of N.

where N is the set of nodes (or rather, node names) and B is the set of booleans. (There is no loss of generality in considering only booleans because enumerated types can be encoded using booleans.)

Second, there is a fixed m such that any subset of m nodes determines a **view** $v = \{n_1, \ldots, n_m\}$ of M. In other words, V is the set of m-element subsets of N. (For example, $m = 2$ for GERMAN and $m = 3$ for FLASH[7].) For each $v \in V$, the abstraction function f_v retains all boolean and pointer variables, discards all array entries except those indexed by a node in v, and sets any pointer-valued

---

[7] There is a slight complication here: in the case of FLASH, one of the 3 nodes in a view must be the home node.

variable or array entry to a special value `Other` $\notin N$ if its value is $\notin v$. More precisely, we define f_v as follows:

$$\begin{cases} f_v(s)(\mathbf{x}) = s(\mathbf{x}) & \text{for } \mathbf{x} : B \\ f_v(s)(\mathbf{y}) = s(\mathbf{y}) \downarrow v & \text{for } \mathbf{y} : N \\ f_v(s)(\mathbf{z}) = \lambda i \in v : s(\mathbf{z})(i) & \text{for } \mathbf{z} : \mathtt{array} \ [N] \ \mathtt{of} \ B \\ f_v(s)(\mathbf{w}) = \lambda i \in v : s(\mathbf{w})(i) \downarrow v & \text{for } \mathbf{w} : \mathtt{array} \ [N] \ \mathtt{of} \ N \end{cases}$$

where $j \downarrow v = \mathbf{if} \ j \in v \ \mathbf{then} \ j \ \mathbf{else} \ \mathtt{Other}$.

Third, since all nodes are symmetric with respect to each other in M (i.e., the set N is a *scalarset* [8]), we can take all $\widetilde{M_v}$'s to be isomorphic copies of the same abstract system $\widetilde{M_r}$ ("r" for "representative"). For instance, for GERMAN, we can take $\widetilde{M_r}$ to be the STS corresponding to ABSGERMAN (i.e., Figure 3). For each $v \in V$, $\widetilde{M_v}$ is obtained from $\widetilde{M_r}$ by renaming the nodes using any 1-1 mapping from r to v, where r also denotes the set of (non-`Other`) nodes in $\widetilde{M_r}$.

Now let us see what Theorem 3 says, given the above. Its conclusion (9) says that the property $P = \forall v \in V : f_v^{-1}(\mathcal{R}(\widetilde{M_v}))$ is an invariant of M. But what does P say? P is true of a state s of M iff for any $v \in V$, any invariant of $\widetilde{M_v}$ is true of s when projected via f_v^{-1} onto the view v (remember that the set of reachable states is also the strongest invariant). For example, the property `CtrlProp` has been proved (by model checking) to be an invariant of ABSGERMAN and hence also an invariant of any isomorphic copy $\widetilde{M_v}$ of ABSGERMAN. Since `CtrlProp` contains 2 node quantifiers and $\widetilde{M_v}$ contains 2 nodes, (9) allows us to conclude that `CtrlProp` is an invariant of M. The same reasoning applies to all desired properties and noninterference lemmas in the GERMAN and FLASH proofs. Note again that the reasoning depends on the fact that there are at least as many nodes in $\widetilde{M_v}$ as there are nested node quantifiers in the invariant.

But, in order to invoke the conclusion (9) of Theorem 3, we must discharge its antecedents (7) and (8) for each view $v \in V$. Since $\widetilde{M_v}$ is a renamed copy of $\widetilde{M_r}$ and all nodes are symmetric in M, there is no loss of generality in considering only the case when $v = r$. We will discuss only (8), since (7) is similar but simpler. Consider any step (s, s') of M. Note that the transition relation T can be decomposed as follows:

$$T = \bigcup_{r_1 \in R_1} \bigcup_{i \in N} T_i^{r_1} \cup \bigcup_{r_2 \in R_2} \bigcup_{(i,j) \in N \times N} T_{i,j}^{r_2}$$

where each $T_i^{r_1}$ (respectively, $T_{i,j}^{r_2}$) corresponds to an instance of a ruleset with name r_1 (r_2) and node parameters i (i and j). So the proof of (8) entails a case split into which ruleset instance, $T_i^{r_1}$ or $T_{i,j}^{r_2}$, the step (s, s') belongs to. The former case is split further into subcases $i \in r$ or $i \notin r$; the latter into subcases $(i \in r$ and $j \in r)$ or $(i \notin r$ and $j \in r)$ or $(i \in r$ and $j \notin r)$ or $(i \notin r$ and $j \notin r)$. We will do one subcase for GERMAN as an example of the apparently circular reasoning; all other cases in the GERMAN and FLASH proofs are similar.

Consider the ruleset `RecvInvAck` in GERMAN when i $\notin r$. Suppose it fires. If we can prove that the state change it effects in M is (via f_r) permitted by `ABS_RecvInvAck` or `ABS_Skip` in $\widetilde{M}_r$, then we have discharged (8) for this subcase. Since `RecvInvAck` fires, its precondition:

```
Chan3[i].Cmd = InvAck & CurCmd != Empty
```

must be true in the current state s. Now comes the crucial point: (8) allows us to assume that the aforementioned property $P = \forall v \in V : f_v^{-1}(\mathcal{R}(\widetilde{M}_v))$ is true at s. So we can project the noninterference lemma `Lemma_1` on i and any node j in r. There are two further cases to consider: if `ExGntd` is true, the projected `Lemma_1` implies that the state change is permitted by `ABS_RecvInvAck` (in particular, the precondition of `ABS_RecvInvAck` is true); otherwise, if `ExGntd` is false, `RecvInvAck` has no effect whatever after f_r (because i $\notin r$) and hence is trivially permitted by `ABS_Skip`. QED.

5   What Remains to Be Done

The first priority is clearly *mechanization*. We have carried out by hand the reasoning steps in Section 4.2 (i.e., the discharging of (7) and (8) and the application of (9)). Though they are quite simple, it would be much better if they are checked by a theorem prover. Another task that should be completely automatable is the construction of the initial abstract models as described in Sections 2 and 3. Such abstraction is very tedious and may allow errors to creep in when the protocol description is long. Ideally, we want to formalize not only the reasoning steps in Section 4.2 but also the theory developed in Section 4.1 in a theorem prover, so that we can have a completely formal proof.

It is also desirable to be able to reason about liveness, which we cannot do now. We have put some thoughts into this and believe that it is doable, but of course the devil will be in the details. Since Theorem 3 is quite general and does not depend on any intrinsic property of the index set V, it should be possible to use it to reason about parameterized systems where the parameter sets are not scalarsets but have additional structures (such as successor and ordering) [14].

6   Comparison with Other Works

This paper owes most of its intellectual debts to McMillan's work on compositional model checking [10] and its application to FLASH [12]. The abstractions we used, the reliance on apparently circular reasoning, and the counterexample-guided discovery of noninterference lemmas are all deeply influenced by McMillan's work. His framework is also more general than ours by encompassing liveness properties [11], though we believe that our framework can be generalized to handle liveness as well. Relative to his work, we think we make two main contributions. First, we show that practical parameterized verification can be done using any model checker (not just Cadence SMV) plus some simple reasoning. The freedom to choose model checkers is important in practice, as experience shows that for cache coherence protocols explicit-state model checkers are often superior to symbolic model checkers. Second, we develop a simple theory based on the classical notion of simulation proofs to justify the apparently circular reasoning. We believe this de-mystifies compositional model checking and opens the way to formalizing the theory and its application in a theorem prover.

Park and Dill [16] proved the safety properties of FLASH using machine-assisted theorem proving in PVS. Their proof is also based on the notion of simulation proofs, but uses the formulation of simulation in Definition 1, which requires an inductive invariant. Not surprisingly, they spent a significant amount (perhaps most) of their efforts on formulating and proving the inductive invariant. In contrast, the conjunction of the noninterference lemmas in Figure 4 falls far short of an inductive invariant. Also, it took them roughly two weeks to come up with the inductive invariant and to do the proof, which is a lot longer than the one day we spent.

Predicate abstraction has been used to verify GERMAN (without data paths) by Baukus, Lakhnech, and Stahl [2] and FLASH by Das, Dill, and Park [3]; the former also handles liveness. There are two main problems to be solved when applying predicate abstraction to parameterized verification: how to discover a suitable set of predicates, and how to map a finite set of predicates onto an unbounded set of state variables. To solve the second problem, the above two papers use complex predicates containing quantifiers, some of which are almost as complex as an invariant. This makes the discovery of such predicates non-obvious and probably as hard as the formulation of noninterference lemmas. More recently, a conceptual breakthrough was made by Lahiri and Bryant [9], who developed a theory of and the associated symbolic algorithms for *indexed predicates*, where the indices are implicitly universally quantified over. They used their techniques to verify a version of GERMAN with unbounded FIFO queues. We believe that there are close connections between their work and this paper, which we want to explore in the future.

Pnueli, Ruah, and Zuck [17] proposed an automatic (though incomplete) technique for parameterized verification called *invisible invariants*, which uses a small instance with N_0 nodes to generate an inductive invariant that works for instances of any size, where the bound N_0 depends on the forms of protocol and property descriptions. For GERMAN (without data paths), $N_0 = 4$. Although their technique is very attractive for being automatic, there are reasons to believe that it would not work for FLASH. First, their theory does not seem to allow the protocol to use node pointer arrays indexed by nodes, which FLASH has. Second, even if the theory can be made to work, the bound N_0 for FLASH is likely to be much greater than 4. Given the remarks in Section 3, this makes it very doubtful that FLASH can be verified using their method. We believe that the large bound results from the automatic nature of their method, which forces them to use general arguments that depend only on the form of the protocol and property descriptions. In our framework, human insights about specific protocols can limit the number of nodes needed by means of noninterference lemmas.

Emerson and Kahlon [6] verified GERMAN (without data paths) by first reducing it to a snoopy bus protocol and then invoking a theorem of theirs asserting that if a snoopy bus protocol of a certain form is correct for 7 nodes then it is correct for any number of nodes. Unfortunately, no such cut-off results are known for protocols as complex as FLASH (or, for that matter, for GERMAN directly), nor is it clear how FLASH can be reduced to protocols for which cut-off results are known.

Acknowledgements

We are grateful to Steven German for his comments, which greatly helped to improve this paper.

References

1. Apt, K.R., Kozen, D.: Limits for automatic program verification of finite-state concurrent systems. *Information Processing Letters* (1986) 22(6):307–309.
2. Baukus, K., Lakhnech, Y., Stahl, K.: Parameterized verification of a cache coherence protocol: safety and liveness. VMCAI (2002) 317–330.
3. Das, S., Dill, D.L., Park, S.: Experience with predicate abstract. CAV (1999) 160–171.
4. Della Penna, G., Intrigila, B., Tronci, E., Zilli, M.V.: Exploiting transition locality in the disk based Murphi verifier. FMCAD (2002) 202–219.
5. Dill, D.L., Drexler, A.J., Hu, A.J., Yang, C.H.: Protocol verification as a hardware design aid. IEEE Int. Conf. on Computer Design: VLSI in Computers and Processors (1992) 522-525.
6. Emerson, E.A., Kahlon, V.: Exact and efficient verification of parameterized cache coherence protocols. CHARME (2003) 247–262.
7. German, S.M.: Personal communications (2000).
8. Ip, C.N., Dill, D.L.: Better verification through symmetry. CHDL (1993) 87–100.
9. Lahiri, S.K., Bryant, R.E.: Constructing quantified invariants via predicate abstraction. VMCAI (2004) 267–281.
10. McMillan, K.L.: Verification of infinite state systems by compositional model checking. CHARME (1999) 219–234.
11. McMillan, K.L.: Circular compositional reasoning about liveness. CHARME (1999) 342–345.
12. McMillan, K.L.: Parameterized verification of FLASH cache coherence protocol by compositional model checking. CHARME (2001) 179–195.
13. McMillan, K.L.: Exploiting SAT solvers in unbounded model checking. CAV tutorial (2003) (http://www-cad.eecs.berkeley.edu/~kenmcmil/cav03tut.ppt).
14. McMillan, K.L., Qadeer, S., Saxe, J.B.: Induction in compositional model checking. CAV (2000) 312–327.
15. Milner, R.: An algebraic definition of simulation between programs. IJCAI (1971) 481–489.
16. Park, S., Dill, D.L.: Verification of the FLASH cache coherence protocol by aggregation of distributed transactions. SPAA (1996) 288–296.
17. Pnueli, A., Ruah, S., Zuck, L.: Automatic deductive verification with invisible invariants. TACAS (2001) 82–97.

A Partitioning Methodology for BDD-Based Verification

Debashis Sahoo[1], Subramanian Iyer[2], Jawahar Jain[3], Christian Stangier[3], Amit Narayan, David L. Dill[1], and E. Allen Emerson[2]

[1] Stanford University, Stanford CA 94305, USA
[2] University of Texas at Austin, Austin, TX 78712, USA
[3] Fujitsu Labs of America, Sunnyvale, CA 94085, USA

Abstract. The main challenge in BDD-based verification is dealing with the memory explosion problem during reachability analysis. In this paper we advocate a methodology to handle this problem based on state space partitioning of functions as well as relations. We investigate the key questions of how to perform partitioning in reachability based verification and provide suitable algorithms. We also address the problem of instability of BDD-based verification by automatically picking the best configuration from different short traces of the reachability computation. Our approach drastically decreases verification time, often by orders of magnitude.

1 Introduction

Verification and synthesis of sequential circuits require efficient techniques to represent and analyze the state space of the design under consideration [6, 13]. It is well known that in sequential circuits the number of reachable states can be exponential in the number of state elements present in the circuit. A popular approach to deal with this *state explosion problem* consists of implicitly representing and manipulating functions using *Reduced Ordered Binary Decision Diagrams* (OBDDs) [2]. Though often efficient, there are cases, where the OBDD representation is not compact. Unfortunately, some practical application areas seem to exhibit this worst case complexity frequently. To overcome this problem of explosive memory requirements, the use of *Partitioned-OBDDs* (POBDDs) has been suggested [9]. By partitioning the state space into disjoint subspaces, and representing as well as processing all functions in each subspace independently of other subspaces, efficiency in time and space can be obtained.

The partitioned reachability techniques suggested in [11] do not sufficiently address the practical issues involved with partitioning, and as a result do not scale well on many difficult circuits. In [8], dynamically partitioned OBDDs were introduced as a capable data structure that extend the usefulness of POBDDs for reachability and model checking. In this paper, we address the various issues related to partitioning, including but not limited to data structure issues, and demonstrate techniques that perform better than OBDDs as well as classical

A.J. Hu and A.K. Martin (Eds.): FMCAD 2004, LNCS 3312, pp. 399–413, 2004.

Partitioned-OBDDs. These techniques use heuristics to improve the existing approaches.

Since OBDDs form a special case of POBDDs, where the whole function is represented in a single partition, we focus our attention on analyzing the deficiencies in the classical approach to partitioning. This will set the stage for introducing our algorithms and proving their effectiveness.

What Is Missing in the Classical Approach?

Often OBDDs suffice for concise symbolic representation of boolean functions. Note, such functions are not the subject of this paper as further improving efficiency in their verification will not address the main bottleneck of the current BDD-based verification. In such cases, an OBDD approach can be more efficient as they avoid the partitioning overhead. However, for many practical applications, the function representations are too large for efficient *monolithic* representation as a single OBDD. If we accept this premise, then partitioning should show a distinct advantage. In this context, some problems arise naturally, which have not been addressed effectively in the literature. For example, the key questions include what functions should be considered as a basis for generating partitions, how many partitions should be created, when should the partitioning commence, how should the processing of partitions be prioritized, etc. We posit that these questions are fundamental to creating any practical technique that exploits partitions, and hence, are fundamental for any technique to make the BDD-based verification more practical and accordingly provide efficient algorithms to address the same.

Further, BDD approaches have a high sensitivity to parameter configuration. We develop a trace-centric approach to address this instability in BDD-based verification by automatically picking the best configuration from multiple short previews of the reachability computation.

Our fully automated approach completes all circuits but two in the VIS Verilog benchmark suite. An impressive gain over previous partitioned techniques is also seen.

Related Work

Algorithms for POBDD-based reachability were presented in [11]. They do not however adequately address some of the key questions relating to the actual application of partitioning, which are addressed here.

In [4] a technique is discussed where the set of reachable states is decomposed into two or more sets during the intermediate stages of computation and reachability is performed on these decompositions separately. However, after a few steps of reachability, results from these different sets are combined to obtain a monolithic OBDD representation of the reachable state set.

Recently, a method for distributed model checking was studied by [7]. It parallelizes the classical model checking algorithm [5] using the window-based partitioning first mentioned in [11]. Such distributed techniques can further help increase the practicality of the approach presented here.

In the remainder of the paper we address the various questions raised above, present the results, and discuss their significance. We start by presenting relevant background information in Section 2. The basic rationale and an overall picture of our approach are in Section 3, followed by algorithmic details. Section 4 has experimental results that confirm that our approach is indeed more efficient and stable, in both time and space, then previous POBDD [11] as well as state-of-the-art OBDD approaches. Section 5 is a summary of the paper.

2 Preliminaries

Partitioned-OBDDs

The idea of partitioning was used to discuss a function representation scheme called Partitioned-OBDDs in [9], which was further extensively developed in [12].

Definition 1. *[12] Given a Boolean function $f : B^n \to B$, defined over n inputs $X_n = \{x_1, \ldots, x_n\}$, the partitioned-OBDD (henceforth, POBDD) representation χ_f of f is a set of k function pairs, $\chi_f = \{(w_1, f_1), \ldots, (w_k, f_k)\}$ where, $w_i : B^n \to B$ and $f_i : B^n \to B$, are also defined over X_n and satisfy the following conditions:*

1. w_i and f_i are represented as OBDDs respecting the variable ordering π_i, for $1 \leq i \leq k$.
2. $w_1 \vee w_2 \vee \ldots \vee w_k = 1$
3. $w_i \wedge w_j = 0$, for $i \neq j$
4. $f_i = w_i \wedge f$, for $1 \leq i \leq k$

The set $\{w_1, \ldots, w_k\}$ is denoted by W. Each w_i is called a *window function* and represents a *partition* of the Boolean space over which f is defined. Each partition is represented separately as an OBDD and can have a different variable order. Most OBDD-based algorithms can be adapted easily for POBDDs.

Partitioned-OBDDs are canonical and various Boolean operations can be efficiently performed on them just like OBDDs. In addition, they can be exponentially more compact than OBDDs for certain classes of functions. The practical utility of this representation is also demonstrated by constructing OBDDs for the outputs of combinational circuits [12]. An excellent comparison of the computational power of various BDD-based representations and partitioned-OBDDs may be found in [1].

Reachability and Invariant Checking

The standard reachability algorithm is based on a breadth-first traversal of finite-state machines [6, 10, 16]. The algorithm takes as inputs the set of initial states, $I(s)$, expressed in terms of the present state variables, s, and a transition relation, $T(s, s', i)$ that relates the next state s' a system can reach from a state s on an input i. The transition relation, $T(s, s', i)$, is obtained by taking a conjunction of the transition relations, $s'_k = f_k(s, i)$, of the individual state elements, i.e., $T(s, s', i) = \prod(s'_k = f_k(s, i))$. Given a set of states, $R(s)$, that the system can reach, the set of next states, $N(s')$, is calculated using the equation $N(s') = \exists_{s,i}[T(s, s', i) \wedge R(s)]$. This calculation is also known as *image computation*. The set of reached states is computed by adding $N(s)$ (obtained by replacing variables s' with s) to $R(s)$ and iteratively performing the above image computation step until a fixed point is reached.

State space partitioning induces a partitioning on transition relations. The transition relation, T_{jk}, comprised of transitions from states in partition j to states in partition k, can be derived by conjoining T with the respective window functions expressed appropriately in terms of present and next state variables, as $T_{jk}(s, s', i) = w_j(s)w_k(s')T(s, s', i)$. Each such T_{jk} can have an implicitly conjoined [3] representation.

```
POBDD-Reachability(TR, InitStates) {
    Initialize Rch to InitStates
    Create partitioned rep for Rch
    do {
        for (each partition i)
            Calculate LeastFixedPoint(Rch) in partition i
        for (each partition i)
            Communicate states from i to all partitions
    } until (No new state is added to Rch);
}
```

Fig. 1. POBDD-based Reachability Algorithm

The flow of the POBDD-based-reachability algorithm is as shown in Fig. 1. Essentially, the algorithm performs as many steps as possible of image computation within each partition i using T_{ii}. This is called a step of *least fixed point* within the partition. When no more images can be thus computed, it synchronizes between partitions. This step is termed as *communication*, and is performed from partition i to each partition j using T_{ij}.

An invariant is a proposition that is to hold at every reachable state, and therefore invariants can be checked as newer states are added during the reachability computation.

In the next section, we will present techniques for the efficient construction of POBDDs. We address the issues of when, where, as well as how partitioning should be performed.

3   The Partitioning Methodology

The problem of reachability is about representation of sets of states and relations, as well as operations performed on them. The key operation is successive image computation on fragments of the state space until all reachable states have been explored. Thus, there is a need to develop an approach which can be efficient for both aspects – creating subspaces so as to represent functions succinctly as well as doing image computation.

In this context, the following questions naturally arise:

1. Is partitioning required at all?
2. If we must partition, what constitutes the "axis of partitioning"? In other words, along what lines should the partitioning be performed? e.g., what splitting variables should be used for creating windows?
3. As computation is performed, is the partitioning effective or is more partitioning required?
4. If the blowup is likely to be temporary (local), can the partitioning be likewise?
5. Once partitions are generated, in what order should they be processed?

These issues give more heuristic challenges on the POBDDs which can lead to a successful strategy in managing the behavior of BDDs in verification. Further due to the dynamic nature of partitioning, our approach can reduce the memory explosion in many circumstances. In contrast, the monolithic approach can exert no control on the program to prevent it from generating huge data structures that overflow memory.

We begin by discussing the algorithms for construction and utilization of partitioned representations, which address the questions raised above. Then, we detail the essential points of a trace-centric approach in the next section. This is used to impose some stability on the performance of the OBDDs with respect to the selection and setting of appropriate parameter values. At the end we give a complete reachability algorithm based on all the heuristics described in this paper. We now describe the mechanism for the construction and practical application of Partitioned OBDDs.

3.1   Whether to Partition: Initial Partitioning

Since reachability needs manipulation of image BDD using transition relation, if either of them shows signs of blowup then partitioning seems to be the prudent choice. Figure 2 shows how partitioning is invoked. If the transition relation is small, then many initial steps of reachability identical to the classical approach using a single BDD can be performed and partitioning can be delayed. Reachability is performed using OBDDs until such time as a "blowup" in BDD size is detected. This may be measured either absolutely as a maximum size of the symbolic representation of the image or in a relative way as the ratio of the representation of the reached states before and after any image computation. We adopt the latter approach with a threshold factor chosen *a priori*. However, if the transition relation cannot be easily constructed, then it is advantageous to partition quickly.

3.2   How to Partition: Choice of Partitioning Variable

After a "blowup" is detected, we select n splitting variables and the corresponding 2^n partitioning windows are created. The choice of the splitting variables is

```
InitialPartitioning(T, I) {
    If (T is large) {
        R := I
        Do Partitioning using T as basis.
    } else {
        R := Do Reachability from I using T until Blowup.
        Do Partitioning using R and T as basis.
    }
    return Partitioned R;
}
```

Fig. 2. Initial Partitioning Algorithm

critical to the the effectiveness of the partitioning approach. The goal is to create small and relatively balanced partitions that represent *non-compatible* functions. A set of functions is said to be *non-compatible* if the totality of their individual representations using different orders is far more compact, than their combined representation as a whole. The splitting variable is selected by means of a cost function, for e.g., as described in [11]. For each variable, the cost function takes into account the relative BDD sizes of the positive and negative co-factors with respect to the BDD size of the original graph.

```
SelectPartitioningVars(basis BDD F) {
    for (each method i := 1 to m) {
        get ordered splitting variable list using F.
        select top k variables.
        for (each subspace j := 1 to 2^k) {
            cost[i][j] := size of the cofactor F_j.
        }
        cost of method i := Σ_j cost[i][j]
    }
    select method with lowest cost.
    return corresponding vars.
}
```

Fig. 3. Selecting Partitioning Variable

However, the measurement of graph sizes for determining a blowup and for recognizing its subsidence can be done with respect to the BDD size of the transition relation or the image representation or both. We try to get separate splitting variable choices from each of these three methods. We select that choice which gives the smallest co-factor graphs after reordering as illustrated in the Figure 3. Intuitively, this selects a variable that creates two partitions as non-compatible as possible.

3.3   Are More Partitions Required: Global Dynamic Repartitioning

Whenever a BDD size blowup is detected during computation in a partition, dynamic repartitioning [8] is performed, as illustrated in Figure 4. Repartitioning is performed by splitting the given partition by co-factoring the entire state space based on one or more suitable, newly calculated, splitting choices until the blowup has been ameliorated. Initially, the partitioning is done using one splitting variable. To prevent excessive overhead in the new splitting variable selection, they are obtained by recalculating the cost of only the top few choices provided by the partitioning variable selection method discussed before. At this point, each new partition is checked to see whether the blowup has subsided. If not, repartitioning is recursively performed on that partition. A threshold on maximum number partitions is kept to prohibit the method to produce exponential number of partitions.

```
DynamicPartition(basis BDD F, partition i){
    v := SelectPartitioningVars(F)
    create partition i₁ from i with v := 0
    if (blowup in i₁)
        DynamicPartition(F_{v:=0}, i₁)
    create partition i₂ from i with v := 1
    if (blowup in i₂)
        DynamicPartition(F_{v:=1}, i₂)
}
```

Fig. 4. Dynamic Partitioning

It must be noted that the variable selection algorithm ensures that superfluous partitions are not created and that the ones created are somewhat balanced. In practice this imposes a bound on how many partitions are actually created.

3.4   Partition Only Image: Local Partitioning

During each step of image computation, many steps of alternating composition and conjunction are performed. Often it is found that the blowup in the BDD sizes during such a *micro-step* of image computation is a temporary phenomenon which eventually subsides by the time the image computation is completed. In such a case the invocation of dynamic global repartitioning could create a large number of partitions, whose BDD sizes become eventually very small. Hence, it is advantageous to create these partitions *locally* only for that particular image computation and then recombine them before the end of the image computation. If local partitioning does not reduce the blowup, then dynamic global repartitioning can be done. To create the local partitions, we cofactor using the ordered list of splitting variables that was generated earlier. Figure 5 describes how this is done.

```
ComputeImage(TR, state set R, variable list L){
    do {
        one microstep of image
        if (blowup) {
            varList := top k vars from L
            create partitions using varList
            for (each new partition)
                recursively do all remaining micro steps
        }
    }while(microsteps remain)
}
```

Fig. 5. Computing Image with Local partitioning

3.5   How to Order Partitions: Scheduling

In this section we describe our technique for state space traversal which schedules partitions based on their difficulty of traversal. The goal of the scheduling is to discover error states as early as possible in the state space traversal. The expectation is that the probability of catching an error is higher as more of the state space is covered. We characterize partitions in terms of how quickly it has been possible to cover state space symbolically in that partition. This is measured in terms of a cost for processing the partitions. The details of how this cost is computed is described in the following. Once this characterization of the level of difficulty is available, we schedule the partitions for processing in ascending order of their costs. Thus, the state space can be explored in a way that speeds up the rate at which new states are discovered. Notice that in the "worst" case, this processes all the partitions and thus traverses the entire state space if the design is correct

Scheduling Cost Metrics. We will now describe two metrics that are used for assigning a scheduling cost for processing the partitions.

Density Based Scheduling: Similar to [14] we define the *density* of a partition as the ratio of the number of reachable states discovered in that partition to the size of the BDD representing the reachable states. It may be noted that large function representation sizes, i.e. BDD sizes, are the most important bottleneck in symbolic verification techniques. Thus, in the interest of greater and faster state space coverage, it is advisable to first process partitions with a higher *density*.

Time Based Scheduling: Note that each partition may require many fixed point computations. Hence, another useful metric takes into account the time required for the latest fixed point computation within each partition. The partition with faster fixed point computation is intuitively more attractive as it may be more amenable to symbolic manipulation using BDDs. Therefore, it is advantageous to select partitions which have historically been known to take lesser time. In the above calculations the time spent in communicating either to or from any partition was excluded.

The cost for processing a partition is the ratio of the time taken for the most recent fixed point computation to the density of that partition. Intuitively, this prioritizes partitions that are more amenable to symbolic traversal. In our reachability algorithm (Figure 6), priority queues are used to schedule partitions in increasing order of their cost.

```
Reachability(T, I) {
    R := InitialPartitioning(T, I)
    Initialize Priority Queues in Scheduler S;
    do {
        Get LFPList from S.LFPQueue
        for each partition i in LFPList
            Calculate LeastFixedPoint in i and update S
        Get CommList from S.CommQueue
        for each partition i in CommList
            Communicate from i to all parts and update S
    }until (No new state is added to R);
}
```

Fig. 6. Scheduling-based Reachability Algorithm

4   Addressing Instability in BDD-Based Verification

Instability in BDD based verification refers to the sensitivity of performance to various parameters like the size of the clusters in the implicitly conjoined transition relation, the selection of variable reordering methods etc. It is observed that a single choice seldom works uniformly for all cases and therefore, such parameters need to be tweaked manually. The performance of BDD based methods can vary widely and unexpectedly based on these settings.

In a partitioned scheme, there are an even greater number of specific choices available for state space traversal. The degrees of freedom include the number of partitions, when and whether to dynamically decompose partitions further, how to schedule the image computations involving multiple partitions, etc. Hence, we propose a *trace-centric* approach to parameter selection which can dynamically fine-tune the partitioning choices and balance the various options available to a BDD based method.

A small set of identical computations are separately executed, each using a different choice of the various options. Each of these is referred to as a *trace*. The length of a trace is how far it proceeded into the entire computation. A large number of traces may lead to a high cost in overhead. Therefore, we elect to look at just a few traces with orthogonal settings. These traces are only observed until the size of the OBDDs exceeds a pre-determined threshold.

The traces are compared with one another on various factors, for e.g., the blowup of OBDDs when performing the image operation, the number of image operations completed, number of states traversed, etc. The configuration for the full run is adopted from that of the most efficient trace. Needless to say that if a trace completes the reachability in the allowed space and time, no further computation is required. We have found that even very simple dynamic examinations can be dramatically effective in stabilizing the performance of BDDs.

Also, we find that the overhead of generating multiple traces is minor when balanced against the savings. Even if graph size is reduced by a factor of 2 (in the more efficient configuration), it proves to be important. This is because during the reachability multiple reorderings are triggered, and even saving one large reordering of 1 million node graph compensates calculation of 3 different traces with maximum BDD threshold of 100k BDD nodes.

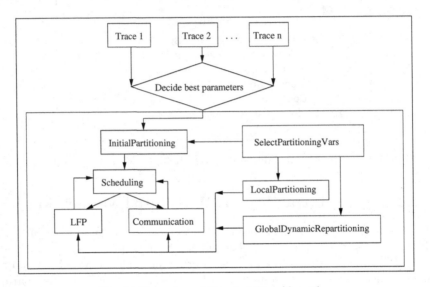

Fig. 7. Trace-based Reachability Algorithm

5   The Complete Reachability Algorithm

The complete reachability algorithm is shown in Figure 7. The input to the reachability algorithm is a transition relation T and initial states I. The algorithm first picks a best parameter configuration by running a few short traces with orthogonal settings. Then it runs the *InitialPartitioning* procedure described in section 3.1. After this the algorithm performs POBDD-based state traversal guided by the scheduling heuristics described in section 3.5. There are two important steps in the POBDD-based state traversal algorithm. The first one is computing a fixed point (called LFP) inside a partition and the other one is to compute image of a function in other partitions (called Communication from one partition to other partitions). The scheduler selects the partition to process next for the above operations. The scheduler implements two priority queues, one for each of the above operations described. Each partition is assigned a cost described in section 3.5. The local partitioning described in section 3.4 and the global dynamic repartitioning described in section 3.3 is enabled during the fixed point and communication. The *SelectPartitioningVars* heuristics described in section 3.2 is called when partitioning is needed.

6   Experiments

Our implementation of the POBDD-data structure and algorithms uses VIS-2.0, which is a state-of-the-art public domain BDD-based formal verification package. We have chosen VIS for its Verilog support and its powerful OBDD-package (i.e. CUDD [15]). As our techniques affect only the BDD-data structures and algorithms, they can – with moderate effort – be implemented in other packages as well. These techniques work with any method of image computation; for this implementation, both OBDDs and POBDDs use the IWLS95 method.

We found that lazy_sift reordering method works better for most cases. All the experiments use lazy_sift BDD reordering method.

Benchmarks
For experiments on reachability and invariant checking, we chose various public domain circuits: the VIS-Verilog [17] benchmark suite and ISCAS89 benchmark suite. We choose only invariant checking properties in VIS-Verilog benchmark suite. For sake of brevity, results are omitted for the smaller examples and presented only on those circuits where VIS requires more than 250,000 BDD nodes.

Results
We compare the methodology proposed in this paper with three other approaches: the non-partitioned approach of VIS, the static partitioning approach and our own partitioning approach without computation traces. We find that the computation of small traces outperforms, sometimes significantly, all other approaches.

Comparison vs. Non-partitioned Approach, Invariant Checking
Table 1 compares the non-partitioned approach of VIS with the proposed method on the time and space needed to check invariant properties from the VIS-Verilog benchmark suite. The time includes cpu time for simultaneous check of all properties of a given circuit. The memory required is measured in terms of the cumulative peak live nodes for all BDDs that are maintained.

The first column shows the memory required when running VIS. The second column lists the memory for our trace-centric partitioning method, and the next column shows the corresponding space gain. In the runtime comparison, the first column shows time taken by VIS in seconds. The second column lists the effect of our improved partitioning method when combined with a trace-centric approach. The last column shows the time gain of the trace centric partitioning over VIS.

Table 1. Comparison of OBDD-VIS with POBDD-VIS on VIS-benchmarks for all circuits where VIS requires more than 250K BDD nodes (T/O = timeout = 1 day, M/O = memout = 512MB). The time includes cpu time for simultaneous check of all properties of a given circuit

	Space (BDD nodes)			Time (sec)		
	Vis	Proposed	Gain	Vis	Proposed	Gain
palu	371K	7K	53.0	186	5	37.2
s1269b	2.6M	38K	68.4	1189	27	44.0
sp_product	919K	70K	13.1	1299	440	3.0
FIFOs	975K	131K	7.4	1704	1521	1.1
vsaR	5.2M	1.3M	4.0	5281	2409	2.2
blackjack	3.2M	1.1M	2.9	16298	11739	1.4
ns3	4.7M	1.0M	4.7	18592	19093	1.0
am2910	11.7M	67K	>174	M/O	222	>392
ball	18.8M	17K	>1106	T/O	168	>518
spinner32	1.4M	248K	> 5.6	T/O	335	>260
rotate32	827K	240K	> 3.4	T/O	293	>297
vcrc32_8	20.5M	2.4M	> 8.5	T/O	3871	>23
am2901	20.8M	2.9M	> 7.2	T/O	20247	> 4.3
b12	4.2M	800K	> 5.3	T/O	T/O	–
vsa16a	11.1M	4.8M	> 2.3	T/O	T/O	–

Table 2. Comparison of OBDD-VIS with POBDD-VIS on ISCAS89 benchmark

	Space (BDD nodes)			Time (sec)		
	Vis	Proposed	Gain	Vis	Proposed	Gain
s1269	2.4M	31K	77	2305	28	82
s3330	1.3M	263K	4.9	**T/O**	948	>92
prolog	976K	138K	7.1	**T/O**	592	>147
s4863	438K	264K	1.7	1382	1717	0.8
	3.3M	1.7M	1.9	**T/O**	**T/O**	–
s1423	States covered			2e+10	1e+13	419
	Time for 2.3e+10 states			87000	633	137

In both time as well as space, the trace-centric partitioning approach provides dramatic gains. Our approach completes all circuits except two in the VIS Verilog benchmark suite. Notably, it verified six circuits where the VIS failed to finish. For some circuits such as *palu, s1269b, am2910, ball*, verification was completed by the very first POBDD trace of 100k nodes. In most cases, there is an order of magnitude or more improvement in both time as well as in space.

Comparison vs. Non-partitioned Approach, Reachability Analysis
In identical format, Table 2 compares our method with Vis-2.0 on formal reachability analysis for some ISCAS89 benchmark circuits. The proposed POBDD implementation works better in first three circuits. In s4863, the time required in computing traces made the method slightly slower than VIS.

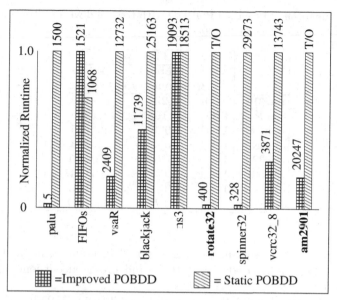

Fig. 8. Comparison of Dynamic trace-centric and Static Partitioning Approaches on all Large designs (time>1000s) of VIS-benchmarks. The actual runtime in seconds is shown at the top of each bar

We also found that in s1423 our method covers more states than VIS does in the same time. Also notice that the partitioned approach covers the same number of states as VIS in a small fraction of the time required.

Comparison vs. Static Partitioning

Figure 8 compares the run time of our trace-centric POBDD method to the static POBDD approach of [11]. The initial number of partitions for both methods were kept identical to have a level playing field. The graph shows the normalized runtimes by size of the bar. The actual runtime in seconds is shown at the top of each bar. One can observe that the proposed method noticeably improves on the static partitioning scheme for most of the circuits, especially when the time taken is large. In once case that could not be completed by the static partitioning approach, the current method is able to complete reachability.

Traces vs. No Traces

Table 3 compares proposed POBDD approach with and without traces. The proposed POBDD with trace finishes one more circuit that the method without trace. It has noticable improvements on three other circuits, viz., *spinner32*, *rotate32*, *vcrc32_8* . Table 3 shows that the partitioning methodology is definitely improved by using short traces.

7   Conclusions

We have discussed an efficient methodology for improving difficult instances of reachability based verification using the approach of state space partitioning.

Table 3. Comparison of Proposed POBDD with trace and without trace on all designs where VIS runs out of time or memory

		Time (sec)	
	Vis	Proposed (without trace)	Proposed (with trace)
am2910	M/O	222	222
ball	T/O	168	168
spinner32	T/O	9305	335
rotate32	T/O	5537	293
vcrc32_8	T/O	51576	3871
am2901	T/O	T/O	20247
b12	T/O	T/O	T/O
vsa16a	T/O	T/O	T/O

We have investigated relevant problems posed in creating a partitioned data structure during BDD-based verification, and provided efficient and practical algorithms for the same.

We have also addressed the issue of instability in BDD-based approaches where parameters are seldom found to work well uniformly. We developed a trace-centric approach to selection of such parameters. The resulting method dramatically improves the space and run time, often from one to three orders of magnitude, on various public-domain benchmark circuits that are otherwise known to be difficult.

It is found that methods based on a monolithic representation of the state sets often encountered space explosion early on in the computation, after which they could not make much progress due to memory limitations. However, the trace-centric partitioning method scaled well, and could finish most circuits in the VIS Verilog benchmark suite.

Acknowledgement

Professor E. Allen Emerson acknowledges CCR-009-8141 and CCR-020-5483 grants.

References

1. B. Bollig and I. Wegener. Partitioned BDDs vs. other BDD models. In *IWLS*, 1997.
2. R. Bryant. Graph-based Algorithms for Boolean Function Manipulation. *IEEE Transactions on Computers*, C-35:677–691, August 1986.
3. J. R. Burch, E. M. Clarke, and D. E. Long. Symbolic Model Checking with Partitioned Transition Relations. In *Proc. of the Design Automation Conf.*, pages 403–407, 1991.
4. G. Cabodi, P. Camurati, and Stefano Quer. Improved reachability analysis of large finite state machines. *ICCAD*, pages 354–360, 1996.

5. E.M. Clarke and E.A. Emerson. Design and synthesis of synchronization skeletons using branching time temporal logic. In *Proc. IBM Workshop on Logics of Programs*, volume 131 of *Lecture Notes in Computer Science*, pages 52–71. Springer-Verlag, 1981.
6. O. Coudert, C. Berthet, and J. C. Madre. Verification of sequential machines based on symbolic execution. In *Proc. of the Workshop on Automatic Verification Methods for Finite State Systems*, 1989.
7. Orna Grumberg, Tamir Heyman, and Assaf Schuster. Distributed symbolic model checking for μ-calculus. In *Computer Aided Verification*, pages 350–362, 2001.
8. S. Iyer, D. Sahoo, C. Stangier, A. Narayan, and J. Jain. Improved symbolic Verification Using Partitioning Techniques. In *Proc. of CHARME 2003*, volume 2860 of *Lecture Notes in Computer Science*, 2003.
9. J. Jain, J. Bitner, D. S. Fussell, and J. A. Abraham. Functional partitioning for verification and related problems. *Brown/MIT VLSI Conference*, 1992.
10. Kenneth L. McMillan. *Symbolic Model Checking*. Kluwer Academic Publishers, 1993.
11. A. Narayan, A. Isles, J. Jain, R. Brayton, and A. Sangiovanni-Vincentelli. Reachability Analysis Using Partitioned-ROBDDs. In *ICCAD*, pages 388–393, 1997.
12. A. Narayan, J. Jain, M. Fujita, and A. Sangiovanni-Vincentelli. Partitioned-ROBDDs - A Compact, Canonical and Efficiently Manipulable Representation for Boolean Functions. In *ICCAD*, pages 547–554, 1996.
13. C Pixley. Introduction to a computational theory and implementation of sequential hardware equivalence. 1990.
14. K. Ravi and F. Somenzi. High-density reachability analysis. In *ICCAD*, pages 154–158, 1995.
15. Fabio Somenzi. CUDD: CU Decision Diagram Package ftp://vlsi.colorado.edu/pub, 2001.
16. H. J. Touati, H. Savoj, B. Lin, R. K. Brayton, and A. L. Sangiovanni-Vincentelli. Implicit State Enumeration of Finite State Machines using BDD's. In *ICCAD*, pages 130–133, 1990.
17. VIS. Vis verilog benchmarks http://vlsi.colorado.edu/~vis/, 2001.

Invariant Checking
Combining Forward and Backward Traversal

Christian Stangier and Thomas Sidle

Fujitsu Labs of America Inc.
{cstangier,tsidle}@fla.fujitsu.com

Abstract. In invariant checking two directions of state space traversal are possible: Forward from initial states or backward starting from potential error states. It is not clear in advance, which direction will be computationally easier or will terminate in fewer steps. This paper presents a dynamic approach based on OB-DDs for interleaving forward and backward traversal. The approach increases the chance for selecting the shorter direction and at the same time limits the overhead due to redundant computation. Additionally, a second approach using two OB-DDs with different variable orders is presented, providing improved completion at the cost of some additional overhead. These approaches result in a dramatic gain in efficiency over unidirectional traversal. For the first time all benchmarks of the VIS-Verilog suite have been finished using a BDD-based method.

1 Introduction

Despite other recent developments OBDD-based invariant checking is still a method of choice for checking assertions in circuit design. Its advantage is that it is a falsifying as well as a verifying technique (as opposed to e.g. bounded model checking). This can become important, for example in the case of abstraction refinement, where after a series of false negatives and subsequent refinements a property finally proves correct.

The dilemma one faces with OBDD-based invariant checking is that two ways of traversal are possible: Forward from the initial states or backward from possible error states. Consider the above mentioned abstraction refinement: The design under consideration could be oversimplified s.t. its sequential depth is very shallow. In this case forward traversal would be preferable. On the other hand the number of states from which an error state can be reached could be very small, making backward traversal the preferable choice.

Unfortunately, one cannot decide in advance which direction to choose for a more efficient computation, although the *right* choice can be drastically more efficient. One direction might reach a fixpoint in fewer steps or the computational complexity could be a lot less than for the other direction.

The drastic differences in runtime for the different directions are shown in the plot in Figure 1. Here the runtime in seconds for forward and backward invariant checking using our benchmark set is shown (The benchmarks have been ordered to increase visibility).

For the first 15 benchmarks forward traversal is clearly the better choice as 10 benchmarks time out and 5 more require very large runtime for backward traversal.

A.J. Hu and A.K. Martin (Eds.): FMCAD 2004, LNCS 3312, pp. 414–429, 2004.

The next 20 benchmarks show comparable results for both directions. For the last 16 benchmarks we see an almost symmetrical behavior just that now the backward direction is preferable because all benchmarks in forward direction time out (Both methods time out for the very last benchmark).

A dramatic improvement in runtime could be achieved if one would be able to always choose the better direction, i.e. forward for the first 25 cases and backward for the remaining 31 cases. As stated earlier this decision can not be made before the actual computation is performed.

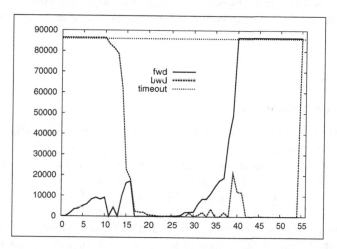

Fig. 1. Plot of forward vs. backward runtime in seconds for 56 VIS-Verilog benchmarks.

The methods we will develop in this paper are heuristic in nature. They will decide *on-the-fly* which traversal direction to choose, maximizing the probability for an optimal choice and minimizing redundant computation. As an alternative method and a solution to the increased complexity of two state traversals represented in a single OBDD we present a method using multiple OBDDs with different variable orders. A key algorithm to enable the use of multiple OBDDs is presented as well.

The overall contribution of these methods is an increased gain in the performance of OBDD-based invariant checking. The results are exceptionally good and possibly for the first time all VIS-Verilog invariant benchmarks have been solved by an automatic OBDD-based method.

Related Work

Mixing forward and backward traversal for verification is not new per se and has been used by others with different approaches. Iwashita and Kawata [9] use forward and backward traversal for forward model checking. Cabodi, Camurati and Quer [5] use forward traversal to prune states for exact backward traversal. Govindaraju and Dill [8] use repeated runs of forward and backward over-approximations for verification. Cabodi, Nocco and Quer [6] propose a backward verification procedure based on prioritized traversal.

In contrast to the methods mentioned above our approach performs forward and backward traversal *simultaneously* in one single pass. The other approaches use one sweep of traversal to approximate or to prune the search space and then another sweep in the other direction to perform the actual verification or they even iterate this process. Our approach instead is a direct replacement for a standard forward traversal algorithm.

The remainder of this paper is structured as follows: In the next section we describe the basic concepts of state space traversal, partitioned transition relations and image computation. The next two sections present our new techniques for interleaving forward and backward traversal. In Section 5 we give experimental proof of the concepts developed before. The last section draws conclusions and gives an outlook on future work.

2 Preliminaries

Symbolic State Space Traversal

The increasing complexity of sequential systems requires efficient techniques to be able to perform reachability analysis.

Since the set of reachable states can be quite large, an explicit representation of this set, e.g. in form of a list, cannot be suitable under any circumstances. Coudert, Berthet and Madre [4] have investigated the characteristic function of state sets which can be considered as a Boolean function and therefore be represented by an OBDD [1]. They have shown that this symbolic representation form goes well together with the operations which have to be performed for the computation of the reachable states: If reachable states are computed according to a breadth-first-traversal then the representation via the characteristic function allows to compute all corresponding successor states within a single computation. For this reason, one also uses the term *symbolic breadth-first traversal*. Once more, the complexity of the computation depends on the OBDD-size of the occurring state sets.

Invariant Checking

Invariant checking is a straightforward formal verification application based on state space traversal. Properties that should globally hold at all times are checked (e.g. *overflow=0*). If during state space traversal a state is reached that violates the property the traversal is terminated returning *failed*. If the traversal reaches a fixpoint without finding a property violating state, *passed* is returned.

Partitioned Transition Relations

The computation of the reachable states is a core task for optimization and verification of sequential systems. The essential part of OBDD-based traversal techniques is the transition relation:

$$\mathrm{TR}(x, y, e) = \prod_i \delta_i(x, e) \equiv y_i,$$

which is the conjunction of the transition relations of all latches (δ_i denotes the transition function of the ith latch, x, y, e represent present state, next state and input variables). This *monolithic* transition relation is represented as a single OBDD and usually is much too large to allow computation of the reachable states. Sometimes a monolithic transition relation is even too large for a representation with OBDDs. Therefore, more sophisticated reachable states computation methods make use of a *partitioned* transition relation [2], i.e. a cluster of OBDDs each of them representing the transition relation of a group of latches. A transition relation partitioned over sets of latches $P_1, \ldots, P_j$ can be described as follows:

$$\mathrm{TR}(x, y, e) = \prod_j \mathrm{TR}_j(x, y, e) \text{ , where } \mathrm{TR}_j(x, y, e) = \prod_{i \in P_j} \delta_i(x, e) \equiv y_i.$$

Image Computation Using AndExist

The reachable states computation consists of repeated image computations $\mathrm{Img}(\mathrm{TR}, R)$ of a set of already reached states R:

$$\mathrm{Img}(\mathrm{TR}, R) = \exists_{x,e}(\mathrm{TR}(x, y, e) \cdot R)$$

With the use of a partitioned transition relation the image computation can be iterated over P_i and the $\exists$ operation can be applied during the product computation *(early quantification)*:

$$\mathrm{Img}(\mathrm{TR}, R) = \exists_{v^j}(\mathrm{TR}_j \cdot \ldots \cdot \exists_{v^2}(\mathrm{TR}_2 \cdot \exists_{v^1}(\mathrm{TR}_1 \cdot R)\ldots),$$

where v^i are those variables in $(x \cup e)$ that do not appear in the following TR_k, $(i < k \leq j)$.

The so called *AndExist* [2] or *AndAbstract* operation performs the AND operation on two functions (here partitions) while simultaneously applying existential quantification ($\exists_{x_i} f = (f_{x_i=1} \vee f_{x_i=0})$) on a given set of variables, i.e. the variables that not in the support of the remaining partitions. Unlike the conventional AND operation the AndExist operation only has an exponential upper bound for the size of the resulting OBDD, but for many practical applications it prevents a blow-up of OBDD-size during the image computation.

The standard method for finding a schedule for conjunction the partitions is the so called *IWLS95-method* [10]. It uses a greedy scheme to minimize the number of variables involved in the AndExist operation. The IWLS95 method also is the standard method for partitioning used in the VIS-package [3].

3   Interleaved Invariant Checking

As described before forward traversal and backward traversal are both equally applicable to the invariant checking problem. Experience shows that there are often drastic differences in the complexity of the invariant checking problem depending on the traversal direction. The plot in Figure 1 and the data in Table 4 strongly support the above statement.

The difficulty lies in the fact that it is impossible to detect in advance which method is to be used preferably. Our proposed solution to this dilemma is a heuristic that combines forward and backward traversal by deciding on-the-fly in which direction to proceed.

Combining Forward and Backward Traversal

Figure 2 shows a schematic for combining forward and backward traversal in BFS search. The forward search extends the explored reachable state space by adding so-called *onion rings* in BFS manner starting from the initial states I. The backward search extends the state set from which failing states can be reached by repeating pre-image computations starting with the property violating states P.

In the case of a failing property (Figure 2a) the two searches will eventually intersect. The number of onion-rings determines the depth of the error. Two special cases may occur:

- The reachable state space covers all possible states i.e. 2^n states if n state bits are given. Thus, including all states violating the property under consideration.
- The failing states set covers all 2^n possible states, thus including all initial and reachable states.

In the case of a passing property (Figure 2b) the two searches will reach fixpoints without intersecting. Whenever one search terminates with reaching a fixpoint the property is proven to be correct.

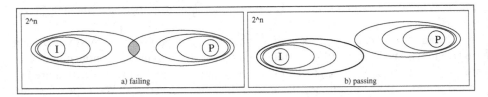

Fig. 2. Schematic of a) failing and b) passing property.

Advantages and Challenges in Combined Traversal

Using a combined traversal approach has the following advantages:

- Because the cost of computation can differ drastically between the two directions, one should use the freedom to choose the cheaper one.
- One traversal direction might reach a fixpoint in fewer computation steps than the other one. This direction should be chosen preferably.
- In the case of a failing property both traversals will eventually intersect, thus no computation is redundant; all of it contributes to the solution.

Of course, none of the above is known in advance. On the other hand certain challenges when doing combined traversal must be dealt with:

– In the case of a passing property one direction will reach a fixpoint before the other one. The computations done in the direction that did not complete do not contribute to the solution and are thus redundant.
– The cost of the computation for the two directions might be so unbalanced that even trying one direction could turn out to be extremely expensive.
– By having two state sets to be represented as an OBDD the overall complexity of the problem increases.

In the following we will describe our interleaving heuristic that tries to maximize the advantages of combined traversal, while at the same time dealing with its challenges.

The Interleaving Heuristic

The heuristic determines the traversal direction dynamically by evaluating the cost associated with computing an image or a pre-image. The cost metric is the largest OBDD-size during the iteration over the partitioned transition relation in (pre-)image computation.

In the first step an image is computed in both directions to obtain initial costs. In the following steps the computation proceeds in the direction, which had the lower cost in its last execution, i.e. execution is done in one direction until the cost exceeds the cost of the last image done in the other direction.

Note, that so far no manual parameter setting is required in the decision making, resulting in a fully dynamic and self-adjusting process. Normally, the costs for forward and backward traversals differ widely. As a result the heuristic will very likely chose the *better* direction. To exploit this unbalancedness even more we introduced a threshold limiting the maximum cost of an image computation. If this threshold is exceeded during an operation this image computation is aborted and the heuristic disables bidirectional traversal and returns to unidirectional traversal in the direction not aborted. This threshold is intended to avoid prohibitively expensive computation for one directions and is set conservatively to a very large value, enabling it only for the case when one direction exceeds its share of the available memory disproportionately.

We introduced the *maxcost* threshold to avoid that one traversal direction causes a memory overflow. The maxcost threshold, when set more aggressively can be used as a parameter to tune the application. For circuits, where the cost for different traversal directions is very unbalanced a lower threshold can drastically reduce the time that is spent for computing an image in the more expensive direction. Also, for circuits that show a certain systematic behavior a lower threshold improves efficiency.

For a sketch of the main loop of the interleaving algorithm see Figure 3.

Error Trace Generation

The computation of an error trace (or *counter example*) in case of a failing property is slightly more complex for interleaving than for plain forward or backward traversal. For a schematic refer to Figure 4. In the case of a failing property the states computed forward traversal and the states computed backward traversal overlap (shaded area in Fig. 4). From this intersection an arbitrary *pivot* state p is chosen. This state is reachable

```
while(!fwd_terminated && !bwd_terminated &&
        !Intersect(reach, fail)){
    if(steps == 0){
        newreach = image(reach);
        newfail = preimage(fail);
        update(newreach, reach, fwd_cost, fwd_limit_exceeded, fwd_terminated);
        update(newfail , fail , bwd_cost, bwd_limit_exceeded, bwd_terminated);
    } else if(fwd_limit_exceeded){
        newfail = preimage(fail);
        update(newfail , fail , bwd_cost, bwd_limit_exceeded, bwd_terminated);
    } else if(bwd_limit_exceeded){
        newreach = image(reach);
        update(newreach, reach, fwd_cost, fwd_limit_exceeded, fwd_terminated);
    } else if(fwd_cost < bwd_cost){
        newreach = image(reach);
        update(newreach, reach, fwd_cost, fwd_limit_exceeded, fwd_terminated);
    } else { /* bwd_cost ≤ fwd_cost) */
        newfail = preimage(fail);
        update(newfail , fail , bwd_cost, bwd_limit_exceeded, bwd_terminated);
    }
    steps++;
}
```

Fig. 3. Sketch of the Interleaving Algorithm.

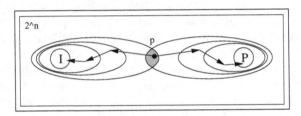

Fig. 4. Schematic of the error trace computation.

from the initial state as well as a state violating the property can be reached from it. The error trace will lead from an initial state in I to p and from there to a state in P. The computation of the error-trace requires that for both traversals the *onion rings* i.e. the frontier states of each iteration are being stored. The first part of the error trace (from I to p) is computed using pre-image computation starting from p going backward to I and restricting the result to the onion rings. For each iteration an arbitrary state from the particular onion ring is chosen.

The second part of the error trace (from p to P) is computed in a similar manner using image computation starting from p going to P.

Both parts are then combined to form a complete error trace.

Storing the onion rings of the computation adds overhead to the computation. It is hard to predict the amount of overhead as it depends on the depth of the error-trace and the complexity of the states sets represented in the onion rings. Experiments suggest that this overhead is smaller for interleaving than for an unidirectional approach. A reason for this could lie in the fact that the interleaving chooses the *cheaper* direction and thus storing the onion rings becomes more efficient as well.

4   Interleaving Using OBDDs with Different Variable Orders

Limitations of the Previous Approach

The approach described in the previous section has some inherent drawbacks:

First, the presence of two transition relations and two completely different state sets (reachable and failing states) complicates the whole representation and may lead to a large overhead in OBDD size.

Secondly, the AndExist operation during image computation tends to dominate the variable reordering process and thus the resulting variable order. Having two searches and two AndExist operations with very different requirements to the variable order taking place in OBDD may hurt performance drastically. Either by resulting in large OBDDs sizes for one direction or by some *back-and-forth* reordering triggered by the two different AndExist operations.

The obvious solution to this problem would be to use two different OBDDs with differing variable orders: One OBDD for the forward traversal and the other OBDD for the backward traversal.

Unfortunately, this solution comes with some caveats that have to be taken care of.

Advantages and Challenges when Using Two OBDDs in Interleaving

The main advantage of using two OBDDs lies in the fact that only one traversal is performed in each OBDD and thus only one major state set has to be represented. As a result variable reordering will produce better results because it is targeted to only one AndExist operation.

This advantage will in many cases outweigh the disadvantages that are inherent to a multi-OBDD approach:

Loss of sharing: Two OBDDs with different variable orders cannot share any nodes. In a worst case this may lead to a blow-up in the factor of 2. But, in the best case the representation of two different functions can be exponentially smaller.

Overhead: Initializing and maintaining two OBDDs generates overhead. For smaller cases this could be significant.

Splitting of memory: The available memory has to be allocated to the two OBDDs. This could be problematic as it is not obvious how much memory will be required by each OBDD. Also, various caches and stacks come into play.

The Communication Problem

Despite the challenges mentioned above the main problem here is the communication between the two OBDDs. Communication between OBDDs is required for the computation of intersection between the reachable state set and the failing state set. Computing the intersection is needed to detect a failing property (see Figure 2a). A solution to this problem is crucial as otherwise all advantages of multiple OBDDs might be lost.

Intersection of two OBDDs with different variable orders is known to be exponential in the worst case. In the following we present an algorithm that only checks for the existence of an intersection and thus is able to *tunnel* the communication from one OBDD to the other.

The CrossIntersect Algorithm

Unlike OBDDs with only one variable order, for which all important operations have polynomial time and space algorithms, OBDDs with different variable orders have no polynomial algorithms for general operations. Thus, we have to check in each case for the existence of an efficient algorithm or define a subproblem, whose solution would be sufficient. Fortune, Hopcroft and Schmidt [7] have shown that equivalence between a read-once FreeBDD and an OBDD can be done in polynomial time. The algorithm for checking intersection is based on their algorithm.

The algorithm checks whether the OBDDs F representing f and G representing g share an assignment evaluating to 1. In this case the algorithm returns *true*, if no such assignment exists the algorithm returns *false*. For a sketch of the CrossIntersect algorithm see Figure 5.

The algorithm traverses w.l.o.g F in BFS order, testing symbolically all fulfilling assignments. Because g is represented in G in a different variable order it can not simply be traversed in parallel. Instead g is decomposed by the current branching variable in the recursion of f. If at the current recursion point (F', G') the top node of F' has index x_i the following recursion pairs will be: $(F'_{|x_i=0}, G'_{|x_i=0})$ and $(F'_{|x_i=1}, G'_{|x_i=1})$ The algorithm terminates returning *true*, whenever a pair $(true, true)$ can be reached.

The runtime for this algorithm can be exponential in the worst case. This happens e.g. when g has an exponential OBDD size in the variable order of OBDD F and f is *dense* i.e. each variable is tested on every path in F.

Whenever f is not dense the computation becomes much simpler and in all our experiments we never experienced problematic behavior. We expect the crossIntersect algorithm to have an average runtime that is comparable to the runtime of the ITE-operation for OBDDs. For this reason we implemented the computed table of our algorithm analogously to the ITE-operation as a cache, thus limiting the maximal memory consumption of the computed table.

For the above mentioned applications it is sufficient to know whether the OBDDs intersect. Computation of the intersection itself is not required. As a side product of the algorithm, a single satisfying assignment of the intersection can easily be computed.

The 2-OBDD approach utilizes the same heuristics and metrics as the single OBDD interleaving method.

5   Experimental Results

Benchmarks

For our experiments we chose the public domain VIS-Verilog [13] benchmark suite, which can be downloaded from the VIS webpage.

Out of all available invariant properties in the VIS-Verilog benchmark suite we chose the largest 110 properties, leaving those out that require less than 10 seconds for VIS to finish. Passing and failing properties are equally distributed (53 passing and 57 failing).

```
CrossIntersectRecur (f,g){
    // Trivial cases
    if ( f==0-sink || g==0-sink ) return 0;
    if ( f==1-sink && g!=0-sink ) return 1;
    if ( g==1-sink && f!=0-sink) return 1;

    if(lookup(f,g)) return 0;// Lookup computed table

    // Recursive step
    // Find first index on which f depends
    topf = f→index; // Index of root node of f
    g1 = Compose(g, topf, 1);

    res1 = IntersectRecur(f→then , g1);
    if (res1) return 1;

    g0 = Compose(g, topf, 0);

    res0 = CrossIntersectRecur(f→else, g0);
    if (res0) return 1;

    insert(f, g, 0) // Insert result 0 in computed table
    return 0; // No intersection found
}
```

Fig. 5. Sketch of the CrossIntersect Algorithm.

Experimental Setup

Our implementation of the interleaving approach is based on VIS-2.0 [3]. All standard parameters remained unchanged. In the 2-OBDD approach, both OBDDs share the same settings.

All experiments were run on 2.2GHz Intel Xeon CPUs running Linux (kernel 2.4.18 SMP). Usage of virtual memory was limited to 500MB and the CPU-time was limited to 86400secs (= 1 day).

Results

For experimental results on CPU-time see Table 4. All properties, where all methods require less than 100s are omitted, although shown in the total time. Unfortunately, the CPU times differ so much that we were not able to compact the table further, without removing significant entries.

Properties that exceeded the 500MB memory limit are denoted by -*m/o*- and those exceeding the CPU limit are denoted by -*t/o*-. All CPU times are rounded to the full second. The first two columns describes the circuit and the property in the order they appear in the invariant file and the number of flip-flops after simplifying the circuit according to the property. The second and third column show CPU time for plain VIS (forward) and a modified VIS version running strictly backward. The next two columns show the CPU time for the interleaved approach using a single OBDD and the improvement over VIS. The last two columns show the CPU time for the interleaved approach using the two OBDD approach and the improvement over VIS.

For the computation of the improvement a CPU time of 86400s is assumed, if the property timed out. If a property terminated due to memory exception, the CPU time spent so far is added to the total time, but no comparison to other methods is made.

Table 1. Overall results of forward, backward, interleaving and 2-OBDD interleaving for the 55 largest cases.

	Best-choice	Worst-choice	Not Finished
Forward	33%	53%	29%
Backward	40%	42%	20%
Interl.	51%	7%	4%
2-DD-Interl.	33%	4%	0%

Table 2. Overall peaknode sizes for forward, backward, interleaving and 2-OBDD interleaving.

	Peaknodes	Memory out
Forward	298M	2
Backward	242M	3
Interl.	111M	0
2-DD-Interl.	$\leq$ 135M	0

The last two rows show overall computation time and the number of properties not finished.

The most noteworthy result of Table 4 is that the 2-OBDD interleaving approach is capable of finishing all benchmarks. None of the benchmarks requires more than 12 hours of CPU time, undercutting the CPU time limit by half. The result is an almost 5 times improvement in computation time over standard VIS (3.8 times over VIS-backward).

The interleaving approach using a single OBDD is performing comparable well. It outperforms 2-DD-interleave for some of the medium sized benchmarks. This approach performs less efficient on the larger benchmarks and is not capable of finishing ns3_7 and ns3_8.

An interesting observation can be made when comparing the overall performance and the best and worst choices. Table 1 compares the overall performance of the four different method for the 55 largest cases (Those shown in Table 4). It highlights the dilemma one is facing in forward and backward invariant checking. Table 1 compares best choices, worst choices and unfinished cases. Here *best choice* means that the specific method results in the best runtime or lies within 10% or 5s from the best runtime. The same applies for *worst choice*.

While forward is in 33% the best choice, in more than half of the cases (53%) it is the worst choice. Backward represents equally the best choice (40%) and the worst choice (42%). Interleaving is in more than half of the cases (51%) the best choice and only in 7% it is among the worst choices. Interleaving using 2-OBDDs is the best choice only in 33%, but only very rarely it is the worst choice (4%) and all of the benchmarks finish.

In Summary: If looking for the highest probability of making the best choice of a method *Interleaving* should be the preferred method. But, if overall stability especially for larger cases is the goal Interleaving with multiple OBDDs is the method of choice.

Table 3. Comparison of runtime and peaknodes for combined properties for forward and 2-OBDD interleaving.

	CPU-time/s			Peak-nodes		
	VIS	Interleave-2DDs		VIS	Interleave-2DDs	
FIFOs	1835	1524	1.2x	1092K	2721K	0.4x
am2901	m/o	139	-n/a-	-m/o-	522K	-n/a-
am2910	t/o	35	2468.5x	8241K	107K	76.9x
b12	t/o	10322	8.4x	5846K	177K	32.8x
b12abs	901	1038	0.9x	28K	47K	0.6x
ball	t/o	24499	3.5x	3499K	5750K	0.6x
blackjack	17577	14915	1.2x	2608K	4893K	0.5x
crc	t/o	3	30857.4x	9080K	41K	219.2x
matrix	60	28	2.1x	47K	75K	0.6x
mm_product	79	543	0.1x	224K	1467K	0.2x
ns3	5565	21003	0.3x	1887K	6953K	0.3x
palu	168	8	22.1x	355K	68K	5.2x
rotate32	t/o	6	14895.7x	718K	51K	14.0x
s1269b	1258	8	167.7x	1632K	61K	26.6x
soapLTL4	60	140	0.4x	76K	4025K	0.0x
soap	53	5938	0.0x	84K	286K	0.3x
sp_product	2536	2053	1.2x	1763K	71K	24.6x
spinner32	19342	6	3453.9x	4326K	1923K	2.2x
vsaR	3331	31	107.4x	2661K	119K	22.3x
vsa16a	m/o	74	-n/a-	-m/o-	105K	-n/a-
Total (of 28) :	617,169	82,480	7.5x	77M	29M	2.6x
Not completed:	7	0		7	0	

Memory Consumption

For a summary of the OBDD peaknode sizes of all benchmarks see Table 2 (Detailed results for peaknode size can be found in Table 5).

The results clearly show the superiority of the interleaving approaches over the unidirectional ones. Not only are the interleaving approaches capable of avoiding any memory exception, they obviously choose the computation of lesser complexity.

Currently, we are not able to record the exact peaknode sizes for the 2-OBDD approach. The number given is the sum of the maximum peaknode size of each OBDD separately and thus may be an over-approximation as the peaks may not occur simultaneously. However, the overhead of 21% introduced by using two different OBDDs seems acceptable and does not hurt performance.

Combined Properties

Forward invariant checking can profit from checking several properties simultaneously. This can be done as long as the properties are based on the same model. For each step the reachable states are checked against the various properties. The process is terminated when the last property fails or the reachable states computation is completed.

Table 4. Comparison of runtime in seconds for forward, backward, interleaving and 2-OBDD interleaving.

	FF	VIS	VIS-bwd	Interleave		Interleave-2DDs	
FIFOs_1	142	2141	1826	19059	0.1x	8540	0.3x
am2901_1	68	-m/o-	99	92	-n/a-	155	-n/a-
am2910_1	99	-t/o-	10	33	2586.7x	28	3130.3x
b12_1	112	39	1982	44	0.9x	49	0.8x
b12_2	110	-t/o-	12021	5240	16.5x	5838	14.8x
b12_3	112	40	2085	44	0.9x	49	0.8x
b12_4	110	-t/o-	11719	5100	16.9x	5836	14.8x
b12abs_2	34	77	706	131	0.6x	208	0.4x
ball_1	78	-t/o-	4	5	16301.1x	5	15999.2x
ball_2	78	-t/o-	4	5	16614.5x	5	15999.1x
ball_3	78	-t/o-	3	5	18383.1x	6	15158.0x
ball_4	78	-t/o-	3	4	21072.1x	5	17631.7x
ball_5	78	-t/o-	4	5	16614.5x	5	17999.1x
ball_6	78	-t/o-	-t/o-	55754	1.5x	38224	2.3x
ball_7	78	1413	-t/o-	12222	0.1x	2054	0.7x
blackjack_1	103	5047	-t/o-	13917	0.4x	20123	0.3x
blackjack_2	103	3772	-t/o-	40062	0.1x	20151	0.2x
blackjack_3	103	8244	-m/o-	2698	3.1x	2587	3.2x
blackjack_4	103	5956	-t/o-	20779	0.3x	12831	0.5x
blackjack_5	103	3422	-m/o-	12744	0.3x	14016	0.2x
crc_1	32	-t/o-	1	2	50820.6x	2	41140.5x
eight_1	44	1	166	1	0.6x	2	0.5x
eight_2	44	1	307	1	0.6x	2	0.5x
mm_product_1	48	74	607	603	0.1x	629	0.1x
ns3_1	100	16266	22820	6690	2.4x	4762	3.4x
ns3_10	100	8543	2106	1282	6.7x	29827	0.3x
ns3_11	97	17492	9	9	1901.3x	10	1822.1x
ns3_12	97	14598	9	9	1604.2x	10	1459.8x
ns3_2	100	49011	21151	44718	1.1x	11192	4.4x
ns3_3	100	18764	2068	11585	1.6x	7147	2.6x
ns3_4	100	11208	3793	2603	4.3x	3617	3.1x
ns3_5	100	10121	62219	8092	1.3x	39804	0.3x
ns3_6	100	22134	-t/o-	7115	3.1x	19847	1.1x
ns3_7	100	9124	-t/o-	-t/o-	0.1x	26714	0.3x
ns3_8	100	4380	81444	-t/o-	0.1x	30490	0.1x
ns3_9	100	17094	18129	4495	3.8x	22438	0.8x
palu_1	37	136	249	19	7.2x	15	8.9x
rotate32_1	64	-t/o-	3	3	31998.1x	3	26180.2x
s1269b_1	36	2049	2	2	1138.2x	3	660.9x
s1269b_5	36	2263	1	2	1191.3x	3	754.5x
soapLTL4_1	142	69	-t/o-	353	0.2x	727	0.1x
soap_1	140	92	-m/o-	3216	0.0x	3874	0.0x
soap_2	140	39	83311	63	0.6x	103	0.4x
soap_3	140	62	78707	446	0.1x	929	0.1x
sp_product_1	100	6024	707	1501	4.0x	1019	5.9x
spinner32_1	65	37749	3	3	15099.8x	5	6990.6x
usb_phy_4	76	7	2595	19	0.4x	18	0.4x
vsaR_1	66	8617	111	52	166.7x	34	252.7x
vsa16a_1	172	-t/o-	14	22	3857.5x	28	3064.1x
vsa16a_2	172	-m/o-	14	19	-n/a-	26	-n/a-
vsa16a_4	172	-t/o-	14	22	3909.6x	30	2870.5x
vsa16a_5	172	-t/o-	13	23	3840.1x	27	3260.4x
vsa16a_6	172	305	26	24	12.7x	31	10.0x
vsa16a_7	172	545	204	26	21.1x	36	15.1x
vsa16a_8	172	300	45	24	12.4x	30	10.1x
Total (of 110):		1,606,120	1,264,305	454,789	3.5x	335,172	4.8x
Not completed:		16	11	2		0	

Table 5. Comparison of peaknodes for forward, backward, interleaving and 2-OBDD interleaving.

	FF	VIS	VIS-bwd	Interleave		Interleave-2DDs	
FIFOs_1	142	1186K	2771K	4660K	0.3x	2818K	0.4x
am2901_1	68	-m/o-	189K	316K	-n/a-	394K	-n/a-
am2910_1	99	9318K	43K	91K	102.1x	106K	87.6x
b12_1	112	23K	1685K	45K	0.5x	46K	0.5x
b12_2	110	6098K	1112K	209K	29.2x	609K	10.0x
b12_3	112	23K	1685K	45K	0.5x	46K	0.5x
b12_4	110	6098K	1112K	209K	29.2x	609K	10.0x
b12abs_2	34	9K	24K	10K	1.0x	17K	0.6x
ball_1	78	13283K	12K	27K	475.2x	27K	481.6x
ball_2	78	13048K	12K	27K	466.8x	27K	473.1x
ball_3	78	8117K	13K	24K	334.9x	8K	1014.6x
ball_4	78	8609K	13K	22K	383.3x	8K	1076.1x
ball_5	78	13398K	12K	27K	479.3x	27K	485.8x
ball_6	78	13124K	13383K	11239K	1.2x	7819K	1.7x
ball_7	78	584K	14193K	4279K	0.1x	1032K	0.6x
blackjack_1	103	1600K	14639K	4347K	0.4x	5514K	0.3x
blackjack_2	103	1623K	21331K	10709K	0.2x	7365K	0.2x
blackjack_3	103	2131K	-m/o-	1645K	1.3x	1315K	1.6x
blackjack_4	103	1567K	20410K	10091K	0.2x	5615K	0.3x
blackjack_5	103	1752K	-m/o-	10680K	0.2x	6752K	0.3x
crc_1	32	12237K	11K	22K	544.0x	27K	446.5x
eight_1	44	8K	383K	17K	0.5x	21K	0.4x
eight_2	44	8K	1005K	11K	0.8x	16K	0.5x
mm_product_1	48	215K	1238K	1247K	0.2x	1456K	0.1x
ns3_1	100	5636K	1651K	1941K	2.9x	2459K	2.3x
ns3_10	100	3053K	1453K	1110K	2.8x	14056K	0.2x
ns3_11	97	6150K	25K	31K	194.8x	44K	138.0x
ns3_12	97	4834K	24K	29K	162.0x	44K	108.8x
ns3_2	100	7785K	718K	7756K	1.0x	5113K	1.5x
ns3_3	100	6605K	665K	3573K	1.8x	3761K	1.8x
ns3_4	100	3615K	709K	1192K	3.0x	2244K	1.6x
ns3_5	100	3368K	16025K	1998K	1.7x	13622K	0.2x
ns3_6	100	7185K	17742K	2106K	3.4x	9889K	0.7x
ns3_7	100	3130K	770K	17945K	0.2x	10286K	0.3x
ns3_8	100	2822K	11484K	3059K	0.9x	10011K	0.3x
ns3_9	100	7113K	8728K	2177K	3.3x	12299K	0.6x
palu_1	37	400K	997K	101K	3.9x	111K	3.6x
rotate32_1	64	941K	27K	27K	34.6x	37K	24.9x
s1269b_1	36	2077K	22K	28K	72.7x	43K	48.0x
s1269b_5	36	2077K	19K	28K	72.7x	43K	48.0x
soapLTL4_1	142	117K	12177K	378K	0.3x	633K	0.2x
soap_1	140	152K	-m/o-	4360K	0.0x	3863K	0.0x
soap_2	140	85K	5426K	214K	0.4x	204K	0.4x
soap_3	140	119K	12180K	530K	0.2x	1045K	0.1x
sp_product_1	100	4195K	784K	937K	4.5x	1281K	3.3x
spinner32_1	65	6325K	24K	29K	213.2x	56K	111.3x
usb_phy_4	76	26K	427K	69K	0.4x	76K	0.3x
vsaR_1	66	4848K	269K	130K	37.2x	111K	43.5x
vsa16a_1	172	17234K	53K	53K	323.7x	105K	163.2x
vsa16a_2	172	-m/o-	53K	53K	-n/a-	105K	-n/a-
vsa16a_4	172	21701K	53K	53K	407.5x	105K	205.5x
vsa16a_5	172	22961K	53K	53K	431.2x	105K	217.4x
vsa16a_6	172	274K	53K	53K	5.1x	105K	2.6x
vsa16a_7	172	412K	338K	55K	7.5x	107K	3.8x
vsa16a_8	172	274K	63K	53K	5.1x	105K	2.6x
Total (of 110):		298M	242M	111M	2.7 x	135M	2.2x
Not completed:		16	11	2		0	

This technique is not applicable to backward invariant checking because the starting points for the backward traversal differ.

We implemented a technique in the 2-DD interleaving approach that enables simultaneous check of several properties.

A comparison of the experiments can be found in Table 3. Due to the increased effort needed for reachability computation the clustersize of the transition relation has been enlarged to 8000 nodes. Results with runtime smaller than 60s are not shown.

The table shows impressive improvements. While forward invariant checking cannot finish 25% of the circuits, the interleaving approach is capable of finishing all circuits and it requires 7.5 times less CPU-time than the forward approach, resulting in an overall runtime of 82480s. At the the same time interleaving requires 2.6 times less memory than the unidirectional approach. This experiment shows impressive the superiority of the interleaving approach, where properties are computed in a *cooperative* way.

6   Conclusions and Future Work

This paper presented methods for combining forward and backward traversal for invariant checking.

The interleaving method works fully automatic, adapts dynamically and does not need any parameter tuning. Additionally, an extension of interleaving using multiple OBDDs, together with and algorithm for communication between those OBDDs has been presented.

The overall result is an increased range of applicability for OBDD based invariant checking, underlined by the fact that all benchmarks of the VIS-Verilog benchmarks suite could be successfully finished.

Currently we start application of the interleaving methods to real designs from industry. The results seem very promising suggesting an ever larger improvement because the circuits are more homogenous than the public benchmarks.

Another area that we will explore is the integration of interleaving into abstraction refinement methods that require many iterations of invariant checking.

Finally, we are planning to unify the two approaches in the way that an automatic – possibly dynamic – decision can be made whether to use one or two OBDDs.

References

1. R. E. Bryant, *Graph-Based Algorithms for Boolean Function Manipulation*, IEEE Transactions on Computers, C-35, 1986.
2. J. R. Burch, E. M. Clarke and D. E. Long, *Symbolic Model Checking with partitioned transition relations*, Proc. of Int. Conf. on VLSI, 1991.
3. R. K. Brayton, G. D. Hachtel, A. L. Sangiovanni-Vincentelli, F. Somenzi, A. Aziz, S. Cheng, S. A. Edwards, S. P. Khatri, Y. Kukimoto, A. Pardo, S. Qadeer, R. K. Ranjan, S. Sarwary, T. R. Shiple, G. Swamy and T. Villa, *VIS: A System for Verification and Synthesis*, Proc. of Computer Aided Verification (CAV'96), 1996.

4. O. Coudert, C. Berthet and J. C. Madre, *Verification of Synchronous Machines using Symbolic Execution*, Proc. of Workshop on Automatic Verification Methods for Finite State Machines, LNCS 407, Springer, 1989.
5. G. Cabodi, P. Camurati and S. Quer, *Efficient State Space Pruning in Symbolic Backward Traversal*, Proc. of ICCD, 1994.
6. G. Cabodi, S. Nocco and S. Quer, *Mixing Forward and Backward Traversals in Guided-Prioritized BDD-Based Verification*, Proc. of CAV, 2002.
7. S. Fortune, J. Hopcroft and E. Schmidt, *The Complexity of Equivalence and Containment for Free Single Variable Program Schemes*, Proc. of ICALP, 1978.
8. S. G. Govindaraju and D. L. Dill, *Verification by approximate forward and backward reachability*, Proc. ICCAD, 1998.
9. H. Iwashita and T. Nakata, *Forward Model Checking Techniques Oriented to Buggy Designs*, Proc. ICCAD, 1997.
10. R. K. Ranjan, A. Aziz, R. K. Brayton, C. Pixley and B. Plessier, *Efficient BDD Algorithms for Synthesizing and Verifying Finite State Machines*, Proc. of Int. Workshop on Logic Synthesis (IWLS'95), 1995.
11. F. Somenzi, *CUDD: CU Decision Diagram Package*, ftp://vlsi.colorado.edu/pub/ .
12. D. E. Thomas and P. Moorby, *The Verilog Hardware Description Language*, Kluwer, 1991.
13. VIS Verilog Benchmarks, vlsi.colorado.edu/~vis/

Variable Reuse for Efficient Image Computation

Zijiang Yang[1] and Rajeev Alur[2]

[1] Department of Computer Science
Western Michigan University, Kalamazoo, MI 49008
[2] Department of Computer and Information Science
University of Pennsylvania, Philadelphia, PA 19104

Abstract. *Image computation*, that is, computing the set of states reachable from a given set in one step, is a crucial component in typical tools for BDD-based symbolic reachability analysis. It has been shown that the size of the intermediate BDDs during image computation can be dramatically reduced via conjunctive partitioning of the transition relation and ordering the conjuncts for facilitating early quantification. In this paper, we propose to enhance the effectiveness of these techniques by reusing the quantified variables. Given an ordered set of conjuncts, if the last conjunct that uses a variable u appears before the first conjunct that uses another variable v, then v can be renamed to u, assuming u will be quantified immediately after its last use. In general, multiple variables can share the same identifier so the BDD nodes that are inactive but not garbage collected may be activated. We give a polynomial-time algorithm for generating the optimum number of variables that are required for image computation and show how to modify the image computation accounting for variable reuse. The savings for image computation are demonstrated on ISCAS'89 and Texas'97 benchmark models.

1 Introduction

In model checking, a finite-state model of a design is automatically verified with respect to temporal requirements to reveal inconsistencies [8, 10, 9]. The key step in a model checker is to compute the set of reachable states of a model. The reachable set is usually computed by iterative applications of image computation, where the image $Img(S)$ of a set S of states contains all states that can be reached from some state in S by executing one step of the model. In the past decade, a lot of research has centered around improving the image computation [4, 5, 11, 18, 17, 16, 6, 7]. In particular, for BDD-based symbolic model checkers, *conjunctive partitioning* and *early quantification* have significantly enhanced the applicability of model checkers. In this paper, we present a new technique, called *variable reuse*, that works synergetically with conjunctive partitioning and early quantification, leading to further savings in computational requirements of reachability analysis.

Consider a system M whose state can be described by n boolean variables $X = \{x_1, \ldots x_n\}$. A set S of states of M, then, can be viewed as a boolean

A.J. Hu and A.K. Martin (Eds.): FMCAD 2004, LNCS 3312, pp. 430–444, 2004.

function of variables in X. If $X' = \{x'_1, \ldots x'_n\}$ denotes the set of *next-state* variables, then the dynamics of M is captured by the transition relation $T(X, Y, X')$, where $Y = \{y_1, \ldots y_l\}$ is the set of auxiliary variables such as the combinational variables and the primary inputs. The transition relation T is, thus, a boolean function over $m = 2n + l$ variables. The image computation can be defined as $Img(S) = [\exists X, Y. S(X) \wedge T(X, Y, X')][X' \to X]$, where $[X' \to X]$ denotes the renaming operation of replacing each next-state variable x'_i by the corresponding current-state variable x_i [4, 15]. A popular representation for the boolean functions for the purpose of symbolic reachability analysis is ordered binary decision diagrams [3], or its variants. For realistic designs, representing the transition relation T as a monolithic BDD is not possible. Consequently, symbolic analyzers such as COSPAN [14], SMV [15], and VIS [2], employ a partitioned representation of T as a set $\{C_1, \ldots C_k\}$ of transition relations such that T is the conjunction $C_1 \wedge \cdots \wedge C_k$. Instead of computing the conjunction T a priori, the conjunction $S \wedge C_1 \wedge \cdots \wedge C_k$, which constrains T by the current set S, is computed during each image computation [5, 15].

During image computation, all the variables in $X \cup Y$ are quantified, and since quantification normally leads to smaller BDDs, *early quantification* is employed, that is, variables are quantified as soon as logically possible. Let Q_i be the set variables u in $X \cup Y$ such that the conjunct C_i depends on u, but none of the subsequent conjuncts $C_{i+1}, \ldots C_k$ depend on u. Then, the image computation $Img(S)$ can be rewritten as $\exists Q_k \cdots (\exists Q_2 (\exists Q_1. S \wedge C_1) \wedge C_2) \cdots][X' \to X]$. Thus, starting with S, at each step i, we take conjunction with the cluster C_i while quantifying the variables in Q_i. This scheme leads to significantly smaller intermediate BDDs. The effectiveness of this scheme depends on (1) *clustering*, that is, determining the clusters $\{C_1, \ldots C_k\}$ from the original description of the design, and (2) *ordering*, that is, sequencing the clusters $C_1, \ldots C_k$ so that as many variables get quantified out as early as possible. There has been a steady progress on good heuristics for clustering and ordering (see [11, 18, 17, 16, 6, 7] for sampling of this research).

Let us suppose that we have committed to a specific clustering as well as specific ordering of the clusters. Consider a variable u in Q_i, that is to be quantified at i-th step, and a variable v that does not appear in $S, C_1, \ldots C_i$. Then, the variable v can be renamed to u. In general, we partition the set $X \cup Y \cup X'$ of variables so that for every pair of variables within the same partition, the range of clusters that the two variables belong to are disjoint (we assume that all variables in X appear in the first cluster, and all variables in X' appear in the last cluster). Then, only a single variable identifier is needed per partition, and the image computation can proceed as before, but after renaming each variable to the unique identifier for its partition.

After formulating the problem of reducing the number of variables needed for image computation, we develop an algorithm for partitioning the variables into minimal number of sets. Our algorithm is quadratic in the number of variables. Our experiments with ISCAS'89 and Texas'97 benchmarks show a significant reduction in the number of variables by 40% to 68% . In fact, the number of variables is much closer to the number n of variables in X than to the number m of variables in $X \cup Y \cup X'$. Since the reduced number of variables is the minimum necessary for image computation, we believe that the reduced number of variables is a better measure of complexity of the design compared to the number of state variables or the total number of variables.

After reducing the number of variables, image computation needs to be modified to account for renaming. A priori, it is difficult to estimate whether such a modification will improve or degrade the performance. On one hand there are clear advantages. Once a variable has been existentially quantified, the BDD nodes that are associated with the variable become inactive. However, the nodes are not garbage collected immediately. With variable reuse, the quantified variable will be reused in a different role. Instead of creating new BDD nodes and then increasing memory usage, the inactive nodes that are still in memory may be actived. Variable reuse will also benefit variable reordering algorithms because there are fewer BDD variables to be considered. Finally, we expect there is more sharing on BDD nodes because each node may take more than one roles. On the other hand,there is a potential disadvantage. Performance of BDD routines is extremely sensitive to the global ordering of variables, and reusing the same variable identifier in different roles can turn a good ordering into a bad one. Indeed, in presence of dynamic reordering, the computational requirements of image computation are very unpredictable.

We modified the image computation routine of VIS 1.4 model checker to verify the performance on ISCAS'89 and Texas'97 benchmarks. For the algorithm for generating the minimal number of variables, in many cases we obtained significant savings in memory and time, but in some cases, it performs worse than VIS. Consequently, we implemented a modified version of our strategy for partitioning variables which avoids pairing of a current-state variable x_i with a next-state variable x_j with $i \neq j$. The intuition for this lies in the fact that variable ordering and dynamic reordering schemes treat the variables x_i and x_i' as a pair, and renaming x_j' to x_i can be expensive. The modified partitioning requires more number of variables compared to the optimal one, but still significantly less than the number variables used by VIS. Another modification involves ordering of the clusters so as to reduce the number of variables required. In this greedy scheme, we pick the next cluster which will minimize the number of partitions of variables encountered so far, and when there are ties, we resort to the original VIS algorithm for ordering the clusters. With these modifications, we compared our reachability computation with time requirements for VIS 1.4. We get improvements in 29 out of 37 benchmarks, and in 6 cases, additional iterations of the image computation are feasible by our strategy (see Table 2 for details).

The remaining paper is organized as follows. Section 2 describes our strategy intuitively using an illustration. Section 3 formalizes the problem of reducing the number of variables, shows how to modify the image computation accounting for variable reuse, and gives algorithms for reducing the number of variables. Section 4 reports experimental results, and we conclude in Section 5 with directions for possible improvements.

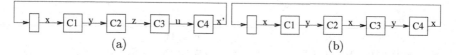

(a)   (b)

Fig. 1. Image computation: (a)without variable reuse, (b)with variable reuse

2   Variable Reuse Technique

Suppose we have fixed the ordering of clusters $C_1, ..., C_k$ and are committed to early quantification during image computation. The support set of the cluster C_i is the set of variables that appear in the BDD of C_i. The support set of S is considered to be X. Consider a variable $u \in X \cup Y$ such that u does not appear in the support sets of $C_{l+1}, ... C_k$, and thus, u can be quantified by step l. Consider a variable w that is not in the support sets of $S, C_1, ..., C_l$, then all occurrences of w in $C_{l+1}, ..., C_k$ can be replaced by u. Repeated applications of such variable replacement causes a variable appear repeatedly in different roles and get quantified repeatedly. As a result, fewer variables are involved in BDD computation. Since size of BDD in many cases is exponential in number of variables, variable reuse can reduce BDD size effectively by taking advantage of already constructed BDD nodes.

Figure 1 (a) shows a simple example for conventional image computation procedure. There are four clusters C_1, C_2, C_3, C_4 and five variables in which x is the current state variable, x' is the next state variable and y, z, u are internal variables. The following five steps are used to compute the set $Img(S(x))$: (1) $S_1(y) := \exists x.S(x) \wedge C_1(x, y)$, (2) $S_2(z) := \exists y.S_1(y) \wedge C_2(y, z)$, (3) $S_3(u) := \exists z.S_2(z) \wedge C_3(z, u)$, (4) $S_4(x') := \exists u.S_3(u) \wedge C_4(u, x')$, and (5) $Img(S(x)) := S_4(x')[x' \to x]$.

However, we observe that after computing $S_1(y)$, x is no longer in scope. Since the variable z has not been used until the computation of S_1 finishes, z can be renamed to x in the cluster C_2. By a similar reasoning, all of x, z and x' can share the same variable identifier, say x, and y and u can have the same name, say y. As shown in Figure 1 (b), only two variables are needed in the following image computation procedure: (1) $S_1(y) := \exists x.S(x) \wedge C_1(x, y)$, (2) $S_2(x) := \exists y.S_1(y) \wedge C_2(y, x)$, (3) $S_3(y) := \exists x.S_2(x) \wedge C_3(x, y)$, and (4) $Img(S(x)) := \exists y.S_3(y) \wedge C_4(y, x)$. Observe that, because we rename x' to x in cluster C_4, the last step of replacement of the next state variable by the current state variable is not needed. Next section discusses algorithms for partitioning the variable set. It turns out that variable partitioning is a low-cost procedure, and can easily be added to image computation.

By examining the modified image computation for our example, we can anticipate two potential benefits. First, the same variables, namely x and y, are involved in all four steps, and consequently, there can be more sharing, and reuse of existing BDD nodes during the computation. Second, with less variables involved, dynamic reordering, a key step in large examples, will take less time. There is a potential drawback, however. A lot of research has been done

```
min_gap()                              set get_mingap_set(P, u)
    A := X ∪ Y ∪ X';                        result := ∅;
    sort A by A[i].high;                    mingap := MAX;
    foreach variable u ∈ A                  foreach set p ∈ P
        p := get_mingap_set(P, u);              gap := u.low − p.high;
        if (p ≠ ∅)                              if (gap>0 && gap<mingap)
            p := p ∪ {u}; p.high := u.high;         mingap := gap; result := p;
        else                               end
            p' := {u}; p'.high = u.high;   return result
            P = P ∪ {p'};              end
    end
end
```

Fig. 2. Minimal gap algorithm

to obtain a good initial variable order and dynamic reordering heuristics. With renaming, the initial order or dynamic reorder heuristics may be no longer effective. For example, if structure of C_1 requires x to be before y, and structure of C_2 requires y to be before z, then after renaming z to x, there is no good ordering.

3   Variable Reuse Algorithms

For a variable $u \in X \cup Y \cup X'$, let $M[u, i] = 1$ if variable u appears in the support set of cluster C_i. We consider $S(X)$ as the 0-th cluster as we wish to compute the conjunction $S \wedge C_1 \wedge \cdots \wedge C_k$. Since prior to the reachability computation, we don't know the exact set $S(X)$ at each image computation, we assume that all the current-state variables appear in $S(X)$. Therefore, $M[u, 0] = 1$ for $u \in X$. We also let $M[u, k] = 1$ if $u \in X'$ because next-state variables cannot be quantified until the end of image computation. For each variable u, let $u.low = min\{i \mid M[u, i] = 1\}$, and $u.high = max\{i \mid M[u, i] = 1\}$. We declare the *range* of u to be the interval $Rng(u) = [u.low, u.high]$. Two variables u and v can be renamed to each other if $Rng(u)$ and $Rng(v)$ are disjoint.

Our goal is to partition the variables $X \cup Y \cup X'$ into disjoint sets $p_1, ..., p_r$ such that $Rng(u) \cap Rng(v) = \emptyset$ if two variables u and v belong to the same partition set p_i. Note that all the variables in a partition set p_i can have the same name, and the number of partitions is the number of variables needed for reachability computation. For a set p of variables, define $p.high = max\{u.high \mid u \in p\}$, $p.low = min\{u.low \mid u \in p\}$, and $Rng(p) = [p.low, p.high]$. The problem can be viewed as an application of constructing a maximal independent set in an interval graph. While maximal independent sets are hard to compute for general graphs, the problem is solvable in polynomial time for interval graphs [12].

3.1   The Minimal Gap Algorithm

Figure 2 shows an algorithm to partition the variables into disjoint sets. Let the A be the set of all the current state, next state and auxiliary variables. We first sort variables by their upper values. The variables with the same upper value are ordered by their lower values. That is, for all $1 \leq i < j \leq m$, either $(A[i].high < A[j].high)$ or $(A[i].high = A[j].high \wedge A[i].low \leq A[j].low)$ holds. The remaining code iterates over the sorted variables to find an existing partition or create a new partition. A variable u can be added to an existing partition p if $Rng(u) \cap Rng(p) = \emptyset$. There may exist several partitions that satisfies the condition. Our strategy is to insert u into a set p such that u and p have the minimal "gap". As implemented in the function get_mingap_set, u can be added to a set p if $u.low - p.high > 0$. This is because $p.high$ is the maximal upper value of a variable in p, therefore, $u.low - p.high > 0$ means the range of u is disjoint from the range of any variable in p. Although u can also be inserted into p if $p.low - u.high > 0$, this is not possible because all the variables in p appear before u in the array ordered by their high values. If no such p disjoint from u exists, get_mingap_set returns the default $\emptyset$, otherwise it returns p for which the value $u.low - p.high$ is the smallest.

Finally the partition P is modified in the function min_gap. If there exists an appropriate set p that u can be added to, u is inserted in p, and the value $p.high$ is updated with $u.high$ (note in this case $u.high$ is guaranteed to be greater than $p.high$). If u cannot be inserted in any existing set, a new set is created for u, and its $high$ field is set to $u.high$ (note that the algorithm does not actually need to keep track of low fields for the partitions).

Theorem 1. *Given a set of variables u with specified ranges $[u.low, u.high]$, the algorithm min_gap shown in Figure 2 creates minimal number of sets such that variables in the same set have pair-wise disjoint ranges.*

Proof: For $i = 1 \ldots m$, let P_i be the (partial) partition created by our algorithm after processing the variables $A[1] \ldots A[i]$. Let us say that P_i is (partially) correct if P_i can be extended to obtain a partition with optimal number of sets. Let i be the smallest index such that P_{i+1} is not correct (if no such i exists, the final partition has optimum number of sets, and we are done). Let $u = A[i+1]$. Thus, $A[i]$ is extensible to an optimal partition, say P_f, but the algorithm makes a mistake while processing u.

First, suppose $Rng(p)$ overlaps $Rng(u)$ for every p in P_i. In this case, P_{i+1} is obtained by adding a new set $\{u\}$ to P_i. Since P_f extends P_i, it must extend P_{i+1} also, a contradiction.

Now suppose our algorithm decides to add u to an existing set p. Note that since the array is sorted, $u.high$ is the smallest among all unprocessed (i.e. not already in P_i) variables. Consequently, the left neighbor of u in the optimal partition P_f is a processed variable (the case that u has no left neighbor in P_f is similar). Suppose the left neighbor of u in P_f belongs to the set $p' \neq p$ in P_i. Both p and p' cannot overlap with u: $p.high > u.low$ and $p'.high > u.low$. The way the algorithm get_mingap_set chooses p, the gap between p and u is less than (or equal to) the gap between p' and u: $p'.high \leq p.high$. Consider P'_{i+1} obtained by adding u to p' in P_i. The only relevant information about a partial partition, for possible ways of adding the unprocessed variables to it, is the sequence of high end-points of the sets in the partition. If we compare the high end-points of the sets in P_{i+1} and P'_{i+1}, they are $\{p'.high, u.high\} \cup \{p''.high \mid p'' \in P_i, p'' \neq p, p'' \neq p'\}$ for P_{i+1}, and $\{p.high, u.high\} \cup \{p''.high \mid p'' \in P_i, p'' \neq p, p'' \neq p'\}$ for P'_{i+1}. Thus, P_{i+1} extends less to the right. It is straightforward to show that P_{i+1} is also extensible, a contradiction. ∎

As far as time complexity of the algorithm is concerned, observe that the number of partitions is at most m, where m is the total number of variables. Consequently, `get_mingap_set` is $O(m)$. As a result, the complexity of `min_gap` is $O(m^2)$.

3.2   Modifying the Image Computation

Let $P = \{p_1, ..., p_r\}$ be the partition sets created by our algorithm. Let l_i be the *leading variable* in p_i to which all the other variables appearing in the same set will be renamed. Let L be a mapping function such that $L(u) = l_i$ if $u \in p_i$. The mapping L naturally extends to sets of variables.

A common strategy for partitioning and ordering of the transition relations proceeds in two steps: obtain clusters of transition relations from the design description usually by combining the BDDs for fine-grain transition relations for the atomic blocks, and then order clusters with a quantification schedule to allow for maximum early quantification. Assume after the second step, we have a sequence of clusters $C_1, \ldots, C_k$ and a sequence of variable sets $Q_1, \ldots, Q_k$ for quantification. The standard image computation algorithm follows: $\exists Q_k \cdots \exists (Q_2(\exists Q_1.S \wedge C_1) \wedge C_2) \cdots][X' \to X]$. We need to introduce a renaming step before the image computation step starts.

Let T_i be the support set of C_i. We compute a BDD C'_i by substituting the variables appearing in C_i with $L(T_i)$, i.e, $C'_i = C_i[T_i \to L(T_i)]$. Similarly, for $Q_i \subseteq T_i$, we obtain a new set $Q'_i = L(Q_i) \subseteq L(T_i)$. The revised image computation is: $\exists Q'_k \cdots \exists (Q'_2(\exists Q'_1.S' \wedge C'_1) \wedge C'_2) \cdots][A \to B]$.

Note that the substitution at the end of image computation becomes $[A \to B]$ instead of $[X' \to X]$, where A and B are obtained as discussed below.

Although any variable in a partition set can be a lead variable, picking the right one leads to more efficient strategy. Following rules are followed in our implementation while choosing a lead variable.

1. *Choose current state variables first.*
   If there exists a current state variable $x_i \in X$ in a partition set, we always choose x_i as the lead variable. Note that two current state variables cannot be in the same partition because $x_i.low = x_j.low = 0$, and thus $Rng(x_i) \cap Rng(x_j) \neq \emptyset$, for $i \neq j$. Such renaming has the benefit that if the matching next state variable x'_i belongs to the same partition, the substitution $[x'_i \to x_i]$ at the end of image computation is not necessary.

2. *Choose next state variable if no current state variable exists.*
   A next state variable $x' \in X'$ should not be renamed to an internal variable $y \in Y$. This is because at the end of image computation we need to convert next state variables to current state variables by $[X' \to X]$. For this reason, we always rename all the internal variables to the next state variable x' in

a partition p. Note a partition can have at most one next state variable because for any $x'_i, x'_j \in X'$, $x'_i.high = x'_j.high$.

3. *Choose any variable if no state variable exists.*

   If there are no current state or next state variables in a partition, any variable can be chosen as a lead variable.

The above rules specify how to choose the lead variables in each partition, and thus, how to fix the renaming map L. Finally, consider the substitution $[X' \rightarrow X]$ at the end of image computation. If x'_i is renamed to x_j by L, where $i \neq j$, we cannot use $[X' \rightarrow X]$ as it is. We first need to rename x_j to x_i, followed by the standard renaming $[X' \rightarrow X]$. A better method is to combine the two conversion steps into one step $[A \subseteq (X \cup X') \rightarrow B \subseteq X]$. The two arrays are defined as follows: for each state variable $x_i \in X$, if $L(x'_i) = x_j$ with $j \neq i$, then $A[i] = x_j$ and $B[i] = x_i$, else $A[i] = x'_i$ and $B[i] = x_i$. It should be noted that BDD packages perform such renaming in parallel.

3.3   The Least Effort Algorithm

Although Minimal Gap Algorithm creates minimal number of partitions, it requires extra effort to get the substitution arrays of A and B, and the substitution $[A \rightarrow B]$ can be expensive. This section presents a greedy algorithm least_effort that has additional constraints in renaming. In particular, it treats the next-state variables specially since variable ordering and dynamic reordering try to keep the variables x_i and x'_i together as a pair. The strategy least_effort uses more variables than min_gap, but no changes are needed for the substitution step $[X' \rightarrow X]$. Therefore, we only need to change variable names in clusters and quantification arrays before reachability computation starts and no modification is required in existing image computation code.

```
set get_constrained_mingap_set(P, u)
   if u ∈ X'
      choose v such that v ∈ X and v matches u;
      choose p such that v ∈ p and p.high < u.low;
      if p = ∅
         choose p such that p.high < u.low and (p ∩ X = ∅);
      else
      p := get_mingap_set(P, u);
   return p
end
```

Fig. 3. Get disjoint partition with constraints

The algorithm least_effort is the same as min_gap except that the function call to get_mingap_set is replaced by get_constrained_mingap_set shown in Figure 3. Note that unlike get_mingap_set, get_constrained_mingap_set treats next state variables differently. For each $x' \in X'$, it first tries to obtain

```
greedy_partition(C)                    int compute_cost(S,C_i,C,P)
  init_var_range();                      foreach v ∈ support_set(C_i)
  P = {{x}| x ∈ X };                       if v.low == UNKNOWN
  while C ≠ ∅                                 v.low = |S| + 1;
    foreach C_i ∈ C                         if v ∉ support_set(∪_{j≠i}C_j
      cost=compute_cost(S,C_i,C,P);            v.high = |S| + 1;
      if cost<MIN                           if ∃P_i|P_i.high < v.low
        picked = C_i; MIN = cost;             P_i.high = v.high;
    end                                     else
    S = S ∪ {picked};C = C − {picked};        num_new_partitions ++;
    modify_partitions(P, picked)          end
  end                                      return num_new_partitions;
end                                      end
```

Fig. 4. The greedy algorithm to order clusters and partition variables

a set that satisfies two constraints: (1) it contains the matching current state variable x, and (2) $p.high < x'.low$. The first constraint gives priority to a set such that x' can be renamed to its matching current state variable. The second constraint ensures that x' can be added to the set.

If the second constraint cannot be satisfied (note that the first constraint can always be met), it tries to find any set p that $(p.high < x'.low)$ and $p \cap X = \emptyset$. The constraint of $p \cap X = \emptyset$ ensures that x' will not be in the same set with a non-matching current state variable. If such a set cannot be found, it returns empty set, and x' will be put in a new partition by itself.

For any auxiliary and current state variables, it uses **get_mingap_set** shown in Figure 2 to get the appropriate set. Note that the algorithm prevents the case that a current state variable is added to a set containing a non-matching next state variable. This is because the variables are sorted by first their high end-points and then their low values. Since $x'.high = k$, $x'.low > 0$, $x.high \leq k$, and $x.low = 0$, we have all current-state variables appearing before all next-state variables in the sorted order. Therefore, all the current-state variables have been allocated to some partition sets before any of the next-state variables are handled.

With the constraint that a next state variable cannot be renamed to a non-matching current state variable, we don't need to adjust existing image computation algorithm. Image computation can use the formula $[\exists Q'_k \cdots \exists (Q'_2 (\exists Q'_1 . S \wedge C'_1) \wedge C'_2) \cdots][X' \rightarrow X]$.

3.4   The Greedy Algorithm for Ordering Clusters and Partitioning Variables

The previous algorithms partition variables assuming a given fixed ordering of clusters. The greedy algorithm presented in this section orders the clusters so as to favor minimal number of partitions at each step.

The function **greedy_partition** in Figure 4 shows the algorithm with the set of clusters C as the input. Initially the sorted cluster array S is empty. The first step is to initialize the range values for variables by function call init_var_range. As explained earlier, current-state variables have a common lower bound 0 and next-state variables have a common upper bound $|C|$. The lower and upper bounds of internal variables, as well as the upper bounds of current-state variables and lower bounds of next-state variables, are UNKNOWN. The initial partition set P consists of $|X|$ singleton sets each containing a distinct current-state variable. The iteration of while picks a cluster from C and adds it to the sorted cluster array S in each step. The partition P is then modified accordingly. The function modify_partition uses the same code as the lines 6 to 10 in min_gap in Figure 2. To decide which cluster to pick, the loop of foreach goes through all the remaining clusters and calculate the effect if the variables from a cluster were added to the existing partitions. The one with the least cost is chosen. Finally the existing partitions are modified by incorporating the variables from newly selected clusters. Since the position of the selected cluster in sorted array is known, the ranges of partitions and variables can be updated.

The function compute_cost in Figure 4 shows how to calculate the number of partitions if variables from cluster C_i were added to partitions. There are four parameters: S, the sorted cluster array; C_i, the cluster under consideration; C, the clusters not sorted yet; P, the current variable partitions. Initially the number of new partitions is 0. If C_i is appended to the sorted cluster array, the index of C_i will be $|S| + 1$. We may set the ranges of the variables based on the location of C_i. The function compute_cost tries to set the lower and upper bounds for variables in the support set of C_i. The lower bound of the variable v is $|S|+1$ if $v.low$ is UNKNOWN. This is because C_i must be the first occurrence of v in the sorted cluster array. If v does not appear in the supports of clusters $C - C_i$, C_i would be the last occurrence of v in S. Therefore, the upper bound of v should be $|S| + 1$. After a variable has been assigned upper (possibly still UNKNOWN) and lower bound, the function looks for a partition P_i such that $P_i.high < v.low$. Note that partitions with open upper bound value UNKNOWN does not satisfy $P_i.high < v.low$. If such partition exists, the upper bound of P_i is increased to the upper bound of v (may be UNKNOWN) because we consider v is to be added to P_i; otherwise, a new partition has to be created. Therefore, number of partitions is increased by 1. However, we do not need to really allocate a new partition because we only need to know how many new partitions have to be created, and no two variables from C_i may reside in the same partition, which makes the knowledge of upper and lower bounds of new partitions unnecessary.

The function compute_cost considers the cost to be the number of new partitions created. In the implementation, we distinguish between *open partitions* and *close partitions*. The partitions with unknown upper bound are close partitions; otherwise they are open partitions. Since open partitions do not accept any new variables, we prefer close partitions. In this case, the cost to add a new cluster c becomes $cost = num\_close\_partitions + weight * num\_close\_partitions$ where $weight > 1$. We also consider the number of variables V_{sorted} that have been assigned to a partition set so far. In such case, the cost becomes $num\_partitions/ |V_{sorted}|$.

Table 1. Number of variables

Circuit Name	Latches	Clusters	Number of variables				min %
			VIS	MG	LE	GD	
three_processor_bin	62	10	142	89	111	100	63%
three_processor	62	12	142	90	115	95	63%
IFetchControl1	59	5	146	90	113	99	62%
IFetchControl2	59	5	145	91	114	91	63%
TWO	64	9	204	93	122	99	46%
PCIabnorm	295	23	617	355	588	359	58%
PCInorm	295	31	612	355	588	342	56%
test4	153	16	315	189	314	213	60%
timestamp	79	7	168	114	168	128	68%
multi_master	382	24	781	479	764	441	63%
p62_L_L_V01	308	34	618	374	598	397	61%
p62_L_S_V02	308	34	618	369	595	396	60%
p62_ND_S_V02	308	35	622	362	597	405	58%
p62_L_L_V02	308	34	618	374	598	397	61%
p62_S_S_V01	308	34	618	374	598	397	61%
p62_LS_LS_V01	308	34	618	374	598	397	61%
p62_S_S_V02	308	34	618	374	598	397	61%
p62_LS_LS_V02	308	34	618	374	598	397	61%
p62_LS_L_V01	308	34	618	369	595	396	60%
p62_V_LS_V02	308	34	622	369	595	396	59%
p62_LS_L_V02	308	34	618	369	595	396	60%
p62_ND_ND_V01	308	35	622	395	599	405	64%
p62_V_S_V01	308	34	622	369	595	396	59%
p62_LS_S_V01	308	34	618	369	595	396	60%
p62_ND_ND_V02	308	35	622	395	599	405	64%
p62_V_S_V02	308	34	622	369	595	396	59%
p62_LS_S_V02	308	34	618	369	595	396	60%
p62_ND_ND_V	308	34	622	395	599	405	64%
p62_L_S_V01	308	34	618	369	595	396	60%
p62_ND_S_V01	308	35	622	375	597	405	60%
s1269	37	8	92	64	70	58	63%
s1512	57	4	143	95	114	95	66%
s1423	74	7	165	122	151	134	74%
s4863	104	33	263	112	132	105	40%
s9234	211	23	461	253	387	267	55%
s13207	638	42	1339	638	1001	710	48%
s15850	522	51	1147	665	1014	706	58%

4   Experimental Results

4.1   Reduction in the Number of Variables

In order to evaluate the effectiveness of our variable renaming algorithms, we ran experiments on ISCAS'89 and Texas'97 benchmarks. All experiments were done on a 800MHz Pentium III processor machine running the Linux operating system with 512MB of main memory. In all the experiments, we used the default VIS options (partition threshold=5000, frontier method for building partition BDDs, and image cluster size=5000).

The performance metric we measured in this section are the number of variables required for reachability computation. Table 1 shows experimental results with the first column indicating circuit names. The second column shows the number of latches in the circuits. Since the current state variables have to be in distinct partitions, the number of latches is the lower bound on the number variables for any of the strategies. The third column indicates the number of clusters. Finally, the last four columns provide the number of variables required for different algorithms.

Column "VIS" lists the number of variables by using original VIS-1.4 code. Columns "MG", "LE" and "GD" report the number of variables by min_gap, least_effort and greedy algorithms, respectively. The last column shows the minimal number of variables for one of our renaming algorithms compared with VIS. We can see that only 40%-74% of VIS variables are actually required for reachability computation.

4.2   Savings During Reachability Computation

As discussed in the introduction, it is difficult to predict the impact of our strategy on memory and time requirements during image computation, and can be estimated only by experiments with benchmarks. We integrated our modifications within VIS. For these experiments, we invoke dynamic variable reordering in the CUDD package (see http://vlsi.colorado.edu/~fabio/CUDD/ for information). A time limit of one hour was used for all experiments. The results are reported in Table 2. It compares VIS 1.4 with the best results obtained from either the modification MG with min_gap, the modification LE with least_effort or the modification GD with greedy. For each algorithm the table lists, the number of steps of image computation, the number of states (this is only to verify that actual reachable sets are identical), and time required.

Of the 37 benchmarks tested, variable renaming optimization performs better than VIS on 29 examples, while VIS does better on 8 examples. The last column indicates the comparison. If the value t is greater than 1, our modification achieves a speedup of $t\times$ (e.g., on three_processor_bin, reachability computation after variable renaming speeds up by 3.61). If the value t is in the format of $+ts$, variable rename algorithm can do t steps further than VIS (e.g., on s1423, reachability computation after variable renaming can do one more step). On the other hand, If the value in the last column is less than 1 or in the format of $-ts$, VIS without variable rename is better. Given the non-robust nature of computational requirements of BDD packages, particularly due to dynamic reordering, we consider these results to be promising.

5   Conclusion

In this paper, we have proposed a technique for reducing the number of auxiliary variables required for image computation in symbolic reachability analysis.

Table 2. Reachability Computation

Circuit	VIS			RENAME			
Name	#step	#states	Time	#step	#states	Time	Speedup
three_processor_bin	32	3.6e+08	145.23	32	3.6e+08	40.25	3.61
three_processor	32	3.6e+08	98.02	32	3.6e+08	26.96	3.64
IFetchControl1	27	4.3e+08	4.69	27	4.3e+08	10.48	0.45
IFetchControl2	27	2.5e+08	2.25	27	2.5e+08	1.70	1.32
TWO	21	1.3e+14	42.76	21	1.3e+14	43.76	0.98
PCIabnorm	35	2.6e+06	23.09	35	2.6e+06	9.78	2.36
PCInorm	30	86528	1.15	30	86528	0.99	1.16
test4	17	4.0e+18	1677.67	18	7.8e+20	3121.66	+1s
timestamp	26	3.2e+22	21.75	26	3.2e+22	9.33	2.33
multi_master	41	1.1e+06	20.56	41	1.1e+06	3.27	6.29
p62_L_L_V01	48	2445	46.09	48	2445	15.11	3.05
p62_L_S_V02	73	1327	13.52	73	1327	15.09	0.90
p62_ND_S_V02	106	143788	316.05	106	143788	260.00	1.22
p62_L_L_V02	71	2398	54.30	71	2398	29.53	1.84
p62_S_S_V01	45	437	45.07	45	437	5.92	7.61
p62_LS_LS_V01	61	2823	123.81	61	2823	39.24	3.16
p62_S_S_V02	42	317	2.82	42	317	2.41	1.17
p62_LS_LS_V02	58	1045	41.57	58	1045	12.37	3.36
p62_LS_L_V01	61	2743	77.27	61	2743	38.57	2.00
p62_V_LS_V02	125	93185	385.94	125	93185	381.38	1.01
p62_LS_L_V02	66	1124	12.78	66	1124	11.31	1.13
p62_ND_ND_V01	25	310073	1178.86	32	1.3e+06	2209.86	+7s
p62_V_S_V01	121	59667	374.39	121	59667	386.23	0.97
p62_LS_S_V01	61	2743	77.51	61	2743	38.48	2.01
p62_ND_ND_V02	36	1.1e+06	1674.22	40	2.3e+06	2138.61	+4s
p62_V_S_V02	106	22309	142.28	106	22309	128.63	1.11
p62_LS_S_V02	66	1124	12.84	66	1124	11.34	1.10
p62_ND_ND_V	25	310073	1181.82	32	1.3e+06	2206.98	+7s
p62_L_S_V01	85	3637	79.04	85	3637	46.06	1.72
p62_ND_S_V01	55	378695	1263.28	68	1.6e+06	2742.20	+13s
s1269	9	1.1e+09	2460.04	9	1.1e+09	2668.87	0.92
s1512	1023	1.6e+12	1292.22	1023	1.6e+12	954.87	1.35
s1423	10	1.6e+09	1120.93	11	7.9e+09	2811.42	+1s
s4863	4	2.1e+19	675.58	4	2.1e+19	454.04	1.49
s9234	8	1.3e+14	1137.86	8	1.3e+14	1285.95	0.88
s13207	10	6.6e+26	2976.30	6	8.1e+22	1970.93	-4s
s15850	2	7.4e+12	595.92	2	7.4e+12	895.19	0.67

This idea complements the previous research on conjunctive partitioning and early quantification. Unlike typical optimization problems in design automation, reducing the number of variables optimally turns out to have a polynomial-time solution. Our experiments concerning reducing the number of variables indicate that the number of auxiliary variables necessary for image computation is quite small compared to the number of state variables. In terms of savings in time, our heuristic improves on the state-of-the-art model checker VIS 1.4 on many benchmarks, sometimes leading to a speed up of 7.61 , and sometimes allowing extra iterations of image computation. There is little effort needed to compute the renaming, and our strategy can be incorporated in other model checkers with minimal effort.

The benefits of the proposed heuristic can potentially be improved in many ways. First, the techniques for generating clusters and ordering clusters can be modified to account for variable renaming strategy. In fact, there seems to be no need to assign variable identifiers for all the variables right from the beginning, but to combine all of these preprocessing steps. Second, and possibly more importantly, the heuristics for choosing the initial order and dynamic reordering during image computation need to be examined carefully in light of our strategy. In particular, the fact that a variable appears in multiple roles can be taken into account while choosing the ordering, and the pairing of a current-state variable with next-state variable can be non-essential in our setting. Finally, similar ideas can be explored in conjunction with recent efforts on bounded model checking using SAT solvers [1, 13].

References

1. A. Biere, A. Cimatti, E. Clarke, M. Fujita, and Y. Zhu. Symbolic model checking using SAT procedures instead of BDDs. In *Proceedings of the 36th ACM/IEEE Design Automation Conference*, pages 317–320, 1999.
2. R. Brayton, G. Hachtel, A. Sangiovanni-Vincentell, F. Somenzi, A. Aziz, S. Cheng, S. Edwards, S. Khatri, Y. Kukimoto, A. Pardo, S. Qadeer, R. Ranjan, S. Sarwary, T. Shiple, G. Swamy, and T. Villa. VIS: A system for verification and synthesis. In *Proceedings of the Eighth International Conference on Computer Aided Verification*, LNCS 1102, pages 428–432. Springer-Verlag, 1996.
3. R.E. Bryant. Graph-based algorithms for boolean-function manipulation. *IEEE Transactions on Computers*, C-35(8), 1986.
4. J.R. Burch, E.M. Clarke, D.L. Dill, L.J. Hwang, and K.L. McMillan. Symbolic model checking: 10^{20} states and beyond. *Information and Computation*, 98(2):142–170, 1992.
5. J.R. Burch, E.M. Clarke, and D.E. Long. Symbolic model checking with partitioned transition relations. In *Proceedings of the IFIP International Conference on Very Large Scale Integration: VLSI'91*, pages 49–58, 1991.
6. P. Chauhan, E. Clarke, S. Jha, J. Kukula, H. Veith, and D. Wang. Using combinatorial optimization methods for quantifier scheduling. In *Proceedings of CHARME'01*, LNCS 2144, pages 293–309, 2001.
7. P. Chauhan, E.M. Clarke, S. Jha, J. Kukula, T. Shiple, H. Veith, and D. Wong. Non-linear quantification scheduling in image computation. In *Proceedings of the International Conference on Computer Aided Design: ICCAD'01*, 2001.
8. E.M. Clarke and E.A. Emerson. Design and synthesis of synchronization skeletons using branching time temporal logic. In *Proc. Workshop on Logic of Programs*, LNCS 131, pages 52–71. Springer-Verlag, 1981.

9. E.M. Clarke, O. Grumberg, and D.A. Peled. *Model checking*. MIT Press, 2000.
10. E.M. Clarke and R.P. Kurshan. Computer-aided verification. *IEEE Spectrum*, 33(6):61–67, 1996.
11. D. Geist and I. Beer. Efficient model checking by automated ordering of transition relation partitions. In *Computer Aided Verification, Proc. 6th Int. Conference*, LNCS 818, pages 299–310. Springer-Verlag, 1994.
12. M. Golumbic. *Algorithmic Graph Theory and Perfect Graph*. Academic Press, 1980.
13. A. Gupta, Z. Yang, P. Ashar, and A. Gupta. SAT-based image computation with applications in reachability analysis. In *Proceedings of the Third International Workshop on Formal Methods in Computer-Aided Design*, LNCS 1954, pages 354–371. Springer, 2000.
14. R. Hardin, Z. Har'El, and R.P. Kurshan. COSPAN. In *Proceedings of the Eighth International Conference on Computer Aided Verification*, LNCS 1102, pages 423–427. Springer-Verlag, 1996.
15. K. McMillan. *Symbolic model checking: an approach to the state explosion problem*. Kluwer Academic Publishers, 1993.
16. I.-H. Moon, J.H. Kukula, K. Ravi, and F. Somenzi. To split or to conjoin: the question in image computation. In *Proceedings of the 37th Design Automation Conference*, pages 26–28, 2000.
17. I.-H. Moon and F. Somenzi. Border-block traingular form and conjunction schedule in image computation. In *Proceedings of the Third International Workshop on Formal Methods in Computer-Aided Design*, LNCS 1954, pages 73–90. Springer, 2000.
18. R. Ranjan, A. Aziz, B. Plessier, C. Pixley, and R. Brayton. Efficient BDD algorithms for FSM synthesis and verification. In *Proceedings of the IEEE/ACM International Workshop on Logic Synthesis*, 1995.

Author Index

Aagaard, Mark D.   98, 113
Akbarpour, Behzad   37
Alur, Rajeev   430
Amla, Nina   260
Arditi, Laurent   128
Awedh, Mohammad   230

Baumgartner, Jason   159
Berry, Gerard   128
Biere, Armin   186
Borrione, Dominique   52
Brim, Luboš   352

Černá, Ivana   352
Chechik, Marsha   306
Chou, Ching-Tsun   382
Cimatti, Alessandro   245
Ciubotariu, Vlad C.   98
Claessen, Koen   337

Dang, Thao   21
Day, Nancy A.   113
Della Penna, Giuseppe   214
Dill, David L.   399
Dillinger, Peter C.   367
Donzé, Alexandre   21

Emerson, E. Allen   399

Giunchiglia, Enrico   201
Grumberg, Orna   275
Gurfinkel, Arie   306

Heljanko, Keijo   186
Higgins, Jason T.   98

Intrigila, Benedetto   214
Iyer, Subramanian   399

Jain, Jawahar   399
Jones, Robert B.   113
Junttila, Tommi   186

Kanzelman, Robert   159
Khalvati, Farzad   98
Kishinevsky, Michael   128
Kuehlmann, Andreas   159

Latvala, Timo   186

Maler, Oded   21
Mannava, Phanindra K.   382
Manolios, Panagiotis   82, 367
Mårtensson, Johan   337
McMillan, Ken L.   260
Melatti, Igor   214
Mony, Hari   159
Moon, In-Ho   144
Moore, J. Strother   67
Moravec, Pavel   352

Narayan, Amit   399
Narizzano, Massimo   201
Nopper, Tobias   290

Park, Seungjoon   382
Paruthi, Viresh   159
Pixley, Carl   144

Ray, Sandip   67
Roveri, Marco   245

Sahoo, Debashis   399
Samer, Marko   322
Schmaltz, Julien   52
Scholl, Christoph   290
Schuster, Assaf   275
Sheeran, Mary   6
Sheridan, Daniel   245
Sidle, Thomas   414
Šimša, Jiří   352
Somenzi, Fabio   230
Stangier, Christian   399, 414

Tacchella, Armando   201
Tahar, Sofiène   37
Tronci, Enrico   214

Veith, Helmut   322
Venturini Zilli, Marisa   214
Vroon, Daron   82

Wolf, Wayne   1

Yadgar, Avi   275
Yang, Zijiang   430

Zarpas, Emmanuel   174

Lecture Notes in Computer Science

For information about Vols. 1–3209

please contact your bookseller or Springer

Vol. 3323: G. Antoniou, H. Boley (Eds.), Rules and Rule Markup Languages for the Semantic Web. X, 215 pages. 2004.

Vol. 3315: C. Lemaître, C.A. Reyes, J. González (Eds.), Advances in Artificial Intelligence – IBERAMIA 2004. XX, 987 pages. 2004. (Subseries LNAI).

Vol. 3312: A.J. Hu, A.K. Martin (Eds.), Formal Methods in Computer-Aided Design. XI, 445 pages. 2004.

Vol. 3308: J. Davies, W. Schulte, M. Barnett (Eds.), Formal Methods and Software Engineering. XIII, 500 pages. 2004.

Vol. 3307: C. Bussler, S.-k. Hong, W. Jun, R. Kaschek, Kinshuk, S. Krishnaswamy, S.W. Loke, D. Oberle, D. Richards, A. Sharma (Eds.), Web Information Systems – WISE 2004 Workshops. XV, 277 pages. 2004.

Vol. 3305: P.M.A. Sloot, B. Chopard, A.G. Hoekstra (Eds.), Cellular Automata. XV, 883 pages. 2004.

Vol. 3302: W.-N. Chin (Ed.), Programming Languages and Systems. XIII, 453 pages. 2004.

Vol. 3299: F. Wang (Ed.), Automated Technology for Verification and Analysis. XII, 506 pages. 2004.

Vol. 3298: S.A. McIlraith, D. Plexousakis, F. van Harmelen (Eds.), The Semantic Web – ISWC 2004. XXI, 841 pages. 2004.

Vol. 3295: P. Markopoulos, B. Eggen, E. Aarts, J.L. Crowley (Eds.), Ambient Intelligence. XIII, 388 pages. 2004.

Vol. 3294: C.N. Dean, R.T. Boute (Eds.), Teaching Formal Methods. X, 249 pages. 2004.

Vol. 3293: C.-H. Chi, M. van Steen, C. Wills (Eds.), Web Content Caching and Distribution. IX, 283 pages. 2004.

Vol. 3292: R. Meersman, Z. Tari, A. Corsaro (Eds.), On the Move to Meaningful Internet Systems 2004: OTM 2004 Workshops. XXIII, 885 pages. 2004.

Vol. 3291: R. Meersman, Z. Tari (Eds.), On the Move to Meaningful Internet Systems 2004: CoopIS, DOA, and ODBASE. XXV, 824 pages. 2004.

Vol. 3290: R. Meersman, Z. Tari (Eds.), On the Move to Meaningful Internet Systems 2004: CoopIS, DOA, and ODBASE. XXV, 823 pages. 2004.

Vol. 3289: S. Wang, K. Tanaka, S. Zhou, T.W. Ling, J. Guan, D. Yang, F. Grandi, E. Mangina, I.-Y. Song, H.C. Mayr (Eds.), Conceptual Modeling for Advanced Application Domains. XXII, 692 pages. 2004.

Vol. 3288: P. Atzeni, W. Chu, H. Lu, S. Zhou, T.W. Ling (Eds.), Conceptual Modeling – ER 2004. XXI, 869 pages. 2004.

Vol. 3287: A. Sanfeliu, J.F. Martínez Trinidad, J.A. Carrasco Ochoa (Eds.), Progress in Pattern Recognition, Image Analysis and Applications. XVII, 703 pages. 2004.

Vol. 3286: G. Karsai, E. Visser (Eds.), Generative Programming and Component Engineering. XIII, 491 pages. 2004.

Vol. 3285: S. Manandhar, J. Austin, U. Desai, Y. Oyanagi, A. Talukder (Eds.), Applied Computing. XII, 334 pages. 2004.

Vol. 3284: A. Karmouch, L. Korba, E.R.M. Madeira (Eds.), Mobility Aware Technologies and Applications. XII, 382 pages. 2004.

Vol. 3281: T. Dingsøyr (Ed.), Software Process Improvement. X, 207 pages. 2004.

Vol. 3280: C. Aykanat, T. Dayar, İ. Körpeoğlu (Eds.), Computer and Information Sciences - ISCIS 2004. XVIII, 1009 pages. 2004.

Vol. 3278: A. Sahai, F. Wu (Eds.), Utility Computing. XI, 272 pages. 2004.

Vol. 3274: R. Guerraoui (Ed.), Distributed Computing. XIII, 465 pages. 2004.

Vol. 3273: T. Baar, A. Strohmeier, A. Moreira, S.J. Mellor (Eds.), <<UML>> 2004 - The Unified Modelling Language. XIII, 454 pages. 2004.

Vol. 3271: J. Vicente, D. Hutchison (Eds.), Management of Multimedia Networks and Services. XIII, 335 pages. 2004.

Vol. 3270: M. Jeckle, R. Kowalczyk, P. Braun (Eds.), Grid Services Engineering and Management. X, 165 pages. 2004.

Vol. 3269: J. Lopez, S. Qing, E. Okamoto (Eds.), Information and Communications Security. XI, 564 pages. 2004.

Vol. 3266: J. Solé-Pareta, M. Smirnov, P.V. Mieghem, J. Domingo-Pascual, E. Monteiro, P. Reichl, B. Stiller, R.J. Gibbens (Eds.), Quality of Service in the Emerging Networking Panorama. XVI, 390 pages. 2004.

Vol. 3265: R.E. Frederking, K.B. Taylor (Eds.), Machine Translation: From Real Users to Research. XI, 392 pages. 2004. (Subseries LNAI).

Vol. 3264: G. Paliouras, Y. Sakakibara (Eds.), Grammatical Inference: Algorithms and Applications. XI, 291 pages. 2004. (Subseries LNAI).

Vol. 3263: M. Weske, P. Liggesmeyer (Eds.), Object-Oriented and Internet-Based Technologies. XII, 239 pages. 2004.

Vol. 3262: M.M. Freire, P. Chemouil, P. Lorenz, A. Gravey (Eds.), Universal Multiservice Networks. XIII, 556 pages. 2004.

Vol. 3261: T. Yakhno (Ed.), Advances in Information Systems. XIV, 617 pages. 2004.

Vol. 3260: I.G.M.M. Niemegeers, S.H. de Groot (Eds.), Personal Wireless Communications. XIV, 478 pages. 2004.

Vol. 3258: M. Wallace (Ed.), Principles and Practice of Constraint Programming – CP 2004. XVII, 822 pages. 2004.

Vol. 3257: E. Motta, N.R. Shadbolt, A. Stutt, N. Gibbins (Eds.), Engineering Knowledge in the Age of the Semantic Web. XVII, 517 pages. 2004. (Subseries LNAI).

Vol. 3256: H. Ehrig, G. Engels, F. Parisi-Presicce, G. Rozenberg (Eds.), Graph Transformations. XII, 451 pages. 2004.

Vol. 3255: A. Benczúr, J. Demetrovics, G. Gottlob (Eds.), Advances in Databases and Information Systems. XI, 423 pages. 2004.

Vol. 3254: E. Macii, V. Paliouras, O. Koufopavlou (Eds.), Integrated Circuit and System Design. XVI, 910 pages. 2004.

Vol. 3253: Y. Lakhnech, S. Yovine (Eds.), Formal Techniques, Modelling and Analysis of Timed and Fault-Tolerant Systems. X, 397 pages. 2004.

Vol. 3252: H. Jin, Y. Pan, N. Xiao, J. Sun (Eds.), Grid and Cooperative Computing - GCC 2004 Workshops. XVIII, 785 pages. 2004.

Vol. 3251: H. Jin, Y. Pan, N. Xiao, J. Sun (Eds.), Grid and Cooperative Computing - GCC 2004. XXII, 1025 pages. 2004.

Vol. 3250: L.-J. (LJ) Zhang, M. Jeckle (Eds.), Web Services. X, 301 pages. 2004.

Vol. 3249: B. Buchberger, J.A. Campbell (Eds.), Artificial Intelligence and Symbolic Computation. X, 285 pages. 2004. (Subseries LNAI).

Vol. 3246: A. Apostolico, M. Melucci (Eds.), String Processing and Information Retrieval. XIV, 332 pages. 2004.

Vol. 3245: E. Suzuki, S. Arikawa (Eds.), Discovery Science. XIV, 430 pages. 2004. (Subseries LNAI).

Vol. 3244: S. Ben-David, J. Case, A. Maruoka (Eds.), Algorithmic Learning Theory. XIV, 505 pages. 2004. (Subseries LNAI).

Vol. 3243: S. Leonardi (Ed.), Algorithms and Models for the Web-Graph. VIII, 189 pages. 2004.

Vol. 3242: X. Yao, E. Burke, J.A. Lozano, J. Smith, J.J. Merelo-Guervós, J.A. Bullinaria, J. Rowe, P. Tiño, A. Kabán, H.-P. Schwefel (Eds.), Parallel Problem Solving from Nature - PPSN VIII. XX, 1185 pages. 2004.

Vol. 3241: D. Kranzlmüller, P. Kacsuk, J.J. Dongarra (Eds.), Recent Advances in Parallel Virtual Machine and Message Passing Interface. XIII, 452 pages. 2004.

Vol. 3240: I. Jonassen, J. Kim (Eds.), Algorithms in Bioinformatics. IX, 476 pages. 2004. (Subseries LNBI).

Vol. 3239: G. Nicosia, V. Cutello, P.J. Bentley, J. Timmis (Eds.), Artificial Immune Systems. XII, 444 pages. 2004.

Vol. 3238: S. Biundo, T. Frühwirth, G. Palm (Eds.), KI 2004: Advances in Artificial Intelligence. XI, 467 pages. 2004. (Subseries LNAI).

Vol. 3236: M. Núñez, Z. Maamar, F.L. Pelayo, K. Pousttchi, F. Rubio (Eds.), Applying Formal Methods: Testing, Performance, and M/E-Commerce. XI, 381 pages. 2004.

Vol. 3235: D. de Frutos-Escrig, M. Nunez (Eds.), Formal Techniques for Networked and Distributed Systems – FORTE 2004. X, 377 pages. 2004.

Vol. 3234: M.J. Egenhofer, C. Freksa, H.J. Miller (Eds.), Geographic Information Science. VIII, 345 pages. 2004.

Vol. 3233: K. Futatsugi, F. Mizoguchi, N. Yonezaki (Eds.), Software Security - Theories and Systems. X, 345 pages. 2004.

Vol. 3232: R. Heery, L. Lyon (Eds.), Research and Advanced Technology for Digital Libraries. XV, 528 pages. 2004.

Vol. 3231: H.-A. Jacobsen (Ed.), Middleware 2004. XV, 514 pages. 2004.

Vol. 3230: J.L. Vicedo, P. Martínez-Barco, R. Muñoz, M. Saiz Noeda (Eds.), Advances in Natural Language Processing. XII, 488 pages. 2004. (Subseries LNAI).

Vol. 3229: J.J. Alferes, J. Leite (Eds.), Logics in Artificial Intelligence. XIV, 744 pages. 2004. (Subseries LNAI).

Vol. 3226: M. Bouzeghoub, C. Goble, V. Kashyap, S. Spaccapietra (Eds.), Semantics of a Networked World. XIII, 326 pages. 2004.

Vol. 3225: K. Zhang, Y. Zheng (Eds.), Information Security. XII, 442 pages. 2004.

Vol. 3224: E. Jonsson, A. Valdes, M. Almgren (Eds.), Recent Advances in Intrusion Detection. XII, 315 pages. 2004.

Vol. 3223: K. Slind, A. Bunker, G. Gopalakrishnan (Eds.), Theorem Proving in Higher Order Logics. VIII, 337 pages. 2004.

Vol. 3222: H. Jin, G.R. Gao, Z. Xu, H. Chen (Eds.), Network and Parallel Computing. XX, 694 pages. 2004.

Vol. 3221: S. Albers, T. Radzik (Eds.), Algorithms – ESA 2004. XVIII, 836 pages. 2004.

Vol. 3220: J.C. Lester, R.M. Vicari, F. Paraguaçu (Eds.), Intelligent Tutoring Systems. XXI, 920 pages. 2004.

Vol. 3219: M. Heisel, P. Liggesmeyer, S. Wittmann (Eds.), Computer Safety, Reliability, and Security. XI, 339 pages. 2004.

Vol. 3217: C. Barillot, D.R. Haynor, P. Hellier (Eds.), Medical Image Computing and Computer-Assisted Intervention – MICCAI 2004. XXXVIII, 1114 pages. 2004.

Vol. 3216: C. Barillot, D.R. Haynor, P. Hellier (Eds.), Medical Image Computing and Computer-Assisted Intervention – MICCAI 2004. XXXVIII, 930 pages. 2004.

Vol. 3215: M.G.. Negoita, R.J. Howlett, L.C. Jain (Eds.), Knowledge-Based Intelligent Information and Engineering Systems. LVII, 906 pages. 2004. (Subseries LNAI).

Vol. 3214: M.G.. Negoita, R.J. Howlett, L.C. Jain (Eds.), Knowledge-Based Intelligent Information and Engineering Systems. LVIII, 1302 pages. 2004. (Subseries LNAI).

Vol. 3213: M.G.. Negoita, R.J. Howlett, L.C. Jain (Eds.), Knowledge-Based Intelligent Information and Engineering Systems. LVIII, 1280 pages. 2004. (Subseries LNAI).

Vol. 3212: A. Campilho, M. Kamel (Eds.), Image Analysis and Recognition. XXIX, 862 pages. 2004.

Vol. 3211: A. Campilho, M. Kamel (Eds.), Image Analysis and Recognition. XXIX, 880 pages. 2004.

Vol. 3210: J. Marcinkowski, A. Tarlecki (Eds.), Computer Science Logic. XI, 520 pages. 2004.